YOWAMU
PEDAL

WATARU WATANABE

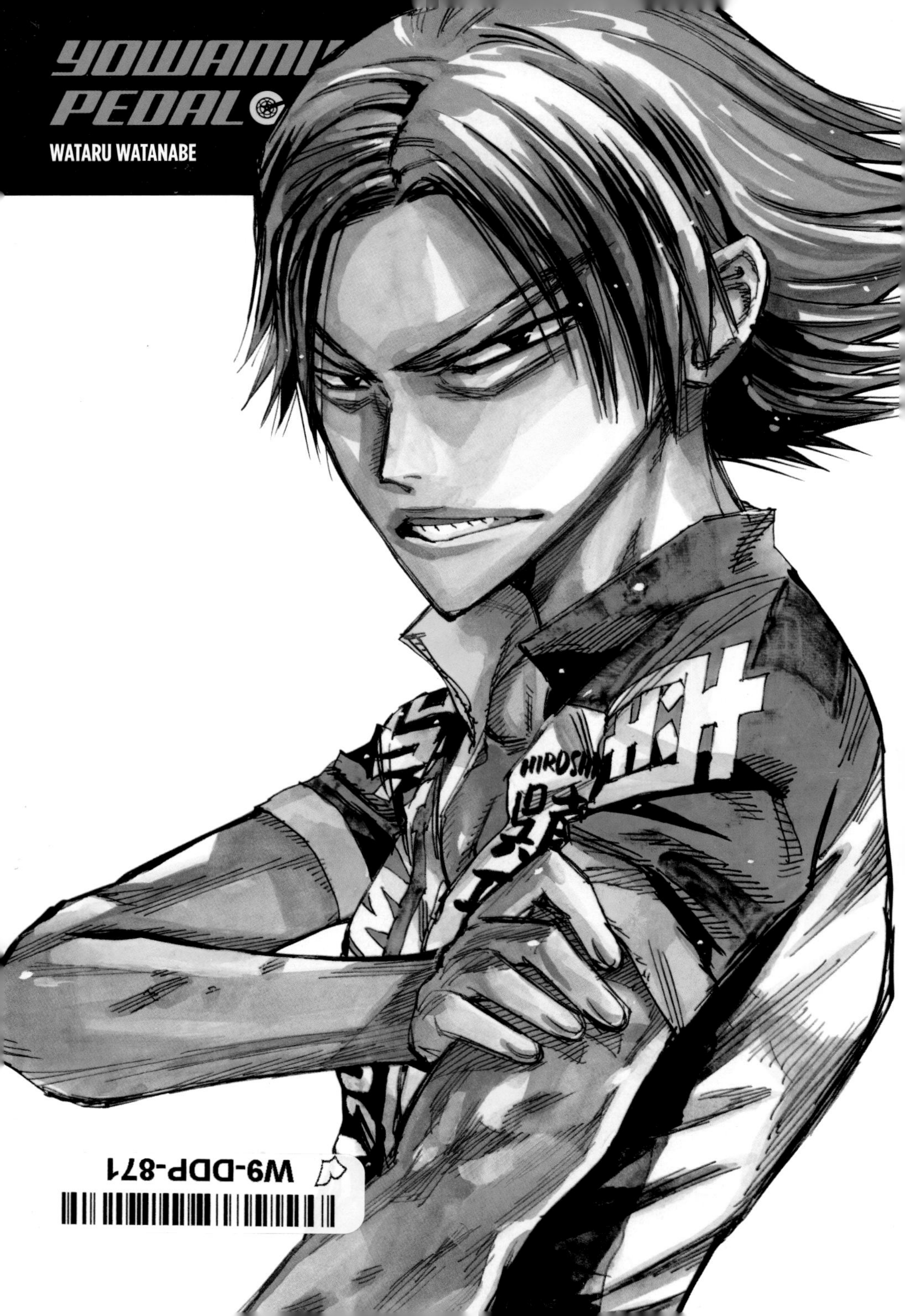

YOWAMUSHI PEDAL

WATARU WATANABE

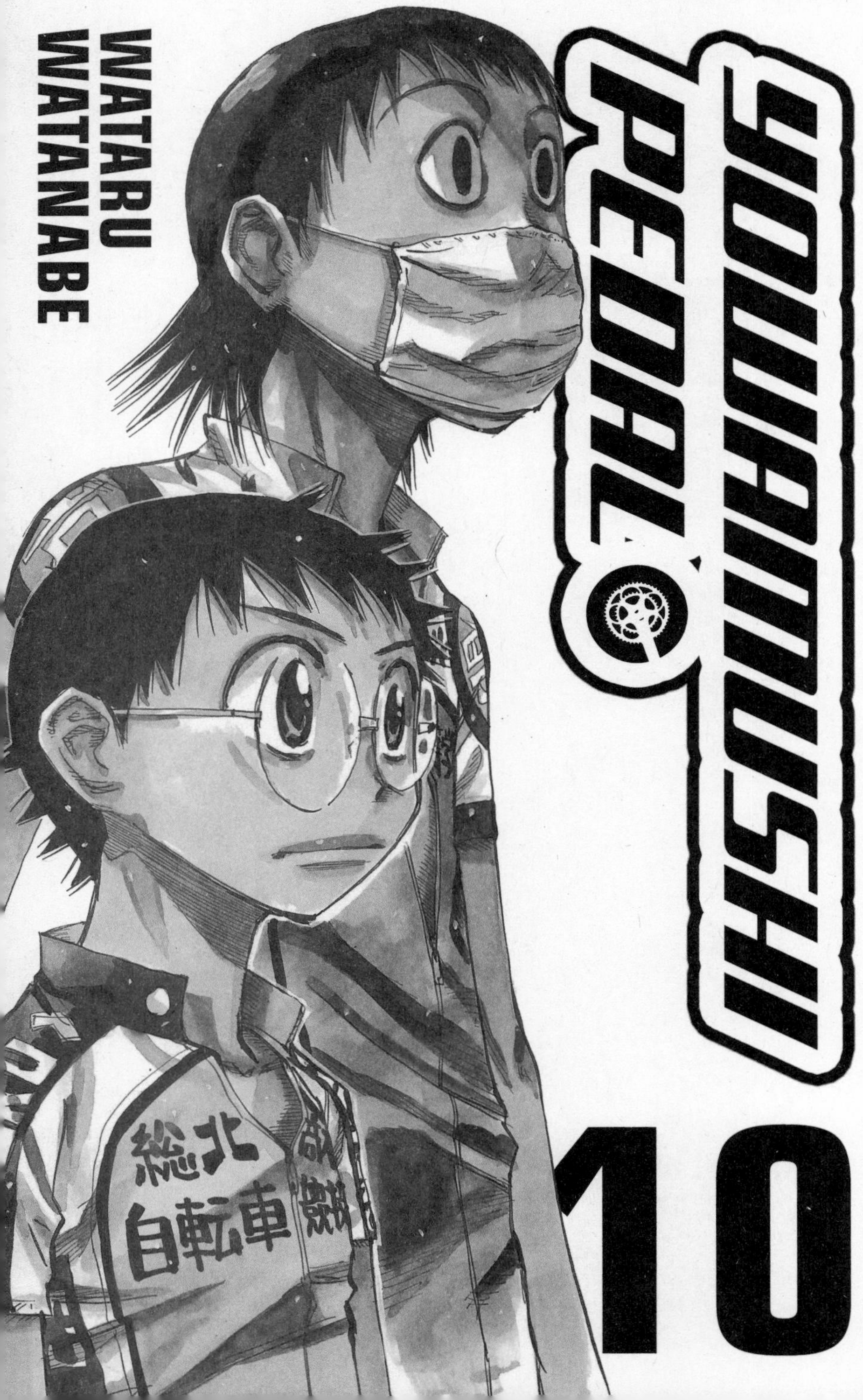
総北
自転車

10

YOWAMUSHI PEDAL

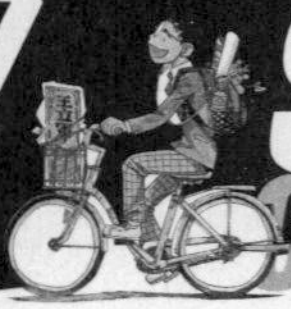

STORY & CHARACTER INTRODUCTION

Inter-High day two reaches its climax! With the Second Stage finish line close at hand, Midousuji pulls off a stunning attack that leaves him riding solo at the front of the race, four seconds ahead of his competitors. As Imaizumi laments his shortcomings as domestique, he entrusts his hopes to Kinjou, the team ace, as he and Fukutomi of Hakone Academy begin their sprint for the finish line! Both aces push themselves beyond their physical limits and begin to close the gap on Midousuji. However, seeing this, Midousuji accelerates even more recklessly! Despite forsaking all else in pursuit of victory, Midousuji is ultimately overtaken by the two aces just before the finish line and places a shocking third place. The long-due showdown between Kinjou and Fukutomi also ends in a slim victory for Fukutomi. As a result, Inter-High day two draws to a close with Fukutomi in first, Kinjou in second, and Midousuji in third place...!! Now, the race plunges onward into its final day!!

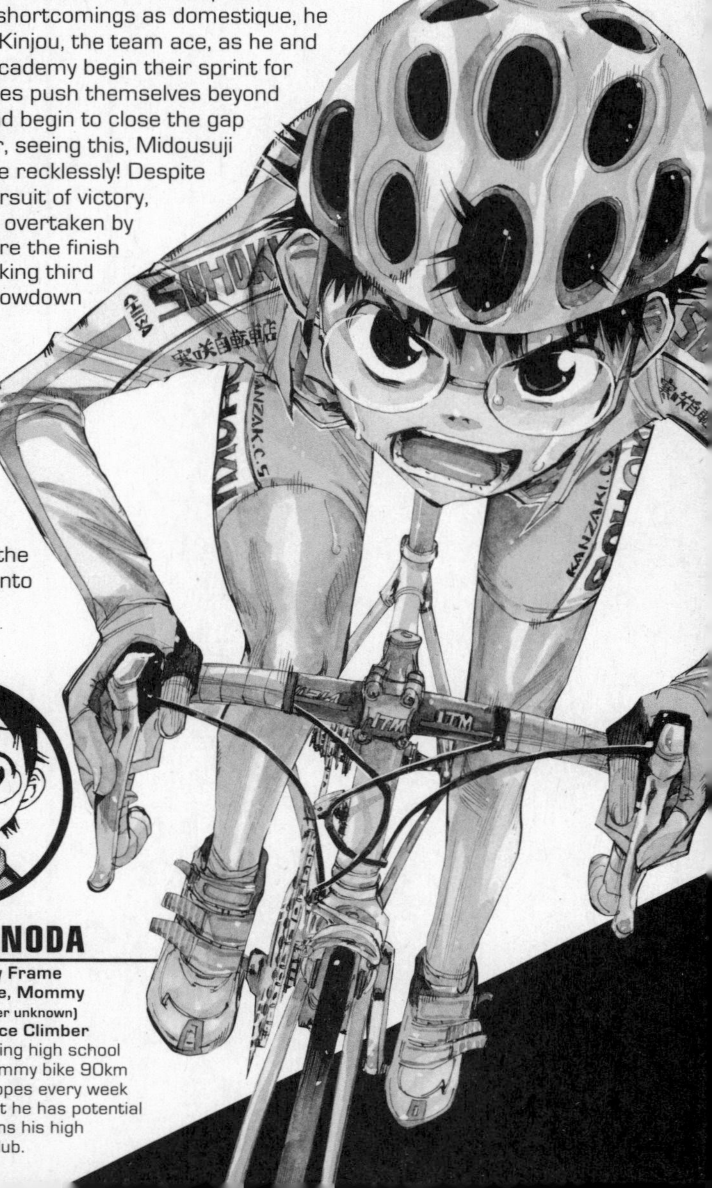

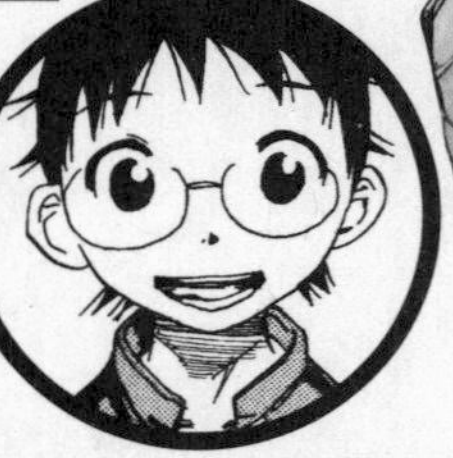

SAKAMICHI ONODA

Preferred Bike: **Chromoly Frame Road Bike, Mommy Bike** (maker unknown)

Cycling Style: **High Cadence Climber**

Sakamichi is an anime-loving high school student who rides his mommy bike 90km round- trip up extreme slopes every week to visit Akiba. Hearing that he has potential as a cyclist, Sakamichi joins his high school's Bicycle Racing Club.

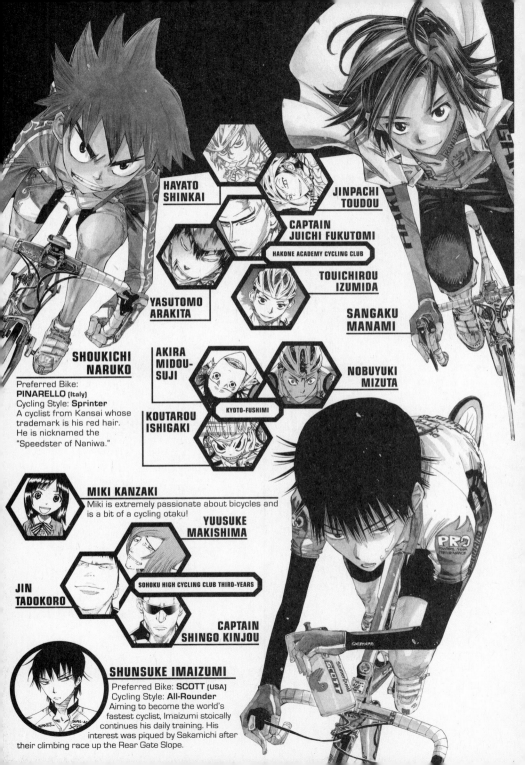

HAYATO SHINKAI

JINPACHI TOUDOU

CAPTAIN JUICHI FUKUTOMI

HAKONE ACADEMY CYCLING CLUB

TOUICHIROU IZUMIDA

YASUTOMO ARAKITA

SANGAKU MANAMI

SHOUKICHI NARUKO

Preferred Bike:
PINARELLO (Italy)
Cycling Style: **Sprinter**
A cyclist from Kansai whose
trademark is his red hair.
He is nicknamed the
"Speedster of Naniwa."

AKIRA MIDOU-SUJI

NOBUYUKI MIZUTA

KYOTO-FUSHIMI

KOUTAROU ISHIGAKI

MIKI KANZAKI

Miki is extremely passionate about bicycles and
is a bit of a cycling otaku!

YUUSUKE MAKISHIMA

JIN TADOKORO

SOHOKU HIGH CYCLING CLUB THIRD-YEARS

CAPTAIN SHINGO KINJOU

SHUNSUKE IMAIZUMI

Preferred Bike: **SCOTT (USA)**
Cycling Style: **All-Rounder**
Aiming to become the world's
fastest cyclist, Imaizumi stoically
continues his daily training. His
interest was piqued by Sakamichi after
their climbing race up the Rear Gate Slope.

VOL.10

YOWAMUSHI PEDAL CONTENTS

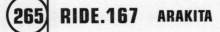

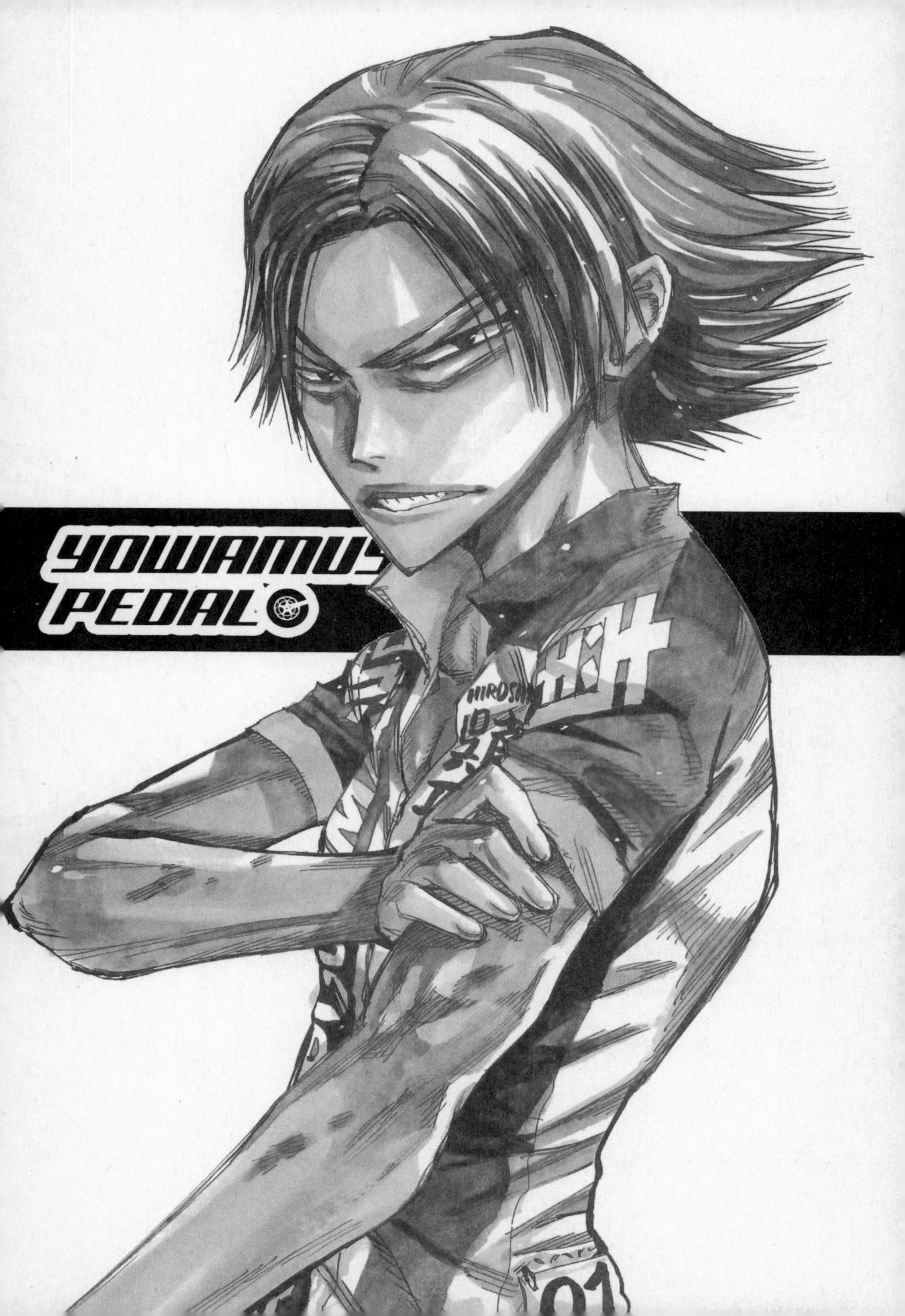
PEDAL

RIDE.155 SOHOKU IN SECOND PLACE

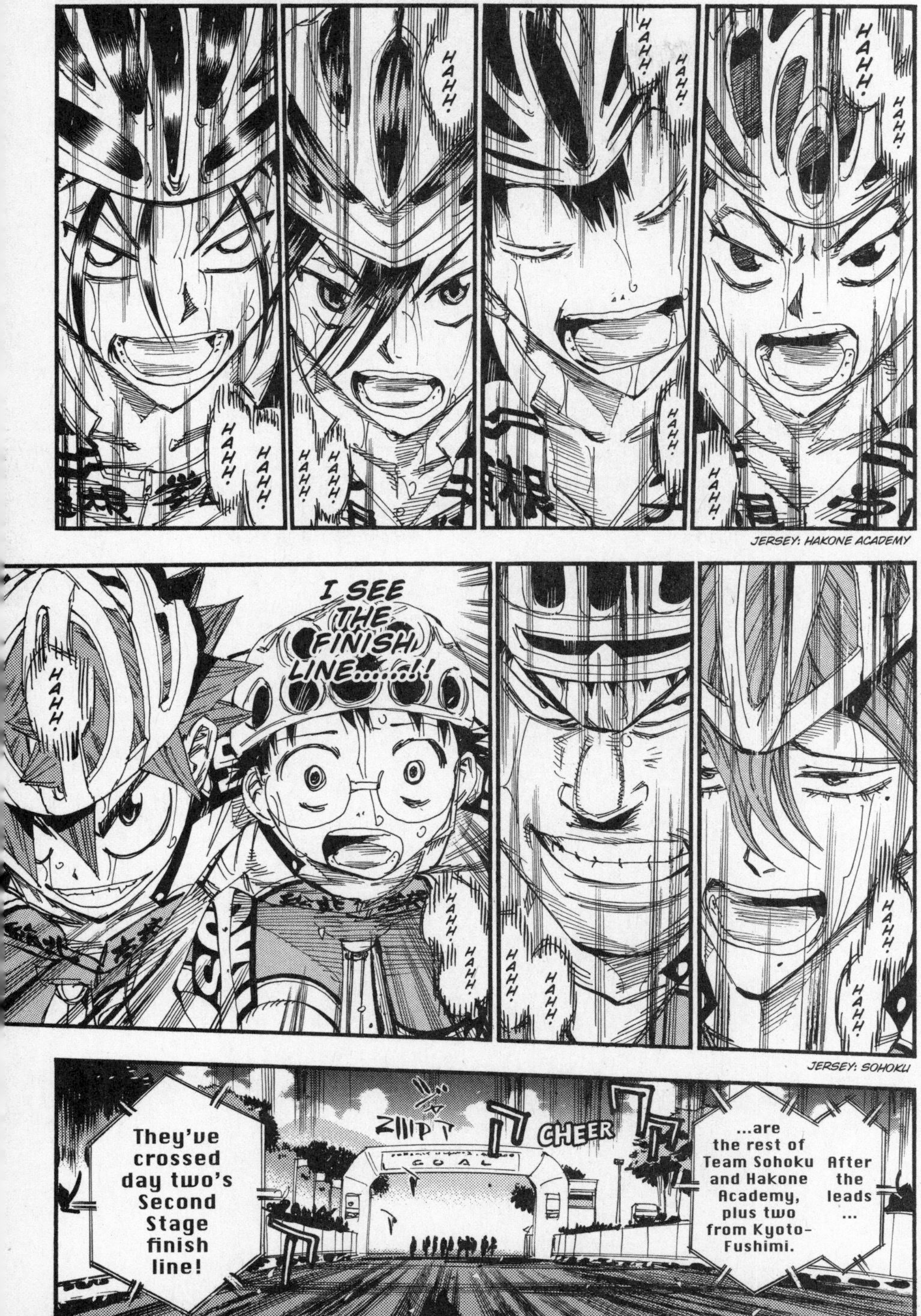
HAHH!
HAHH!
HAHH!
HAHH!
HAHH!
HAHH!
HAHH!
HAHH!
HAHH!
HAHH!
HAHH!
HAHH!
HAHH!
HAHH!
JERSEY: HAKONE ACADEMY
HAHH!
HAHH!
HAHH!
HAHH!
I SEE THE FINISH LINE......!!
HAHH!
JERSEY: SOHOKU
After the leads...
...are the rest of Team Sohoku and Hakone Academy, plus two from Kyoto-Fushimi.
CHEER
ZIIIP
GOAL
They've crossed day two's Second Stage finish line!

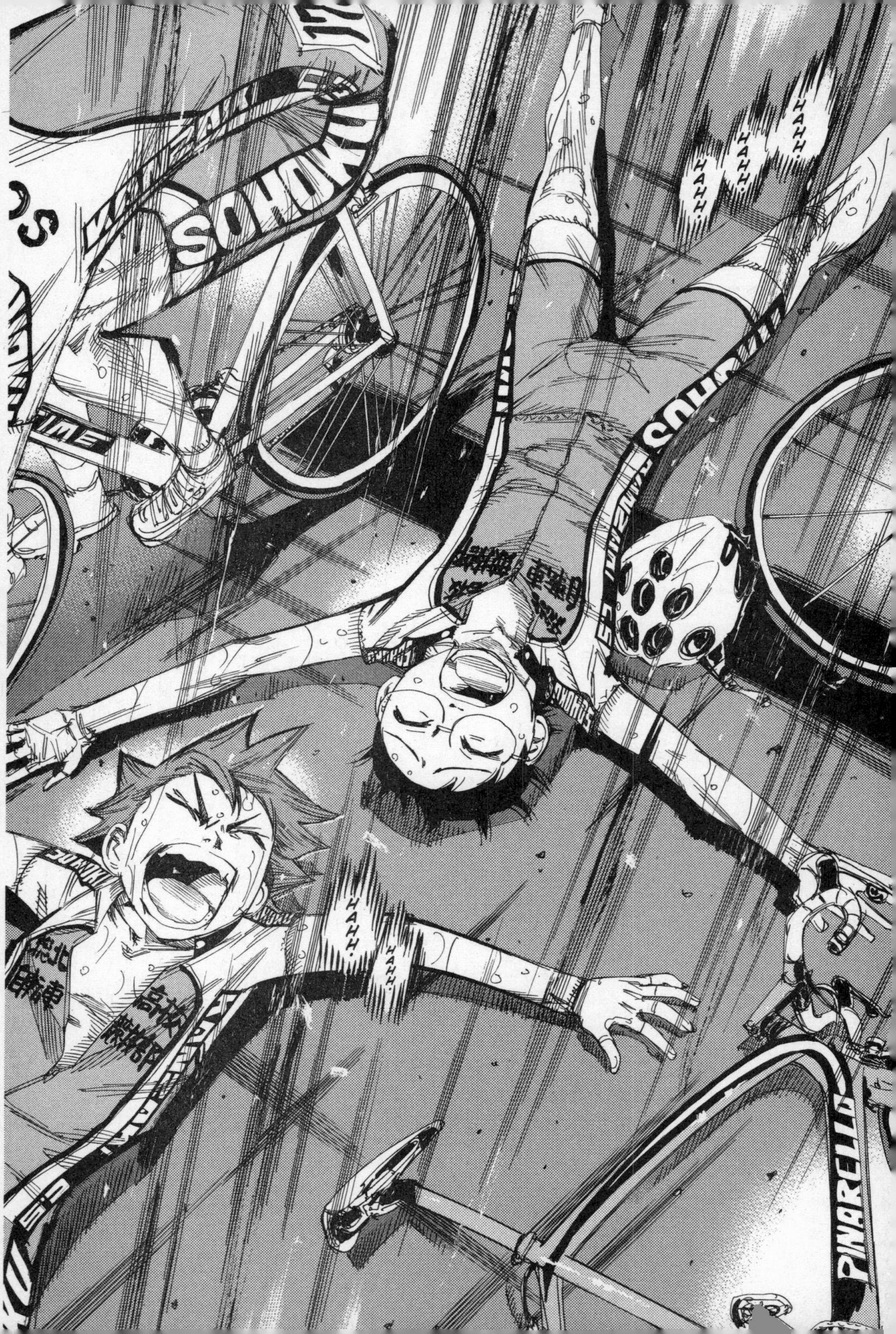
HAHH.
HAHH.
HAHH.
SOHOKU
HAHH.
HAHH.
PINARELLO

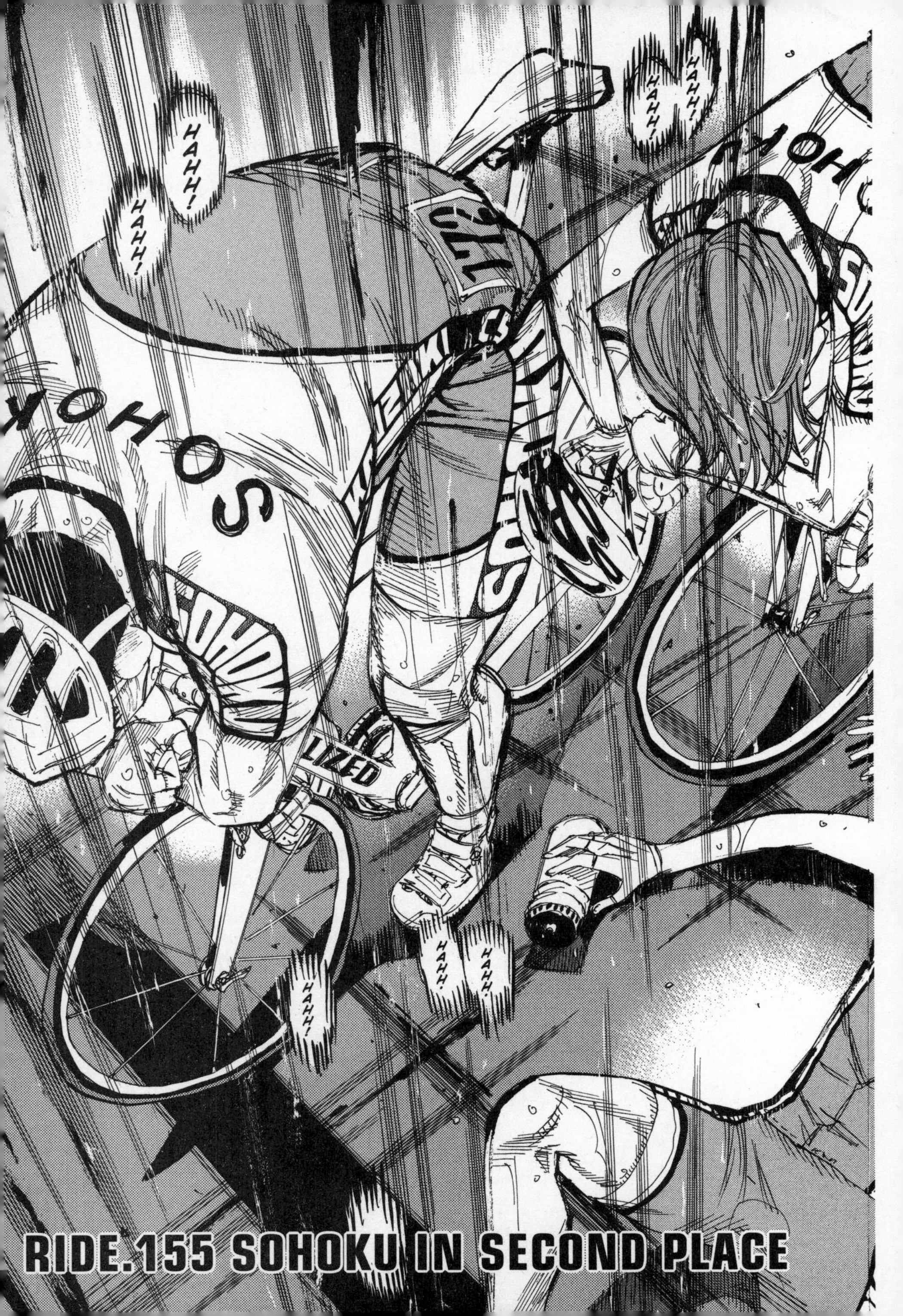
HAHH! HAHH!
HAHH! HAHH!
HAHH. HAHH.
HAHH!

RIDE.155 SOHOKU IN SECOND PLACE

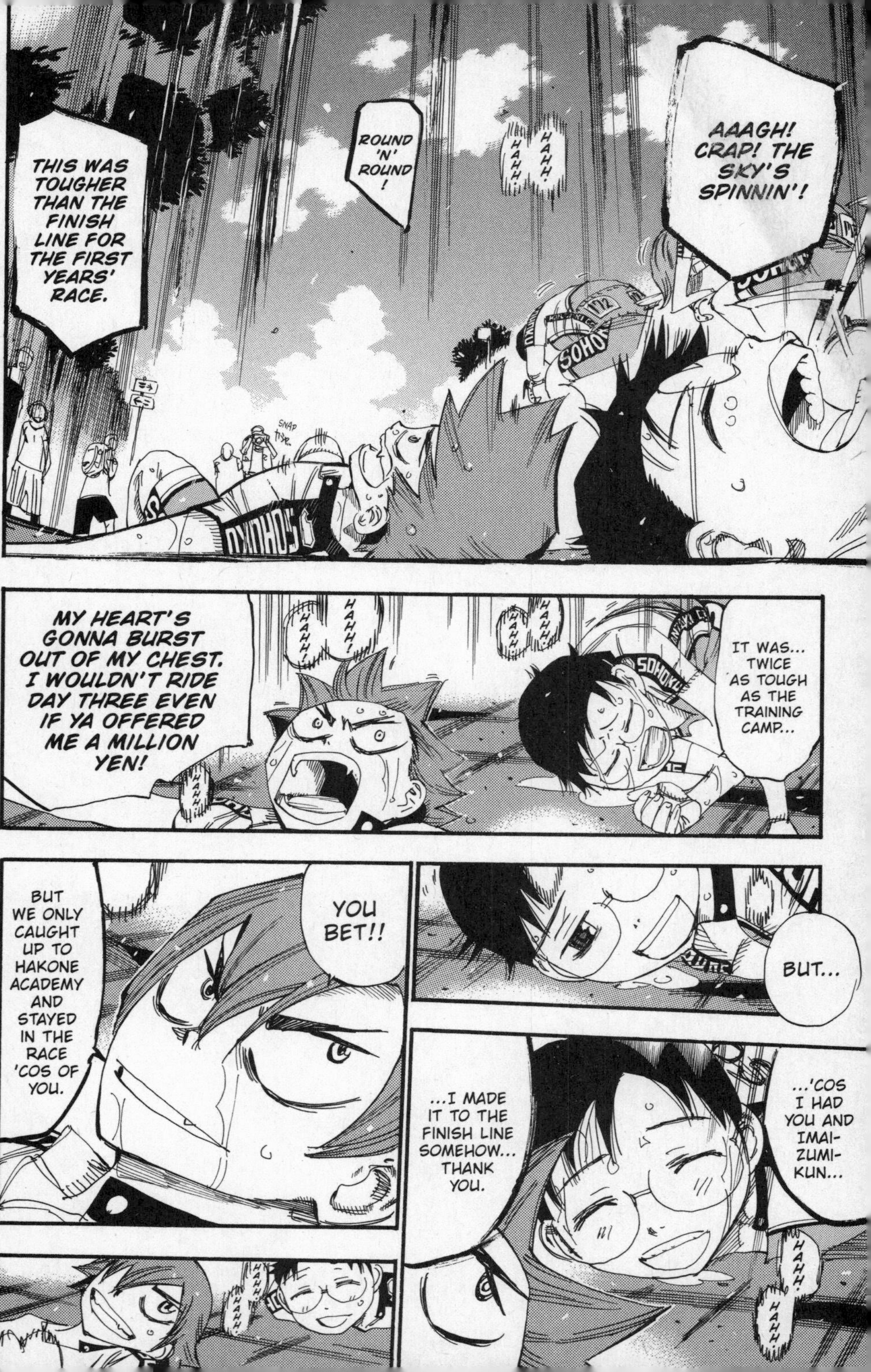
AAAGH! CRAP! THE SKY'S SPINNIN'!
HAHH HAHH
ROUND 'N' ROUND!
THIS WAS TOUGHER THAN THE FINISH LINE FOR THE FIRST YEARS' RACE.
SNAP
IT WAS... TWICE AS TOUGH AS THE TRAINING CAMP...
HAHH HAHH
HAHH HAHH
MY HEART'S GONNA BURST OUT OF MY CHEST. I WOULDN'T RIDE DAY THREE EVEN IF YA OFFERED ME A MILLION YEN!
HAHH
BUT...
...'COS I HAD YOU AND IMAI-ZUMI-KUN...
...I MADE IT TO THE FINISH LINE SOMEHOW... THANK YOU.
YOU BET!!
BUT WE ONLY CAUGHT UP TO HAKONE ACADEMY AND STAYED IN THE RACE 'COS OF YOU.
HAHH HAHH
HAHH

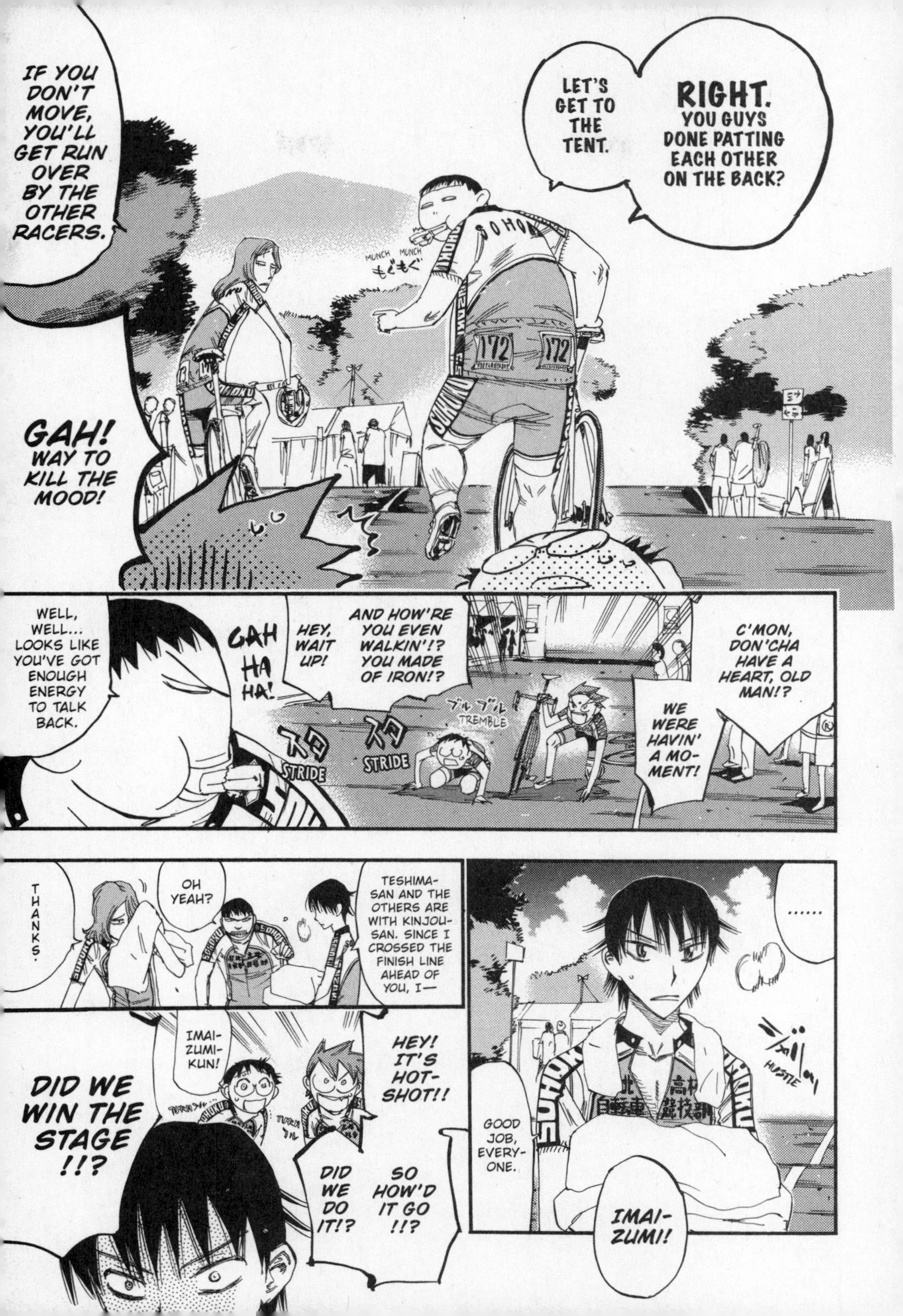
RIGHT. YOU GUYS DONE PATTING EACH OTHER ON THE BACK?
LET'S GET TO THE TENT.
MUNCH MUNCH
もぐもぐ
IF YOU DON'T MOVE, YOU'LL GET RUN OVER BY THE OTHER RACERS.
GAH! WAY TO KILL THE MOOD!
C'MON, DON'CHA HAVE A HEART, OLD MAN!?
WE WERE HAVIN' A MOMENT!
AND HOW'RE YOU EVEN WALKIN'!? YOU MADE OF IRON!?
HEY, WAIT UP!
ブルブル
TREMBLE
スタ
STRIDE
スタ
STRIDE
GAH HA HA!
WELL, WELL... LOOKS LIKE YOU'VE GOT ENOUGH ENERGY TO TALK BACK.
......
ジャリ
HUSTLE
GOOD JOB, EVERYONE.
IMAIZUMI!
TESHIMA-SAN AND THE OTHERS ARE WITH KINJOU-SAN. SINCE I CROSSED THE FINISH LINE AHEAD OF YOU, I—
OH YEAH?
THANKS.
HEY! IT'S HOTSHOT!!
IMAIZUMI-KUN!
SO HOW'D IT GO!!?
DID WE DO IT!?
DID WE WIN THE STAGE!!?

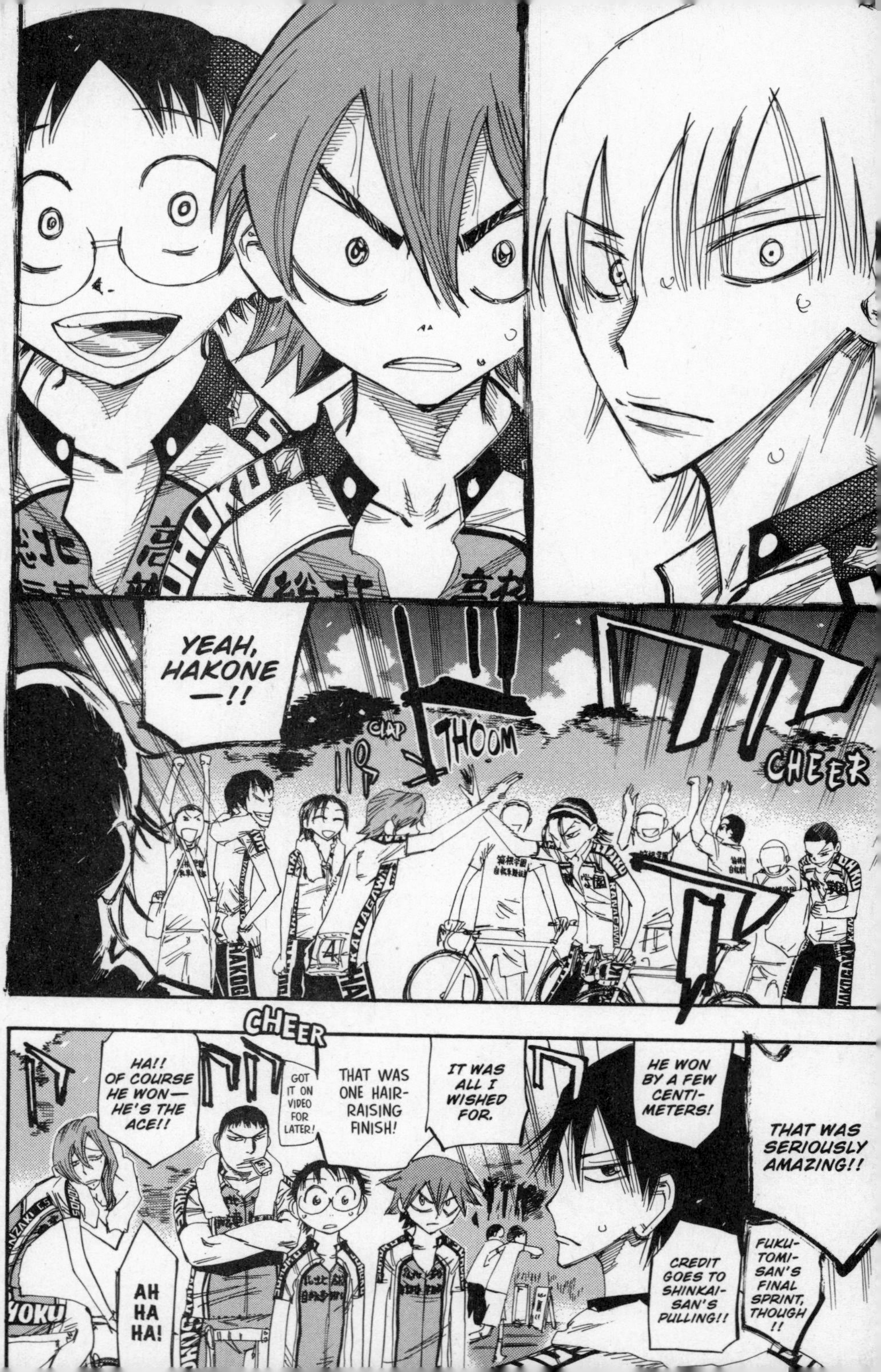
CHEER
THOOM
CLAP
YEAH, HAKONE—!!
THAT WAS SERIOUSLY AMAZING!!
HE WON BY A FEW CENTIMETERS!
FUKUTOMI-SAN'S FINAL SPRINT, THOUGH!!
CREDIT GOES TO SHINKAI-SAN'S PULLING!!
IT WAS ALL I WISHED FOR.
THAT WAS ONE HAIR-RAISING FINISH!
GOT IT ON VIDEO FOR LATER!
CHEER
HA!! OF COURSE HE WON—HE'S THE ACE!!
AH HA HA!

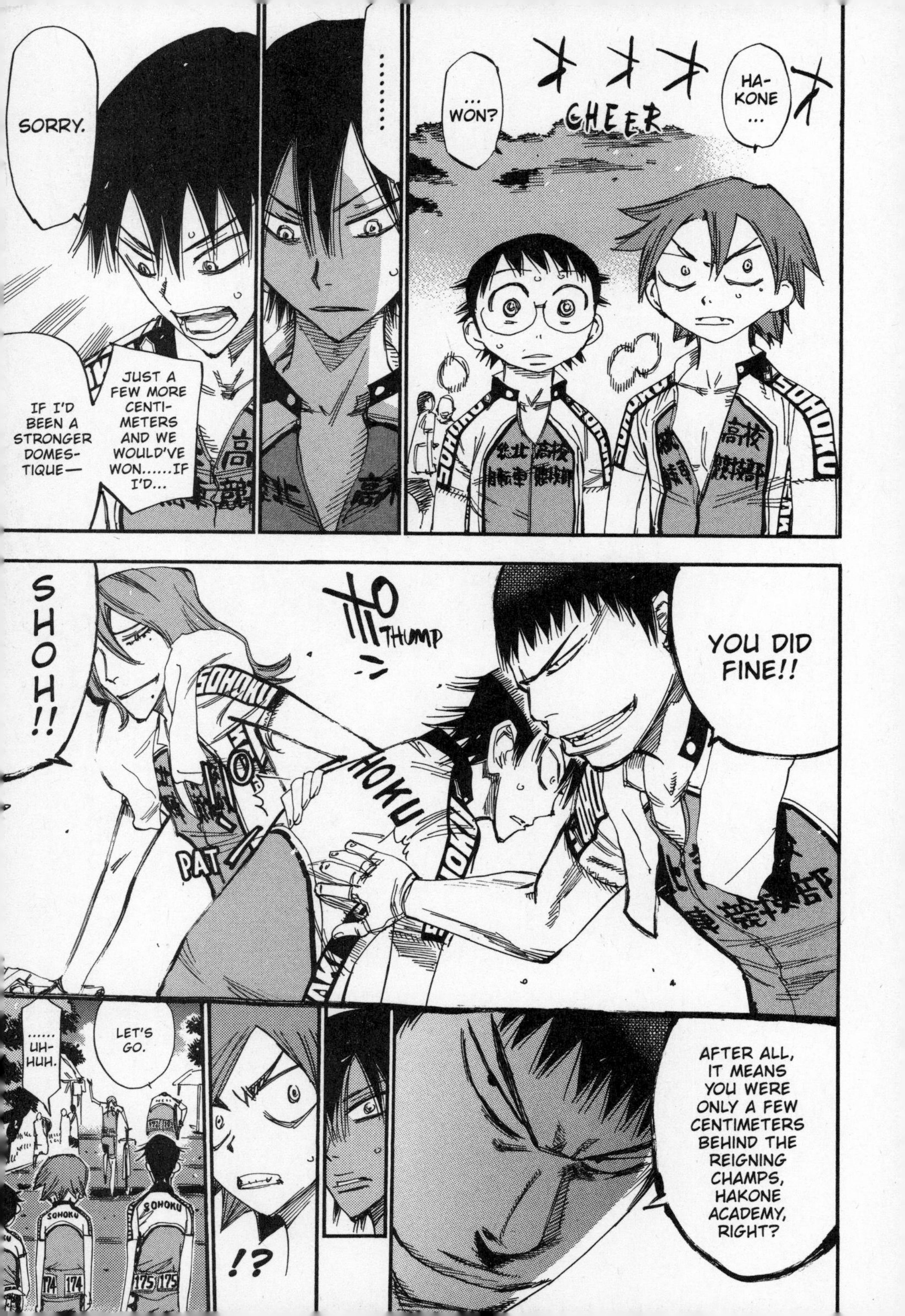
HA-KONE ...
オオオオ
CHEER
... WON?
......
SORRY.
JUST A FEW MORE CENTI-METERS AND WE WOULD'VE WON......IF I'D...
IF I'D BEEN A STRONGER DOMES-TIQUE—
YOU DID FINE!!
THUMP
PAT
SHOH!!
AFTER ALL, IT MEANS YOU WERE ONLY A FEW CENTIMETERS BEHIND THE REIGNING CHAMPS, HAKONE ACADEMY, RIGHT?
!?
LET'S GO.
...... UH-HUH.

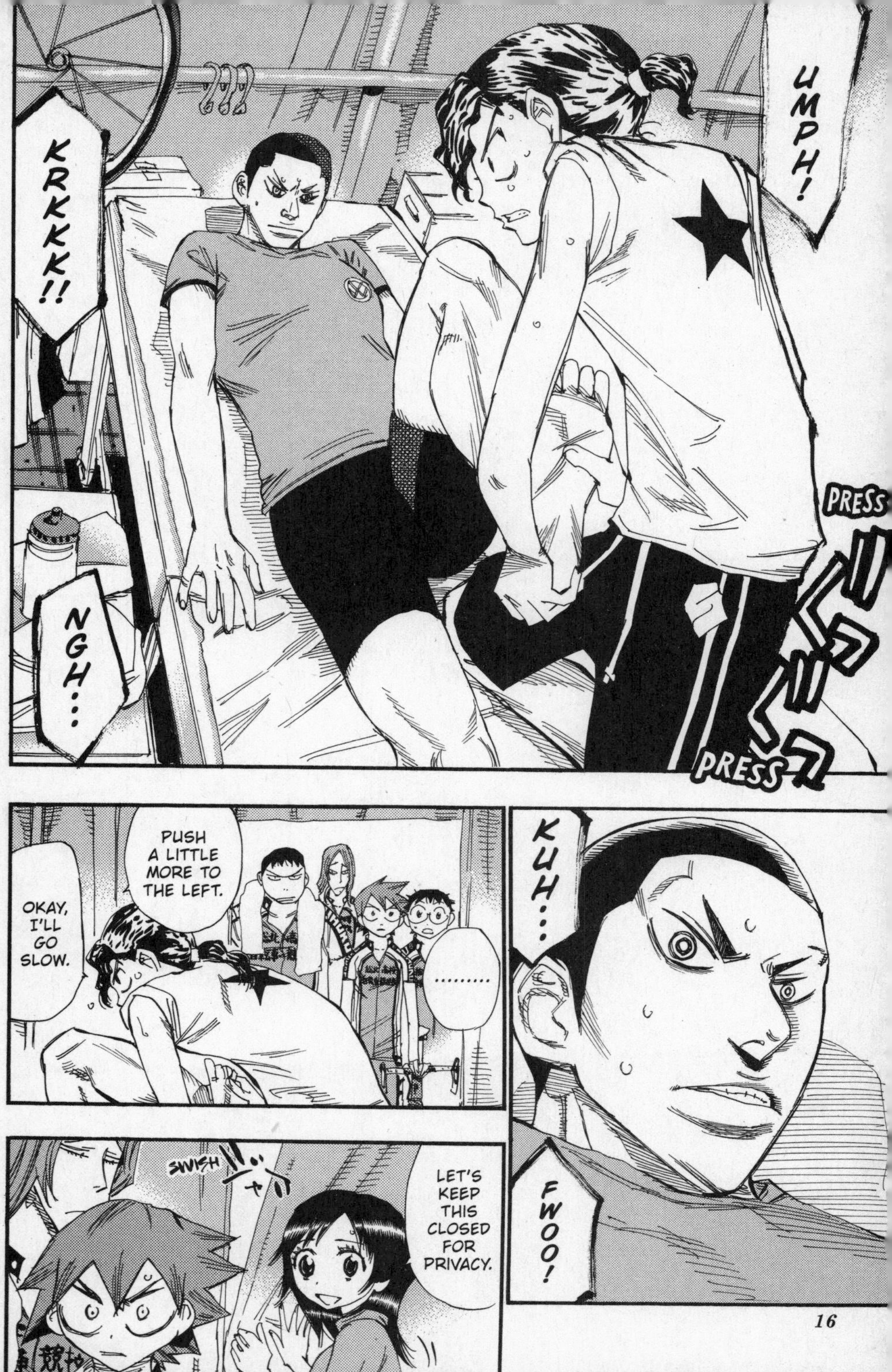
UMPH!
PRESS
PRESS
KRKKKK!!
NGH...
KUH...
FWOO!
PUSH A LITTLE MORE TO THE LEFT.
OKAY, I'LL GO SLOW.
....
LET'S KEEP THIS CLOSED FOR PRIVACY.
SWISH

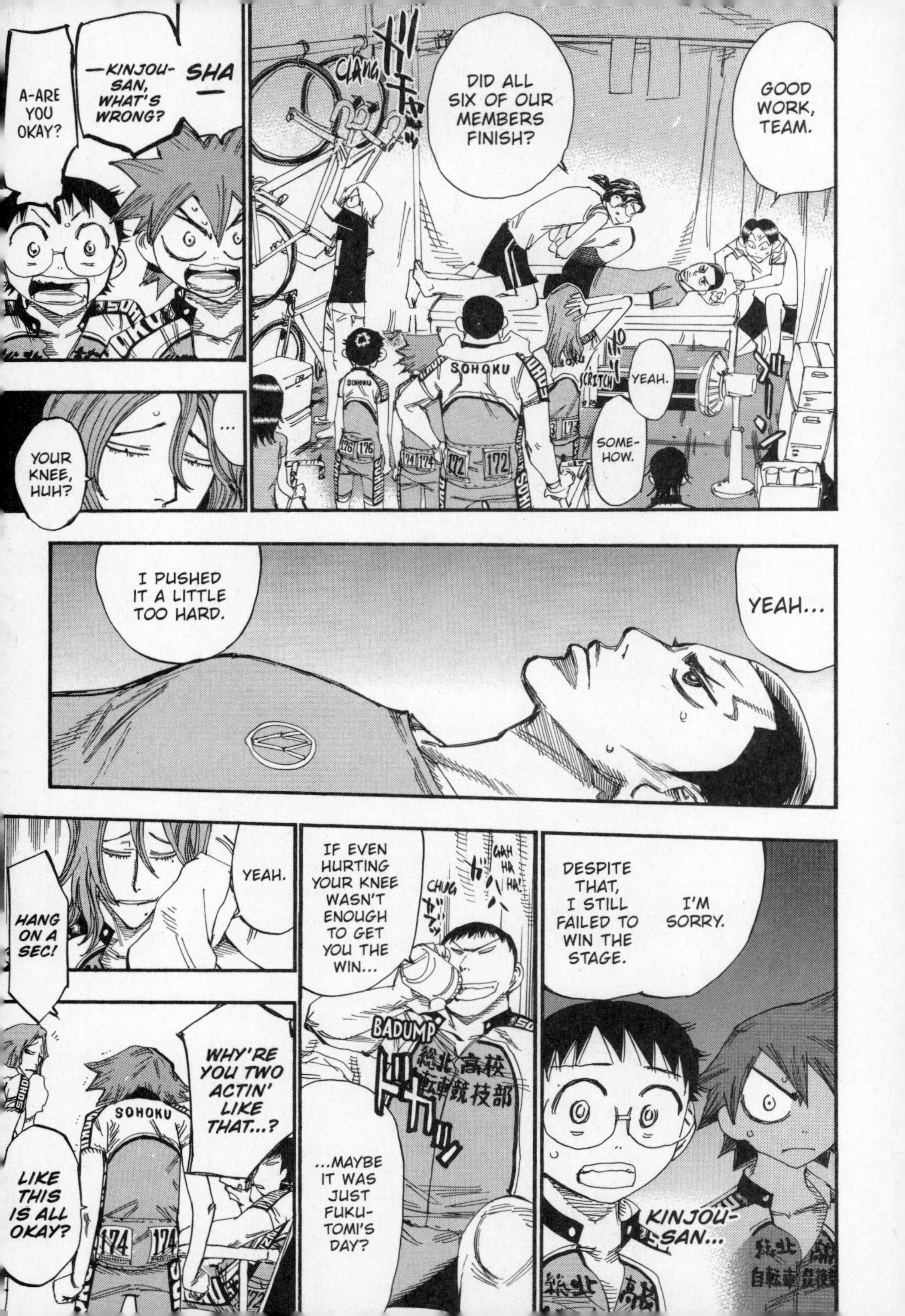
GOOD WORK, TEAM.
DID ALL SIX OF OUR MEMBERS FINISH?
CLANG
YEAH.
SCRITCH
SOME-HOW.
—KINJOU-SAN, WHAT'S WRONG?
SHA
A-ARE YOU OKAY?
...
YOUR KNEE, HUH?
YEAH...
I PUSHED IT A LITTLE TOO HARD.
I'M SORRY.
DESPITE THAT, I STILL FAILED TO WIN THE STAGE.
KINJOU-SAN...
GAH HA HA!
CHUG
IF EVEN HURTING YOUR KNEE WASN'T ENOUGH TO GET YOU THE WIN...
BADUMP
...MAYBE IT WAS JUST FUKUTOMI'S DAY?
YEAH.
HANG ON A SEC!
WHY'RE YOU TWO ACTIN' LIKE THAT...?
LIKE THIS IS ALL OKAY?

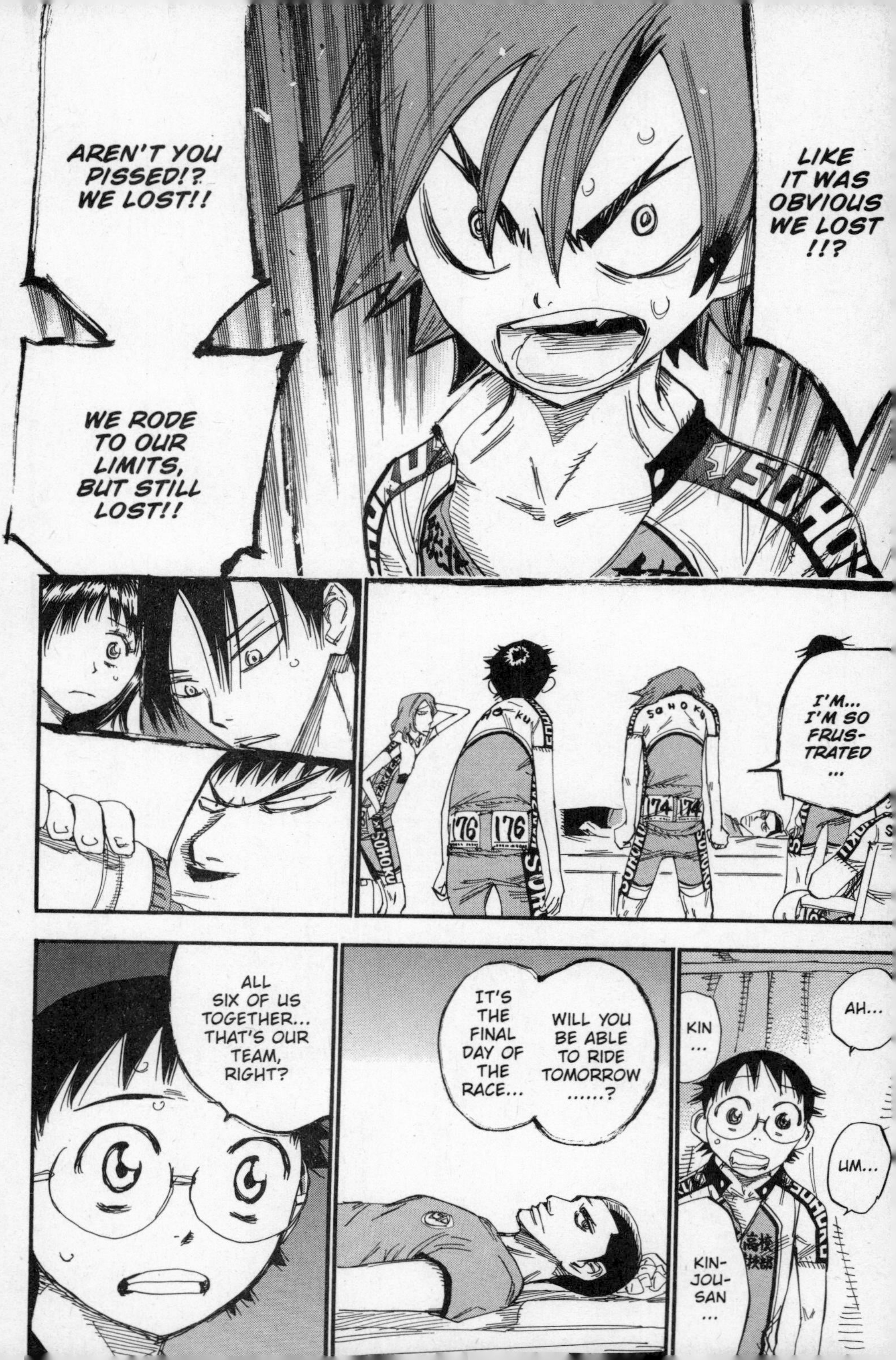
LIKE IT WAS OBVIOUS WE LOST !!?
AREN'T YOU PISSED!? WE LOST!!
WE RODE TO OUR LIMITS, BUT STILL LOST!!
I'M... I'M SO FRUS-TRATED ...
AH...
KIN ...
UM...
KIN-JOU-SAN ...
WILL YOU BE ABLE TO RIDE TOMORROW ......?
IT'S THE FINAL DAY OF THE RACE...
ALL SIX OF US TOGETHER... THAT'S OUR TEAM, RIGHT?

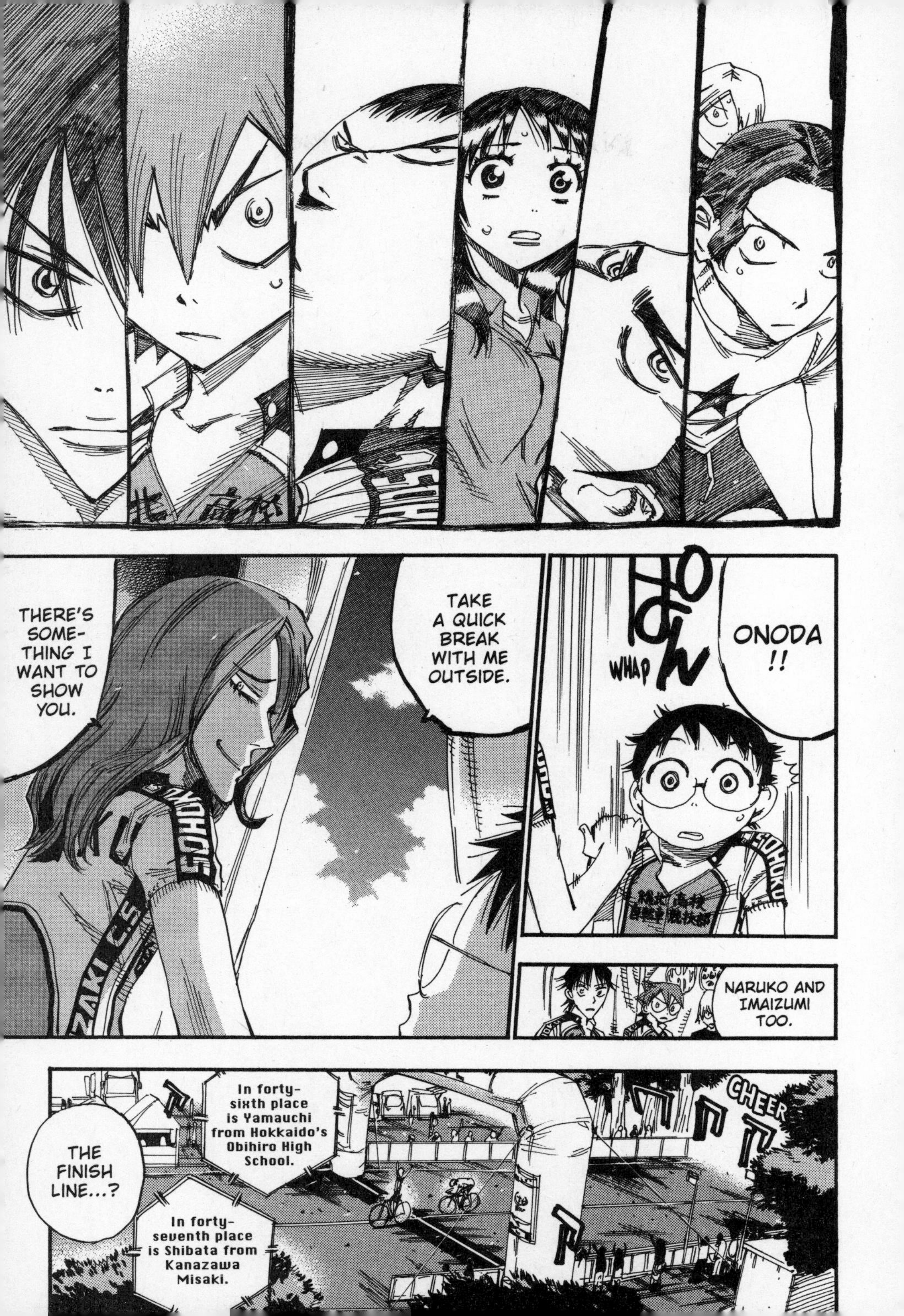
ONODA!!
ぱん
WHAP
NARUKO AND IMAIZUMI TOO.
TAKE A QUICK BREAK WITH ME OUTSIDE.
THERE'S SOMETHING I WANT TO SHOW YOU.
CHEER
In forty-sixth place is Yamauchi from Hokkaido's Obihiro High School.
THE FINISH LINE...?
In forty-seventh place is Shibata from Kanazawa Misaki.

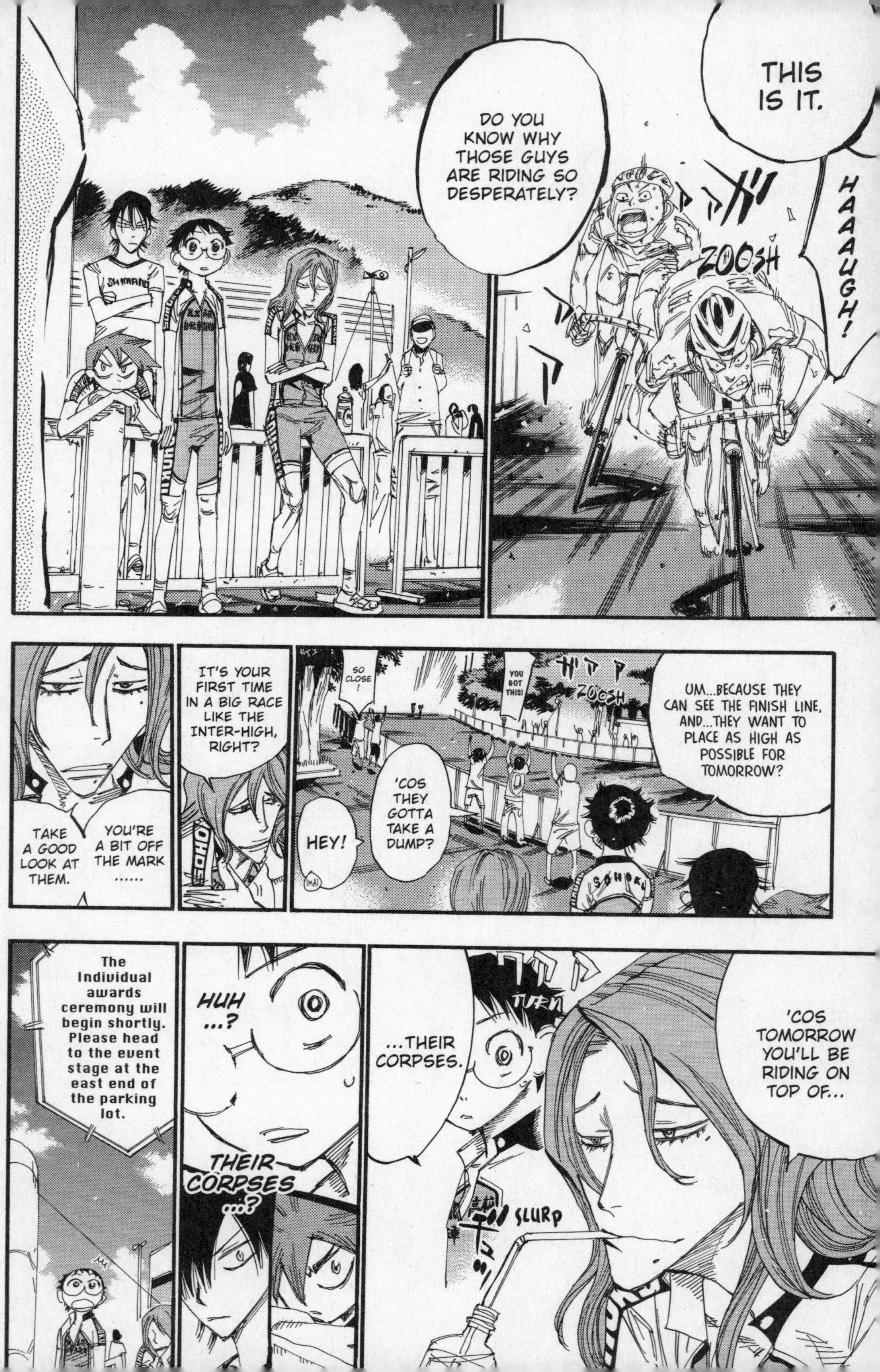
THIS IS IT.
HAAAAUGH!
ZOOSH
DO YOU KNOW WHY THOSE GUYS ARE RIDING SO DESPERATELY?
UM...BECAUSE THEY CAN SEE THE FINISH LINE, AND...THEY WANT TO PLACE AS HIGH AS POSSIBLE FOR TOMORROW?
ZOOSH
YOU GOT THIS!
SO CLOSE!
'COS THEY GOTTA TAKE A DUMP?
HEY!
IMAI
IT'S YOUR FIRST TIME IN A BIG RACE LIKE THE INTER-HIGH, RIGHT?
YOU'RE A BIT OFF THE MARK ......
TAKE A GOOD LOOK AT THEM.
'COS TOMORROW YOU'LL BE RIDING ON TOP OF...
TURN
...THEIR CORPSES.
SLURP
HUH ...?
THEIR CORPSES ...?
The Individual awards ceremony will begin shortly. Please head to the event stage at the east end of the parking lot.

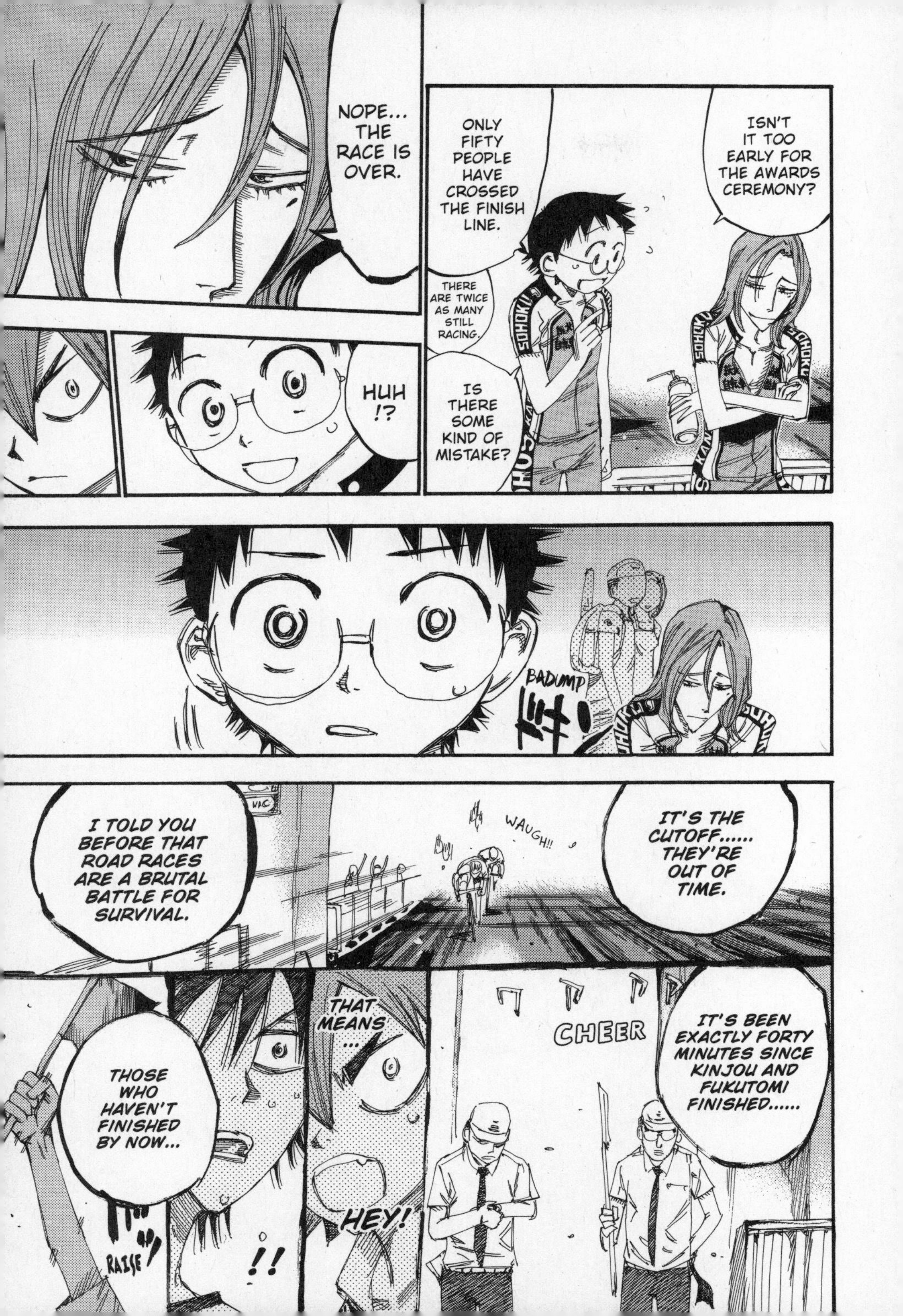
ISN'T IT TOO EARLY FOR THE AWARDS CEREMONY?
ONLY FIFTY PEOPLE HAVE CROSSED THE FINISH LINE.
THERE ARE TWICE AS MANY STILL RACING.
IS THERE SOME KIND OF MISTAKE?
NOPE... THE RACE IS OVER.
HUH !?
BADUMP
IT'S THE CUTOFF...... THEY'RE OUT OF TIME.
WAUGH!!
I TOLD YOU BEFORE THAT ROAD RACES ARE A BRUTAL BATTLE FOR SURVIVAL.
IT'S BEEN EXACTLY FORTY MINUTES SINCE KINJOU AND FUKUTOMI FINISHED......
CHEER
THAT MEANS ...
HEY!
!!
THOSE WHO HAVEN'T FINISHED BY NOW...
RAISE

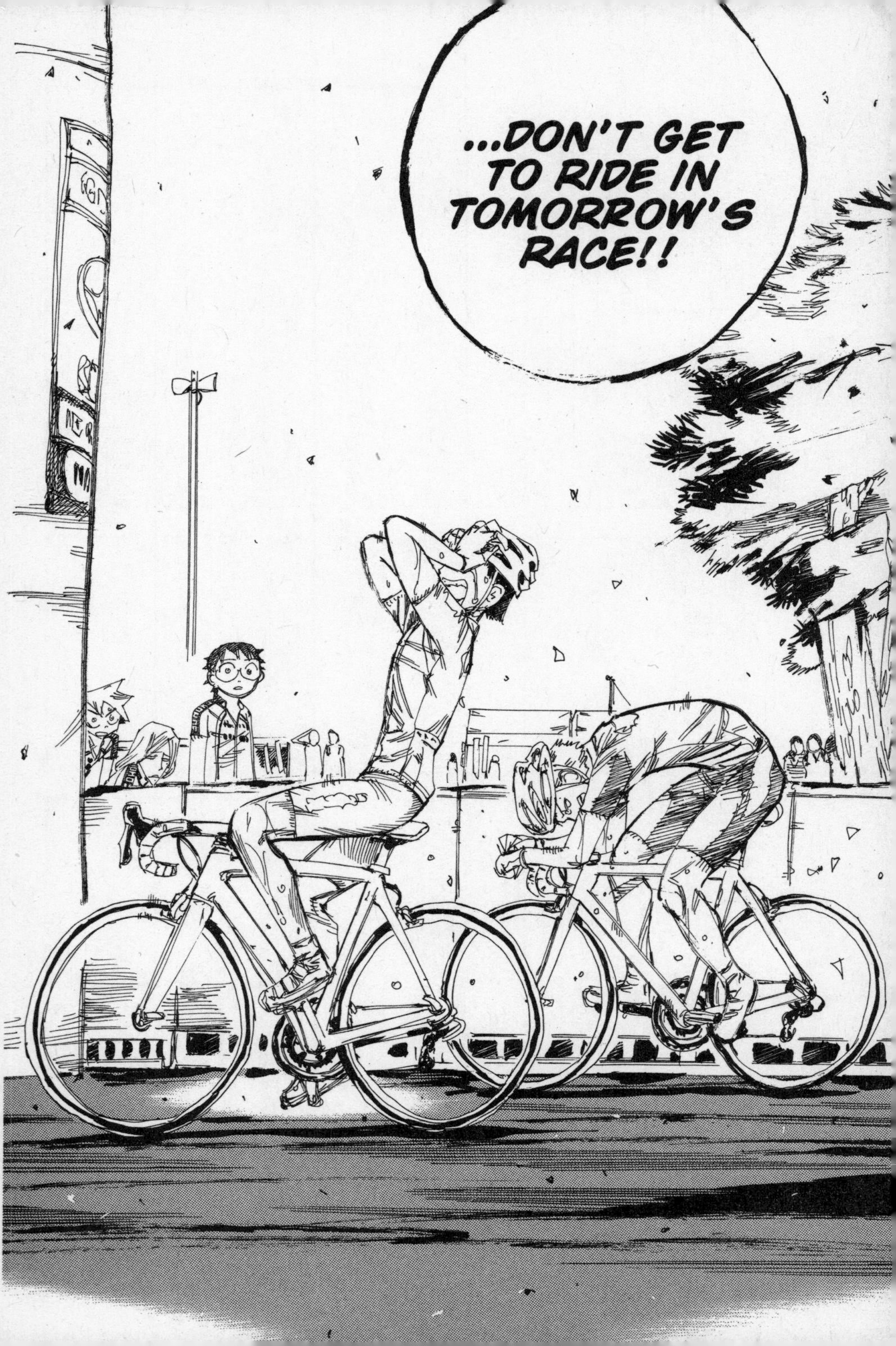
...DON'T GET TO RIDE IN TOMORROW'S RACE!!

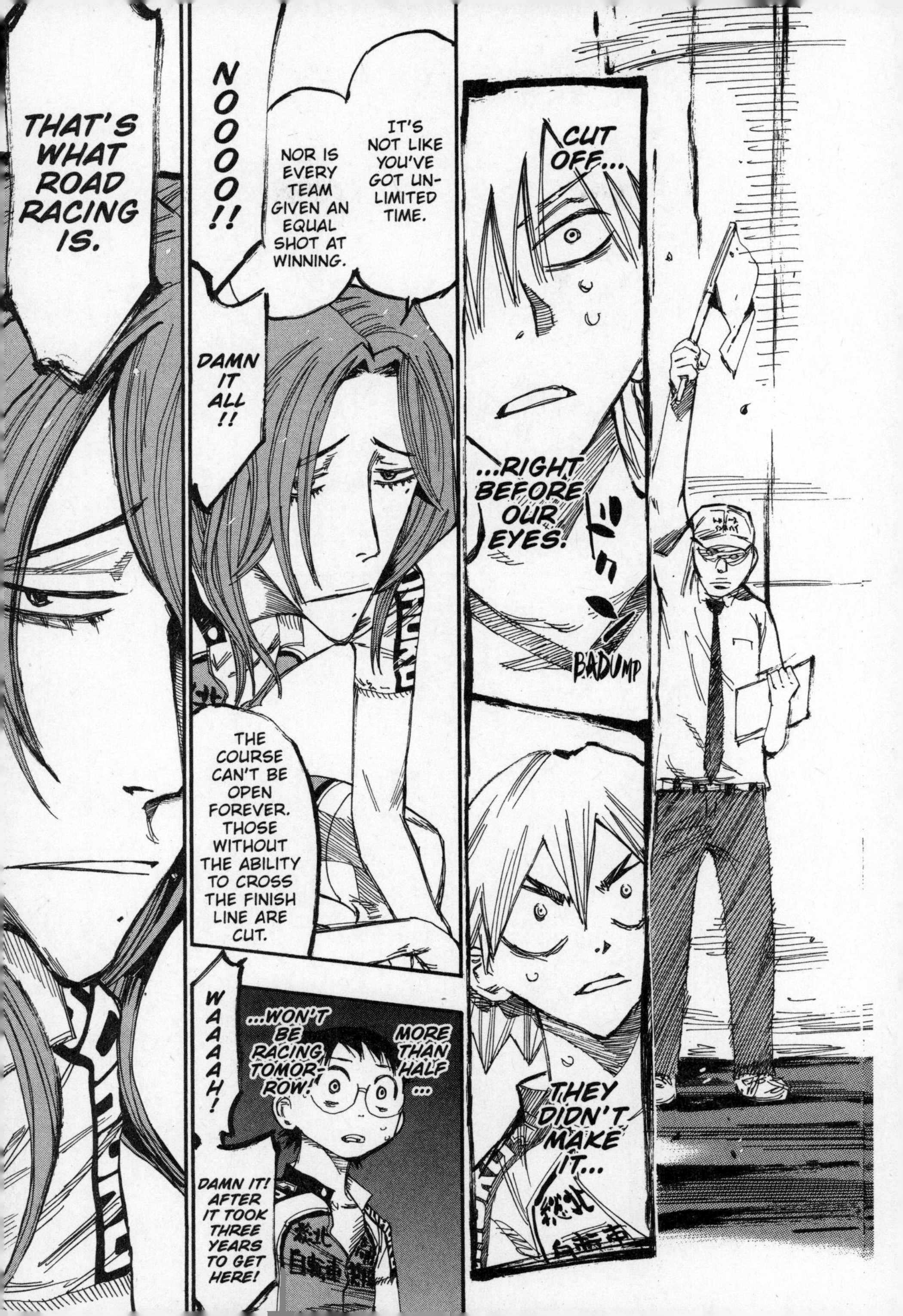
CUT OFF...
...RIGHT BEFORE OUR EYES.
BADUMP
THEY DIDN'T MAKE IT...
IT'S NOT LIKE YOU'VE GOT UN-LIMITED TIME.
NOR IS EVERY TEAM GIVEN AN EQUAL SHOT AT WINNING.
NOOOOO!!
DAMN IT ALL!!
THE COURSE CAN'T BE OPEN FOREVER. THOSE WITHOUT THE ABILITY TO CROSS THE FINISH LINE ARE CUT.
MORE THAN HALF...
...WON'T BE RACING TOMOR-ROW!
WAAAAAH!
DAMN IT! AFTER IT TOOK THREE YEARS TO GET HERE!
THAT'S WHAT ROAD RACING IS.

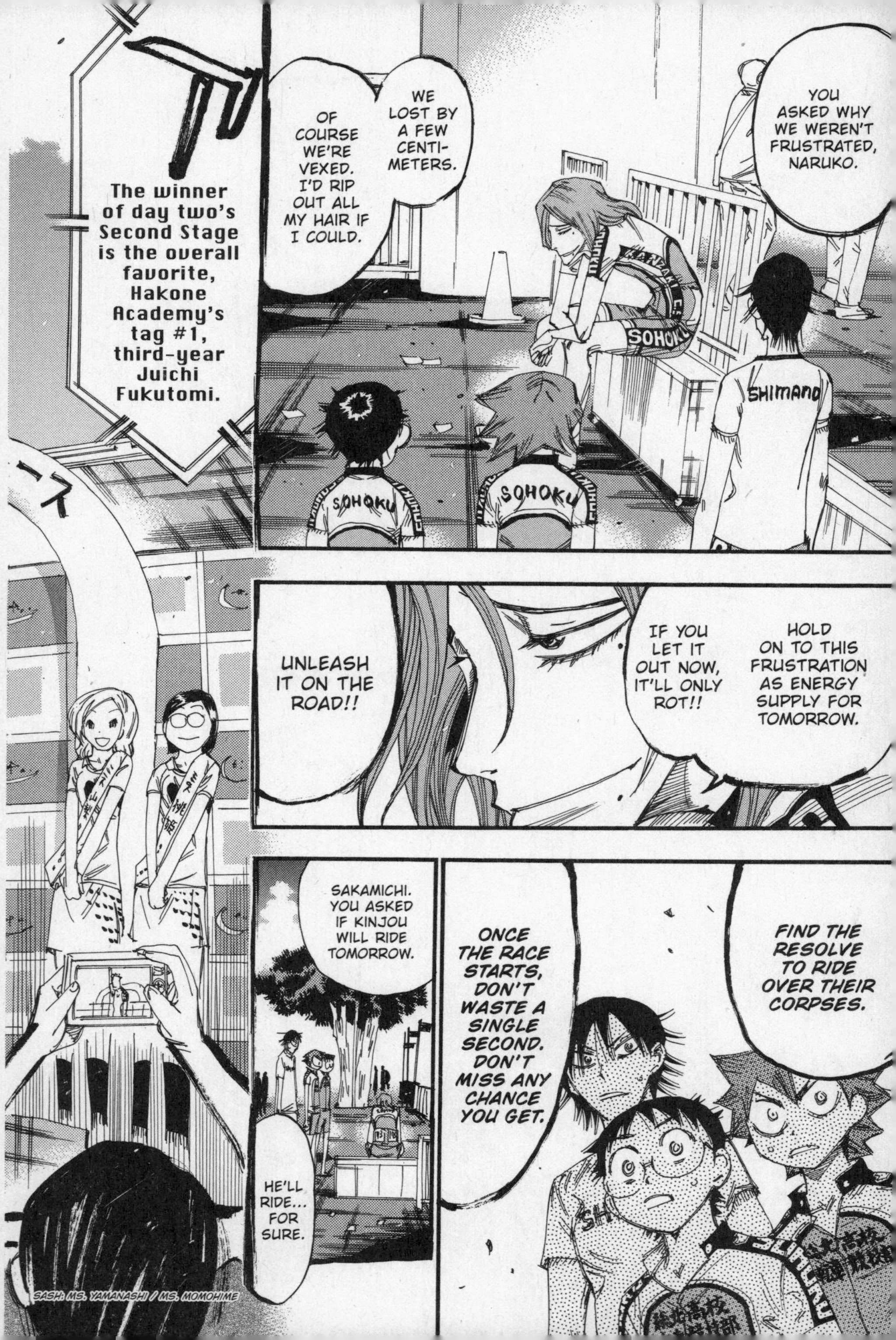
YOU ASKED WHY WE WEREN'T FRUSTRATED, NARUKO.
WE LOST BY A FEW CENTI-METERS.
OF COURSE WE'RE VEXED. I'D RIP OUT ALL MY HAIR IF I COULD.
HOLD ON TO THIS FRUSTRATION AS ENERGY SUPPLY FOR TOMORROW.
IF YOU LET IT OUT NOW, IT'LL ONLY ROT!!
UNLEASH IT ON THE ROAD!!
FIND THE RESOLVE TO RIDE OVER THEIR CORPSES.
ONCE THE RACE STARTS, DON'T WASTE A SINGLE SECOND. DON'T MISS ANY CHANCE YOU GET.
SAKAMICHI. YOU ASKED IF KINJOU WILL RIDE TOMORROW.
HE'LL RIDE... FOR SURE.
The winner of day two's Second Stage is the overall favorite, Hakone Academy's tag #1, third-year Juichi Fukutomi.
SASH: MS. YAMANASHI / MS. MOMOHIME

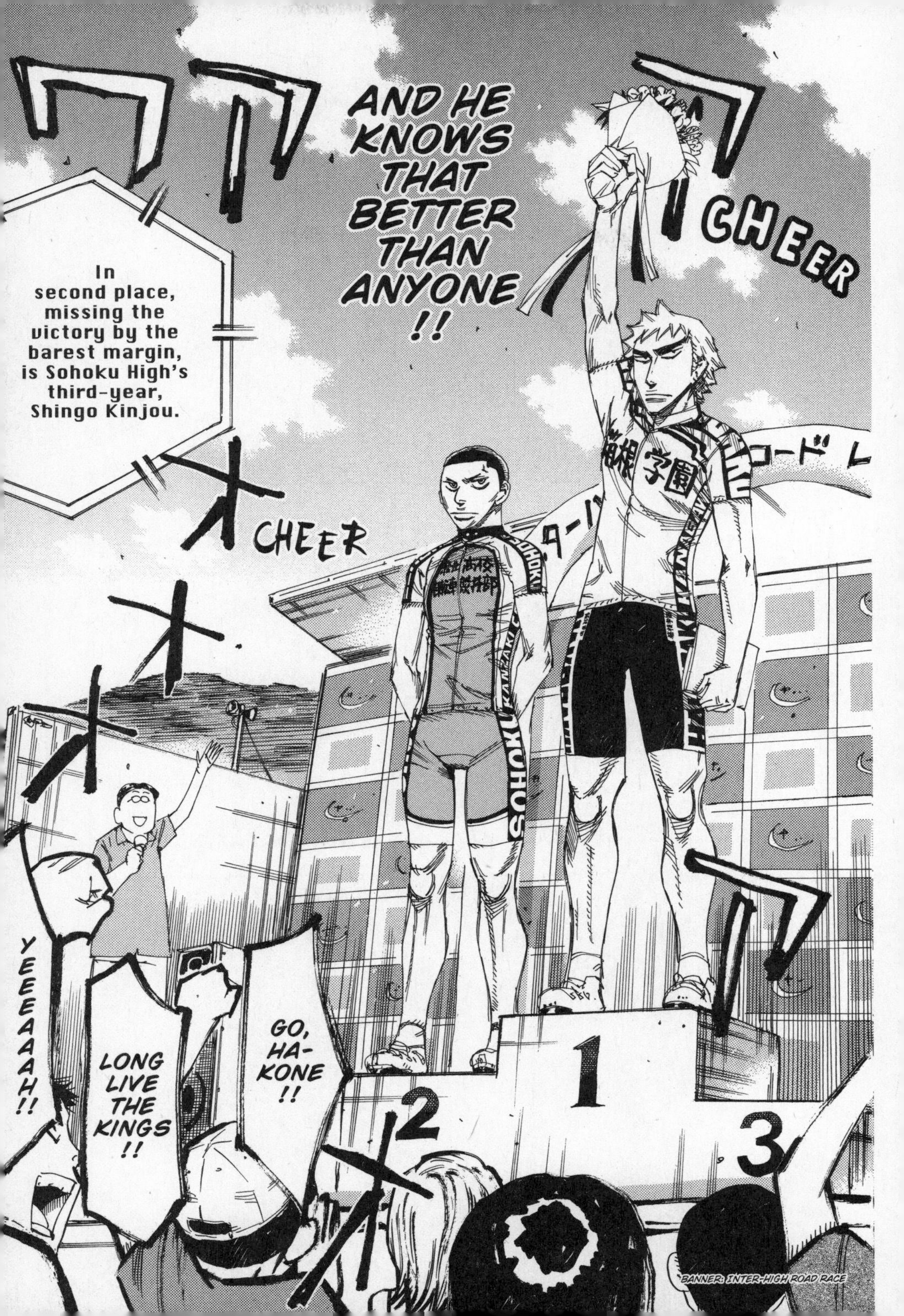
CHEER
AND HE KNOWS THAT BETTER THAN ANYONE!!
In second place, missing the victory by the barest margin, is Sohoku High's third-year, Shingo Kinjou.
CHEER
GO, HA-KONE!!
LONG LIVE THE KINGS!!
YEEEAAAAH!!
BANNER: INTER-HIGH ROAD RACE

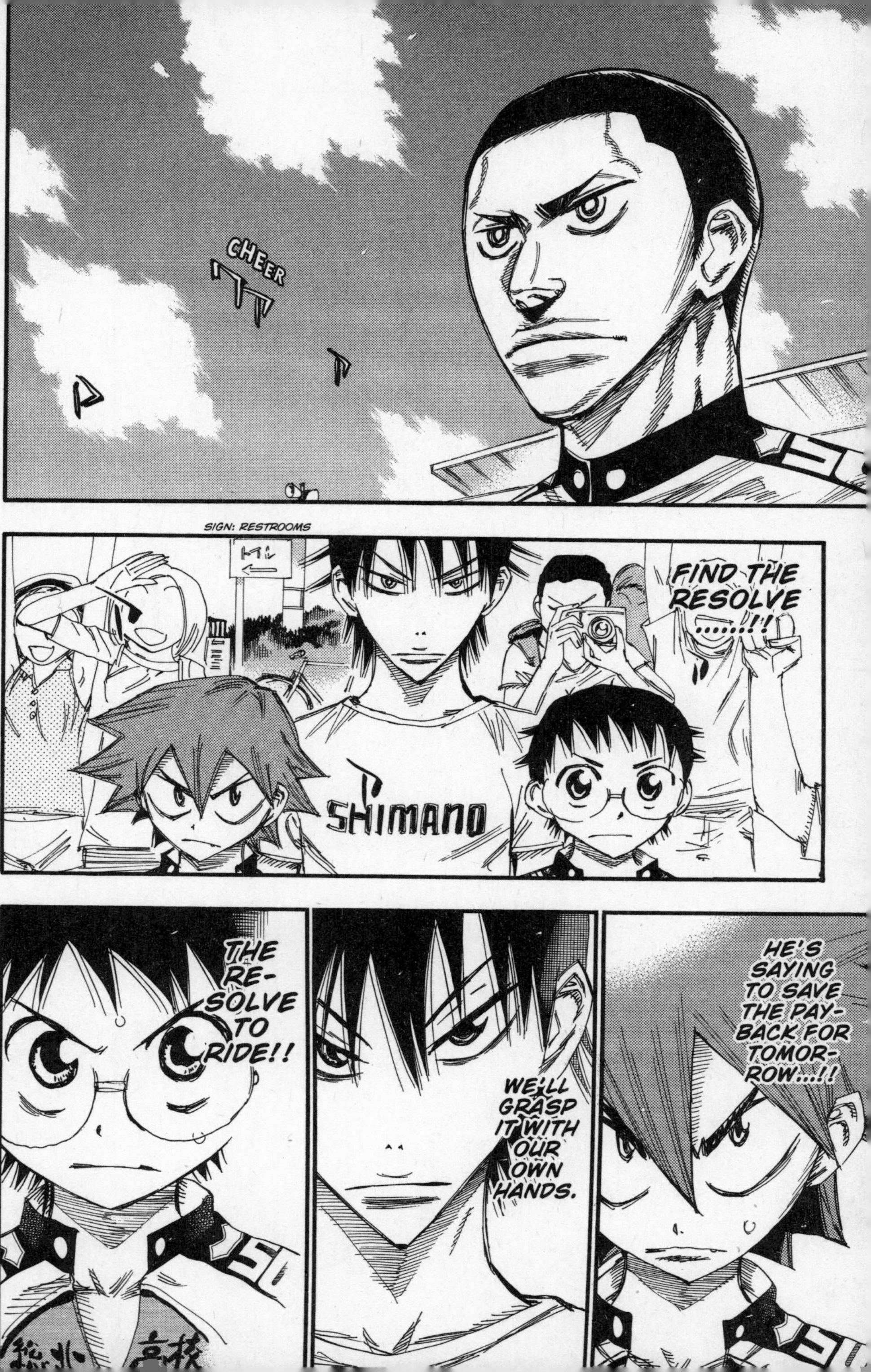
CHEER
SIGN: RESTROOMS
FIND THE RESOLVE ......!!
HE'S SAYING TO SAVE THE PAY-BACK FOR TOMOR-ROW...!!
WE'LL GRASP IT WITH OUR OWN HANDS.
THE RE-SOLVE TO RIDE!!

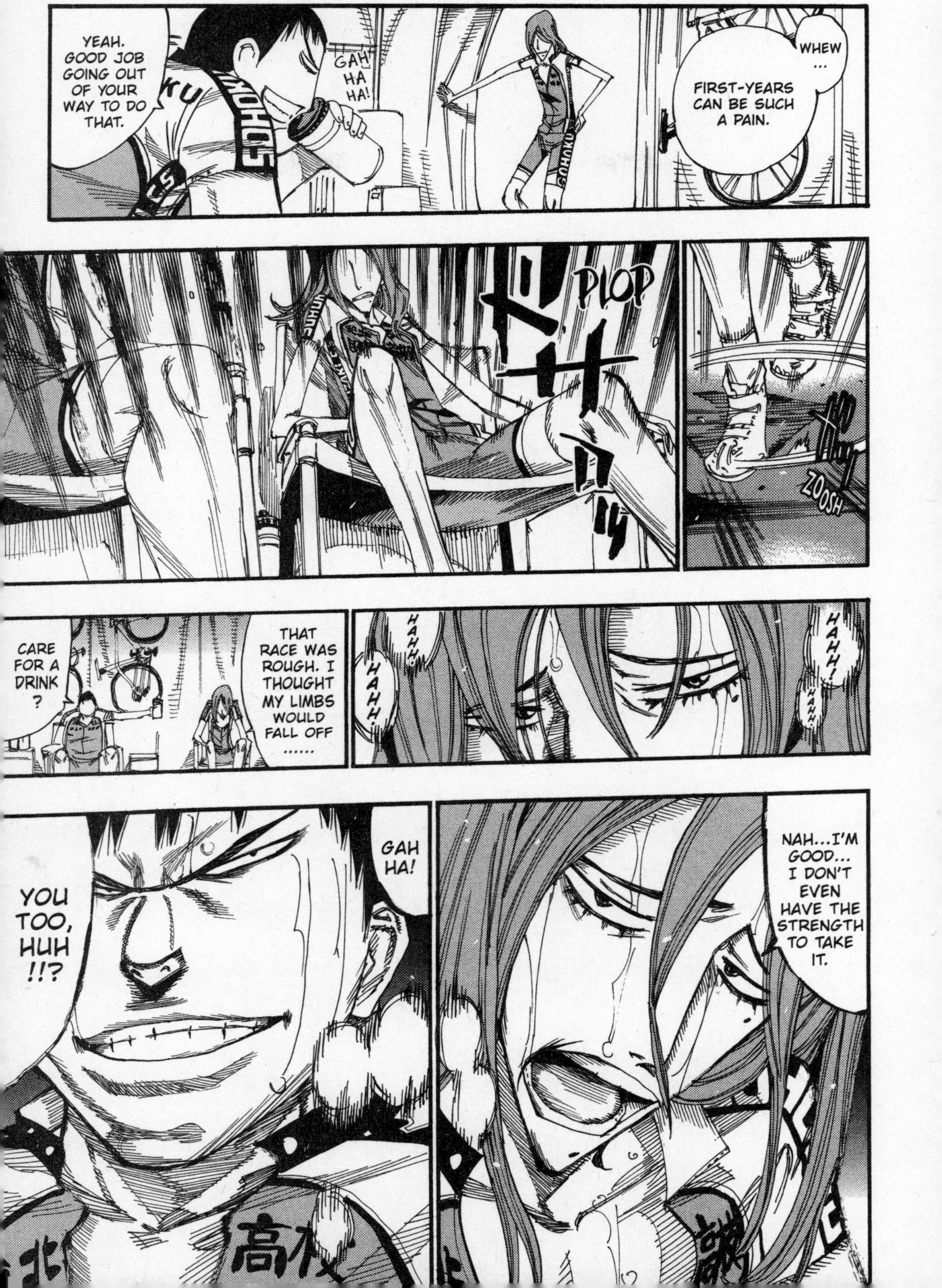
WHEW ...
FIRST-YEARS CAN BE SUCH A PAIN.
GAH HA HA!
YEAH. GOOD JOB GOING OUT OF YOUR WAY TO DO THAT.
ZOOSH
PLOP
HAHH!
HAHH
HAHH
HAHH
THAT RACE WAS ROUGH. I THOUGHT MY LIMBS WOULD FALL OFF ......
CARE FOR A DRINK ?
NAH...I'M GOOD... I DON'T EVEN HAVE THE STRENGTH TO TAKE IT.
GAH HA!
YOU TOO, HUH !!?

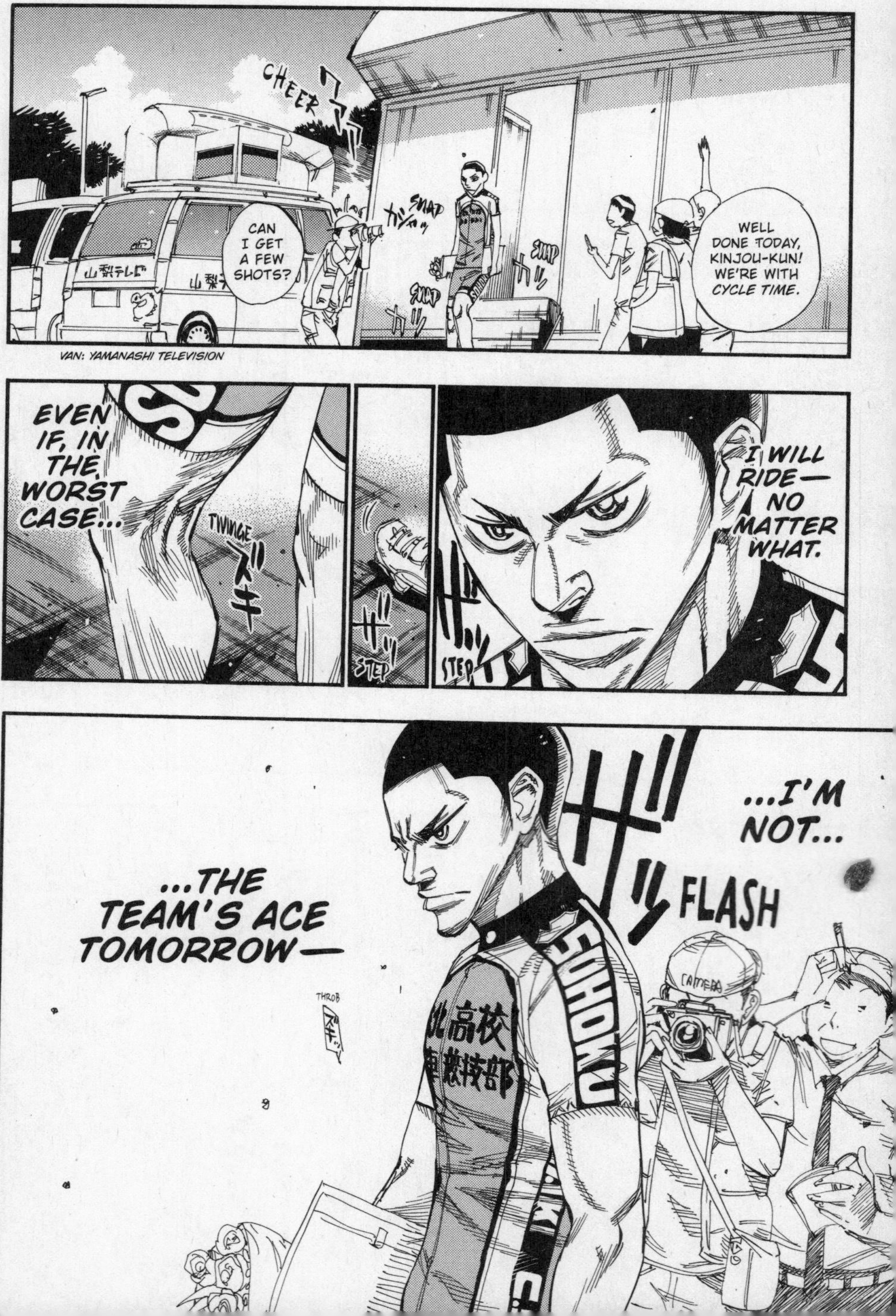
CHEER
WELL DONE TODAY, KINJOU-KUN! WE'RE WITH CYCLE TIME.
SNAP
SNAP
SNAP
CAN I GET A FEW SHOTS?
VAN: YAMANASHI TELEVISION
I WILL RIDE— NO MATTER WHAT.
STEP
STEP
EVEN IF, IN THE WORST CASE...
TWINGE
...I'M NOT...
FLASH
...THE TEAM'S ACE TOMORROW—
THROB

RIDE.156 MIDOUSUJI'S DECISION

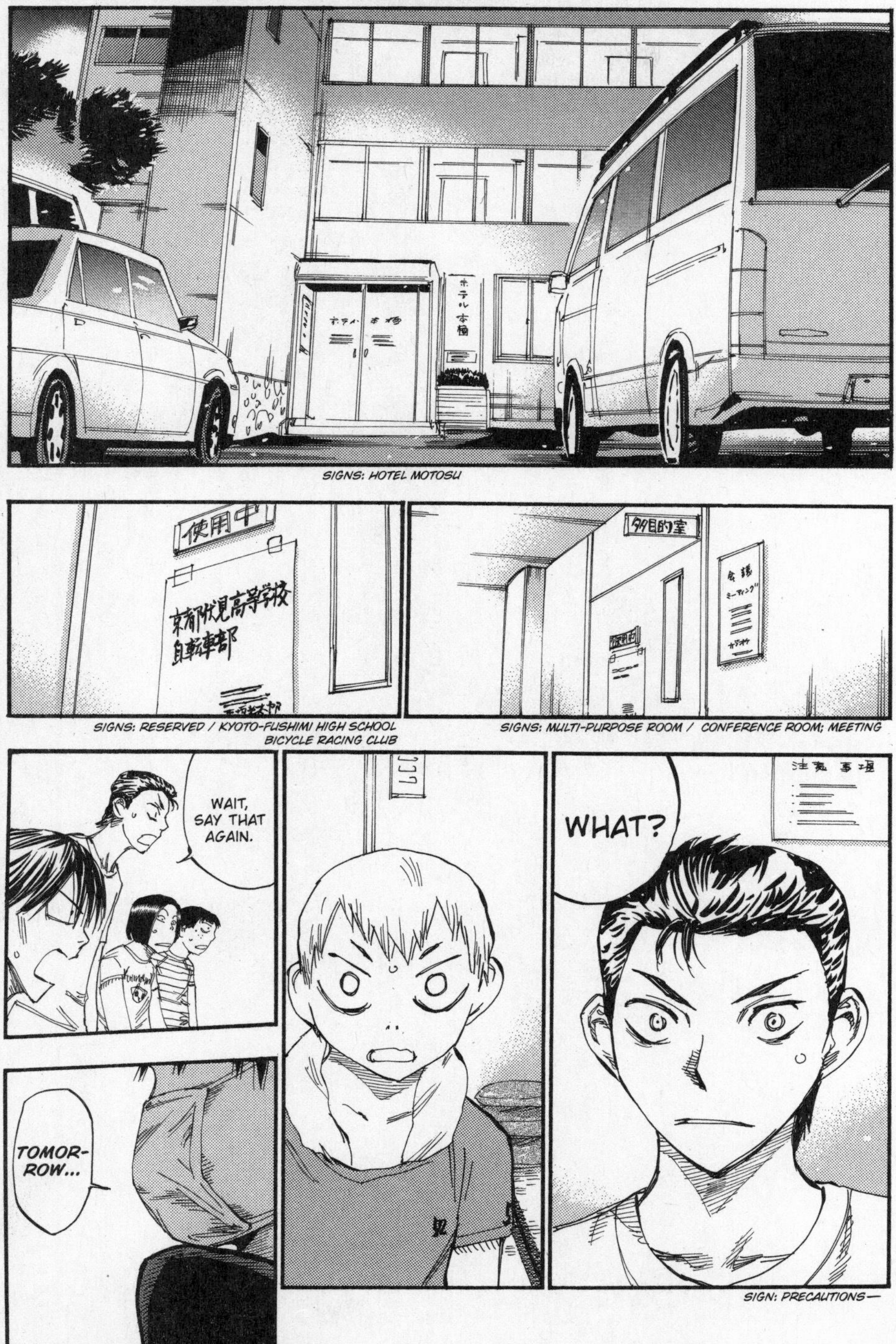
SIGNS: HOTEL MOTOSU
SIGNS: MULTI-PURPOSE ROOM / CONFERENCE ROOM; MEETING
SIGNS: RESERVED / KYOTO-FUSHIMI HIGH SCHOOL BICYCLE RACING CLUB
WHAT?
SIGN: PRECAUTIONS—
WAIT, SAY THAT AGAIN.
TOMOR-ROW...

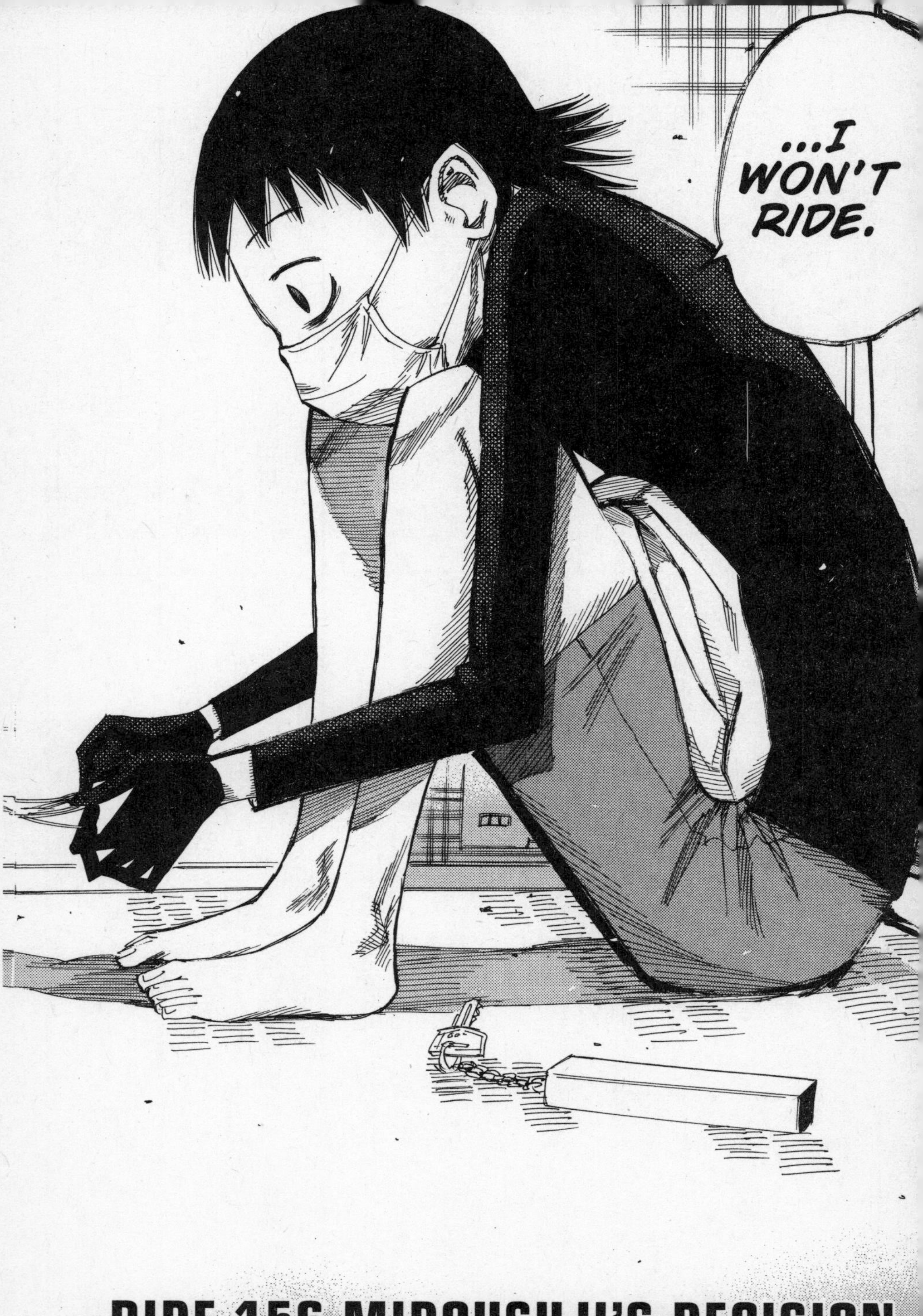
...I WON'T RIDE.

RIDE.156 MIDOUSUJI'S DECISION

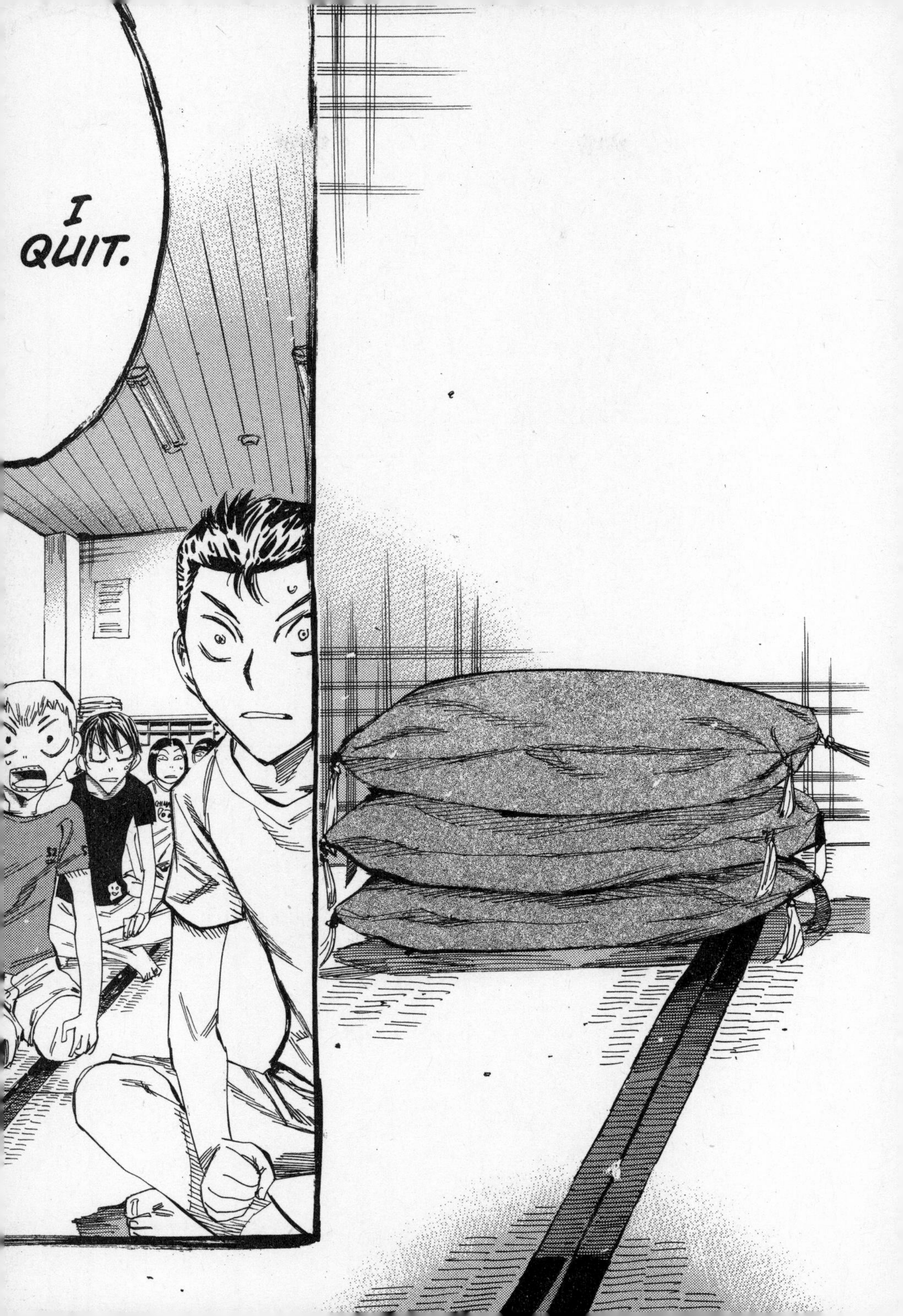
I QUIT.

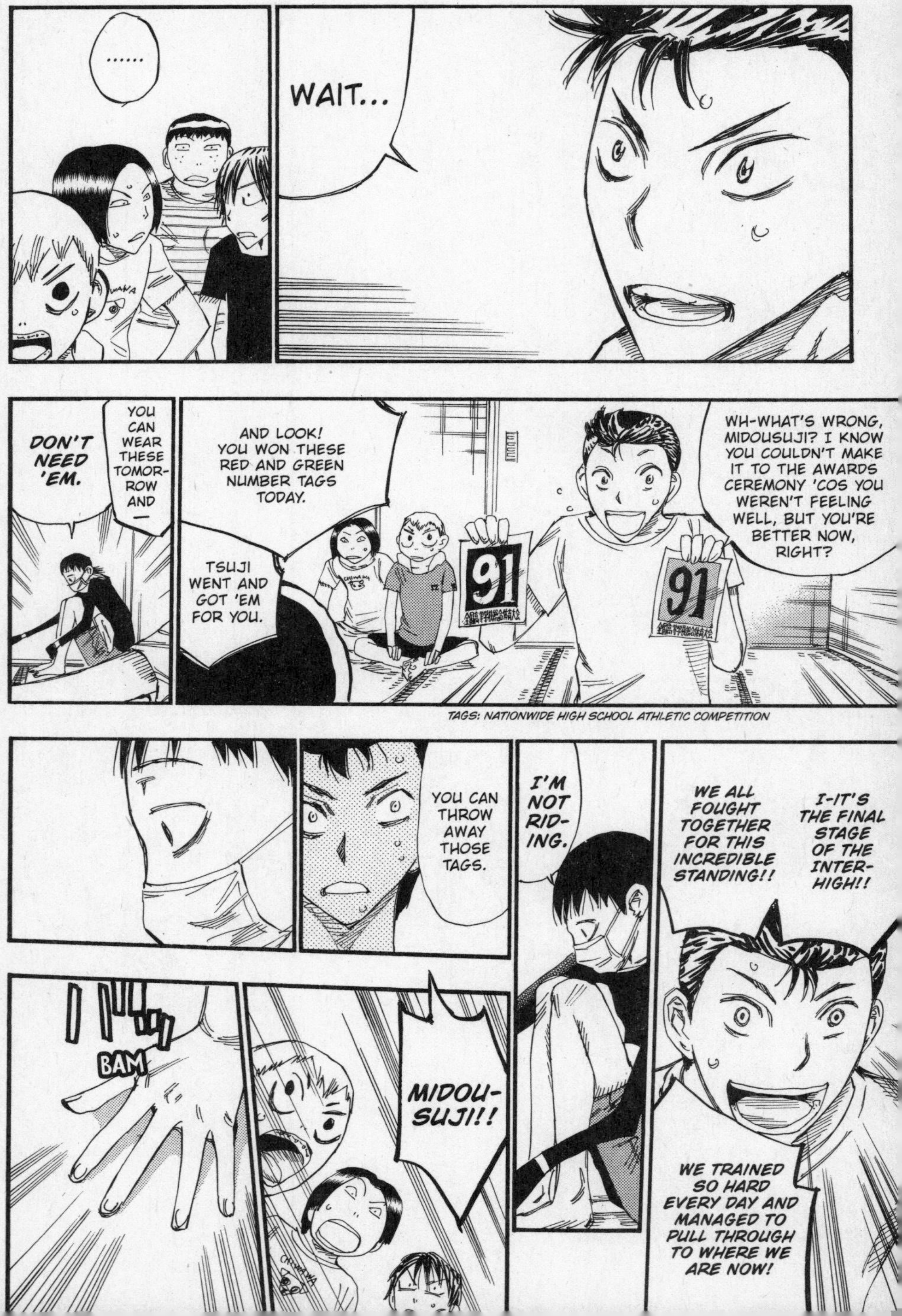
WAIT...
......
WH-WHAT'S WRONG, MIDOUSUJI? I KNOW YOU COULDN'T MAKE IT TO THE AWARDS CEREMONY 'COS YOU WEREN'T FEELING WELL, BUT YOU'RE BETTER NOW, RIGHT?
91
91
AND LOOK! YOU WON THESE RED AND GREEN NUMBER TAGS TODAY.
TSUJI WENT AND GOT 'EM FOR YOU.
YOU CAN WEAR THESE TOMORROW AND—
DON'T NEED 'EM.
TAGS: NATIONWIDE HIGH SCHOOL ATHLETIC COMPETITION
I-IT'S THE FINAL STAGE OF THE INTER-HIGH!!
WE ALL FOUGHT TOGETHER FOR THIS INCREDIBLE STANDING!!
WE TRAINED SO HARD EVERY DAY AND MANAGED TO PULL THROUGH TO WHERE WE ARE NOW!
I'M NOT RIDING.
YOU CAN THROW AWAY THOSE TAGS.
MIDOUSUJI!!
BAM

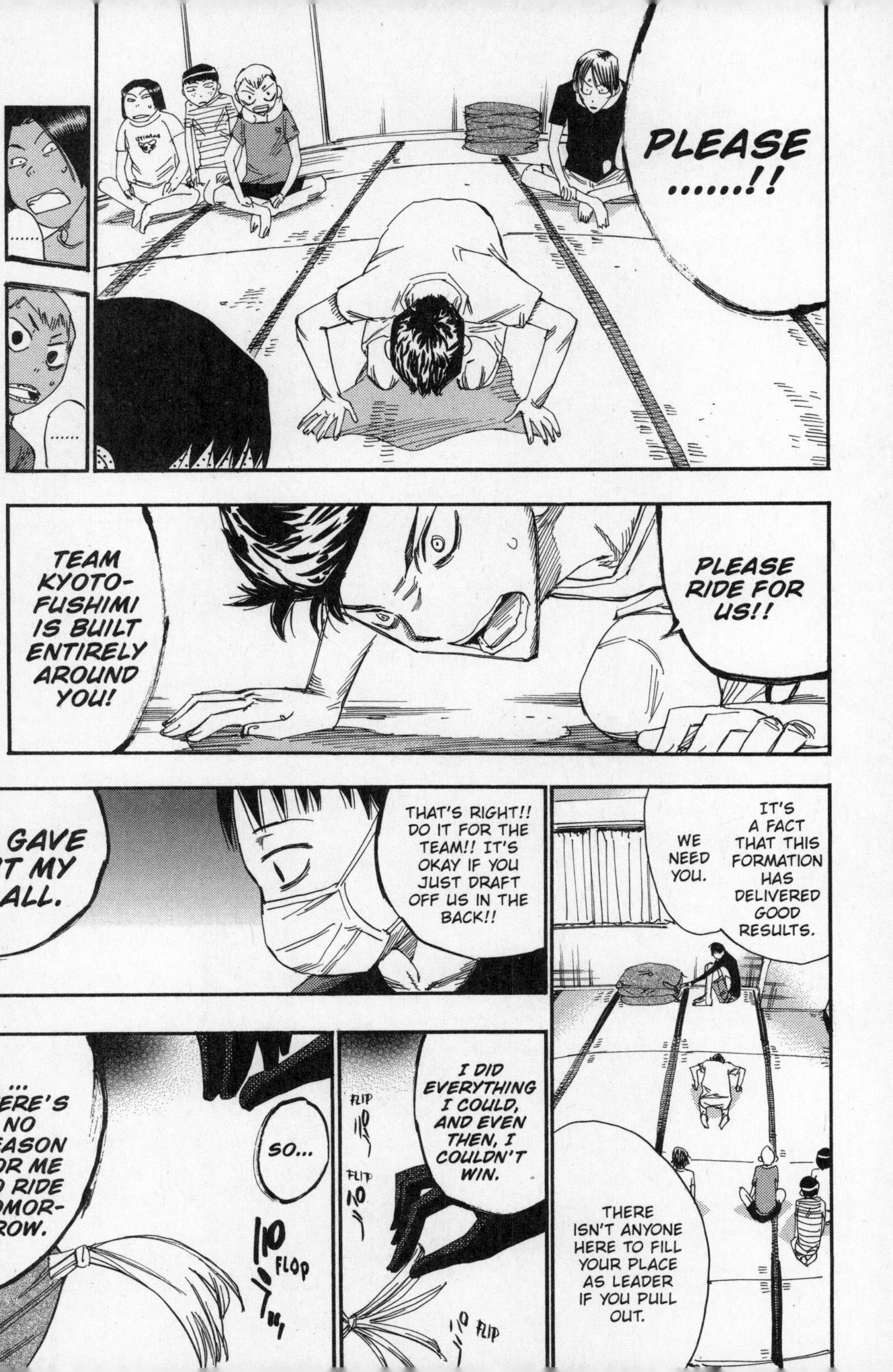
PLEASE ......!!
......
......
PLEASE RIDE FOR US!!
TEAM KYOTO-FUSHIMI IS BUILT ENTIRELY AROUND YOU!
IT'S A FACT THAT THIS FORMATION HAS DELIVERED GOOD RESULTS.
WE NEED YOU.
THERE ISN'T ANYONE HERE TO FILL YOUR PLACE AS LEADER IF YOU PULL OUT.
THAT'S RIGHT!! DO IT FOR THE TEAM!! IT'S OKAY IF YOU JUST DRAFT OFF US IN THE BACK!!
I GAVE IT MY ALL.
I DID EVERYTHING I COULD, AND EVEN THEN, I COULDN'T WIN.
FLIP
FLIP
FLIP
SO...
... THERE'S NO REASON FOR ME TO RIDE TOMORROW.
FLOP

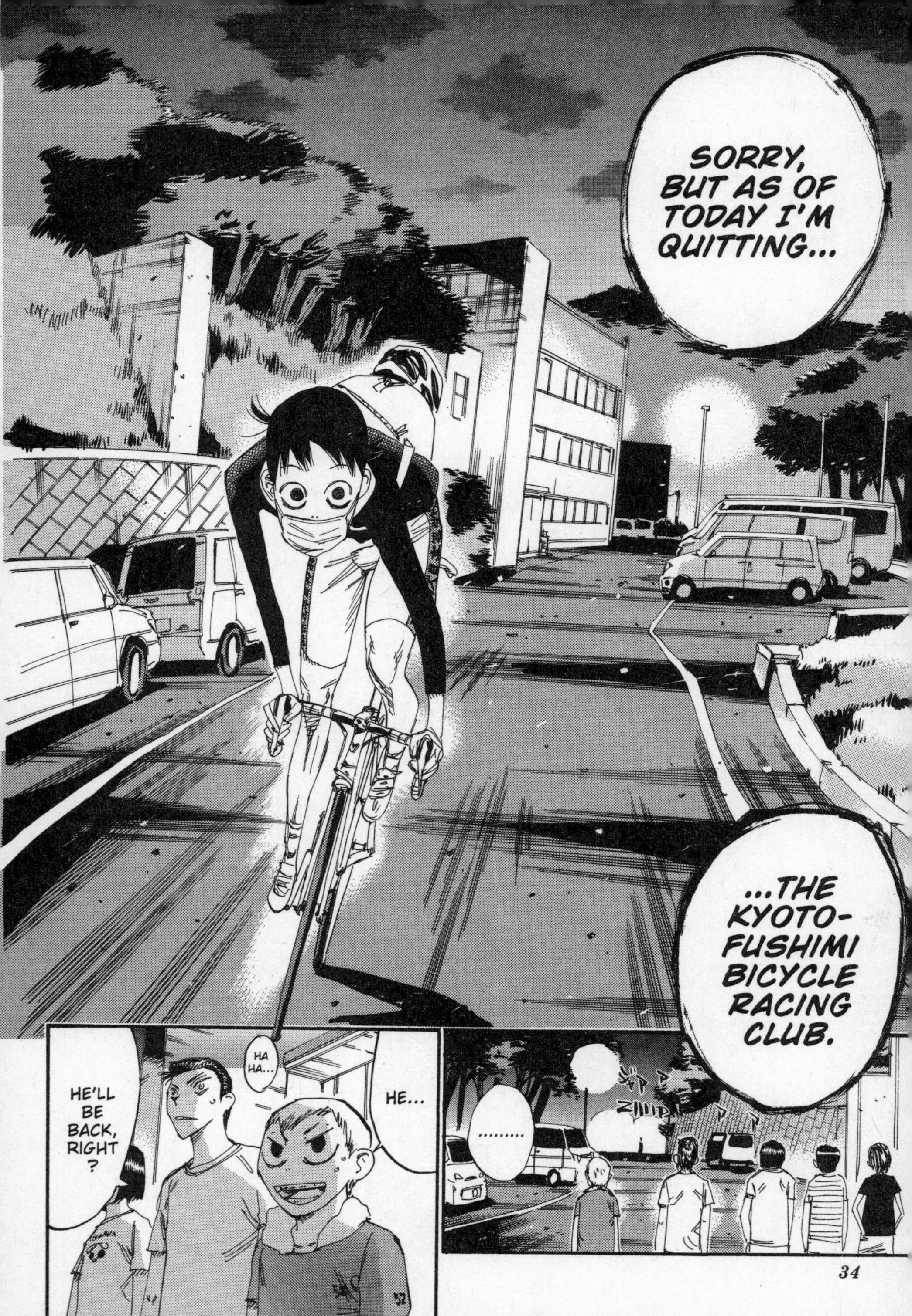
SORRY, BUT AS OF TODAY I'M QUITTING...
...THE KYOTO-FUSHIMI BICYCLE RACING CLUB.
....
ZIIIIP
HA HA...
HE...
HE'LL BE BACK, RIGHT?

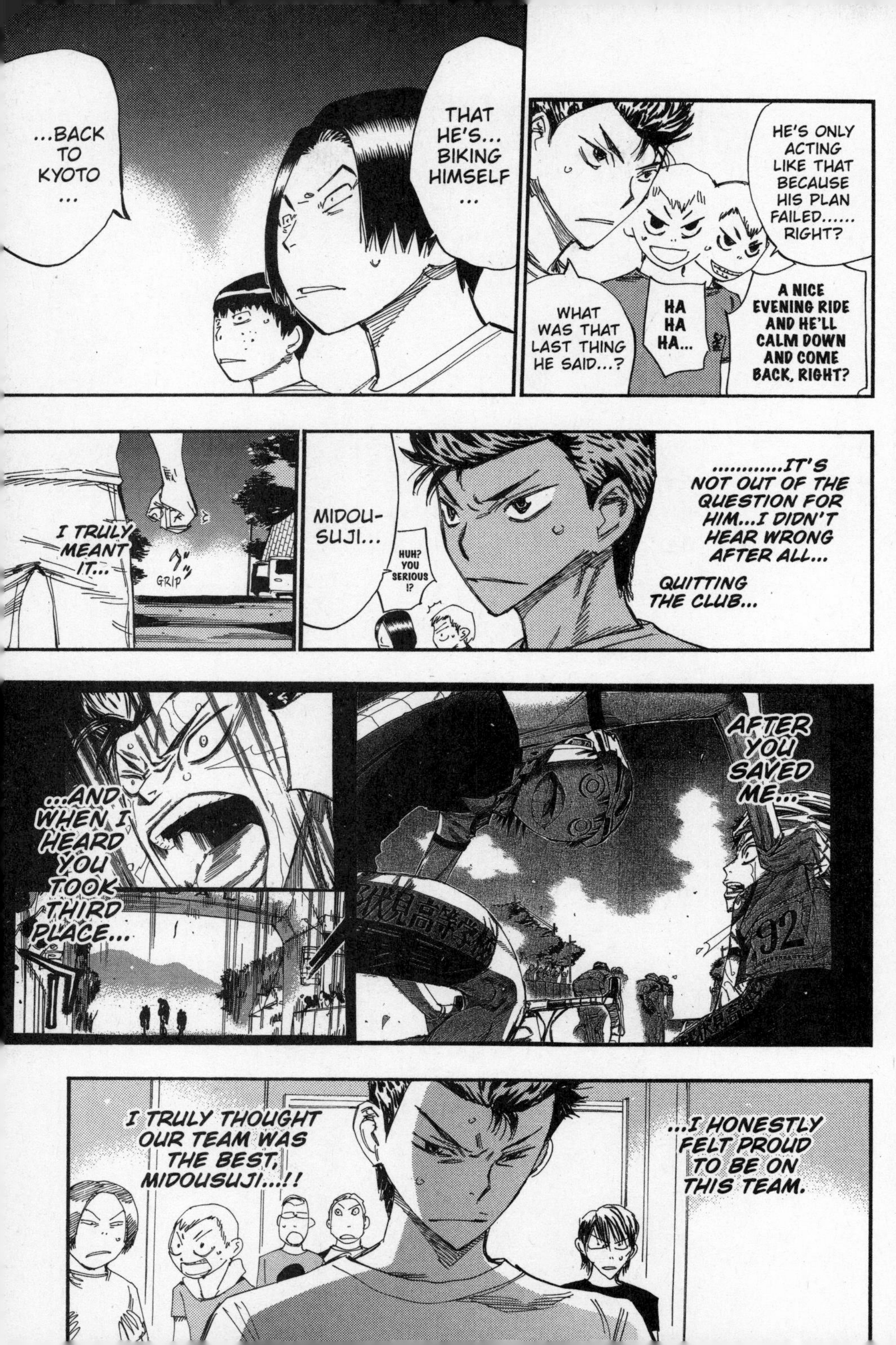
HE'S ONLY ACTING LIKE THAT BECAUSE HIS PLAN FAILED...... RIGHT?
A NICE EVENING RIDE AND HE'LL CALM DOWN AND COME BACK, RIGHT?
HA HA HA...
WHAT WAS THAT LAST THING HE SAID...?
THAT HE'S... BIKING HIMSELF ...
...BACK TO KYOTO ...
............IT'S NOT OUT OF THE QUESTION FOR HIM...I DIDN'T HEAR WRONG AFTER ALL...
QUITTING THE CLUB...
HUH? YOU SERIOUS !?
MIDOUSUJI...
I TRULY MEANT IT...
GRIP
AFTER YOU SAVED ME...
...AND WHEN I HEARD YOU TOOK THIRD PLACE...
...I HONESTLY FELT PROUD TO BE ON THIS TEAM.
I TRULY THOUGHT OUR TEAM WAS THE BEST, MIDOUSUJI...!!

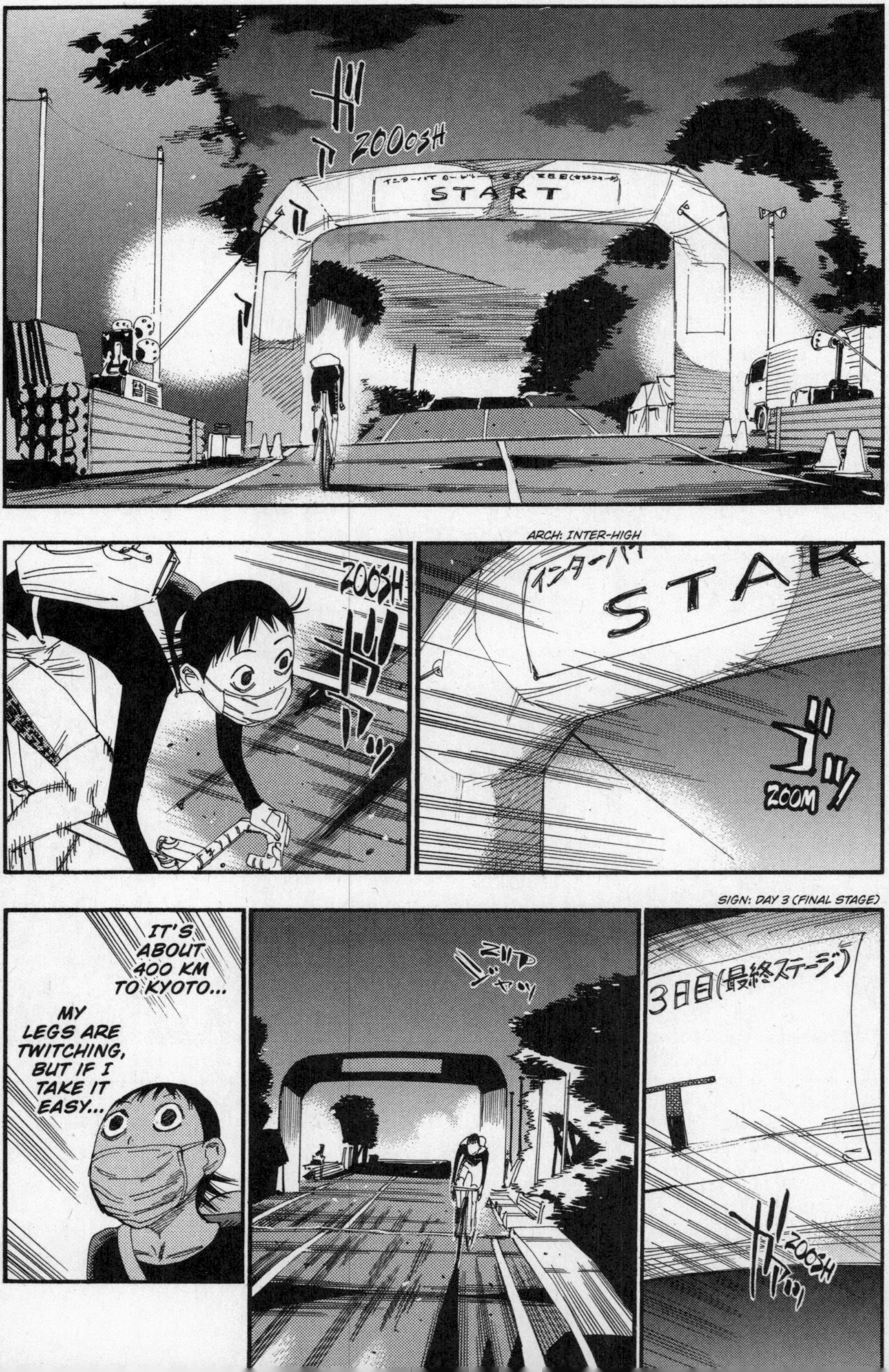
ザ
ZOOOSH
START
ARCH: INTER-HIGH
インターハ
STAR
ゴッ
ZOOM
ZOOSH
ザッ
SIGN: DAY 3 (FINAL STAGE)
3日目(最終ステージ)
ザザ
ZOOSH
ZIP
ジャッ
IT'S ABOUT 400 KM TO KYOTO...
MY LEGS ARE TWITCHING, BUT IF I TAKE IT EASY...

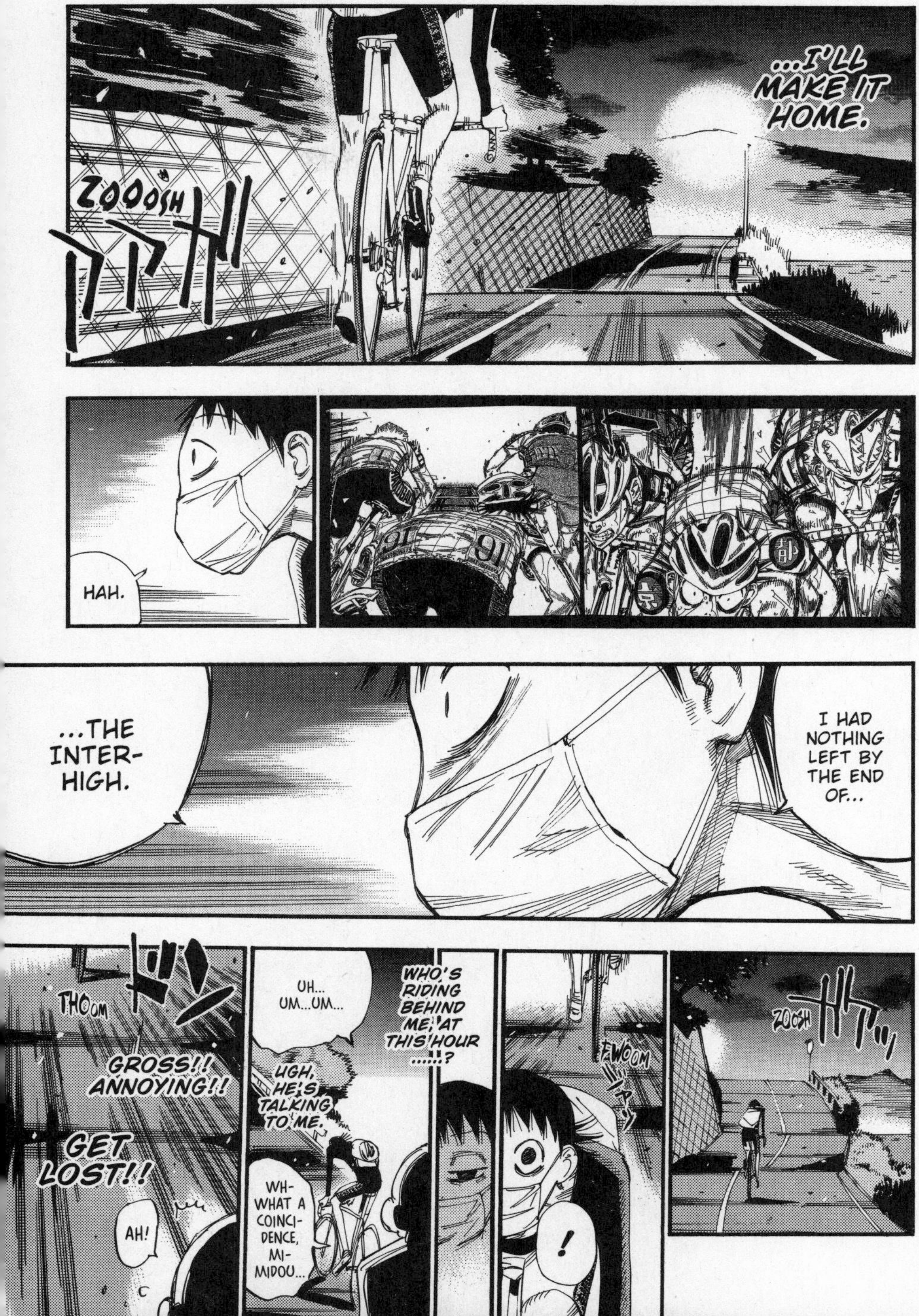
...I'LL MAKE IT HOME.
ZOOOSH
I HAD NOTHING LEFT BY THE END OF...
...THE INTER-HIGH.
HAH.
ZOOSH
FWOOM
!
WHO'S RIDING BEHIND ME, AT THIS HOUR ......?
UH... UM...UM...
UGH, HE'S TALKING TO ME.
WH-WHAT A COINCIDENCE, MI-MIDOU...
THOOM
GROSS!! ANNOYING!!
GET LOST!!
AH!

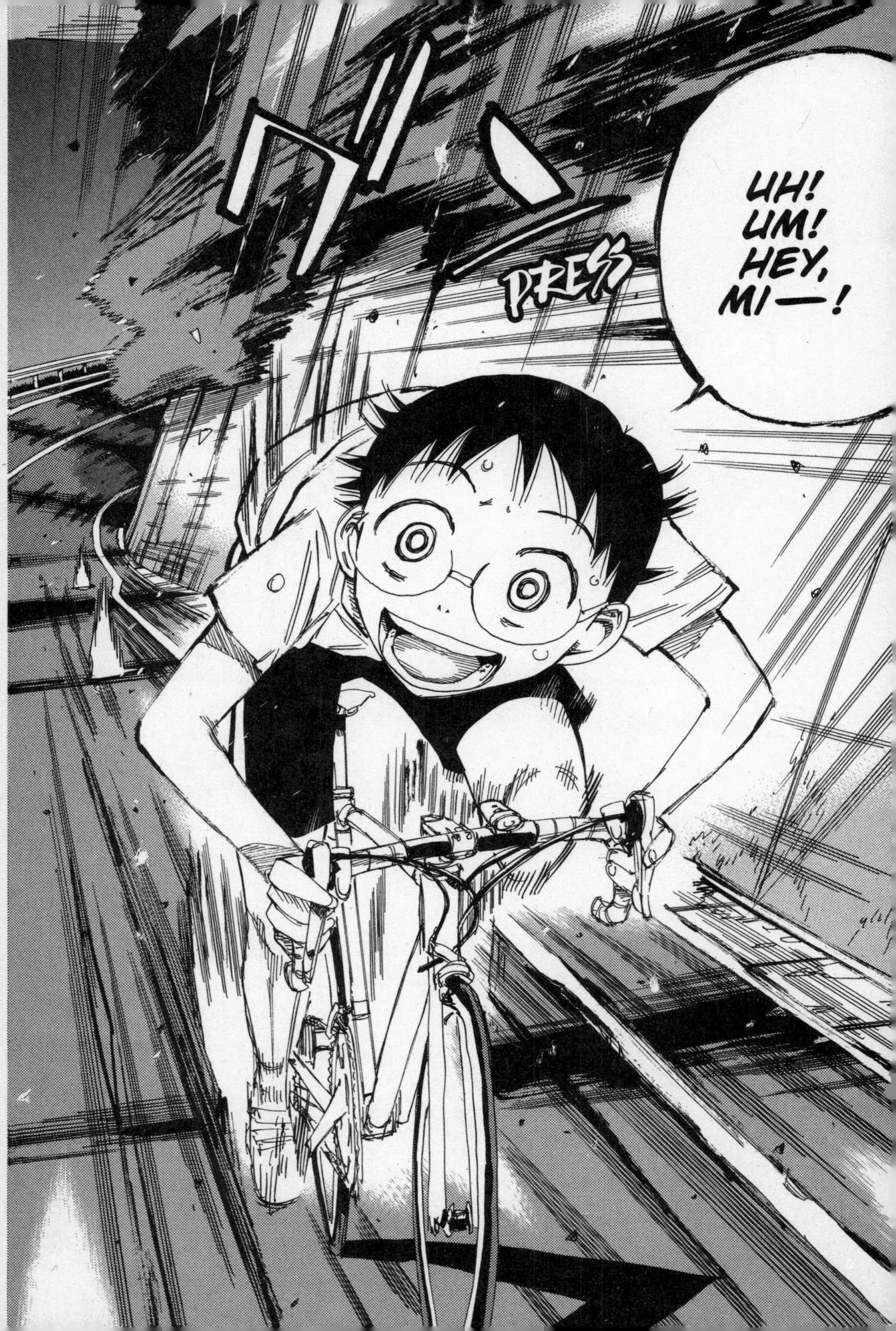
UH! UM! HEY, MI—!
PRESS

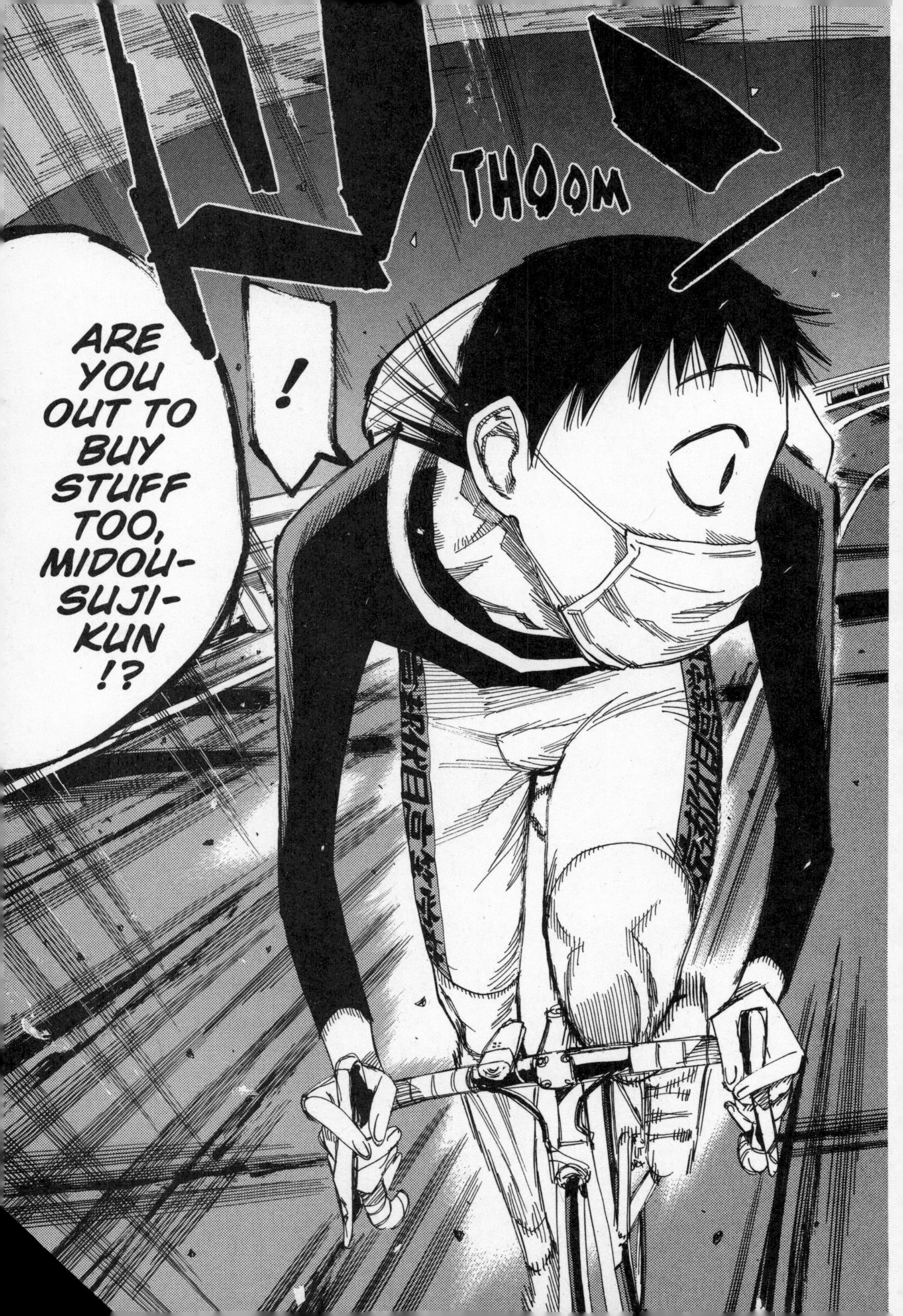
THOOM
!
ARE YOU OUT TO BUY STUFF TOO, MIDOU-SUJI-KUN!?

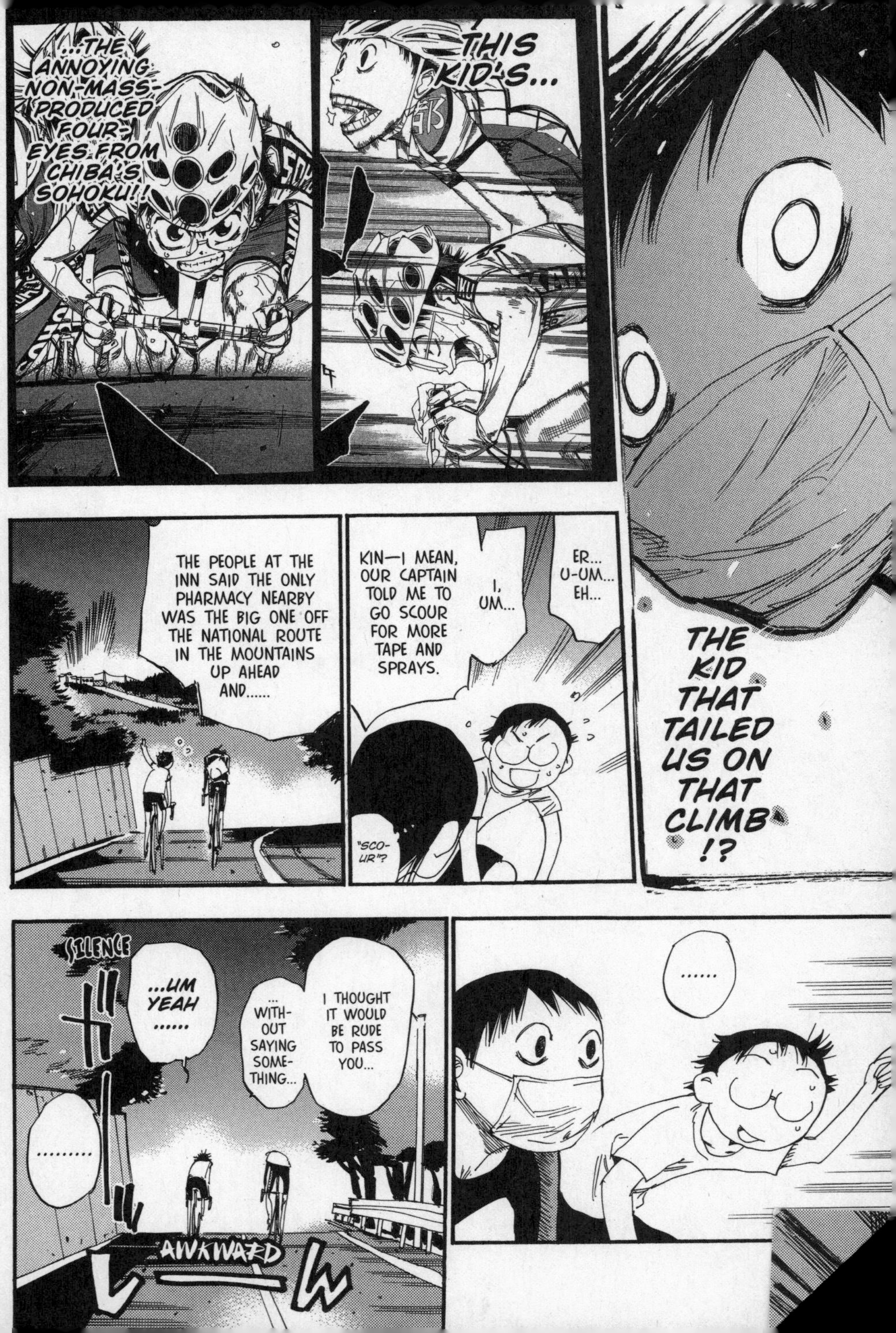
THE KID THAT TAILED US ON THAT CLIMB!?
THIS KID'S...
...THE ANNOYING NON-MASS-PRODUCED FOUR-EYES FROM CHIBA'S SOHOKU!!
ER... U-UM... EH...
I, UM...
KIN—I MEAN, OUR CAPTAIN TOLD ME TO GO SCOUR FOR MORE TAPE AND SPRAYS.
"SCOUR"?
THE PEOPLE AT THE INN SAID THE ONLY PHARMACY NEARBY WAS THE BIG ONE OFF THE NATIONAL ROUTE IN THE MOUNTAINS UP AHEAD AND......
......
I THOUGHT IT WOULD BE RUDE TO PASS YOU...
...WITHOUT SAYING SOMETHING...
...UM YEAH ......
SILENCE
....
AWKWARD

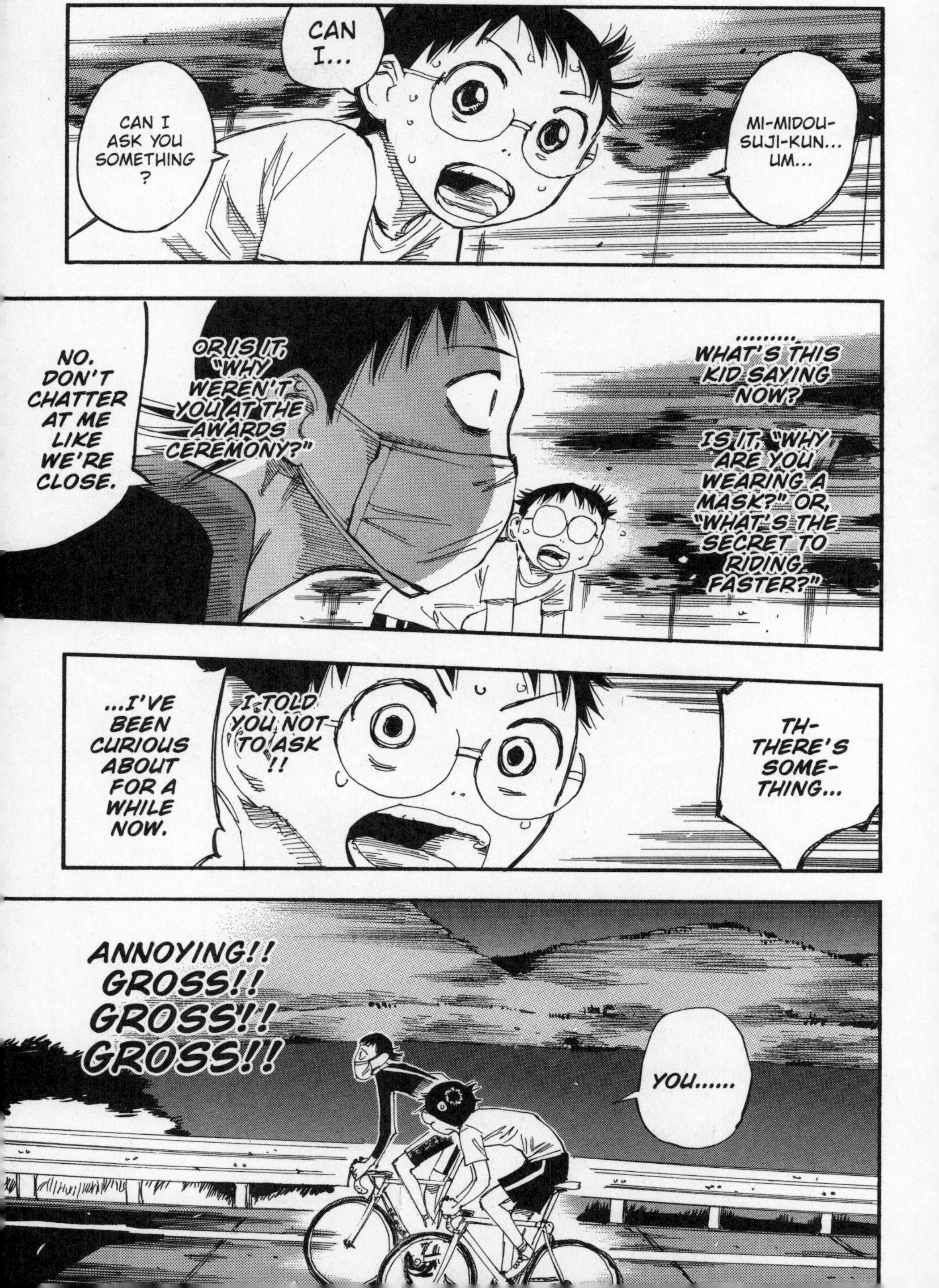

MI-MIDOU-SUJI-KUN... UM...
CAN I...
CAN I ASK YOU SOMETHING ?
.... WHAT'S THIS KID SAYING NOW?
IS IT, "WHY ARE YOU WEARING A MASK?" OR, "WHAT'S THE SECRET TO RIDING FASTER?"
OR IS IT, "WHY WEREN'T YOU AT THE AWARDS CEREMONY?"
NO. DON'T CHATTER AT ME LIKE WE'RE CLOSE.
TH-THERE'S SOME-THING...
I TOLD YOU NOT TO ASK !!
...I'VE BEEN CURIOUS ABOUT FOR A WHILE NOW.
YOU......
ANNOYING!! GROSS!! GROSS!! GROSS!!

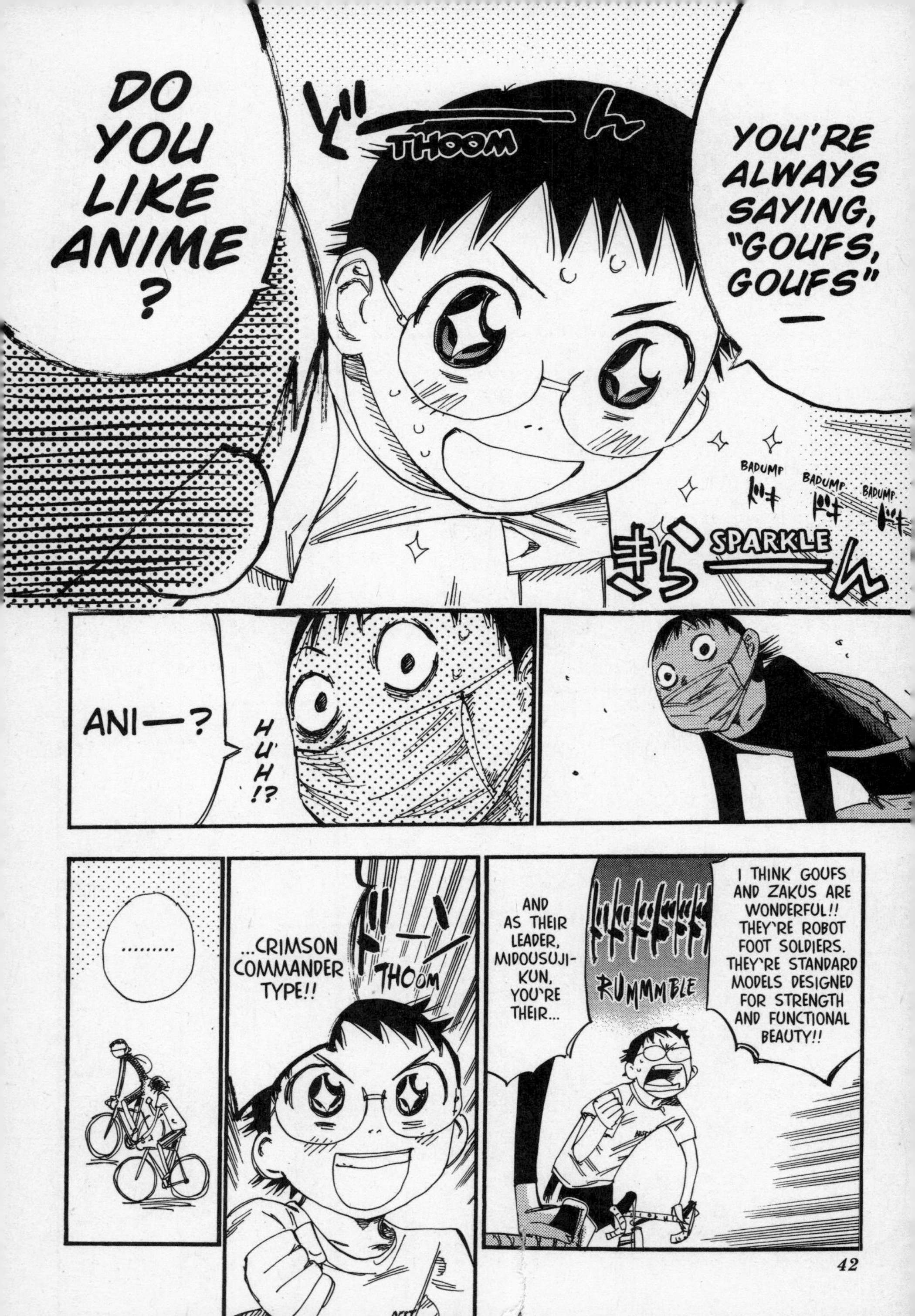
YOU'RE ALWAYS SAYING, "GOUFS, GOUFS" —
DO YOU LIKE ANIME?
THOOM
BADUMP
BADUMP
BADUMP
SPARKLE
ANI—?
HUH!?
I THINK GOUFS AND ZAKUS ARE WONDERFUL!! THEY'RE ROBOT FOOT SOLDIERS. THEY'RE STANDARD MODELS DESIGNED FOR STRENGTH AND FUNCTIONAL BEAUTY!!
RUMMMBLE
AND AS THEIR LEADER, MIDOUSUJI-KUN, YOU'RE THEIR...
...CRIMSON COMMANDER TYPE!!
THOOM
....

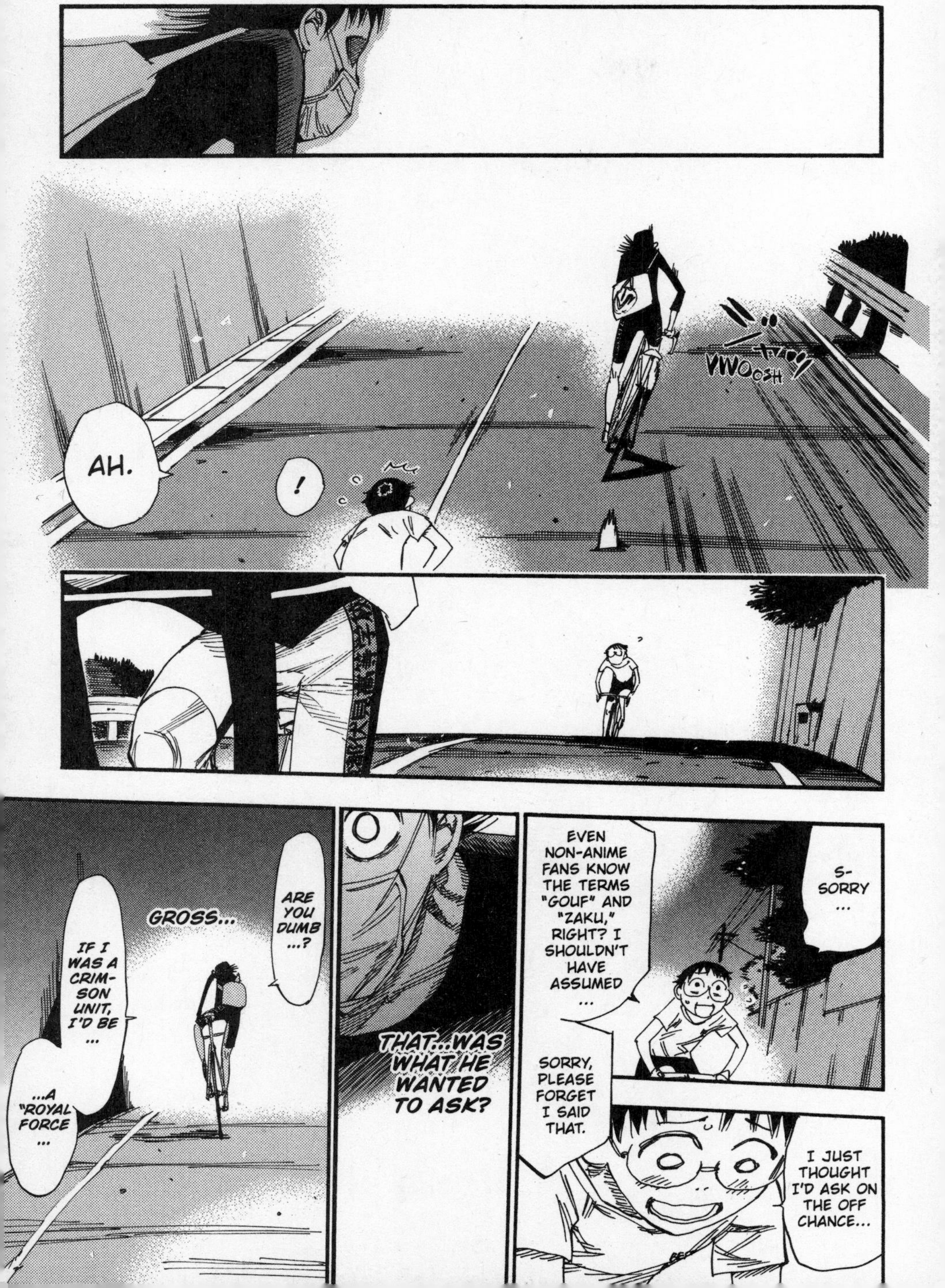
VWOOSH
AH.
!
S-SORRY...
EVEN NON-ANIME FANS KNOW THE TERMS "GOUF" AND "ZAKU," RIGHT? I SHOULDN'T HAVE ASSUMED...
SORRY, PLEASE FORGET I SAID THAT.
I JUST THOUGHT I'D ASK ON THE OFF CHANCE...
THAT...WAS WHAT HE WANTED TO ASK?
ARE YOU DUMB...?
GROSS...
IF I WAS A CRIM-SON UNIT, I'D BE...
...A "ROYAL FORCE"...

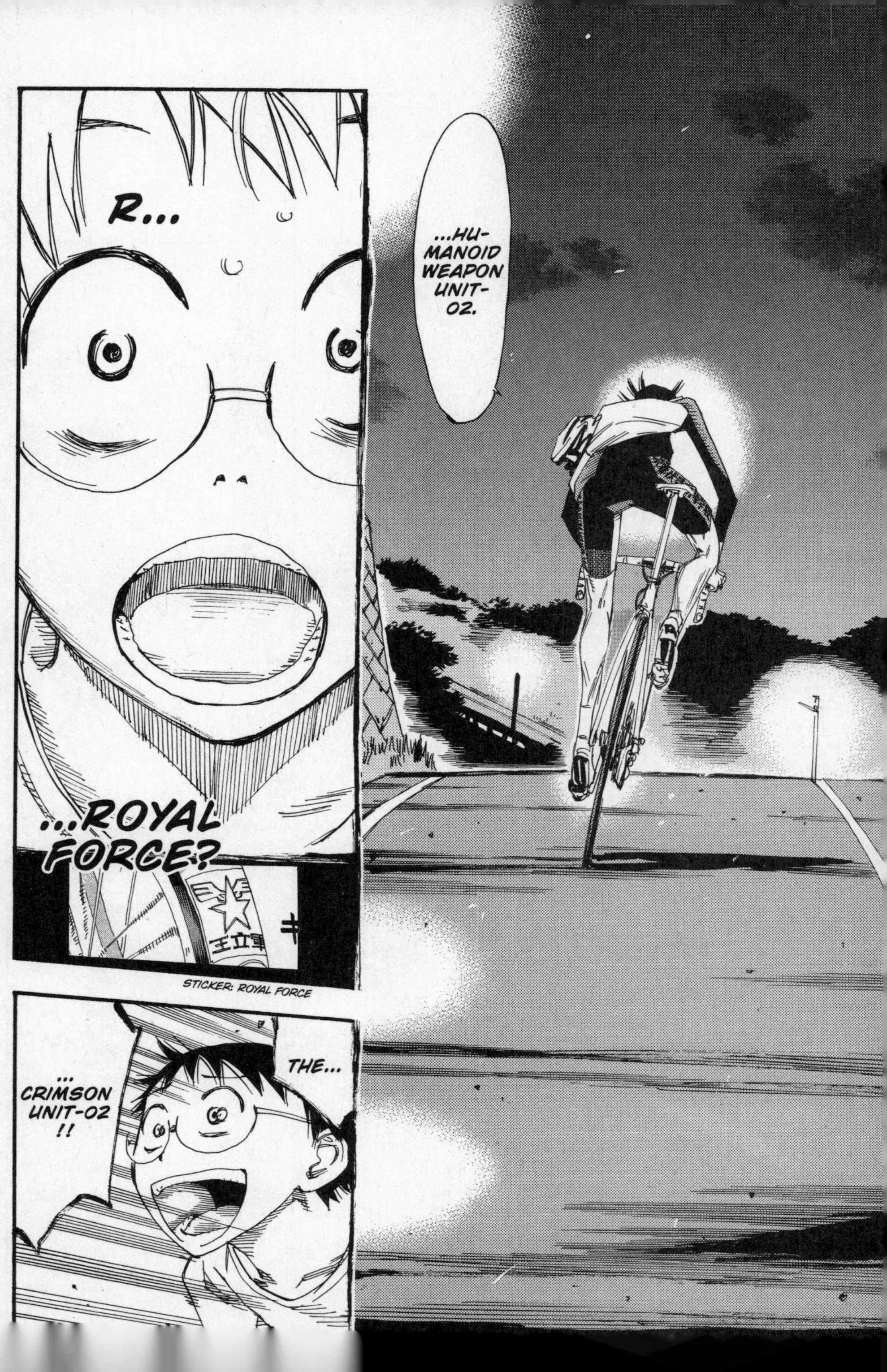
...HU-MANOID WEAPON UNIT-02.
R...
...ROYAL FORCE?
STICKER: ROYAL FORCE
THE...
...CRIMSON UNIT-02!!

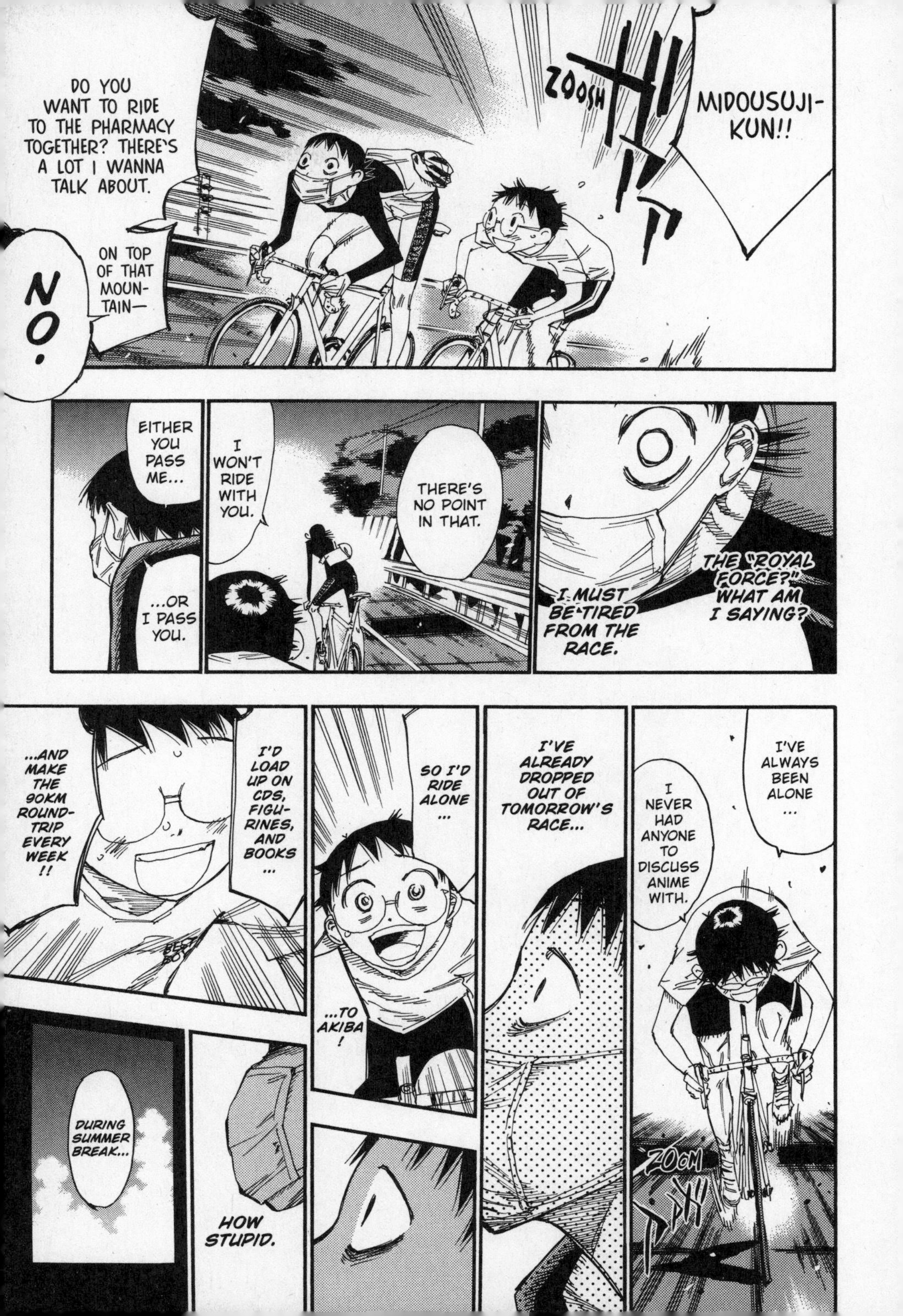
MIDOUSUJI-KUN!!
ZOOSH
DO YOU WANT TO RIDE TO THE PHARMACY TOGETHER? THERE'S A LOT I WANNA TALK ABOUT.
ON TOP OF THAT MOUNTAIN—
NO.
THE "ROYAL FORCE?" WHAT AM I SAYING?
I MUST BE TIRED FROM THE RACE.
THERE'S NO POINT IN THAT.
I WON'T RIDE WITH YOU.
EITHER YOU PASS ME...
...OR I PASS YOU.
I'VE ALWAYS BEEN ALONE ...
I NEVER HAD ANYONE TO DISCUSS ANIME WITH.
ZOOM
I'VE ALREADY DROPPED OUT OF TOMORROW'S RACE...
SO I'D RIDE ALONE ...
...TO AKIBA !
I'D LOAD UP ON CDS, FIGURINES, AND BOOKS ...
...AND MAKE THE 90KM ROUND-TRIP EVERY WEEK !!
HOW STUPID.
DURING SUMMER BREAK...

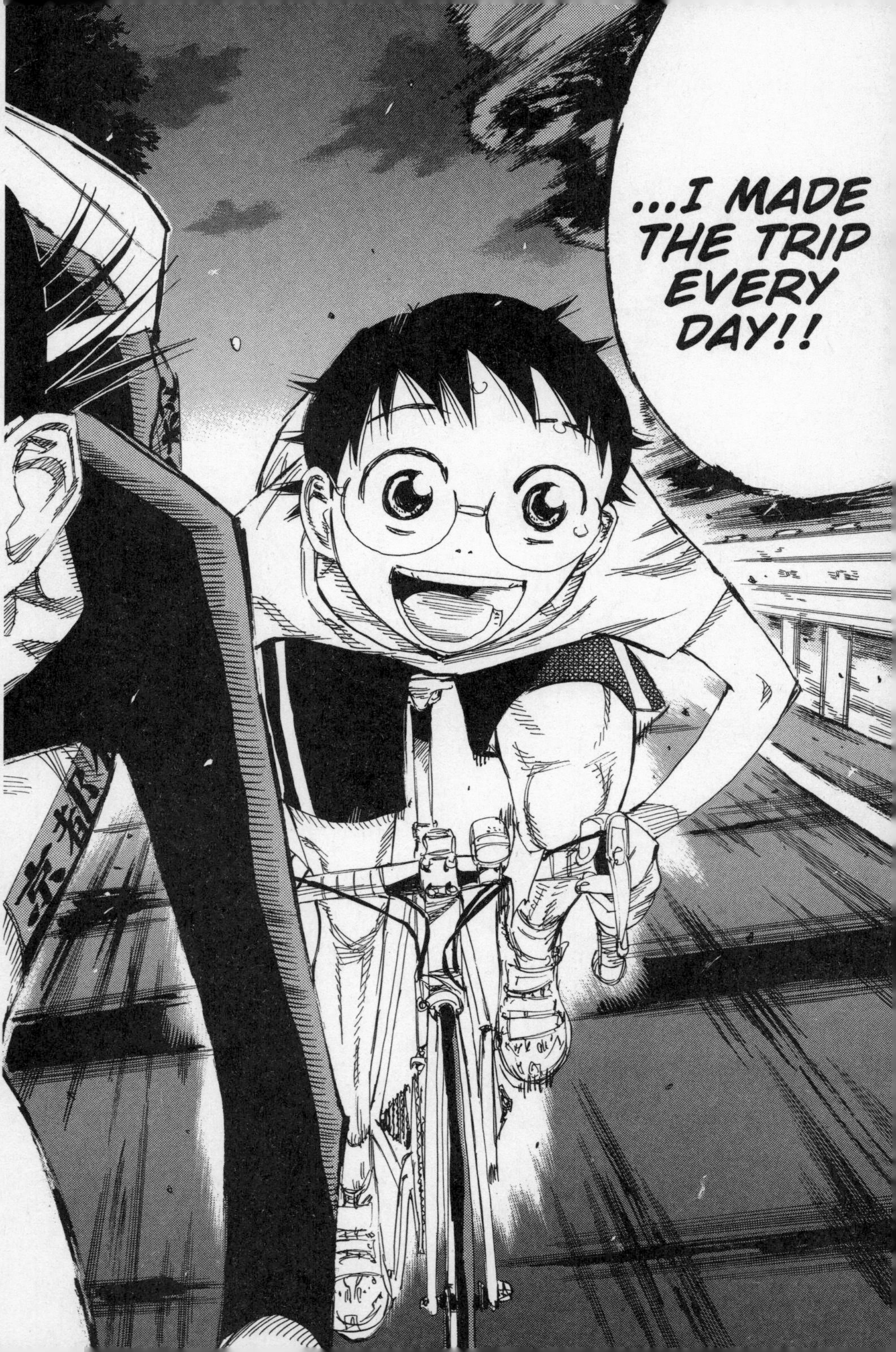
...I MADE THE TRIP EVERY DAY!!
京都

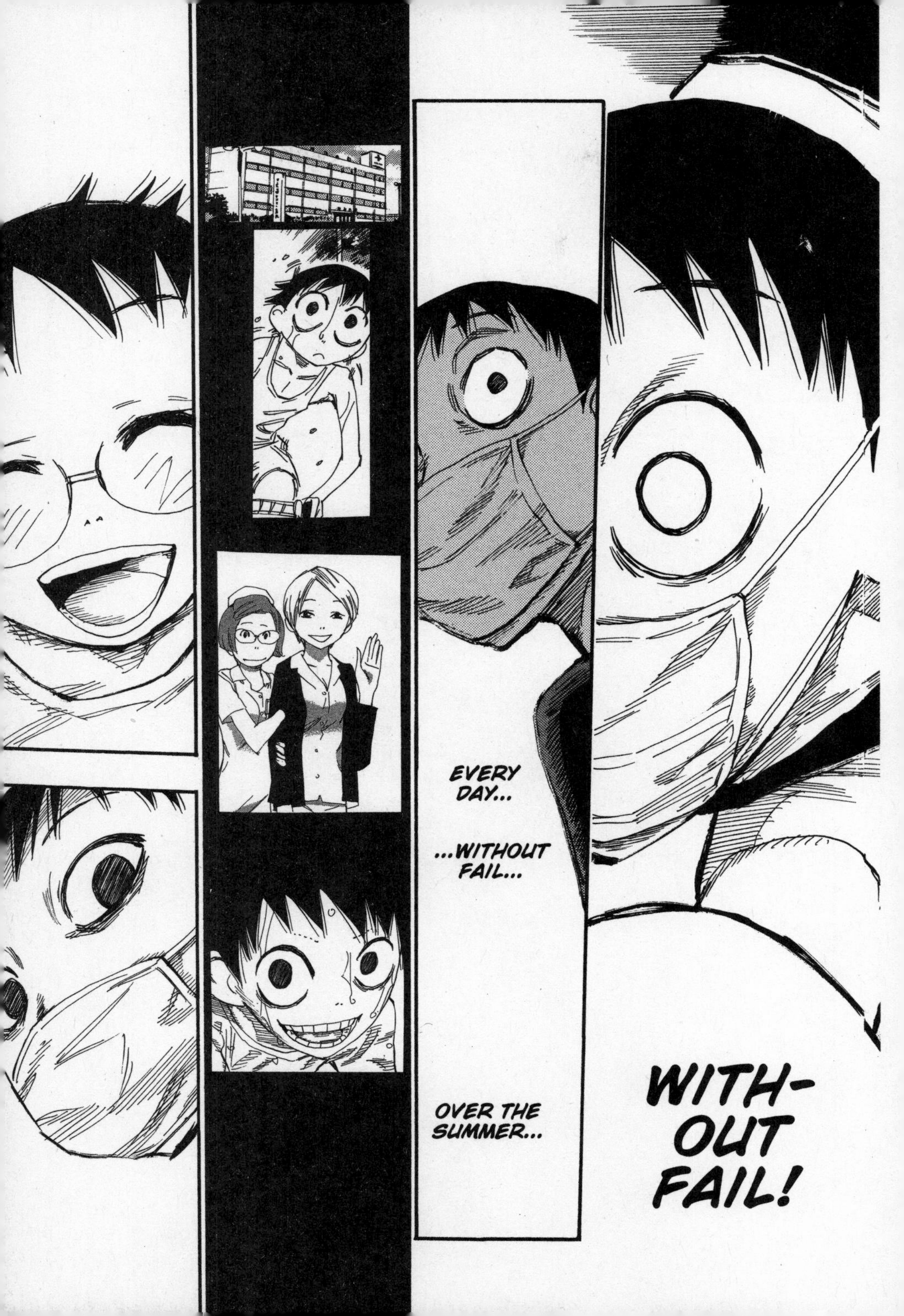
EVERY DAY...
...WITHOUT FAIL...
OVER THE SUMMER...
WITH-OUT FAIL!

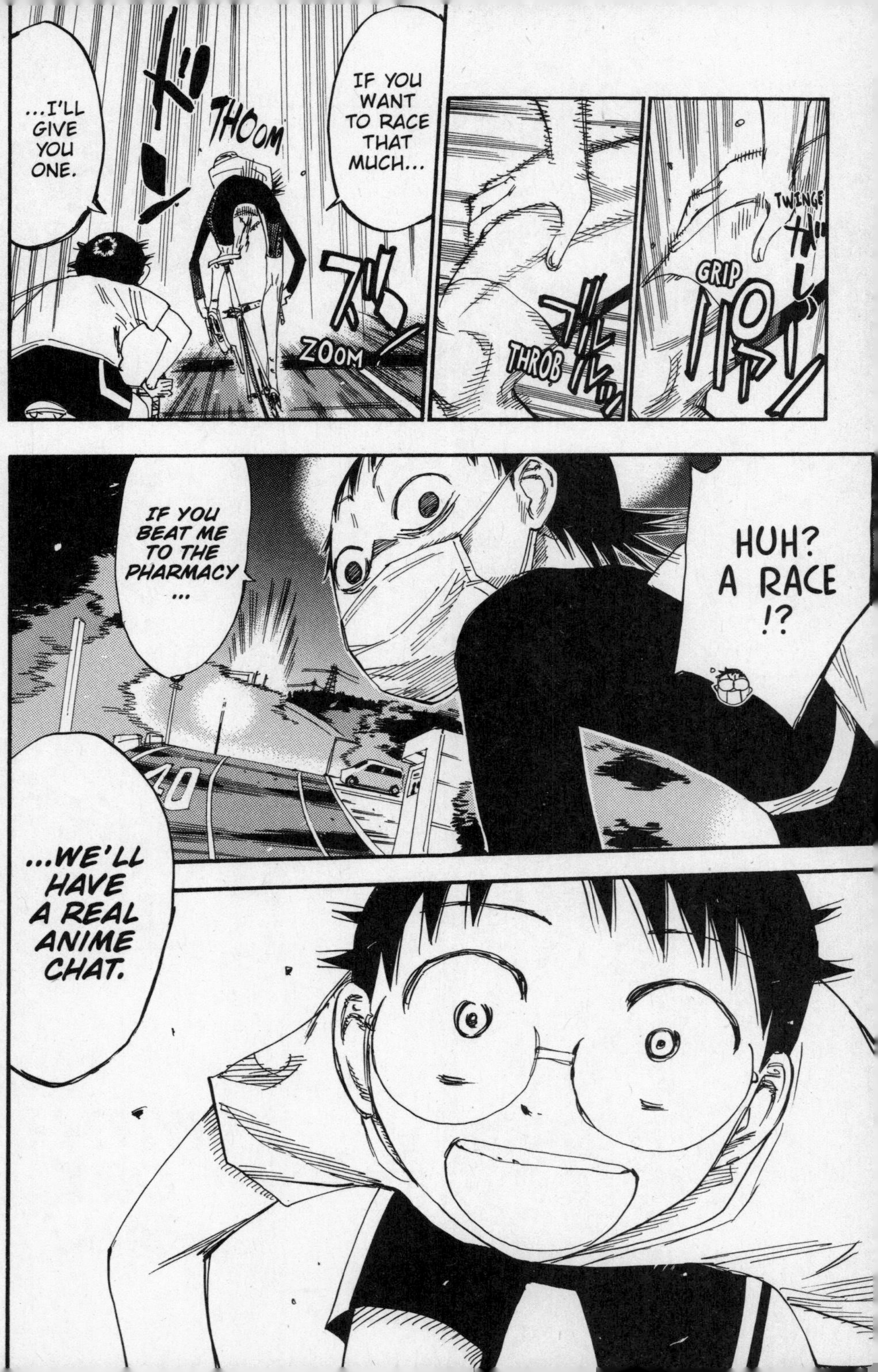
TWINGE
GRIP
THROB
IF YOU WANT TO RACE THAT MUCH...
THOOM
...I'LL GIVE YOU ONE.
ZOOM
HUH? A RACE!?
IF YOU BEAT ME TO THE PHARMACY...
...WE'LL HAVE A REAL ANIME CHAT.

RIDE.157 THE 3KM TO THE PHARMACY

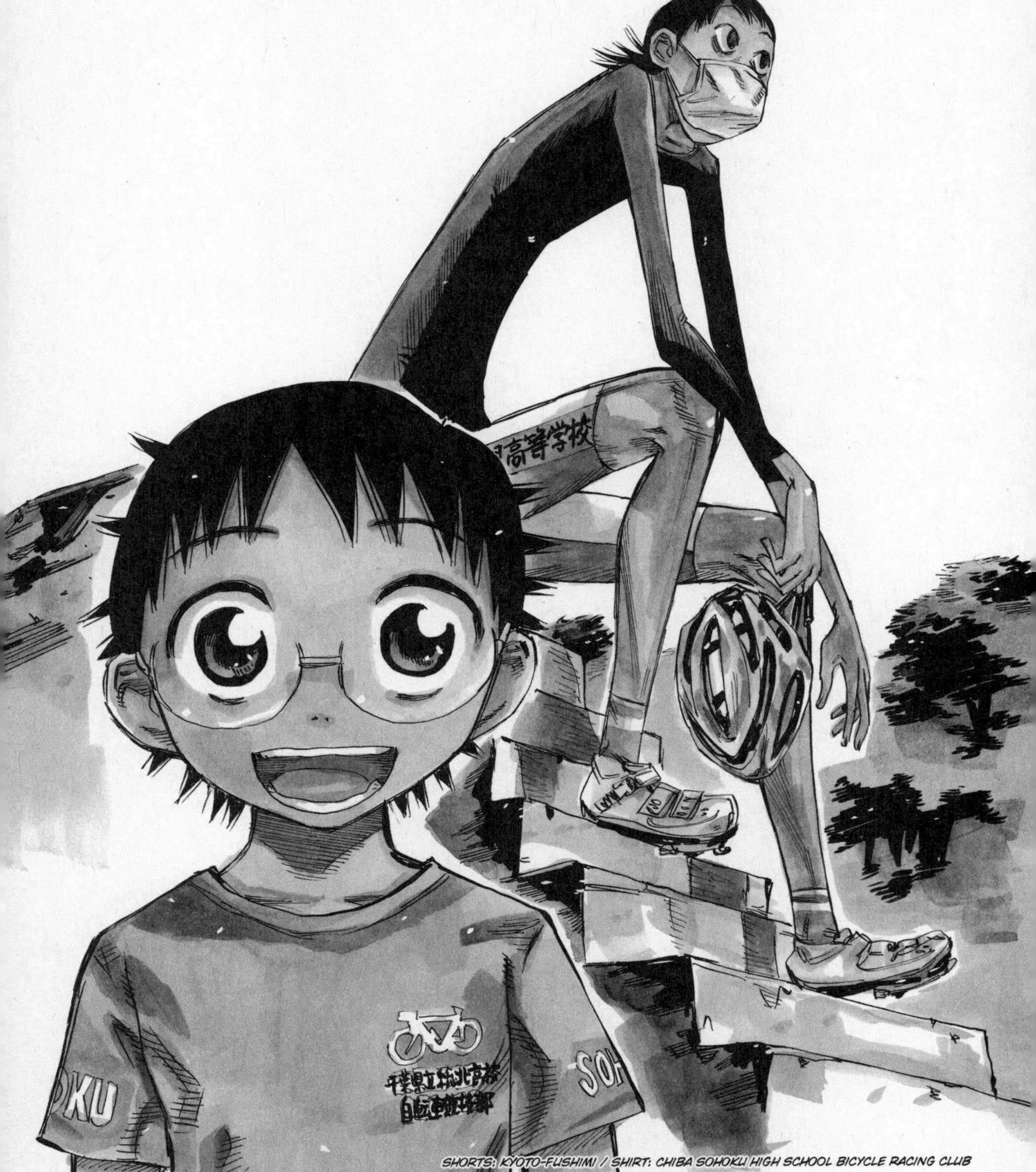

SHORTS: KYOTO-FUSHIMI / SHIRT: CHIBA SOHOKU HIGH SCHOOL BICYCLE RACING CLUB

MIDOUSUJI AKIRA

SAKAMICHI ONODA

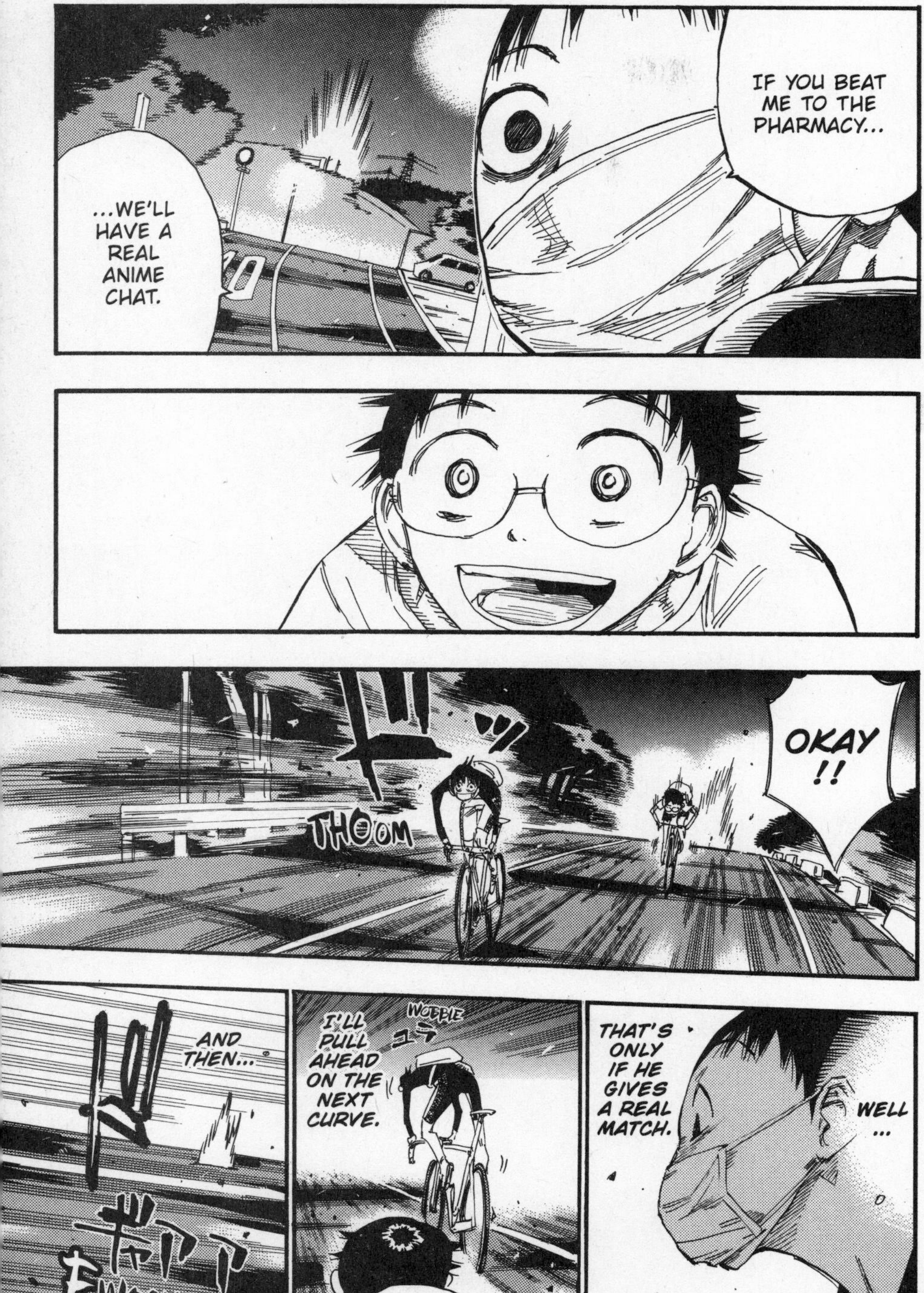
IF YOU BEAT ME TO THE PHARMACY...
...WE'LL HAVE A REAL ANIME CHAT.
OKAY!!
THOOM
WELL ...
THAT'S ONLY IF HE GIVES A REAL MATCH.
WOBBLE
I'LL PULL AHEAD ON THE NEXT CURVE.
AND THEN...
FWOOM

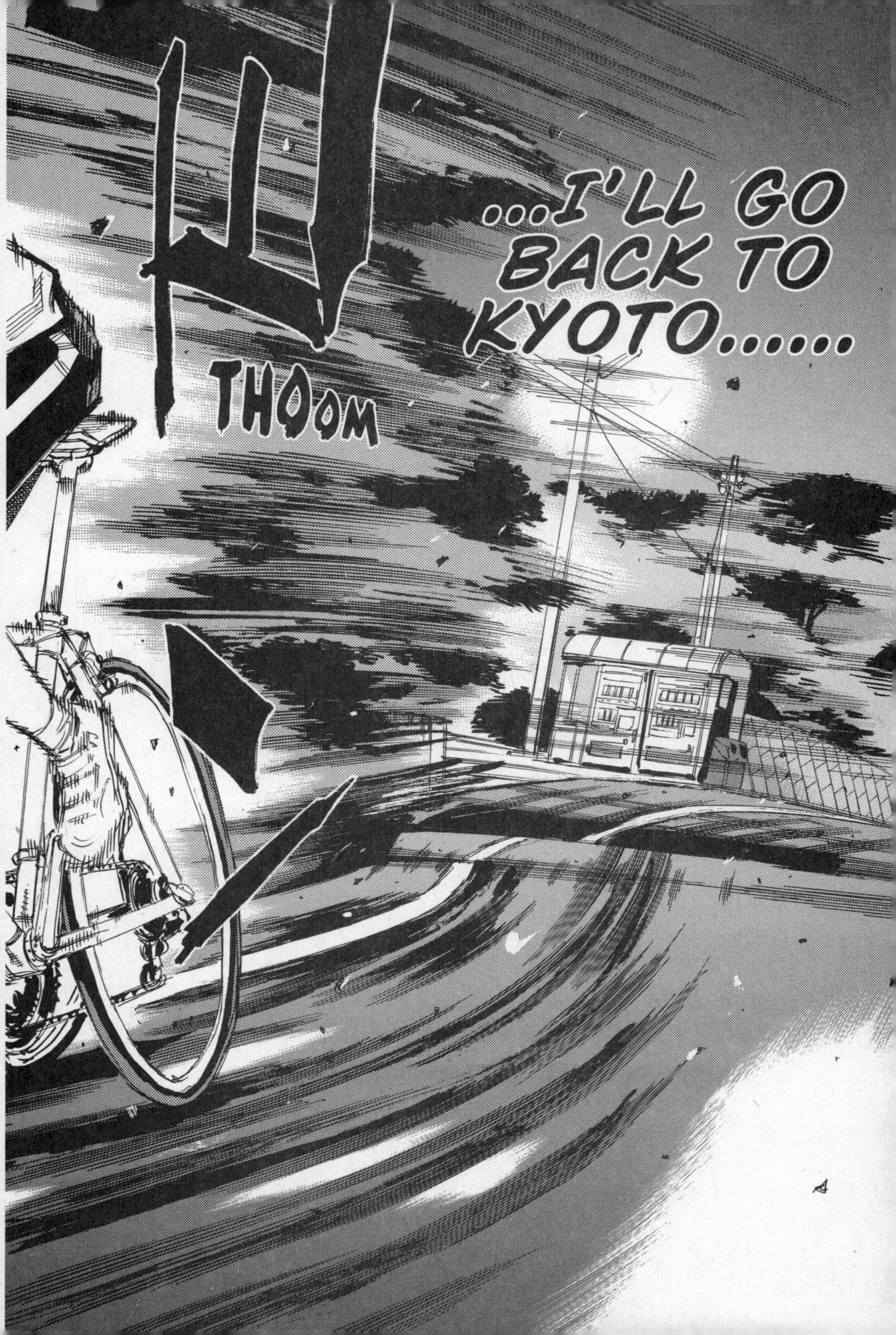
...I'LL GO BACK TO KYOTO......
THOOM

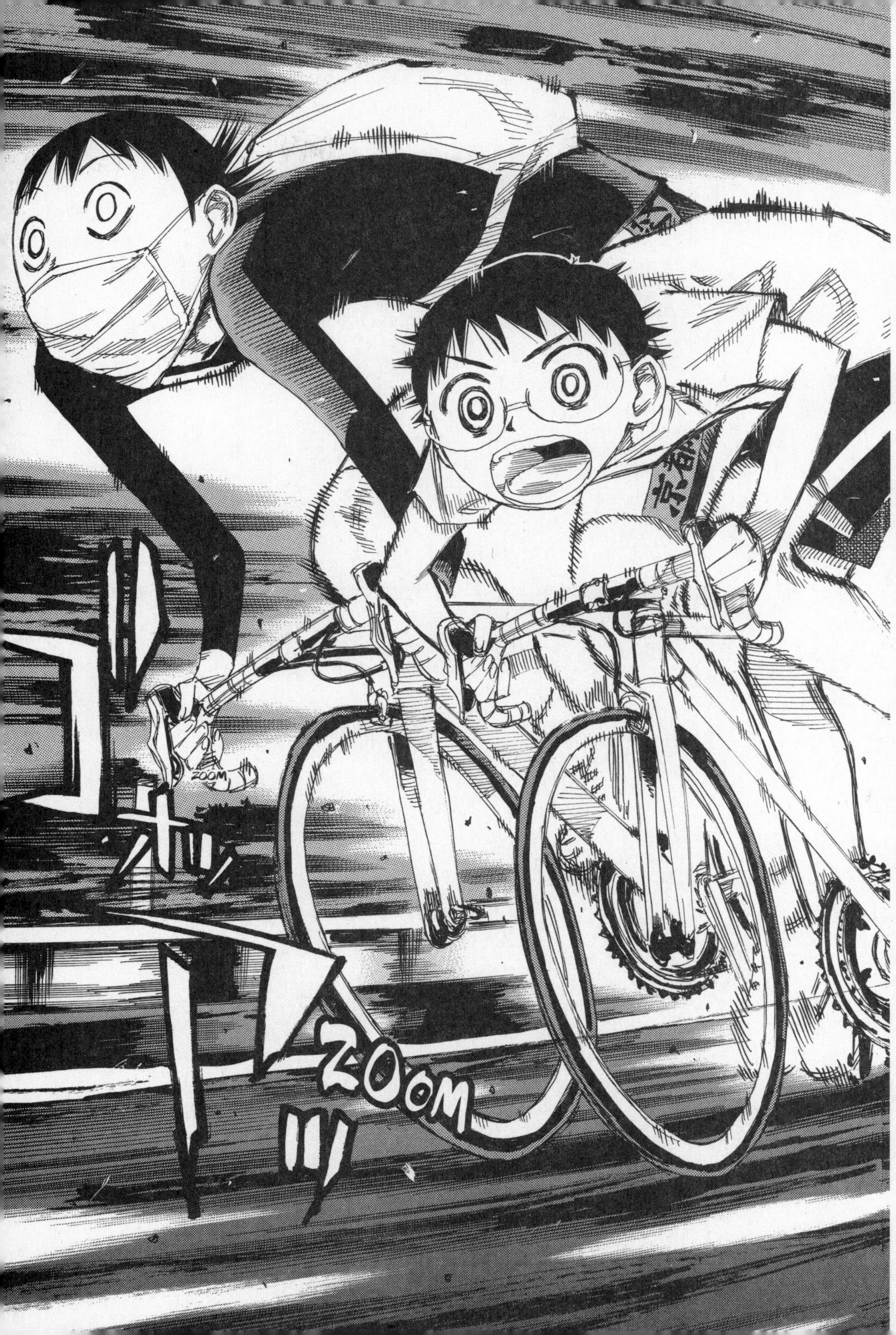
ゴォッ
ZOOM
ZOOM!!

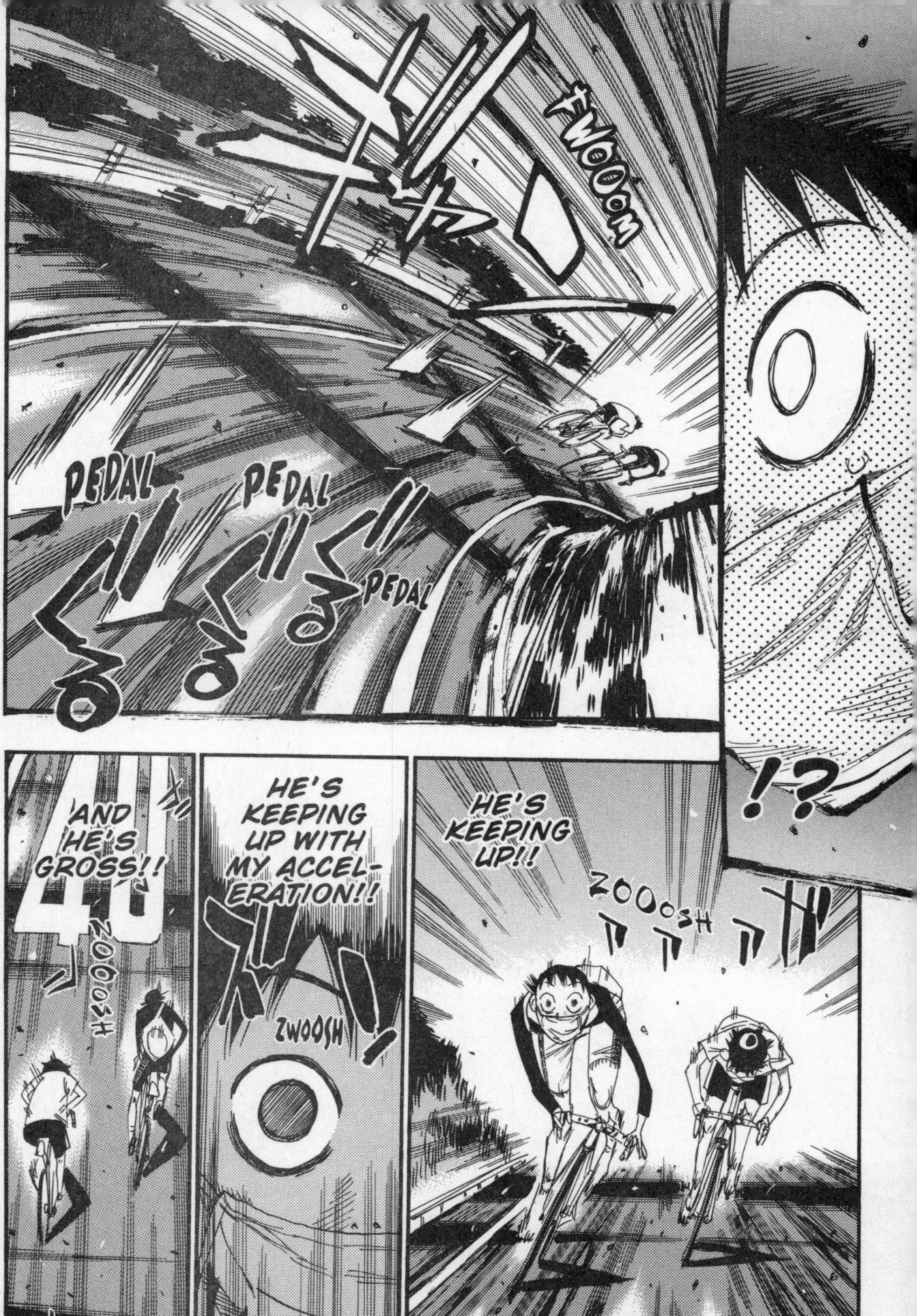
!?
FWOOOM
PEDAL
PEDAL
PEDAL
HE'S KEEPING UP!!
ZOOOSH
HE'S KEEPING UP WITH MY ACCEL-ERATION!!
ZWOOSH
AND HE'S GROSS!!
ZOOOOSH

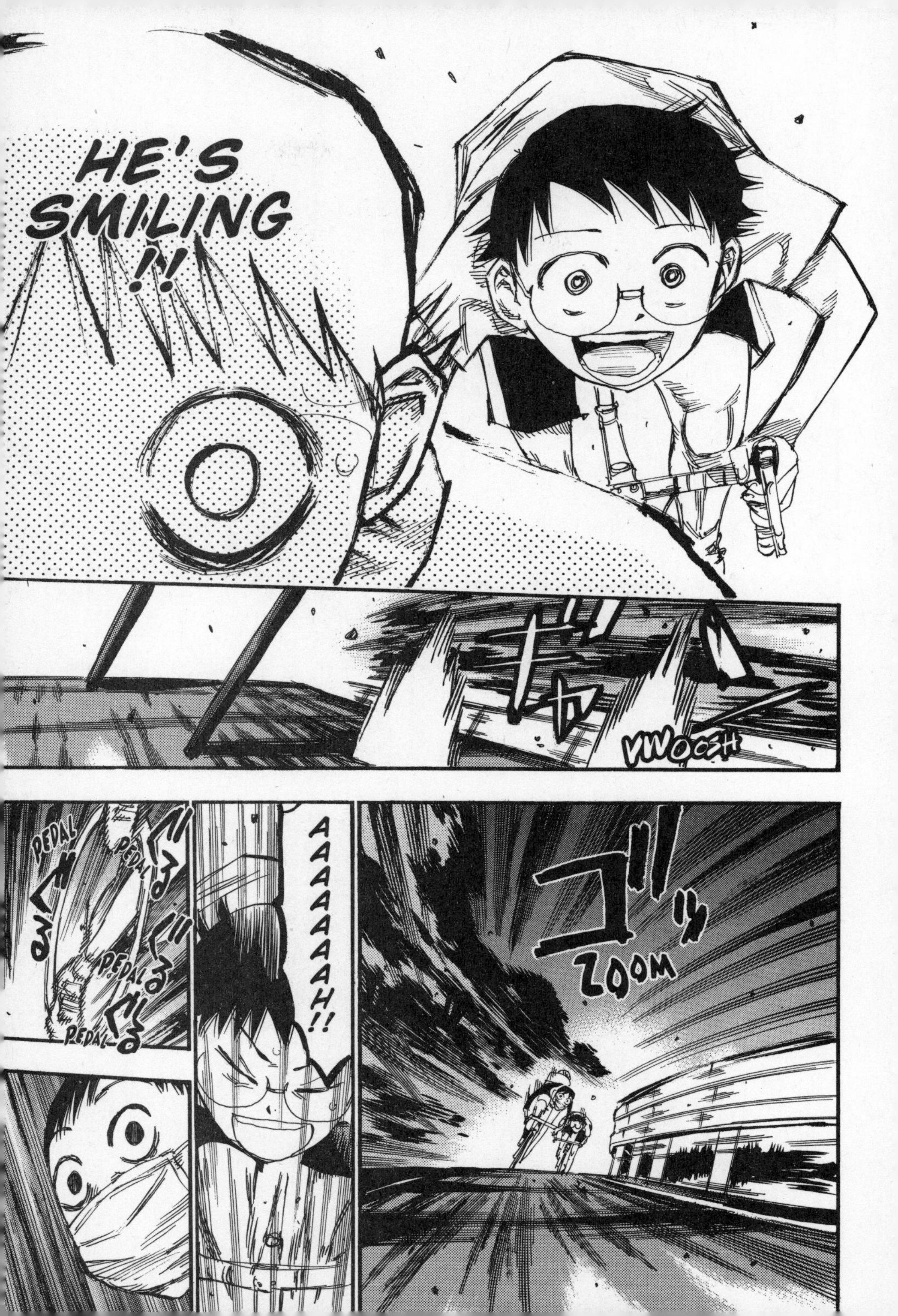
HE'S SMILING!!
VWOOSH
ZOOM
AAAAAAAAH!!
PEDAL
PEDAL
PEDAL
PEDAL

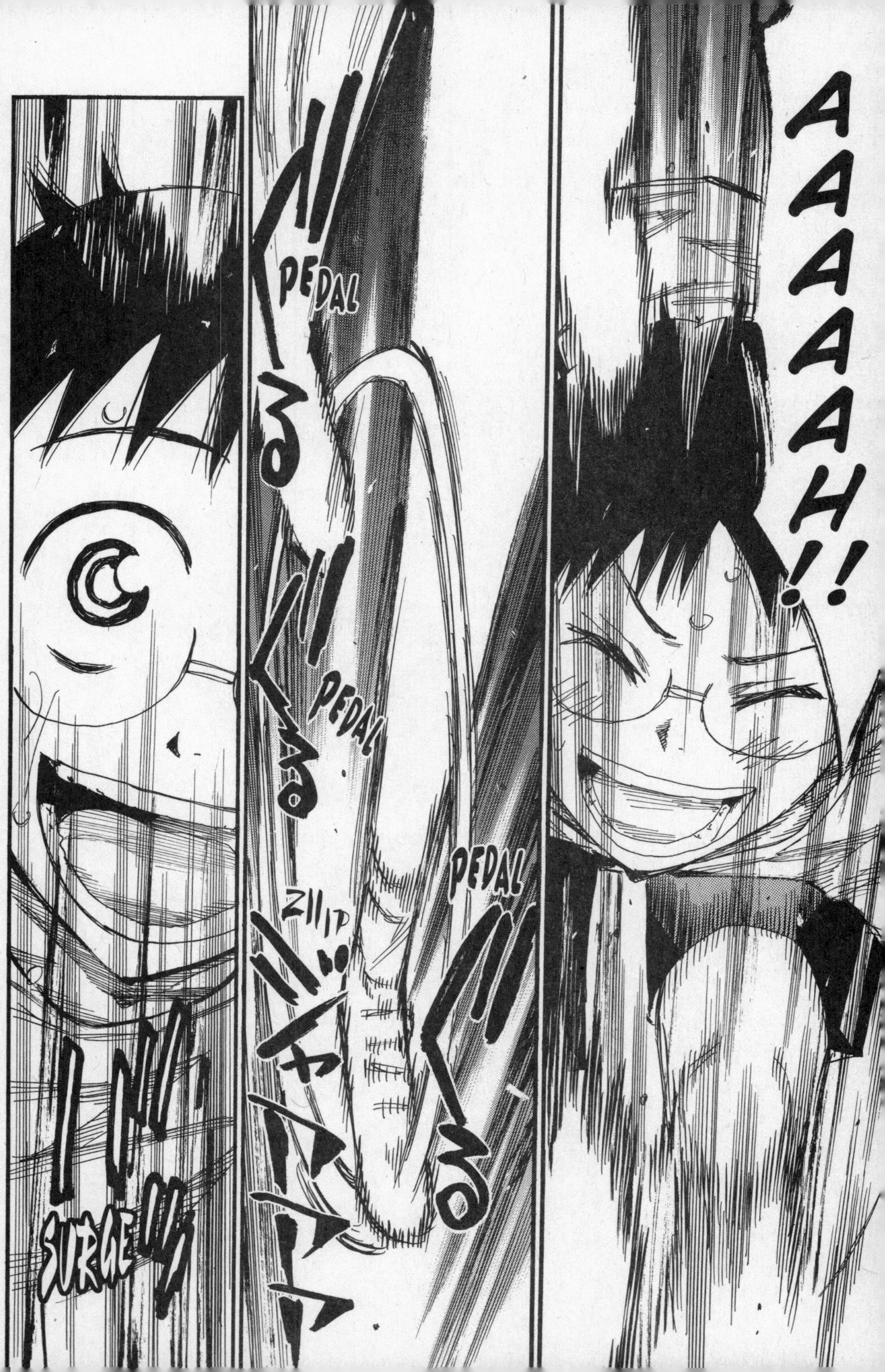
AAAAAAH!!
PEDAL
PEDAL
PEDAL
ZIIIP
SURGE

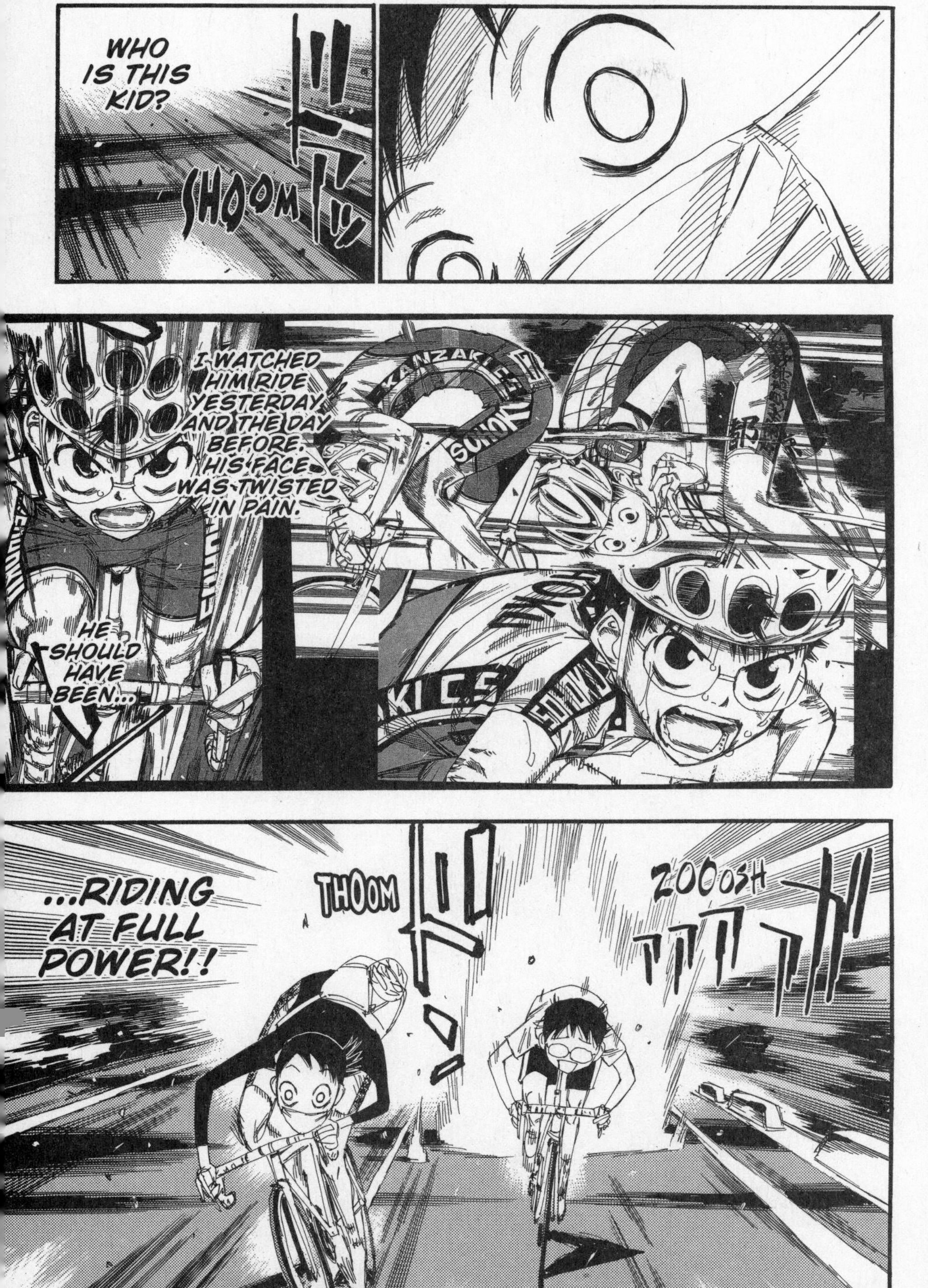

WHO IS THIS KID?
SHOOM
I WATCHED HIM RIDE YESTERDAY AND THE DAY BEFORE. HIS FACE WAS TWISTED IN PAIN.
HE SHOULD HAVE BEEN...
ZOOOSH
THOOM
...RIDING AT FULL POWER!!

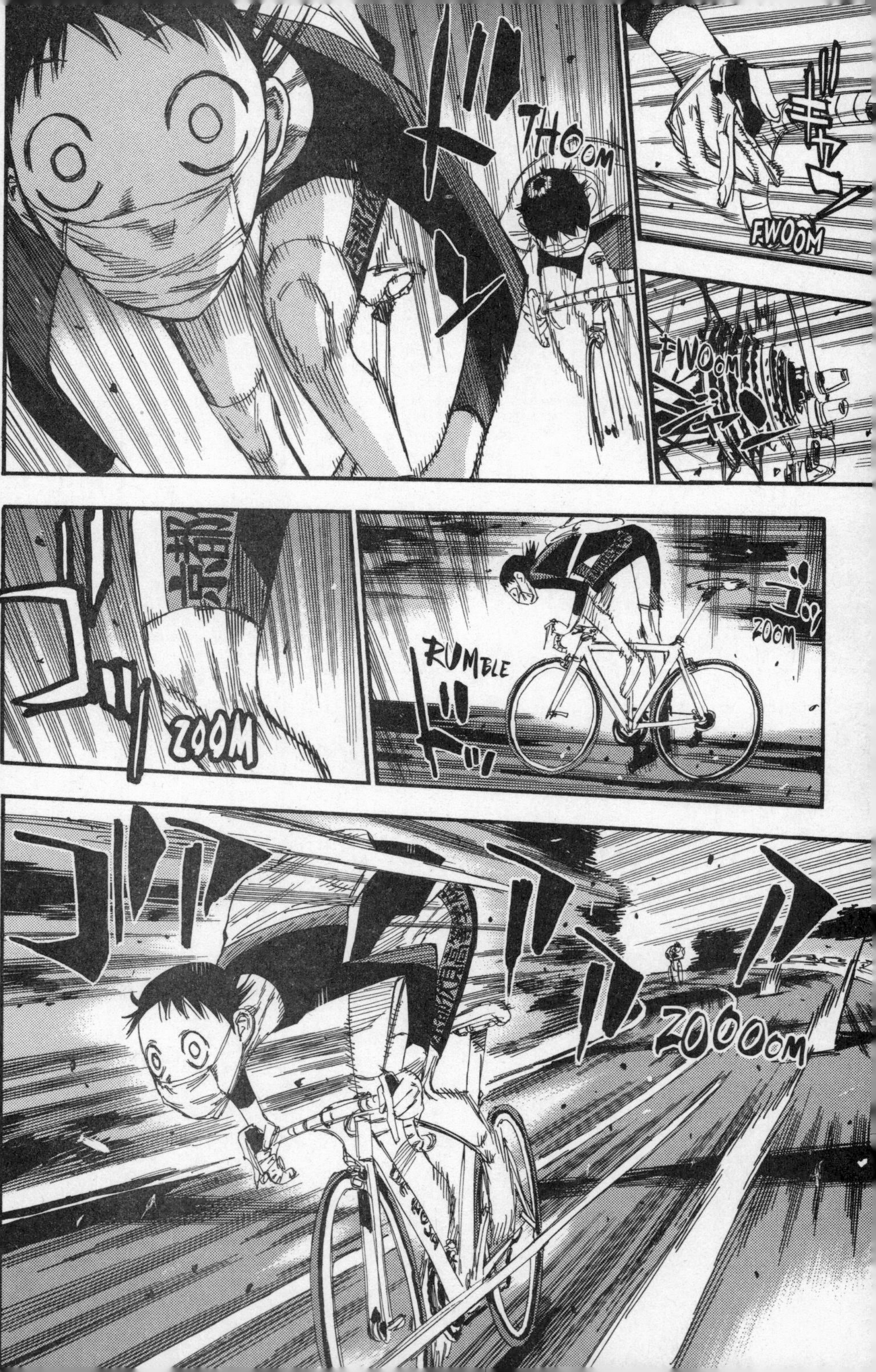
FWOOM
FWOOM
THOOM
ZOOM
RUMBLE
ZOOM
ZOOOOM

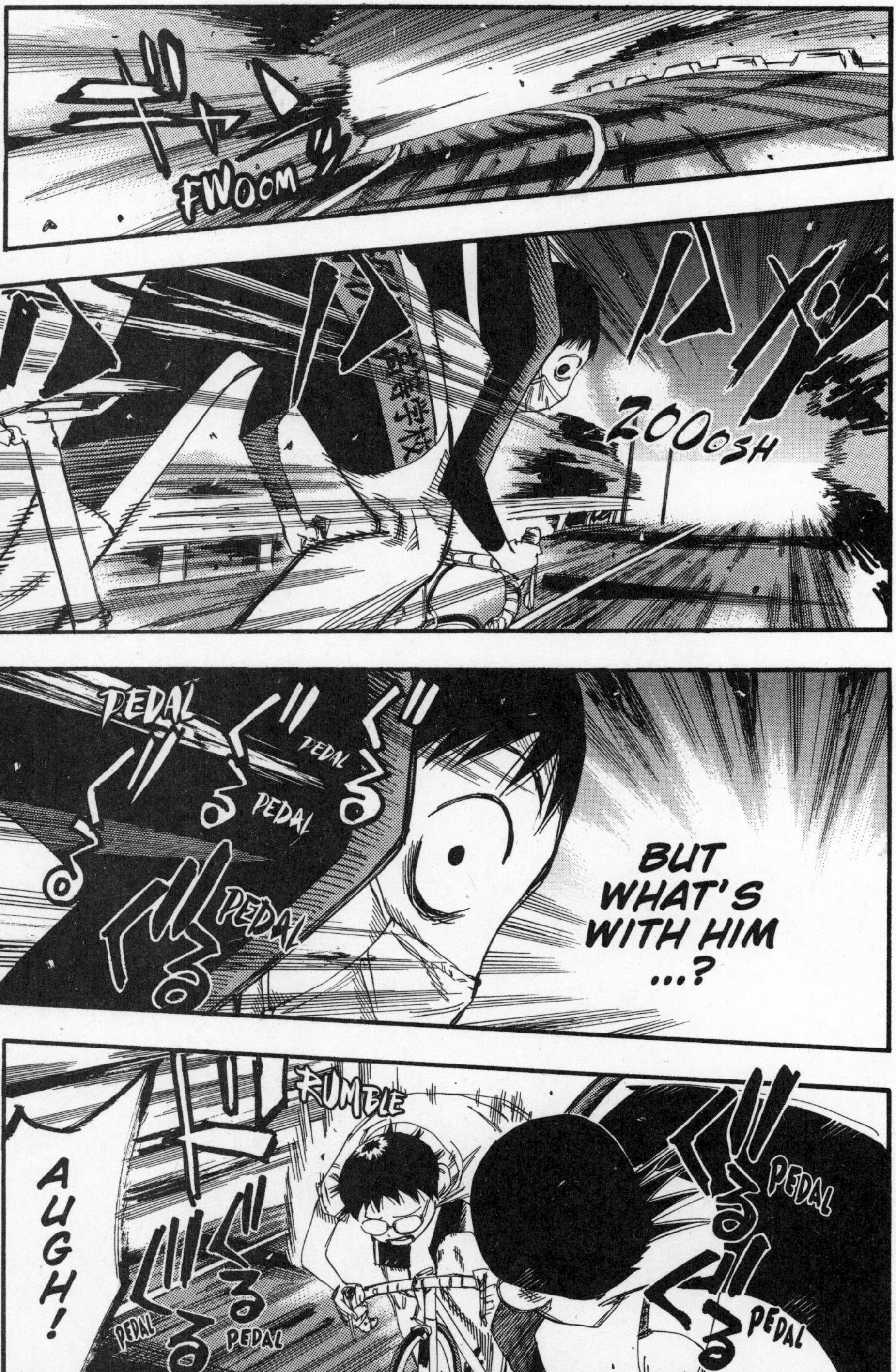
FWOOM
ZOOOOSH
BUT WHAT'S WITH HIM ...?
PEDAL
PEDAL
PEDAL
PEDAL
RUMBLE
PEDAL
PEDAL
AUGH!
PEDAL
PEDAL

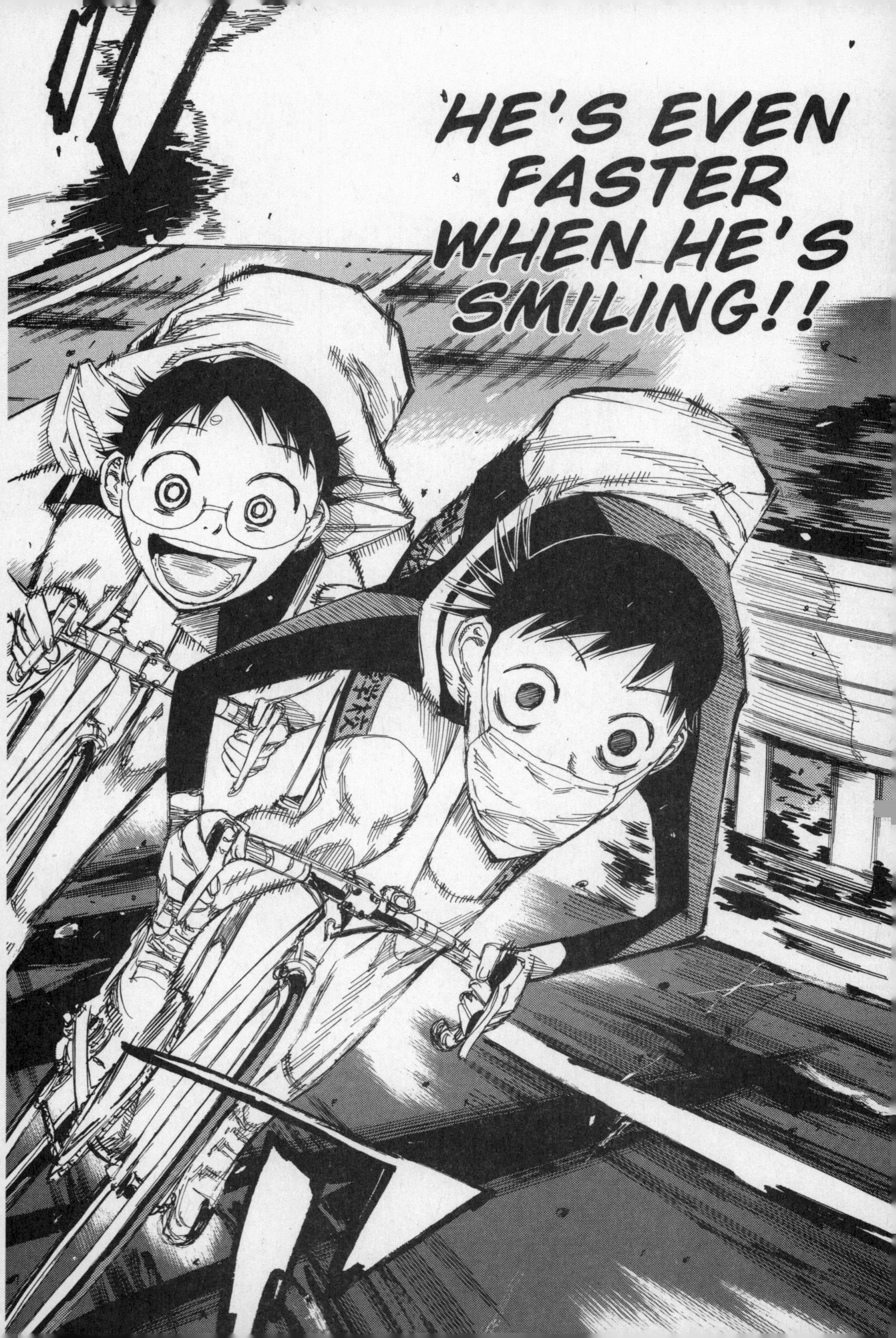
HE'S EVEN FASTER WHEN HE'S SMILING!!

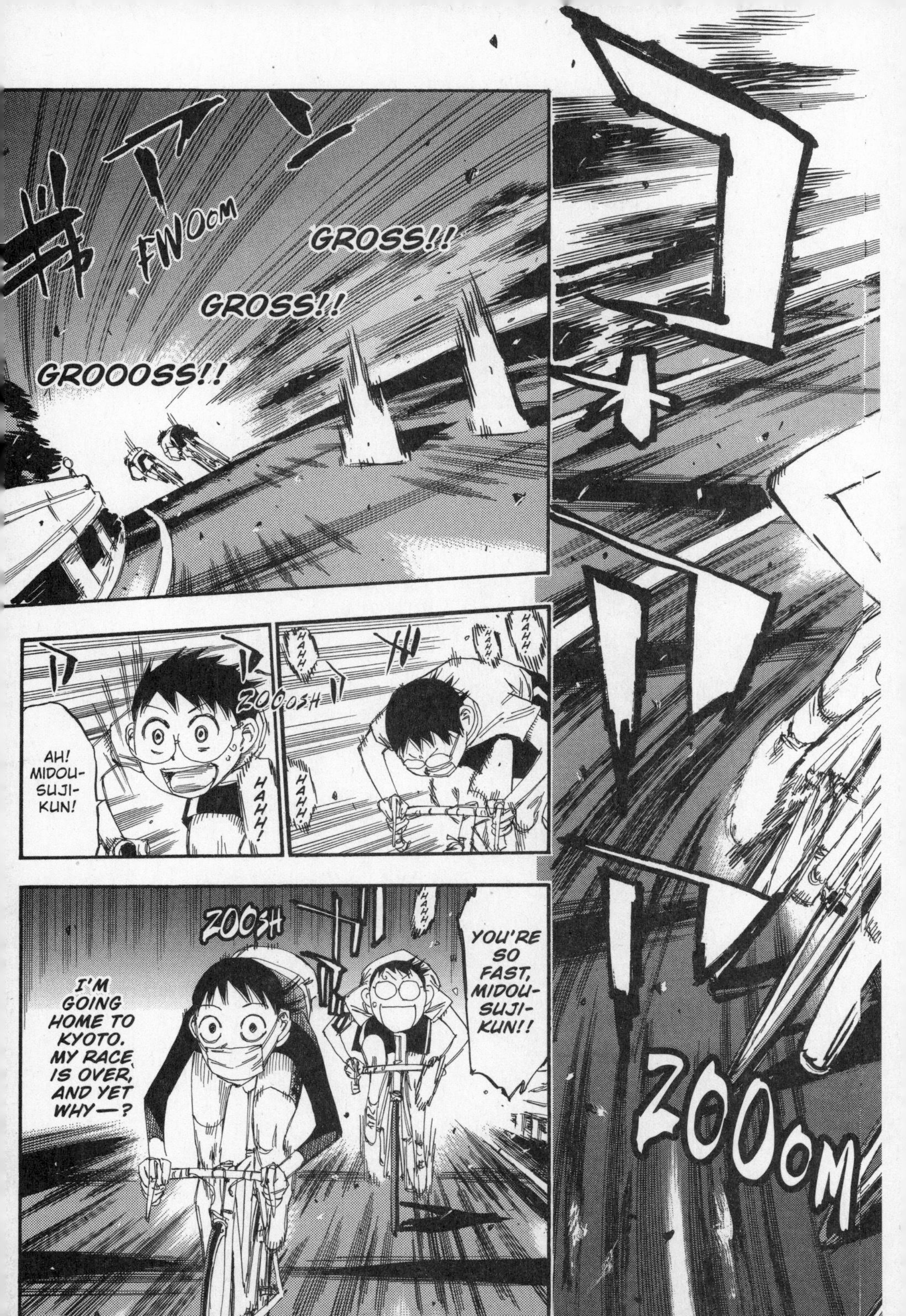
ZOOOM
FWOOM
GROSS!!
GROSS!!
GROOOSS!!
HAHH
HAHH
ZOOOSH
HAHH HAHH!
AH! MIDOUSUJI-KUN!
HAHH
YOU'RE SO FAST, MIDOUSUJI-KUN!!
ZOOSH
I'M GOING HOME TO KYOTO. MY RACE IS OVER, AND YET WHY—?

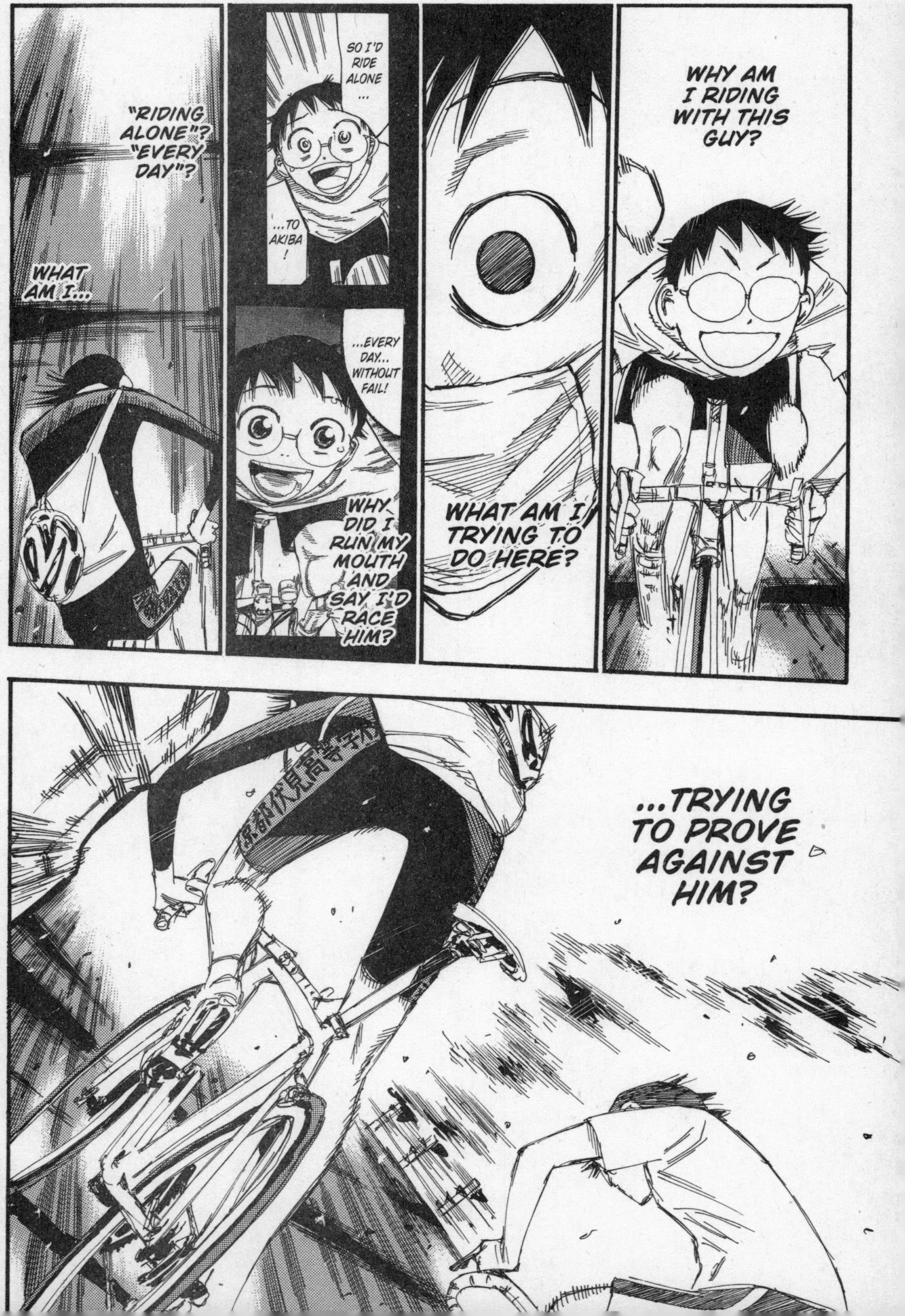
WHY AM I RIDING WITH THIS GUY?
WHAT AM I TRYING TO DO HERE?
SO I'D RIDE ALONE ...
...TO AKIBA!
...EVERY DAY... WITHOUT FAIL!
WHY DID I RUN MY MOUTH AND SAY I'D RACE HIM?
"RIDING ALONE"? "EVERY DAY"?
WHAT AM I...
...TRYING TO PROVE AGAINST HIM?

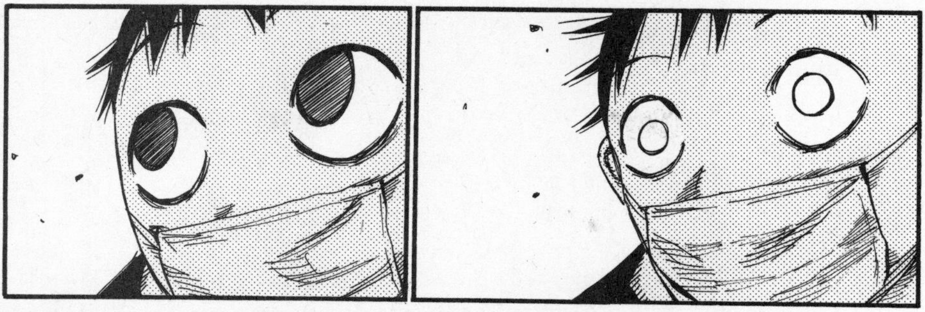

SIGN: MATSUKI TOYOZOU BUILDING: PHARMACY BANNER: ARONAMIN / ALINAMIN G—

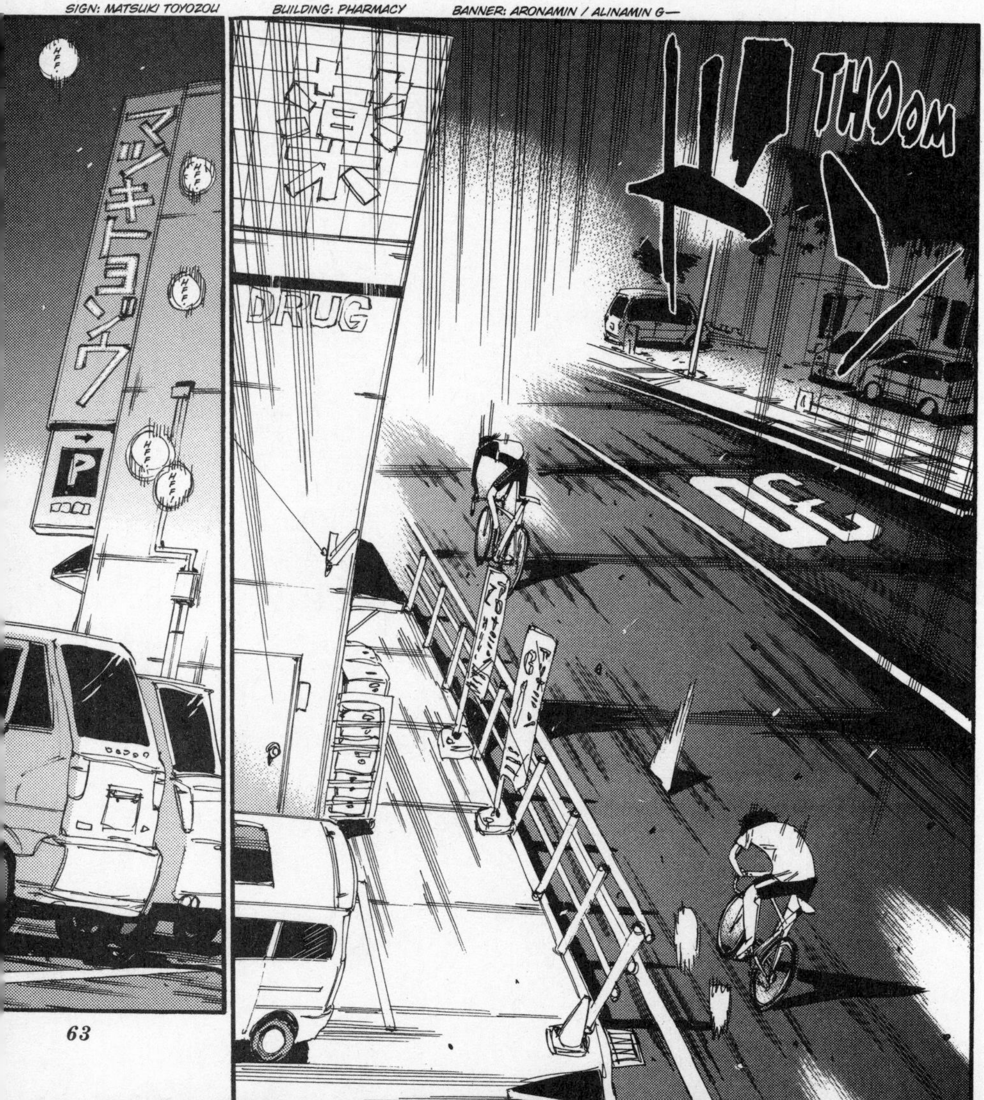
THOOM
DRUG
HFF.
HFF.
HFF.
HFF.
HFF!

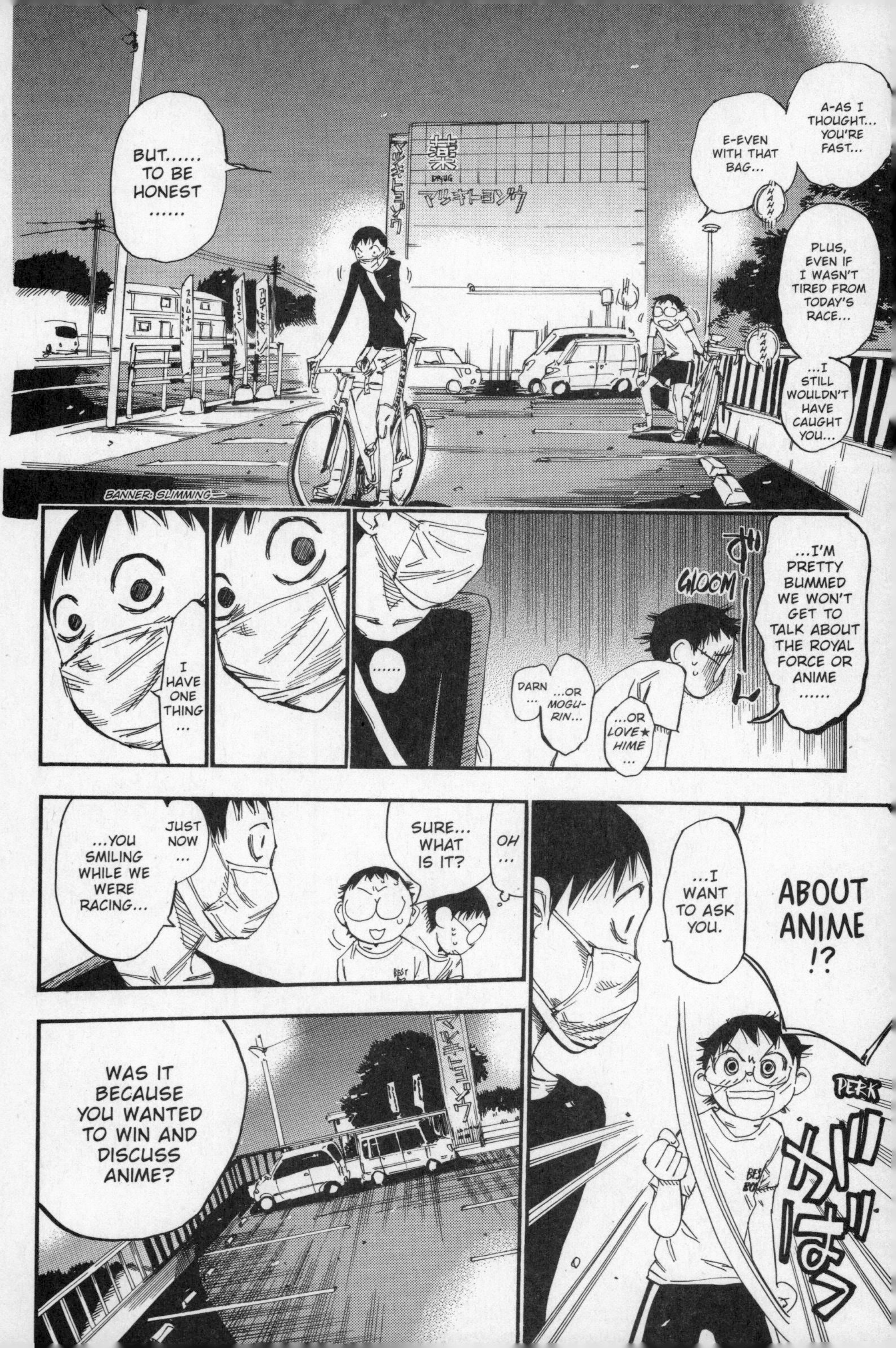
A-AS I THOUGHT... YOU'RE FAST...
HAHH
E-EVEN WITH THAT BAG...
PLUS, EVEN IF I WASN'T TIRED FROM TODAY'S RACE...
HAHH
...I STILL WOULDN'T HAVE CAUGHT YOU...
BUT...... TO BE HONEST ......
BANNER: SLIMMING
...I'M PRETTY BUMMED WE WON'T GET TO TALK ABOUT THE ROYAL FORCE OR ANIME ......
GLOOM
...OR LOVE★HIME ...
...OR MOGURI-RIN...
DARN ...
......
I HAVE ONE THING ...
...I WANT TO ASK YOU.
ABOUT ANIME !?
PERK
OH ...
SURE... WHAT IS IT?
JUST NOW ...
...YOU SMILING WHILE WE WERE RACING...
WAS IT BECAUSE YOU WANTED TO WIN AND DISCUSS ANIME?

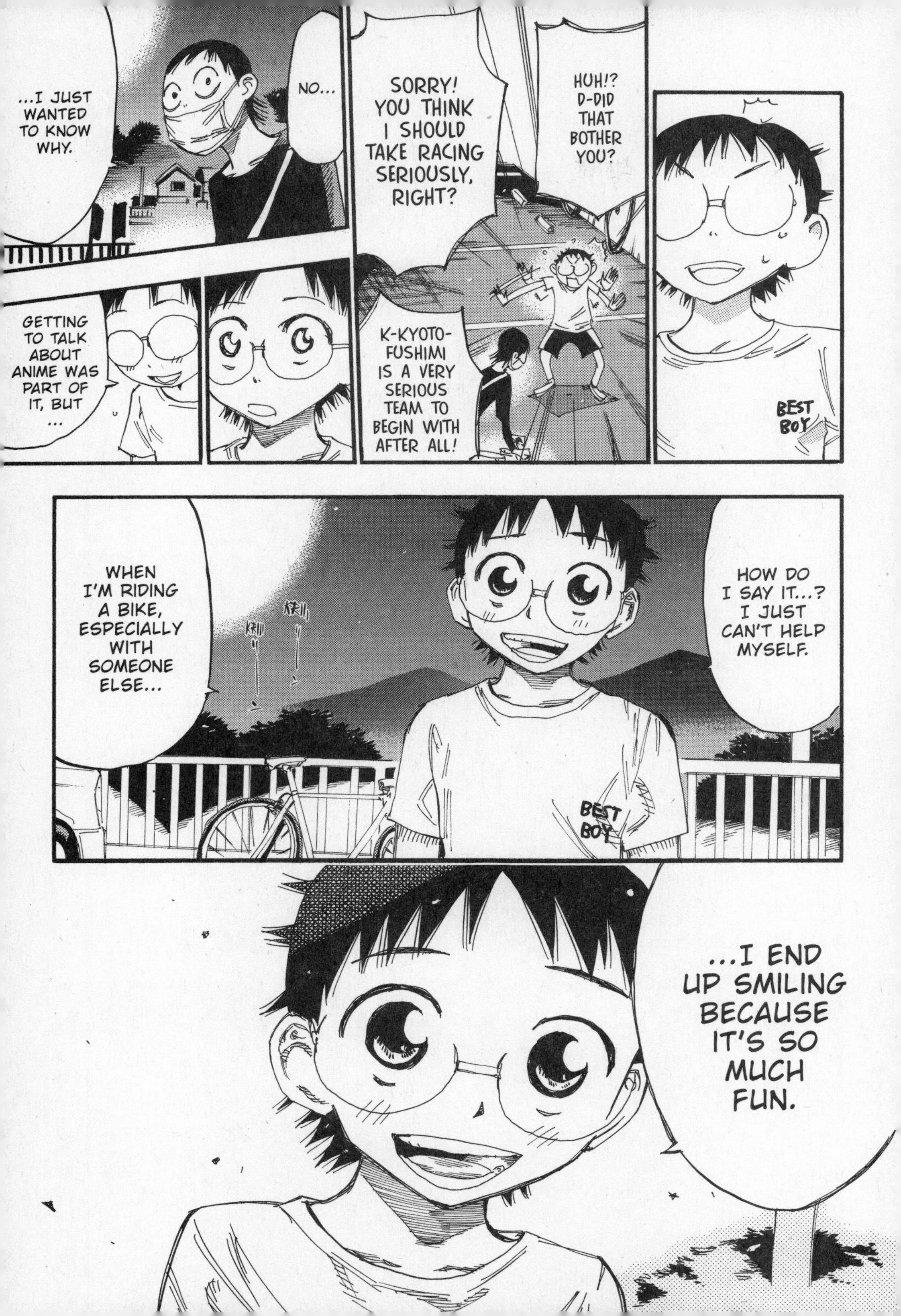
BEST BOY
HUH!? D-DID THAT BOTHER YOU?
SORRY! YOU THINK I SHOULD TAKE RACING SERIOUSLY, RIGHT?
K-KYOTO-FUSHIMI IS A VERY SERIOUS TEAM TO BEGIN WITH AFTER ALL!
NO...
...I JUST WANTED TO KNOW WHY.
GETTING TO TALK ABOUT ANIME WAS PART OF IT, BUT ...
HOW DO I SAY IT...? I JUST CAN'T HELP MYSELF.
WHEN I'M RIDING A BIKE, ESPECIALLY WITH SOMEONE ELSE...
BEST BOY
...I END UP SMILING BECAUSE IT'S SO MUCH FUN.

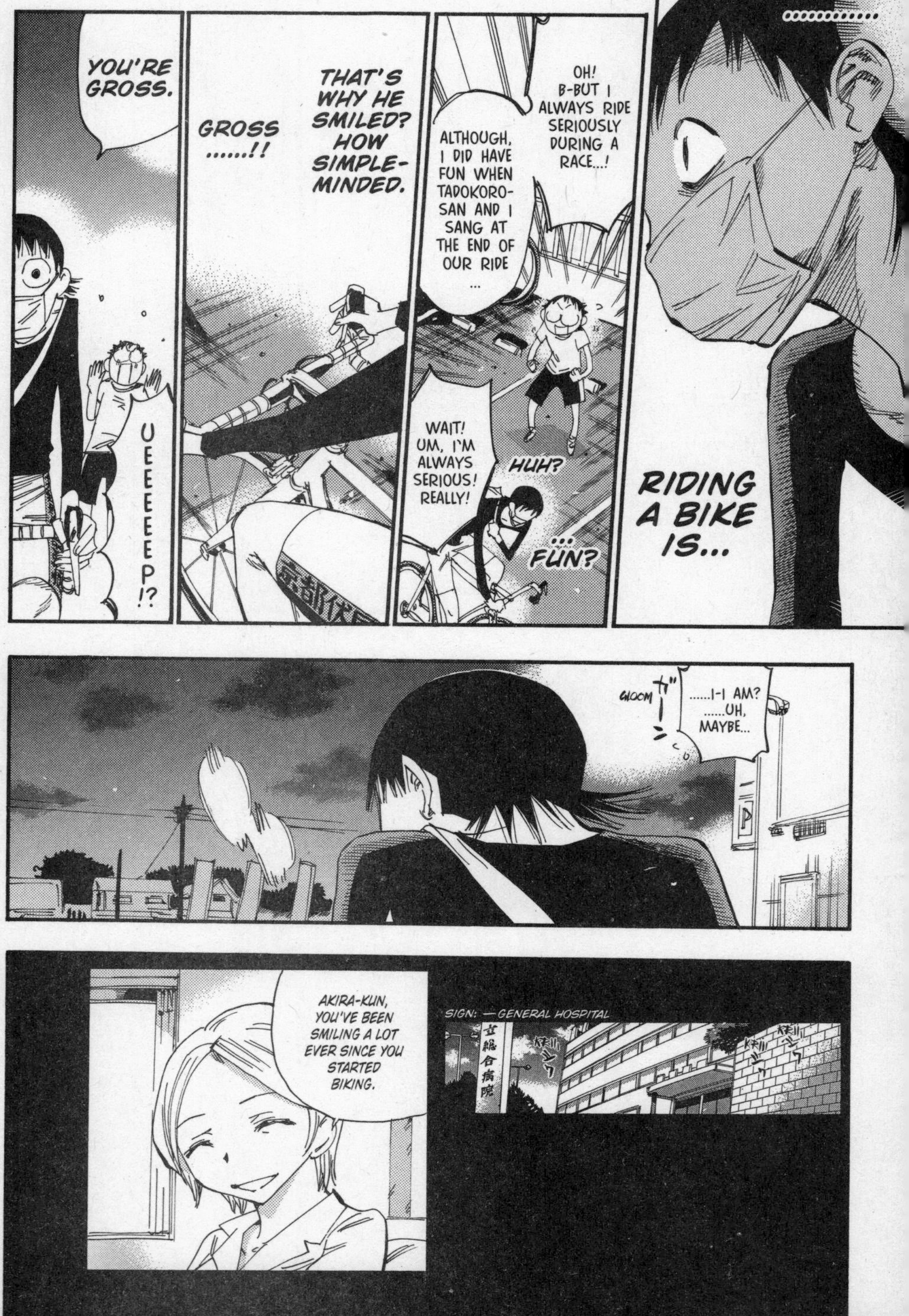
RIDING A BIKE IS...
OH! B-BUT I ALWAYS RIDE SERIOUSLY DURING A RACE...!
ALTHOUGH, I DID HAVE FUN WHEN TADOKORO-SAN AND I SANG AT THE END OF OUR RIDE ...
HUH?
... FUN?
WAIT! UM, I'M ALWAYS SERIOUS! REALLY!
THAT'S WHY HE SMILED? HOW SIMPLE-MINDED.
GROSS ......!!
YOU'RE GROSS.
UEEEEEEEP!?
GLOOM
......I-I AM? ......UH, MAYBE...
SIGN: —GENERAL HOSPITAL
AKIRA-KUN, YOU'VE BEEN SMILING A LOT EVER SINCE YOU STARTED BIKING.

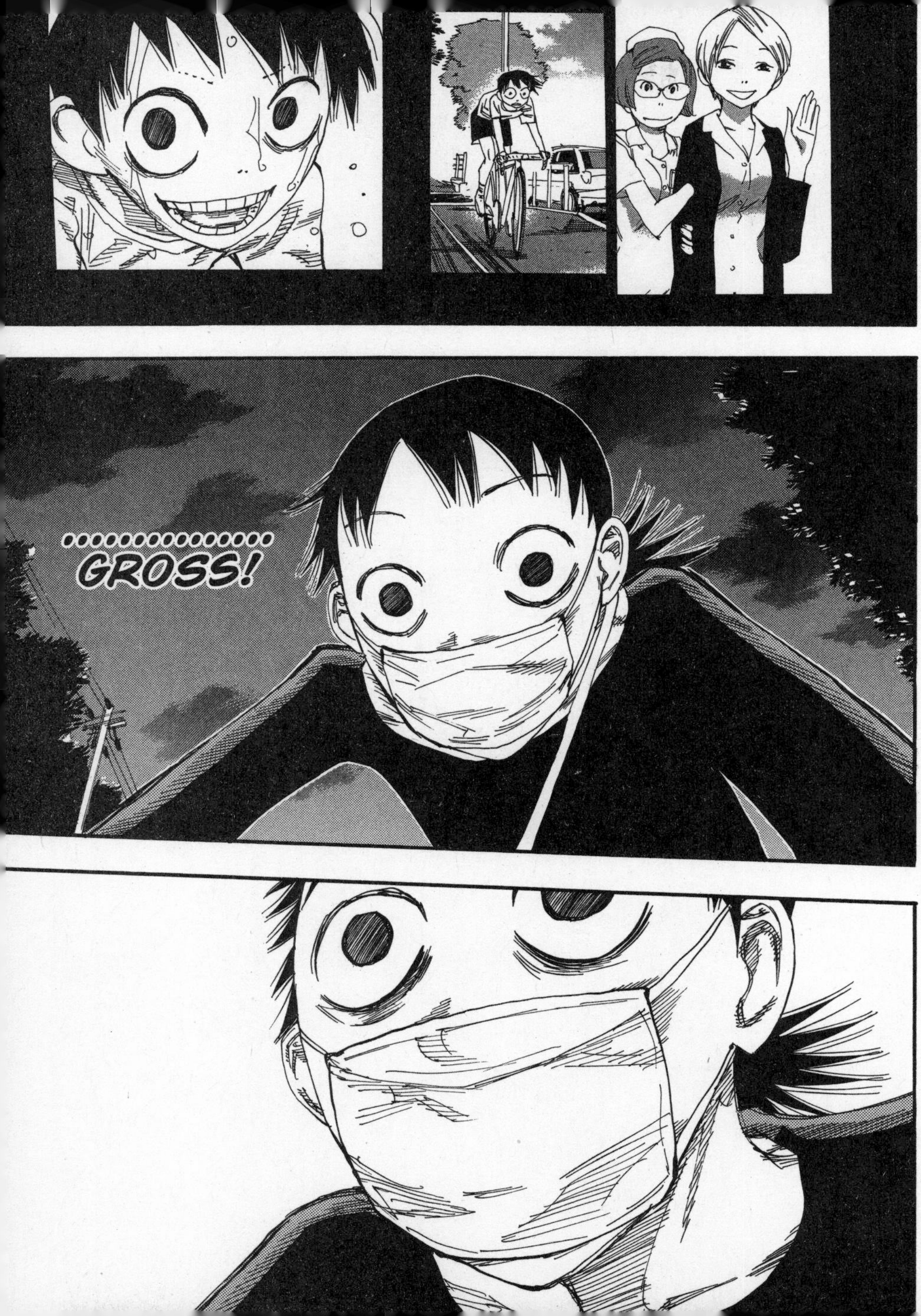
....
GROSS!

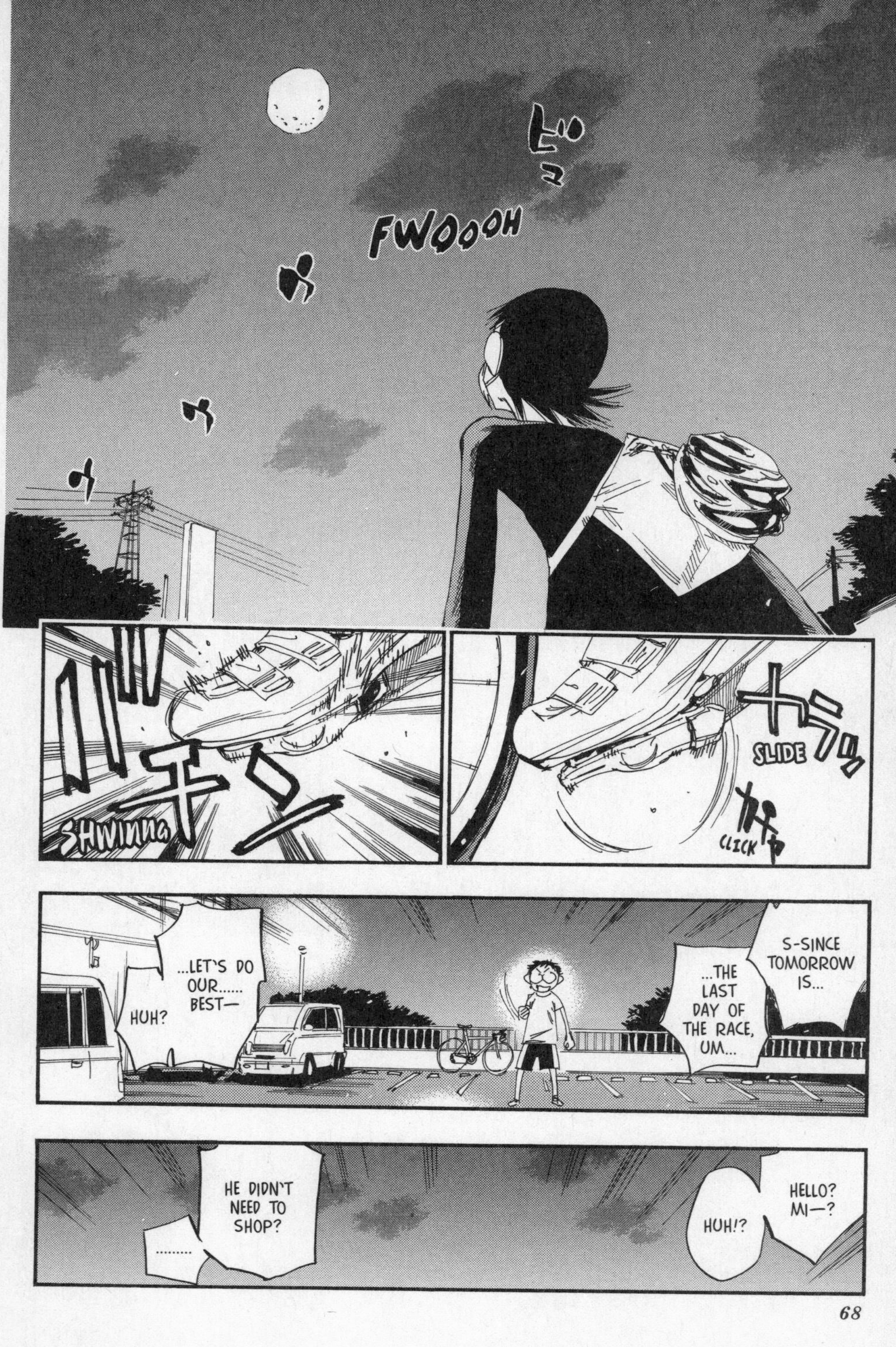
FWOOOH
SLIDE
CLICK
SHWINNG
S-SINCE TOMORROW IS...
...THE LAST DAY OF THE RACE, UM...
...LET'S DO OUR...... BEST—
HUH?
HELLO? MI—?
HUH!?
HE DIDN'T NEED TO SHOP?
....

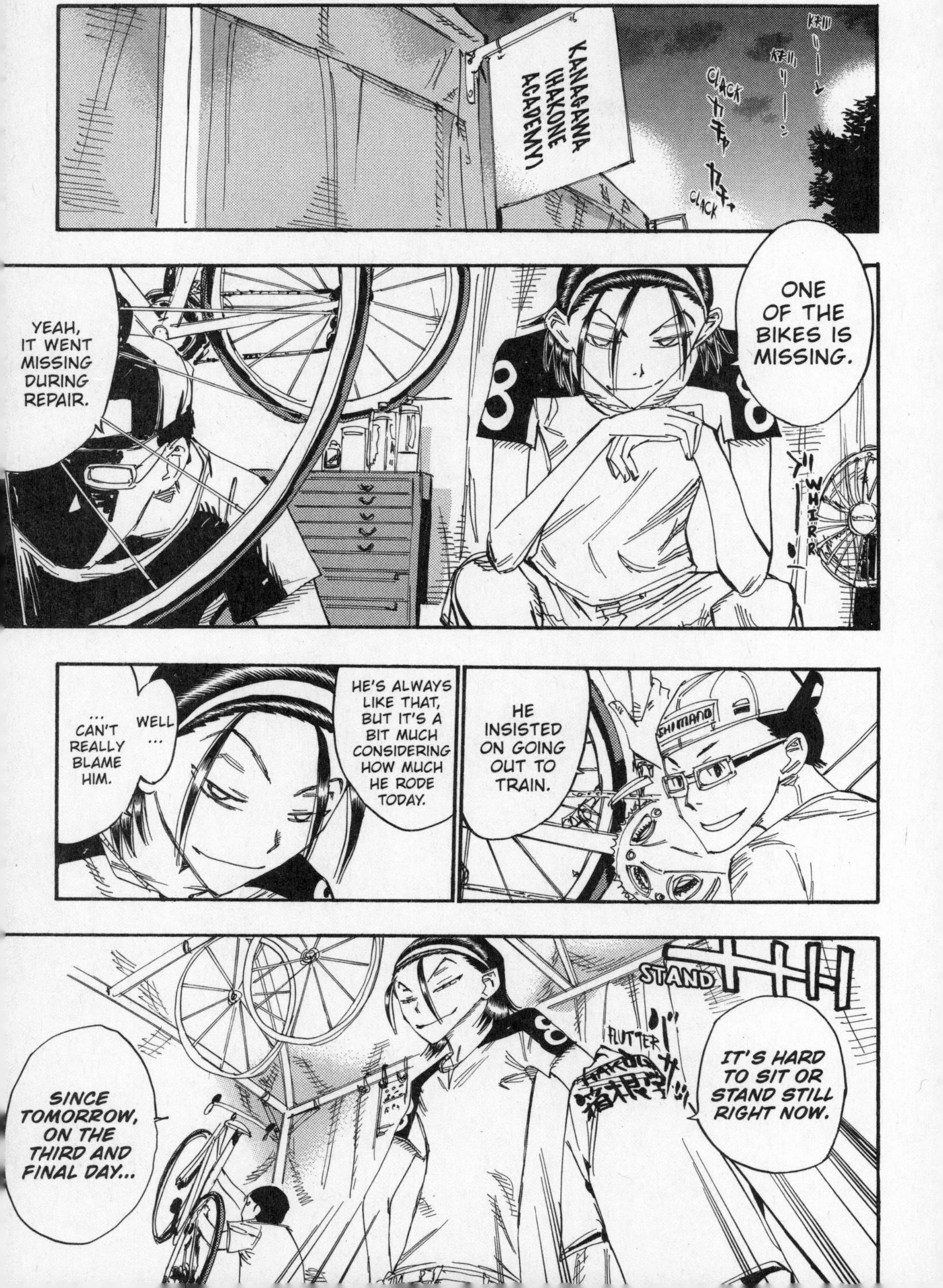
KRII
KRII
CLACK
CLACK
KANAGAWA (HAKONE ACADEMY)
ONE OF THE BIKES IS MISSING.
WHIRR
YEAH, IT WENT MISSING DURING REPAIR.
HE INSISTED ON GOING OUT TO TRAIN.
HE'S ALWAYS LIKE THAT, BUT IT'S A BIT MUCH CONSIDERING HOW MUCH HE RODE TODAY.
WELL ...
... CAN'T REALLY BLAME HIM.
STAND
FLUTTER
IT'S HARD TO SIT OR STAND STILL RIGHT NOW.
SINCE TOMORROW, ON THE THIRD AND FINAL DAY...

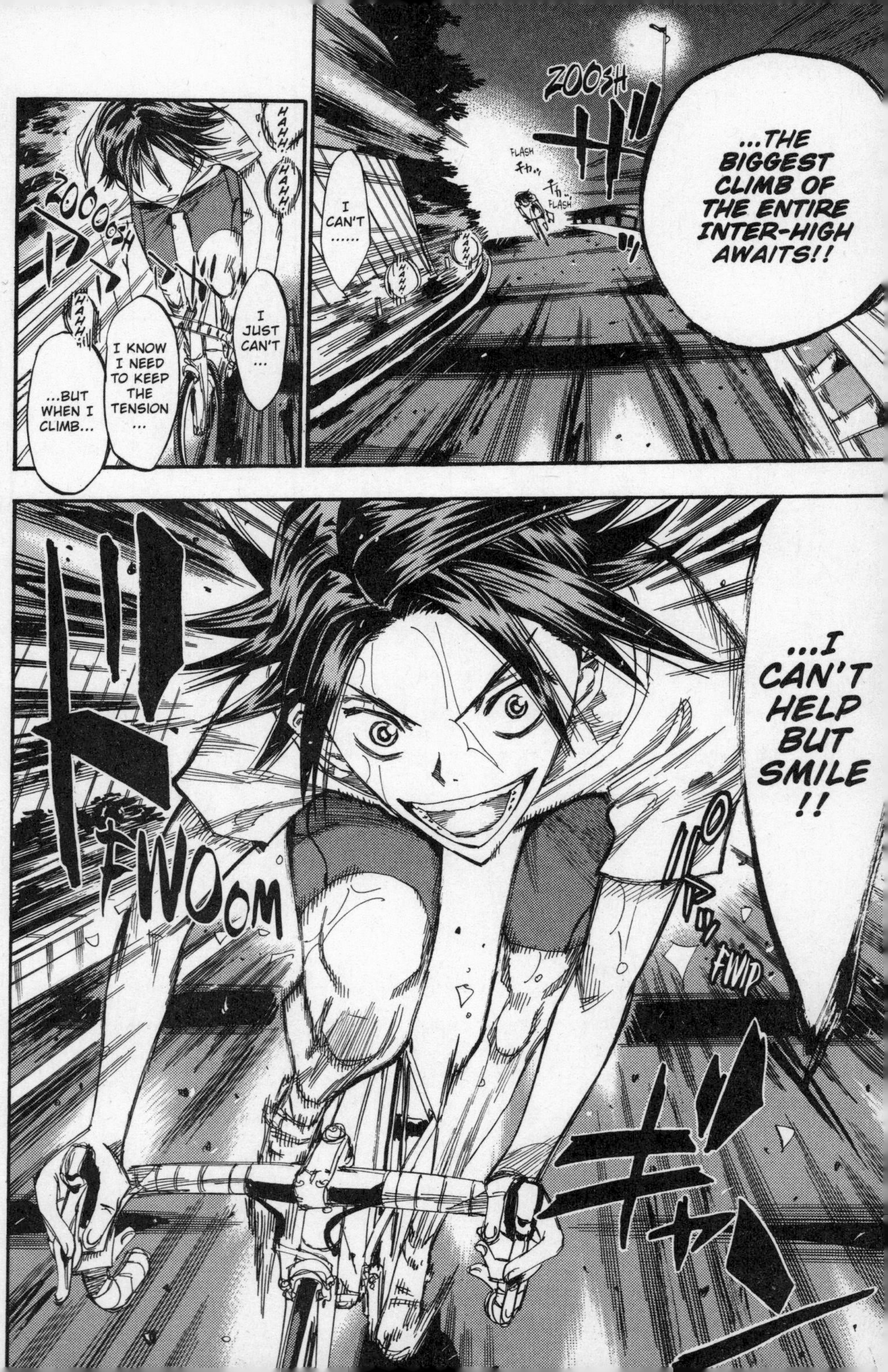ZOOSH
FLASH
FLASH
...THE BIGGEST CLIMB OF THE ENTIRE INTER-HIGH AWAITS!!
I CAN'T ......
HAHH
HAHH
HAHH HAHH HAHH
ZOOOSH
I JUST CAN'T ...
I KNOW I NEED TO KEEP THE TENSION ...
HAHH
...BUT WHEN I CLIMB...
...I CAN'T HELP BUT SMILE!!
FWIP
FWOOM

RIDE.158 DAY THREE GETS UNDERWAY!

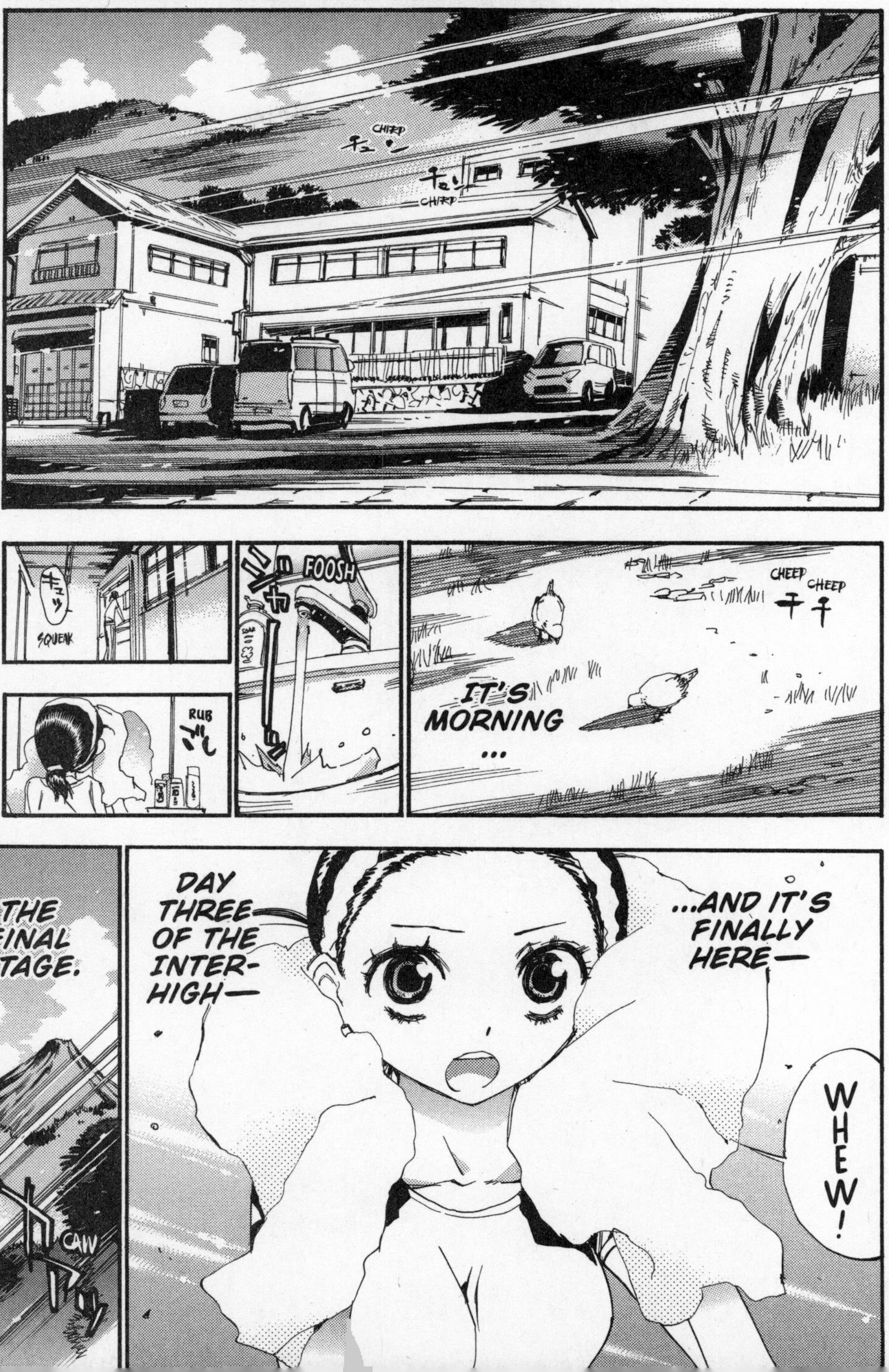
CHIRP
CHIRP
CHEEP CHEEP
IT'S MORNING ...
FOOSH
SQUEAK
RUB
DAY THREE OF THE INTER-HIGH—
...AND IT'S FINALLY HERE—
WHEW!
THE FINAL STAGE.
CAW

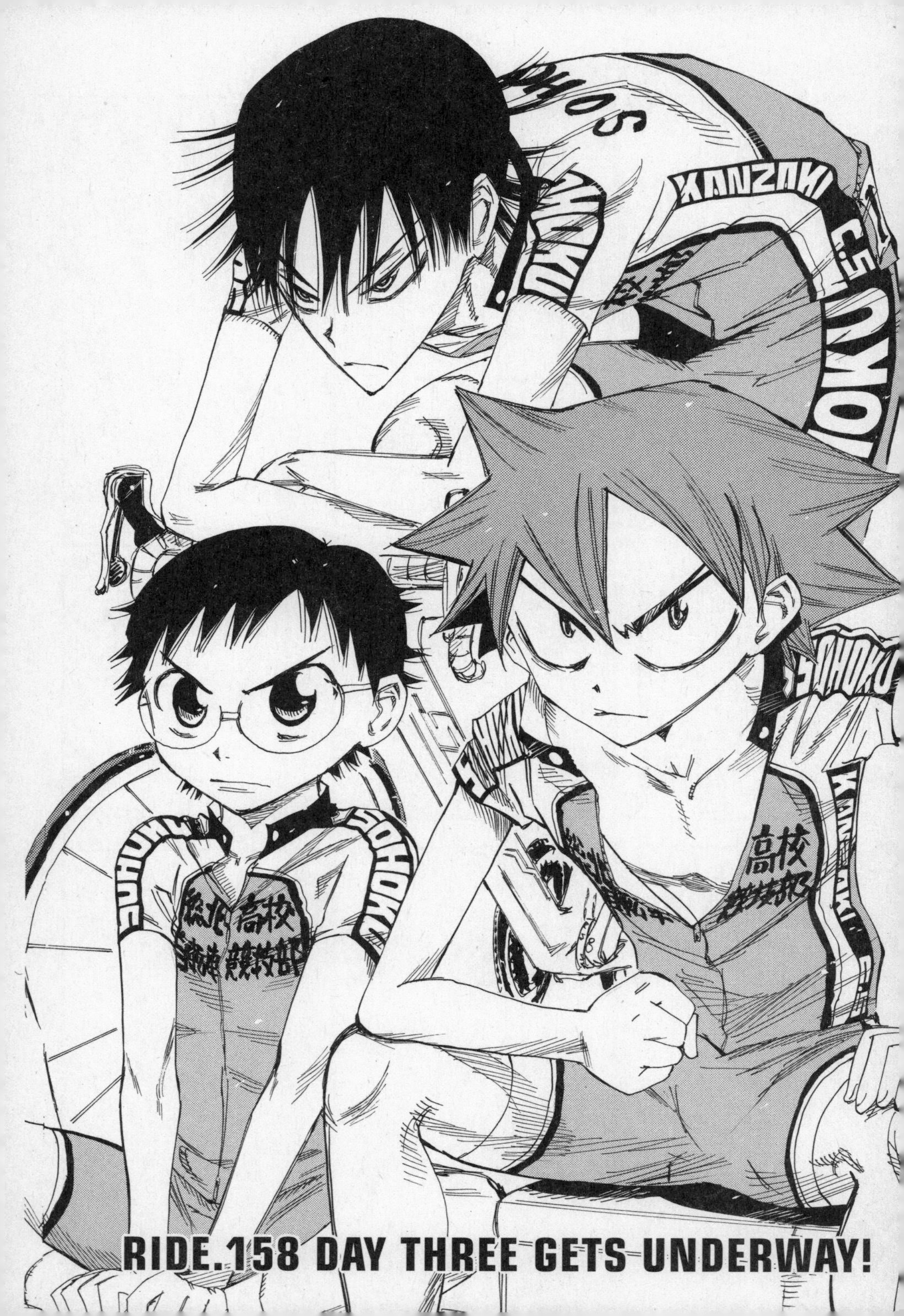

RIDE.158 DAY THREE GETS UNDERWAY!

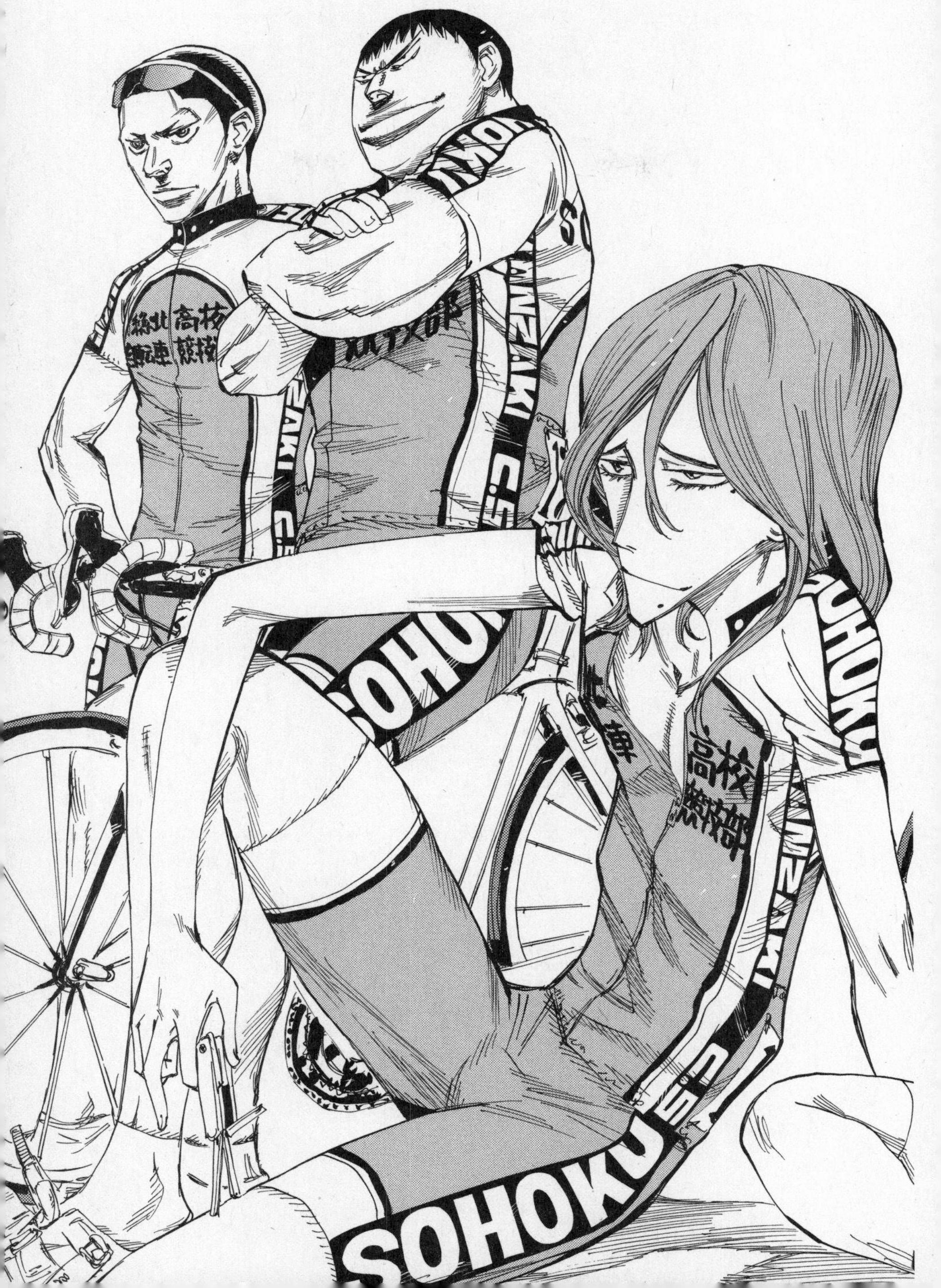
SOHOKU

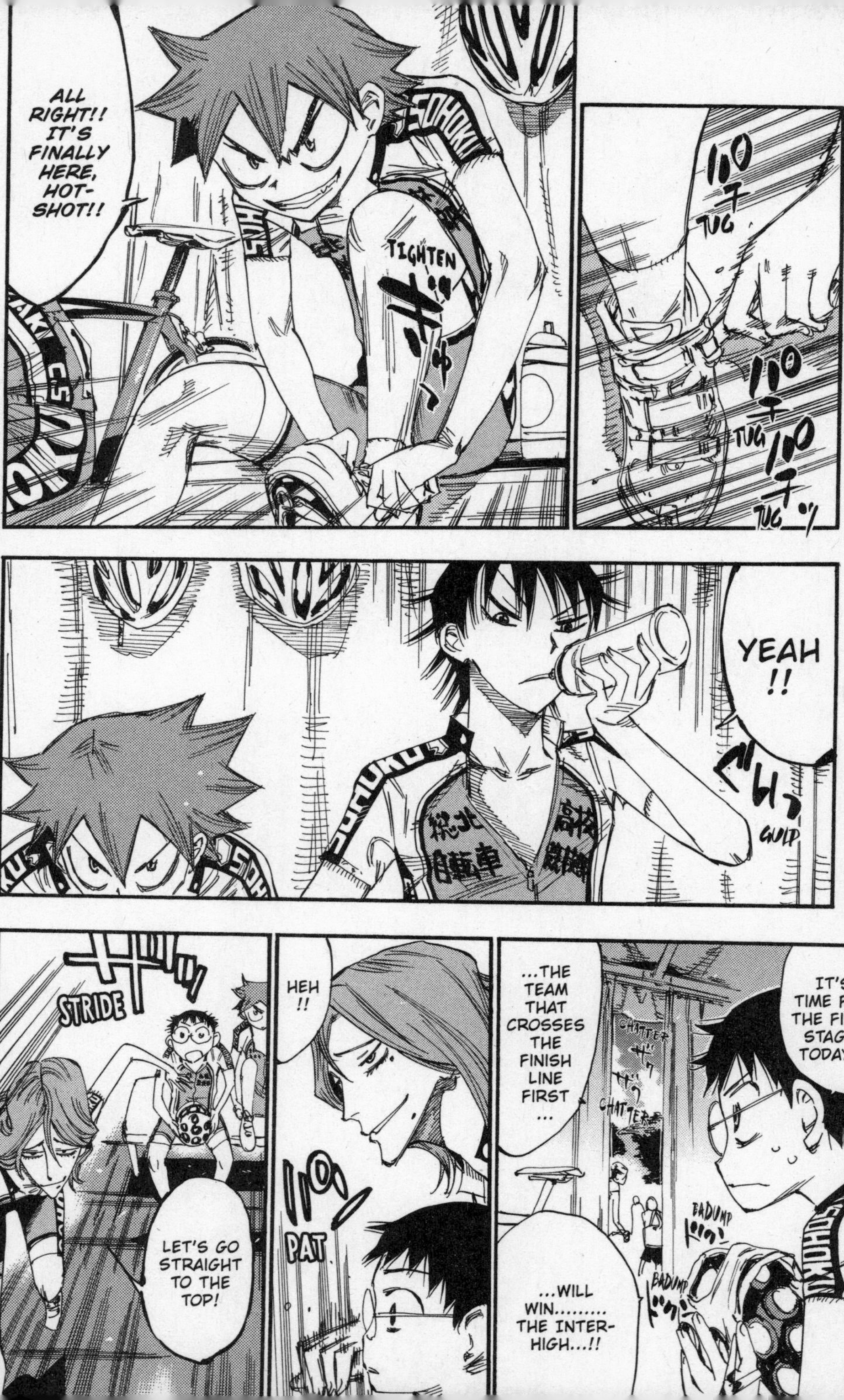
TUG
TUG
TUG
ALL RIGHT!! IT'S FINALLY HERE, HOT-SHOT!!
TIGHTEN
YEAH!!
GULP
IT'S TIME FOR THE FINAL STAGE. TODAY...
...THE TEAM THAT CROSSES THE FINISH LINE FIRST...
CHATTER
CHATTER
BADUMP
BADUMP
...WILL WIN......... THE INTER-HIGH...!!
HEH!!
PAT
STRIDE
LET'S GO STRAIGHT TO THE TOP!

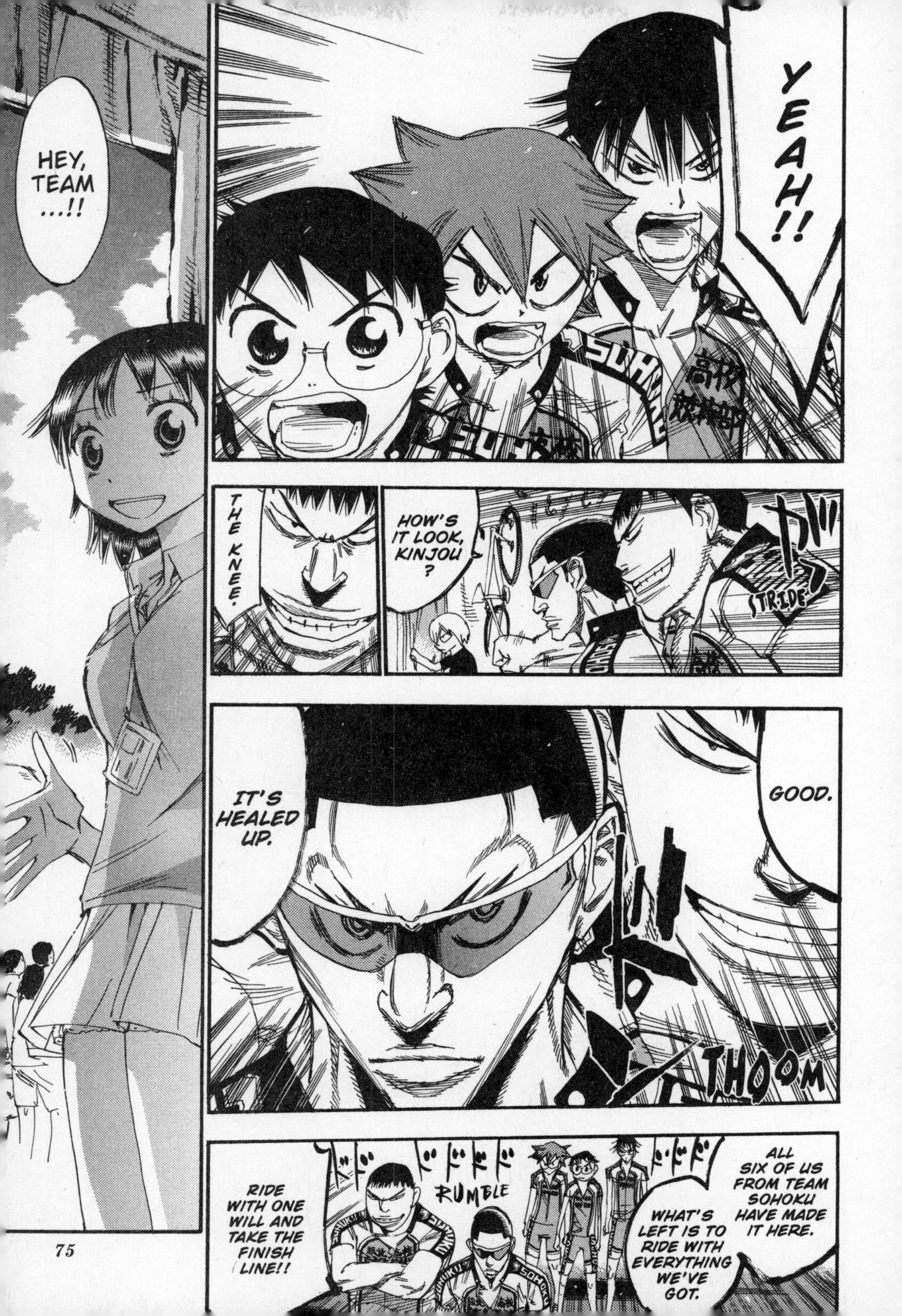
YEAH!!
HOW'S IT LOOK, KINJOU?
STRIDE
THE KNEE.
GOOD.
IT'S HEALED UP.
THOOM
ALL SIX OF US FROM TEAM SOHOKU HAVE MADE IT HERE.
WHAT'S LEFT IS TO RIDE WITH EVERYTHING WE'VE GOT.
RUMBLE
RIDE WITH ONE WILL AND TAKE THE FINISH LINE!!
HEY, TEAM ...!!

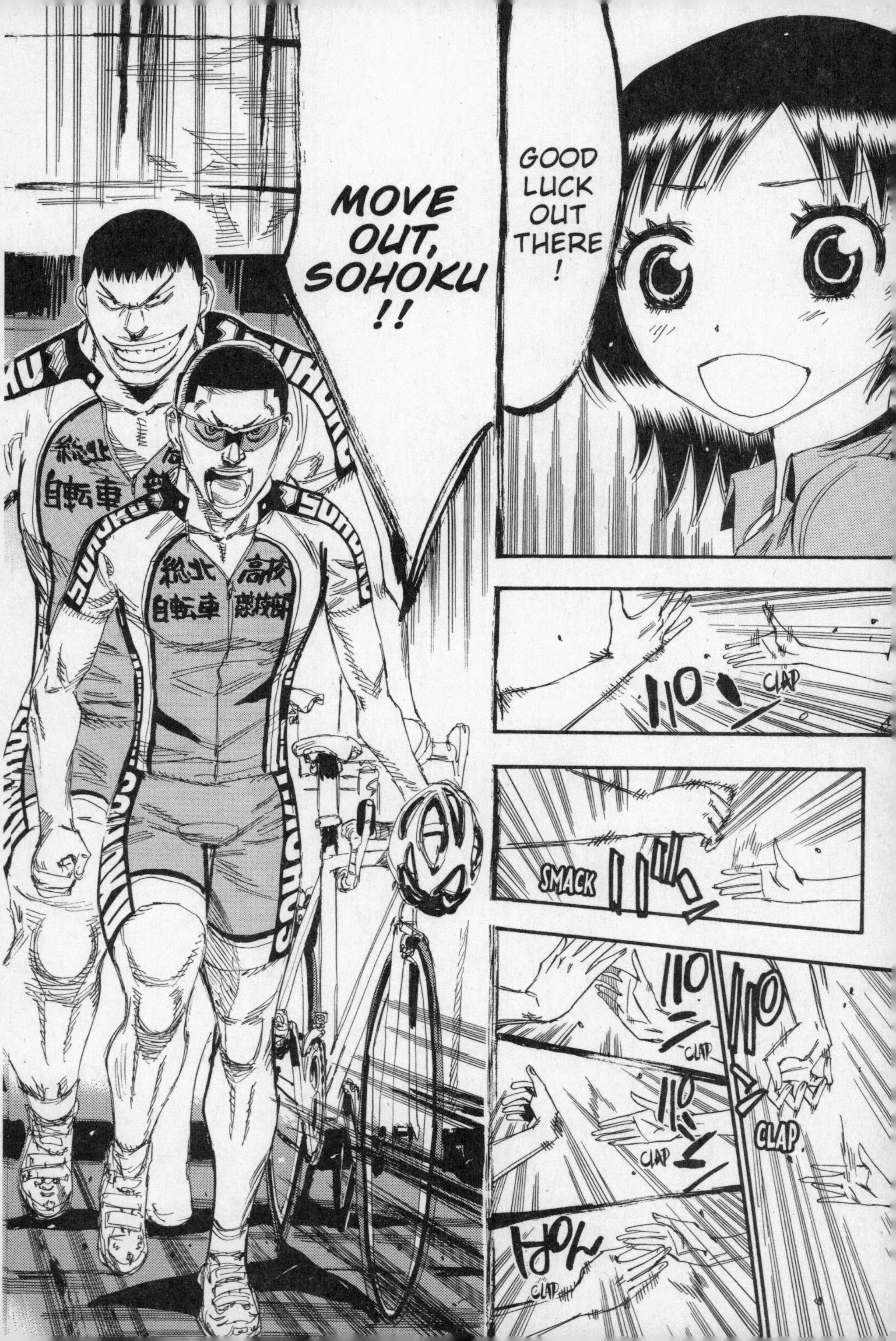
GOOD LUCK OUT THERE!
CLAP
SMACK
CLAP
CLAP
CLAP
CLAP
MOVE OUT, SOHOKU!!
総北高校
自転車競技部

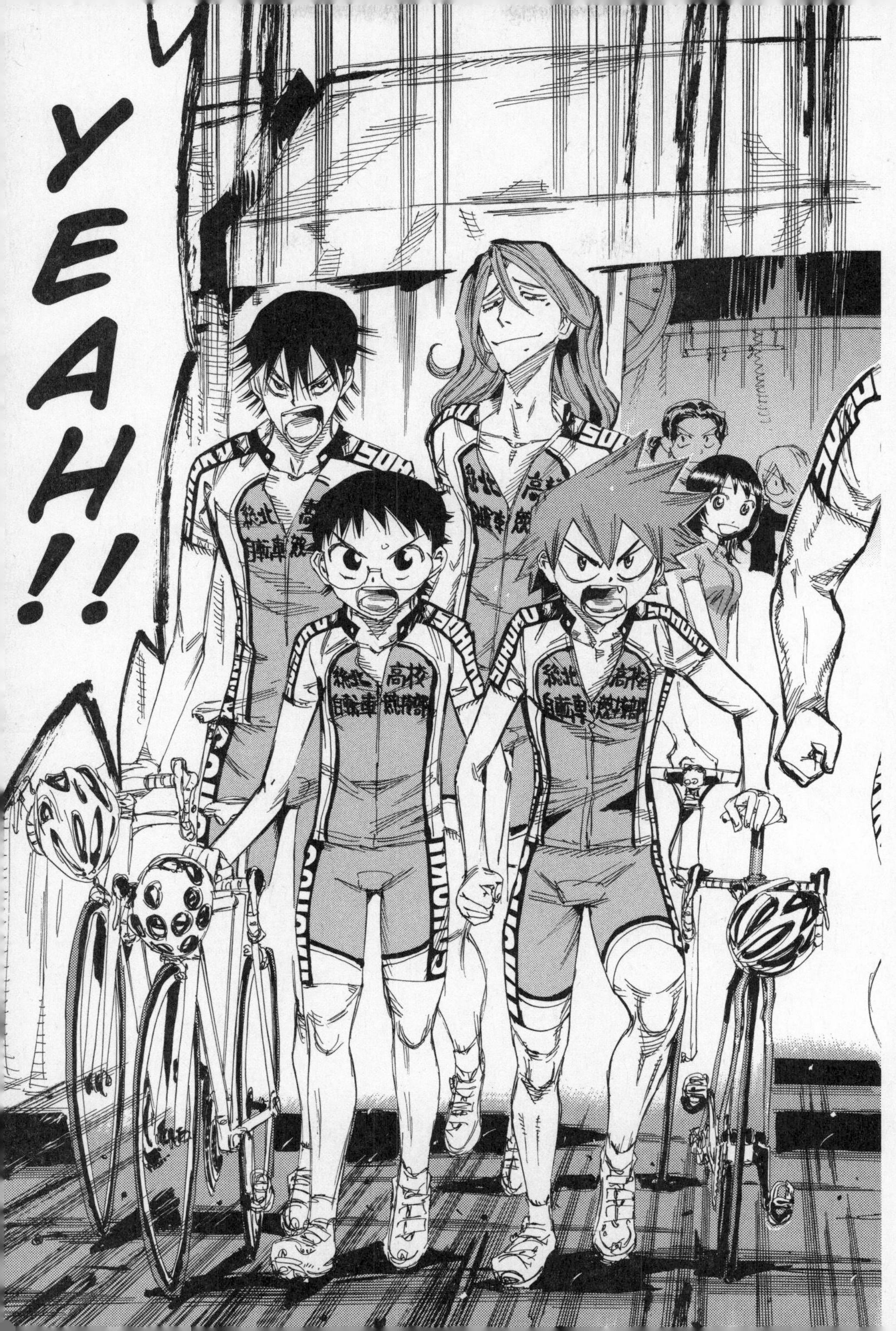
YEAH!!
SOHOKU

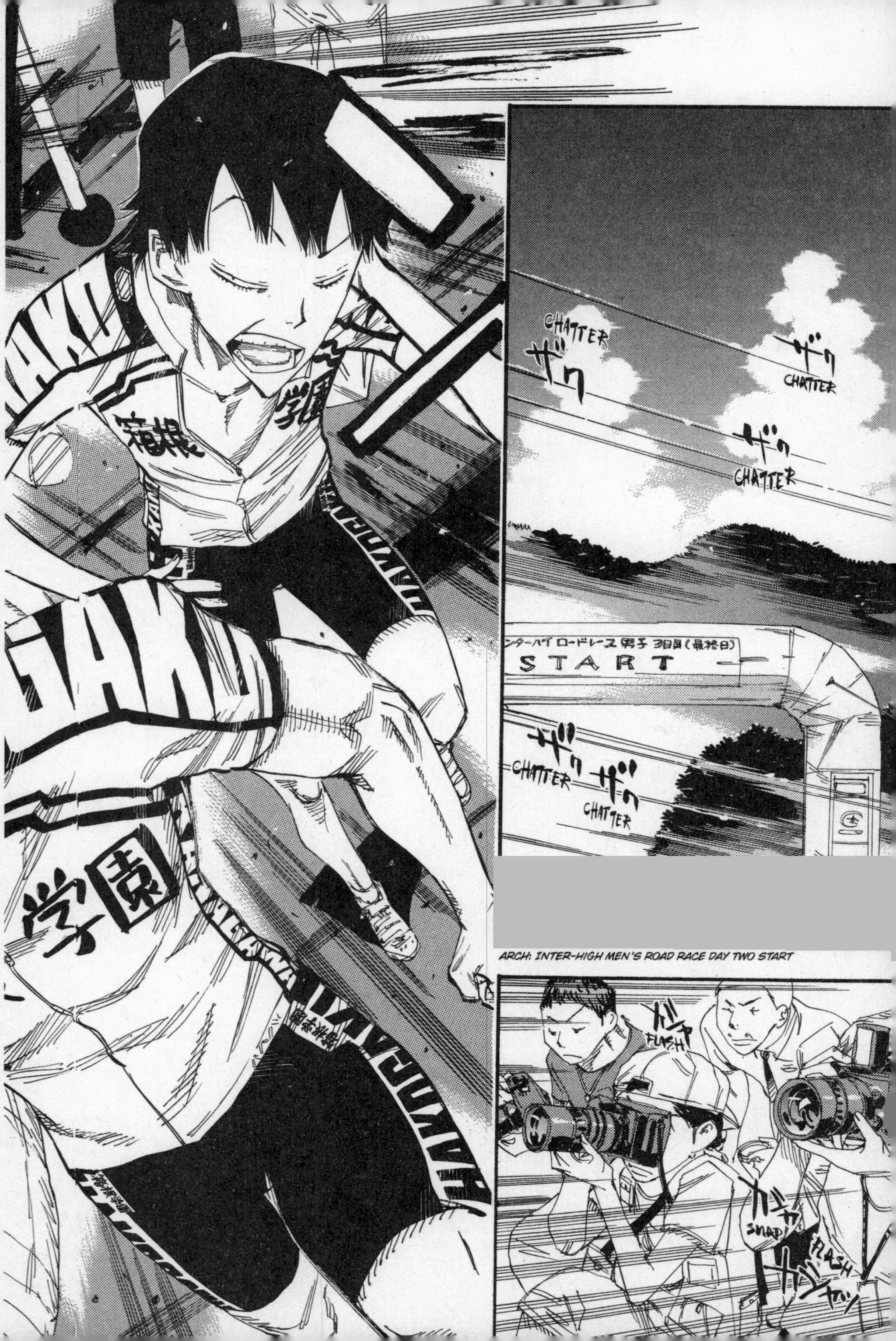
CHATTER
ザワ
ザワ
CHATTER
ザワ
CHATTER
ンターハイ ロードレース 男子 3日目(最終日)
START
ザワ
CHATTER
ザワ
CHATTER
ARCH: INTER-HIGH MEN'S ROAD RACE DAY TWO START
ガシャ
FLASH
SNAP
FLASH
箱根
学園
学園

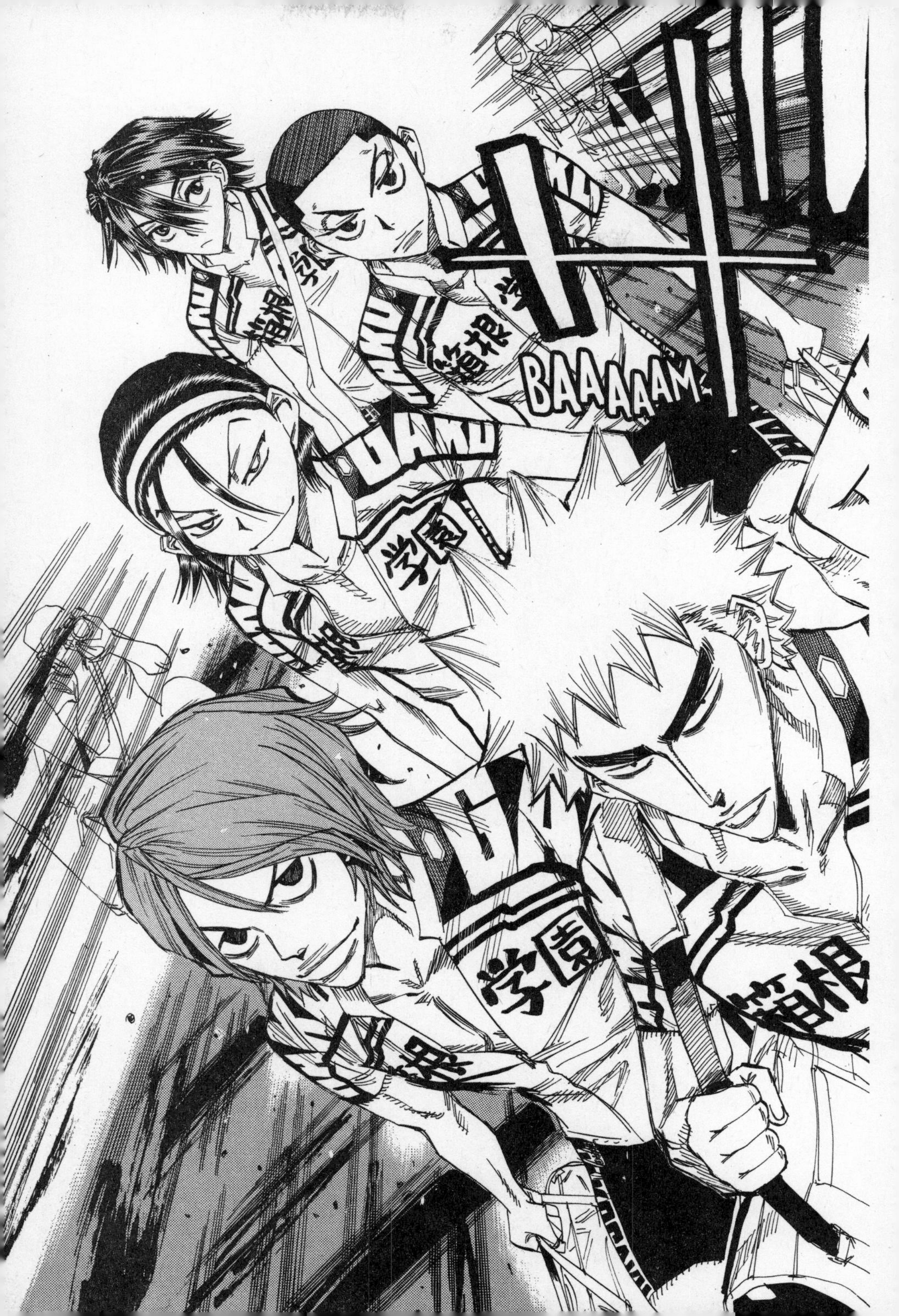
BAAAAAM

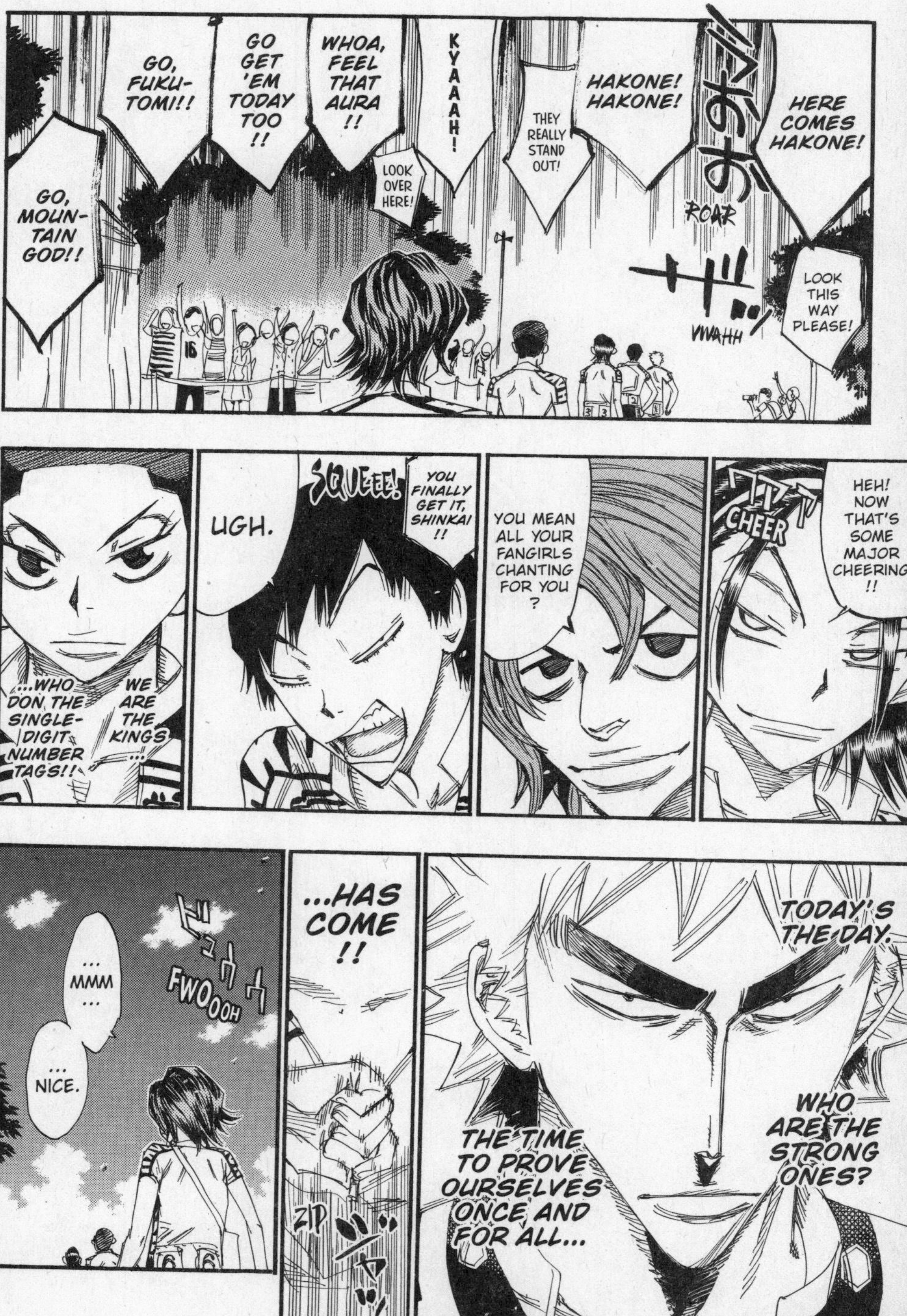
HERE COMES HAKONE!
ROAR
HAKONE! HAKONE!
THEY REALLY STAND OUT!
KYAAAH!
WHOA, FEEL THAT AURA!!
LOOK OVER HERE!
GO GET 'EM TODAY TOO!!
GO, FUKUTOMI!!
GO, MOUNTAIN GOD!!
LOOK THIS WAY PLEASE!
VWAHH
CHEER
HEH! NOW THAT'S SOME MAJOR CHEERING!!
YOU MEAN ALL YOUR FANGIRLS CHANTING FOR YOU?
SQUEEE!
YOU FINALLY GET IT, SHINKAI!!
UGH.
WE ARE THE KINGS...
...WHO DON THE SINGLE-DIGIT NUMBER TAGS!!
TODAY'S THE DAY.
WHO ARE THE STRONG ONES?
THE TIME TO PROVE OURSELVES ONCE AND FOR ALL...
...HAS COME!!
ZIP
FWOOOH
...MMM...
...NICE.

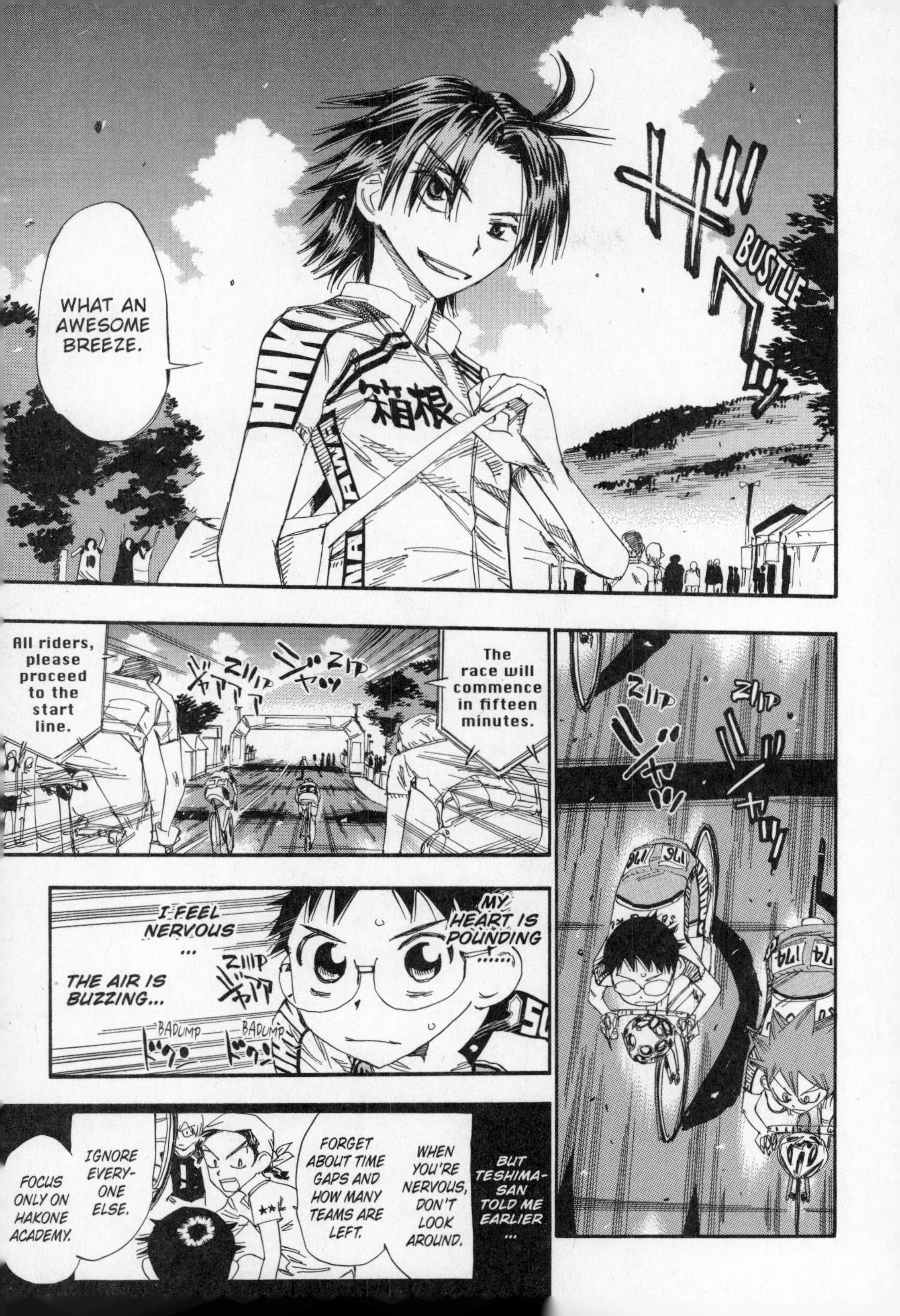
BUSTLE
WHAT AN AWESOME BREEZE.
ZIP
ZIP
The race will commence in fifteen minutes.
ZIP
ZIP
All riders, please proceed to the start line.
MY HEART IS POUNDING......
I FEEL NERVOUS...
ZIP
THE AIR IS BUZZING...
BADUMP
BADUMP
BUT TESHIMA-SAN TOLD ME EARLIER...
WHEN YOU'RE NERVOUS, DON'T LOOK AROUND.
FORGET ABOUT TIME GAPS AND HOW MANY TEAMS ARE LEFT.
IGNORE EVERY-ONE ELSE.
FOCUS ONLY ON HAKONE ACADEMY.

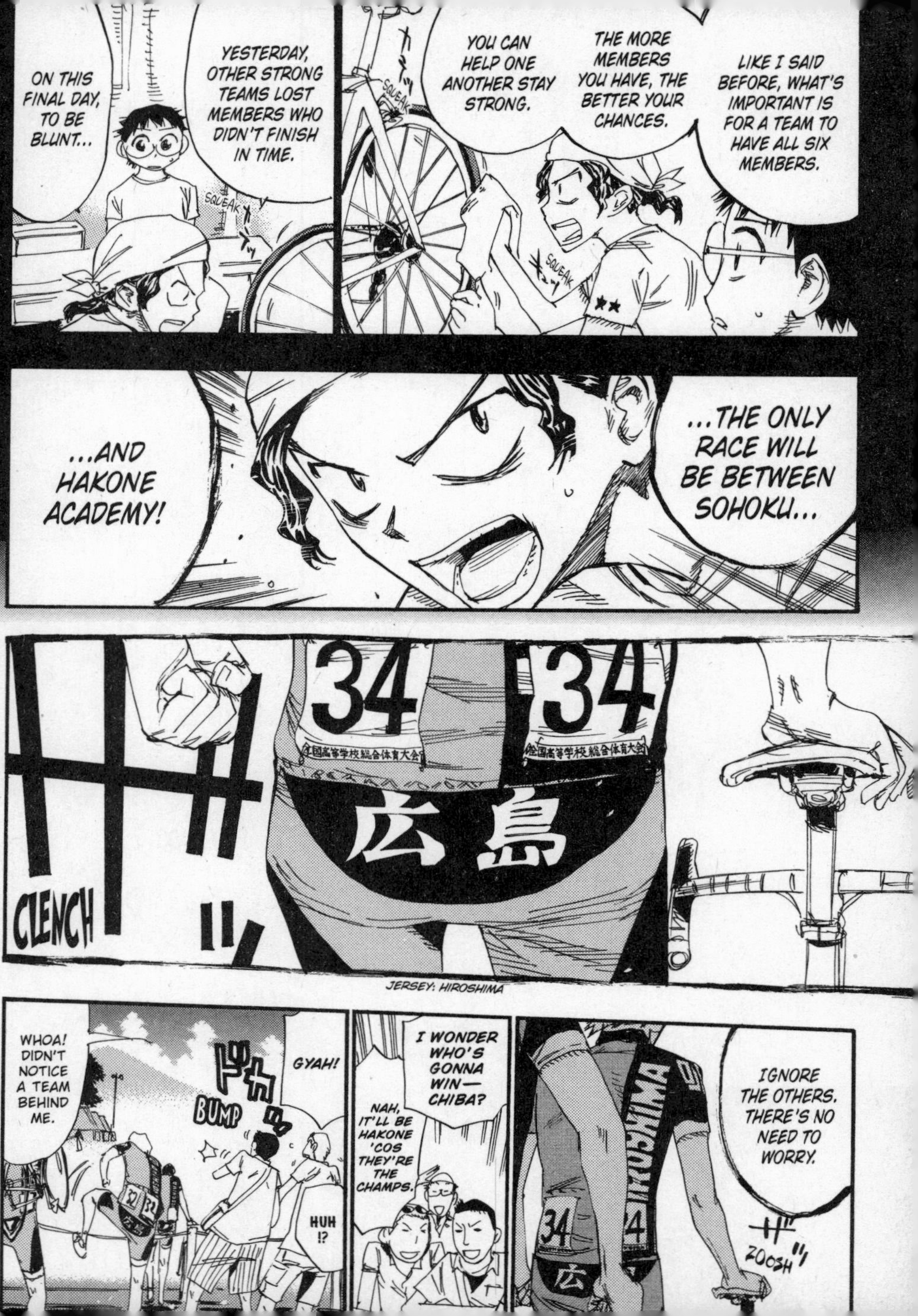
LIKE I SAID BEFORE, WHAT'S IMPORTANT IS FOR A TEAM TO HAVE ALL SIX MEMBERS.
THE MORE MEMBERS YOU HAVE, THE BETTER YOUR CHANCES.
YOU CAN HELP ONE ANOTHER STAY STRONG.
SQUEAK
SQUEAK
YESTERDAY, OTHER STRONG TEAMS LOST MEMBERS WHO DIDN'T FINISH IN TIME.
ON THIS FINAL DAY, TO BE BLUNT...
SQUEAK
...THE ONLY RACE WILL BE BETWEEN SOHOKU...
...AND HAKONE ACADEMY!
34
34
全国高等学校総合体育大会
全国高等学校総合体育大会
広島
CLENCH
JERSEY: HIROSHIMA
IGNORE THE OTHERS. THERE'S NO NEED TO WORRY.
ZOOSH
I WONDER WHO'S GONNA WIN— CHIBA?
NAH, IT'LL BE HAKONE 'COS THEY'RE THE CHAMPS.
GYAH!
WHOA! DIDN'T NOTICE A TEAM BEHIND ME.
BUMP
HUH!?

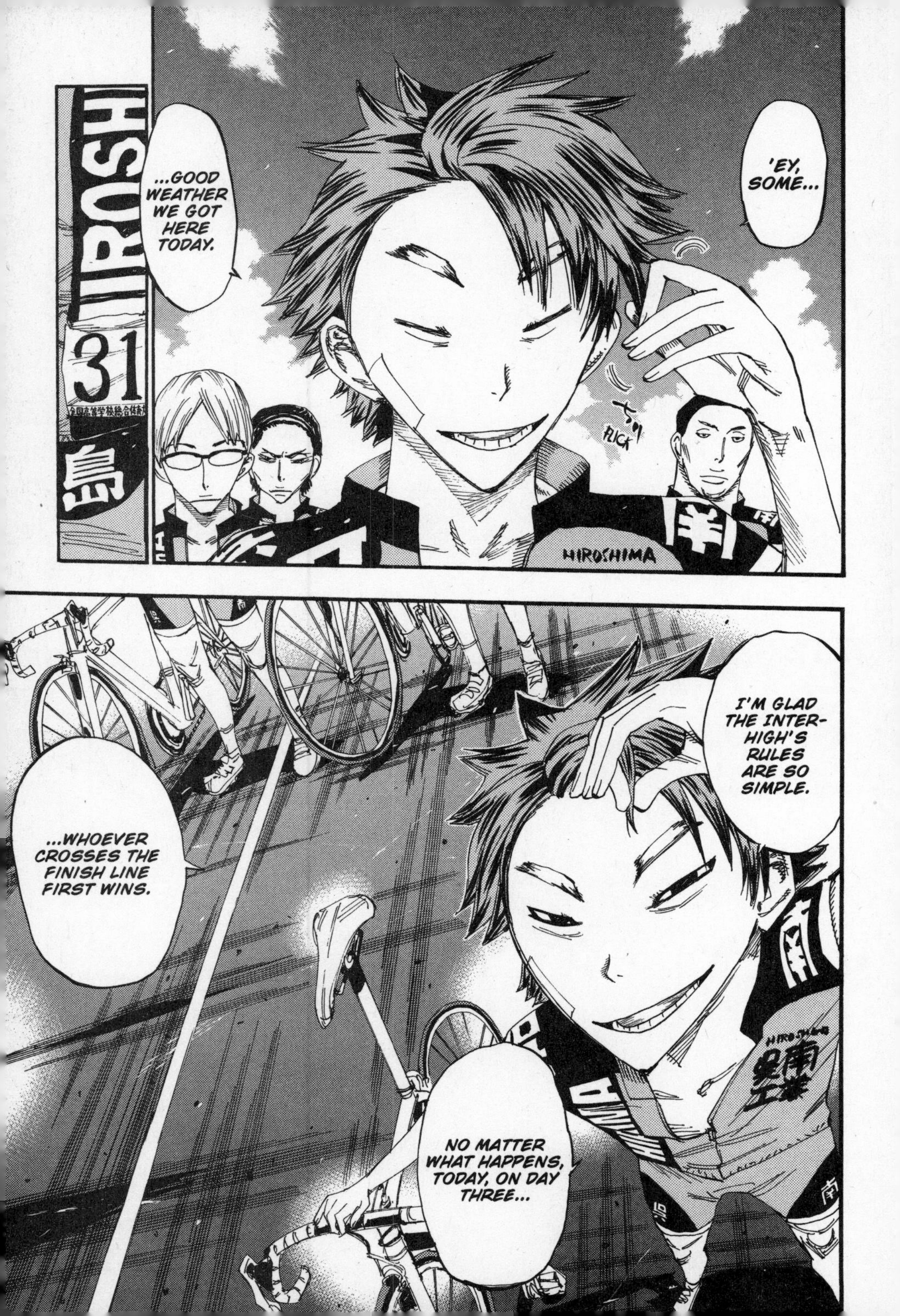
'EY, SOME...
...GOOD WEATHER WE GOT HERE TODAY.
HIROSH
31
島
FLICK
HIROSHIMA
I'M GLAD THE INTER-HIGH'S RULES ARE SO SIMPLE.
...WHOEVER CROSSES THE FINISH LINE FIRST WINS.
NO MATTER WHAT HAPPENS, TODAY, ON DAY THREE...

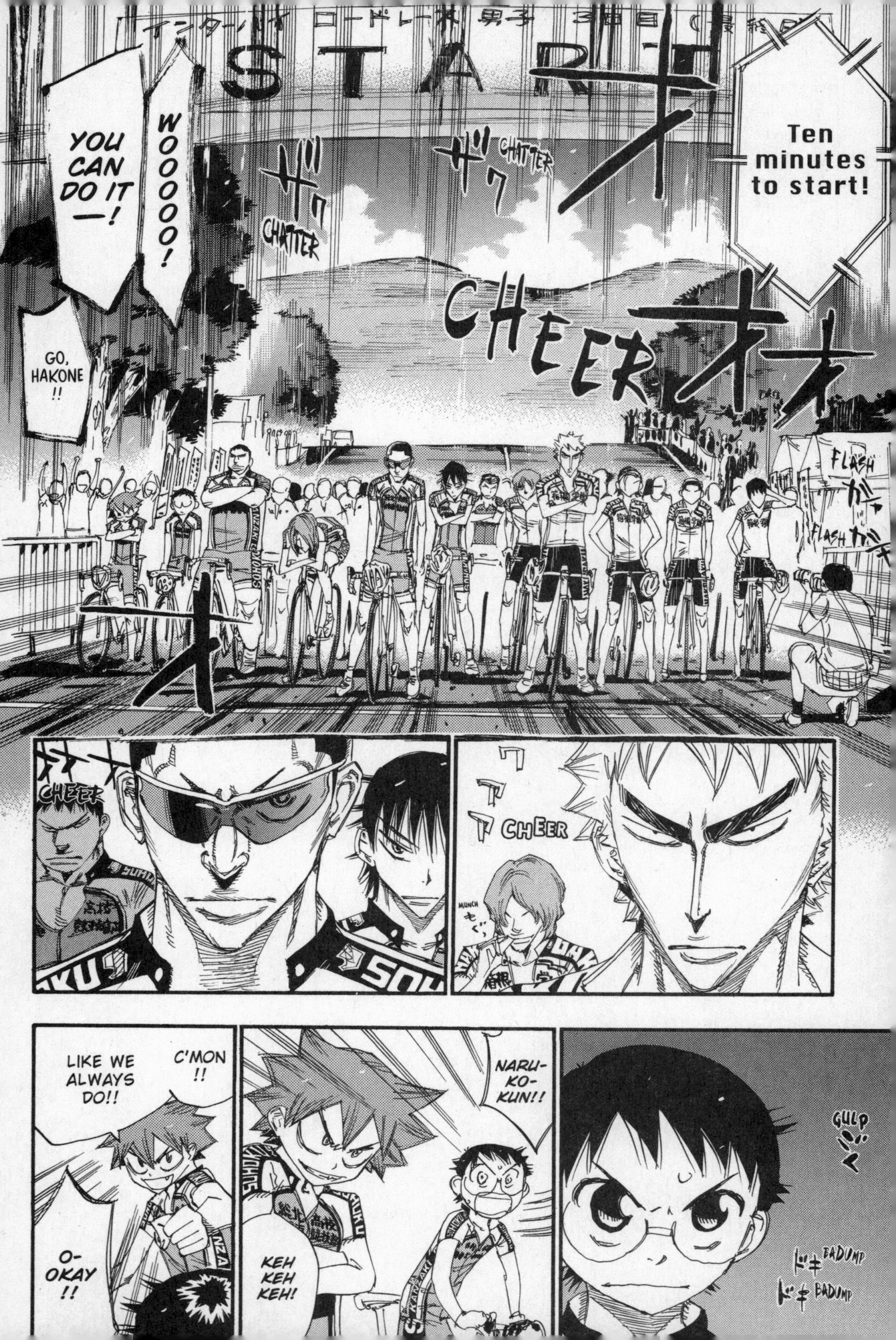
START
Ten minutes to start!
CHATTER
WOOOOOOO!
YOU CAN DO IT—!
CHATTER
CHEER
GO, HAKONE!!
FLASH
FLASH
CHEER
MUNCH
CHEER
GULP
BADUMP
BADUMP
NARUKO-KUN!!
KEH KEH KEH!
C'MON!!
LIKE WE ALWAYS DO!!
O-OKAY!!

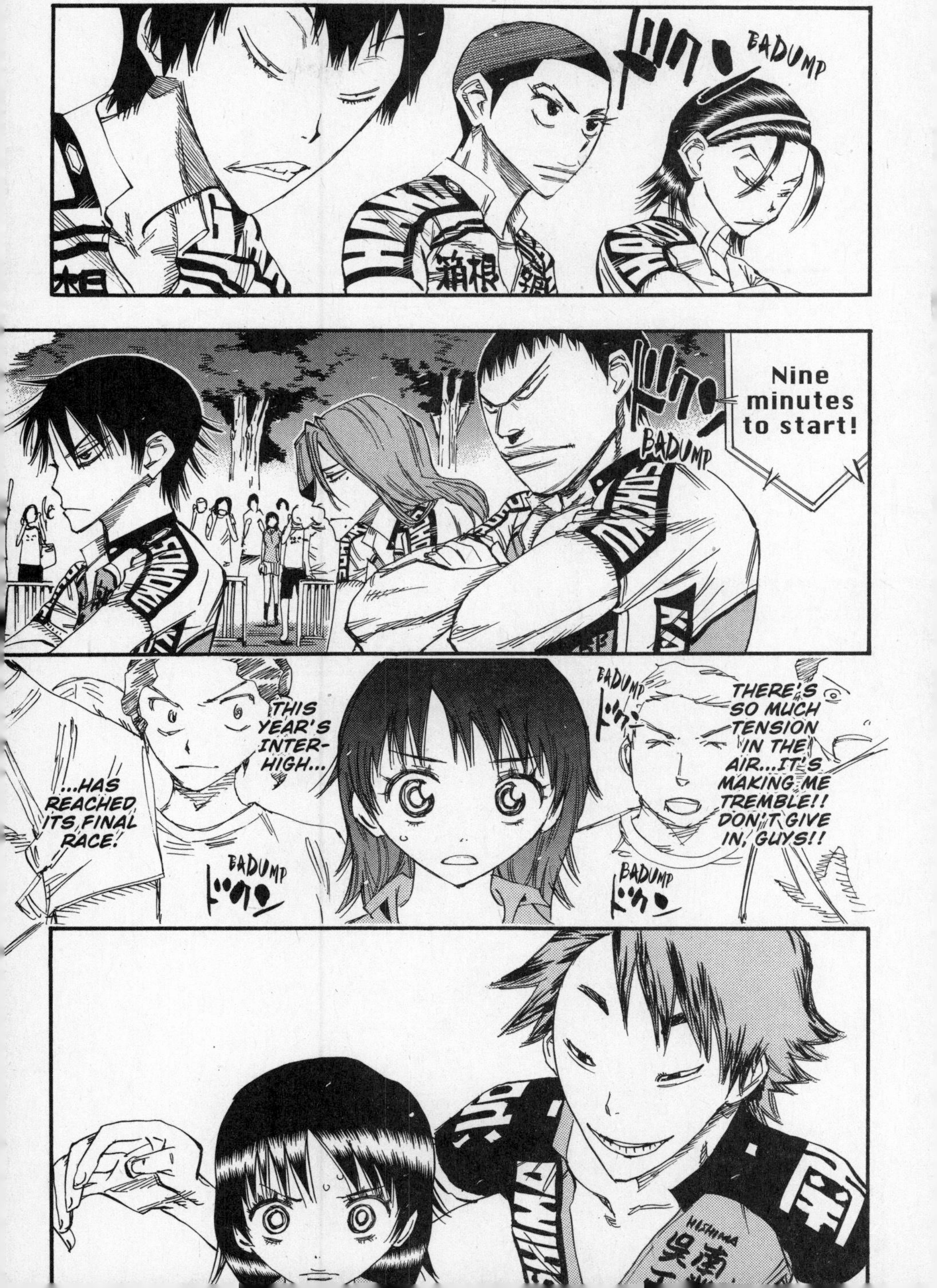
BADUMP
Nine minutes to start!
BADUMP
BADUMP
THERE'S SO MUCH TENSION IN THE AIR...IT'S MAKING ME TREMBLE!! DON'T GIVE IN, GUYS!!
BADUMP
THIS YEAR'S INTER-HIGH...
...HAS REACHED ITS FINAL RACE.
BADUMP

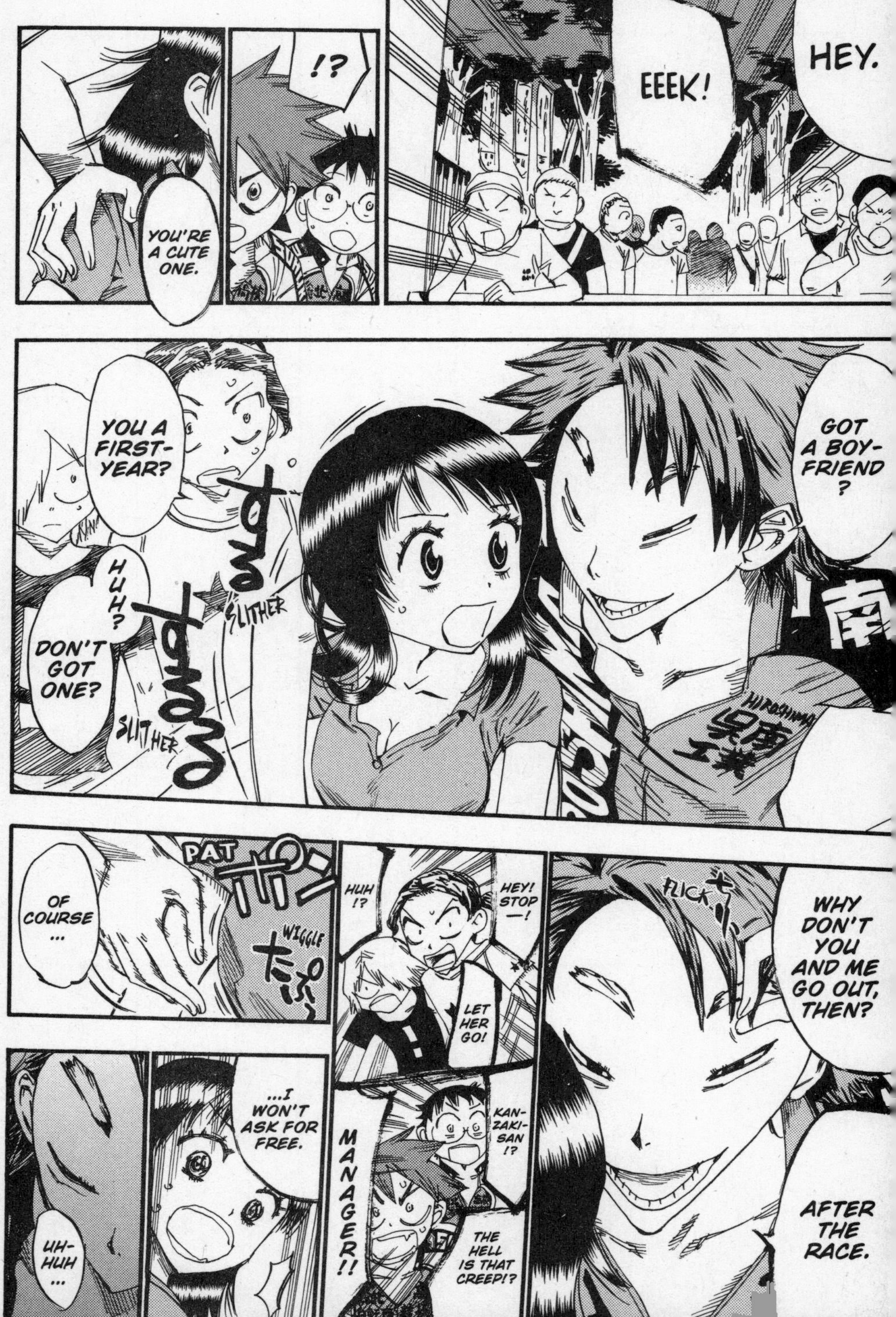
HEY.
EEEK!
!?
YOU'RE A CUTE ONE.
GOT A BOY-FRIEND?
YOU A FIRST-YEAR?
SLITHER
SLITHER
HUH? DON'T GOT ONE?
FLICK
WHY DON'T YOU AND ME GO OUT, THEN?
AFTER THE RACE.
HEY! STOP—!
HUH!?
LET HER GO!
PAT
OF COURSE...
WIGGLE
KANZAKI-SAN!?
THE HELL IS THAT CREEP!?
MANAGER!!
...I WON'T ASK FOR FREE.
UH-HUH...

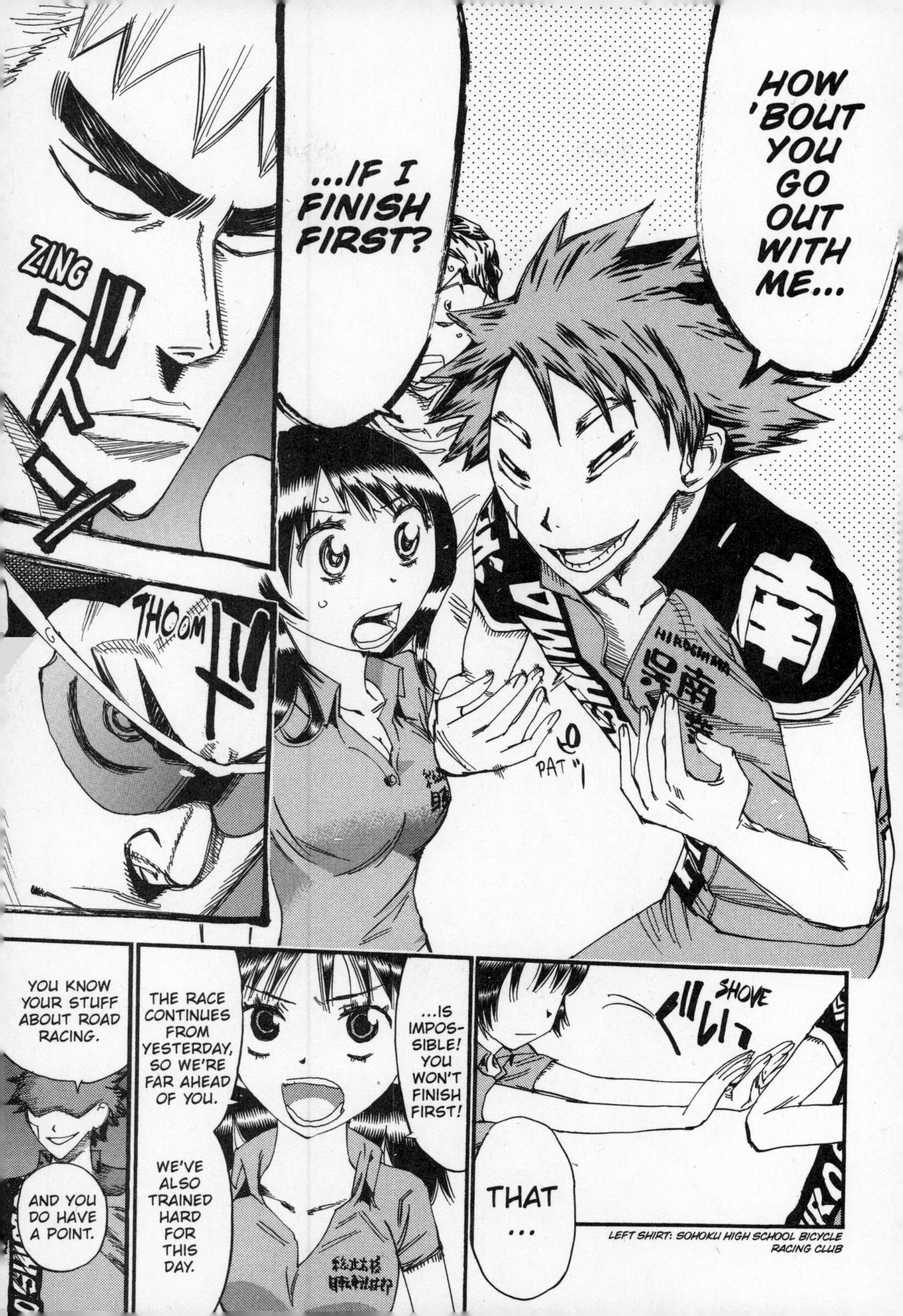
HOW 'BOUT YOU GO OUT WITH ME...
...IF I FINISH FIRST?
PAT
ZING
THOOM
SHOVE
THAT ...
...IS IMPOSSIBLE! YOU WON'T FINISH FIRST!
THE RACE CONTINUES FROM YESTERDAY, SO WE'RE FAR AHEAD OF YOU.
WE'VE ALSO TRAINED HARD FOR THIS DAY.
YOU KNOW YOUR STUFF ABOUT ROAD RACING.
AND YOU DO HAVE A POINT.
LEFT SHIRT: SOHOKU HIGH SCHOOL BICYCLE RACING CLUB

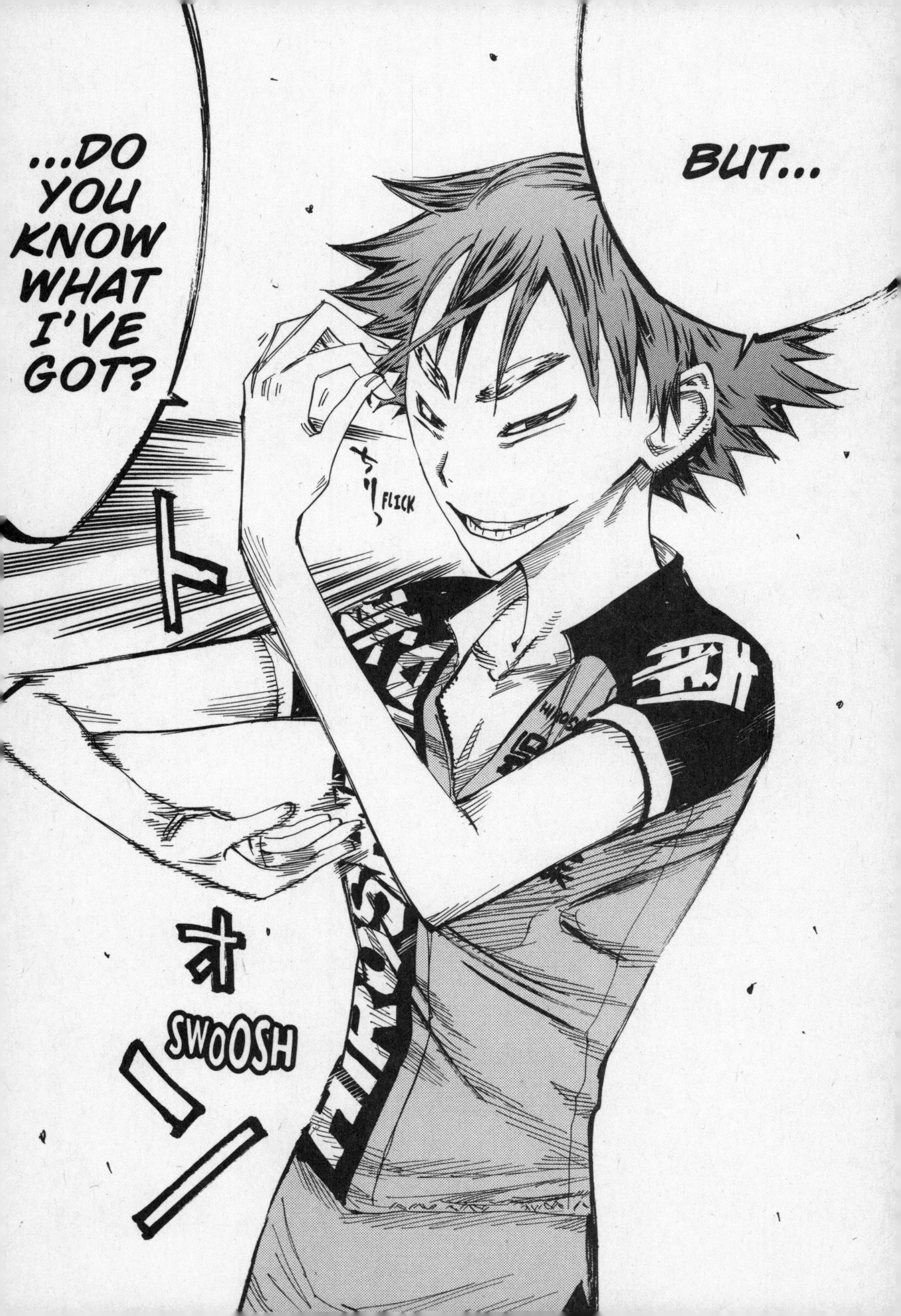
BUT...
...DO YOU KNOW WHAT I'VE GOT?
FLICK
SWOOSH

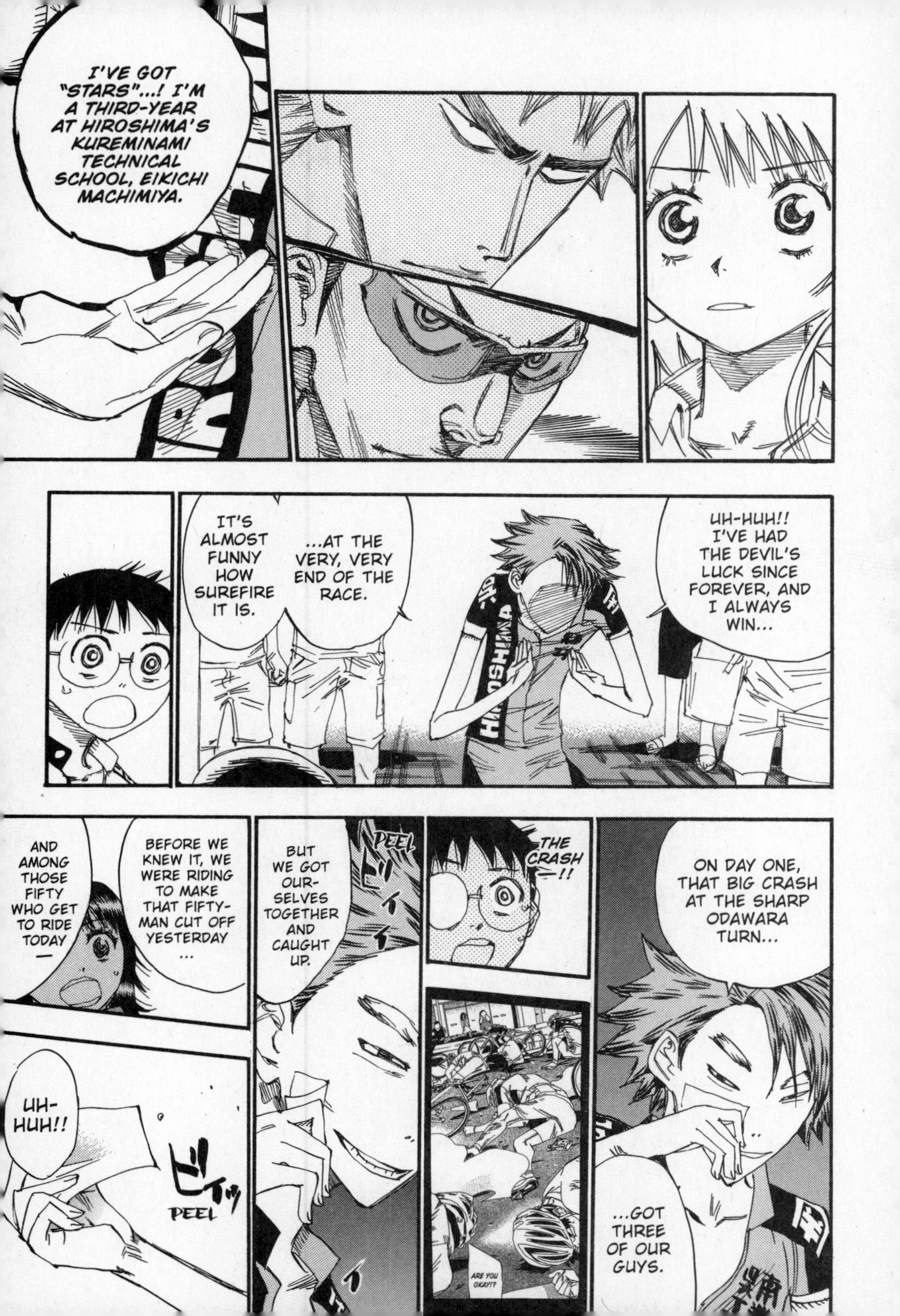
I'VE GOT "STARS"...! I'M A THIRD-YEAR AT HIROSHIMA'S KUREMINAMI TECHNICAL SCHOOL, EIKICHI MACHIMIYA.
UH-HUH!! I'VE HAD THE DEVIL'S LUCK SINCE FOREVER, AND I ALWAYS WIN...
IT'S ALMOST FUNNY HOW SUREFIRE IT IS.
...AT THE VERY, VERY END OF THE RACE.
HIROSHIMA
ON DAY ONE, THAT BIG CRASH AT THE SHARP ODAWARA TURN...
...GOT THREE OF OUR GUYS.
ARE YOU OKAY!?
THE CRASH—!!
PEEL
BUT WE GOT OURSELVES TOGETHER AND CAUGHT UP.
BEFORE WE KNEW IT, WE WERE RIDING TO MAKE THAT FIFTY-MAN CUT OFF YESTERDAY...
AND AMONG THOSE FIFTY WHO GET TO RIDE TODAY—
UH-HUH!!
PEEL

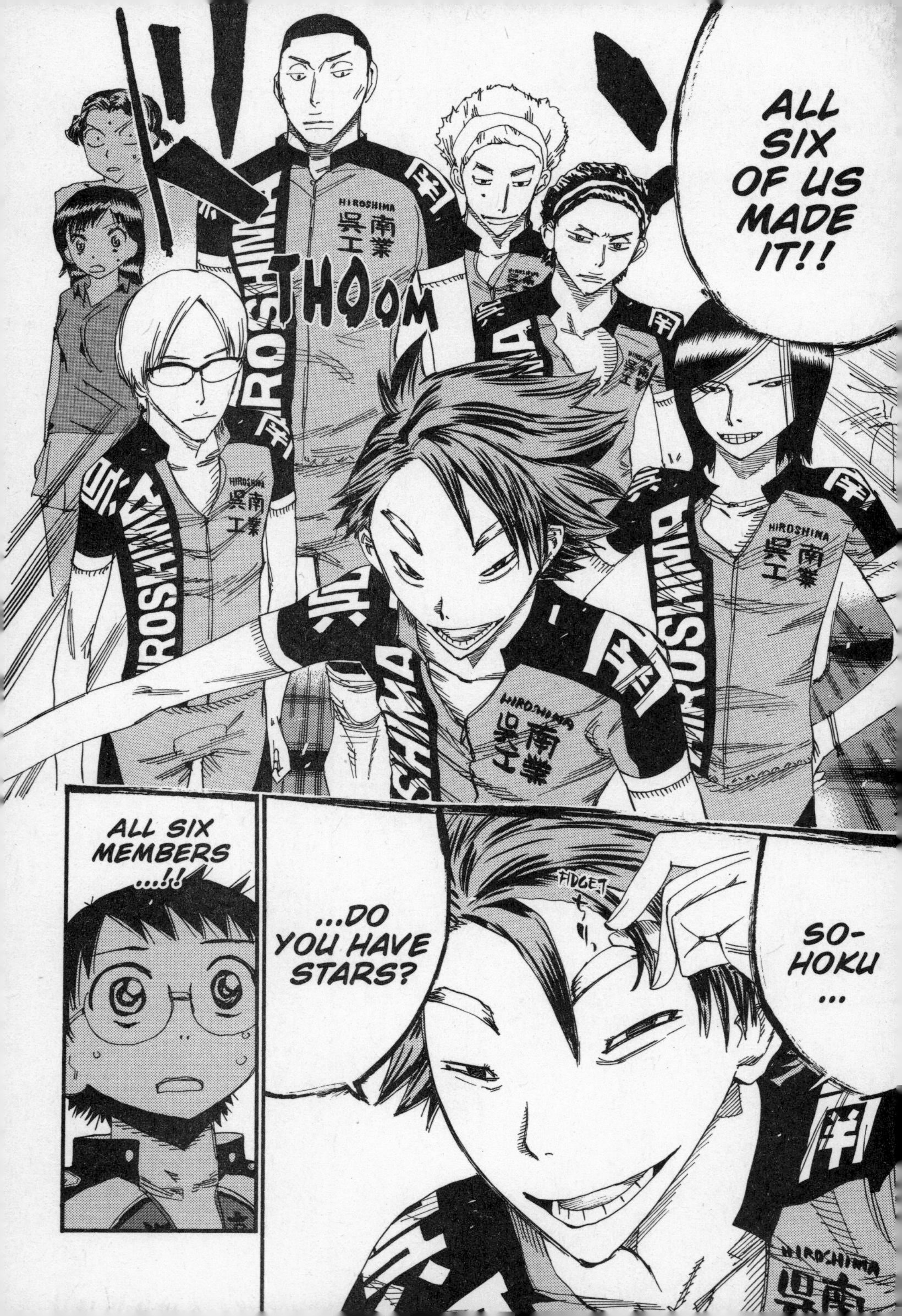
ALL SIX OF US MADE IT!!
THOOM
SO-HOKU ...
FIDGET
...DO YOU HAVE STARS?
ALL SIX MEMBERS ...!!

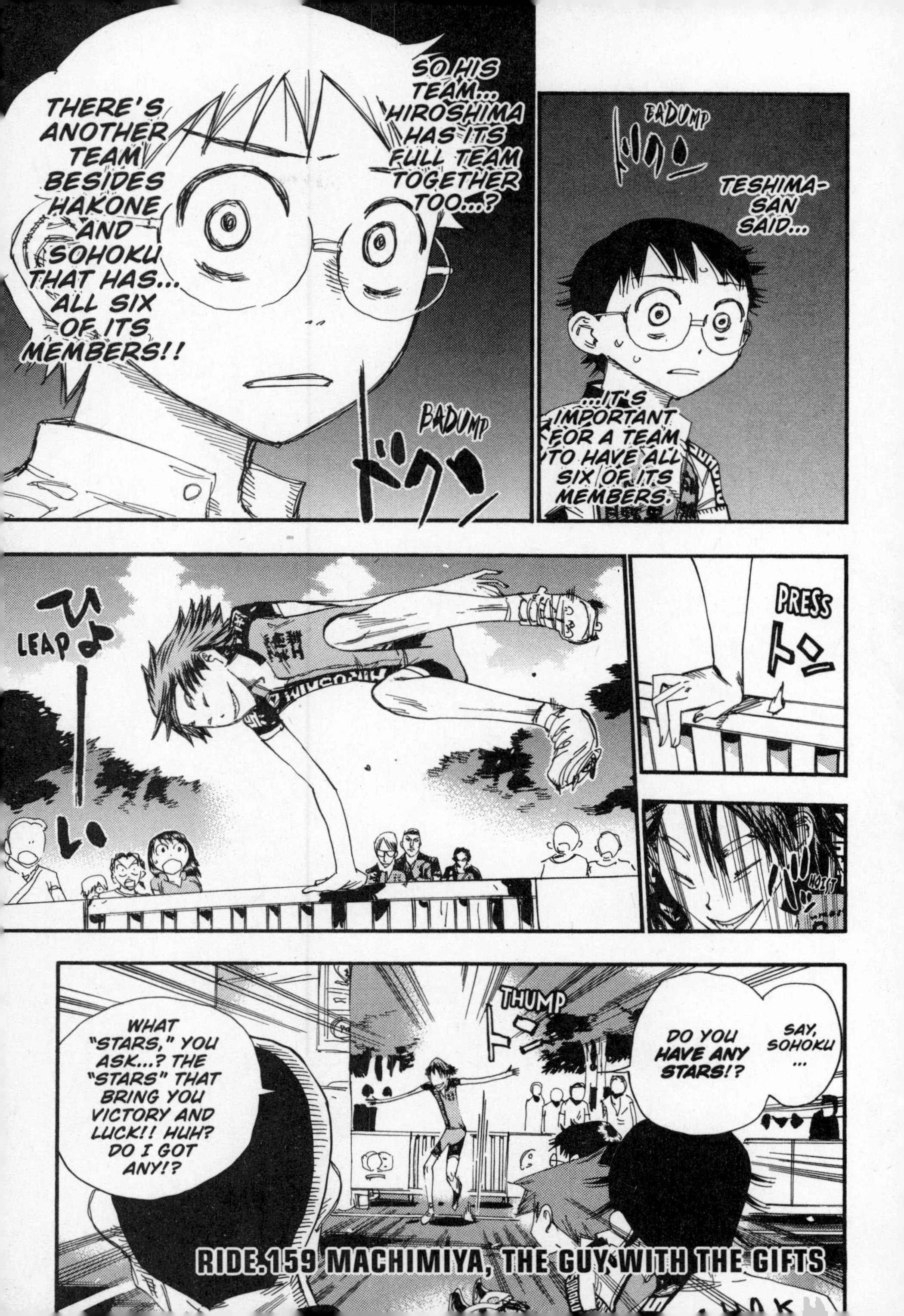
BADUMP
TESHIMA-SAN SAID...
...IT'S IMPORTANT FOR A TEAM TO HAVE ALL SIX OF ITS MEMBERS.
SO HIS TEAM... HIROSHIMA HAS ITS FULL TEAM TOGETHER TOO...?
THERE'S ANOTHER TEAM BESIDES HAKONE AND SOHOKU THAT HAS... ALL SIX OF ITS MEMBERS!!
BADUMP
PRESS
HOIST
LEAP
SAY, SOHOKU ...
DO YOU HAVE ANY STARS!?
THUMP
WHAT "STARS," YOU ASK...? THE "STARS" THAT BRING YOU VICTORY AND LUCK!! HUH? DO I GOT ANY!?
RIDE.159 MACHIMIYA, THE GUY WITH THE GIFTS

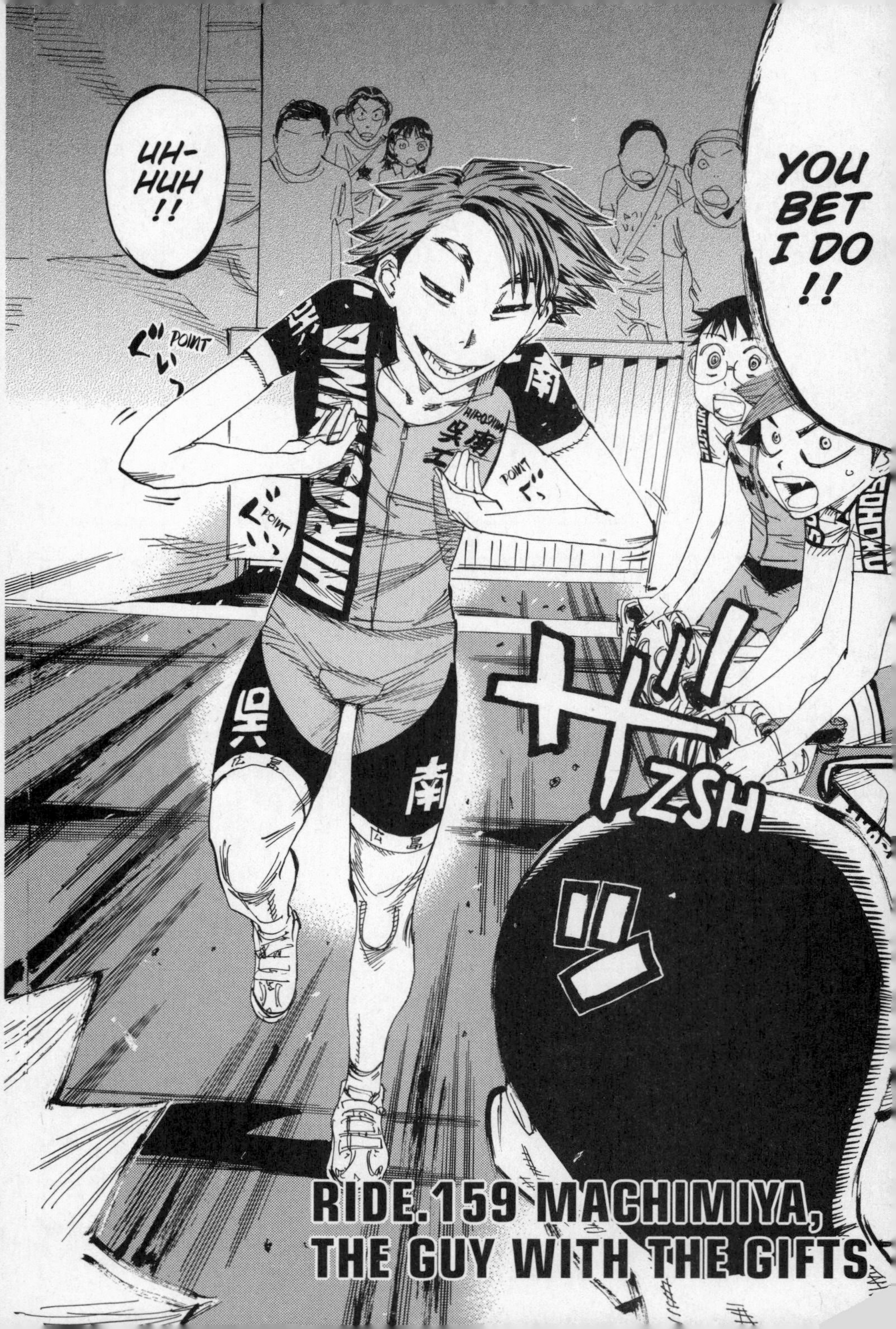
YOU BET I DO!!
UH-HUH!!
POINT
POINT
POINT
ZSH
RIDE.159 MACHIMIYA, THE GUY WITH THE GIFTS

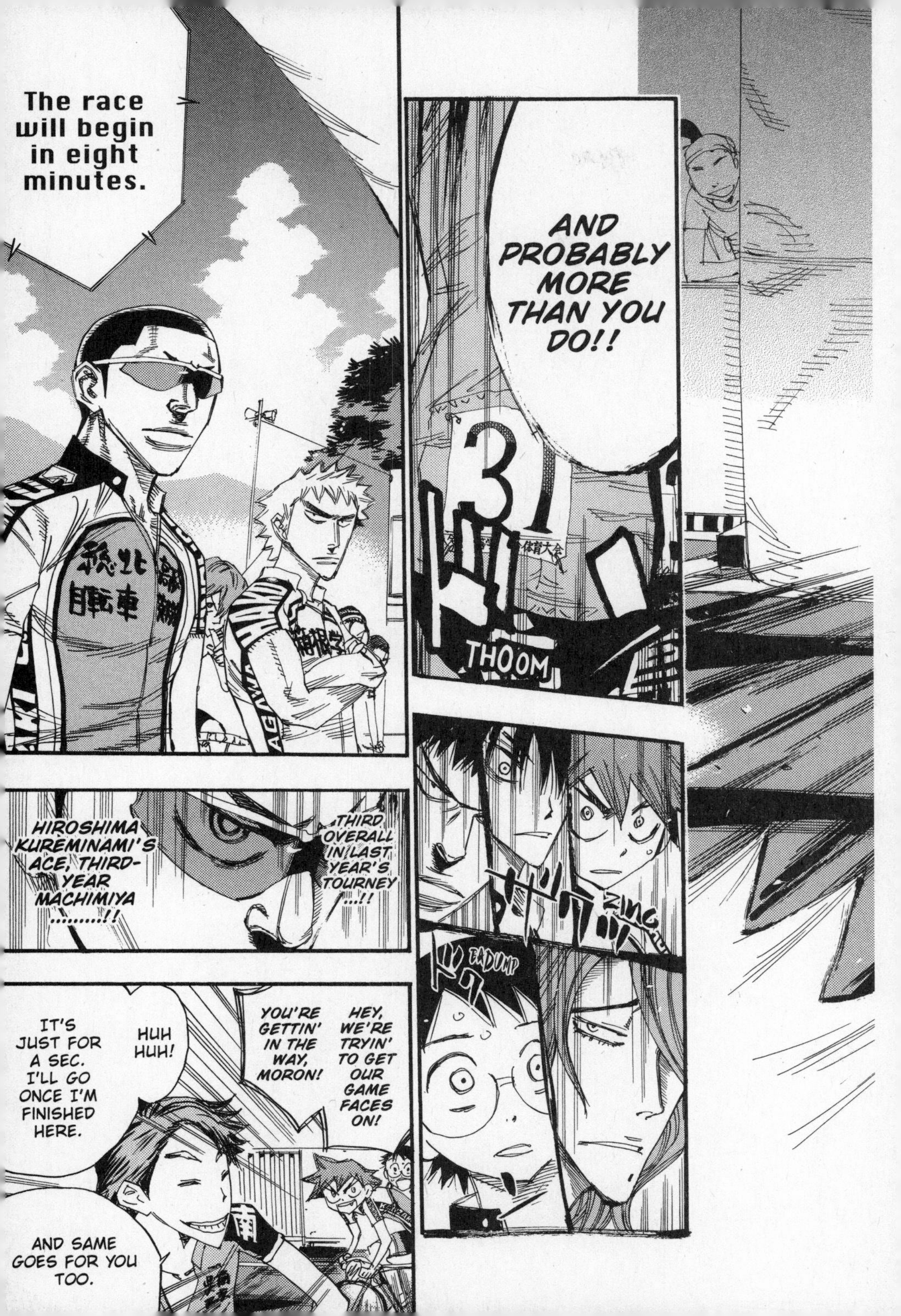
AND PROBABLY MORE THAN YOU DO!!
THOOM
ZING
BADUMP
The race will begin in eight minutes.
THIRD OVERALL IN LAST YEAR'S TOURNEY...!!
HIROSHIMA KUREMINAMI'S ACE, THIRD-YEAR MACHIMIYA..........!!
HEY, WE'RE TRYIN' TO GET OUR GAME FACES ON!
YOU'RE GETTIN' IN THE WAY, MORON!
HUH HUH!
IT'S JUST FOR A SEC. I'LL GO ONCE I'M FINISHED HERE.
AND SAME GOES FOR YOU TOO.

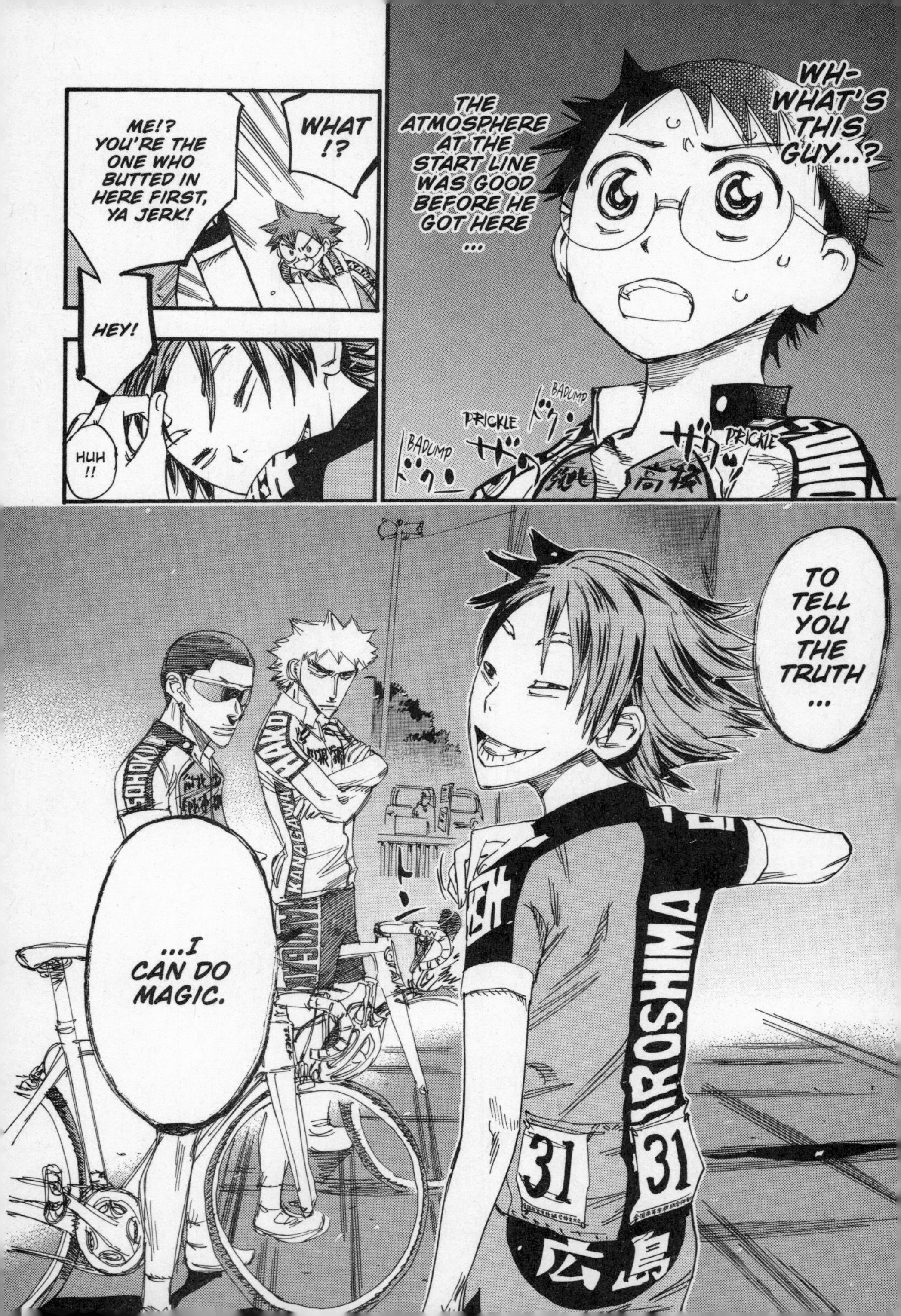
WH- WHAT'S THIS GUY...?
THE ATMOSPHERE AT THE START LINE WAS GOOD BEFORE HE GOT HERE ...
BADUMP
PRICKLE
BADUMP
PRICKLE
高校
WHAT !?
ME!? YOU'RE THE ONE WHO BUTTED IN HERE FIRST, YA JERK!
HEY!
HUH !!
TO TELL YOU THE TRUTH ...
...I CAN DO MAGIC.
ROSHIMA
31
31
広島

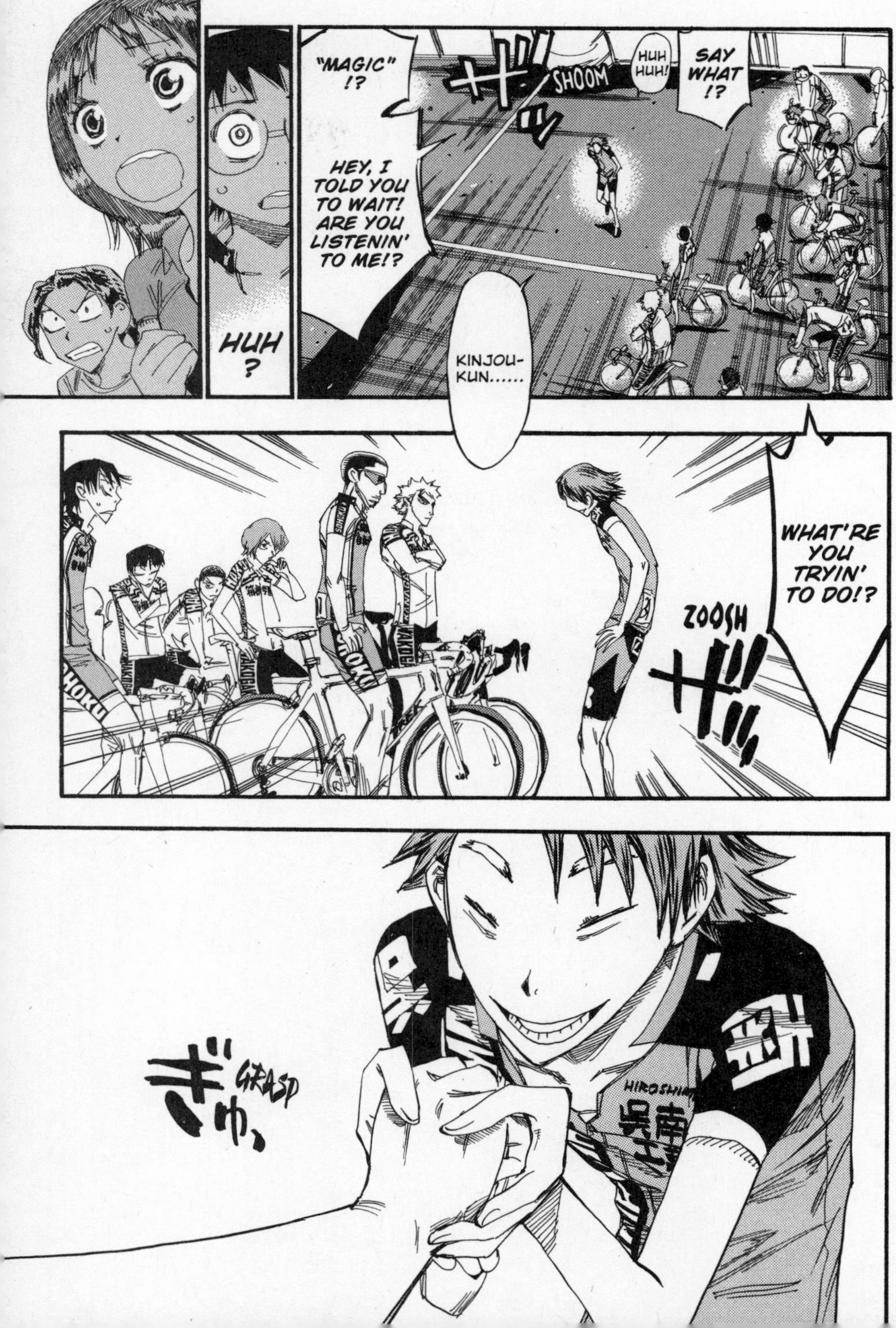
SAY WHAT !?
HUH HUH!
SHOOM
"MAGIC" !?
HEY, I TOLD YOU TO WAIT! ARE YOU LISTENIN' TO ME!?
KINJOU-KUN......
HUH ?
WHAT'RE YOU TRYIN' TO DO!?
ZOOSH
GRASP

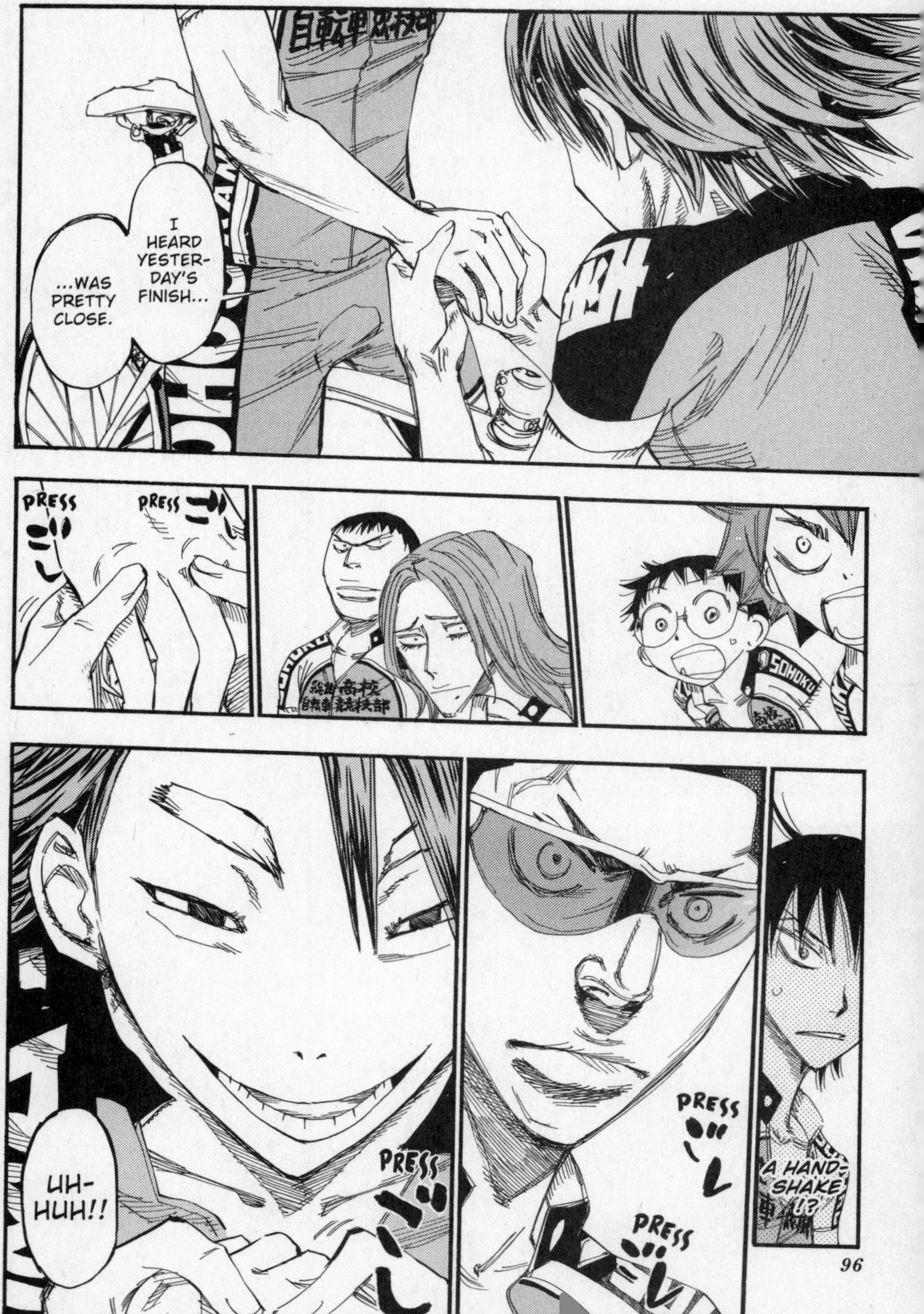
I HEARD YESTER-DAY'S FINISH...
...WAS PRETTY CLOSE.
PRESS
PRESS
A HAND-SHAKE!?
PRESS
PRESS
PRESS
UH-HUH!!

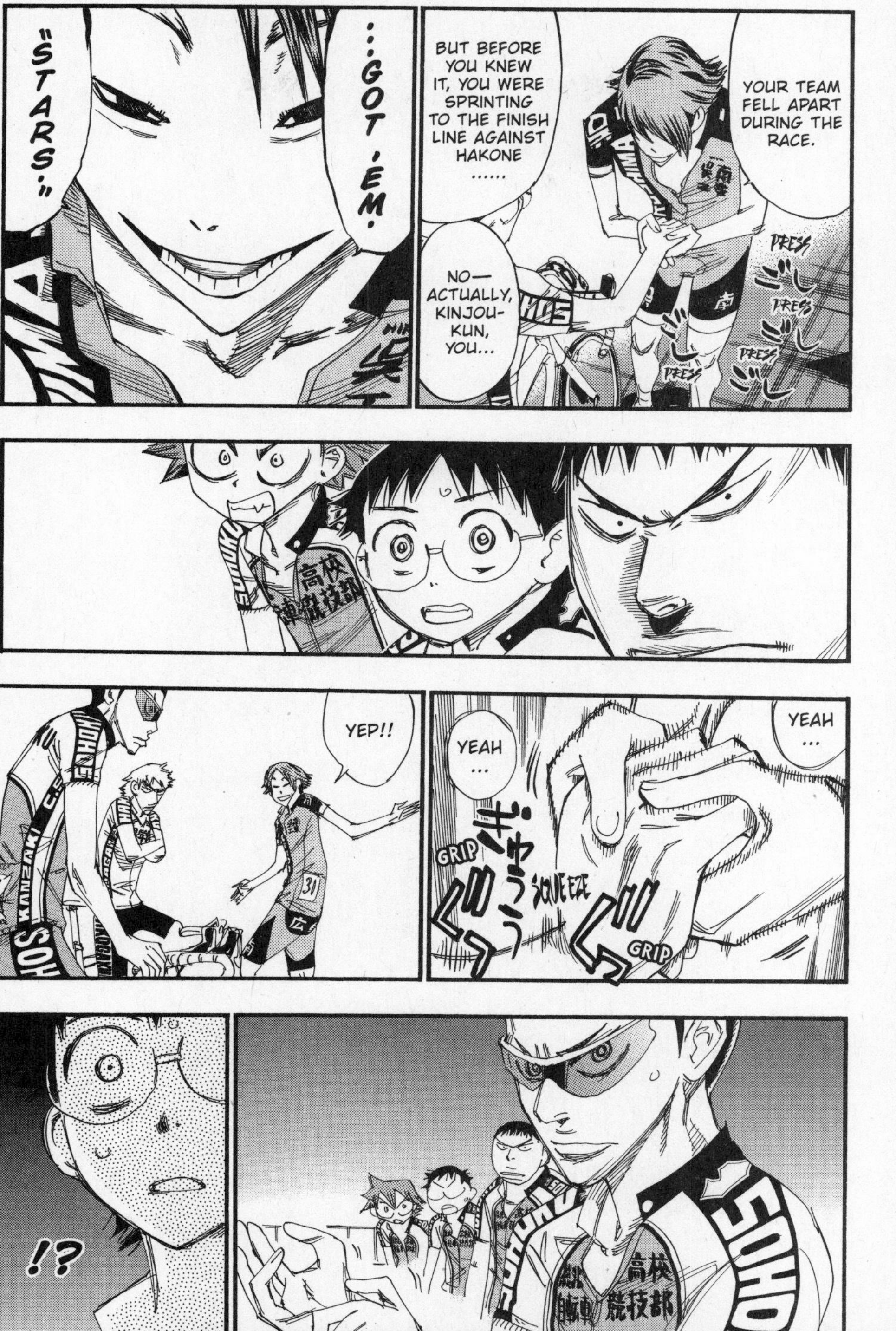
YOUR TEAM FELL APART DURING THE RACE.
BUT BEFORE YOU KNEW IT, YOU WERE SPRINTING TO THE FINISH LINE AGAINST HAKONE ......
NO— ACTUALLY, KINJOU-KUN, YOU...
PRESS
PRESS
PRESS
PRESS
...GOT 'EM.
"STARS."
YEAH ...
YEAH ...
GRIP
SQUEEZE
GRIP
YEP!!
!?

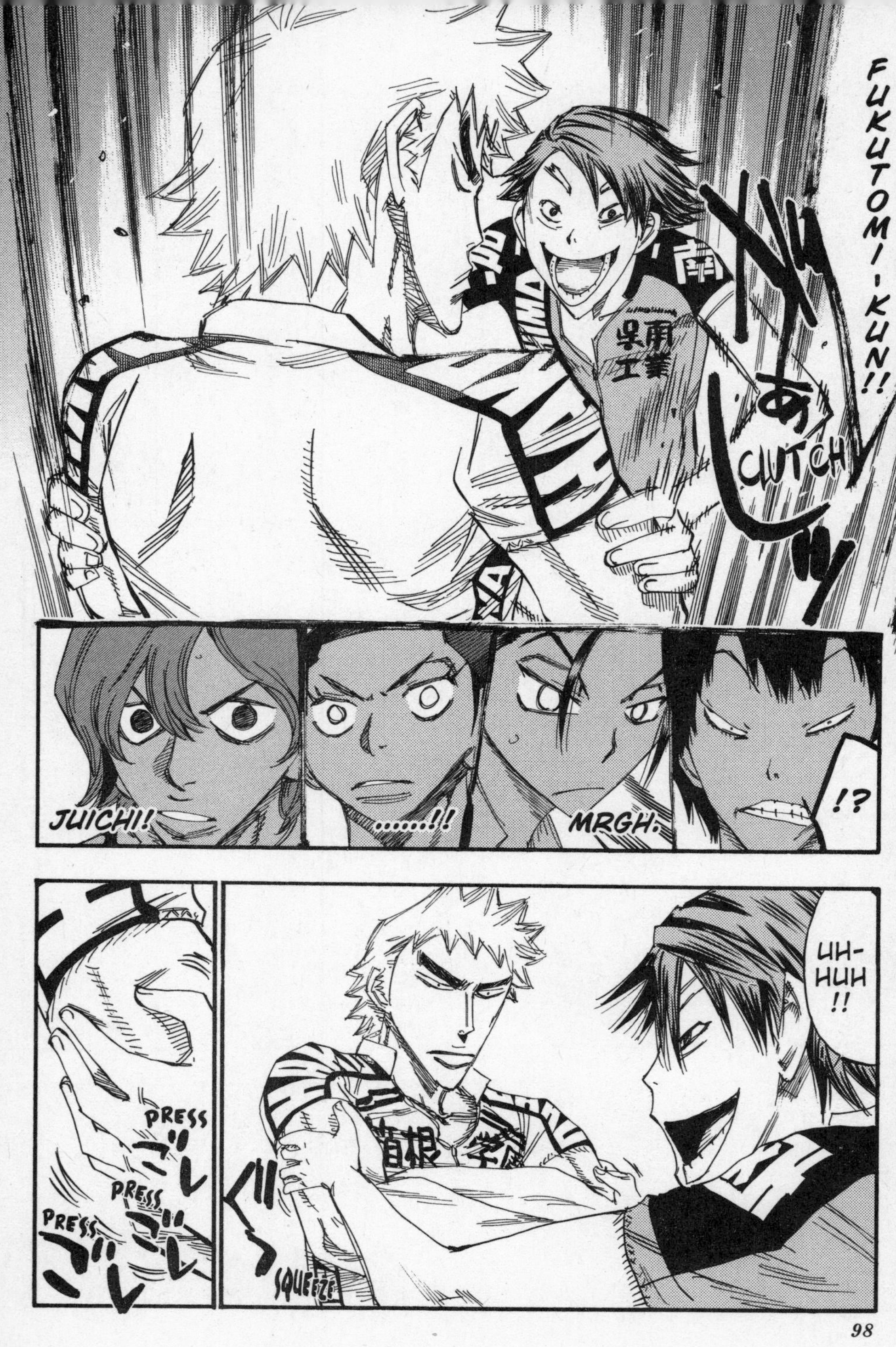
FUKUTOMI-KUN!!
あ
CLUTCH
!?
MRGH.
......!!
JUICHI!
UH-HUH!!
SQUEEZE
PRESS
PRESS
PRESS

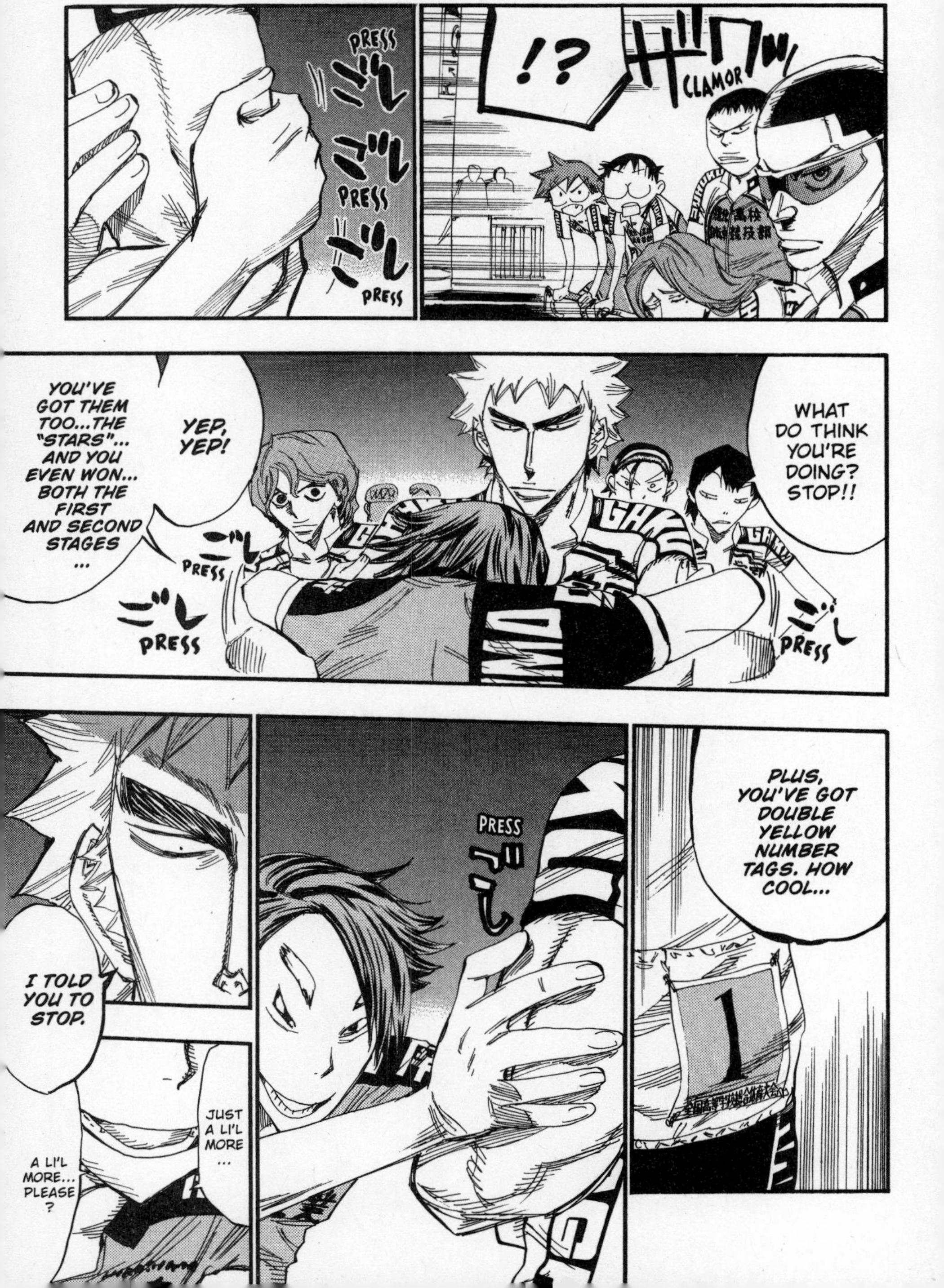
!?
CLAMOR
PRESS
PRESS
PRESS
PRESS
WHAT DO THINK YOU'RE DOING? STOP!!
YEP, YEP!
YOU'VE GOT THEM TOO...THE "STARS"... AND YOU EVEN WON... BOTH THE FIRST AND SECOND STAGES...
PRESS
PRESS
PRESS
PLUS, YOU'VE GOT DOUBLE YELLOW NUMBER TAGS. HOW COOL...
1
PRESS
I TOLD YOU TO STOP.
JUST A LI'L MORE...
A LI'L MORE... PLEASE?

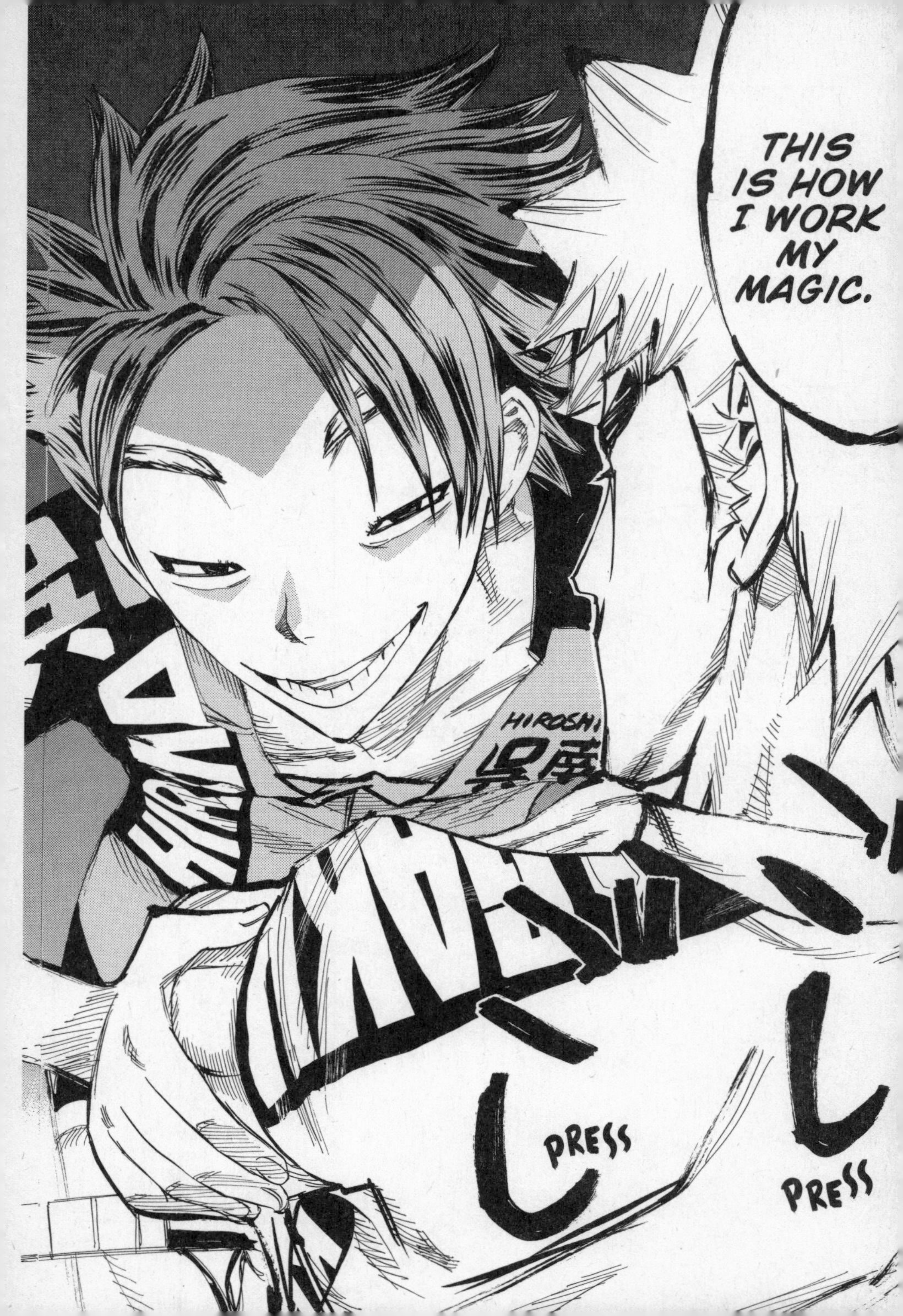
THIS IS HOW I WORK MY MAGIC.
HIROSHI
PRESS
PRESS

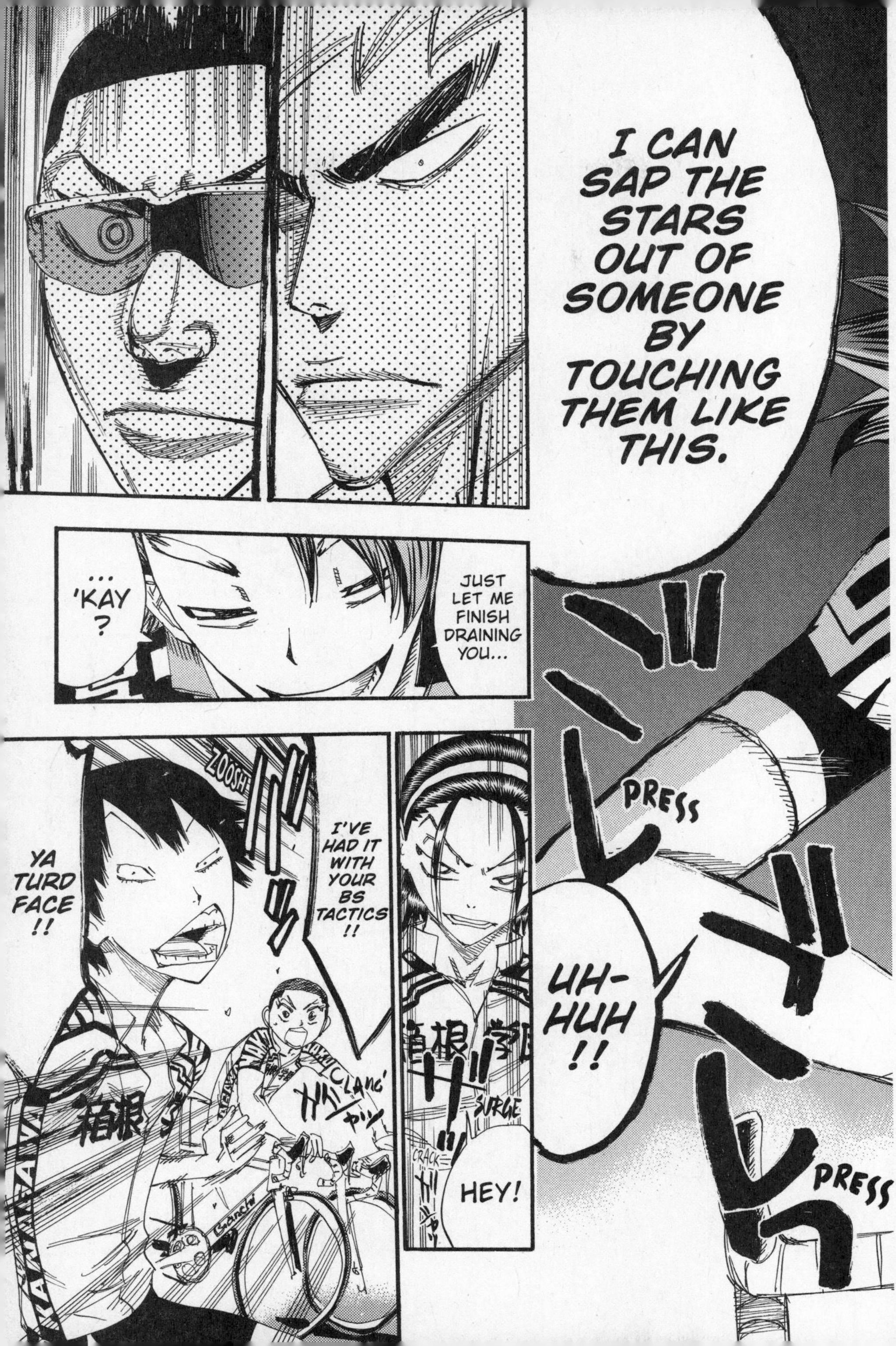
I CAN SAP THE STARS OUT OF SOMEONE BY TOUCHING THEM LIKE THIS.
PRESS
UH-HUH!!
PRESS
JUST LET ME FINISH DRAINING YOU...
...'KAY?
SURGE
HEY!
CRACK
I'VE HAD IT WITH YOUR BS TACTICS!!
YA TURD FACE!!
ZOOSH
CLANG

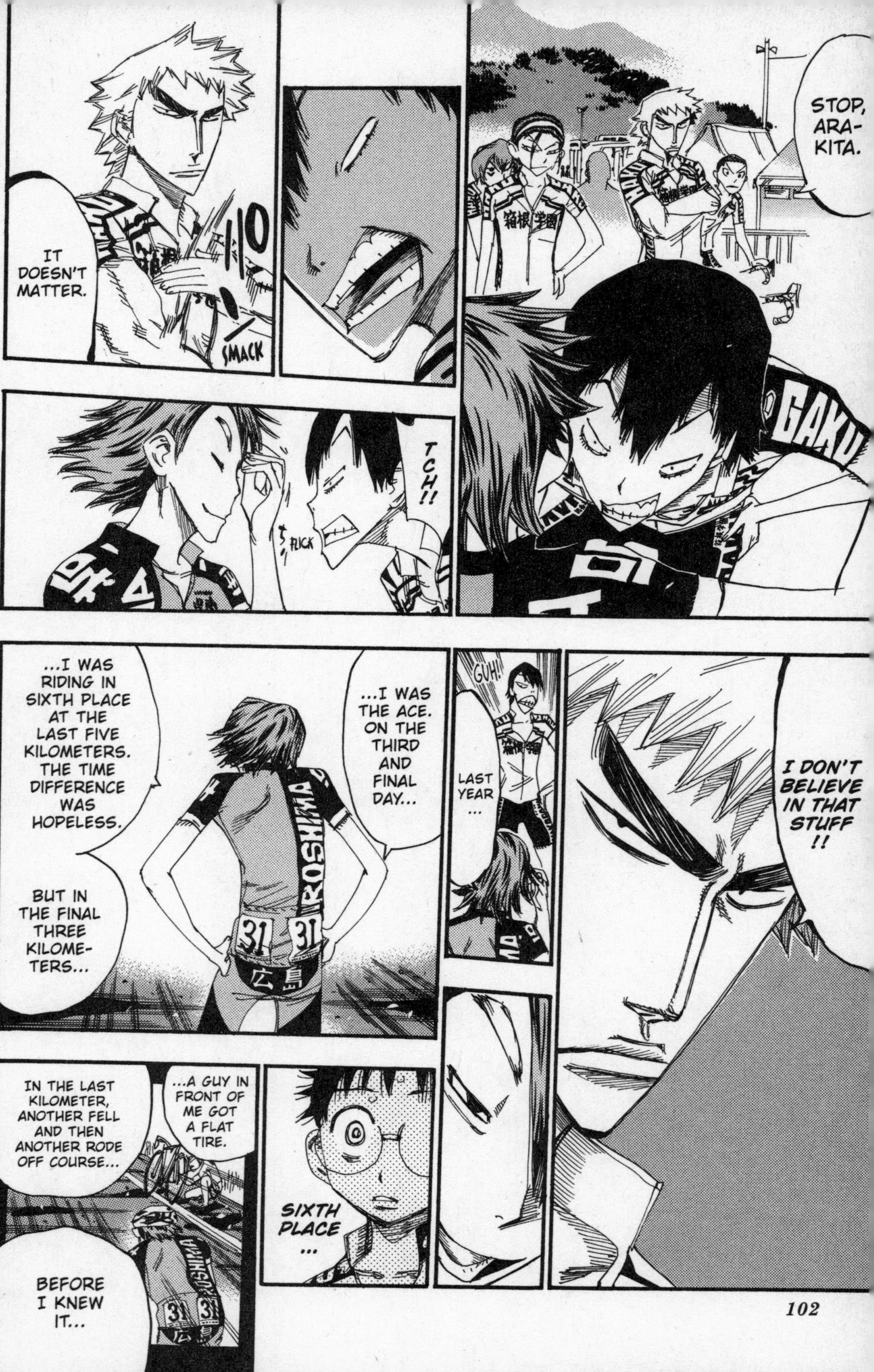
STOP, ARA-KITA.
IT DOESN'T MATTER.
SMACK
TCH!!
FLICK
I DON'T BELIEVE IN THAT STUFF!!
GUH!
LAST YEAR ...
...I WAS THE ACE. ON THE THIRD AND FINAL DAY...
...I WAS RIDING IN SIXTH PLACE AT THE LAST FIVE KILOMETERS. THE TIME DIFFERENCE WAS HOPELESS.
BUT IN THE FINAL THREE KILOME-TERS...
SIXTH PLACE ...
...A GUY IN FRONT OF ME GOT A FLAT TIRE.
IN THE LAST KILOMETER, ANOTHER FELL AND THEN ANOTHER RODE OFF COURSE...
BEFORE I KNEW IT...

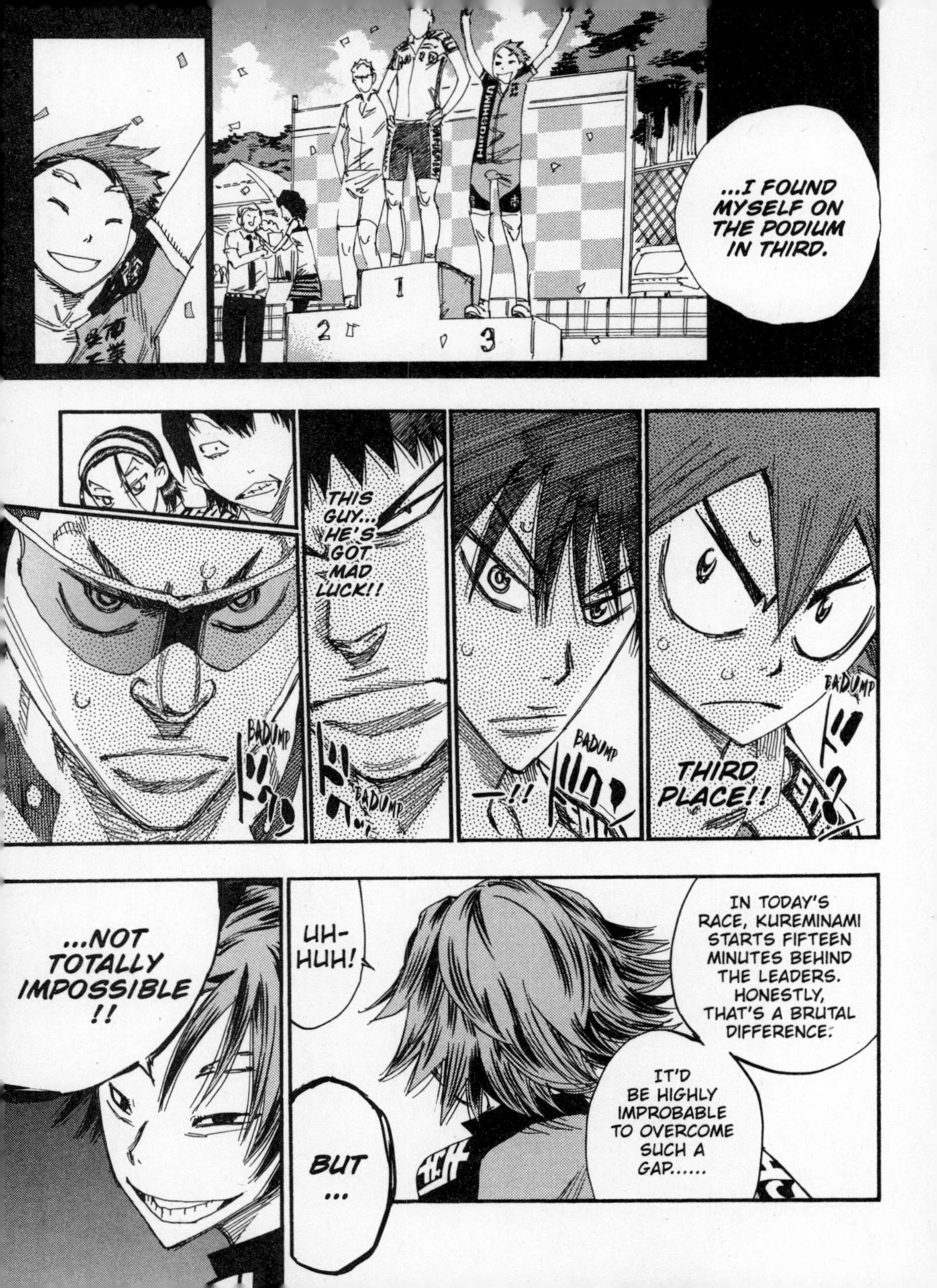
...I FOUND MYSELF ON THE PODIUM IN THIRD.
BADUMP
THIRD PLACE!!
BADUMP
—!!
THIS GUY... HE'S GOT MAD LUCK!!
BADUMP
BADUMP
IN TODAY'S RACE, KUREMINAMI STARTS FIFTEEN MINUTES BEHIND THE LEADERS. HONESTLY, THAT'S A BRUTAL DIFFERENCE.
IT'D BE HIGHLY IMPROBABLE TO OVERCOME SUCH A GAP......
UH-HUH!
BUT...
...NOT TOTALLY IMPOSSIBLE!!

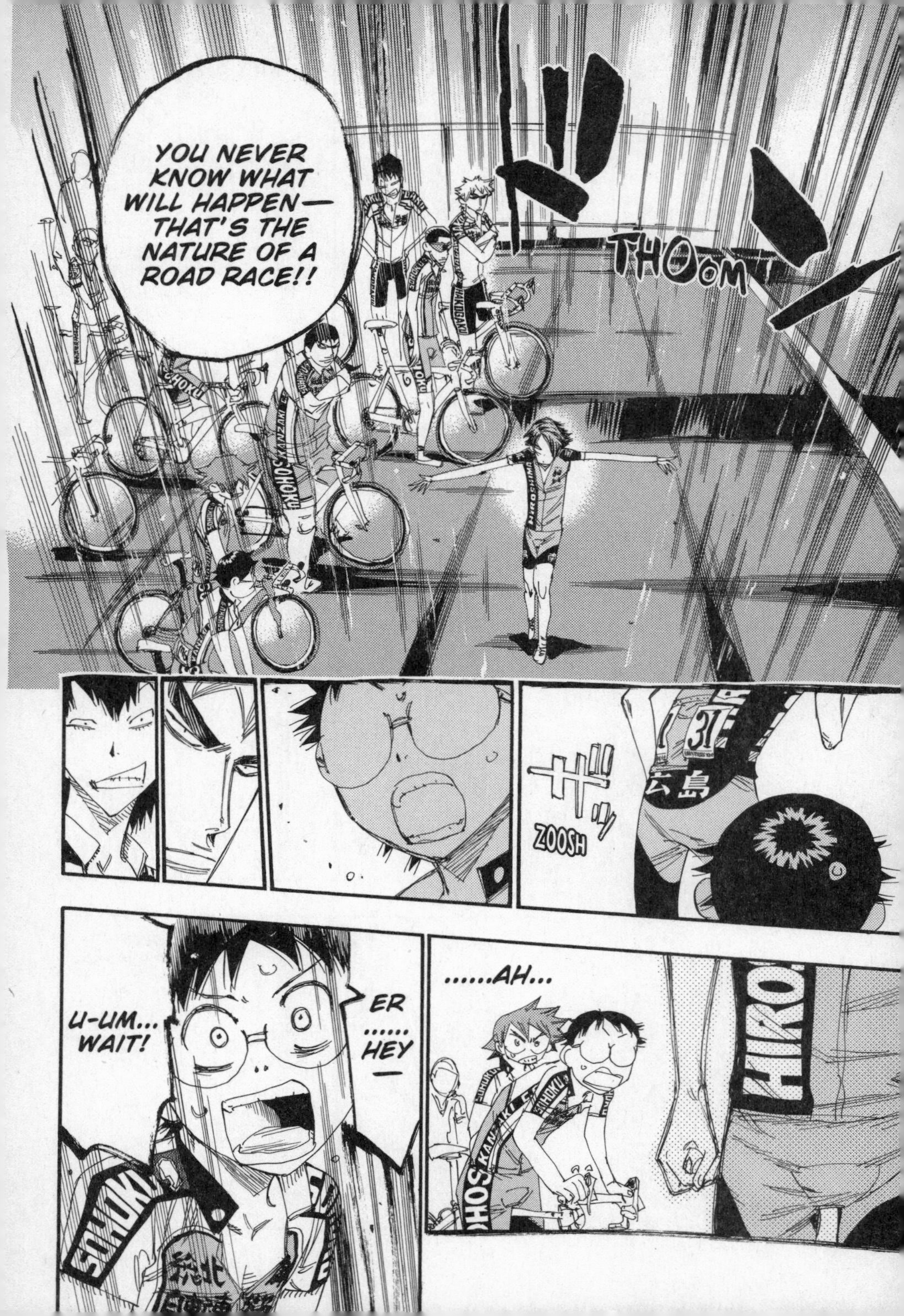
THOOM
YOU NEVER KNOW WHAT WILL HAPPEN—THAT'S THE NATURE OF A ROAD RACE!!
ZOOSH
......AH...
ER ......HEY—
U-UM... WAIT!

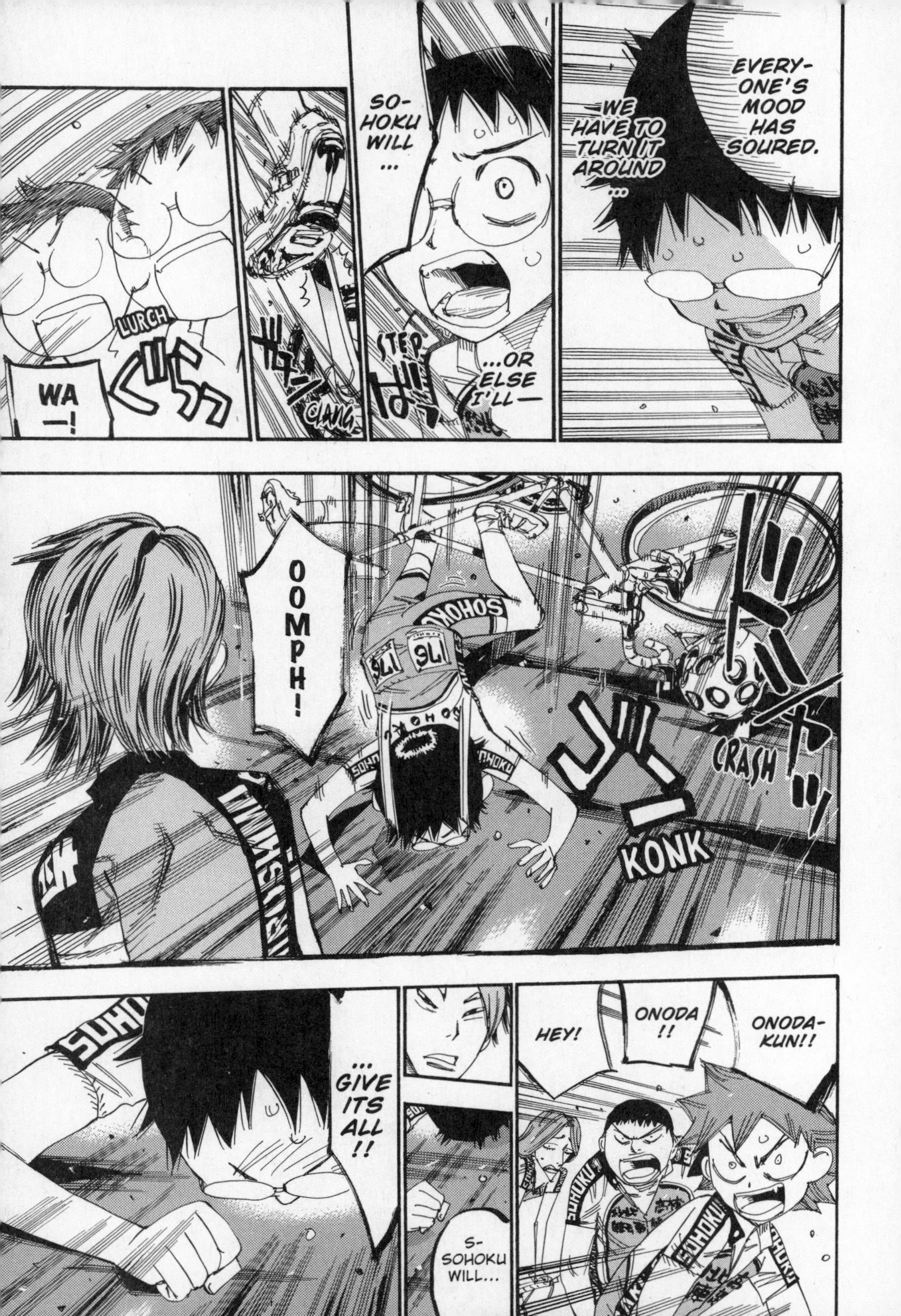
EVERY-ONE'S MOOD HAS SOURED.
WE HAVE TO TURN IT AROUND ...
SO-HOKU WILL ...
STEP
...OR ELSE I'LL—
CLANG
LURCH
WA—!
OOMPH!
CRASH
KONK
ONODA-KUN!!
ONODA!!
HEY!
S-SOHOKU WILL...
...GIVE ITS ALL!!

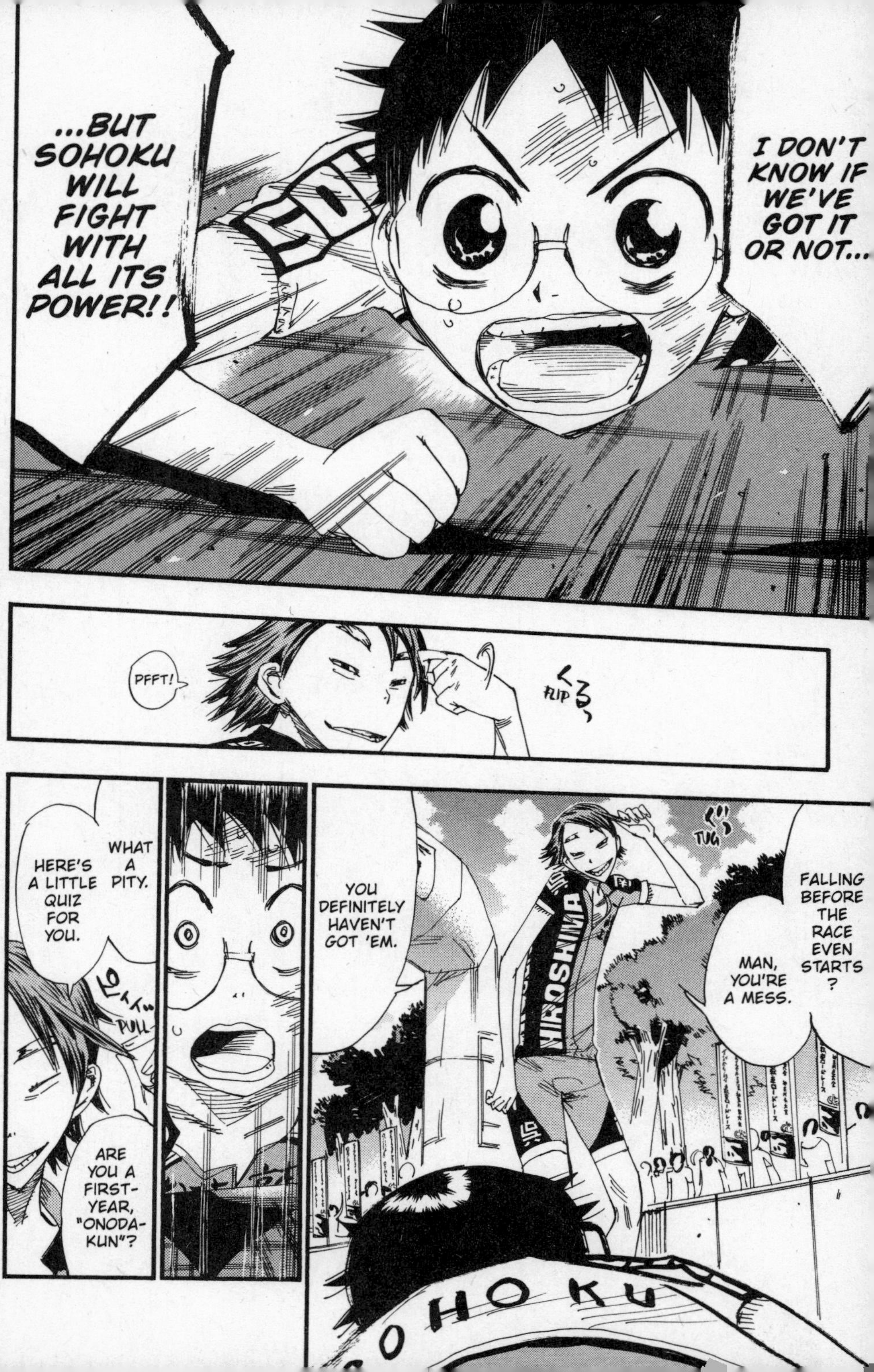
I DON'T KNOW IF WE'VE GOT IT OR NOT...
...BUT SOHOKU WILL FIGHT WITH ALL ITS POWER!!
PFFT!
FLIP
TUG
FALLING BEFORE THE RACE EVEN STARTS?
MAN, YOU'RE A MESS.
YOU DEFINITELY HAVEN'T GOT 'EM.
HIROSHIMA
WHAT A PITY.
HERE'S A LITTLE QUIZ FOR YOU.
PULL
ARE YOU A FIRST-YEAR, "ONODA-KUN"?

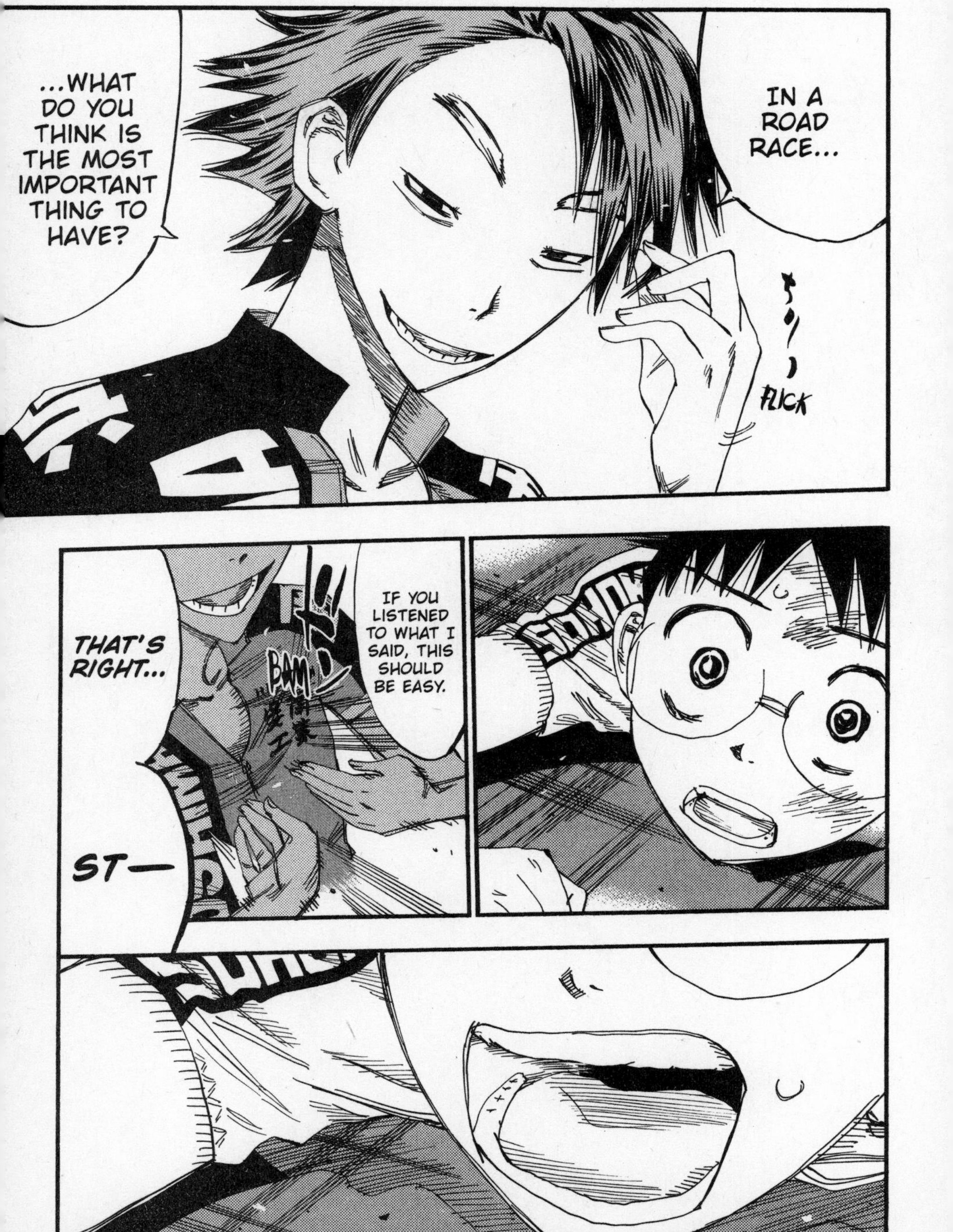
IN A ROAD RACE...
FLICK
...WHAT DO YOU THINK IS THE MOST IMPORTANT THING TO HAVE?
IF YOU LISTENED TO WHAT I SAID, THIS SHOULD BE EASY.
BAM
THAT'S RIGHT...
ST—

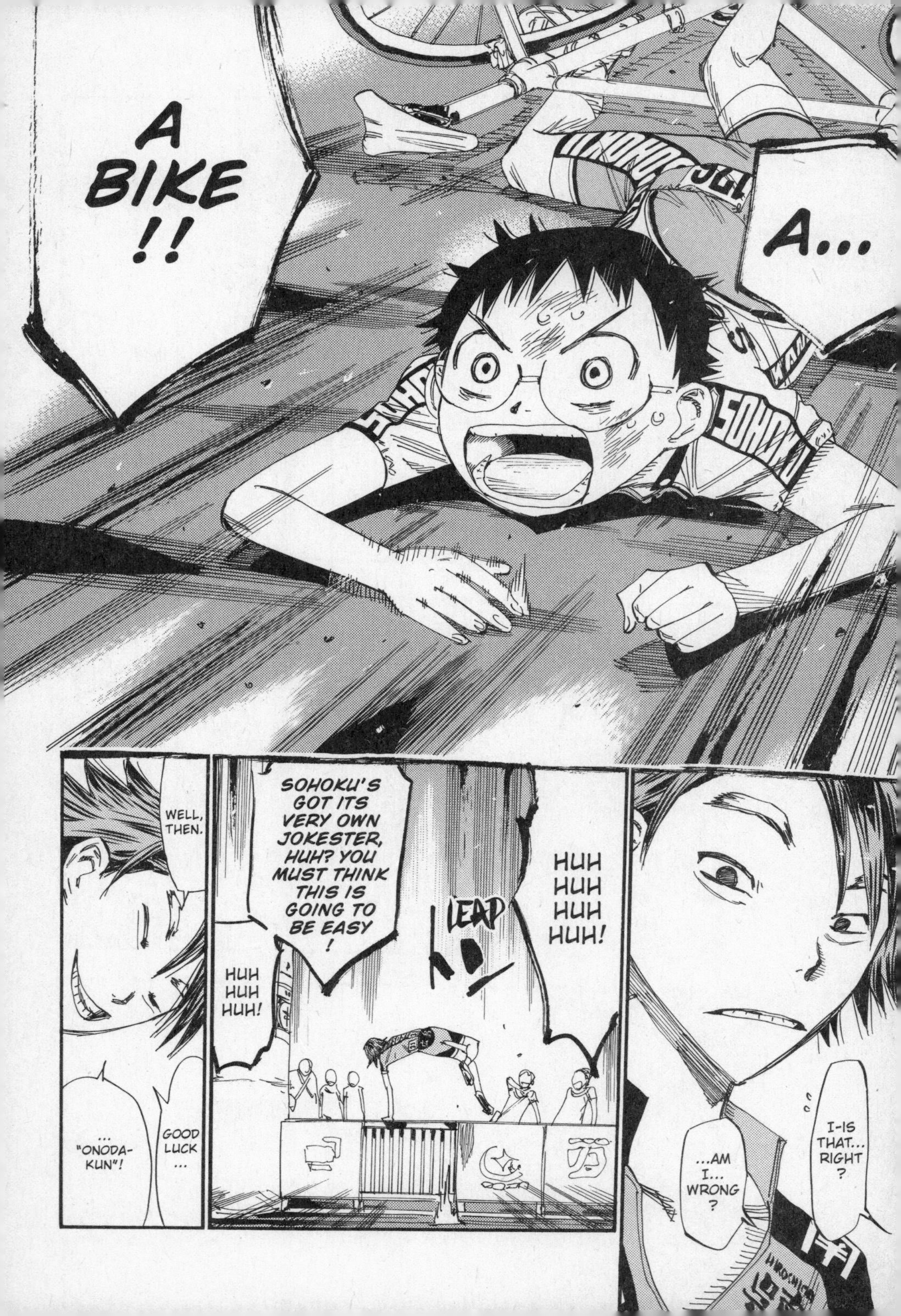
A...
A BIKE !!
I-IS THAT... RIGHT?
...AM I... WRONG?
SOHOKU'S GOT ITS VERY OWN JOKESTER, HUH? YOU MUST THINK THIS IS GOING TO BE EASY!
HUH HUH HUH HUH!
LEAP
HUH HUH HUH!
WELL, THEN.
GOOD LUCK...
..."ONODA-KUN"!

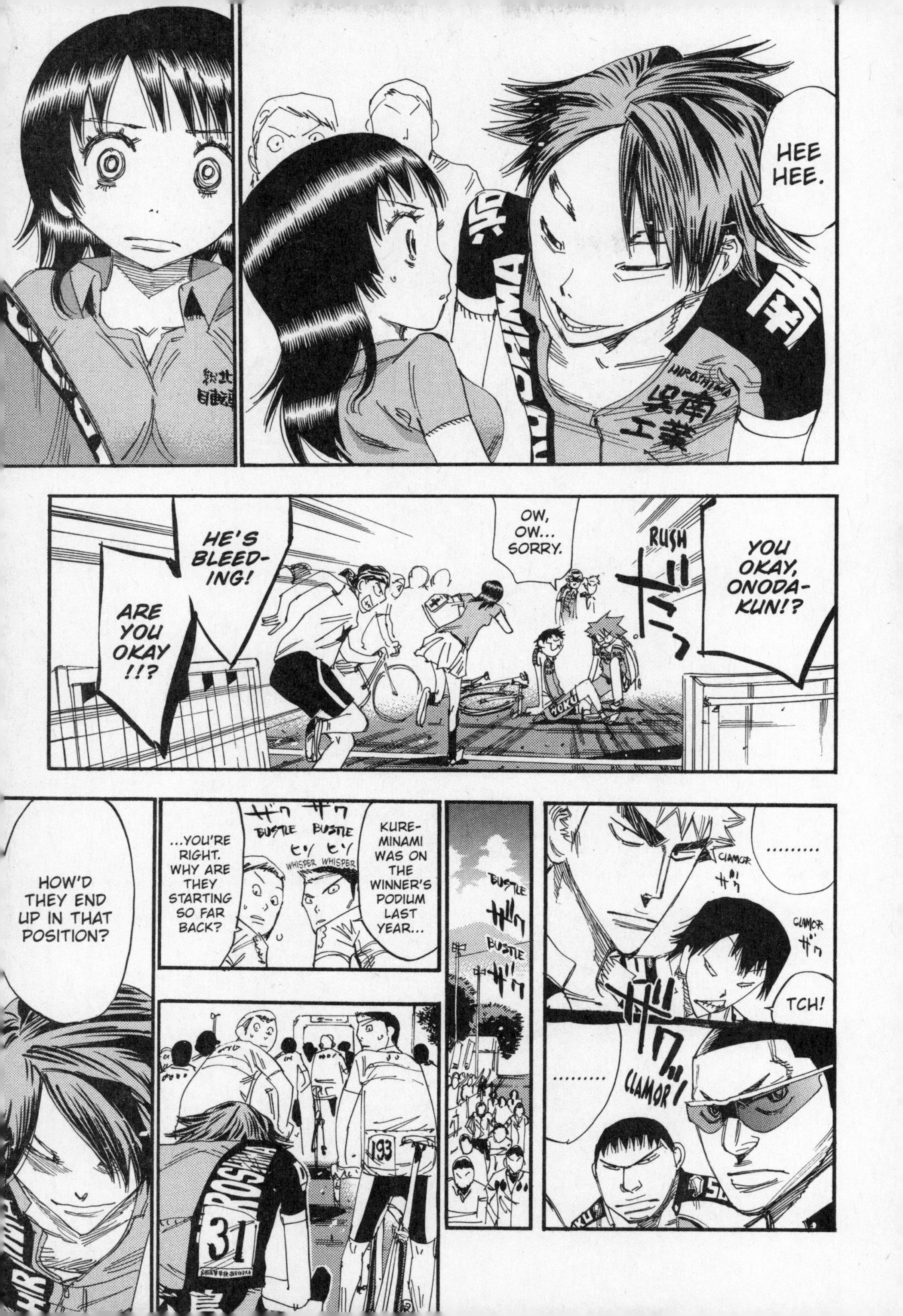
HEE HEE.
YOU OKAY, ONODA-KUN!?
RUSH
OW, OW... SORRY.
HE'S BLEEDING!
ARE YOU OKAY!!?
....
CLAMOR
CLAMOR
TCH!
CLAMOR!
....
BUSTLE
BUSTLE
KURE-MINAMI WAS ON THE WINNER'S PODIUM LAST YEAR...
BUSTLE BUSTLE
WHISPER WHISPER
...YOU'RE RIGHT. WHY ARE THEY STARTING SO FAR BACK?
HOW'D THEY END UP IN THAT POSITION?

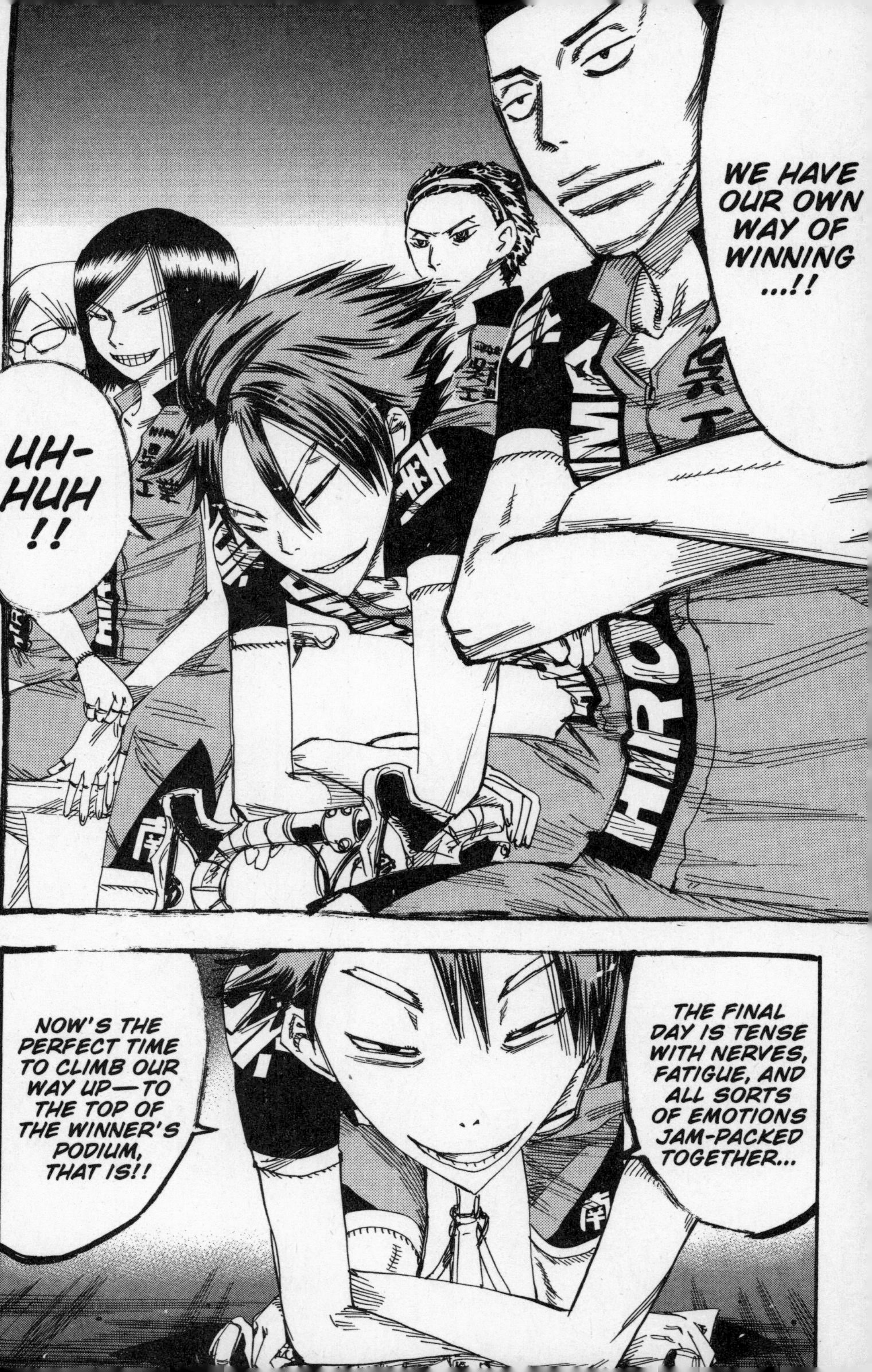
WE HAVE OUR OWN WAY OF WINNING ...!!
UH-HUH!!
THE FINAL DAY IS TENSE WITH NERVES, FATIGUE, AND ALL SORTS OF EMOTIONS JAM-PACKED TOGETHER...
NOW'S THE PERFECT TIME TO CLIMB OUR WAY UP—TO THE TOP OF THE WINNER'S PODIUM, THAT IS!!

RIDE.160 HE'S NOT COMING

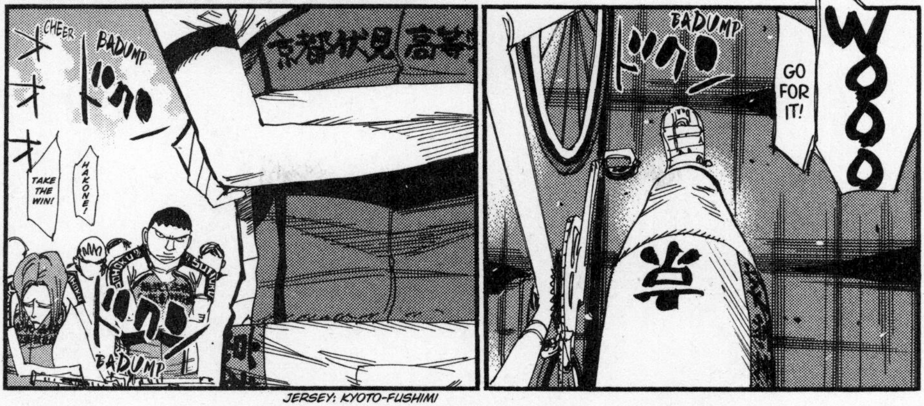
WOOO
GO FOR IT!
BADUMP
HAKONE!
TAKE THE WIN!
CHEER
BADUMP
BADUMP

JERSEY: KYOTO-FUSHIMI

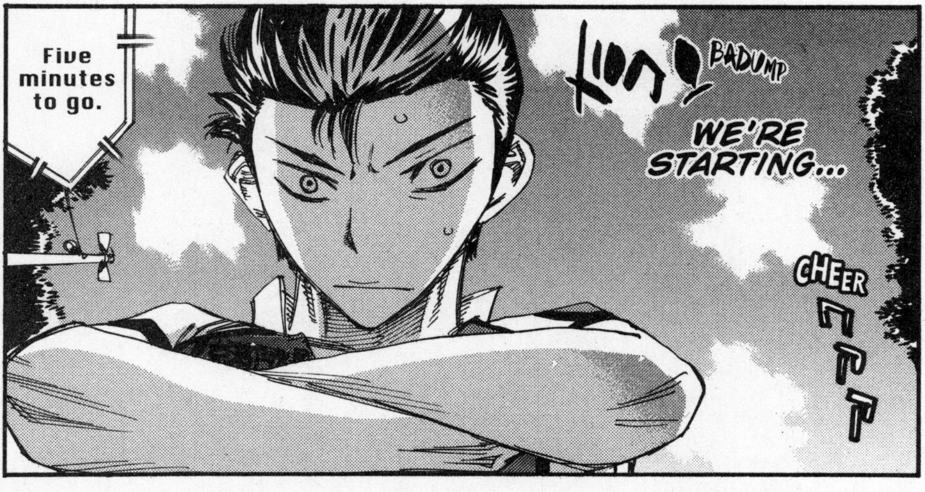
BADUMP
WE'RE STARTING...
CHEER
Five minutes to go.

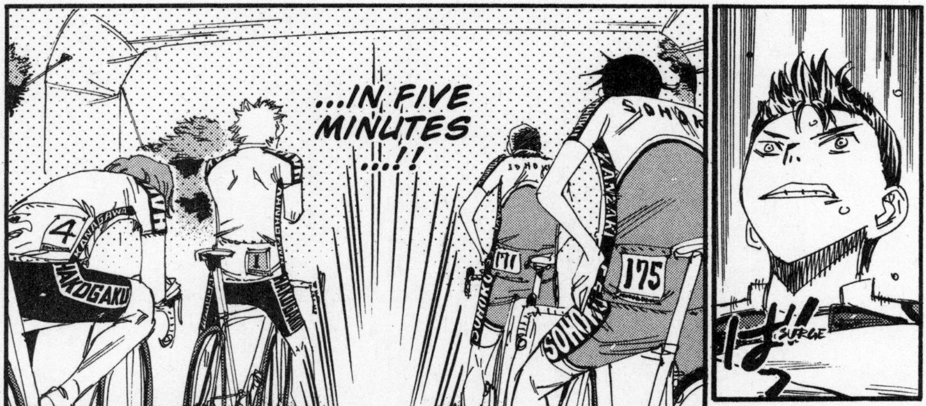
SURGE
...IN FIVE MINUTES ...!!

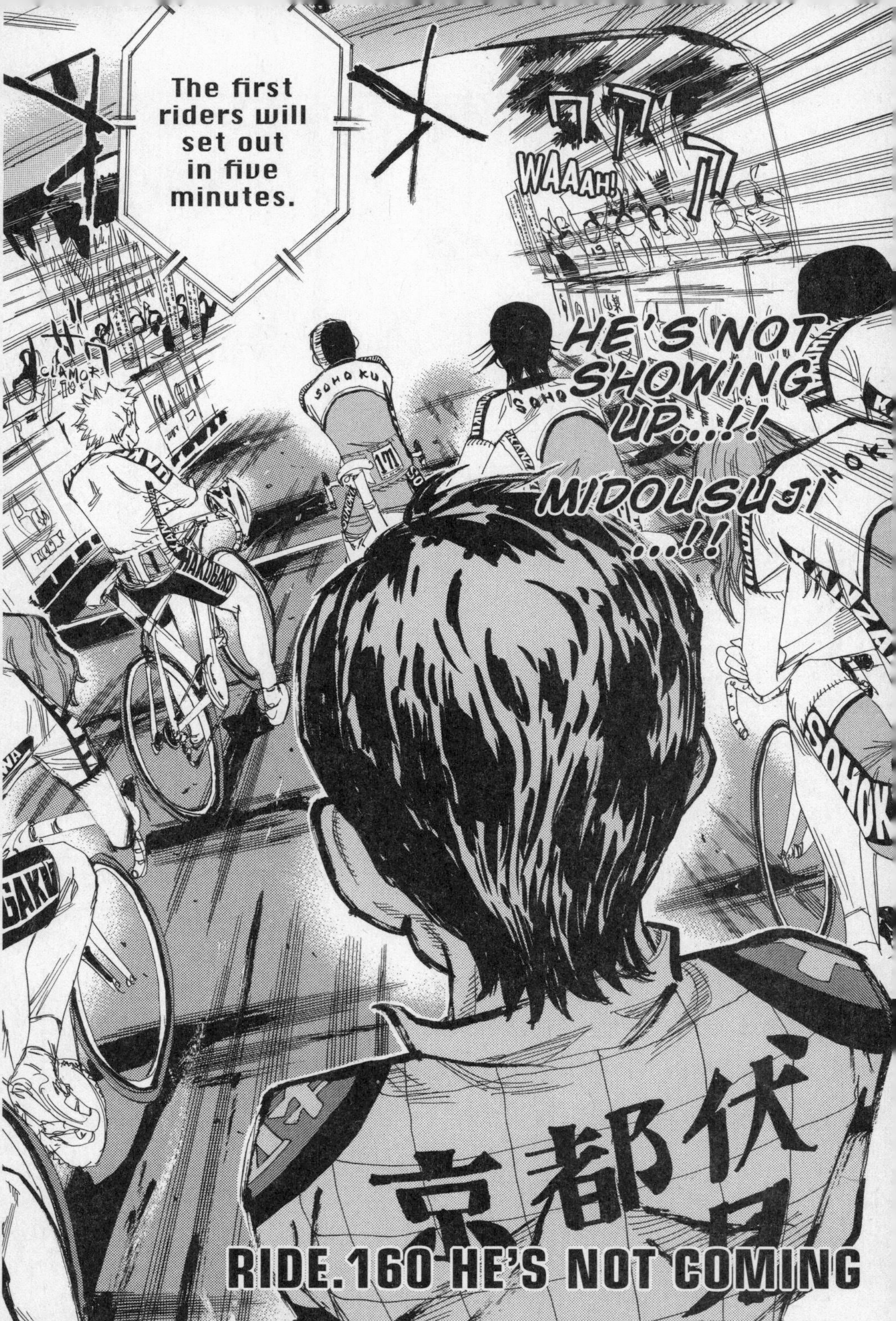
WAAAH!
The first riders will set out in five minutes.
HE'S NOT SHOWING UP...!!
MIDOUSUJI ...!!
CLAMOR
SOHOKU
HAKOGAKU
京都伏

RIDE.160 HE'S NOT COMING

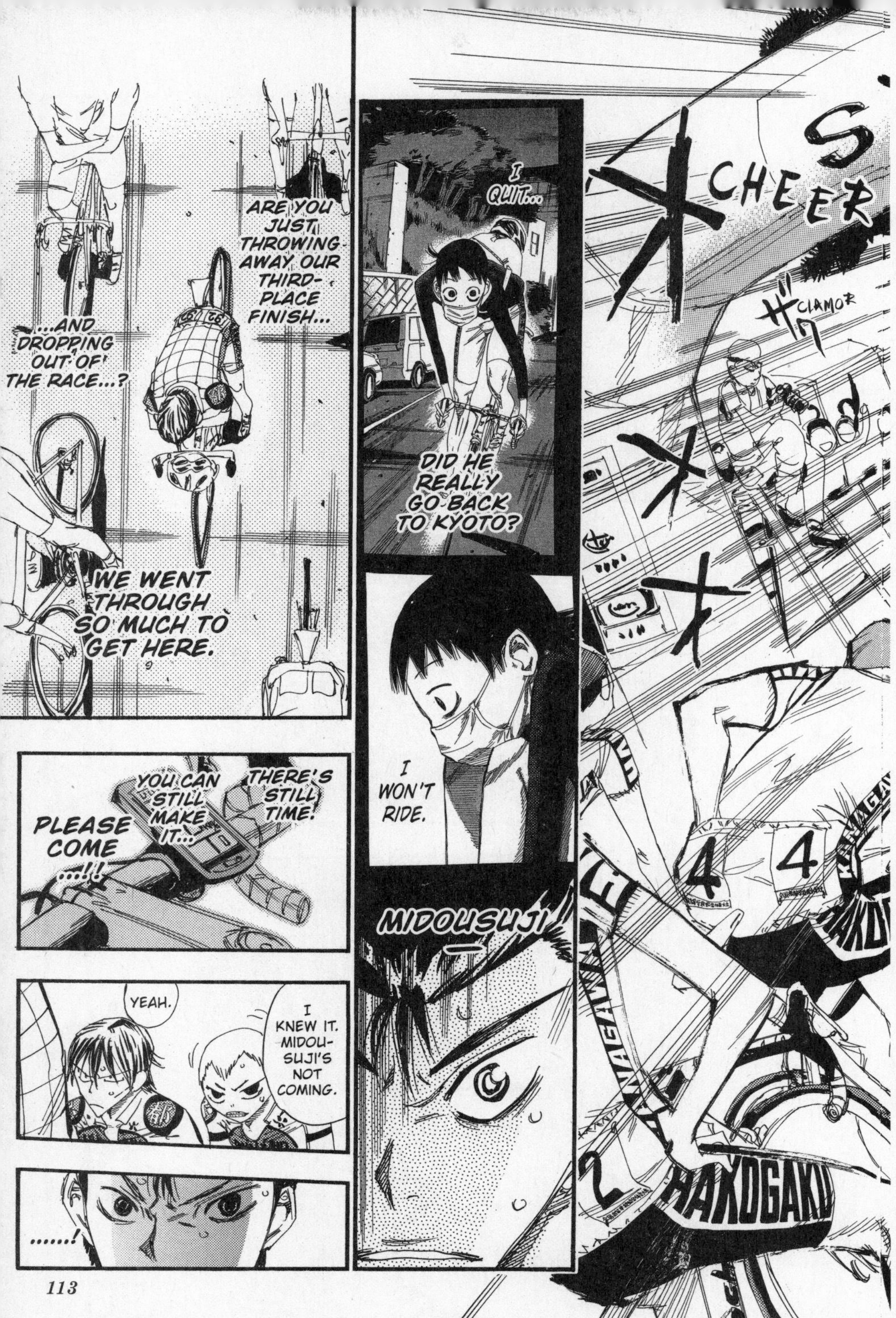
CHEER
CLAMOR
HAKOGAKU
I QUIT...
DID HE REALLY GO BACK TO KYOTO?
I WON'T RIDE.
MIDOUSUJI—
ARE YOU JUST THROWING AWAY OUR THIRD-PLACE FINISH...
...AND DROPPING OUT OF THE RACE...?
WE WENT THROUGH SO MUCH TO GET HERE.
THERE'S STILL TIME!
YOU CAN STILL MAKE IT...
PLEASE COME...!!
I KNEW IT. MIDOUSUJI'S NOT COMING.
YEAH.
......!

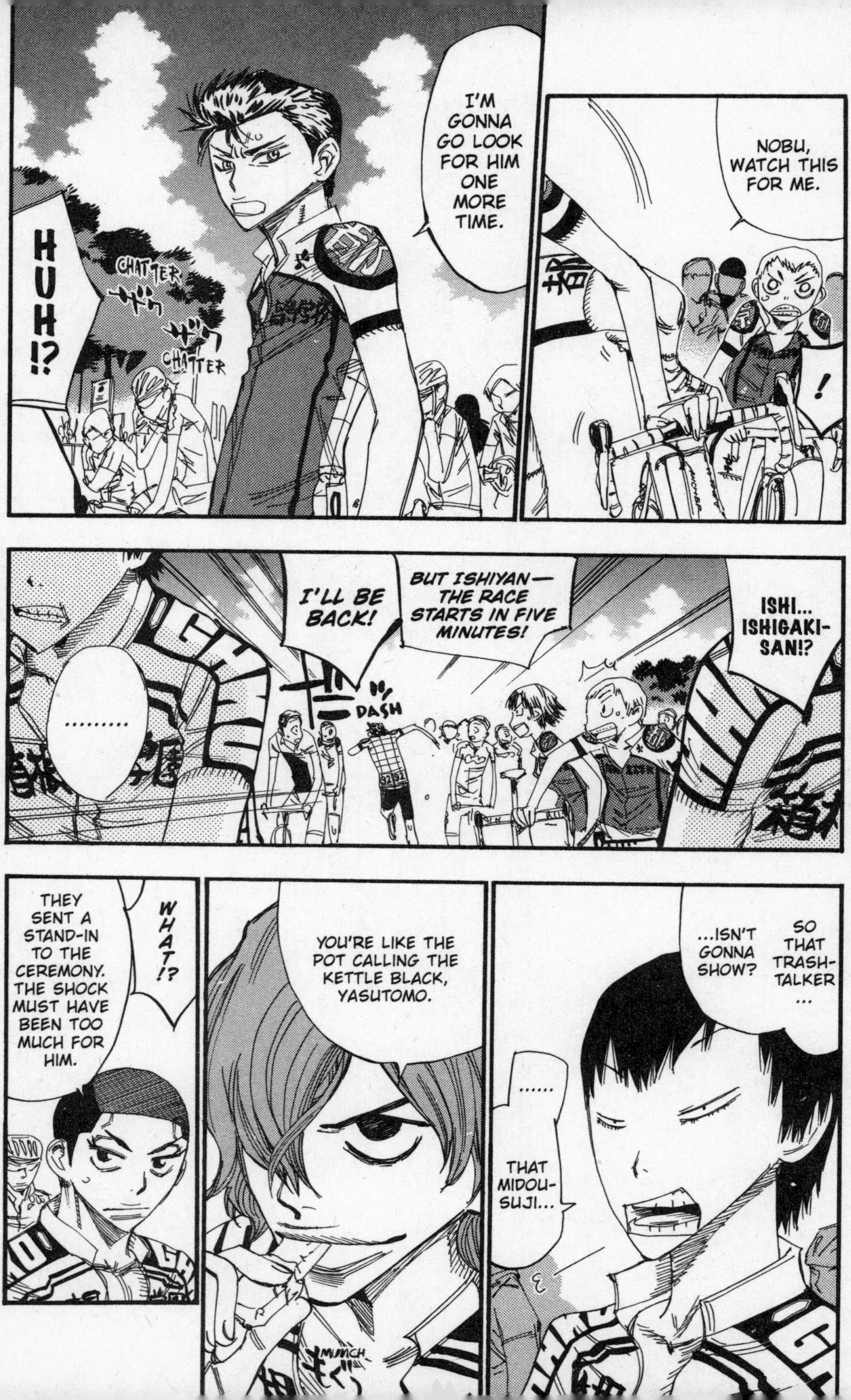
NOBU, WATCH THIS FOR ME.
!
I'M GONNA GO LOOK FOR HIM ONE MORE TIME.
HUH!?
CHATTER
CHATTER
ISHI... ISHIGAKI-SAN!?
BUT ISHIYAN— THE RACE STARTS IN FIVE MINUTES!
I'LL BE BACK!
DASH
....
SO THAT TRASH-TALKER ...
...ISN'T GONNA SHOW?
......
THAT MIDOU-SUJI...
YOU'RE LIKE THE POT CALLING THE KETTLE BLACK, YASUTOMO.
MUNCH
WHAT!?
THEY SENT A STAND-IN TO THE CEREMONY. THE SHOCK MUST HAVE BEEN TOO MUCH FOR HIM.

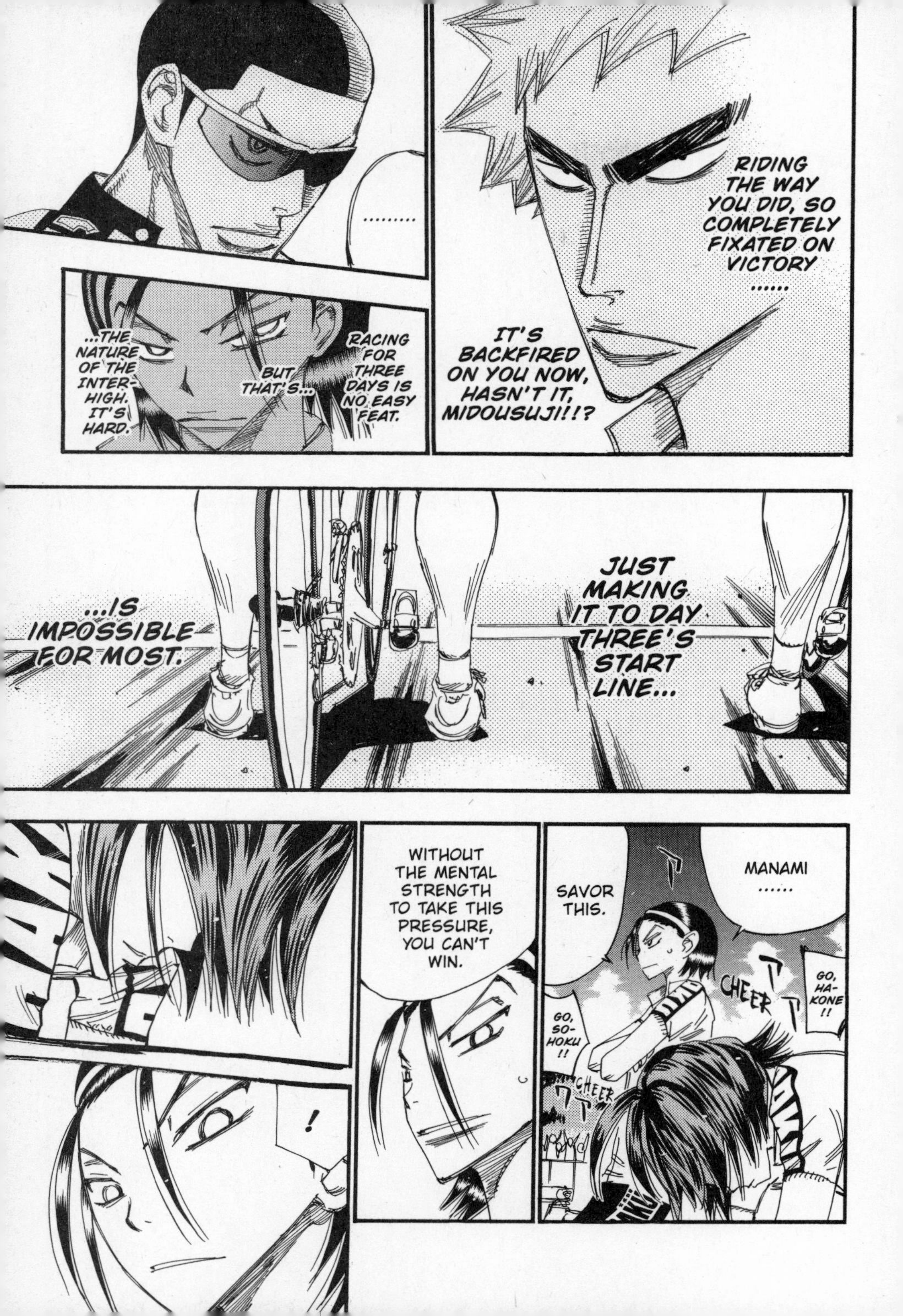
RIDING THE WAY YOU DID, SO COMPLETELY FIXATED ON VICTORY ......
IT'S BACKFIRED ON YOU NOW, HASN'T IT, MIDOUSUJI!!?
....
RACING FOR THREE DAYS IS NO EASY FEAT.
BUT THAT'S...
...THE NATURE OF THE INTER-HIGH. IT'S HARD.
JUST MAKING IT TO DAY THREE'S START LINE...
...IS IMPOSSIBLE FOR MOST.
MANAMI ......
SAVOR THIS.
GO, HAKONE !!
CHEER
GO, SO-HOKU !!
CHEER
WITHOUT THE MENTAL STRENGTH TO TAKE THIS PRESSURE, YOU CAN'T WIN.
!

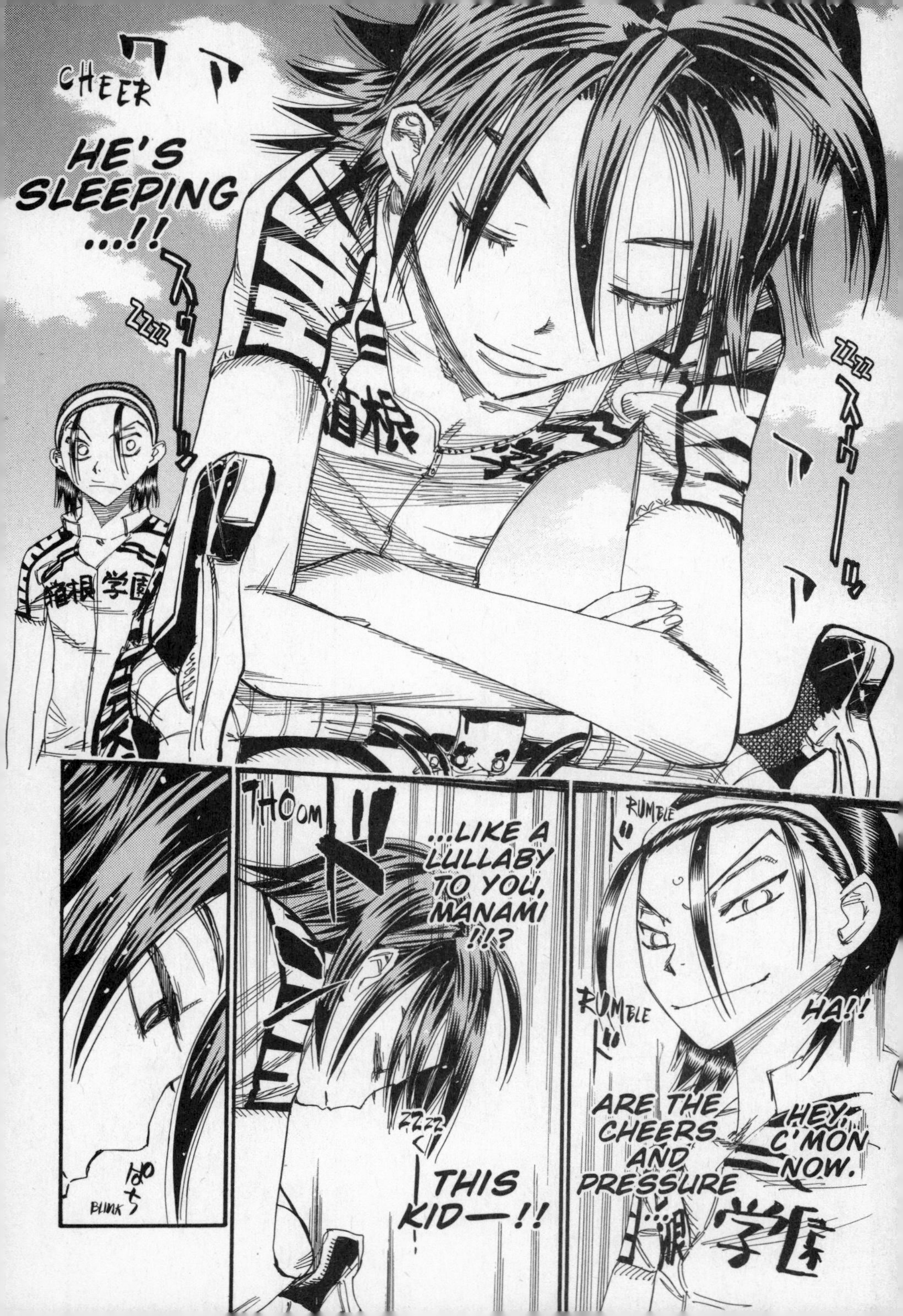
CHEER
HE'S SLEEPING...!!
ZZZ
ZZZ
RUMBLE
HA!!
HEY, C'MON NOW.
ARE THE CHEERS AND PRESSURE
RUMBLE
THOOM
...LIKE A LULLABY TO YOU, MANAMI!!?
ZZZ
THIS KID—!!
BLINK

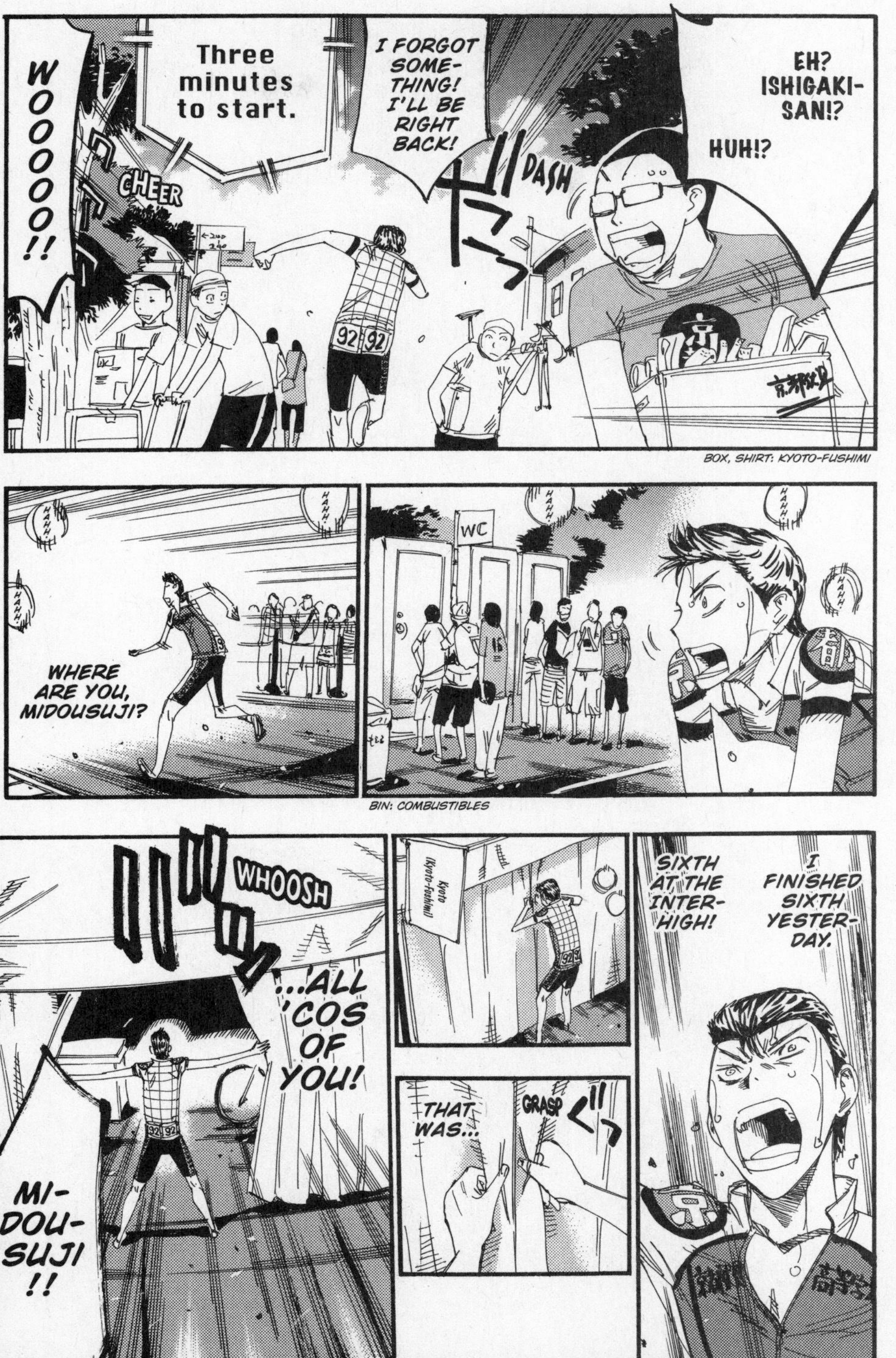
EH? ISHIGAKI-SAN!?
HUH!?
DASH
I FORGOT SOMETHING! I'LL BE RIGHT BACK!
Three minutes to start.
CHEER
WOOOOOOO!!
HAHH
HAHH
DASH
WC
HAHH
HAHH
WHERE ARE YOU, MIDOUSUJI?
I FINISHED SIXTH YESTERDAY.
SIXTH AT THE INTER-HIGH!
Kyoto (Kyoto-Fushimi)
GRASP
THAT WAS...
WHOOSH
...ALL 'COS OF YOU!
MI-DOU-SUJI!!
BOX, SHIRT: KYOTO-FUSHIMI
BIN: COMBUSTIBLES

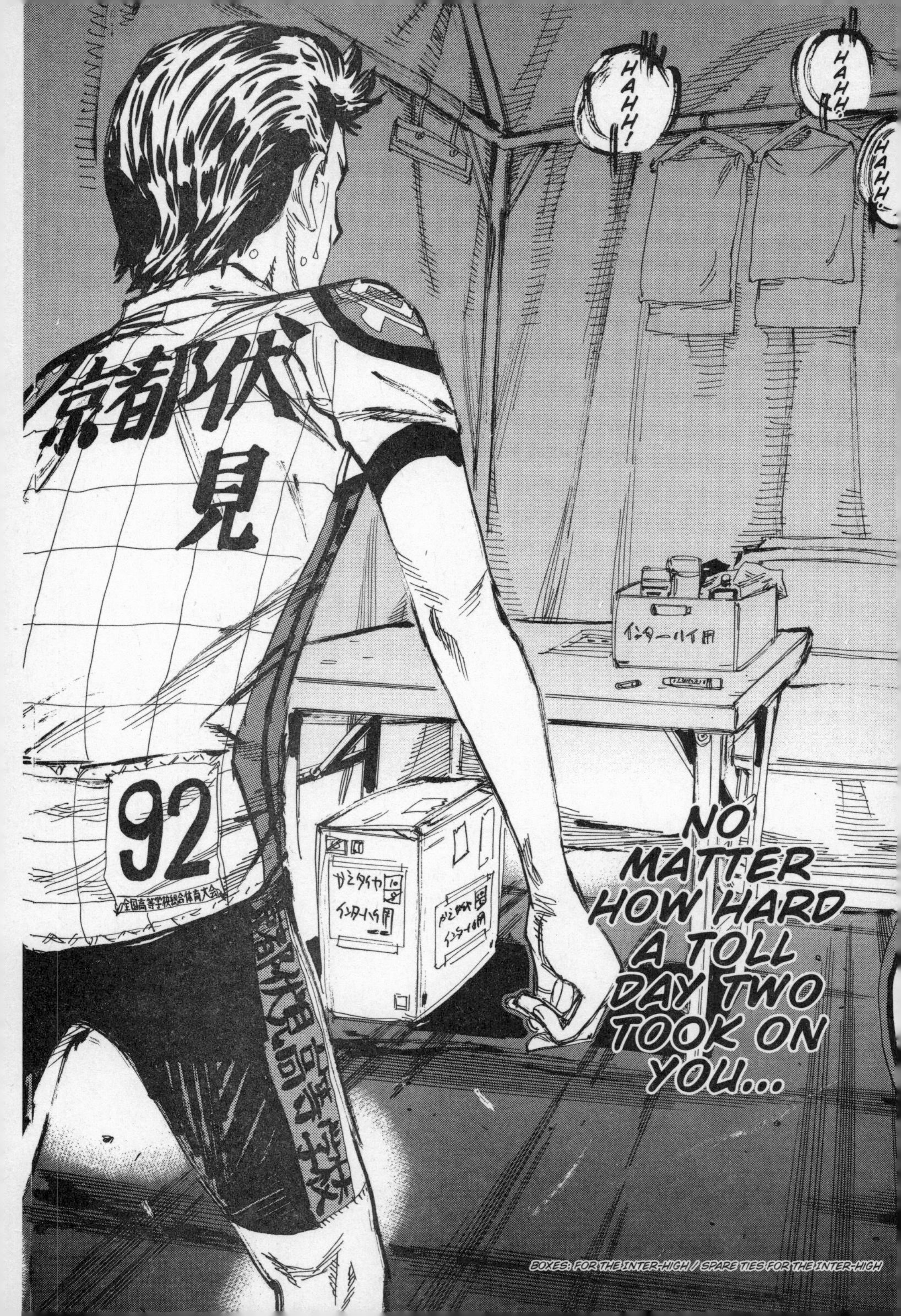

HAHH!
HAHH...
HAHH...
NO MATTER HOW HARD A TOLL DAY TWO TOOK ON YOU...
BOXES: FOR THE INTER-HIGH / SPARE TIES FOR THE INTER-HIGH

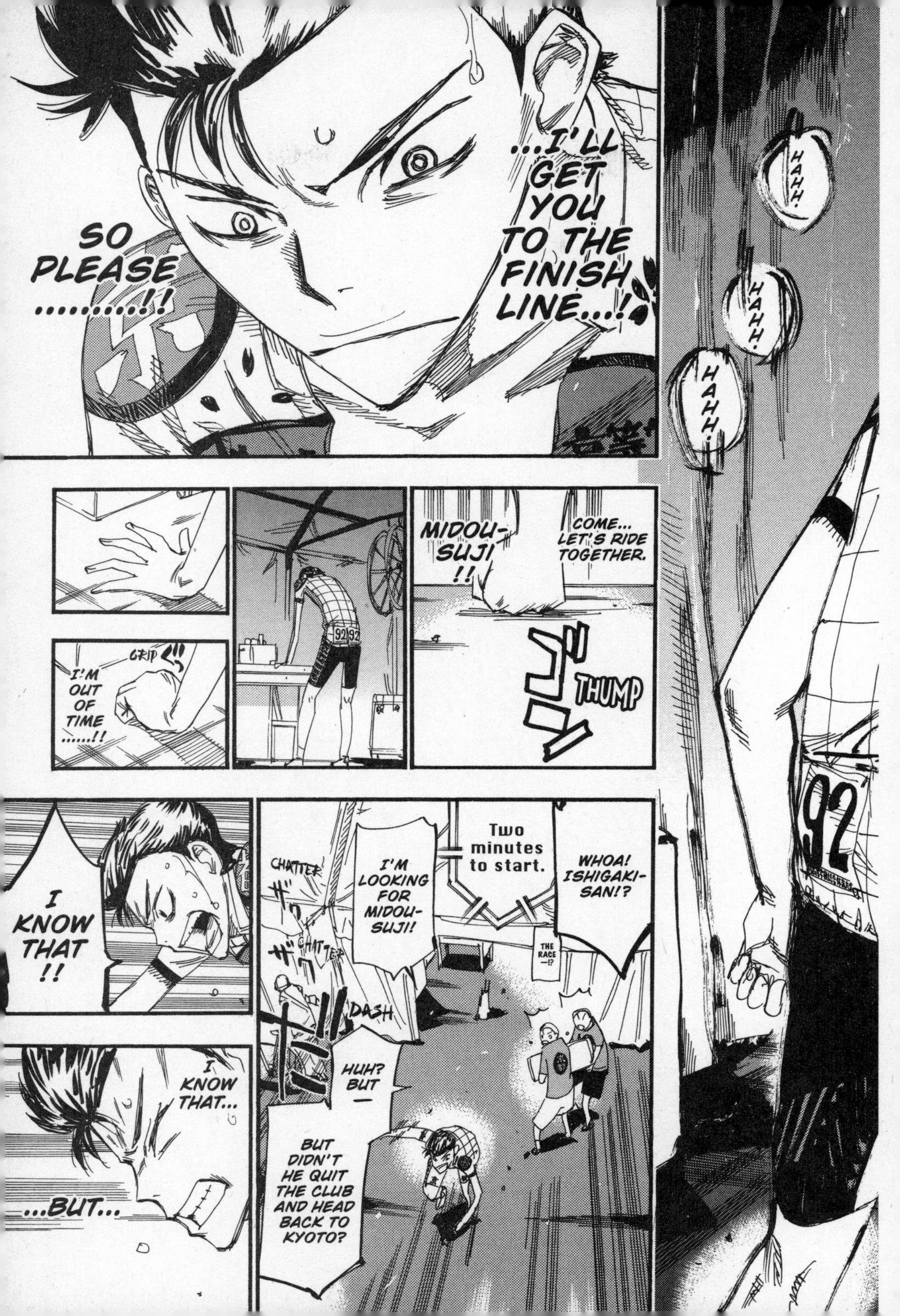
HAHH.
HAHH.
HAHH.
...I'LL GET YOU TO THE FINISH LINE...!
SO PLEASE..........!!
MIDOU-SUJI!!
COME... LET'S RIDE TOGETHER.
THUMP
GRIP
I'M OUT OF TIME......!!
WHOA! ISHIGAKI-SAN!?
THE RACE—!?
Two minutes to start.
I'M LOOKING FOR MIDOU-SUJI!
CHATTER
CHATTER
DASH
HUH? BUT—
BUT DIDN'T HE QUIT THE CLUB AND HEAD BACK TO KYOTO?
I KNOW THAT!!
I KNOW THAT...
...BUT...

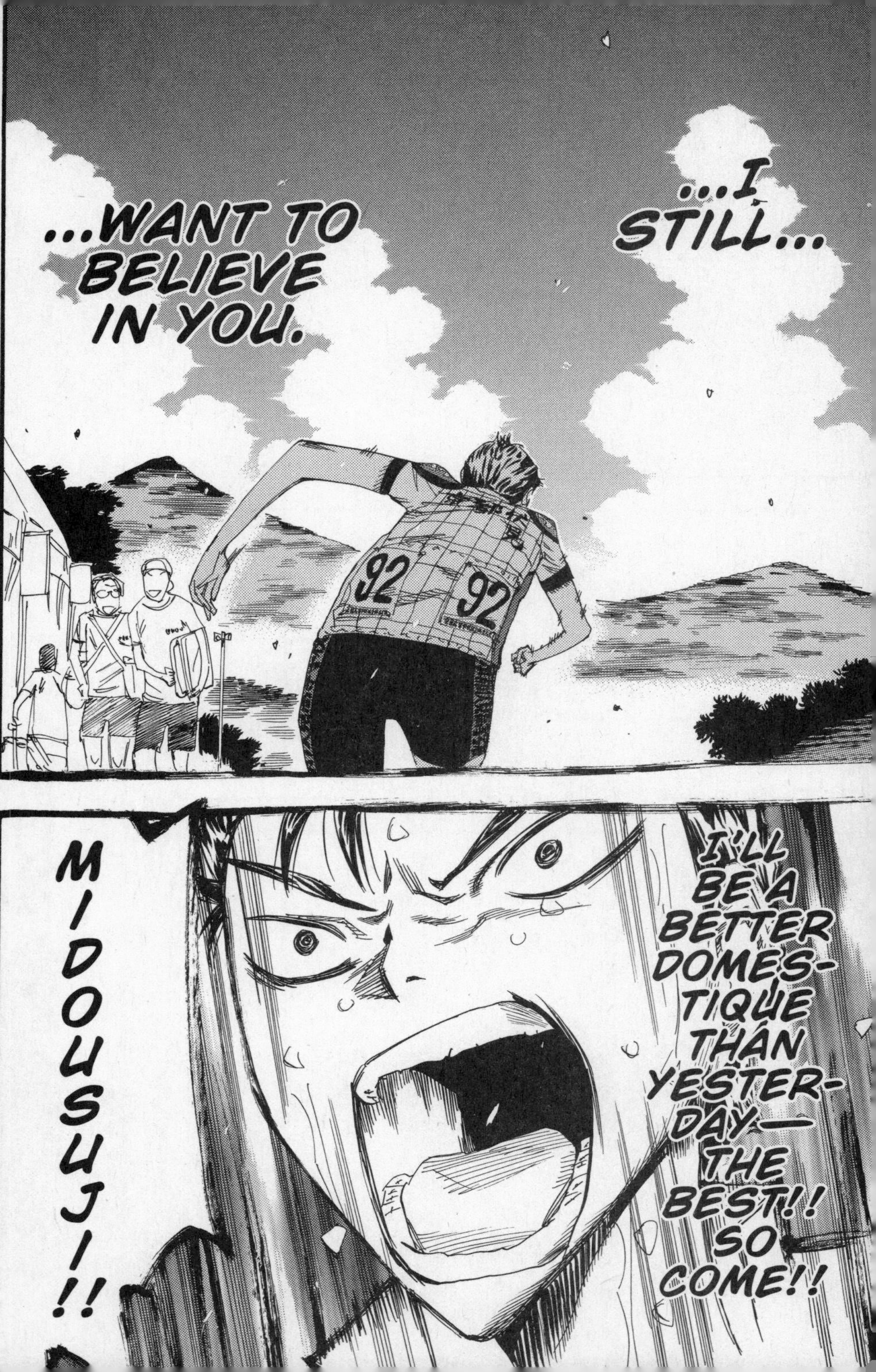
...I STILL...
...WANT TO BELIEVE IN YOU.
I'LL BE A BETTER DOMES-TIQUE THAN YESTER-DAY—THE BEST!! SO COME!!
MIDOUSUJI!!

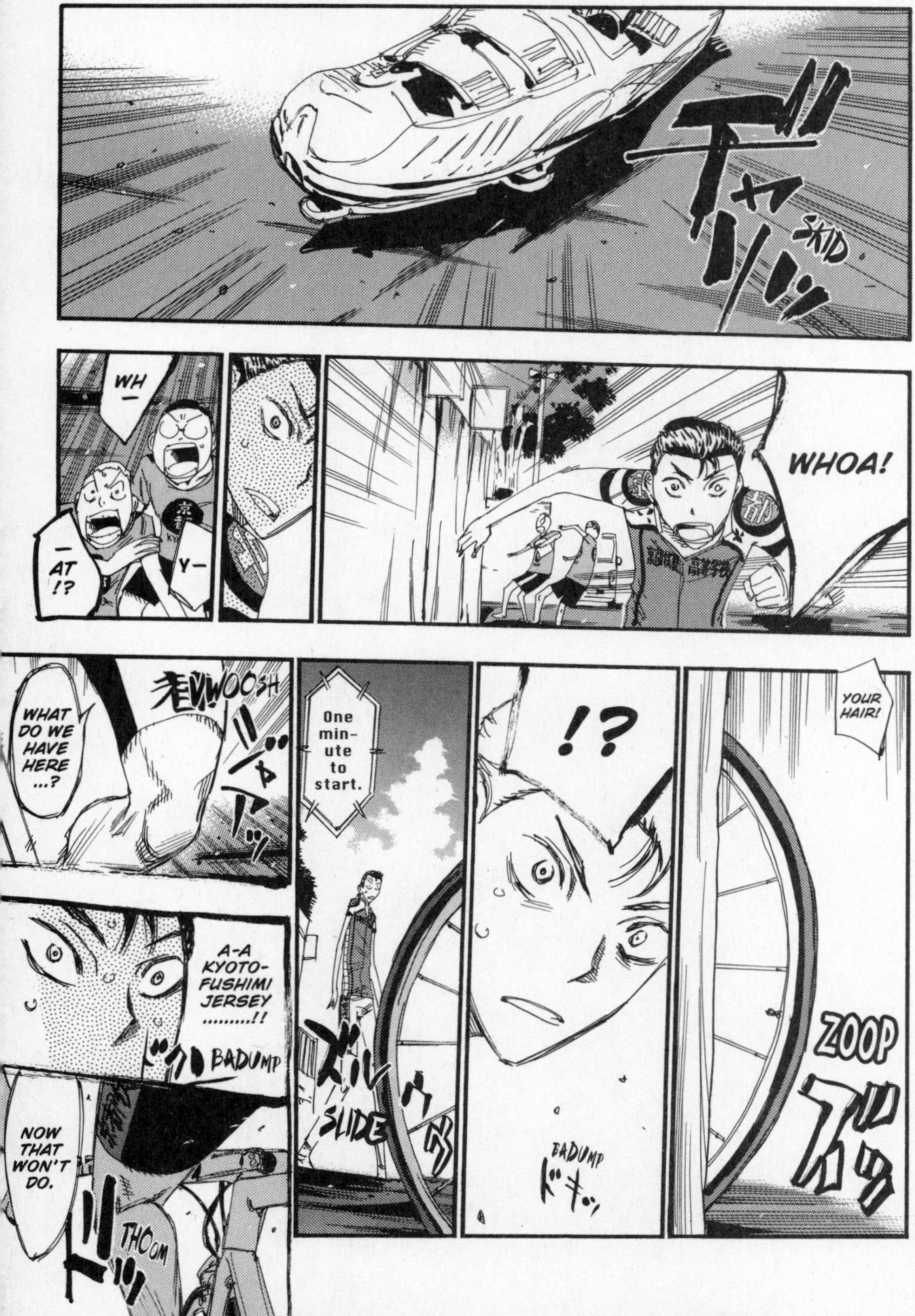
SKID
WHOA!
WH—
Y—
—AT!?
YOUR HAIR!
ZOOP
!?
BADUMP
One minute to start.
SLIDE
WOOSH
WHAT DO WE HAVE HERE ...?
A-A KYOTO-FUSHIMI JERSEY ....!!
BADUMP
NOW THAT WON'T DO.
THOOM

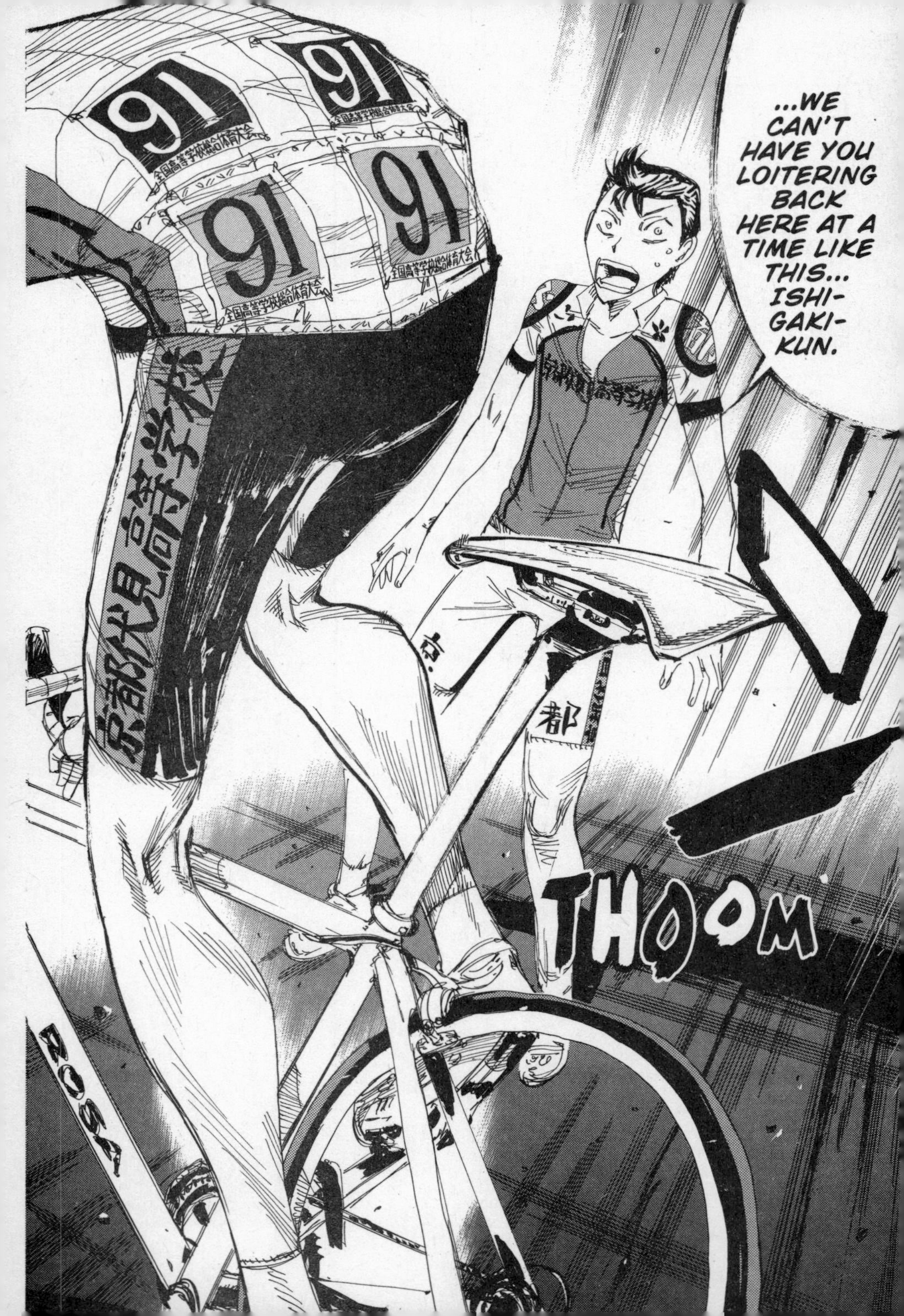
...WE CAN'T HAVE YOU LOITERING BACK HERE AT A TIME LIKE THIS... ISHI-GAKI-KUN.
THOOM

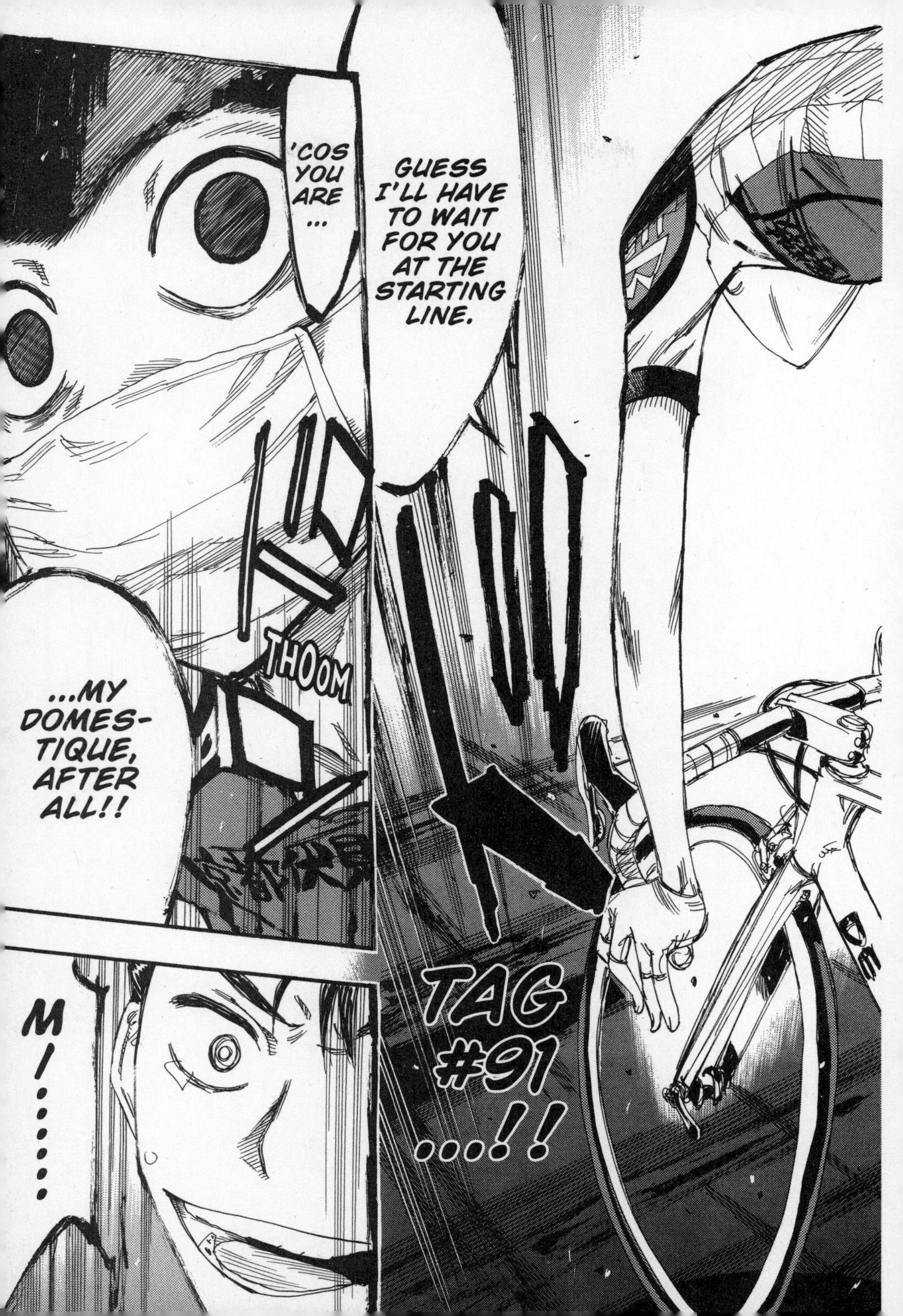
GUESS I'LL HAVE TO WAIT FOR YOU AT THE STARTING LINE.
'COS YOU ARE ...
...MY DOMES-TIQUE, AFTER ALL!!
THOOM
TAG #91 ...!!
M I......

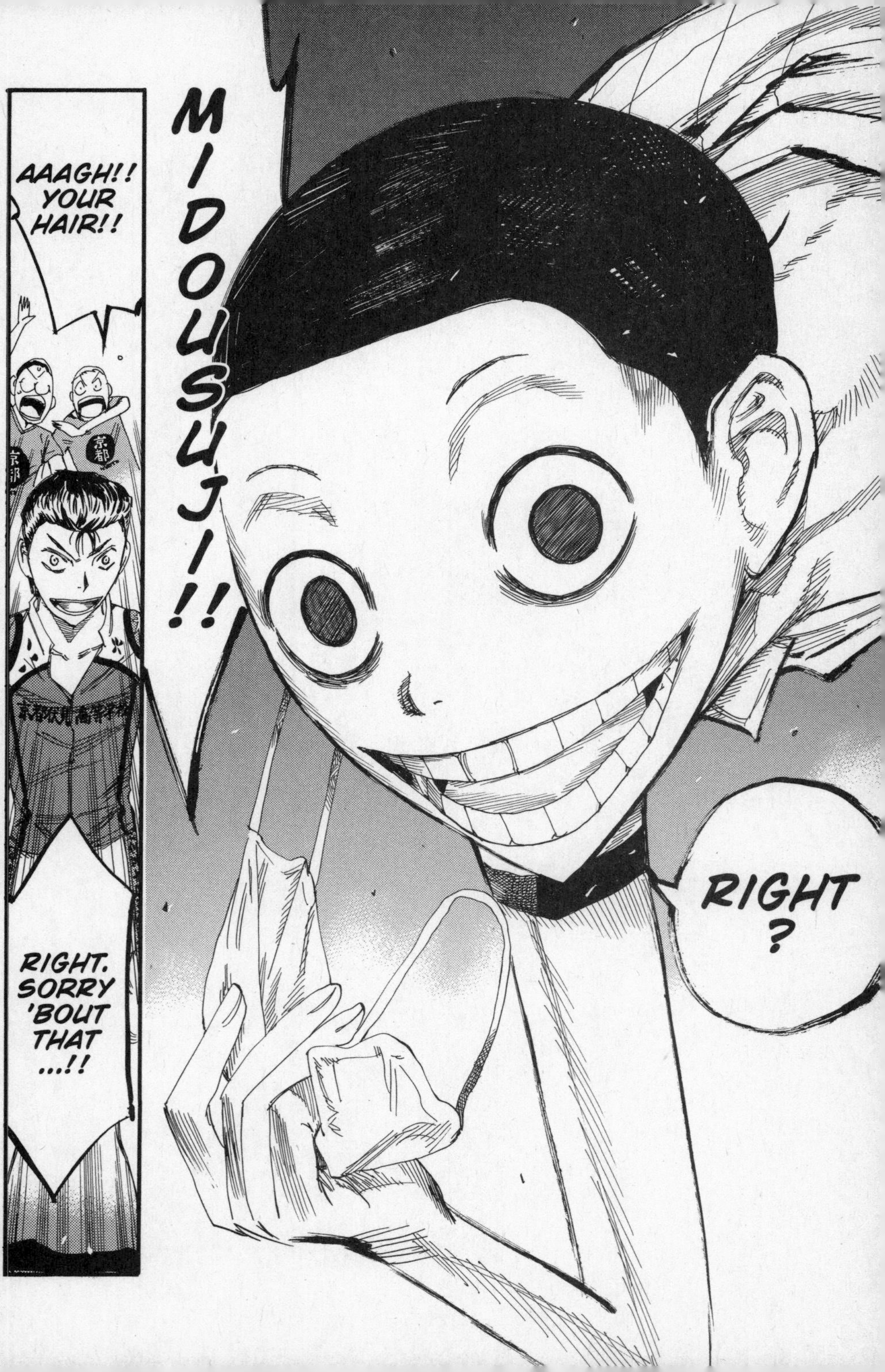
MIDOUSUJI!!
RIGHT?
AAAGH!! YOUR HAIR!!
RIGHT. SORRY 'BOUT THAT ...!!

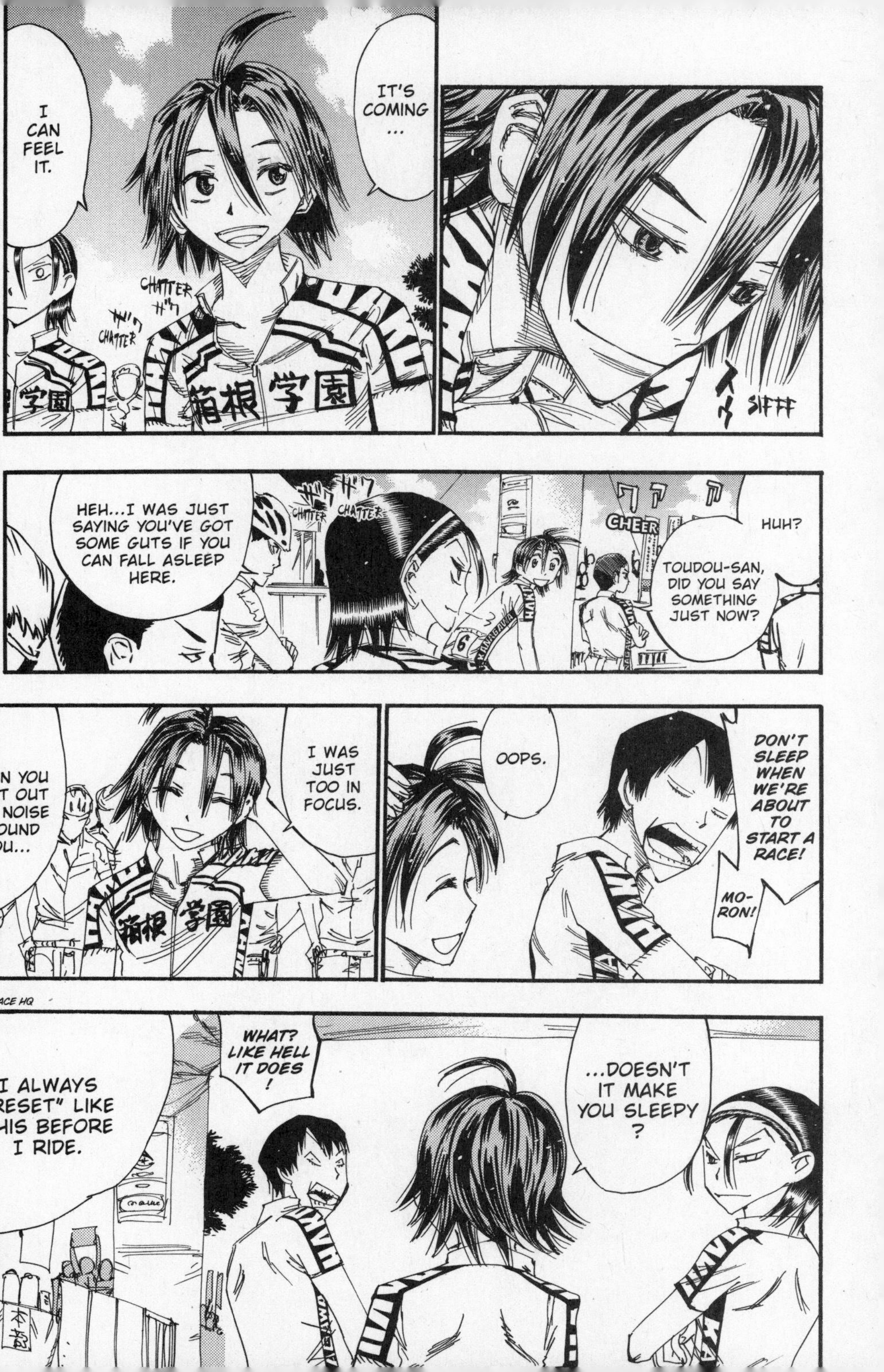
SIFFF
IT'S COMING ...
I CAN FEEL IT.
CHATTER
CHATTER
HUH?
TOUDOU-SAN, DID YOU SAY SOMETHING JUST NOW?
CHEER
CHATTER
CHATTER
HEH...I WAS JUST SAYING YOU'VE GOT SOME GUTS IF YOU CAN FALL ASLEEP HERE.
DON'T SLEEP WHEN WE'RE ABOUT TO START A RACE!
MO-RON!
OOPS.
I WAS JUST TOO IN FOCUS.
WHEN YOU SHUT OUT THE NOISE AROUND YOU...
SIGN: RACE HQ
...DOESN'T IT MAKE YOU SLEEPY?
WHAT? LIKE HELL IT DOES!
I ALWAYS "RESET" LIKE THIS BEFORE I RIDE.

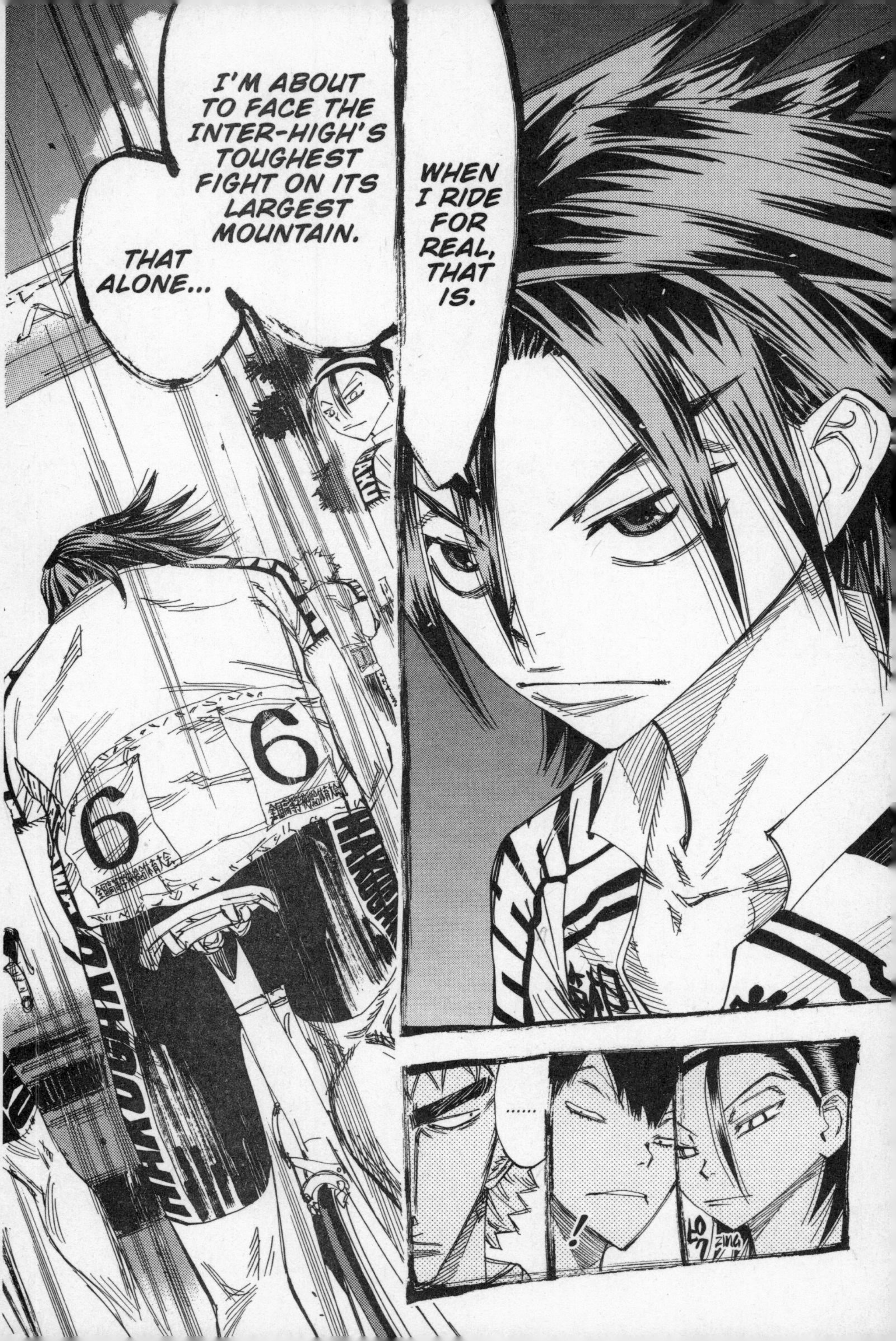
WHEN I RIDE FOR REAL, THAT IS.
I'M ABOUT TO FACE THE INTER-HIGH'S TOUGHEST FIGHT ON ITS LARGEST MOUNTAIN.
THAT ALONE...
......
!
ZING

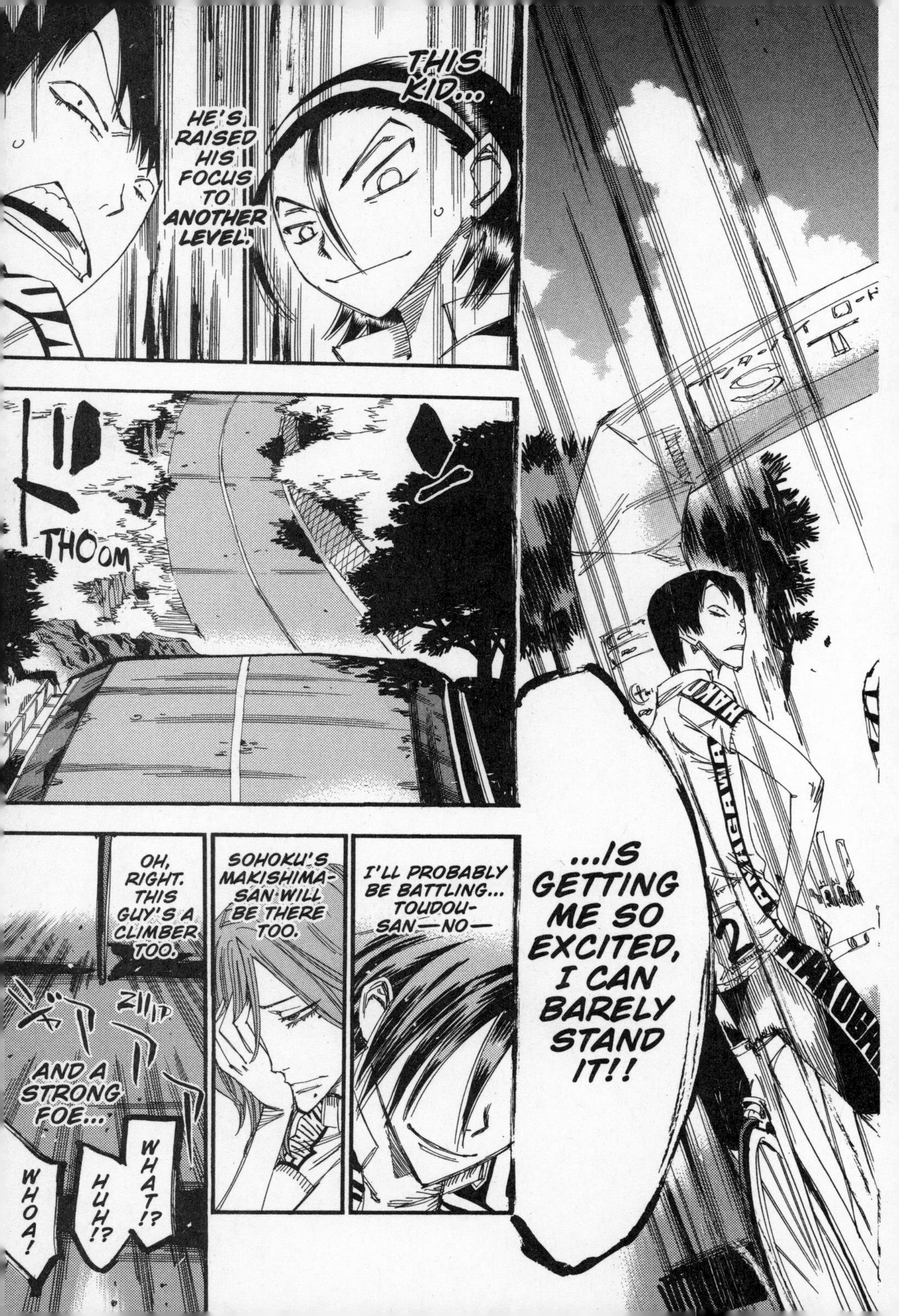
THIS KID...
HE'S RAISED HIS FOCUS TO ANOTHER LEVEL.
THOOM
I'LL PROBABLY BE BATTLING... TOUDOU-SAN—NO—
SOHOKU'S MAKISHIMA-SAN WILL BE THERE TOO.
OH, RIGHT. THIS GUY'S A CLIMBER TOO.
ZIIIP
AND A STRONG FOE...
WHAT!?
HUH!?
WHOA!
...IS GETTING ME SO EXCITED, I CAN BARELY STAND IT!!

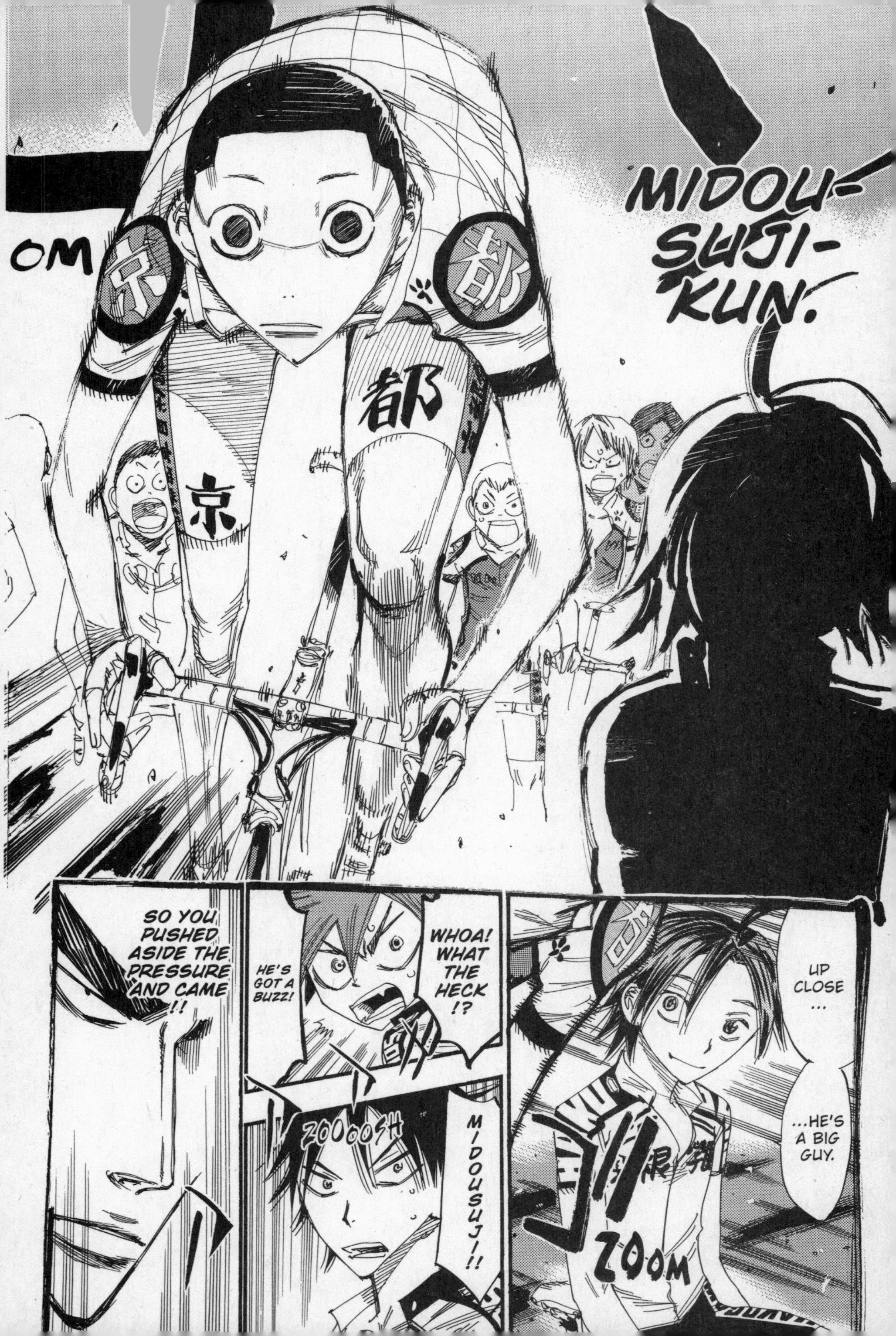
MIDOU-SUJI-KUN.
OM
UP CLOSE ...
...HE'S A BIG GUY.
ZOOM
WHOA! WHAT THE HECK !?
HE'S GOT A BUZZ!
MIDOUSUJI!!
ZOOOOSH
SO YOU PUSHED ASIDE THE PRESSURE AND CAME !!

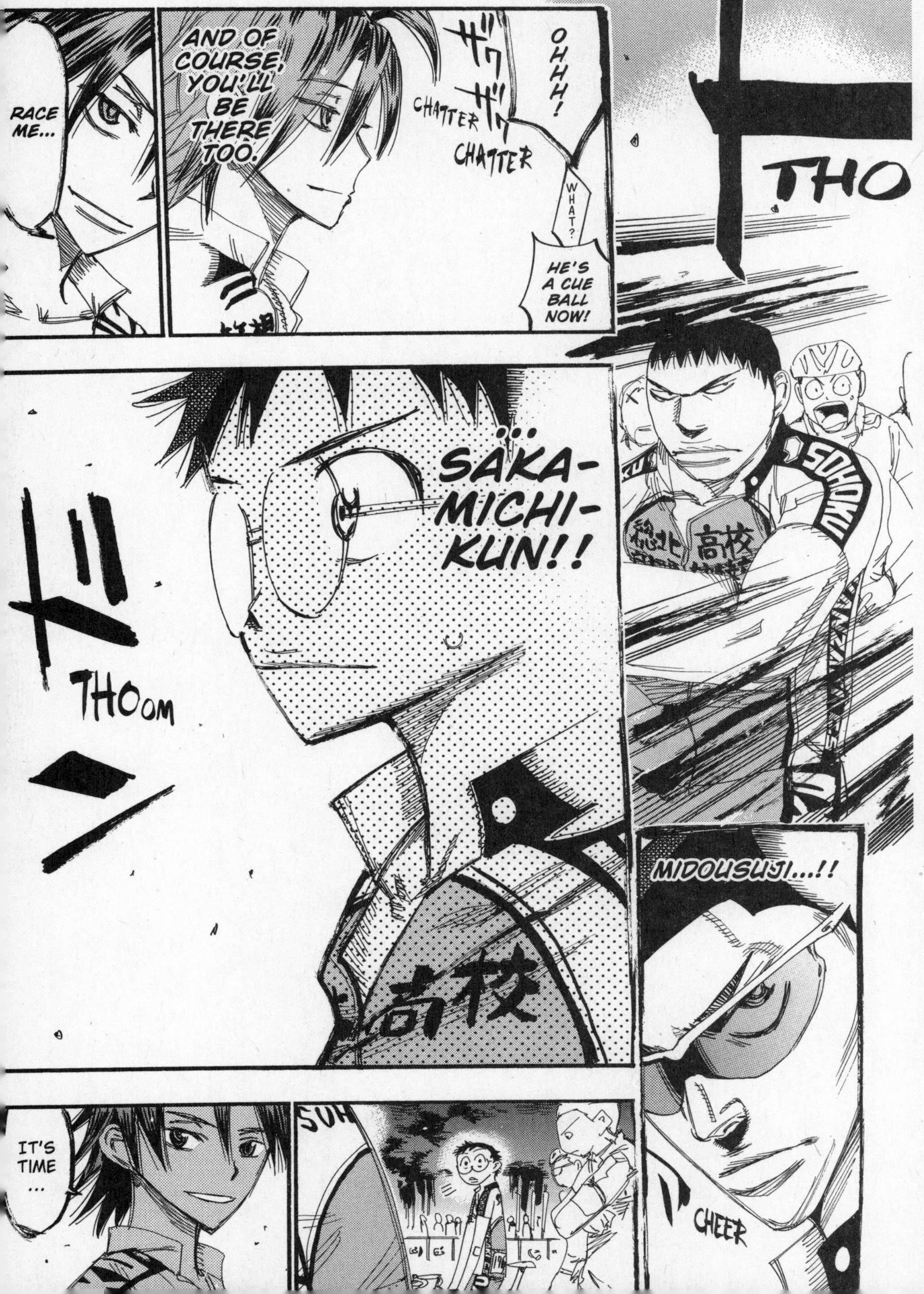
THO
OHHHH!
CHATTER CHATTER
WHAT?
HE'S A CUE BALL NOW!
AND OF COURSE, YOU'LL BE THERE TOO.
RACE ME...
...SAKAMICHI-KUN!!
THOom
MIDOUSUJI...!!
CHEER
SUH
IT'S TIME...

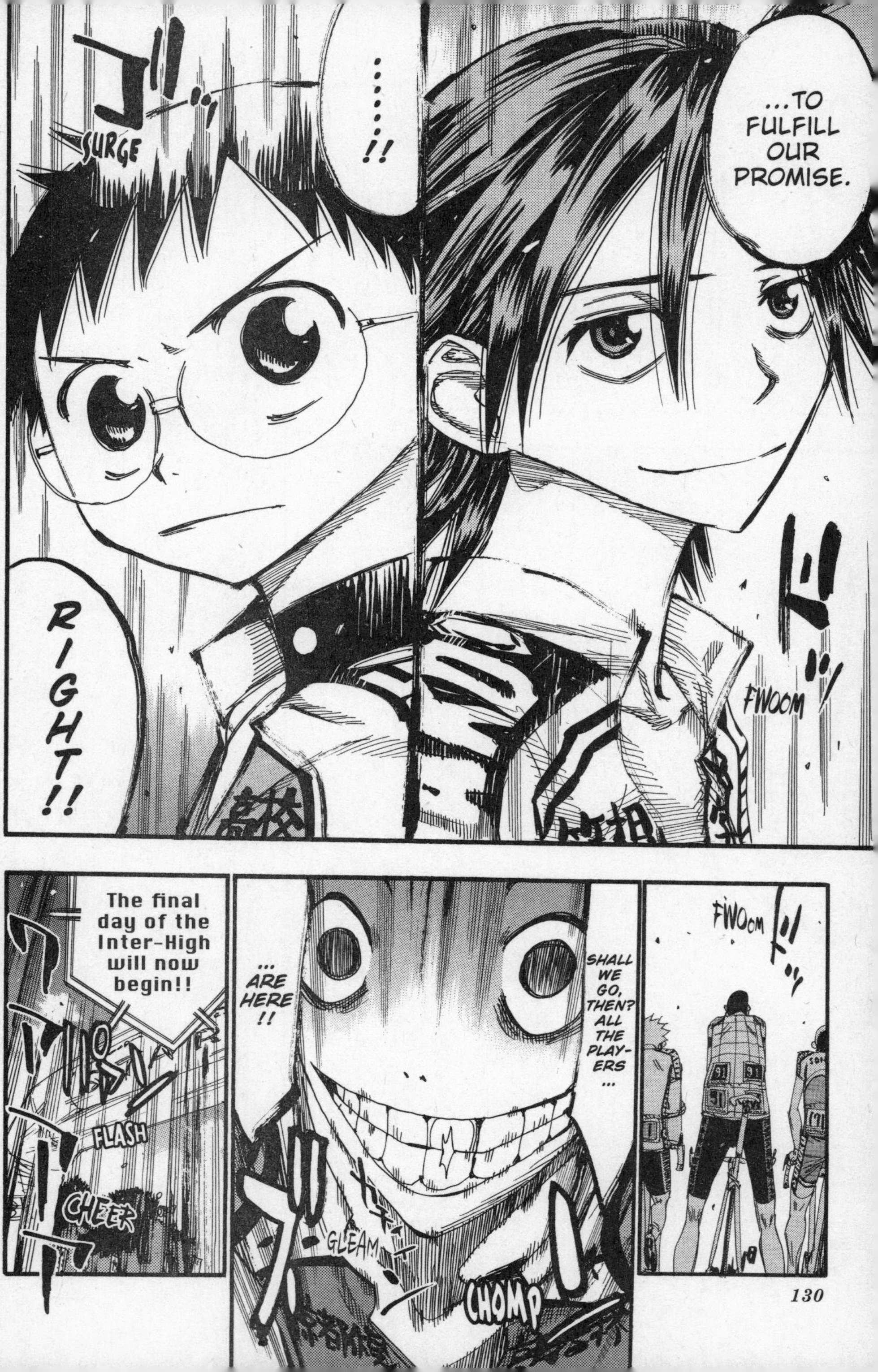
...TO FULFILL OUR PROMISE.
FWOOM
......!!
SURGE
RIGHT!!
SHALL WE GO, THEN? ALL THE PLAYERS ...
FWOOM
... ARE HERE !!
GLEAM
CHOMP
The final day of the Inter-High will now begin!!
FLASH
CHEER

RIDE.161 THE LAST STARTING LINE

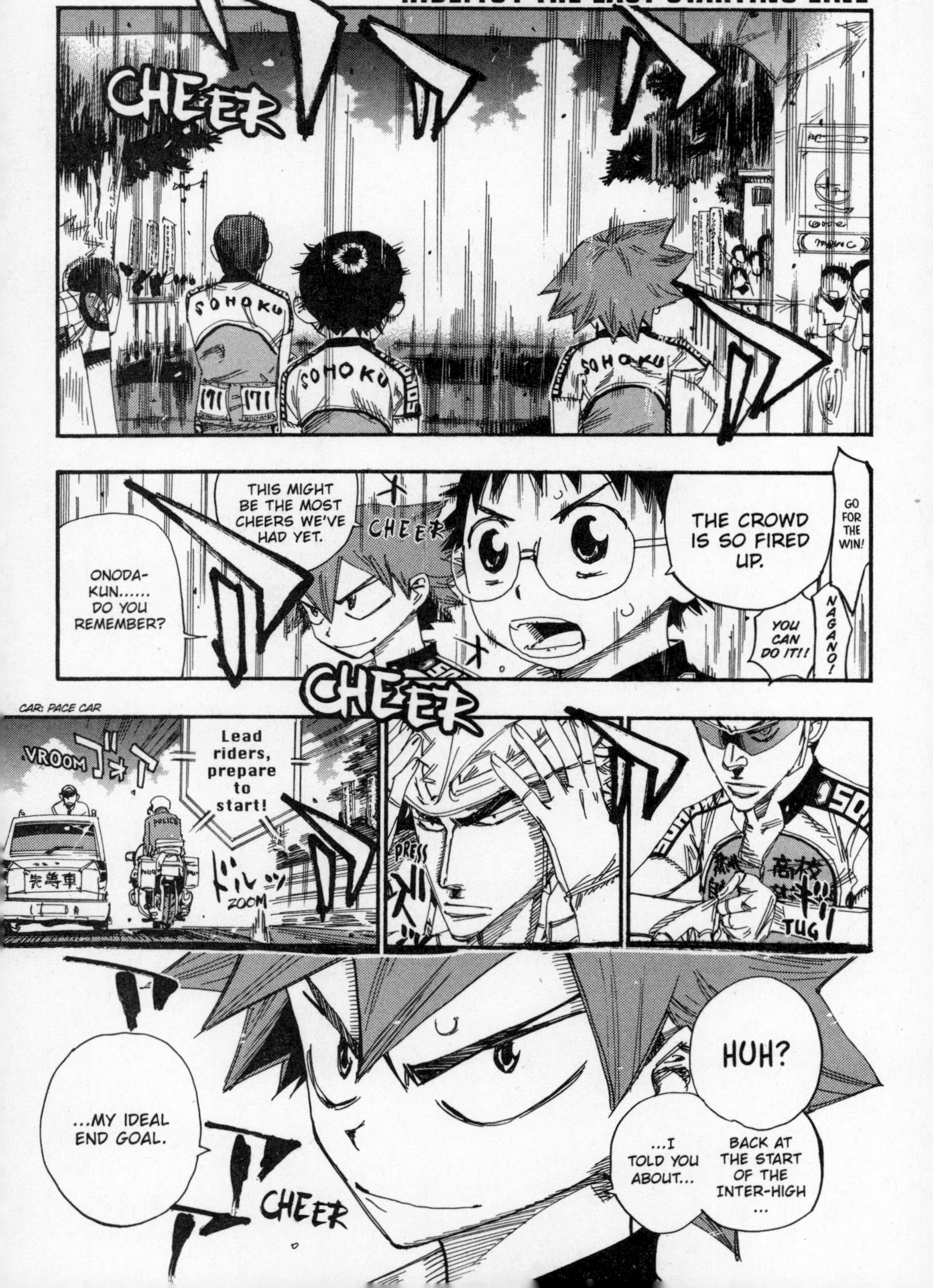
CHEER
GO FOR THE WIN!
NAGANO!
YOU CAN DO IT!!
THE CROWD IS SO FIRED UP.
CHEER
THIS MIGHT BE THE MOST CHEERS WE'VE HAD YET.
ONODA-KUN...... DO YOU REMEMBER?
CHEER
TUG
PRESS
Lead riders, prepare to start!
ZOOM
VROOM
CAR: PACE CAR
HUH?
BACK AT THE START OF THE INTER-HIGH ...
...I TOLD YOU ABOUT...
...MY IDEAL END GOAL.
CHEER

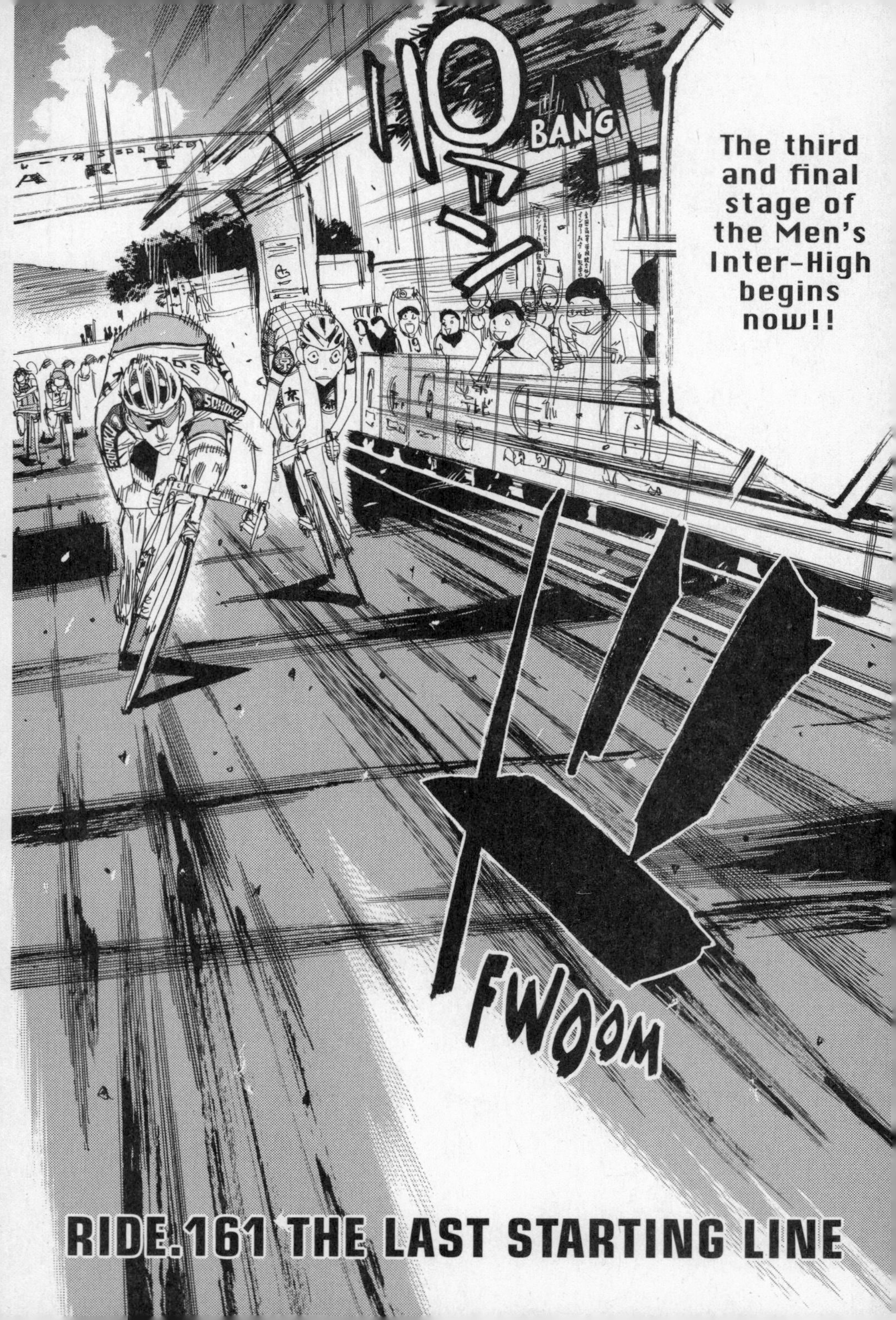
The third and final stage of the Men's Inter-High begins now!!
BANG
FWOOM

RIDE.161 THE LAST STARTING LINE

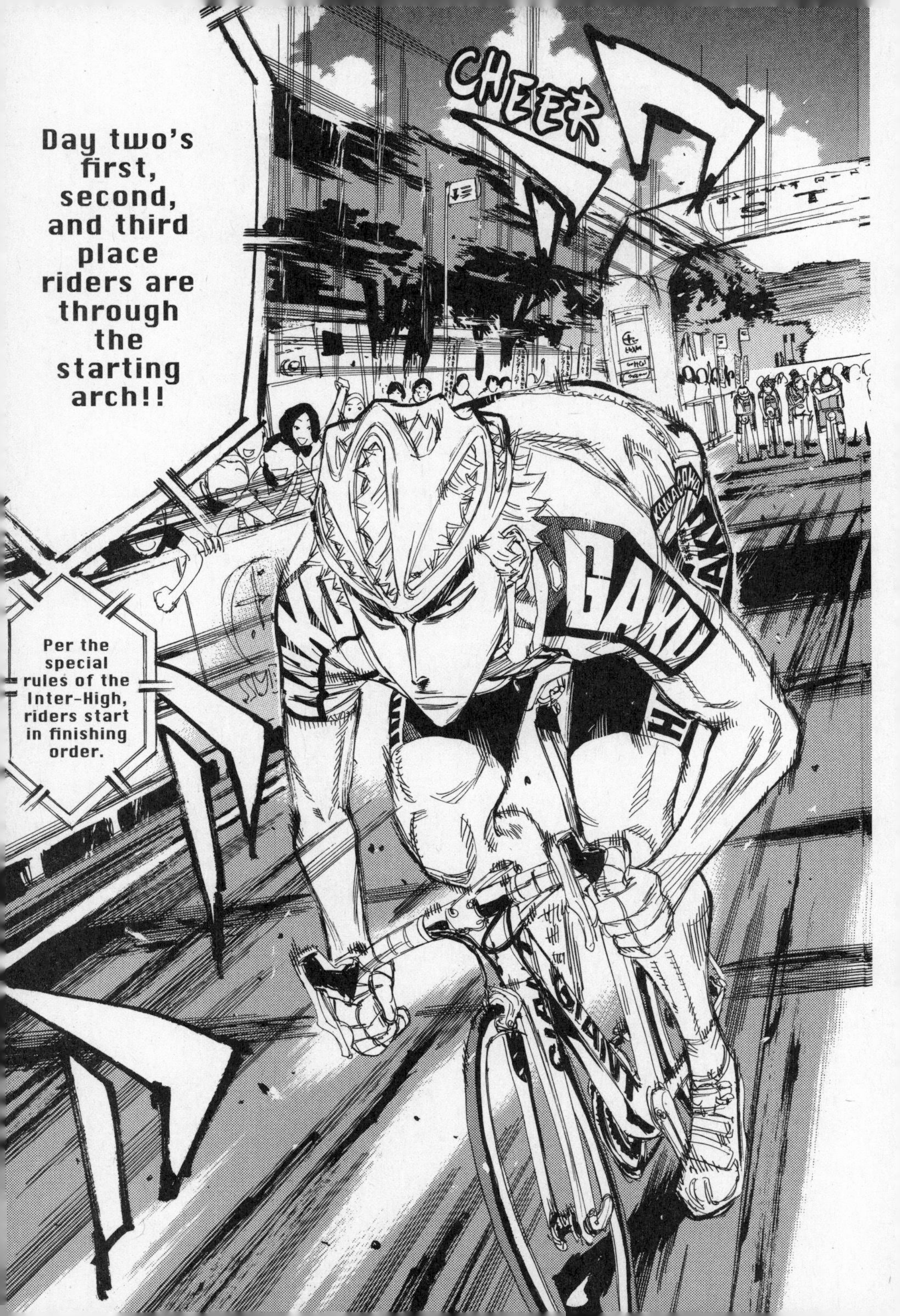
CHEER
Day two's first, second, and third place riders are through the starting arch!!
Per the special rules of the Inter-High, riders start in finishing order.

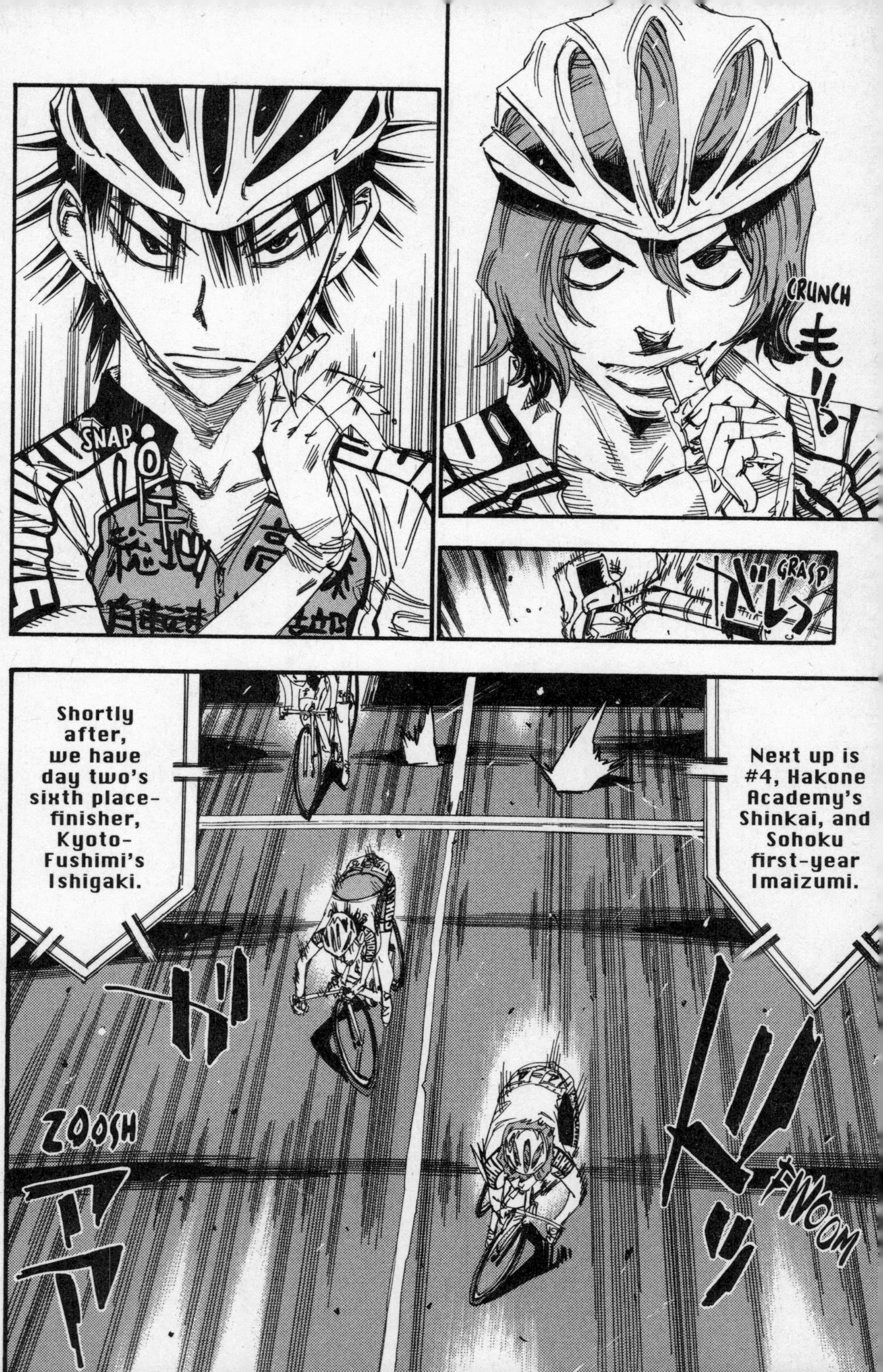
CRUNCH
GRASP
SNAP
Next up is #4, Hakone Academy's Shinkai, and Sohoku first-year Imaizumi.
Shortly after, we have day two's sixth place-finisher, Kyoto-Fushimi's Ishigaki.
FWOOM
ZOOSH

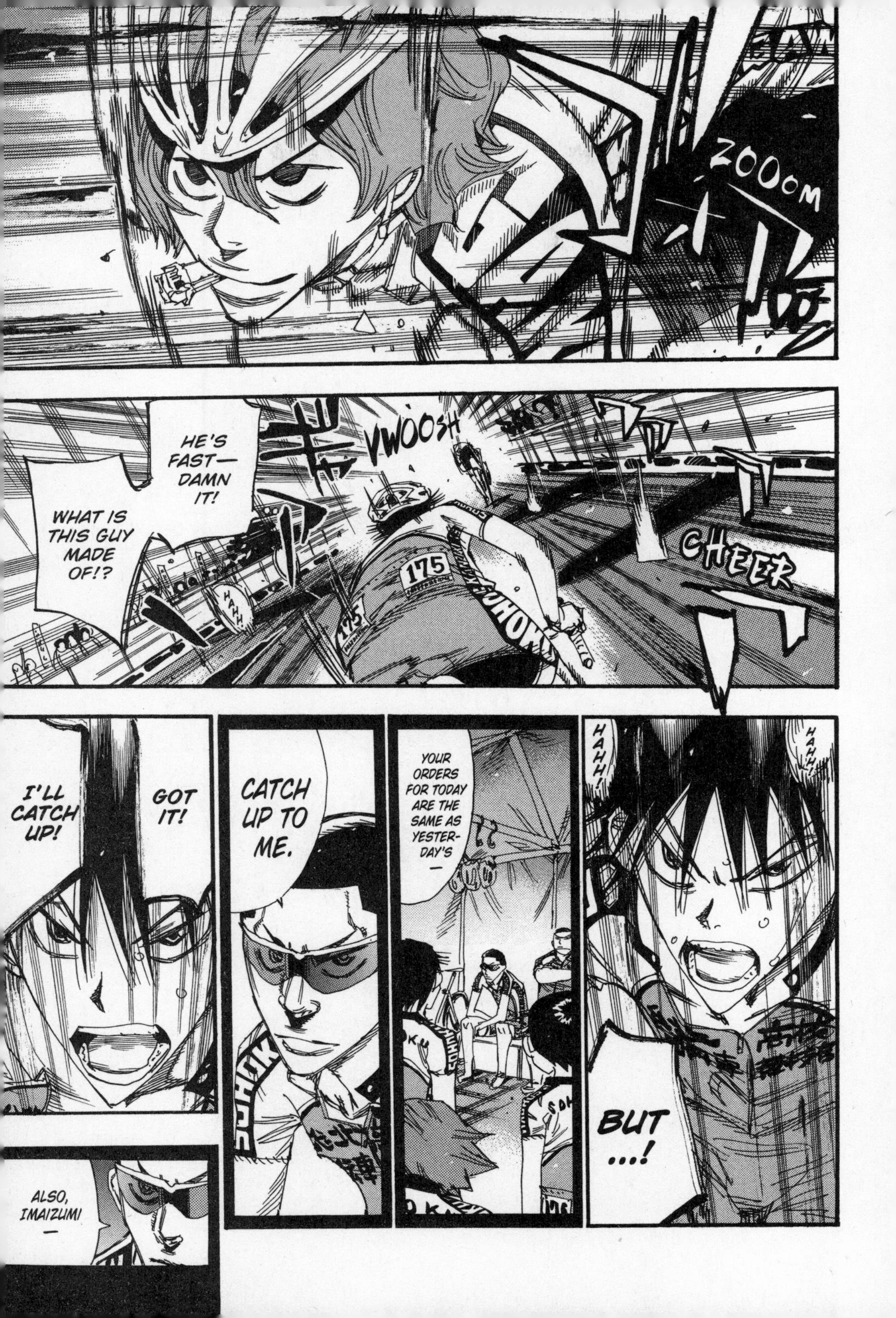
ZOOOM
VWOOSH
CHEER
HE'S FAST—DAMN IT!
WHAT IS THIS GUY MADE OF!?
HAHH
HAHH
HAHH!
BUT ...!
YOUR ORDERS FOR TODAY ARE THE SAME AS YESTER-DAY'S—
CATCH UP TO ME.
GOT IT!
I'LL CATCH UP!
ALSO, IMAIZUMI—

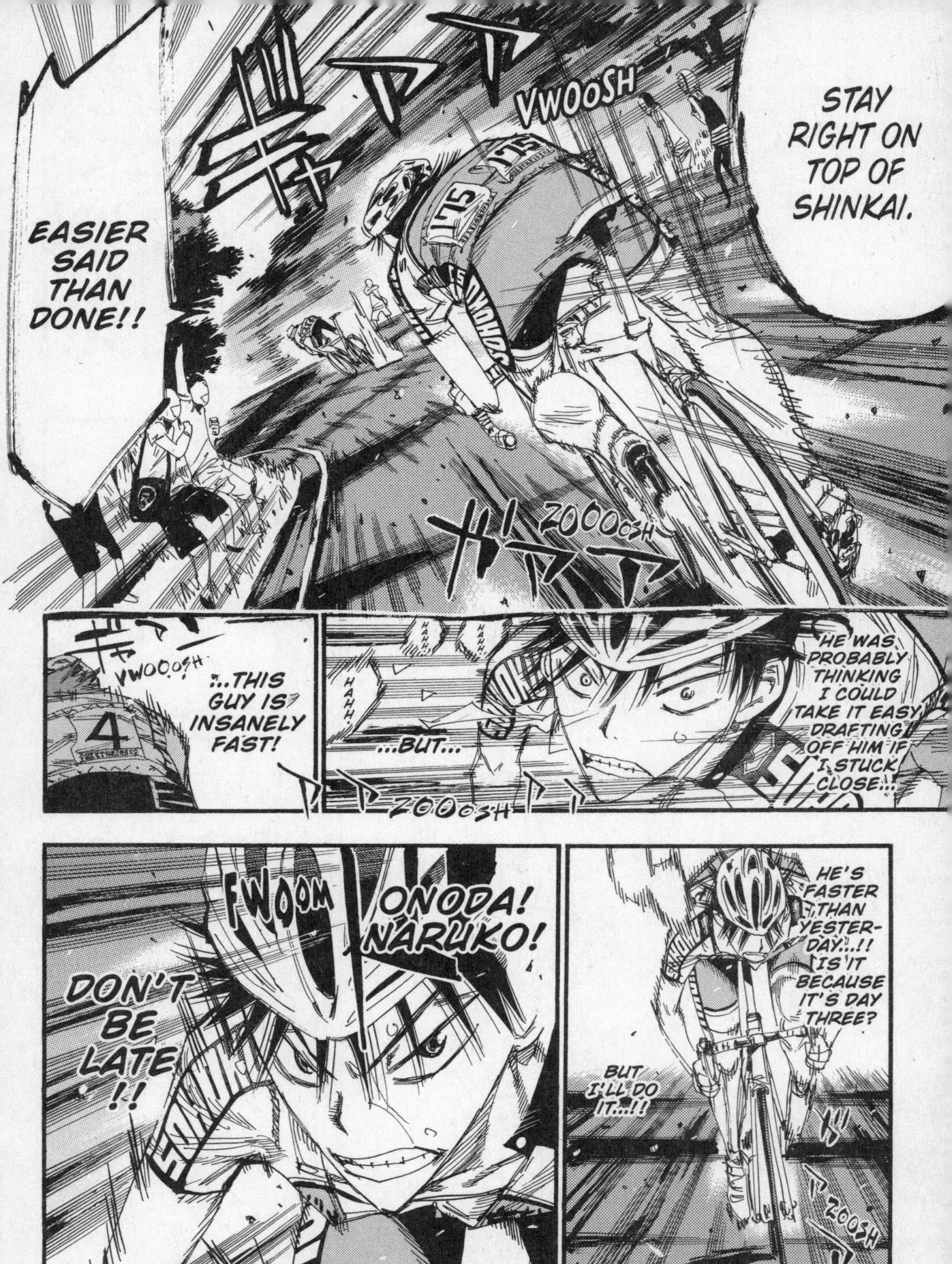
STAY RIGHT ON TOP OF SHINKAI.
VWOOSH
EASIER SAID THAN DONE!!
ZOOOOSH
HAHH
HAHH
HAHH
HE WAS PROBABLY THINKING I COULD TAKE IT EASY DRAFTING OFF HIM IF I STUCK CLOSE...!
...BUT...
ZOOOOSH
VWOOOSH
...THIS GUY IS INSANELY FAST!
HE'S FASTER THAN YESTERDAY...!! IS IT BECAUSE IT'S DAY THREE?
BUT I'LL DO IT...!!
ZOOSH
FWOOM
ONODA! NARUKO!
DON'T BE LATE!!

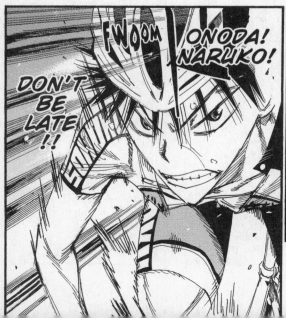

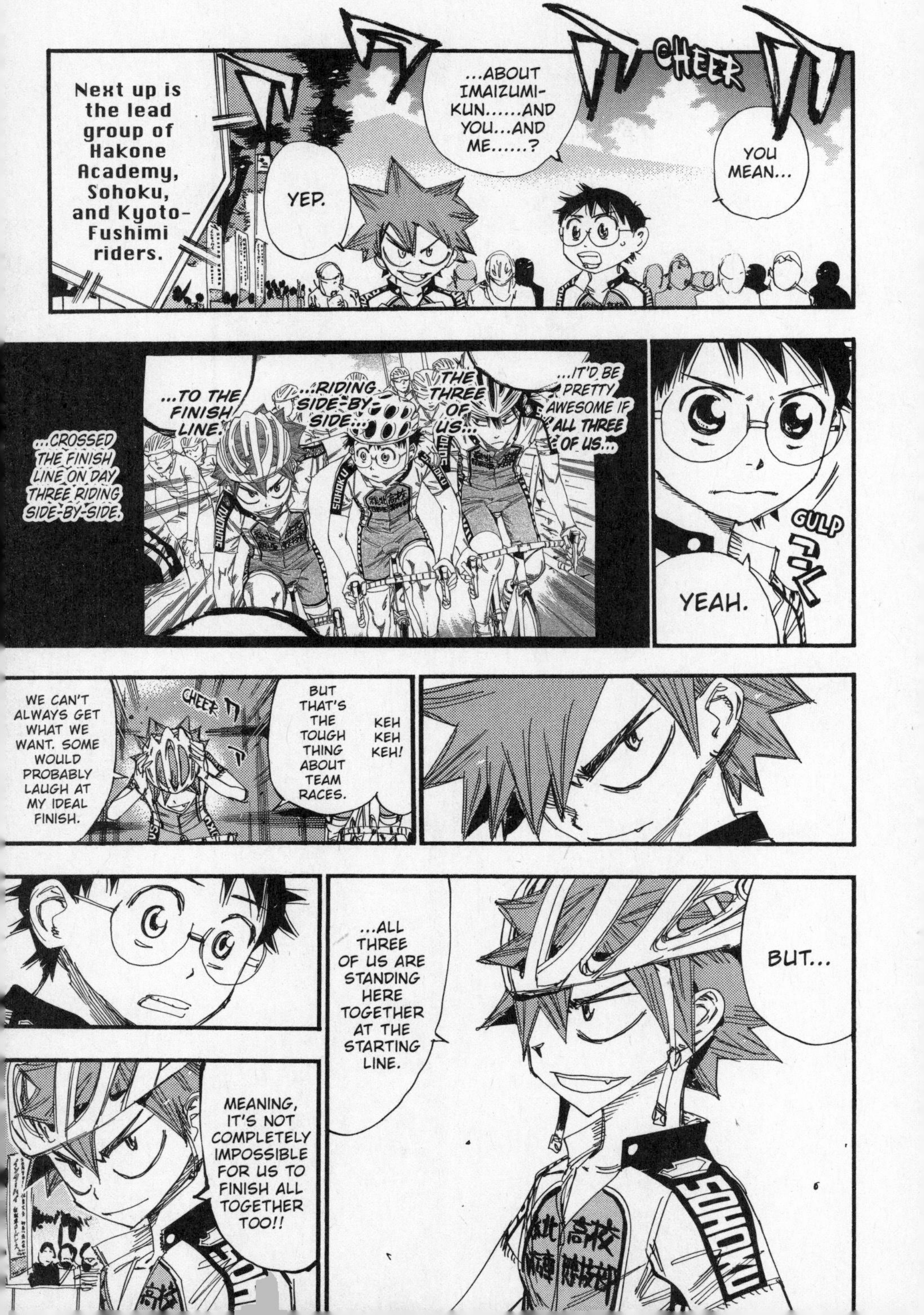
CHEER
YOU MEAN...
...ABOUT IMAIZUMI-KUN......AND YOU...AND ME......?
YEP.
Next up is the lead group of Hakone Academy, Sohoku, and Kyoto-Fushimi riders.
GULP
YEAH.
...IT'D BE PRETTY AWESOME IF ALL THREE OF US...
THE THREE OF US...
...RIDING SIDE-BY-SIDE...
...TO THE FINISH LINE.
...CROSSED THE FINISH LINE ON DAY THREE RIDING SIDE-BY-SIDE.
KEH KEH KEH!
BUT THAT'S THE TOUGH THING ABOUT TEAM RACES.
WE CAN'T ALWAYS GET WHAT WE WANT. SOME WOULD PROBABLY LAUGH AT MY IDEAL FINISH.
CHEER
BUT...
...ALL THREE OF US ARE STANDING HERE TOGETHER AT THE STARTING LINE.
MEANING, IT'S NOT COMPLETELY IMPOSSIBLE FOR US TO FINISH ALL TOGETHER TOO!!

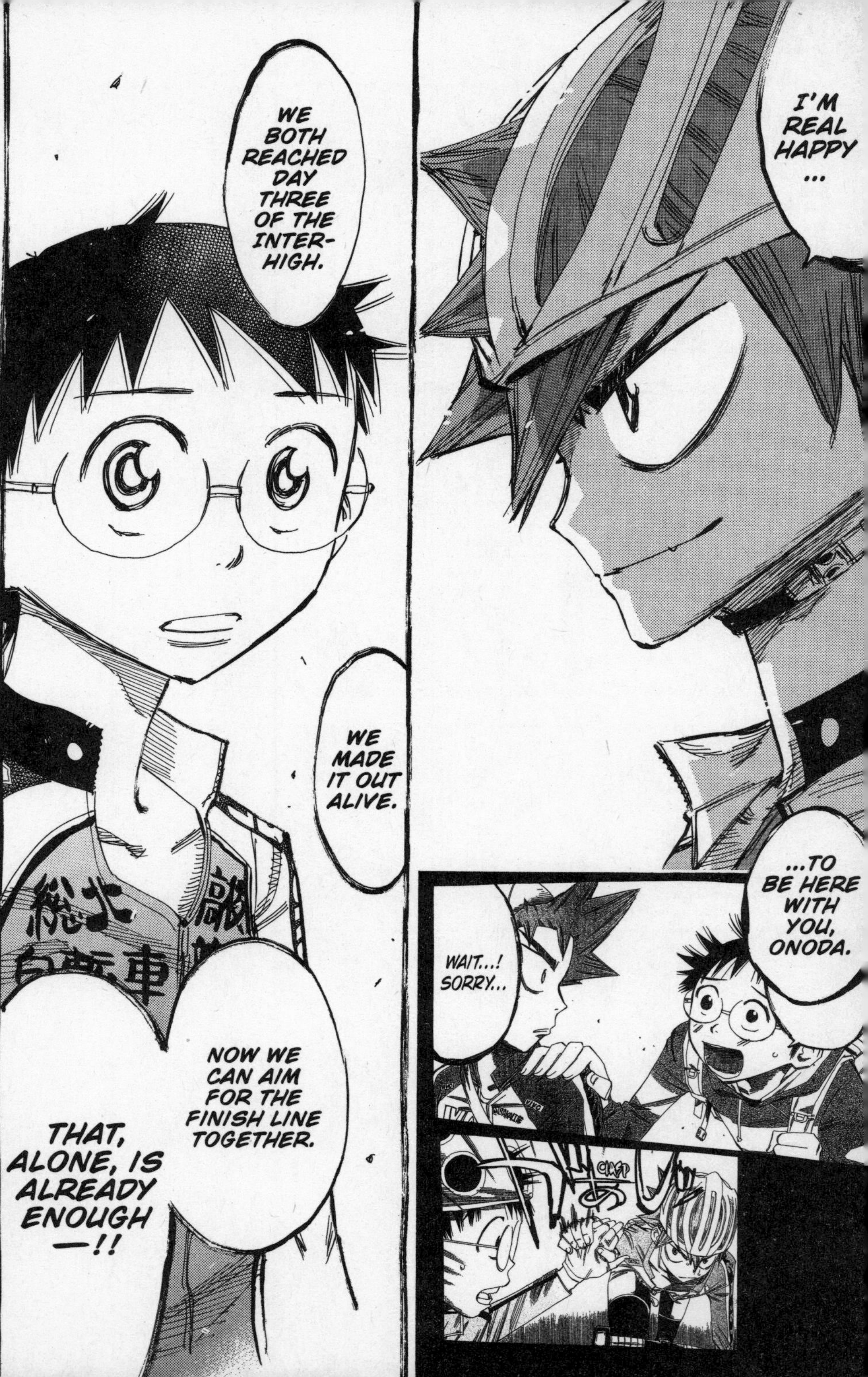
I'M REAL HAPPY ...
...TO BE HERE WITH YOU, ONODA.
WAIT...! SORRY...
CLASP
WE BOTH REACHED DAY THREE OF THE INTER-HIGH.
WE MADE IT OUT ALIVE.
NOW WE CAN AIM FOR THE FINISH LINE TOGETHER.
THAT, ALONE, IS ALREADY ENOUGH—!!

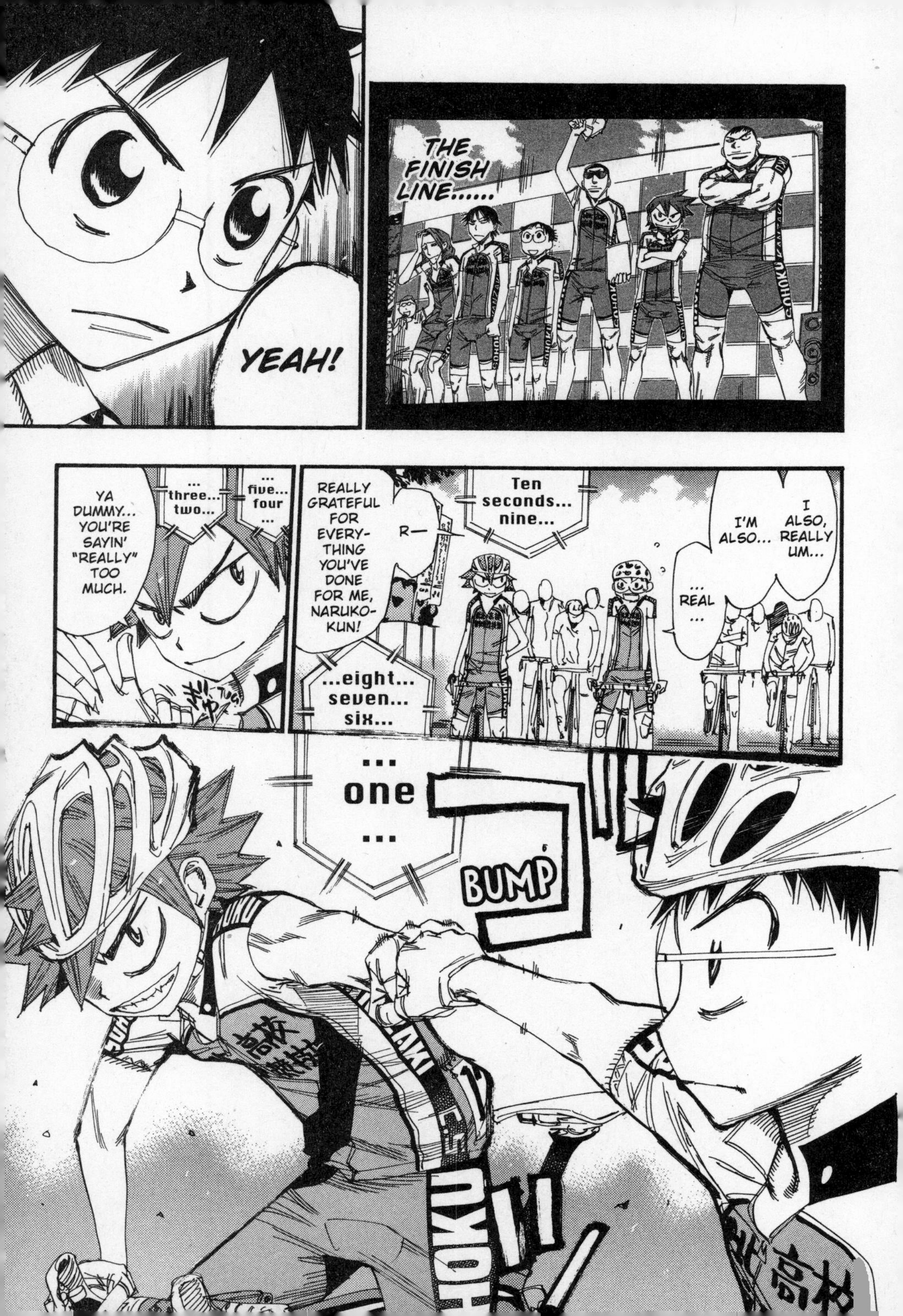
THE FINISH LINE......
YEAH!
Ten seconds... nine...
I ALSO, REALLY UM...
I'M ALSO...
... REAL ...
R—
REALLY GRATEFUL FOR EVERYTHING YOU'VE DONE FOR ME, NARUKO-KUN!
...eight... seven... six...
... five... four ...
... three... two...
YA DUMMY... YOU'RE SAYIN' "REALLY" TOO MUCH.
TUG
... one ...
BUMP

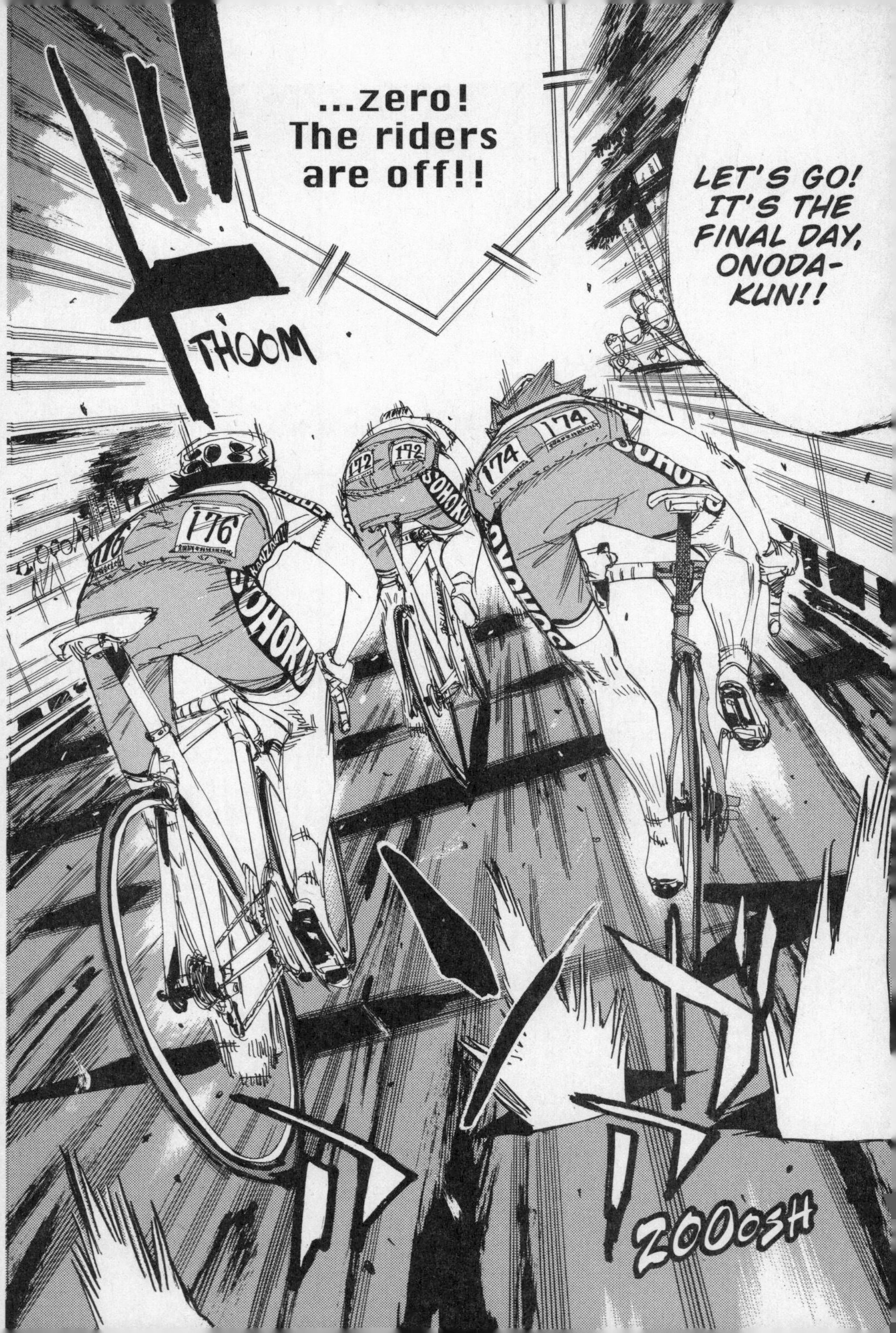
LET'S GO! IT'S THE FINAL DAY, ONODA-KUN!!
...zero! The riders are off!!
THOOM
176
172
174
SOHOKU
ZOOOSH

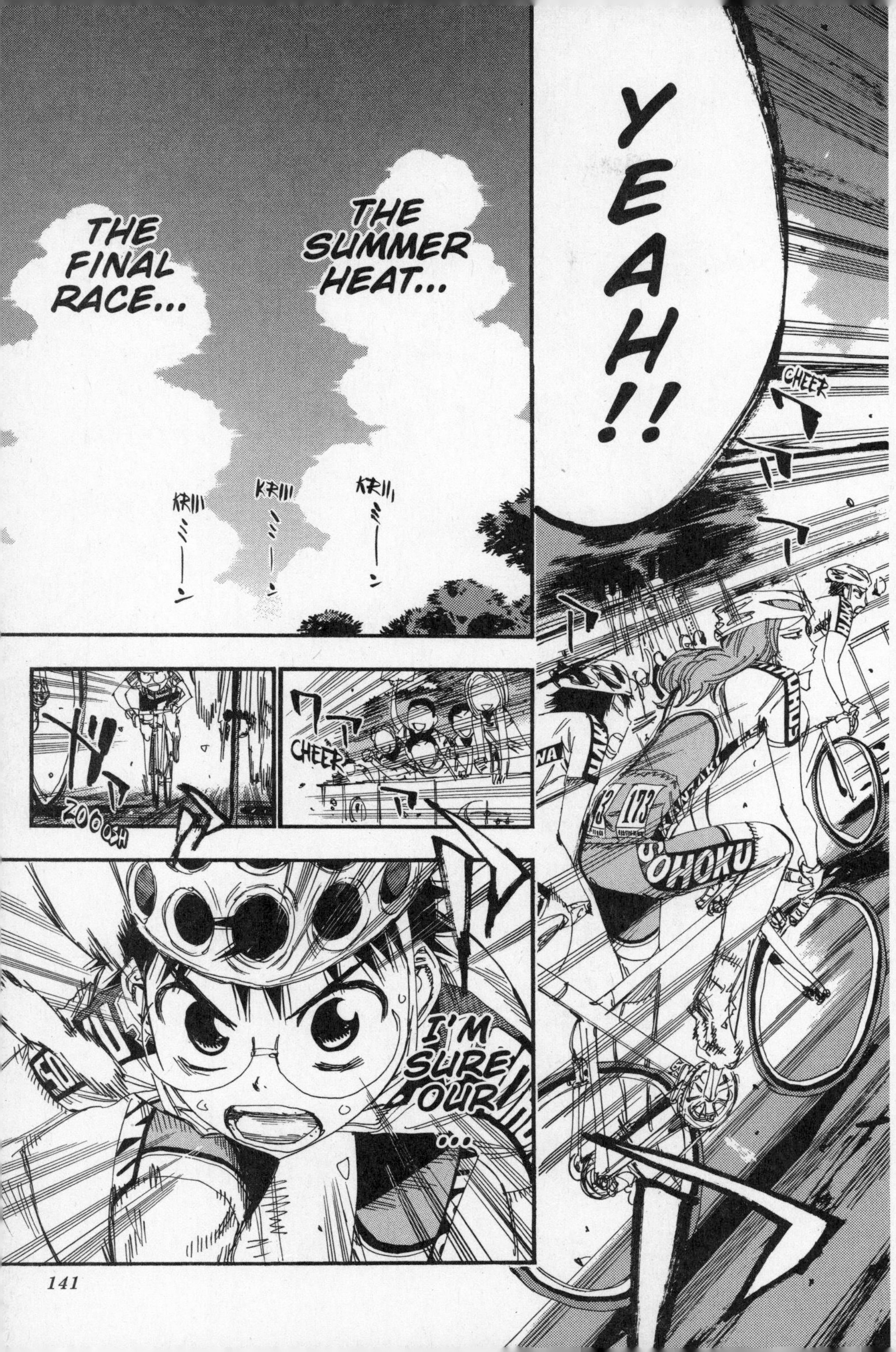
YEAH!!
CHEER
THE SUMMER HEAT...
THE FINAL RACE...
KRIII
KRIII
KRIII
CHEER
ZOOOSH
I'M SURE OUR...

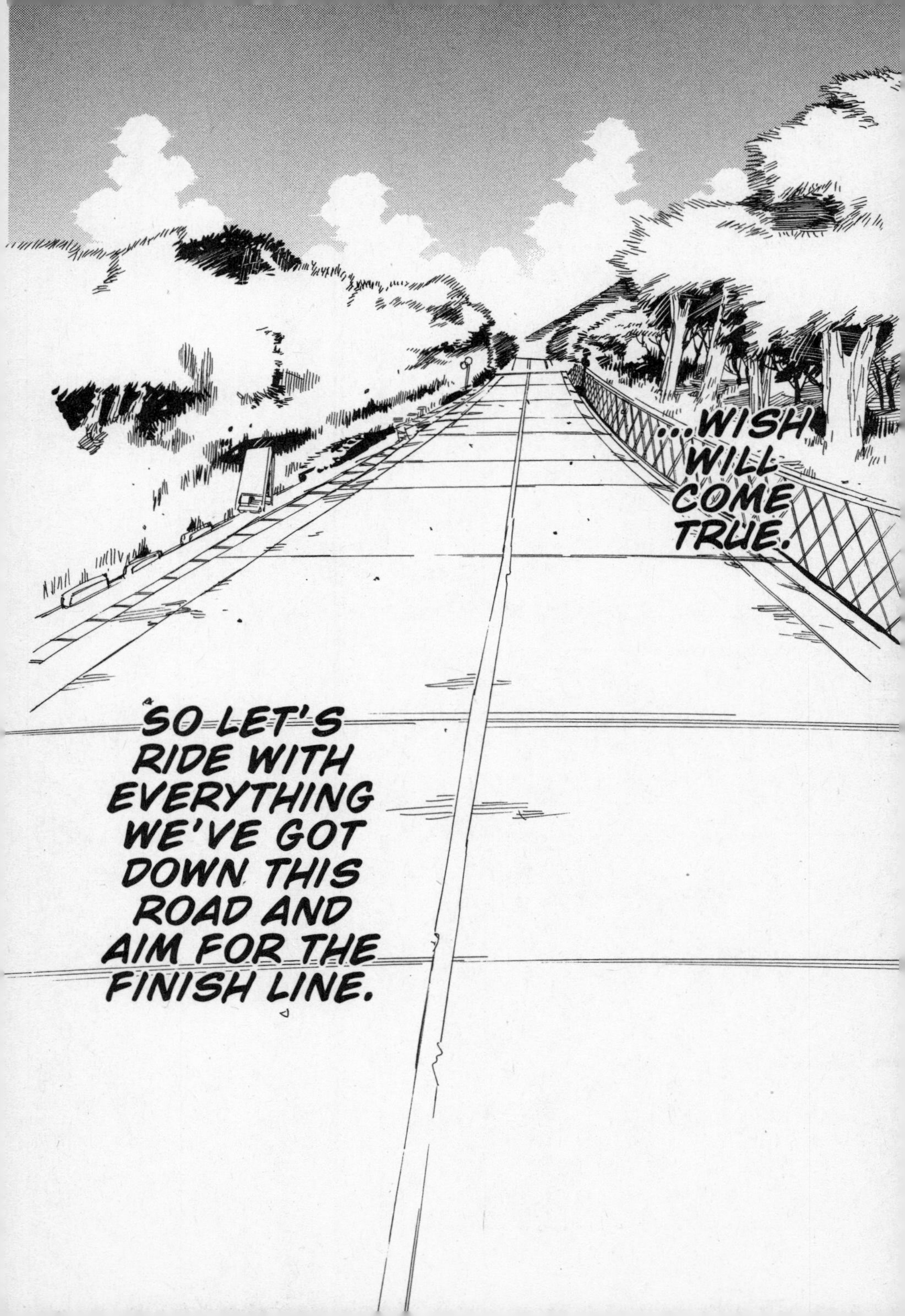
...WISH WILL COME TRUE.
SO LET'S RIDE WITH EVERYTHING WE'VE GOT DOWN THIS ROAD AND AIM FOR THE FINISH LINE.

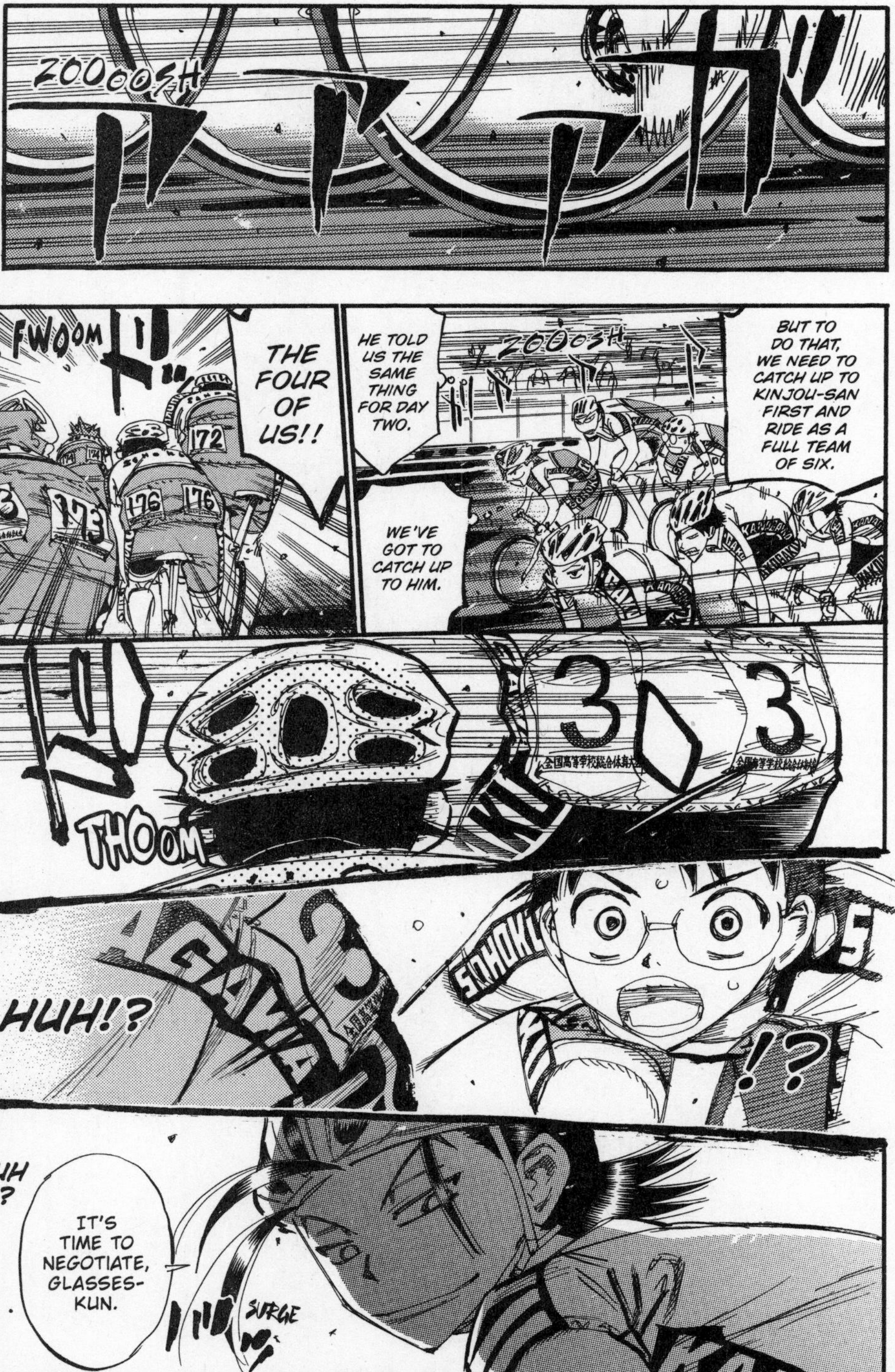
ZOOOOSH
BUT TO DO THAT, WE NEED TO CATCH UP TO KINJOU-SAN FIRST AND RIDE AS A FULL TEAM OF SIX.
ZOOOOSH
HE TOLD US THE SAME THING FOR DAY TWO.
WE'VE GOT TO CATCH UP TO HIM.
FWOOM
THE FOUR OF US!!
THOOM
!?
HUH!?
HUH!?
IT'S TIME TO NEGOTIATE, GLASSES-KUN.
SURGE

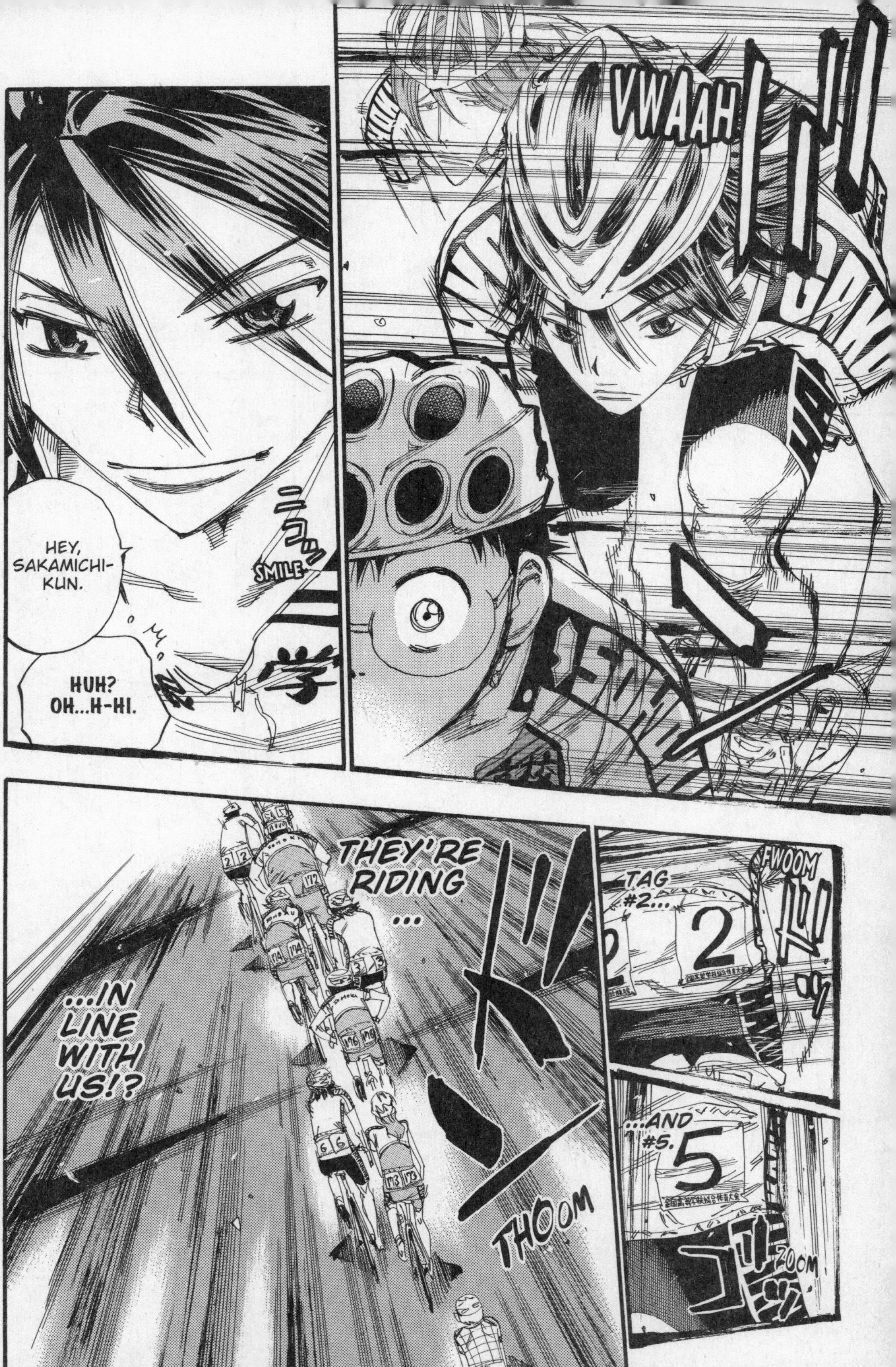
VWAAH
SMILE
HEY, SAKAMICHI-KUN.
HUH? OH...H-HI.
FWOOM
TAG #2...
...AND #5.
ZOOM
THEY'RE RIDING ...
...IN LINE WITH US!?
THOOM

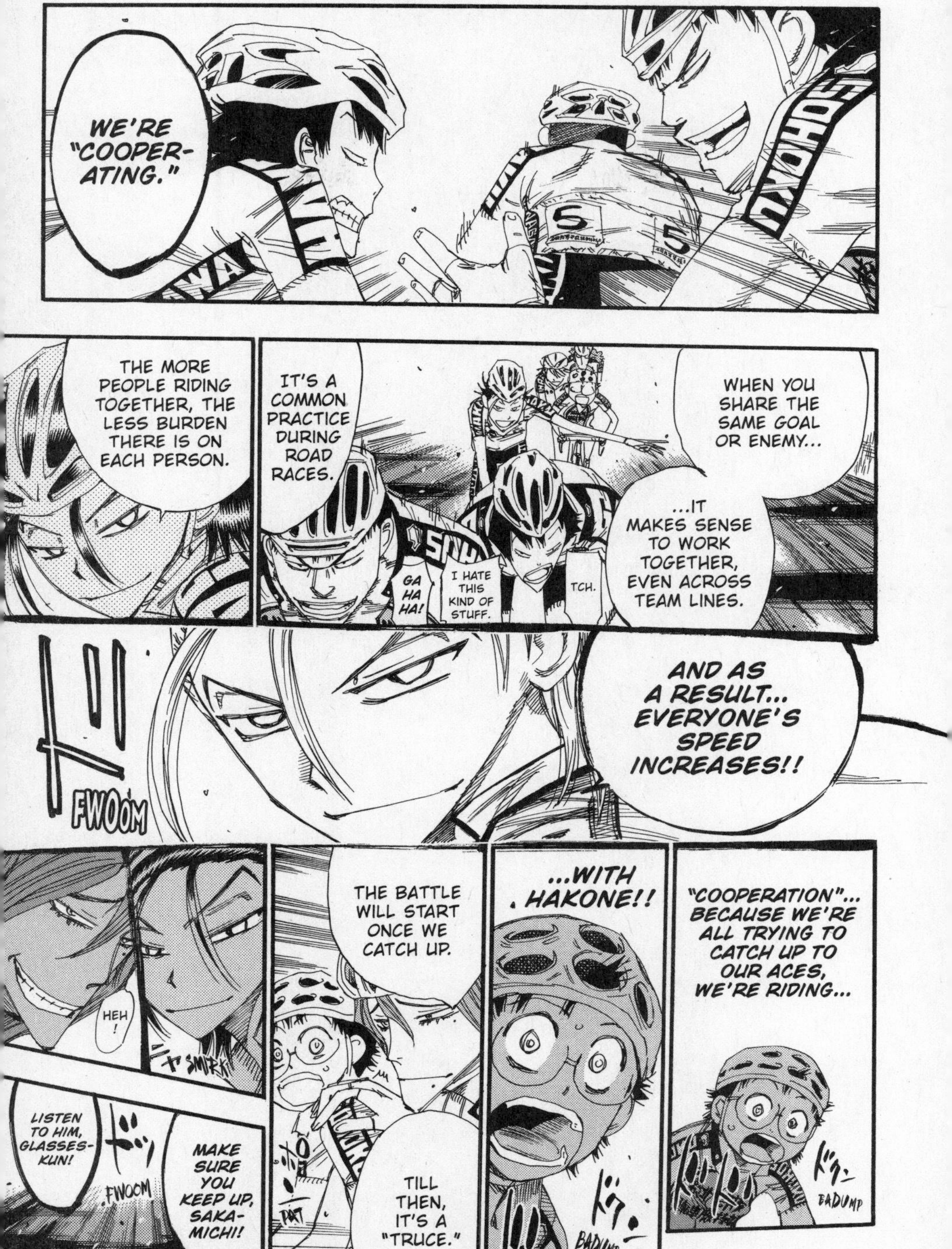
WE'RE "COOPERATING."
WHEN YOU SHARE THE SAME GOAL OR ENEMY...
...IT MAKES SENSE TO WORK TOGETHER, EVEN ACROSS TEAM LINES.
TCH.
I HATE THIS KIND OF STUFF.
GA HA HA!
IT'S A COMMON PRACTICE DURING ROAD RACES.
THE MORE PEOPLE RIDING TOGETHER, THE LESS BURDEN THERE IS ON EACH PERSON.
AND AS A RESULT... EVERYONE'S SPEED INCREASES!!
FWOOM
"COOPERATION"... BECAUSE WE'RE ALL TRYING TO CATCH UP TO OUR ACES, WE'RE RIDING...
BADUMP
...WITH HAKONE!!
BADUMP
THE BATTLE WILL START ONCE WE CATCH UP.
TILL THEN, IT'S A "TRUCE."
PAT
HEH!
SMIRK
MAKE SURE YOU KEEP UP, SAKAMICHI!
FWOOM
LISTEN TO HIM, GLASSES-KUN!

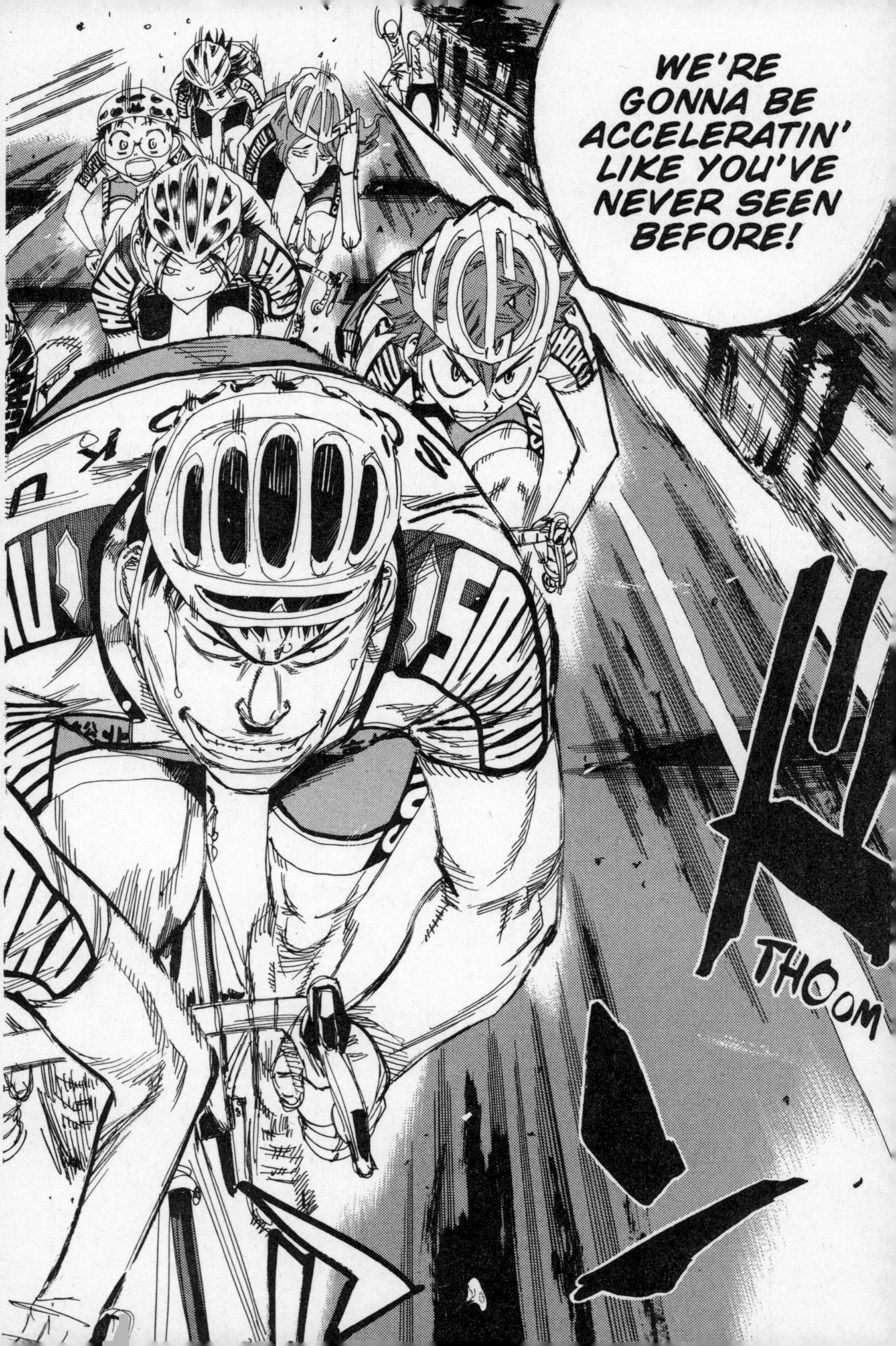
WE'RE GONNA BE ACCELERATIN' LIKE YOU'VE NEVER SEEN BEFORE!
THOOM

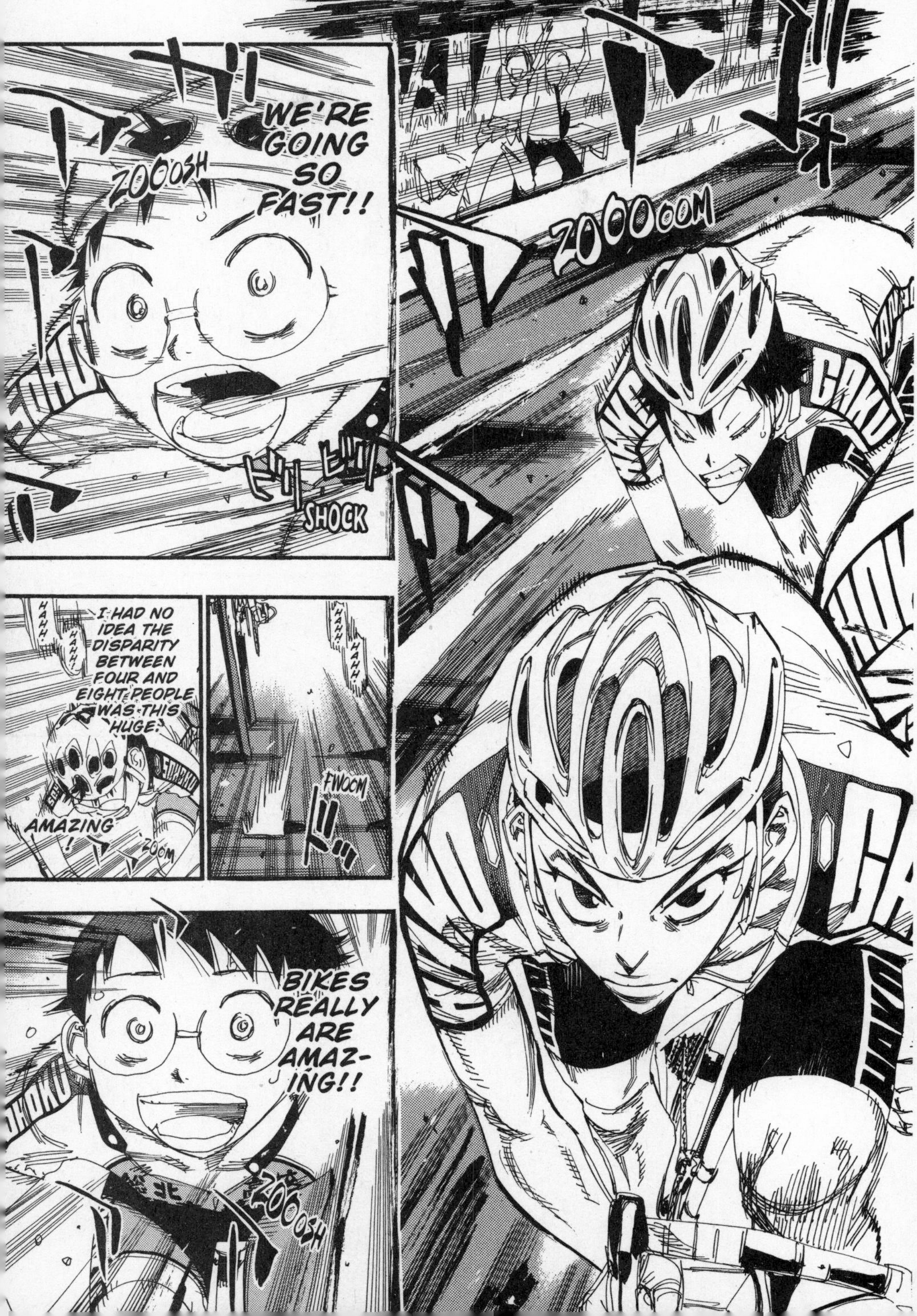

ZOOOOOM
WE'RE GOING SO FAST!!
ZOOOSH
SHOCK
HAHH HAHH
FWOOM
HAHH HAHH
I HAD NO IDEA THE DISPARITY BETWEEN FOUR AND EIGHT PEOPLE WAS THIS HUGE.
AMAZING!
ZOOM
BIKES REALLY ARE AMAZ-ING!!
ZOOOSH

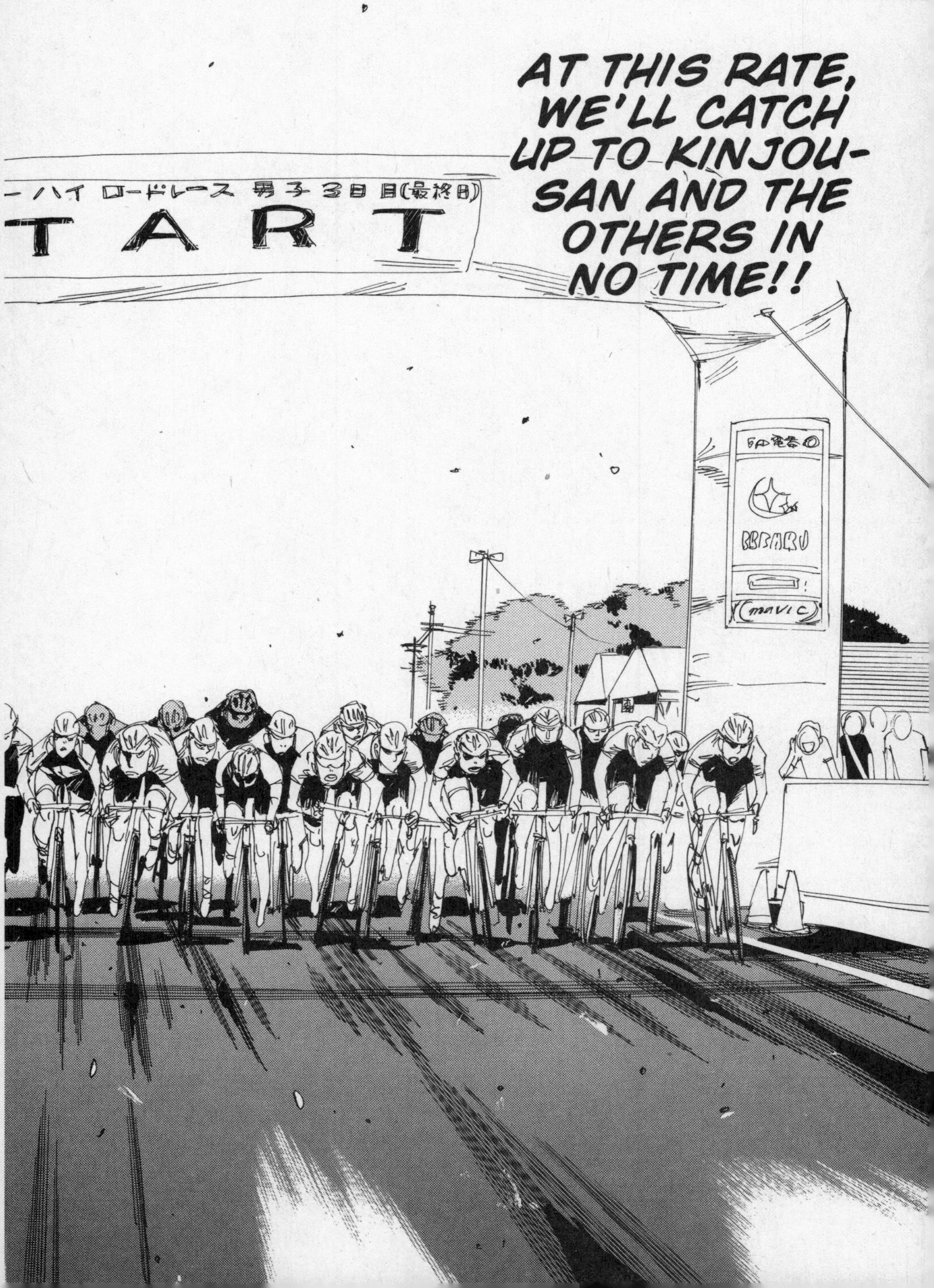
AT THIS RATE, WE'LL CATCH UP TO KINJOU-SAN AND THE OTHERS IN NO TIME!!
TART
mavic

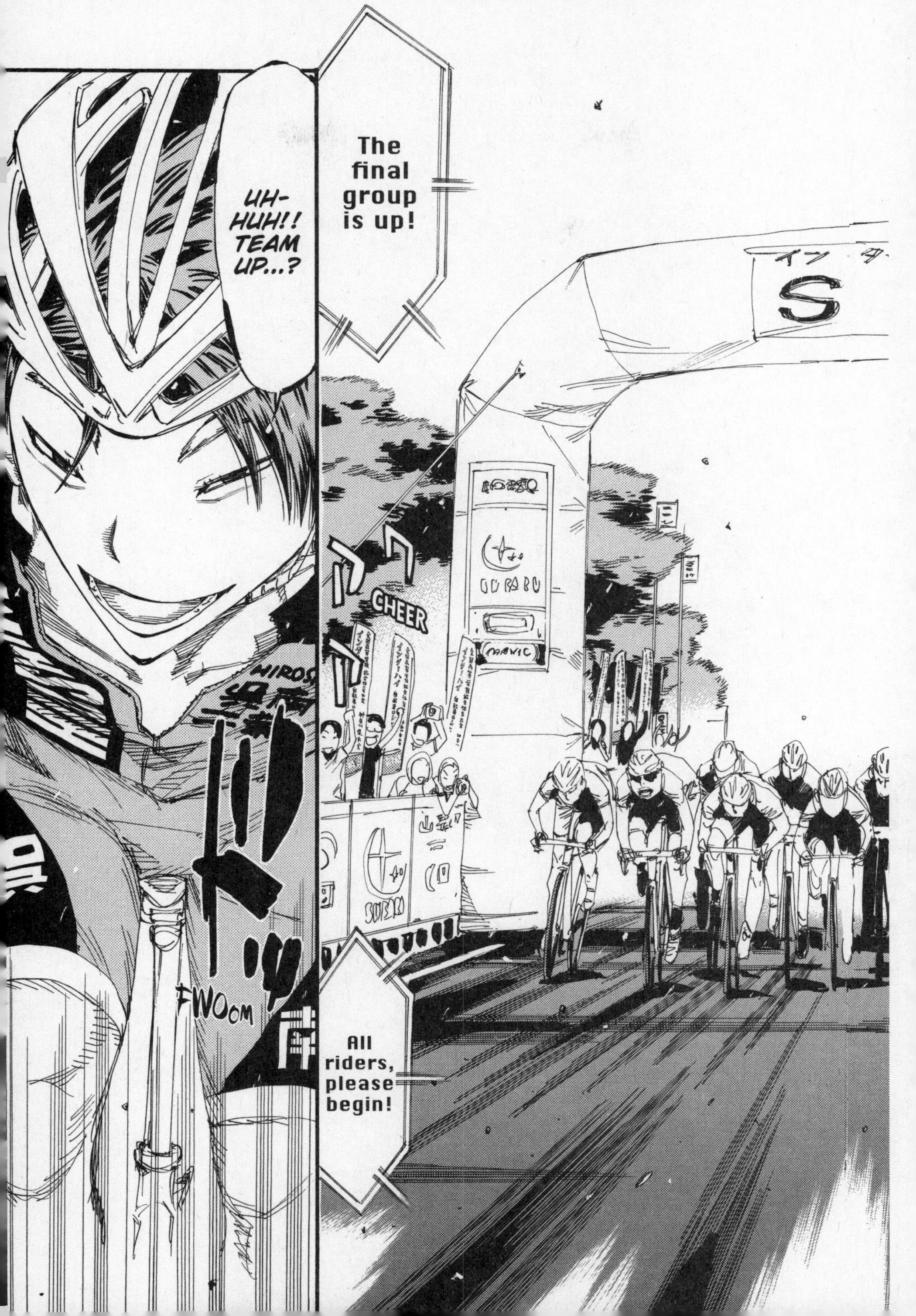
The final group is up!
CHEER
All riders, please begin!
UH-HUH!! TEAM UP...?
FWOOM

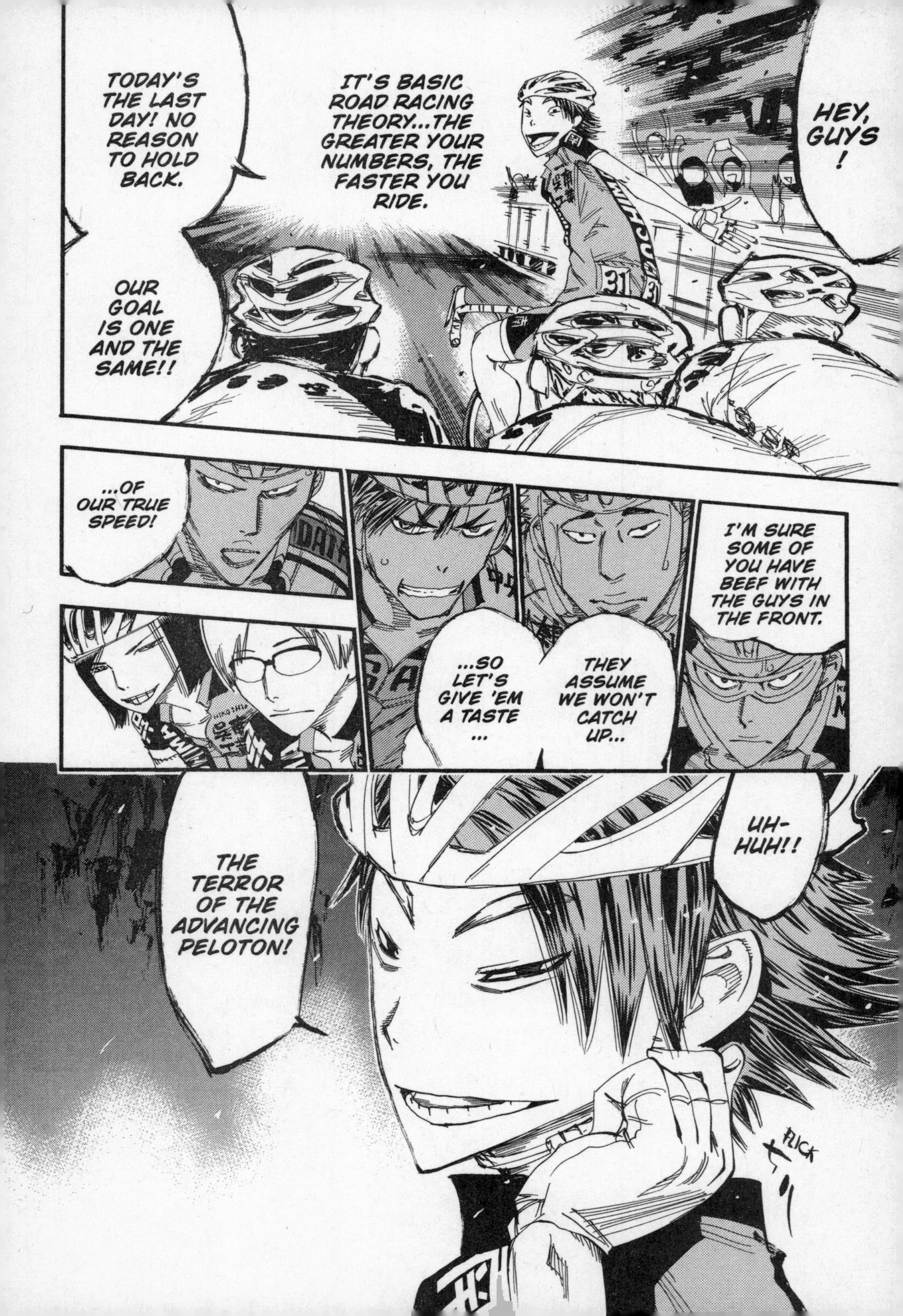
HEY, GUYS!
IT'S BASIC ROAD RACING THEORY...THE GREATER YOUR NUMBERS, THE FASTER YOU RIDE.
TODAY'S THE LAST DAY! NO REASON TO HOLD BACK.
OUR GOAL IS ONE AND THE SAME!!
I'M SURE SOME OF YOU HAVE BEEF WITH THE GUYS IN THE FRONT.
THEY ASSUME WE WON'T CATCH UP...
...SO LET'S GIVE 'EM A TASTE ...
...OF OUR TRUE SPEED!
UH-HUH!!
THE TERROR OF THE ADVANCING PELOTON!
FLICK

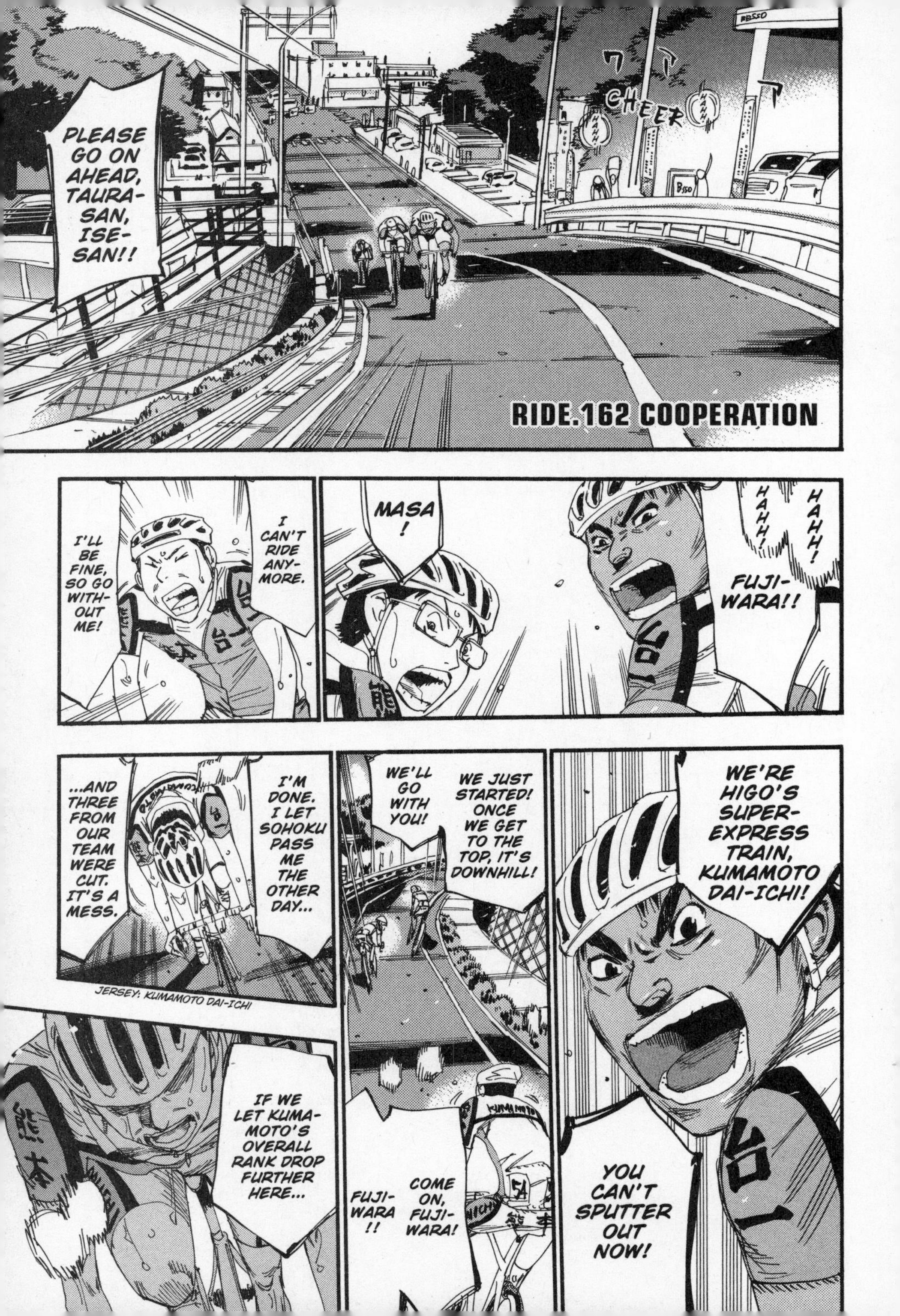
CHEER
HAHH
HAHH
PLEASE GO ON AHEAD, TAURA-SAN, ISE-SAN!!
RIDE.162 COOPERATION
HAHH! HAHH!
FUJIWARA!!
MASA!
I CAN'T RIDE ANYMORE.
I'LL BE FINE, SO GO WITHOUT ME!
WE'RE HIGO'S SUPER-EXPRESS TRAIN, KUMAMOTO DAI-ICHI!
YOU CAN'T SPUTTER OUT NOW!
WE JUST STARTED! ONCE WE GET TO THE TOP, IT'S DOWNHILL!
WE'LL GO WITH YOU!
COME ON, FUJIWARA!
FUJIWARA!!
I'M DONE. I LET SOHOKU PASS ME THE OTHER DAY...
...AND THREE FROM OUR TEAM WERE CUT. IT'S A MESS.
JERSEY: KUMAMOTO DAI-ICHI
IF WE LET KUMAMOTO'S OVERALL RANK DROP FURTHER HERE...

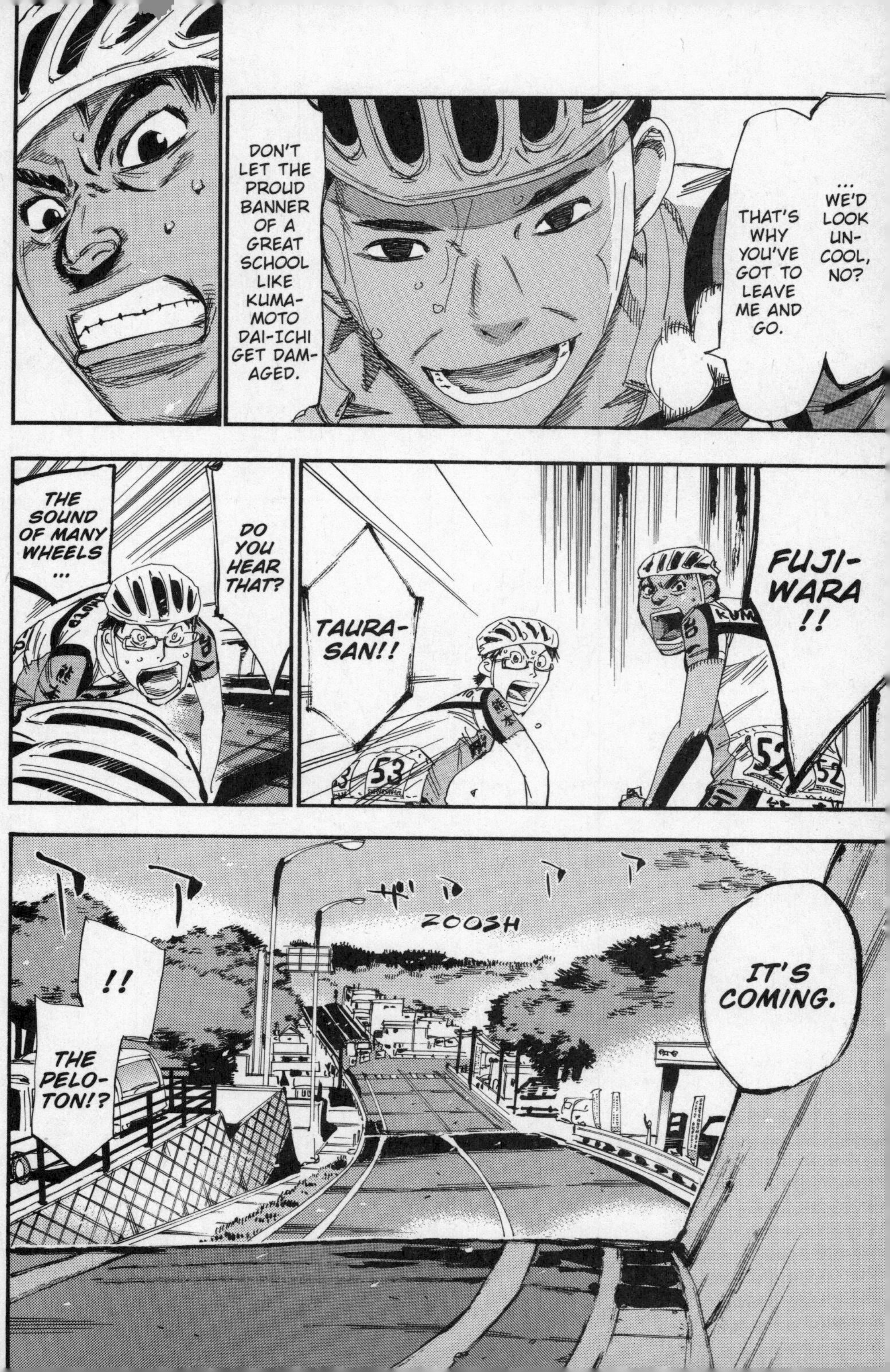
...WE'D LOOK UN-COOL, NO?
THAT'S WHY YOU'VE GOT TO LEAVE ME AND GO.
DON'T LET THE PROUD BANNER OF A GREAT SCHOOL LIKE KUMAMOTO DAI-ICHI GET DAMAGED.
FUJI-WARA!!
TAURA-SAN!!
DO YOU HEAR THAT?
THE SOUND OF MANY WHEELS...
IT'S COMING.
ZOOSH
!!
THE PELO-TON!?

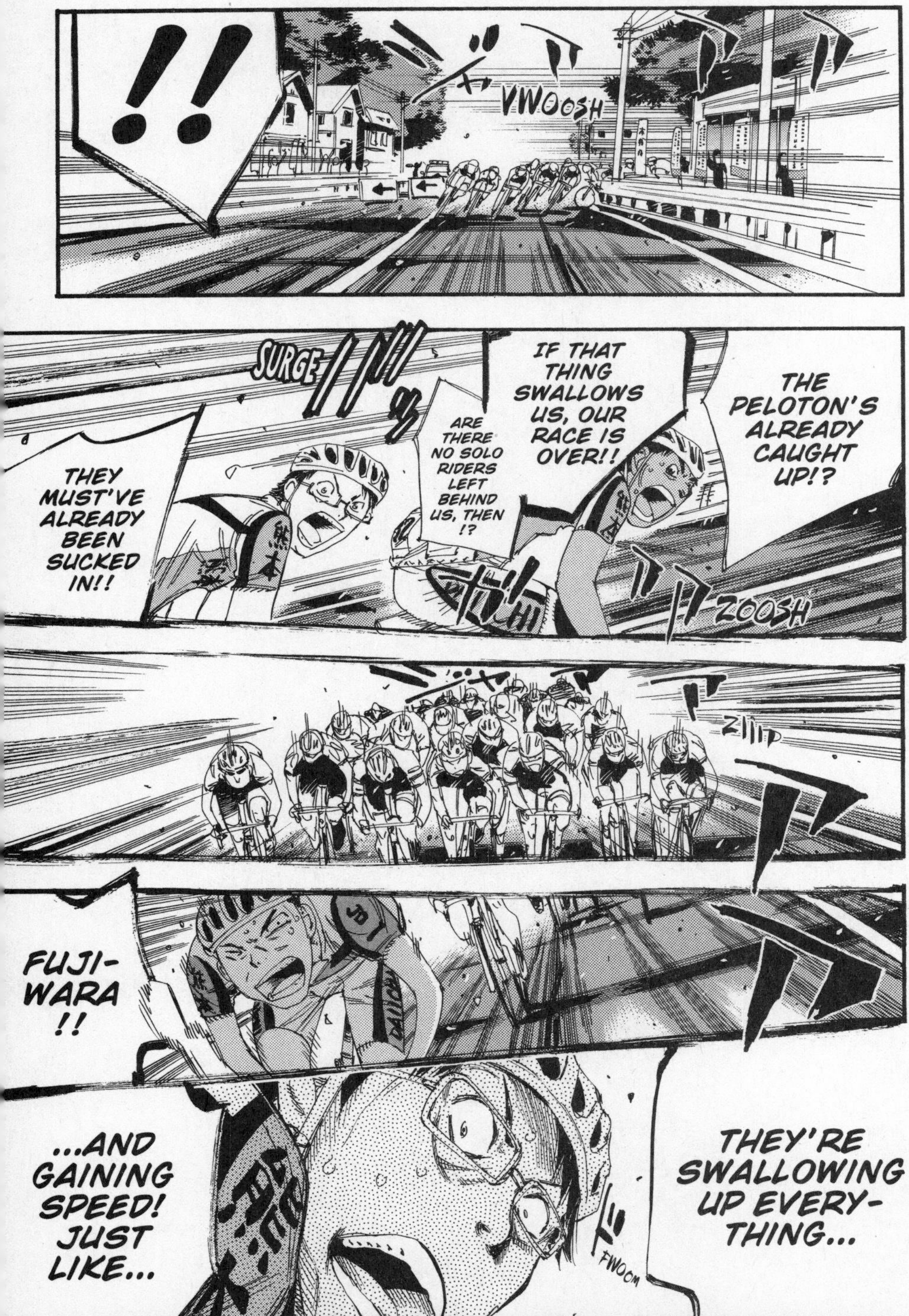
!!
VWOOSH
THE PELOTON'S ALREADY CAUGHT UP!?
IF THAT THING SWALLOWS US, OUR RACE IS OVER!!
ARE THERE NO SOLO RIDERS LEFT BEHIND US, THEN !?
SURGE
THEY MUST'VE ALREADY BEEN SUCKED IN!!
ZOOSH
ZIIIP
FUJI-WARA!!
THEY'RE SWALLOWING UP EVERY-THING...
FWOOM
...AND GAINING SPEED! JUST LIKE...

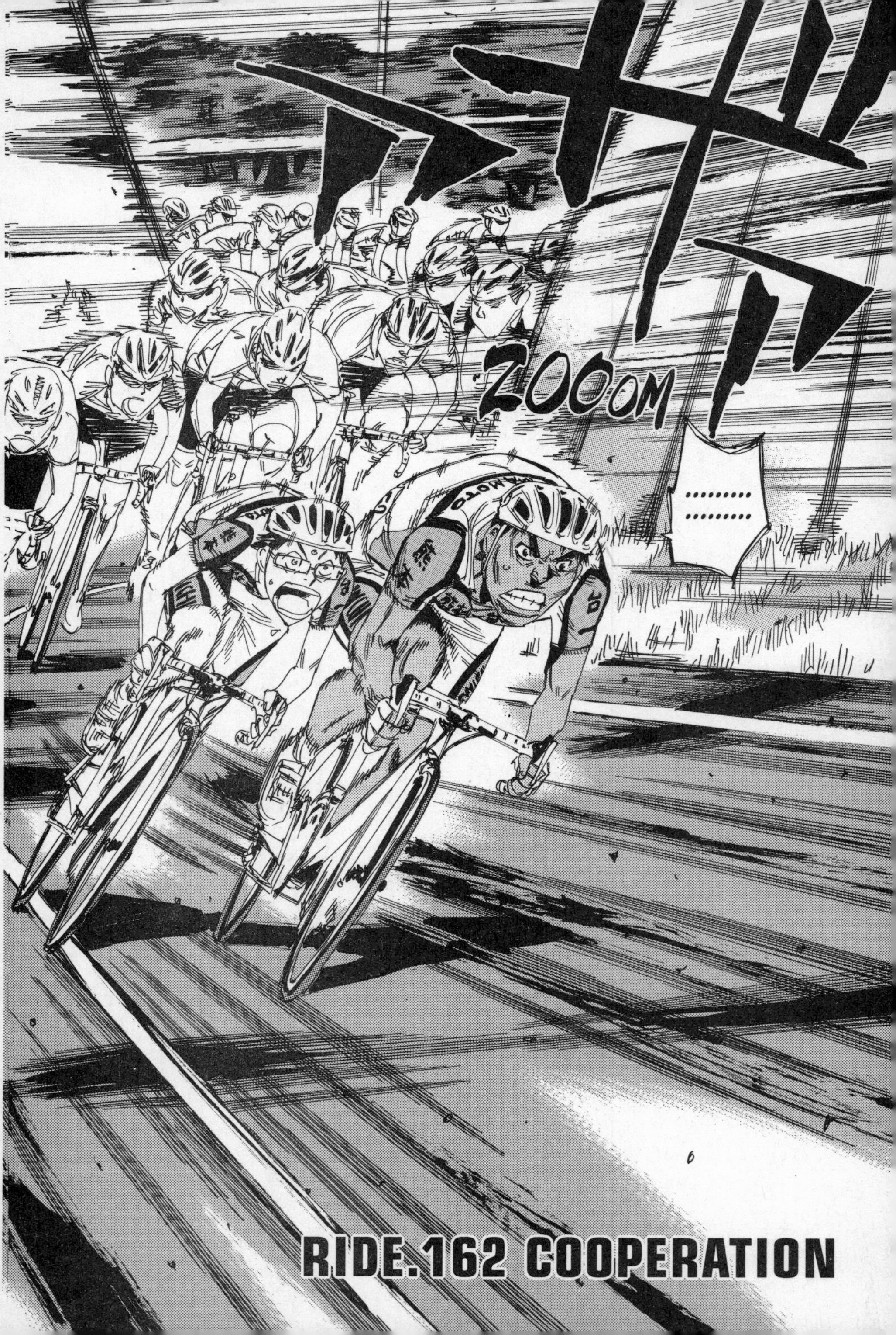
ZOOOM
....
....
RIDE.162 COOPERATION

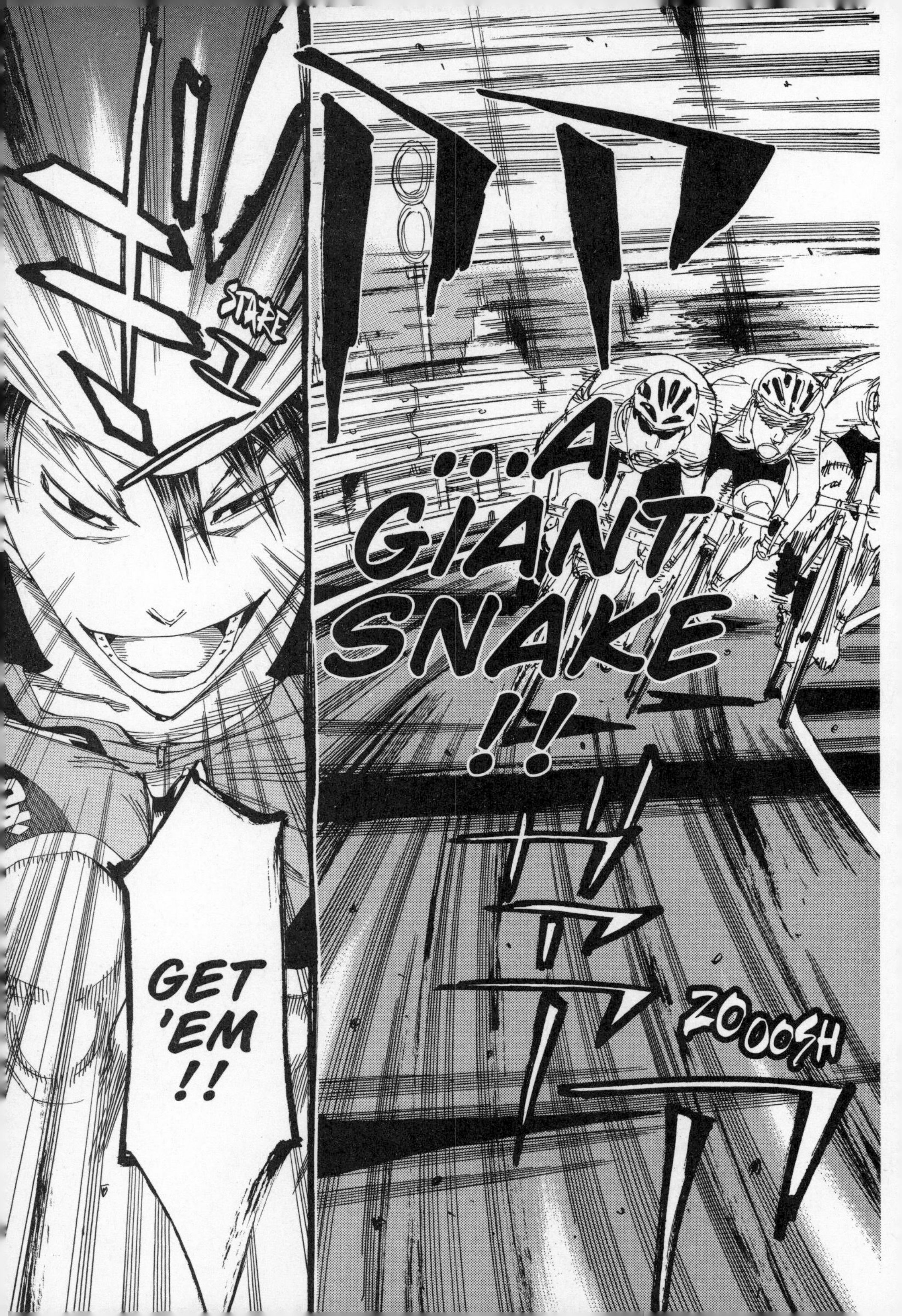
...A GIANT SNAKE!!
ZOOOSH
STARE
GET 'EM!!

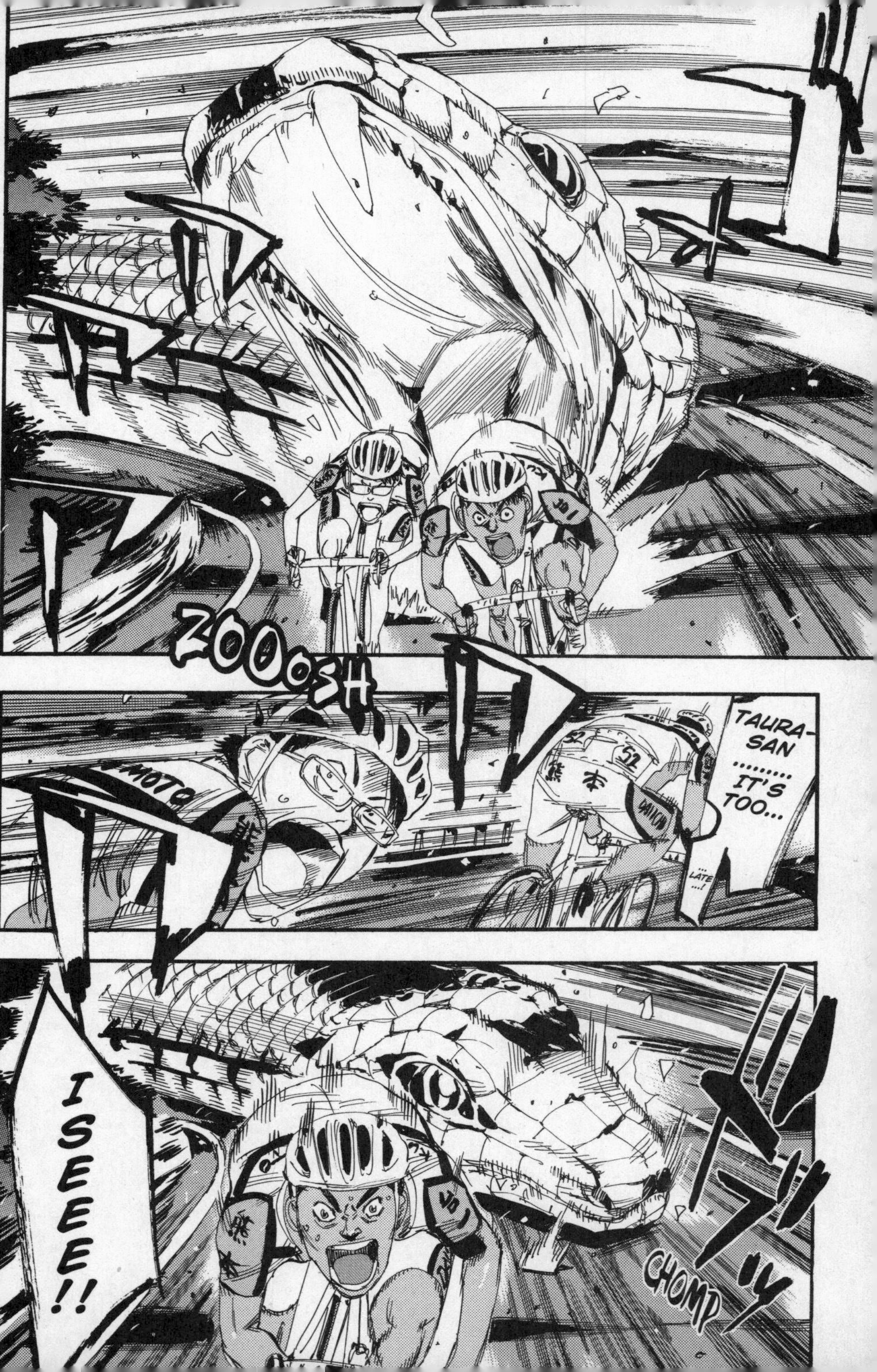
ZOOOOSH
TAURA-SAN .... IT'S TOO...
...LATE...!
I SEEEE!!
CHOMP

PERSIST!!

THE PROUD
KUMA-DAI
TEAM BRIEFLY
RODE IN
THIRD PLACE
YESTERDAY!!
YOU WON'T
CATCH US
HERE!

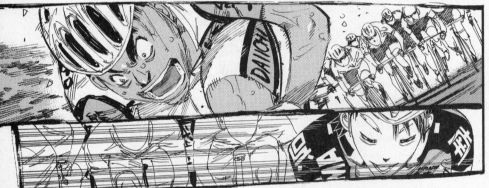

THOOM

AGAIN!!

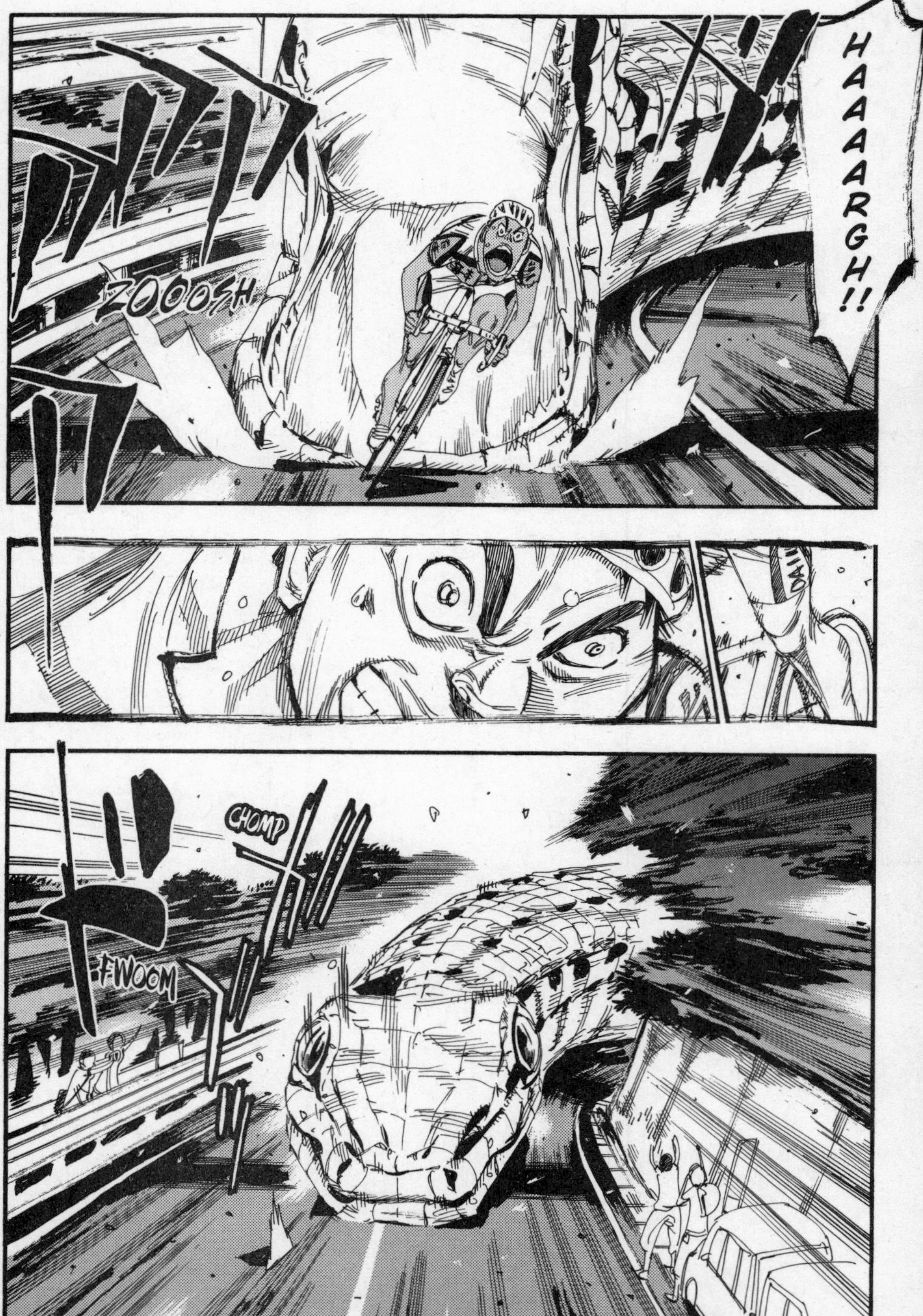
HAAAAARGH!!
ZOOOSH
CHOMP
FWOOM

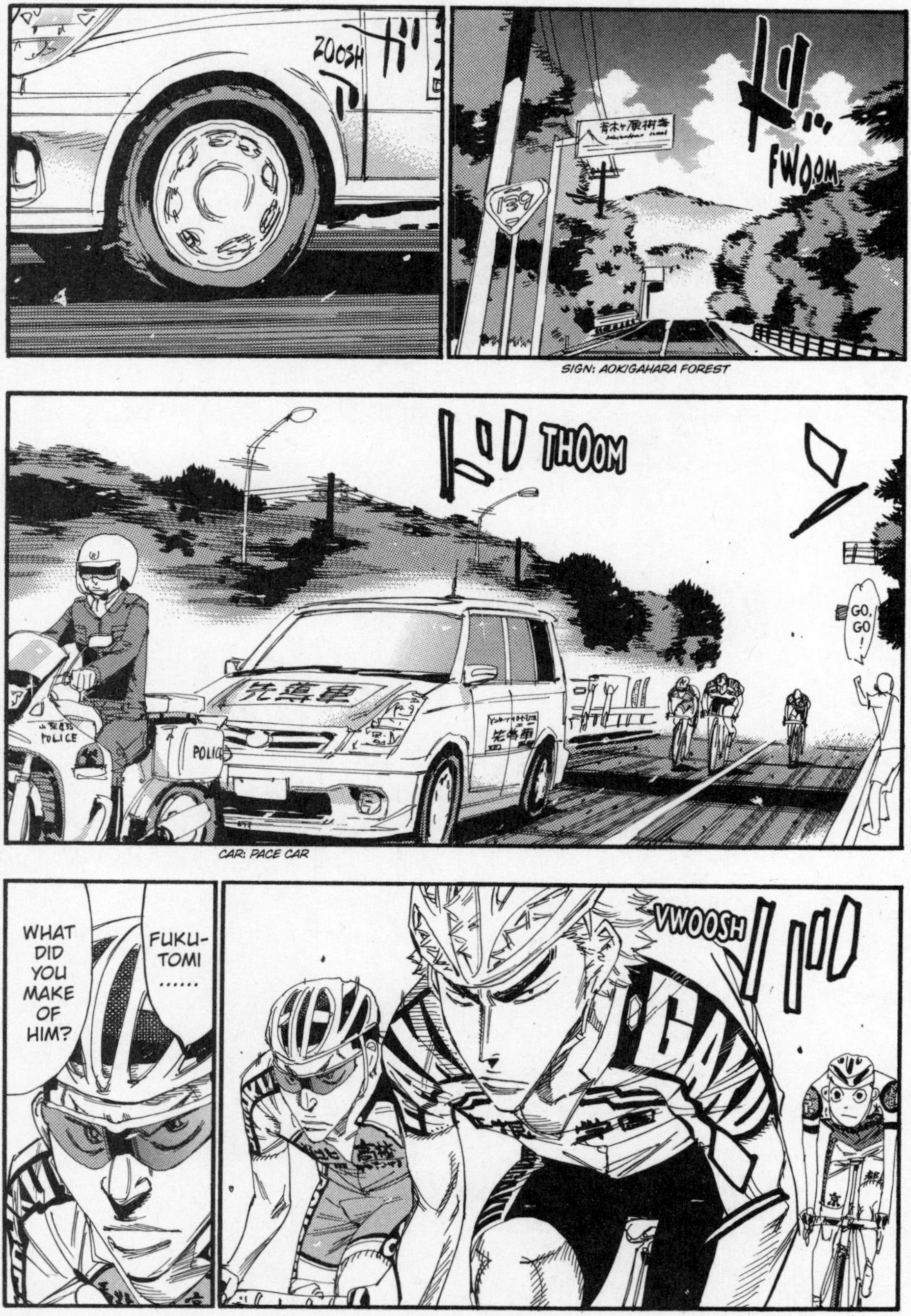
FWOOM
SIGN: AOKIGAHARA FOREST
ZOOSH
THOOM
GO, GO!
CAR: PACE CAR
VWOOSH
FUKU-TOMI ......
WHAT DID YOU MAKE OF HIM?

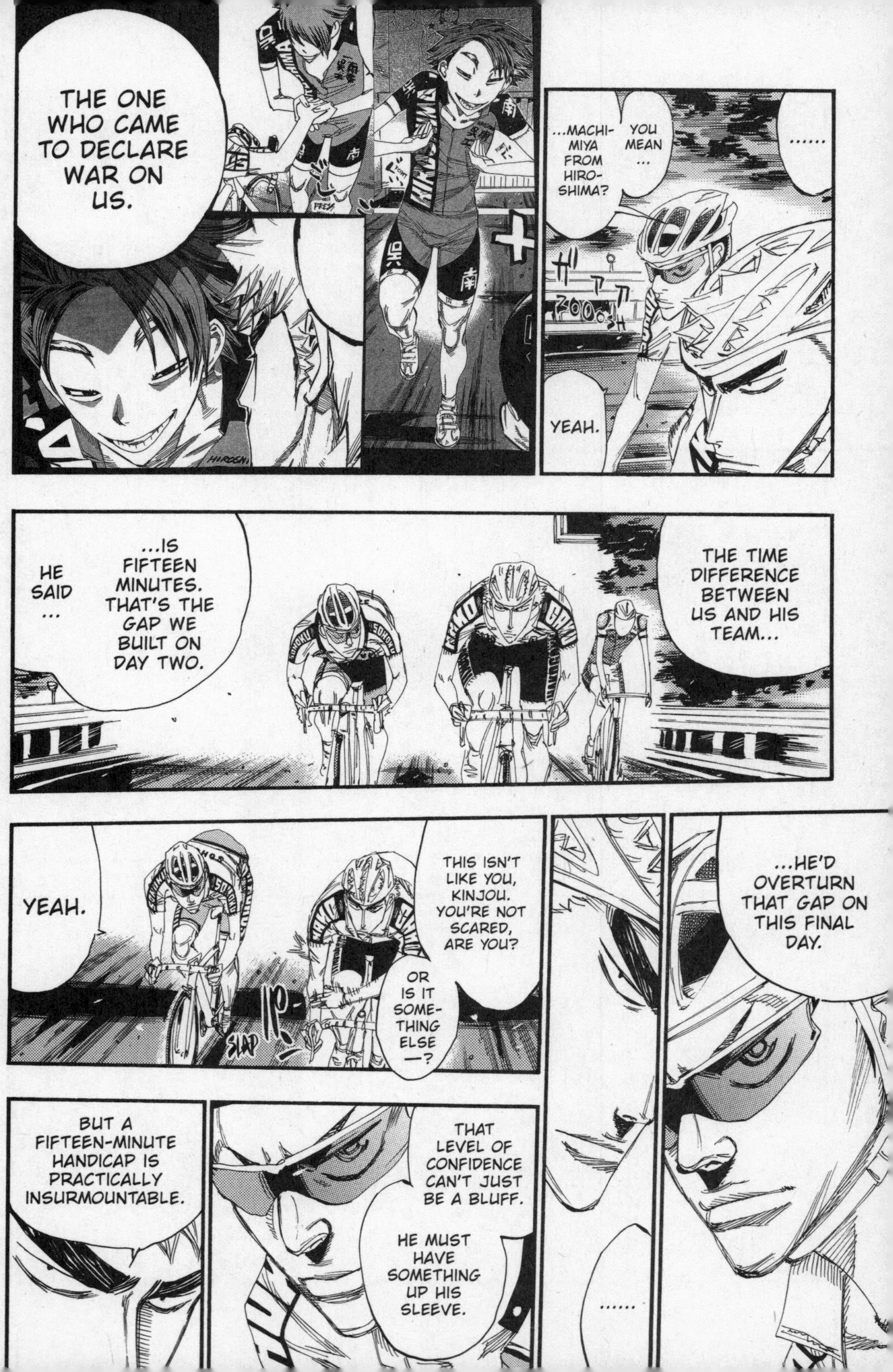
......
YOU MEAN ...
...MACHI-MIYA FROM HIRO-SHIMA?
ZOOOSH
YEAH.
THE ONE WHO CAME TO DECLARE WAR ON US.
THE TIME DIFFERENCE BETWEEN US AND HIS TEAM...
...IS FIFTEEN MINUTES. THAT'S THE GAP WE BUILT ON DAY TWO.
HE SAID ...
...HE'D OVERTURN THAT GAP ON THIS FINAL DAY.
......
THIS ISN'T LIKE YOU, KINJOU. YOU'RE NOT SCARED, ARE YOU?
OR IS IT SOMETHING ELSE—?
SLAP
YEAH.
THAT LEVEL OF CONFIDENCE CAN'T JUST BE A BLUFF.
HE MUST HAVE SOMETHING UP HIS SLEEVE.
BUT A FIFTEEN-MINUTE HANDICAP IS PRACTICALLY INSURMOUNTABLE.

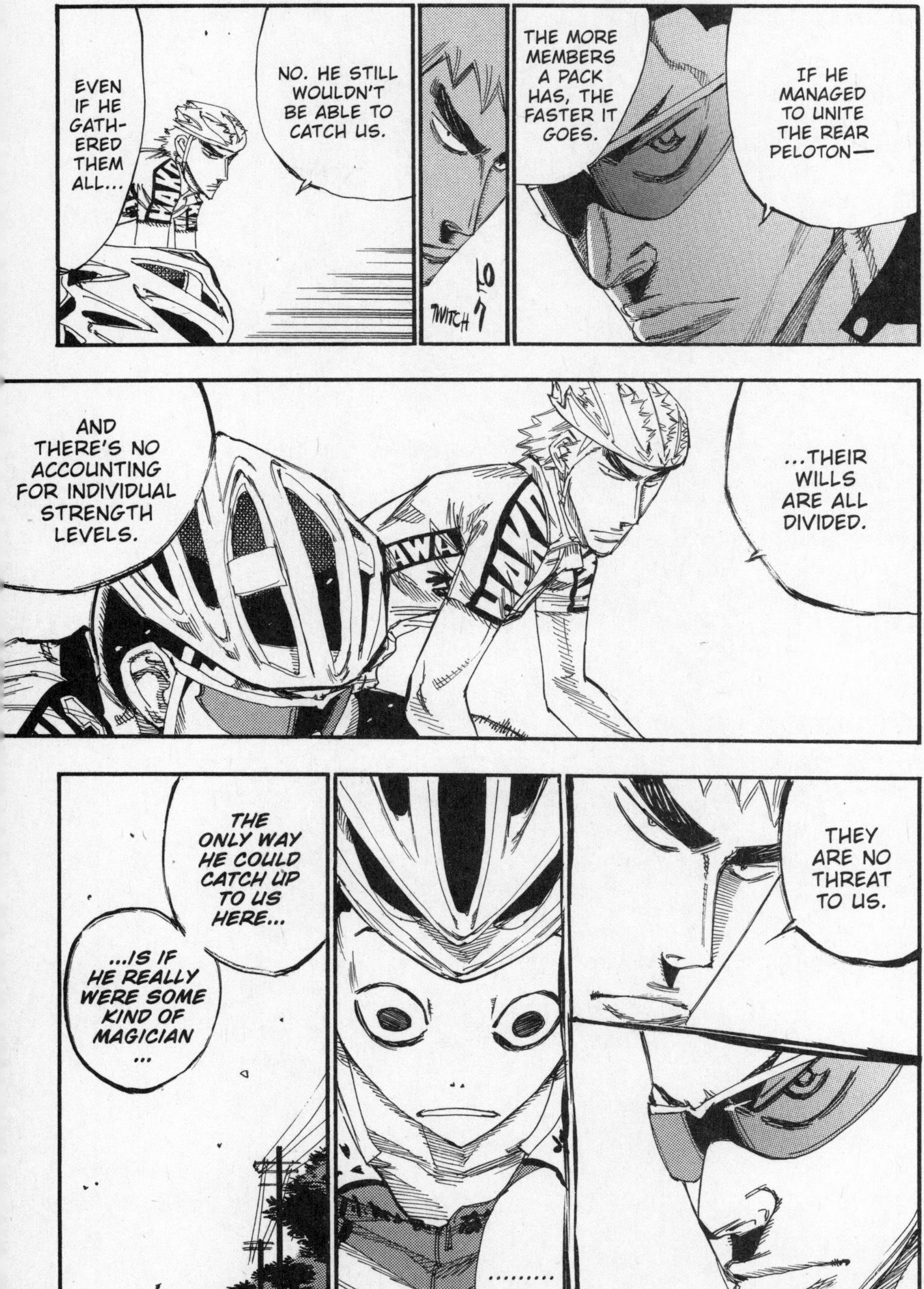
IF HE MANAGED TO UNITE THE REAR PELOTON—
THE MORE MEMBERS A PACK HAS, THE FASTER IT GOES.
TWITCH
NO. HE STILL WOULDN'T BE ABLE TO CATCH US.
EVEN IF HE GATH-ERED THEM ALL...
...THEIR WILLS ARE ALL DIVIDED.
AND THERE'S NO ACCOUNTING FOR INDIVIDUAL STRENGTH LEVELS.
THEY ARE NO THREAT TO US.
....
THE ONLY WAY HE COULD CATCH UP TO US HERE...
...IS IF HE REALLY WERE SOME KIND OF MAGICIAN...

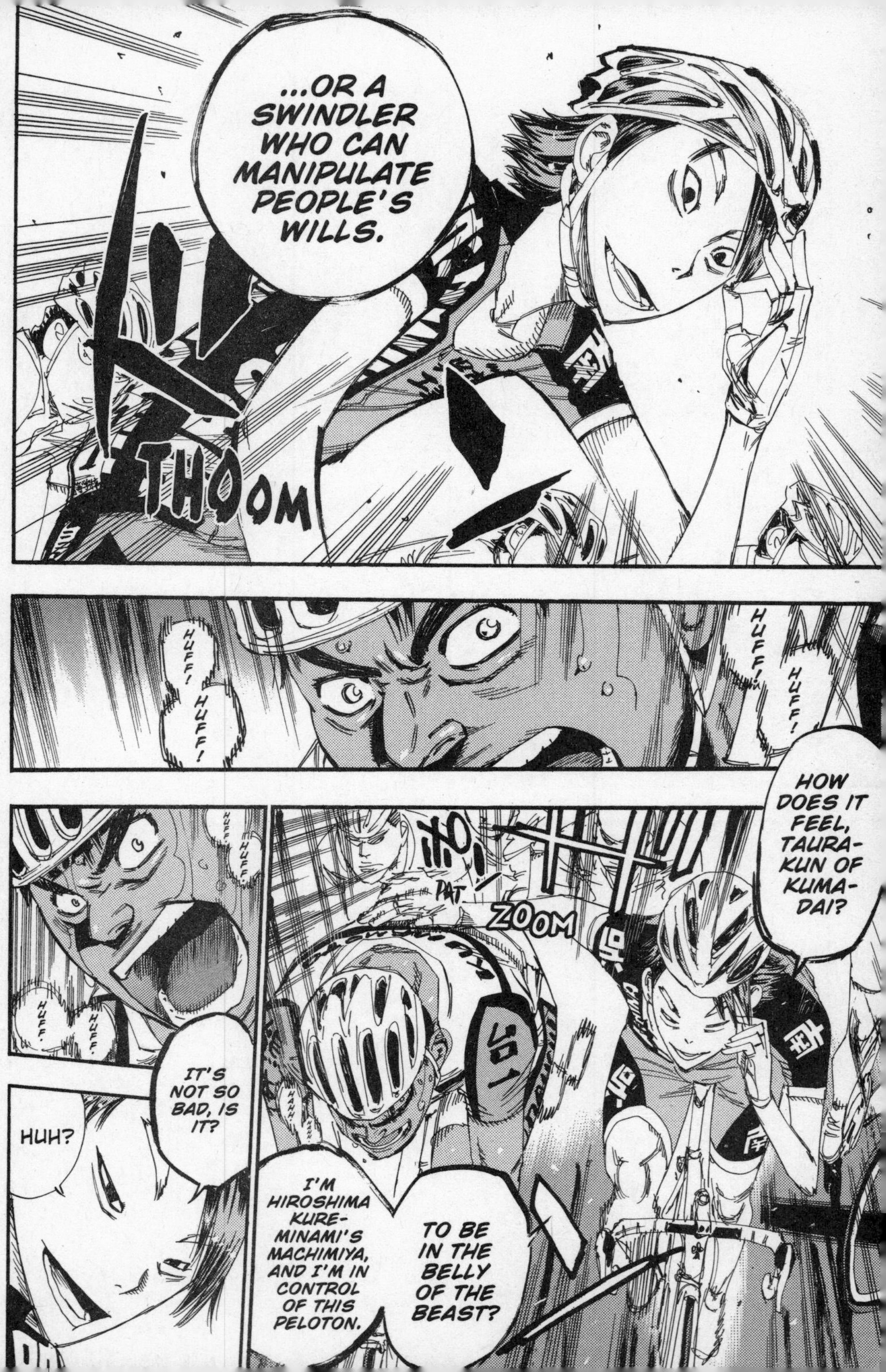
...OR A SWINDLER WHO CAN MANIPULATE PEOPLE'S WILLS.
THOOM
HUFF! HUFF!
HUFF! HUFF!
HOW DOES IT FEEL, TAURA-KUN OF KUMA-DAI?
ZOOM
PAT
TO BE IN THE BELLY OF THE BEAST?
I'M HIROSHIMA KURE-MINAMI'S MACHIMIYA, AND I'M IN CONTROL OF THIS PELOTON.
HUFF HUFF
HUFF. HUFF.
IT'S NOT SO BAD, IS IT?
HUH?

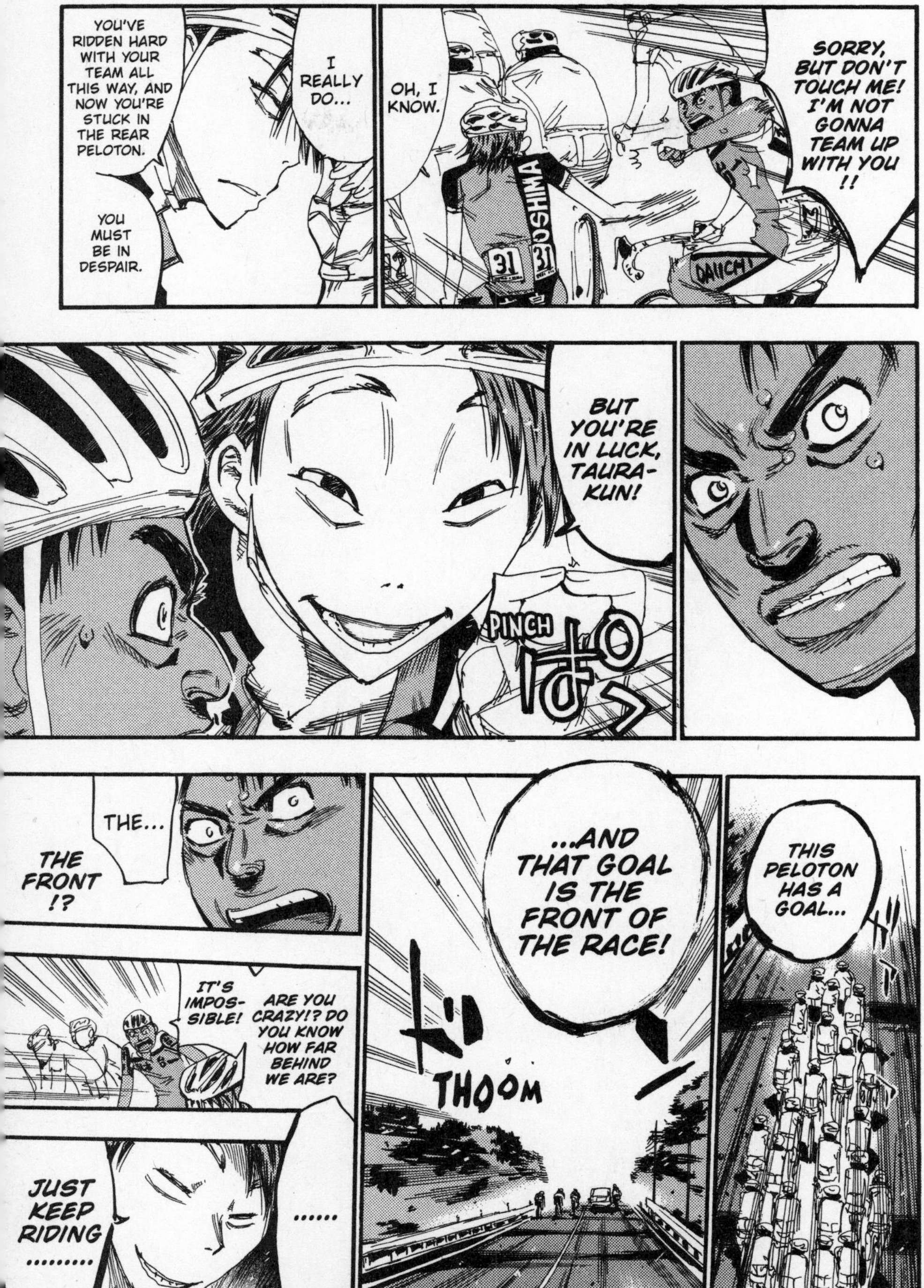
SORRY, BUT DON'T TOUCH ME! I'M NOT GONNA TEAM UP WITH YOU !!
OH, I KNOW.
I REALLY DO...
YOU'VE RIDDEN HARD WITH YOUR TEAM ALL THIS WAY, AND NOW YOU'RE STUCK IN THE REAR PELOTON.
YOU MUST BE IN DESPAIR.
BUT YOU'RE IN LUCK, TAURA-KUN!
PINCH
THIS PELOTON HAS A GOAL...
...AND THAT GOAL IS THE FRONT OF THE RACE!
THOOM
THE...
THE FRONT !?
ARE YOU CRAZY!? DO YOU KNOW HOW FAR BEHIND WE ARE?
IT'S IMPOS-SIBLE!
......
JUST KEEP RIDING ....

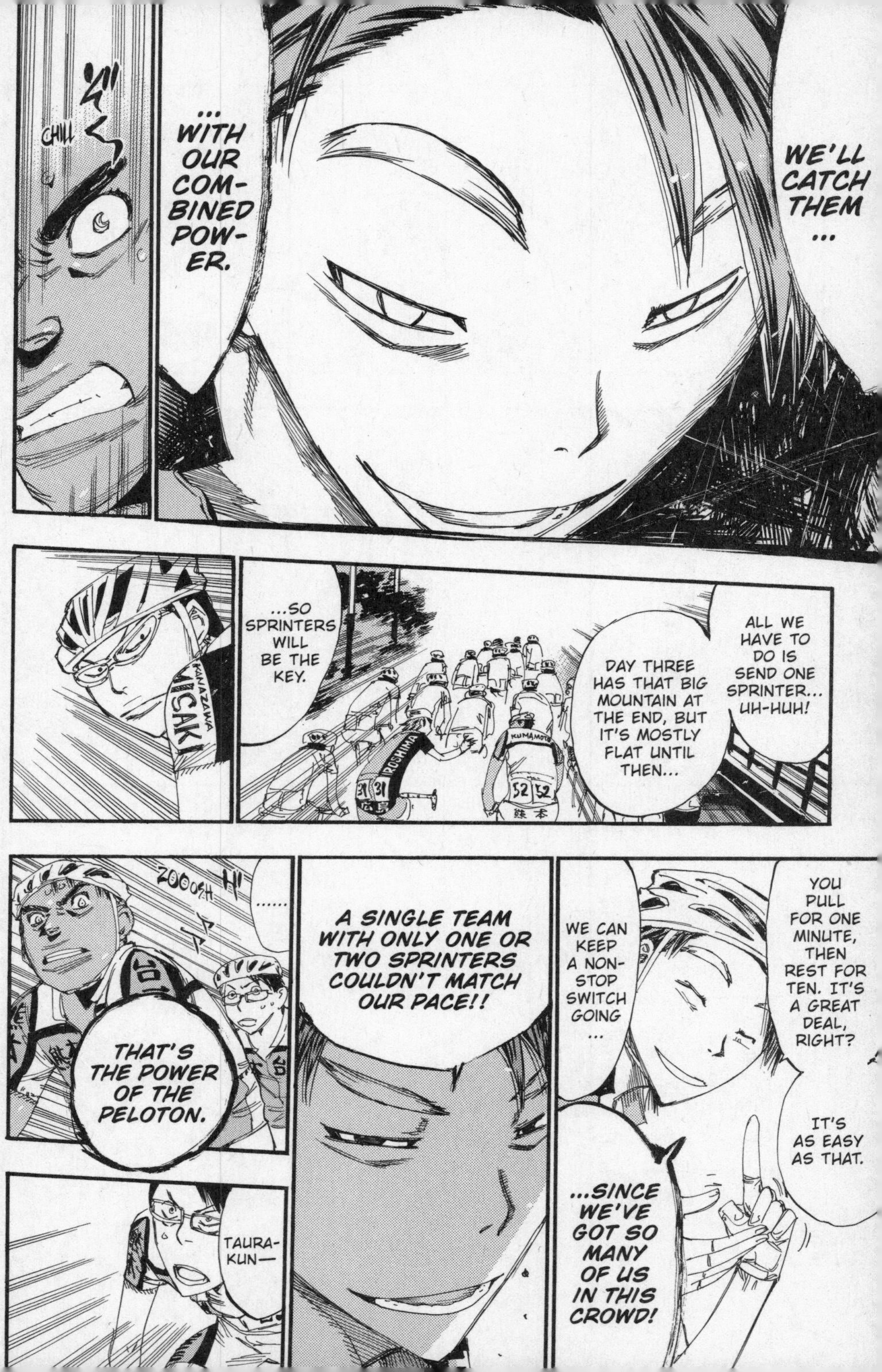
WE'LL CATCH THEM...
...WITH OUR COMBINED POWER.
CHILL
ALL WE HAVE TO DO IS SEND ONE SPRINTER... UH-HUH!
DAY THREE HAS THAT BIG MOUNTAIN AT THE END, BUT IT'S MOSTLY FLAT UNTIL THEN...
...SO SPRINTERS WILL BE THE KEY.
YOU PULL FOR ONE MINUTE, THEN REST FOR TEN. IT'S A GREAT DEAL, RIGHT?
WE CAN KEEP A NON-STOP SWITCH GOING...
IT'S AS EASY AS THAT.
A SINGLE TEAM WITH ONLY ONE OR TWO SPRINTERS COULDN'T MATCH OUR PACE!!
...SINCE WE'VE GOT SO MANY OF US IN THIS CROWD!
......
ZOOOSH
THAT'S THE POWER OF THE PELOTON.
TAURA-KUN—

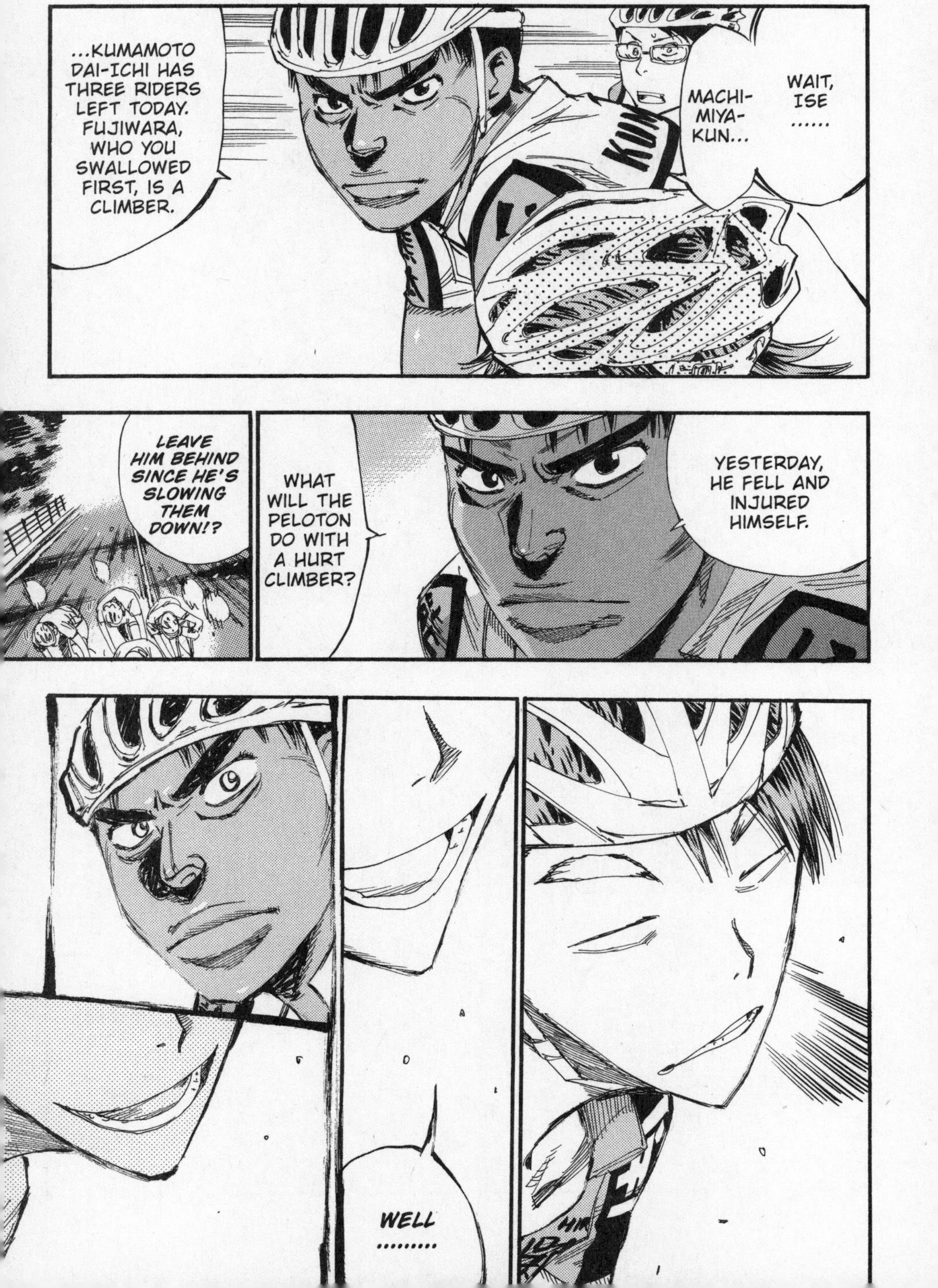
WAIT, ISE ......
MACHI-MIYA-KUN...
...KUMAMOTO DAI-ICHI HAS THREE RIDERS LEFT TODAY. FUJIWARA, WHO YOU SWALLOWED FIRST, IS A CLIMBER.
YESTERDAY, HE FELL AND INJURED HIMSELF.
WHAT WILL THE PELOTON DO WITH A HURT CLIMBER?
LEAVE HIM BEHIND SINCE HE'S SLOWING THEM DOWN!?
WELL ....

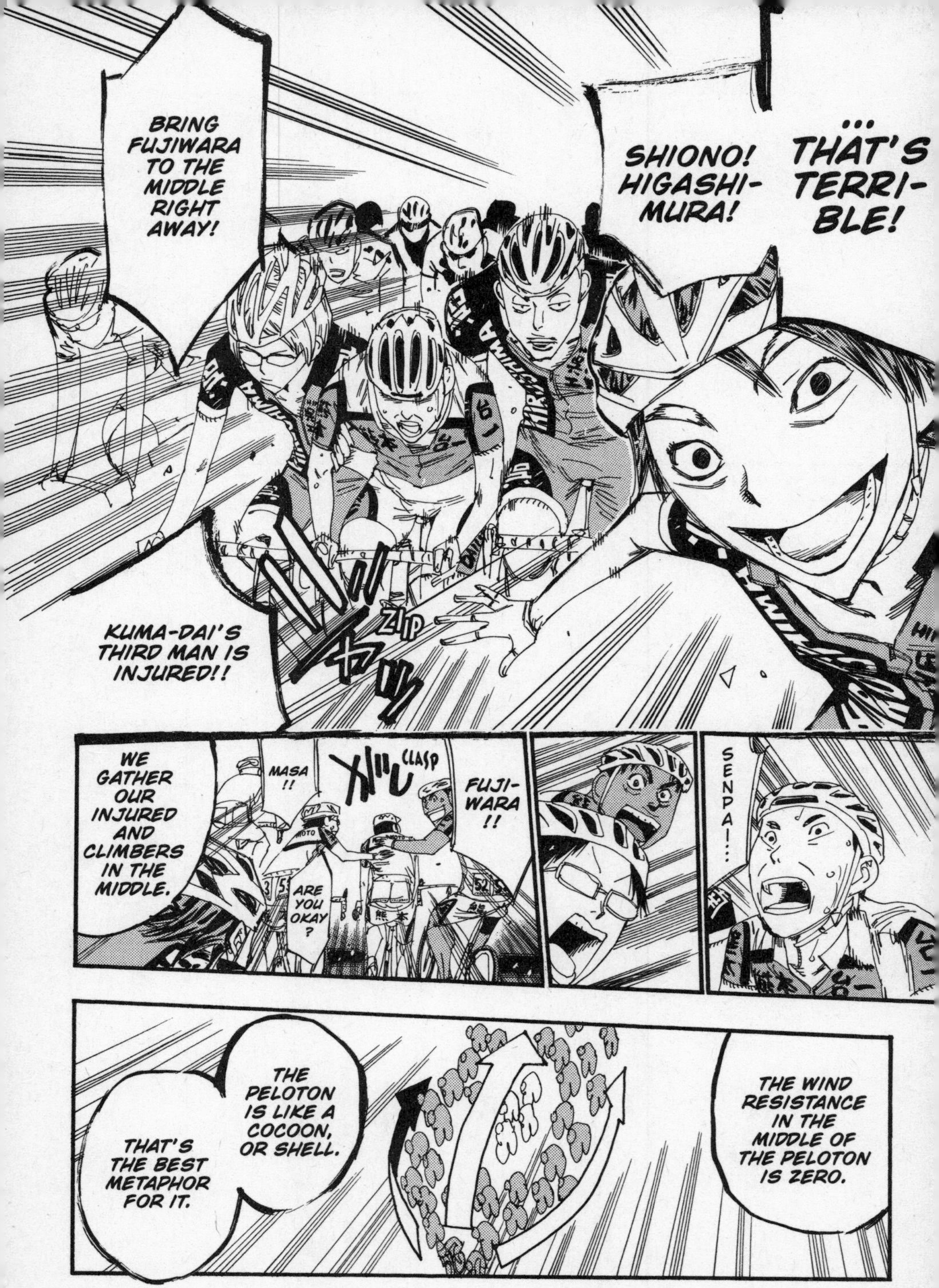
...THAT'S TERRIBLE!
SHIONO! HIGASHIMURA!
BRING FUJIWARA TO THE MIDDLE RIGHT AWAY!
ZIP
KUMA-DAI'S THIRD MAN IS INJURED!!
SENPAI...!
FUJIWARA!!
CLASP
MASA!!
ARE YOU OKAY?
WE GATHER OUR INJURED AND CLIMBERS IN THE MIDDLE.
THE WIND RESISTANCE IN THE MIDDLE OF THE PELOTON IS ZERO.
THE PELOTON IS LIKE A COCOON, OR SHELL.
THAT'S THE BEST METAPHOR FOR IT.

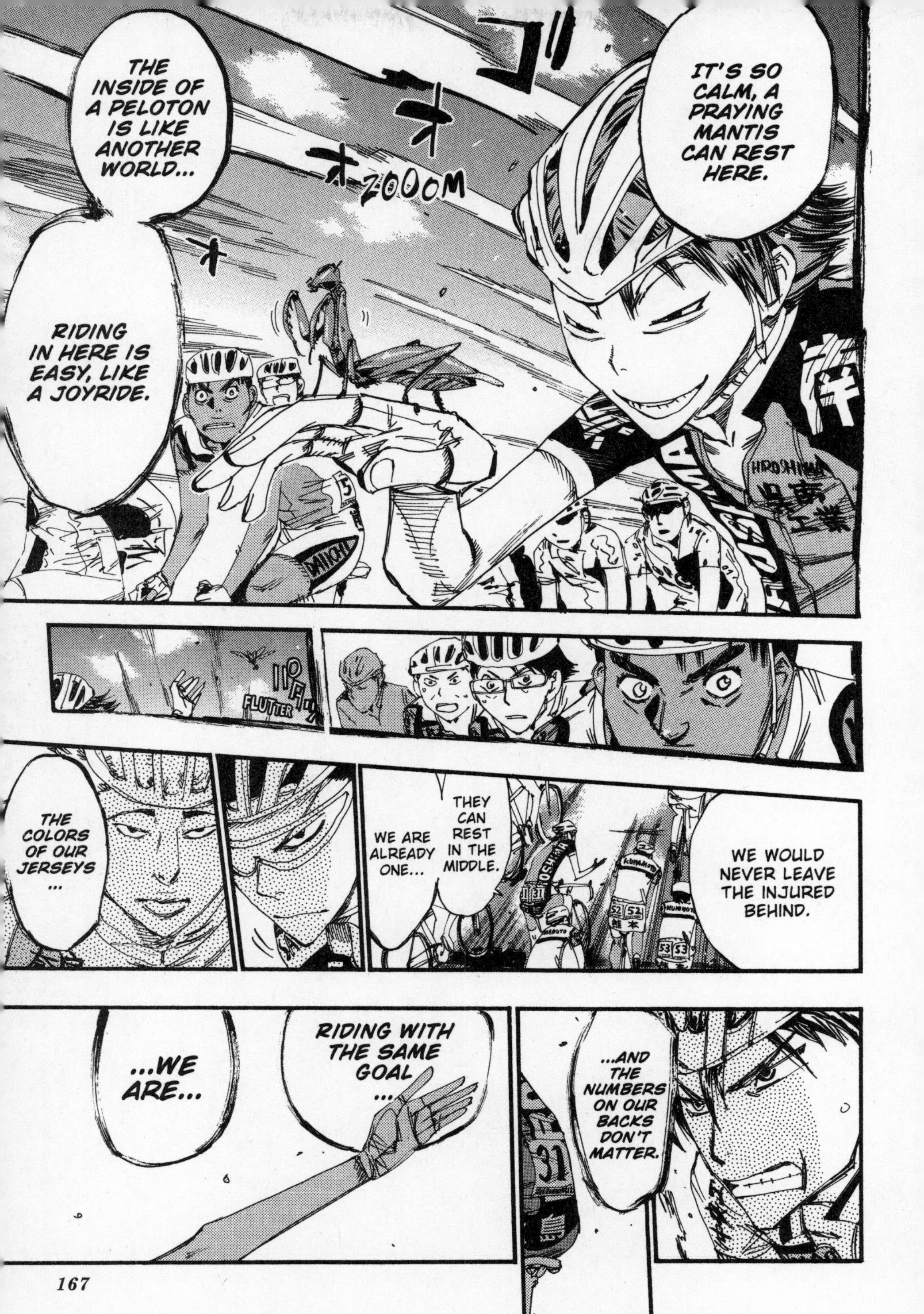
IT'S SO CALM, A PRAYING MANTIS CAN REST HERE.
ZOOOM
THE INSIDE OF A PELOTON IS LIKE ANOTHER WORLD...
RIDING IN HERE IS EASY, LIKE A JOYRIDE.
FLUTTER
WE WOULD NEVER LEAVE THE INJURED BEHIND.
THEY CAN REST IN THE MIDDLE.
WE ARE ALREADY ONE...
THE COLORS OF OUR JERSEYS ...
...AND THE NUMBERS ON OUR BACKS DON'T MATTER.
RIDING WITH THE SAME GOAL ...
...WE ARE...

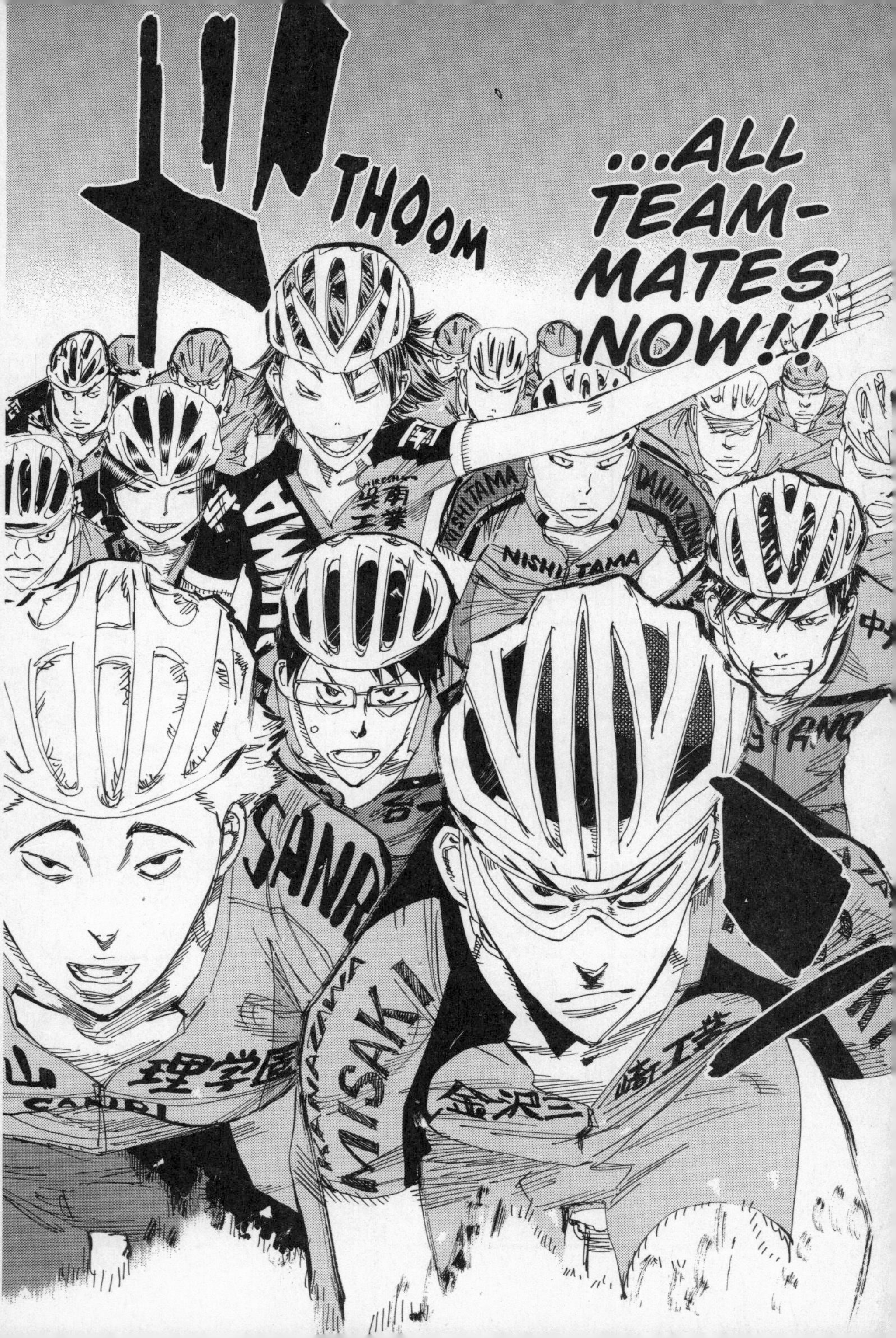
THOOM
...ALL TEAM-MATES NOW!!

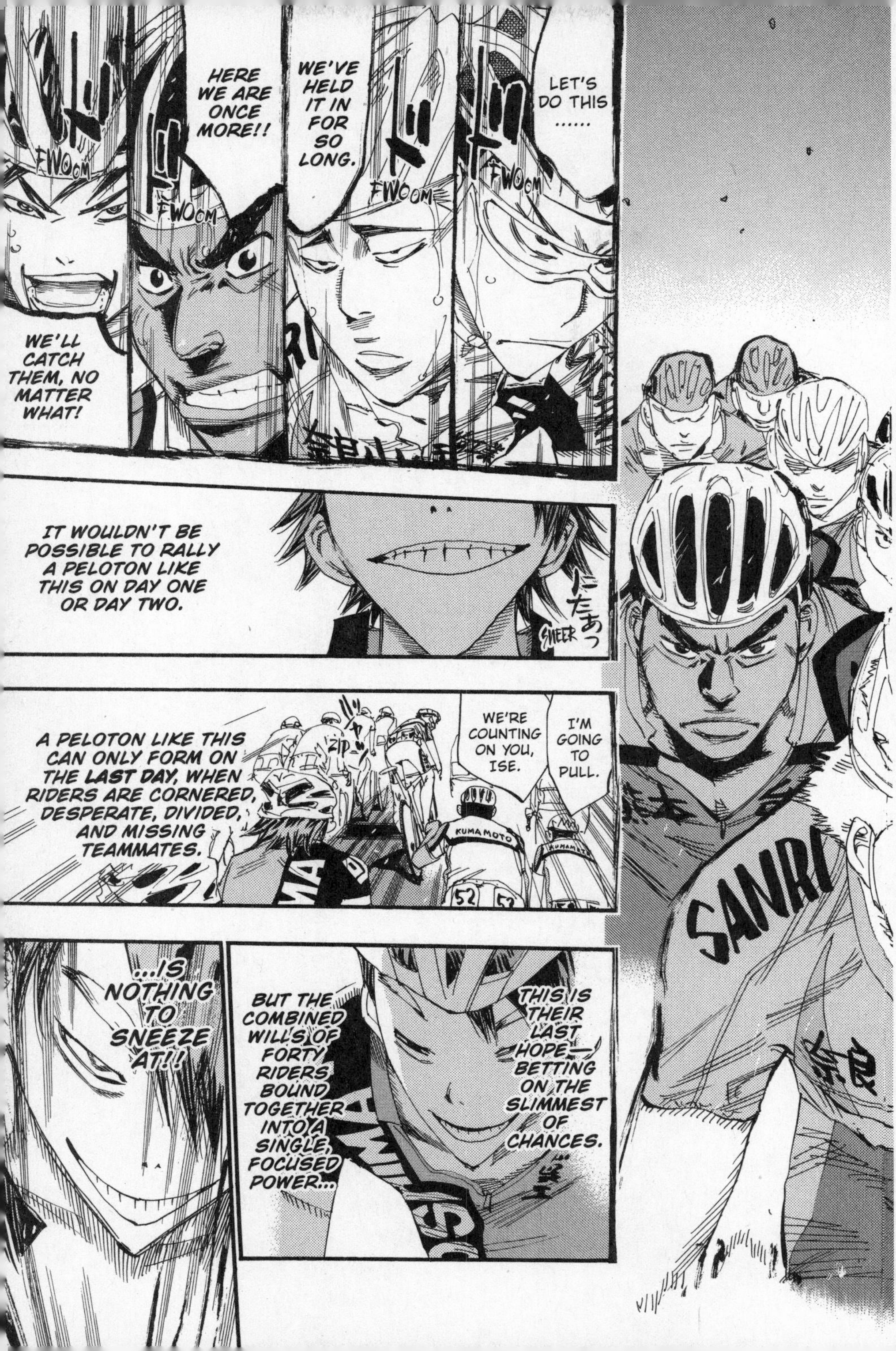
LET'S DO THIS ......
FWOOM
WE'VE HELD IT IN FOR SO LONG.
FWOOM
HERE WE ARE ONCE MORE!!
FWOOM
FWOOM
WE'LL CATCH THEM, NO MATTER WHAT!
IT WOULDN'T BE POSSIBLE TO RALLY A PELOTON LIKE THIS ON DAY ONE OR DAY TWO.
にたぁっ
SNEER
I'M GOING TO PULL.
WE'RE COUNTING ON YOU, ISE.
ZIP
A PELOTON LIKE THIS CAN ONLY FORM ON THE LAST DAY, WHEN RIDERS ARE CORNERED, DESPERATE, DIVIDED, AND MISSING TEAMMATES.
THIS IS THEIR LAST HOPE—BETTING ON THE SLIMMEST OF CHANCES.
BUT THE COMBINED WILLS OF FORTY RIDERS BOUND TOGETHER INTO A SINGLE, FOCUSED POWER...
...IS NOTHING TO SNEEZE AT!!

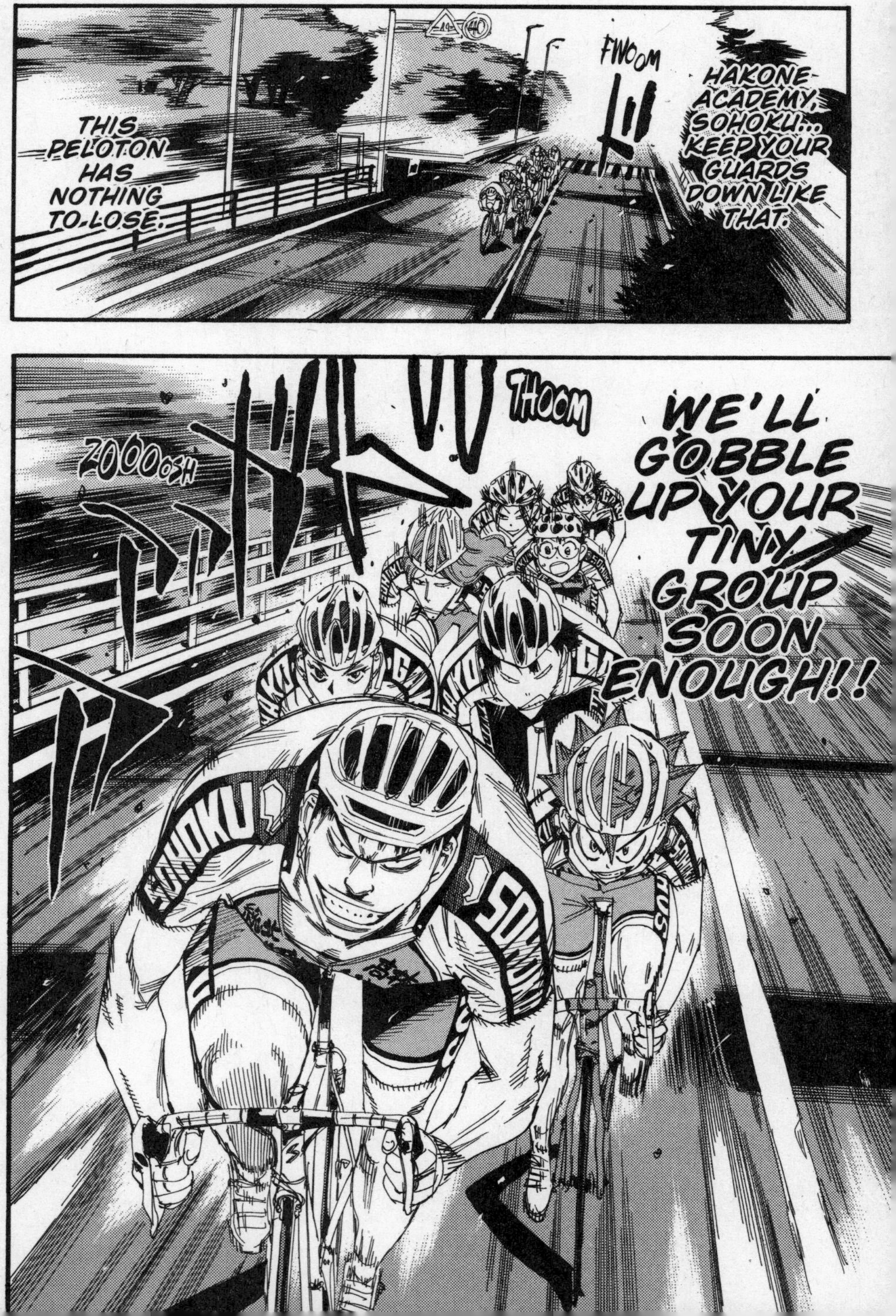
HAKONE ACADEMY, SOHOKU... KEEP YOUR GUARDS DOWN LIKE THAT.
FWOOM
THIS PELOTON HAS NOTHING TO LOSE.
WE'LL GOBBLE UP YOUR TINY GROUP SOON ENOUGH!!
THOOM
ZOOOOSH

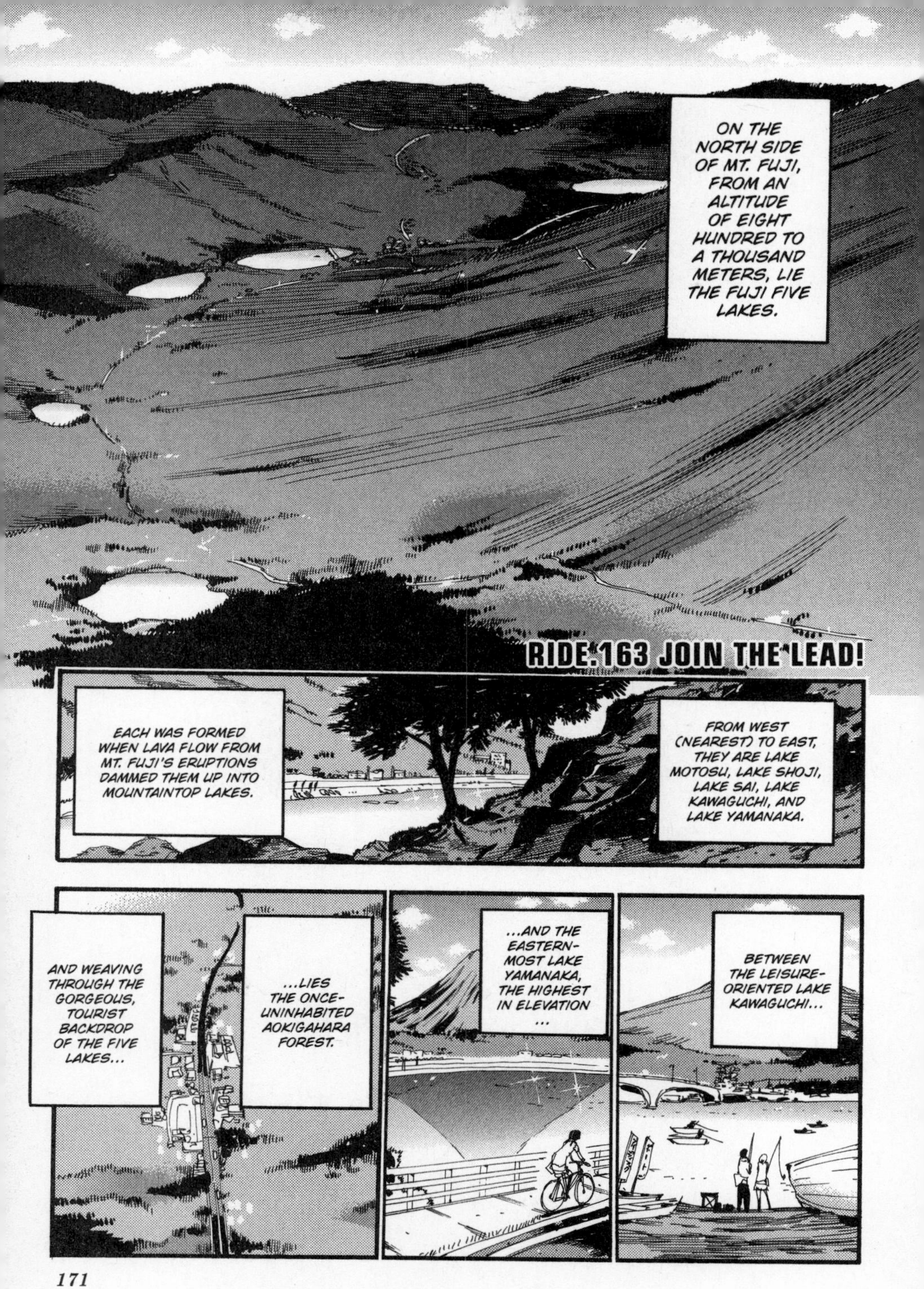
ON THE NORTH SIDE OF MT. FUJI, FROM AN ALTITUDE OF EIGHT HUNDRED TO A THOUSAND METERS, LIE THE FUJI FIVE LAKES.
RIDE.163 JOIN THE LEAD!
FROM WEST (NEAREST) TO EAST, THEY ARE LAKE MOTOSU, LAKE SHOJI, LAKE SAI, LAKE KAWAGUCHI, AND LAKE YAMANAKA.
EACH WAS FORMED WHEN LAVA FLOW FROM MT. FUJI'S ERUPTIONS DAMMED THEM UP INTO MOUNTAINTOP LAKES.
BETWEEN THE LEISURE-ORIENTED LAKE KAWAGUCHI...
...AND THE EASTERN-MOST LAKE YAMANAKA, THE HIGHEST IN ELEVATION...
AND WEAVING THROUGH THE GORGEOUS, TOURIST BACKDROP OF THE FIVE LAKES...
...LIES THE ONCE-UNINHABITED AOKIGAHARA FOREST.

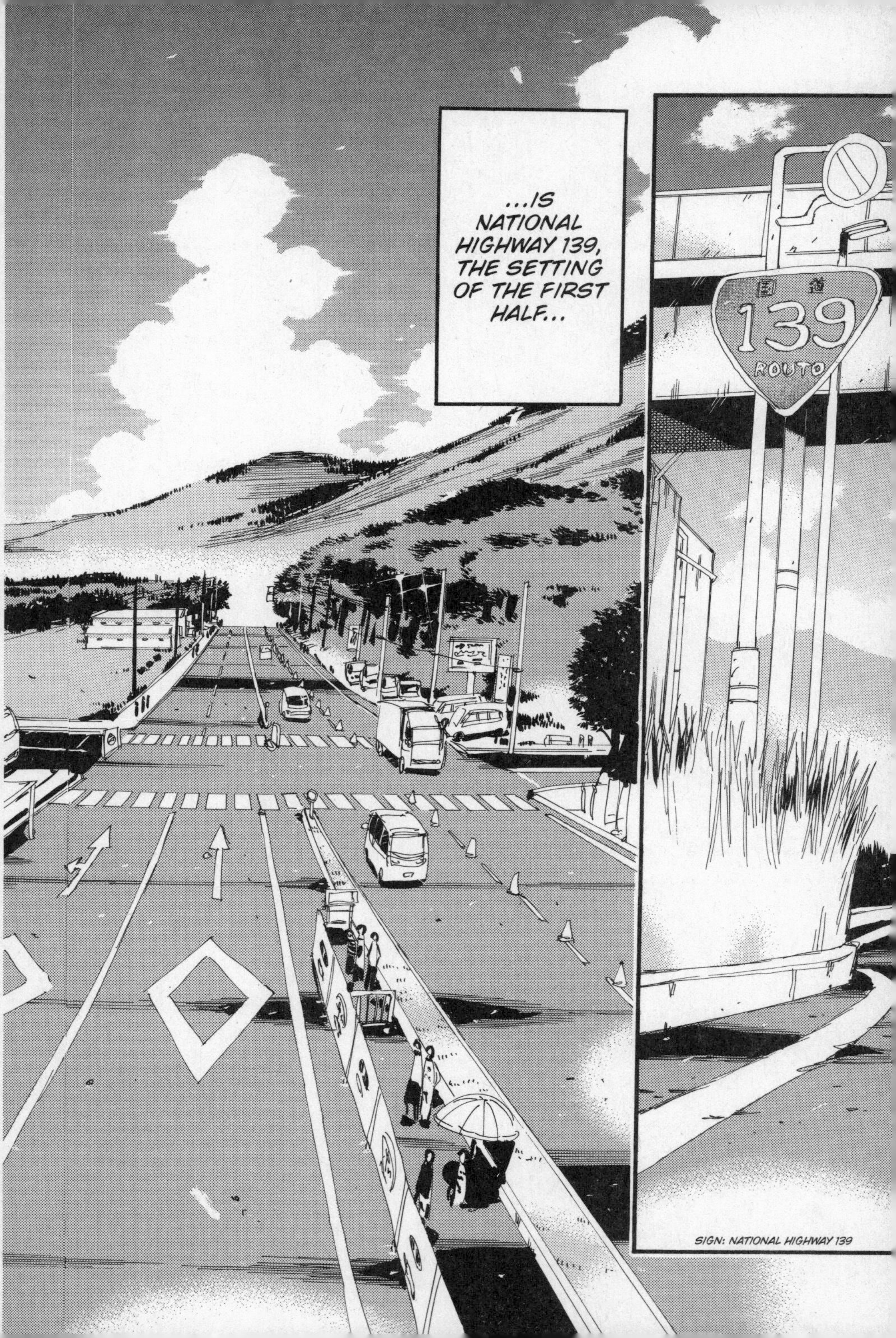
139
ROUTO
SIGN: NATIONAL HIGHWAY 139
...IS NATIONAL HIGHWAY 139, THE SETTING OF THE FIRST HALF...

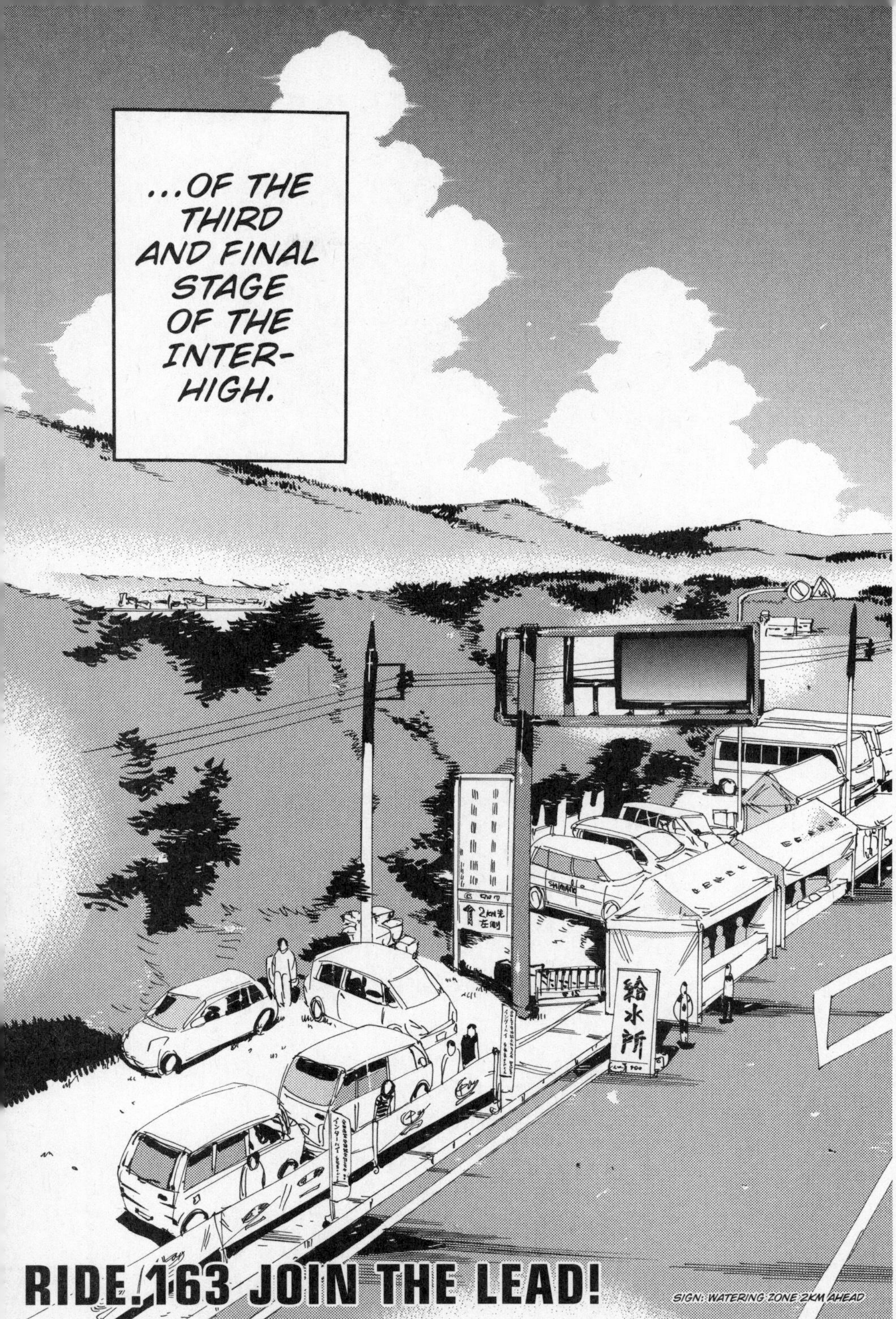
...OF THE THIRD AND FINAL STAGE OF THE INTER-HIGH.
給水所
SIGN: WATERING ZONE 2KM AHEAD

RIDE.163 JOIN THE LEAD!

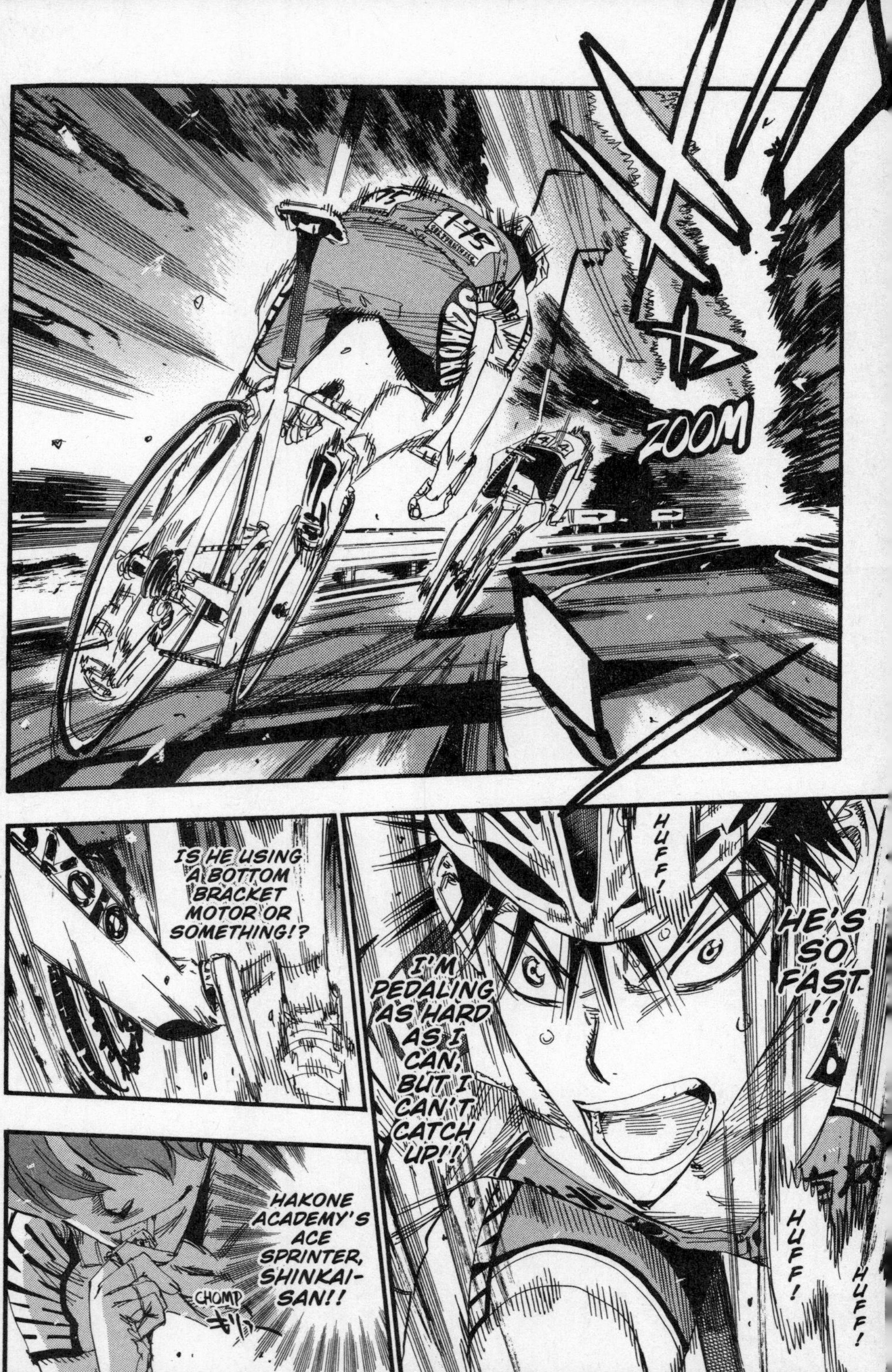
ZOOM
HUFF!
HE'S SO FAST!!
I'M PEDALING AS HARD AS I CAN, BUT I CAN'T CATCH UP!!
HUFF!
HUFF!
IS HE USING A BOTTOM BRACKET MOTOR OR SOMETHING!?
HAKONE ACADEMY'S ACE SPRINTER, SHINKAI-SAN!!
CHOMP

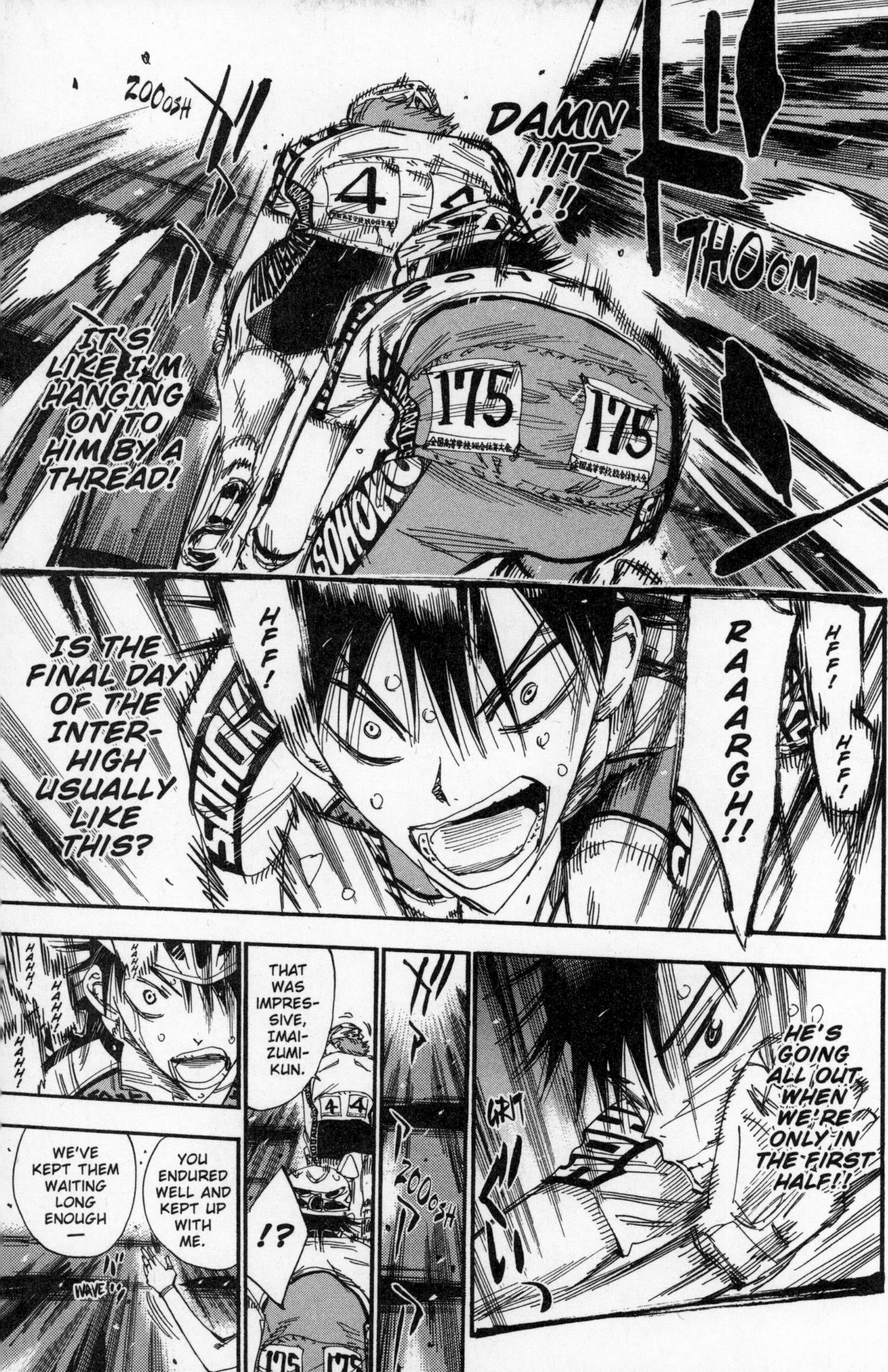
DAMN IIIT!!
THOOM
ZOOOSH
IT'S LIKE I'M HANGING ON TO HIM BY A THREAD!
HFF! HFF!
RAAAARGH!!
HFF!
IS THE FINAL DAY OF THE INTER-HIGH USUALLY LIKE THIS?
HE'S GOING ALL OUT WHEN WE'RE ONLY IN THE FIRST HALF!!
GRIT
ZOOOSH
THAT WAS IMPRESSIVE, IMAIZUMI-KUN.
YOU ENDURED WELL AND KEPT UP WITH ME.
!?
HAHH! HAHH! HAHH! HAHH!
WE'VE KEPT THEM WAITING LONG ENOUGH —
WAVE

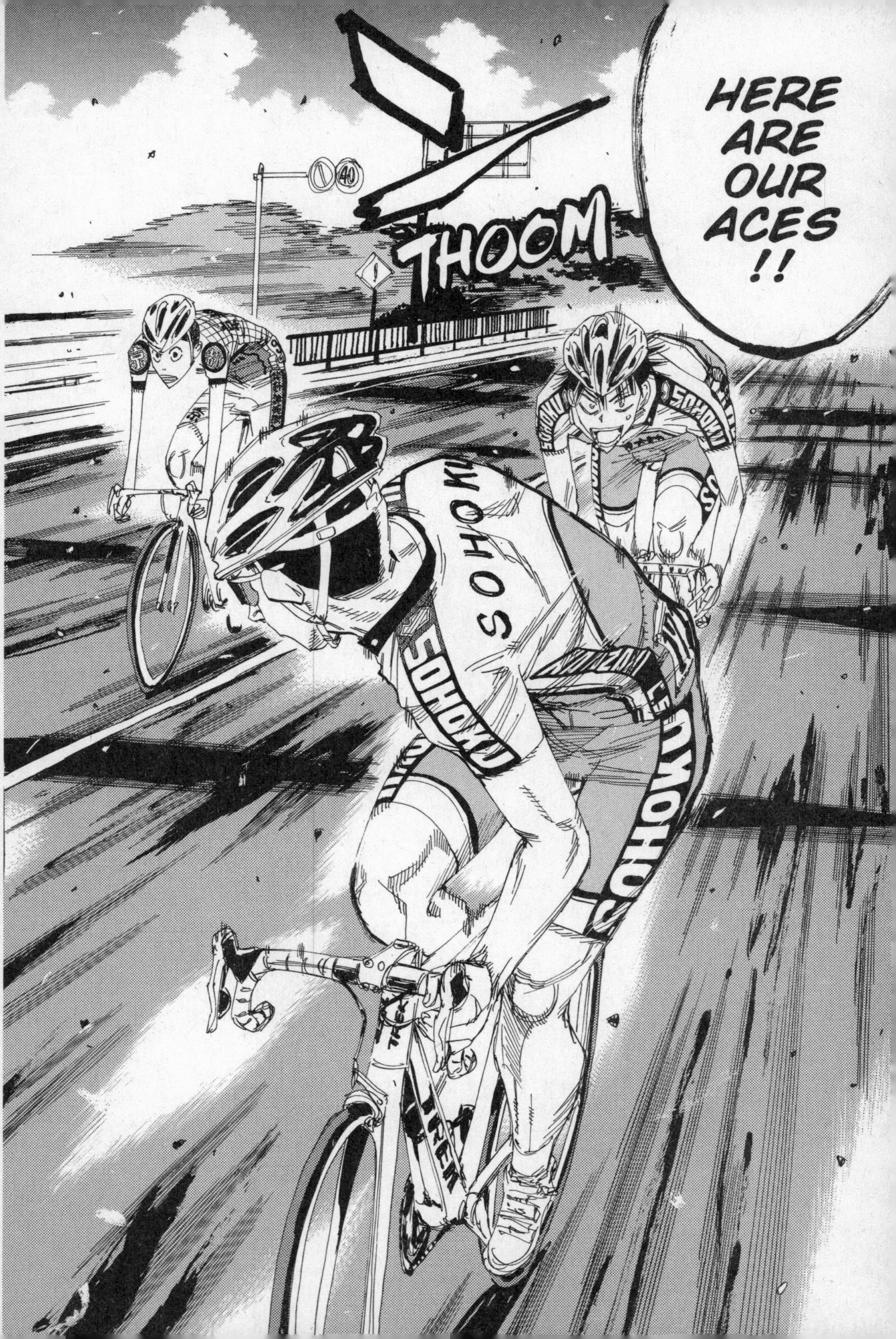
HERE ARE OUR ACES!!
THOOM
SOHOKU

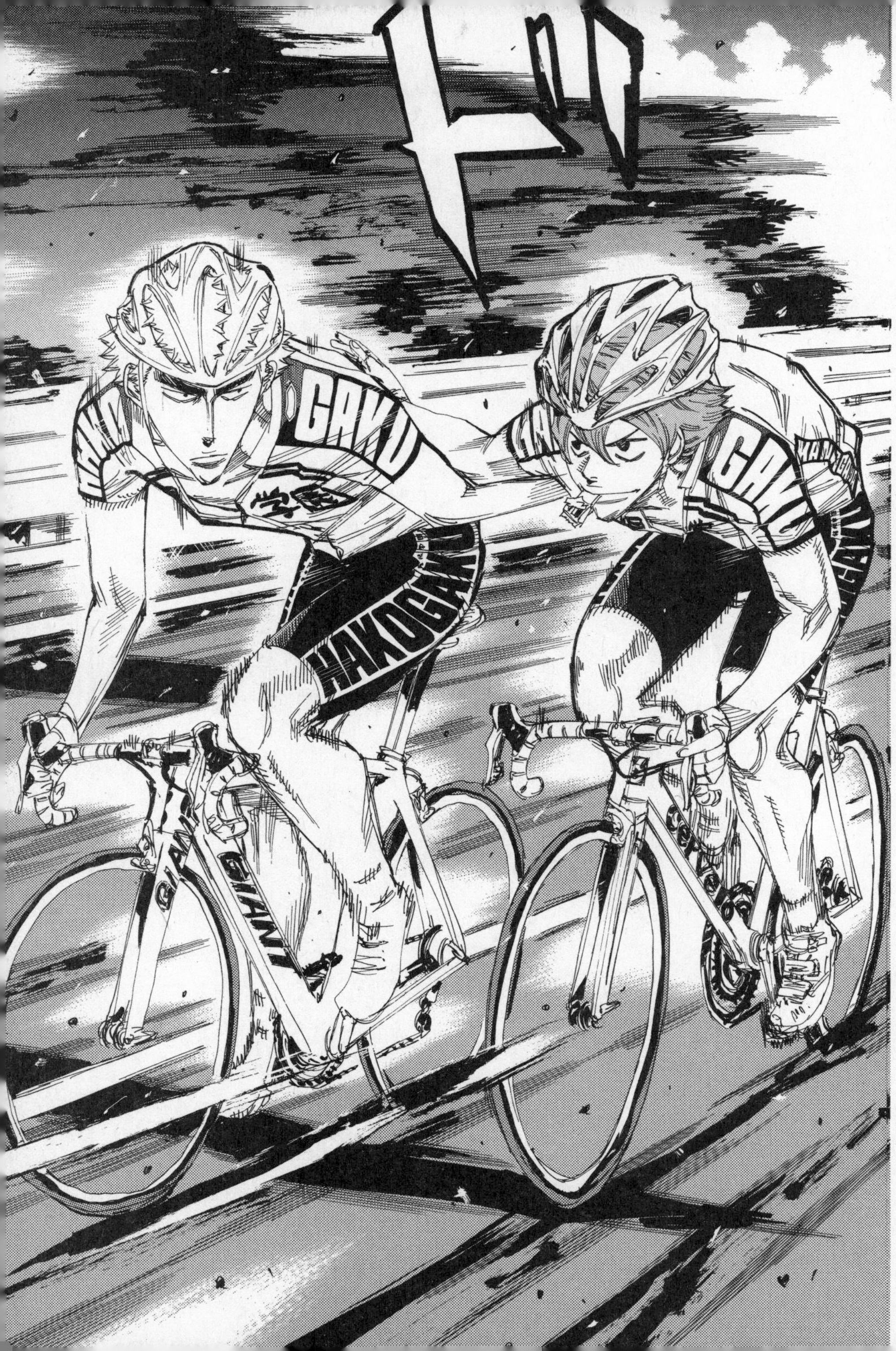
ドッ
GAKU
GAKU
HAKOGAKU

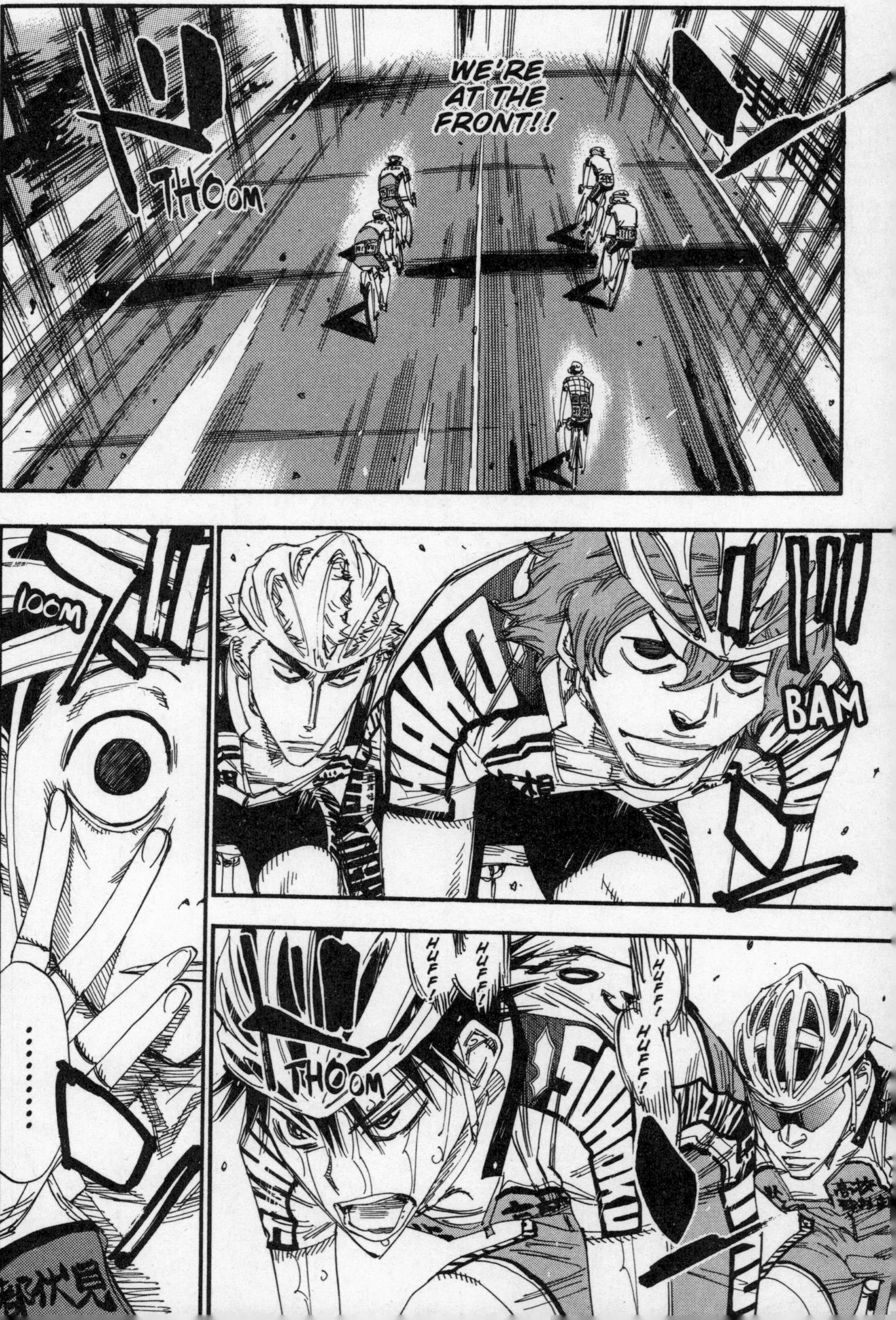
THOOM
WE'RE AT THE FRONT!!
BAM
100M
HUFF! HUFF! HUFF! HUFF! HUFF!
THOOM
......

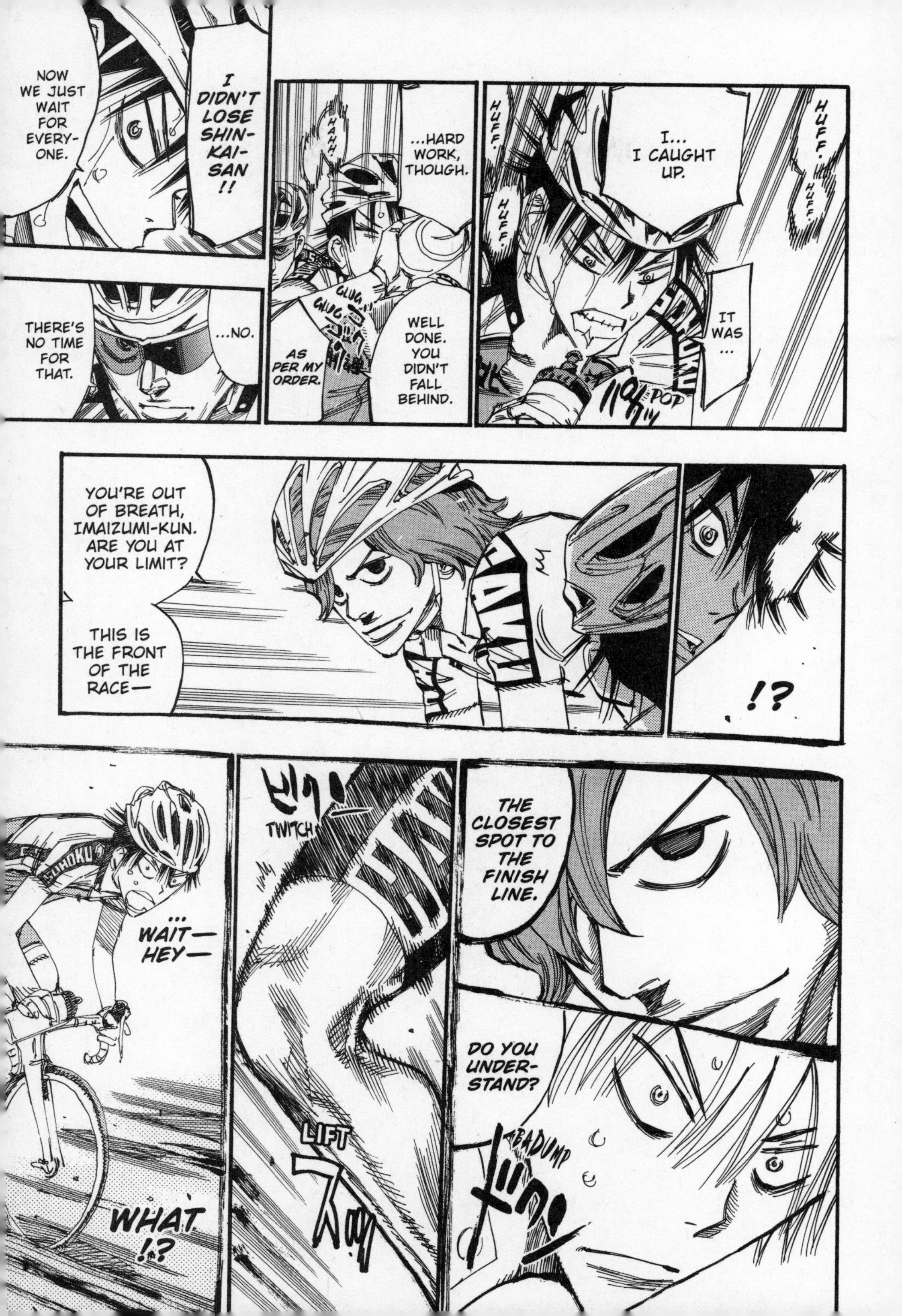
HUFF. HUFF.
I... I CAUGHT UP.
HUFF. HUFF.
IT WAS...
POP
HAHH
...HARD WORK, THOUGH.
GLUG GLUG
WELL DONE. YOU DIDN'T FALL BEHIND.
AS PER MY ORDER.
I DIDN'T LOSE SHIN-KAI-SAN!!
NOW WE JUST WAIT FOR EVERY-ONE.
...NO.
THERE'S NO TIME FOR THAT.
!?
YOU'RE OUT OF BREATH, IMAIZUMI-KUN. ARE YOU AT YOUR LIMIT?
THIS IS THE FRONT OF THE RACE—
THE CLOSEST SPOT TO THE FINISH LINE.
DO YOU UNDER-STAND?
BADUMP
TWITCH
LIFT
...WAIT— HEY—
WHAT!?

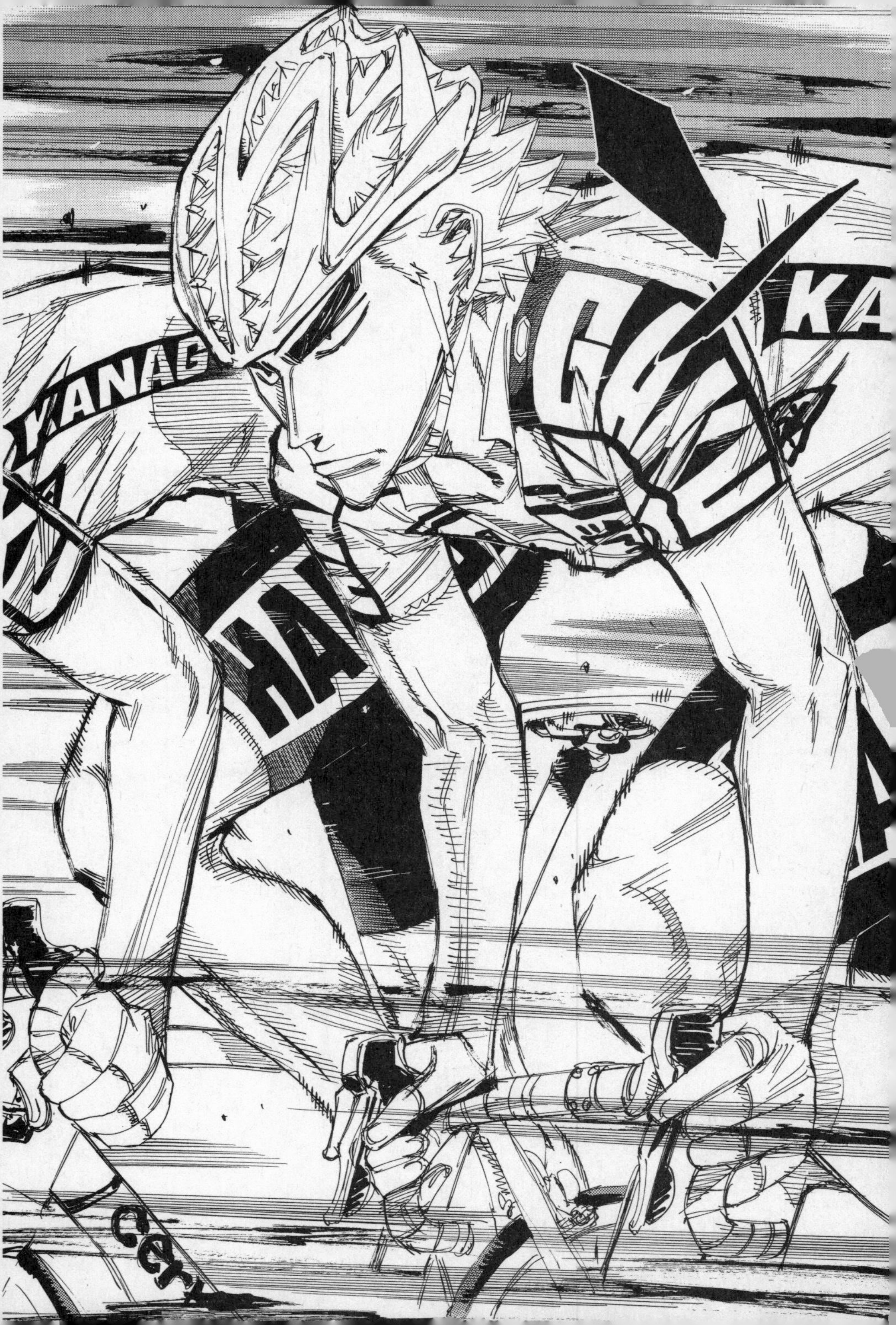

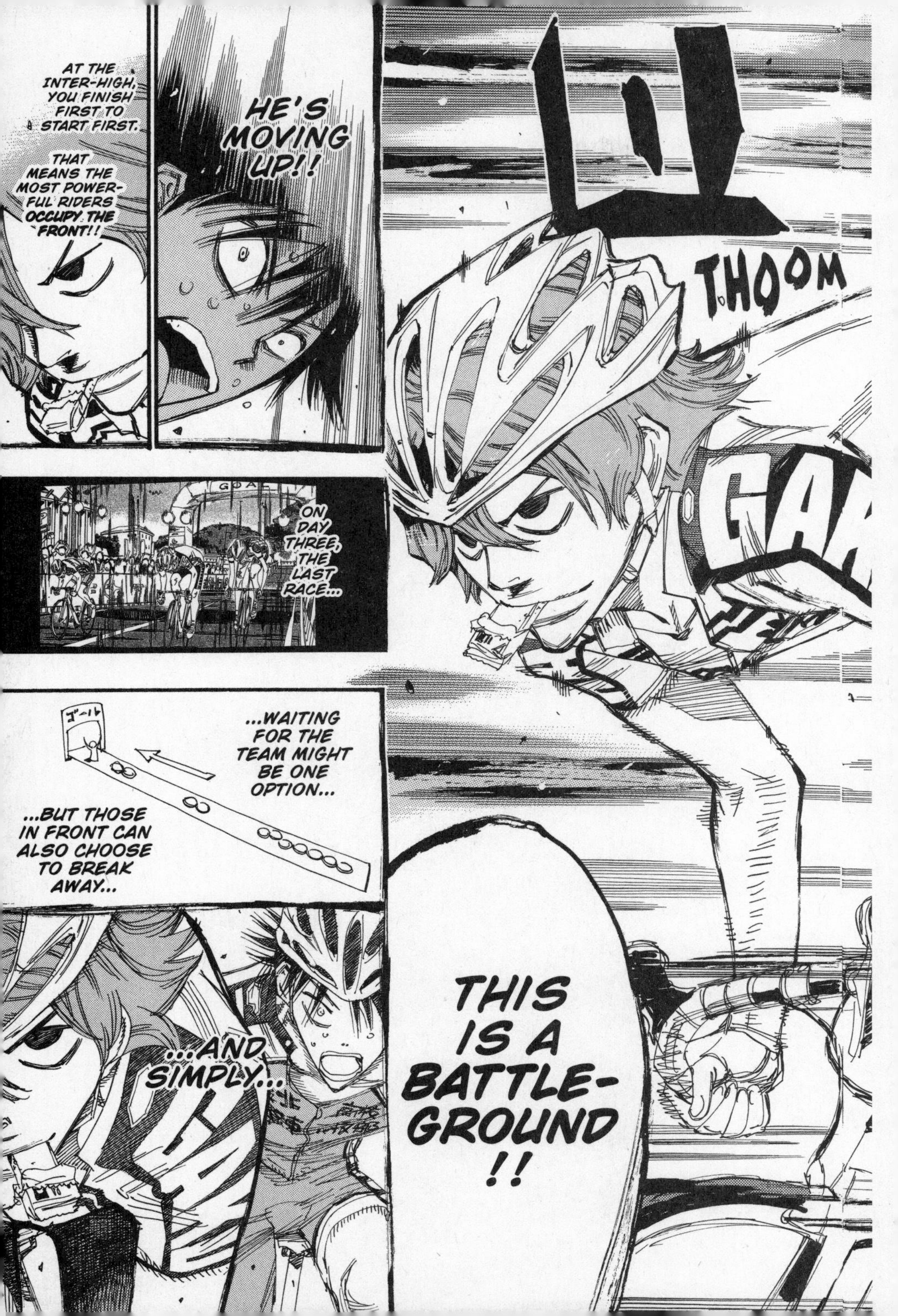
THOOM
HE'S MOVING UP!!
AT THE INTER-HIGH, YOU FINISH FIRST TO START FIRST.
THAT MEANS THE MOST POWER-FUL RIDERS OCCUPY THE FRONT!!
ON DAY THREE, THE LAST RACE...
...WAITING FOR THE TEAM MIGHT BE ONE OPTION...
...BUT THOSE IN FRONT CAN ALSO CHOOSE TO BREAK AWAY...
...AND SIMPLY...
THIS IS A BATTLE-GROUND!!

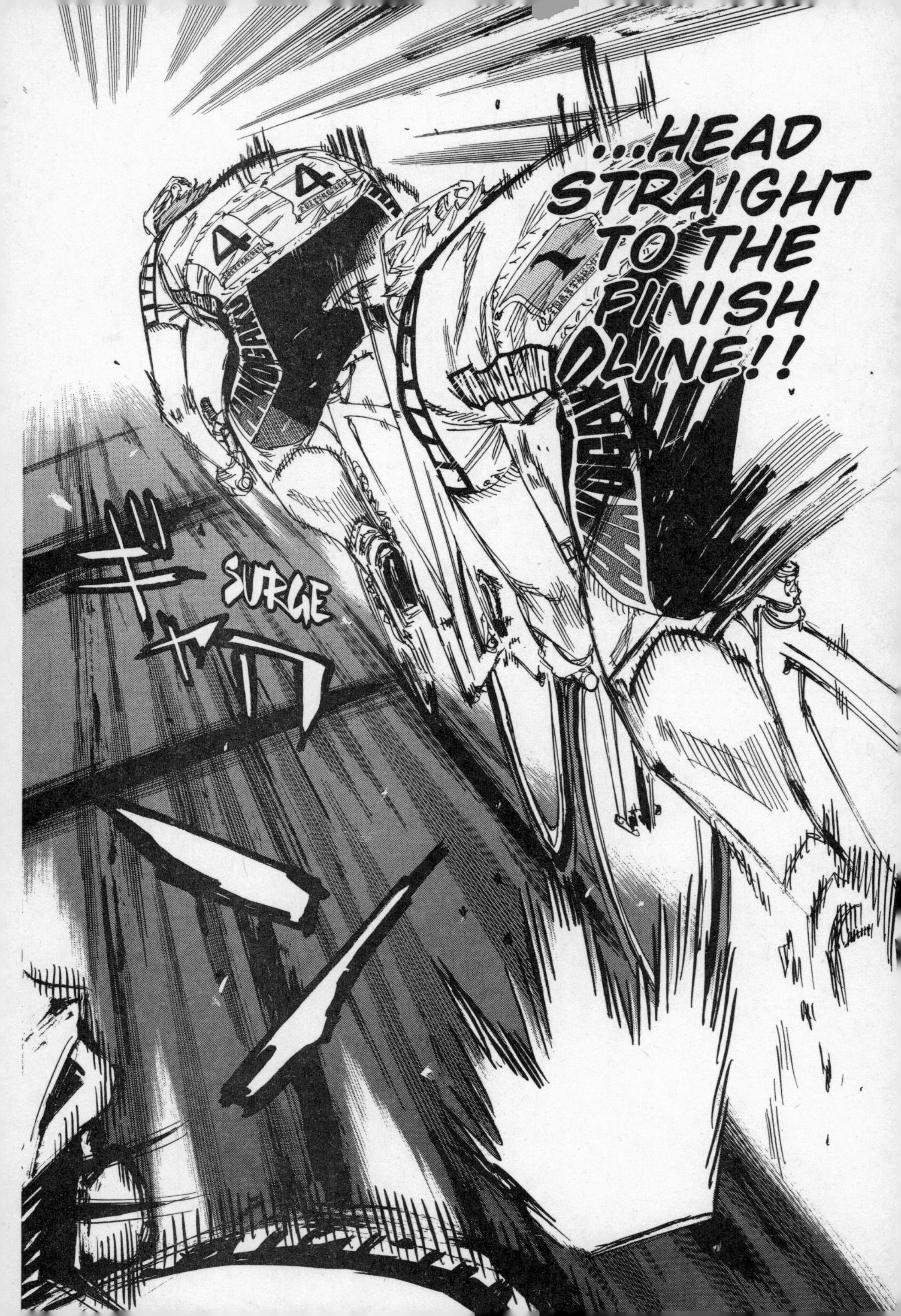
...HEAD STRAIGHT TO THE FINISH LINE!!
SURGE

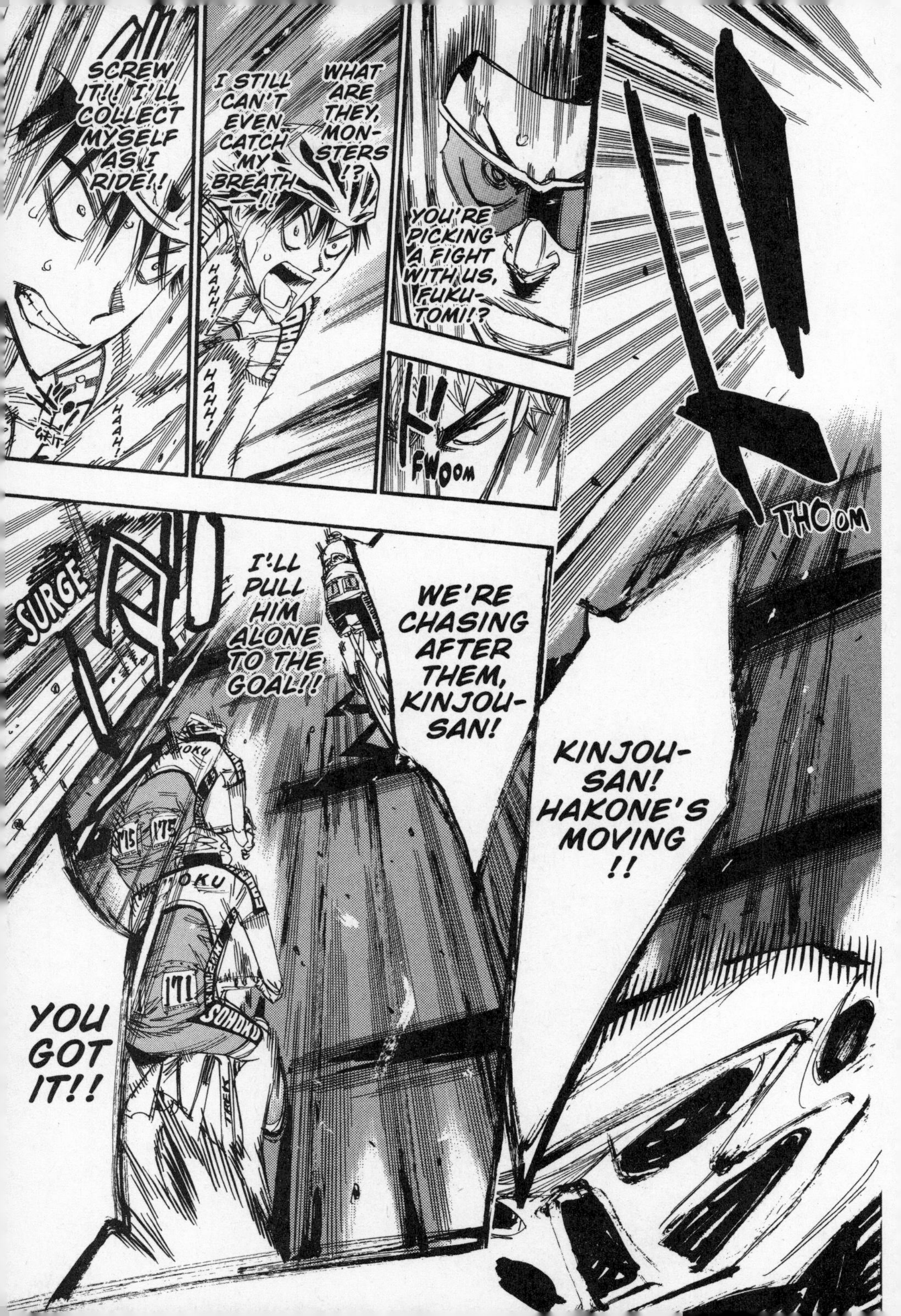
THOOM
KINJOU-SAN! HAKONE'S MOVING!!
YOU'RE PICKING A FIGHT WITH US, FUKUTOMI!?
FWOOM
WHAT ARE THEY, MONSTERS!?
I STILL CAN'T EVEN CATCH MY BREATH!!
HAHH! HAHH!
SCREW IT!! I'LL COLLECT MYSELF AS I RIDE!!
HAAH!
GRIT
WE'RE CHASING AFTER THEM, KINJOU-SAN!
I'LL PULL HIM ALONE TO THE GOAL!!
SURGE
YOU GOT IT!!

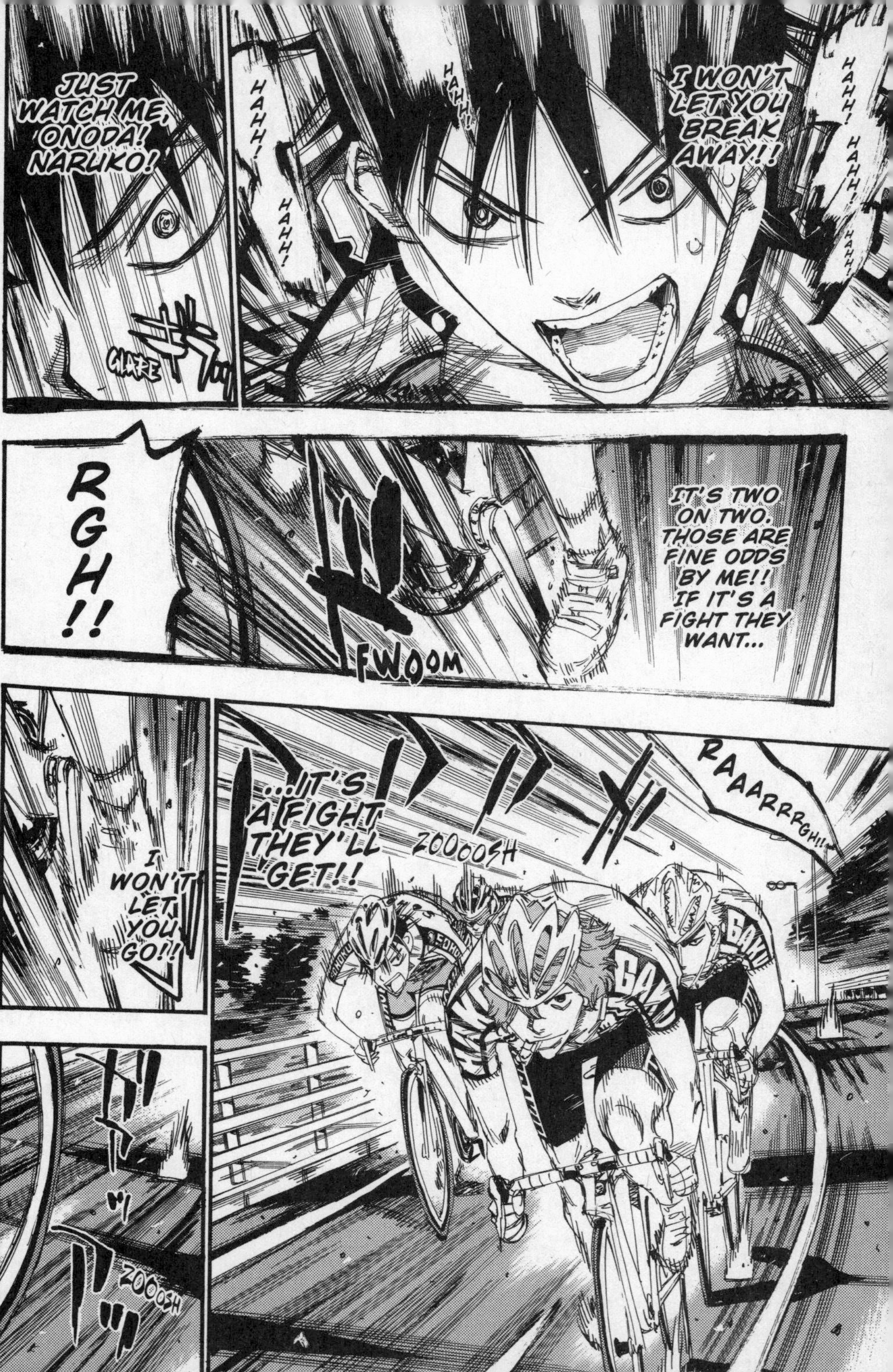
HAHH! HAHH! HAHH! HAHH!
I WON'T LET YOU BREAK AWAY!!
HAHH!
HAHH! HAHH!
JUST WATCH ME, ONODA! NARUKO!
GLARE
IT'S TWO ON TWO. THOSE ARE FINE ODDS BY ME!! IF IT'S A FIGHT THEY WANT...
RGH!!
FWOOM
RAAAARRRGH!!
...IT'S A FIGHT THEY'LL GET!!
ZOOOOSH
I WON'T LET YOU GO!!
ZOOOSH

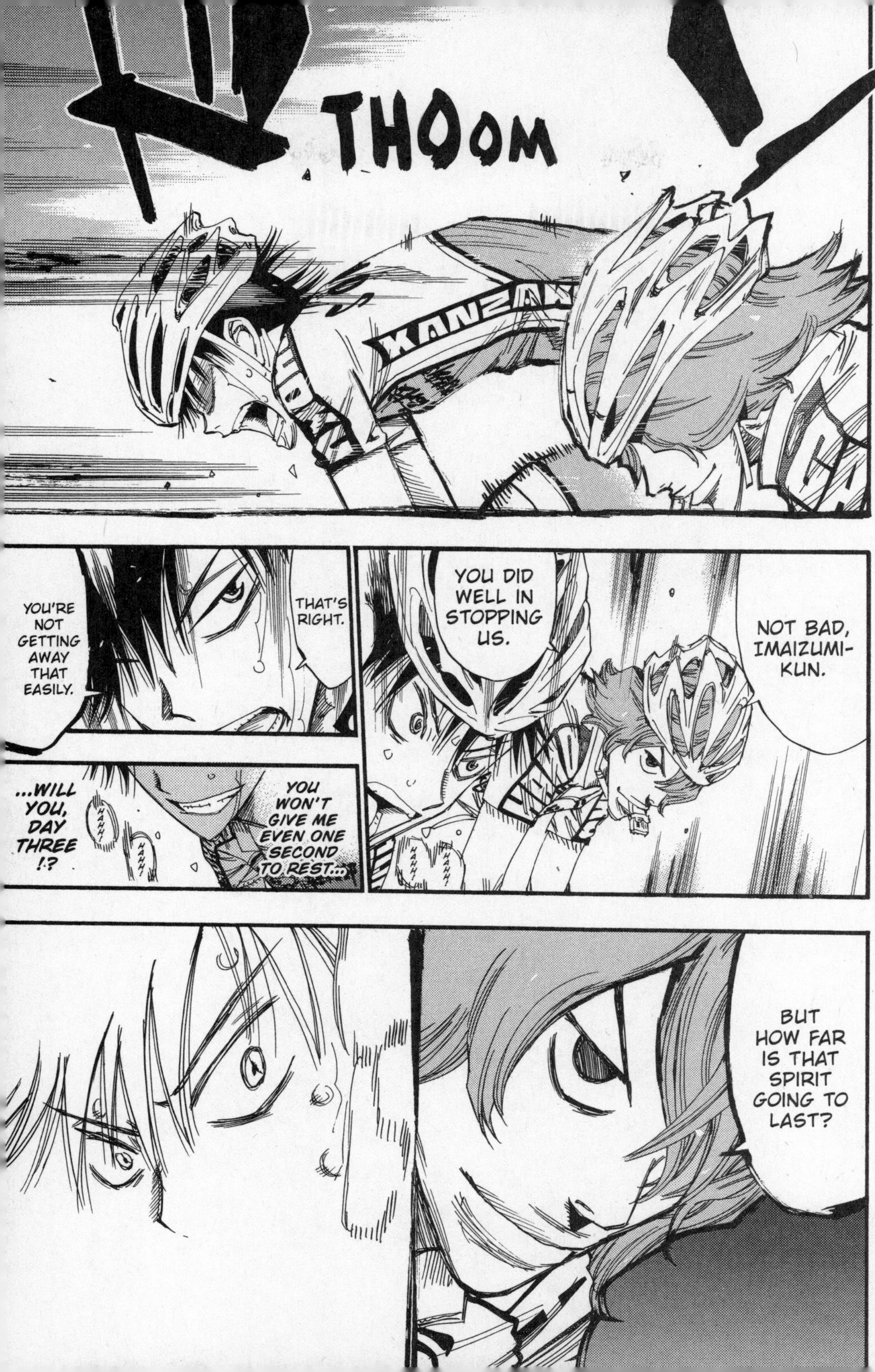
THOOM
NOT BAD, IMAIZUMI-KUN.
YOU DID WELL IN STOPPING US.
THAT'S RIGHT.
YOU'RE NOT GETTING AWAY THAT EASILY.
YOU WON'T GIVE ME EVEN ONE SECOND TO REST...
...WILL YOU, DAY THREE!?
BUT HOW FAR IS THAT SPIRIT GOING TO LAST?

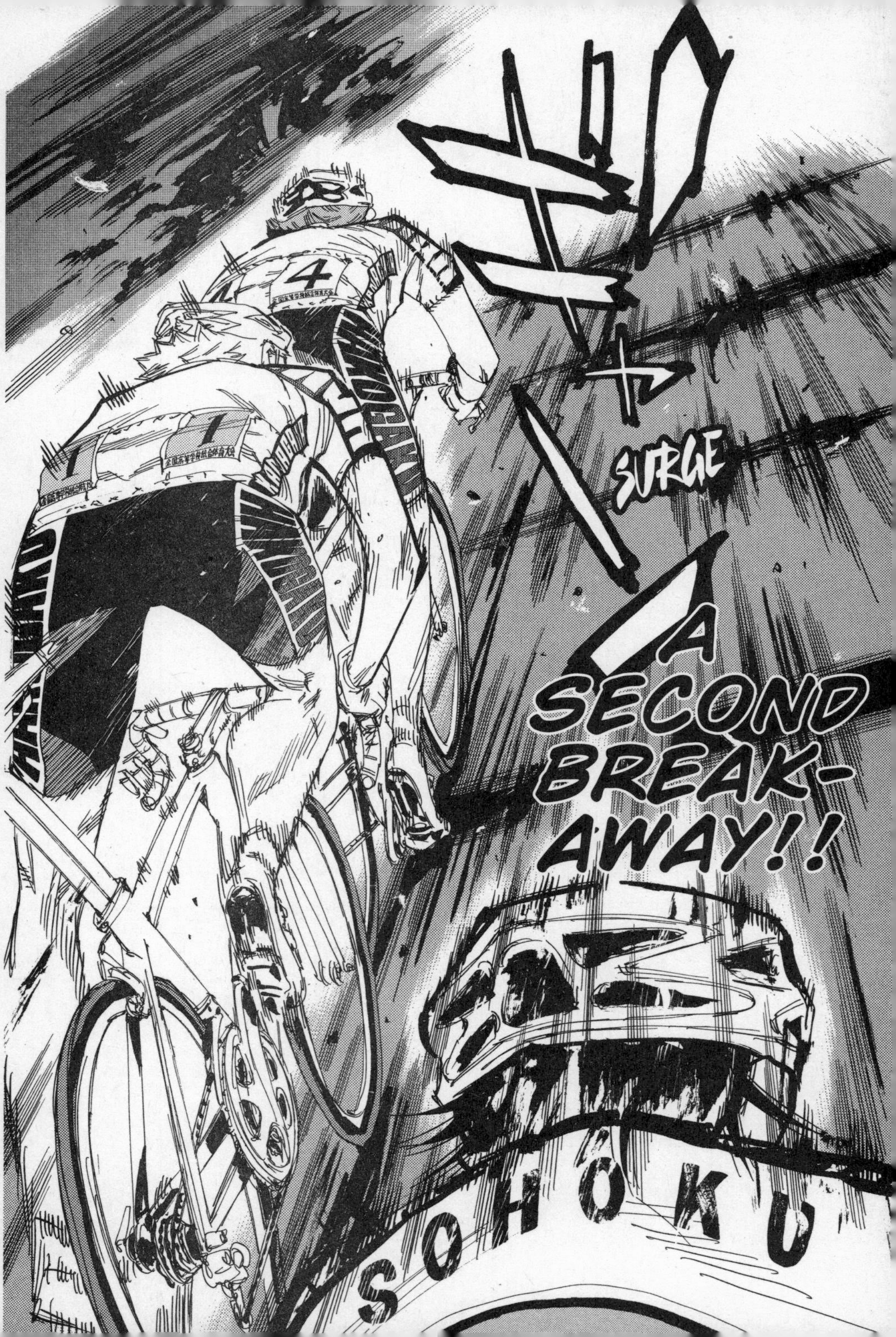
SURGE
A SECOND BREAK-AWAY!!
SOHOKU

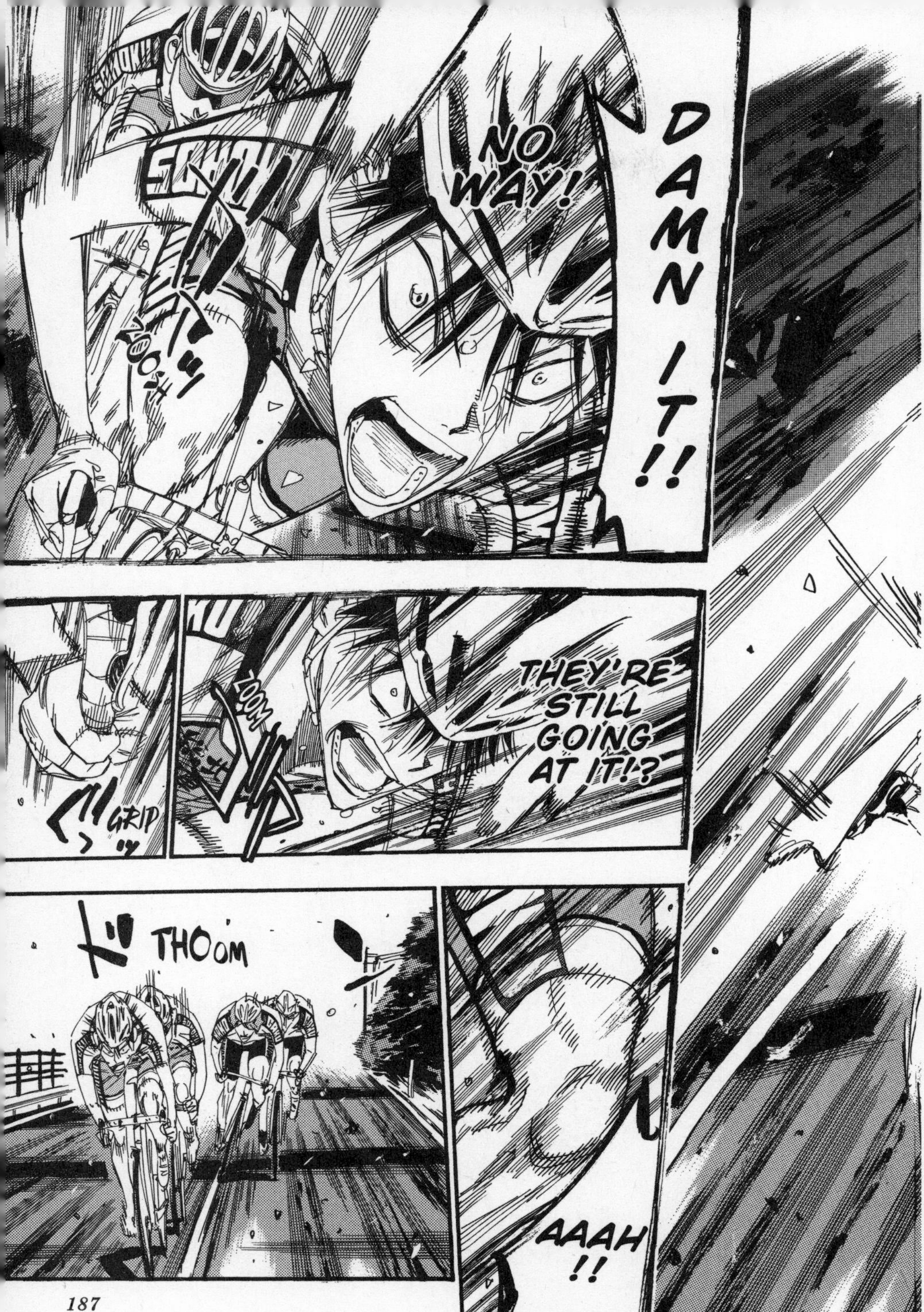
DAMN IT!!
NO WAY!
ZOOM
THEY'RE STILL GOING AT IT!?
ZOOM
GRIP
AAAH!!
THOOM

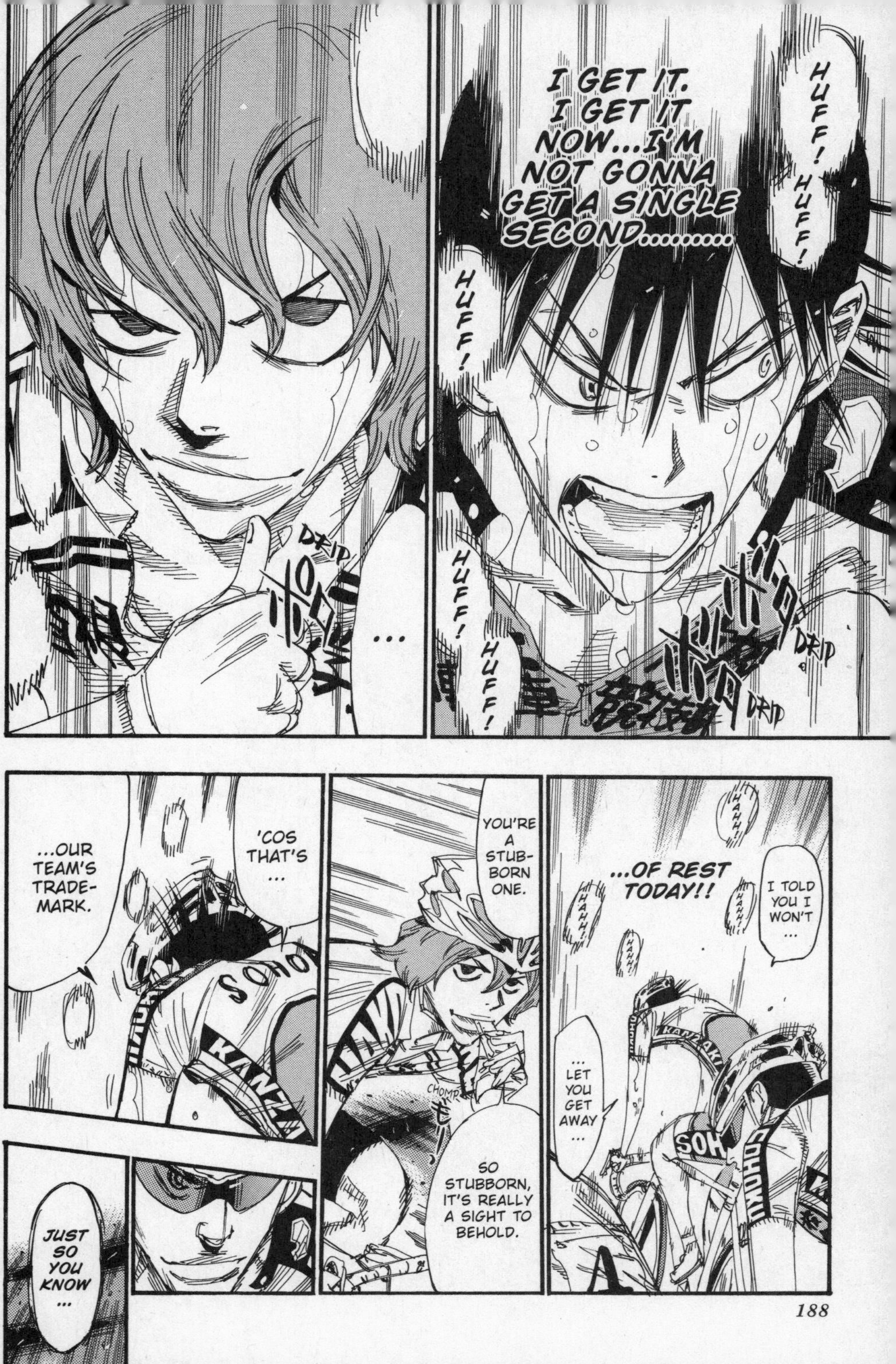
HUFF! HUFF! HUFF!
I GET IT. I GET IT NOW...I'M NOT GONNA GET A SINGLE SECOND..........
HUFF!
HUFF! HUFF! HUFF!
DRIP
DRIP
DRIP
...
HAHH
I TOLD YOU I WON'T ...
...OF REST TODAY!!
HAHH HAHH HAHH
... LET YOU GET AWAY ...
YOU'RE A STUB-BORN ONE.
CHOMP
SO STUBBORN, IT'S REALLY A SIGHT TO BEHOLD.
'COS THAT'S ...
...OUR TEAM'S TRADE-MARK.
JUST SO YOU KNOW ...

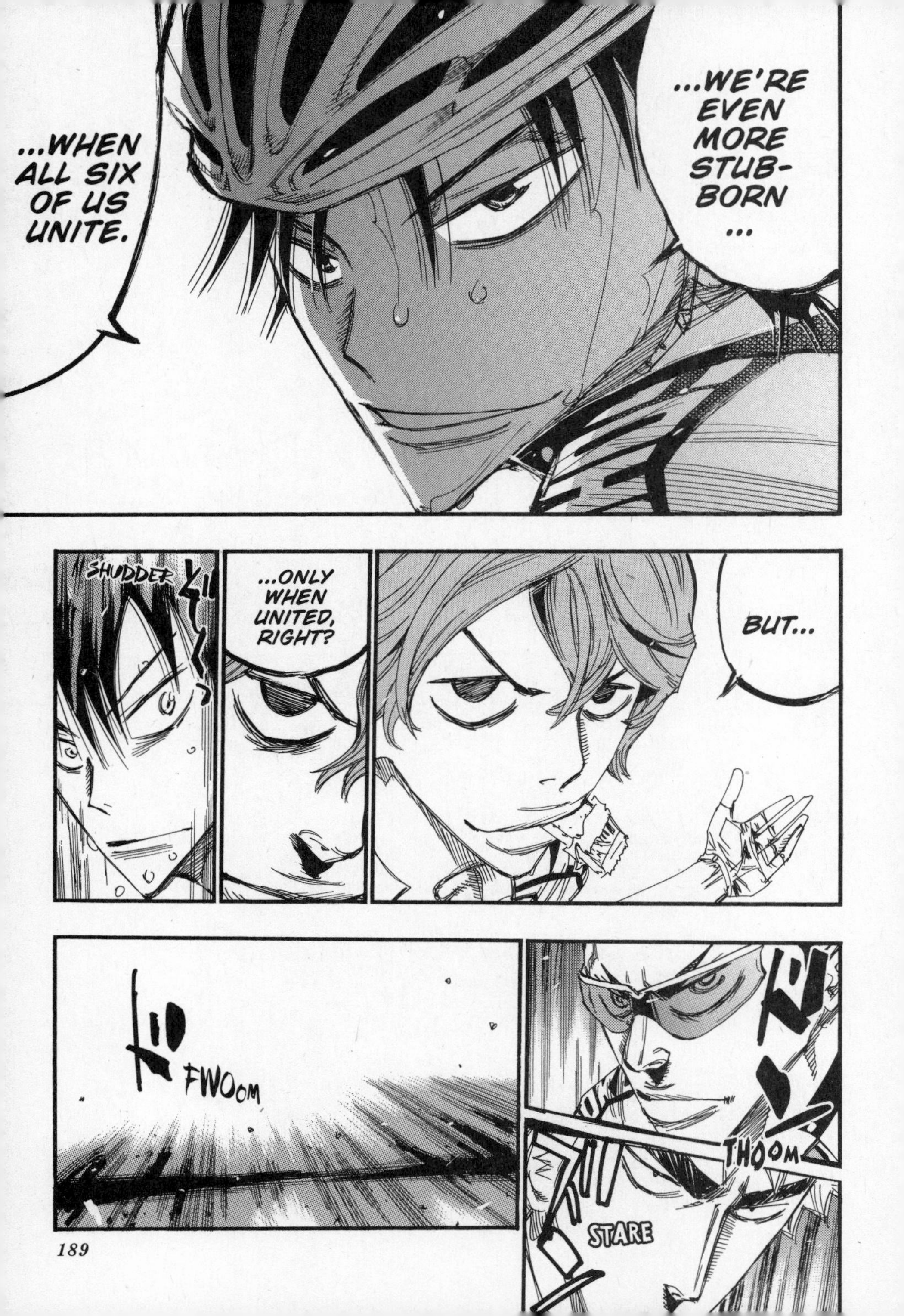
...WE'RE EVEN MORE STUB-BORN...
...WHEN ALL SIX OF US UNITE.
BUT...
...ONLY WHEN UNITED, RIGHT?
SHUDDER
THOOM
STARE
FWOOM

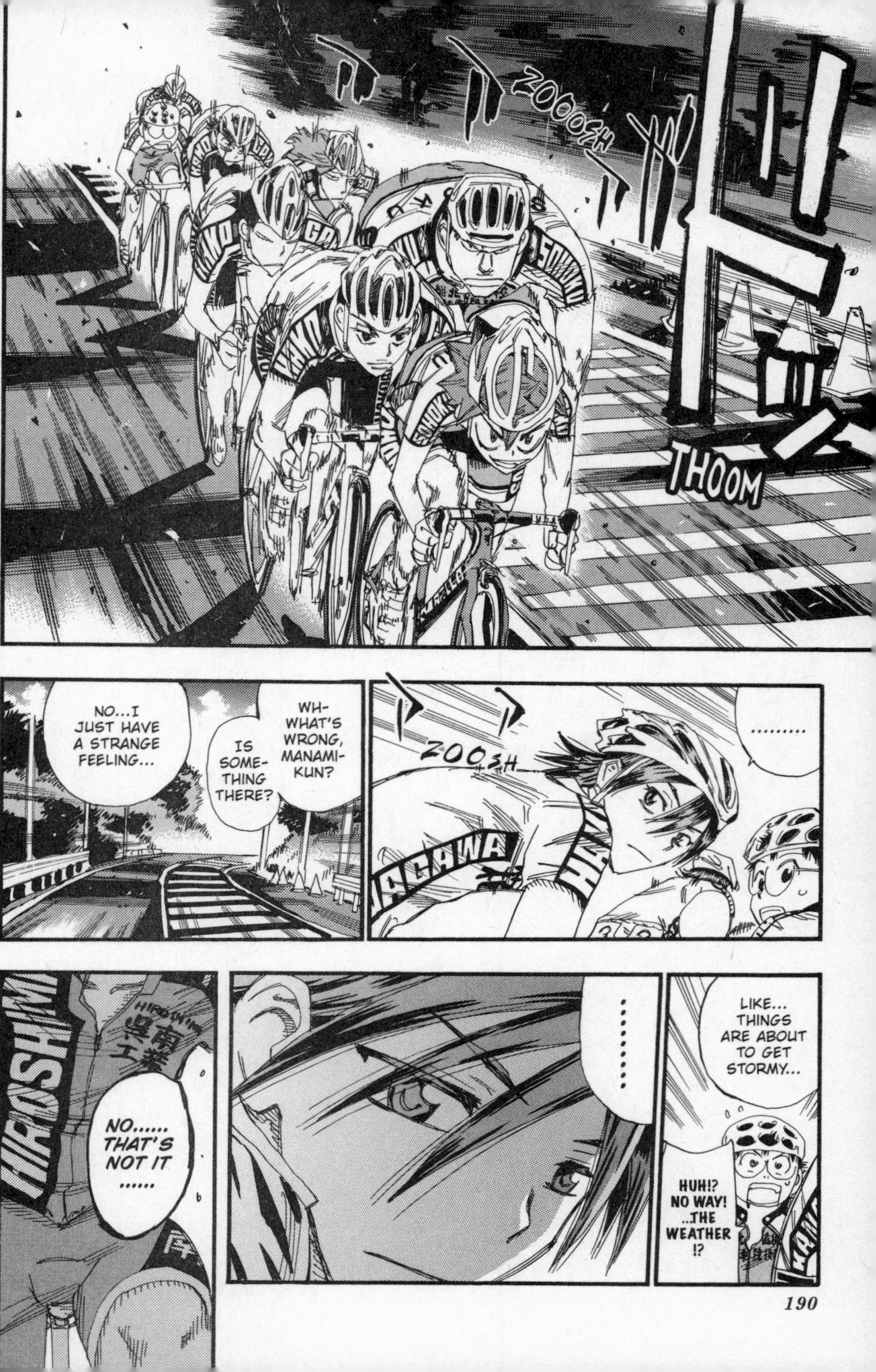
ZOOOSH
THOOM
....
ZOOSH
WH-WHAT'S WRONG, MANAMI-KUN?
IS SOME-THING THERE?
NO...I JUST HAVE A STRANGE FEELING...
LIKE... THINGS ARE ABOUT TO GET STORMY...
HUH!? NO WAY! ...THE WEATHER !?
....
NO...... THAT'S NOT IT ......

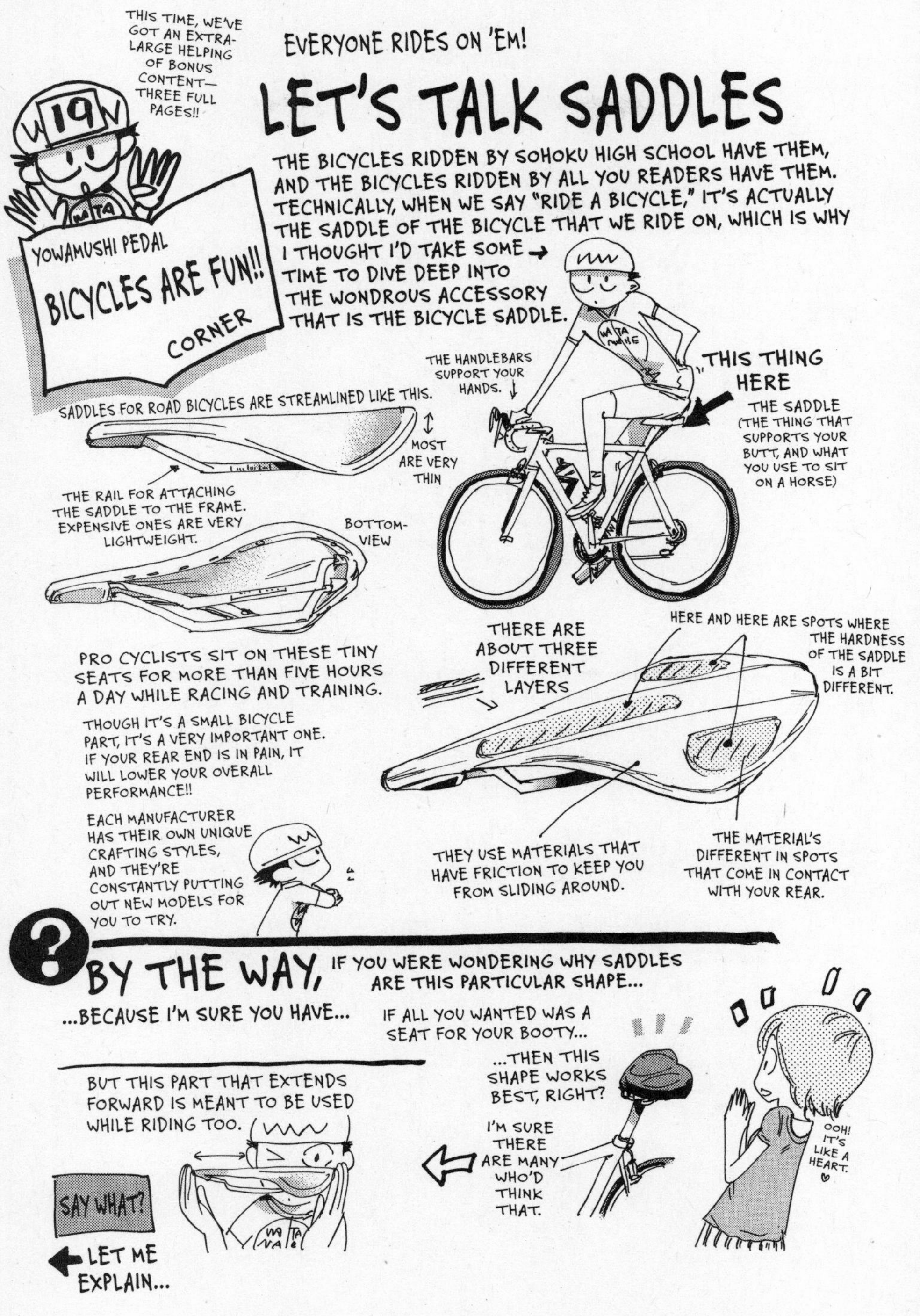
THIS TIME, WE'VE GOT AN EXTRA-LARGE HELPING OF BONUS CONTENT— THREE FULL PAGES!!
19
YOWAMUSHI PEDAL
BICYCLES ARE FUN!!
CORNER
EVERYONE RIDES ON 'EM!
LET'S TALK SADDLES
THE BICYCLES RIDDEN BY SOHOKU HIGH SCHOOL HAVE THEM, AND THE BICYCLES RIDDEN BY ALL YOU READERS HAVE THEM. TECHNICALLY, WHEN WE SAY "RIDE A BICYCLE," IT'S ACTUALLY THE SADDLE OF THE BICYCLE THAT WE RIDE ON, WHICH IS WHY I THOUGHT I'D TAKE SOME TIME TO DIVE DEEP INTO THE WONDROUS ACCESSORY THAT IS THE BICYCLE SADDLE.
THE HANDLEBARS SUPPORT YOUR HANDS.
THIS THING HERE
THE SADDLE (THE THING THAT SUPPORTS YOUR BUTT, AND WHAT YOU USE TO SIT ON A HORSE)
SADDLES FOR ROAD BICYCLES ARE STREAMLINED LIKE THIS.
MOST ARE VERY THIN
THE RAIL FOR ATTACHING THE SADDLE TO THE FRAME. EXPENSIVE ONES ARE VERY LIGHTWEIGHT.
BOTTOM-VIEW
PRO CYCLISTS SIT ON THESE TINY SEATS FOR MORE THAN FIVE HOURS A DAY WHILE RACING AND TRAINING.
THOUGH IT'S A SMALL BICYCLE PART, IT'S A VERY IMPORTANT ONE. IF YOUR REAR END IS IN PAIN, IT WILL LOWER YOUR OVERALL PERFORMANCE!!
EACH MANUFACTURER HAS THEIR OWN UNIQUE CRAFTING STYLES, AND THEY'RE CONSTANTLY PUTTING OUT NEW MODELS FOR YOU TO TRY.
THERE ARE ABOUT THREE DIFFERENT LAYERS
HERE AND HERE ARE SPOTS WHERE THE HARDNESS OF THE SADDLE IS A BIT DIFFERENT.
THEY USE MATERIALS THAT HAVE FRICTION TO KEEP YOU FROM SLIDING AROUND.
THE MATERIAL'S DIFFERENT IN SPOTS THAT COME IN CONTACT WITH YOUR REAR.
BY THE WAY, IF YOU WERE WONDERING WHY SADDLES ARE THIS PARTICULAR SHAPE...
...BECAUSE I'M SURE YOU HAVE...
IF ALL YOU WANTED WAS A SEAT FOR YOUR BOOTY...
...THEN THIS SHAPE WORKS BEST, RIGHT?
OOH! IT'S LIKE A HEART.
I'M SURE THERE ARE MANY WHO'D THINK THAT.
BUT THIS PART THAT EXTENDS FORWARD IS MEANT TO BE USED WHILE RIDING TOO.
SAY WHAT?
LET ME EXPLAIN...

JUST LIKE THERE ARE VARIOUS HANDLEBAR POSITIONS...
ON THE DROPS
ON THE TOPS
ON THE HOODS
...THERE ARE DIFFERENT SADDLE POSITIONS TOO!!
THERE ARE MAINLY TWO TYPES:
A SQUARELY SEATED POSITION ON THE REAR HALF OF THE SADDLE
(IN BROAD TERMS) THIS IS A BASIC PEDALING-FOCUSED POSITION YOU USE WHEN CRUISING.
A FORWARD POSITION ON THE FRONT HALF OF THE SADDLE
(IN BROAD TERMS) THIS IS A POWER-FOCUSED POSITIONS FOR CLIMBING OR OTHER TIMES YOU NEED POWER.
THE BIGGEST DIFFERENCE BETWEEN THESE POSITIONS IS THE MUSCLES THAT EACH POSITION ALLOWS YOU TO UTILIZE MOST.
THIS POSITION MAINLY UTILIZES THIS MUSCLE
IT'S CONNECTED TO YOUR DORSAL MUSCLES, SO YOU CAN USE IT FOR LONG PERIODS.
YOU DON'T USE THIS MUSCLE NORMALLY, SO IF YOU DON'T PAY ATTENTION AND MAKE SURE THAT'S THE MUSCLE YOU'RE PUMPING AS YOU RIDE IN THIS POSITION, YOU COULD UNCONSCIOUSLY SLIP BACK TO USING OTHER MUSCLES. STAY ALERT!
THIS POSITION MAINLY UTILIZES THIS MUSCLE
THIS WILL GIVE YOU AN INSTANTANEOUS BURST OF POWER, BUT IT CAN'T BE SUSTAINED FOR LONG, SO YOU USUALLY END UP EXHAUSTING YOUR ENERGY THIS WAY.
IF YOU USE THE WRONG MUSCLES...
IF YOU JUST KEEP ON USING THE SAME MUSCLES THROUGH YOUR WHOLE RIDE, YOU'LL TIRE THEM OUT REALLY FAST. ROTATING THE MUSCLES YOU USE AS YOUR MAIN POWER SOURCE WILL MAKE ALL OF THEM LAST FOR MUCH LONGER!
PEDAL PEDAL PEDAL PEDAL PEDAL
WHOOSH
HAVE SOME FUN TRYING OUT DIFFERENT RIDING POSITIONS!
SINCE YOU CAN MOVE YOUR SADDLE FORWARD AND BACKWARD ON ITS POST, TEST OUT DIFFERENT POSITIONS TO SEE WHICH WORKS BEST FOR YOU.

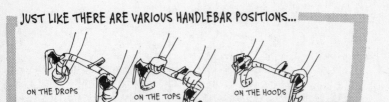

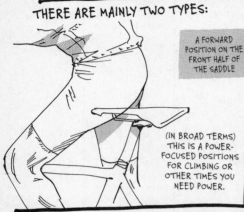

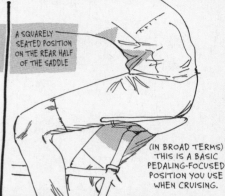

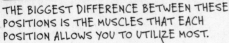

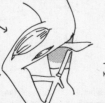

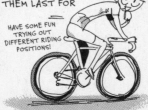

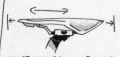

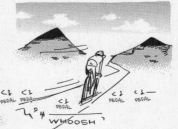

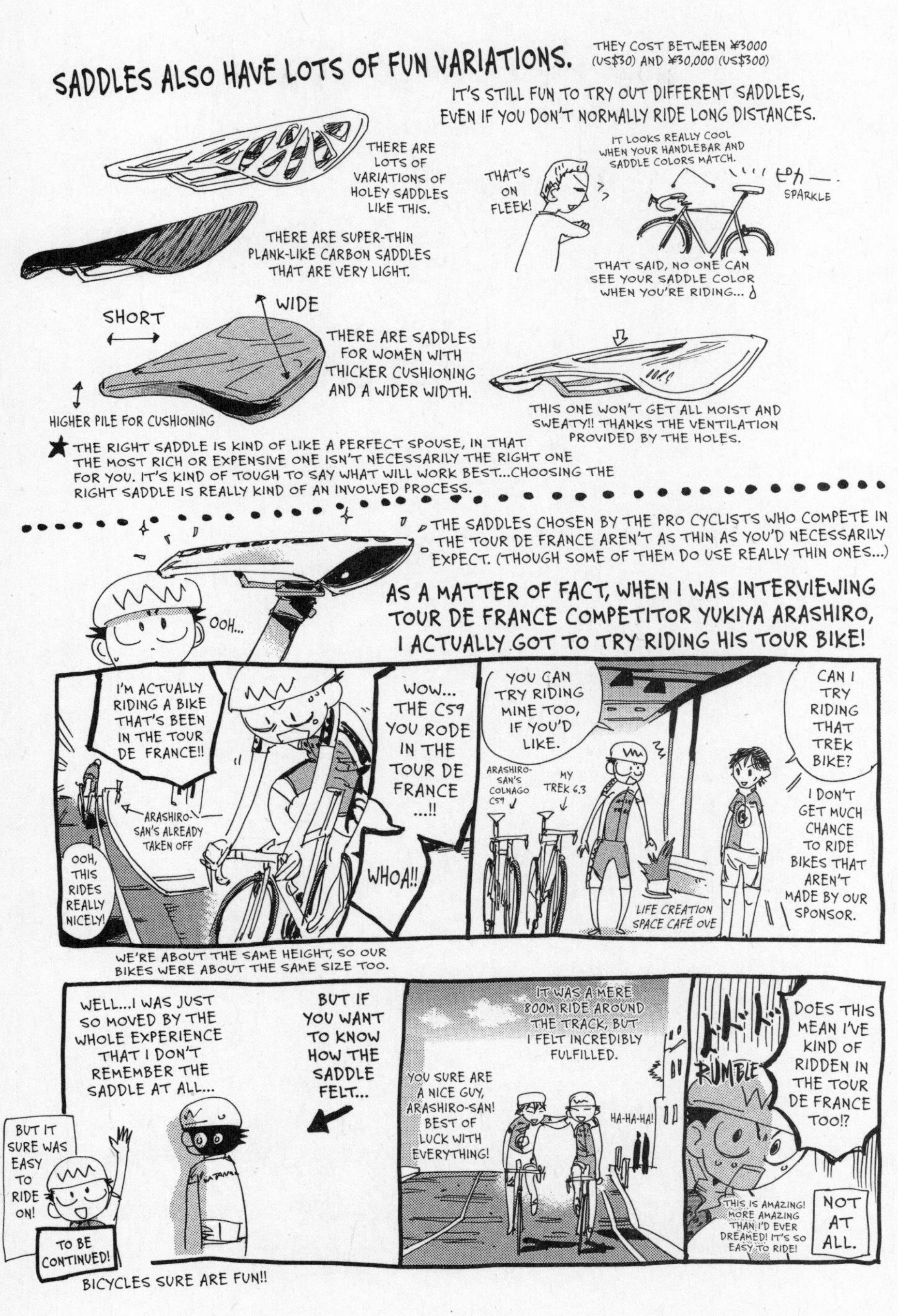
SADDLES ALSO HAVE LOTS OF FUN VARIATIONS.
THEY COST BETWEEN ¥3000 (US$30) AND ¥30,000 (US$300)
IT'S STILL FUN TO TRY OUT DIFFERENT SADDLES, EVEN IF YOU DON'T NORMALLY RIDE LONG DISTANCES.
THERE ARE LOTS OF VARIATIONS OF HOLEY SADDLES LIKE THIS.
THAT'S ON FLEEK!
IT LOOKS REALLY COOL WHEN YOUR HANDLEBAR AND SADDLE COLORS MATCH.
ピカー
SPARKLE
THERE ARE SUPER-THIN PLANK-LIKE CARBON SADDLES THAT ARE VERY LIGHT.
THAT SAID, NO ONE CAN SEE YOUR SADDLE COLOR WHEN YOU'RE RIDING...
SHORT
WIDE
THERE ARE SADDLES FOR WOMEN WITH THICKER CUSHIONING AND A WIDER WIDTH.
HIGHER PILE FOR CUSHIONING
THIS ONE WON'T GET ALL MOIST AND SWEATY!! THANKS THE VENTILATION PROVIDED BY THE HOLES.
★ THE RIGHT SADDLE IS KIND OF LIKE A PERFECT SPOUSE, IN THAT THE MOST RICH OR EXPENSIVE ONE ISN'T NECESSARILY THE RIGHT ONE FOR YOU. IT'S KIND OF TOUGH TO SAY WHAT WILL WORK BEST...CHOOSING THE RIGHT SADDLE IS REALLY KIND OF AN INVOLVED PROCESS.
THE SADDLES CHOSEN BY THE PRO CYCLISTS WHO COMPETE IN THE TOUR DE FRANCE AREN'T AS THIN AS YOU'D NECESSARILY EXPECT. (THOUGH SOME OF THEM DO USE REALLY THIN ONES...)
OOH...
AS A MATTER OF FACT, WHEN I WAS INTERVIEWING TOUR DE FRANCE COMPETITOR YUKIYA ARASHIRO, I ACTUALLY GOT TO TRY RIDING HIS TOUR BIKE!
CAN I TRY RIDING THAT TREK BIKE?
I DON'T GET MUCH CHANCE TO RIDE BIKES THAT AREN'T MADE BY OUR SPONSOR.
YOU CAN TRY RIDING MINE TOO, IF YOU'D LIKE.
ARASHIRO-SAN'S COLNAGO C59
MY TREK 6.3
LIFE CREATION SPACE CAFÉ OVE
WOW... THE C59 YOU RODE IN THE TOUR DE FRANCE ...!!
I'M ACTUALLY RIDING A BIKE THAT'S BEEN IN THE TOUR DE FRANCE!!
WHOA!!
ARASHIRO-SAN'S ALREADY TAKEN OFF
OOH, THIS RIDES REALLY NICELY!
WE'RE ABOUT THE SAME HEIGHT, SO OUR BIKES WERE ABOUT THE SAME SIZE TOO.
DOES THIS MEAN I'VE KIND OF RIDDEN IN THE TOUR DE FRANCE TOO!?
RUMBLE
THIS IS AMAZING! MORE AMAZING THAN I'D EVER DREAMED! IT'S SO EASY TO RIDE!
NOT AT ALL.
IT WAS A MERE 800M RIDE AROUND THE TRACK, BUT I FELT INCREDIBLY FULFILLED.
YOU SURE ARE A NICE GUY, ARASHIRO-SAN! BEST OF LUCK WITH EVERYTHING!
HA-HA-HA!
BUT IF YOU WANT TO KNOW HOW THE SADDLE FELT...
WELL...I WAS JUST SO MOVED BY THE WHOLE EXPERIENCE THAT I DON'T REMEMBER THE SADDLE AT ALL...
BUT IT SURE WAS EASY TO RIDE ON!
TO BE CONTINUED!
BICYCLES SURE ARE FUN!!

YOWAMUSHI PEDAL

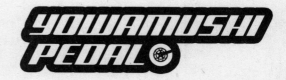

RIDE.164 THE ENCROACHING PELOTON

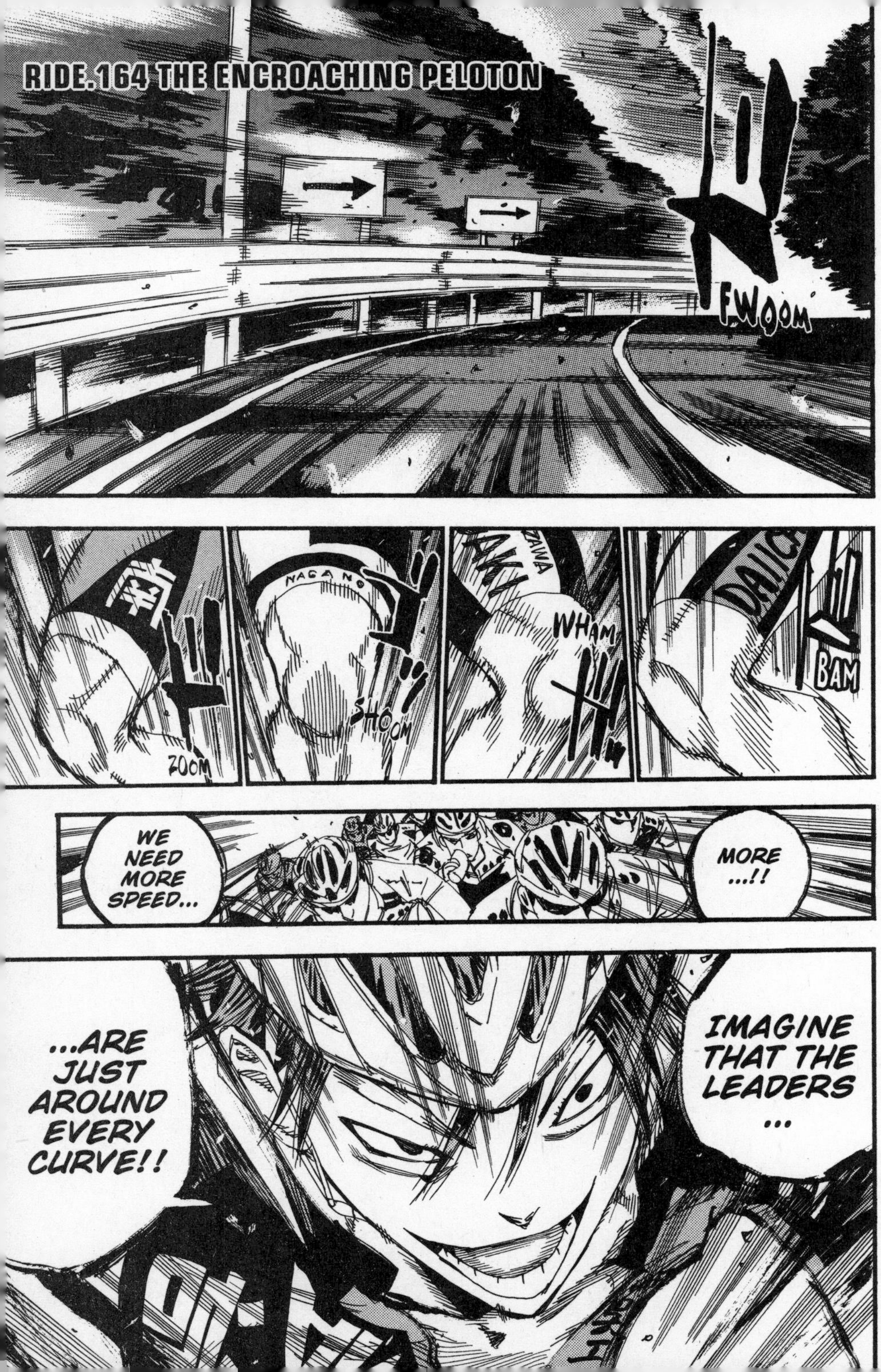
FWOOM
BAM
WHAM
NAGANO
SHOOM
ZOOM
MORE ...!!
WE NEED MORE SPEED...
IMAGINE THAT THE LEADERS ...
...ARE JUST AROUND EVERY CURVE!!

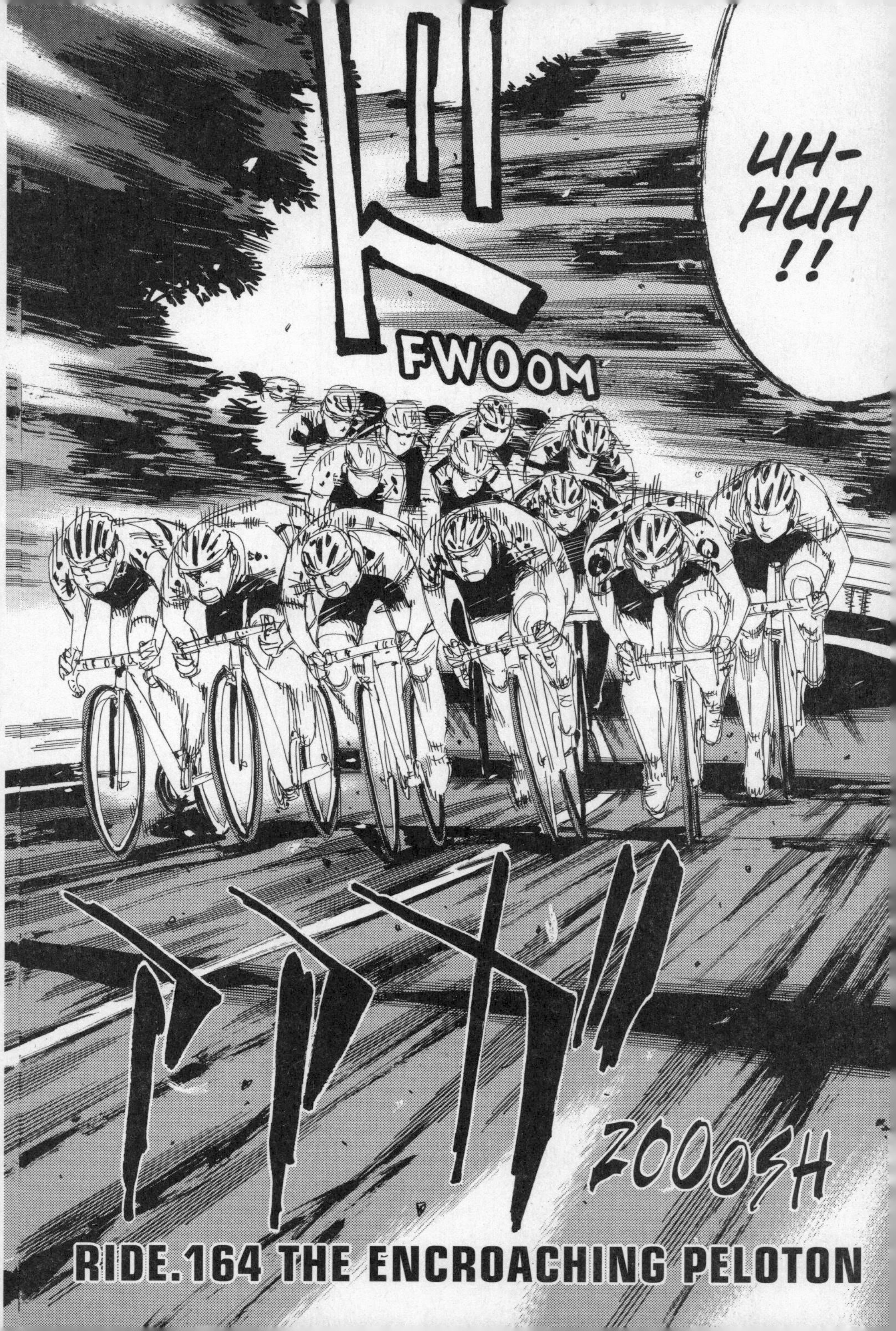
UH-HUH!!
FWOOM
ZOOOSH
RIDE. 164 THE ENCROACHING PELOTON

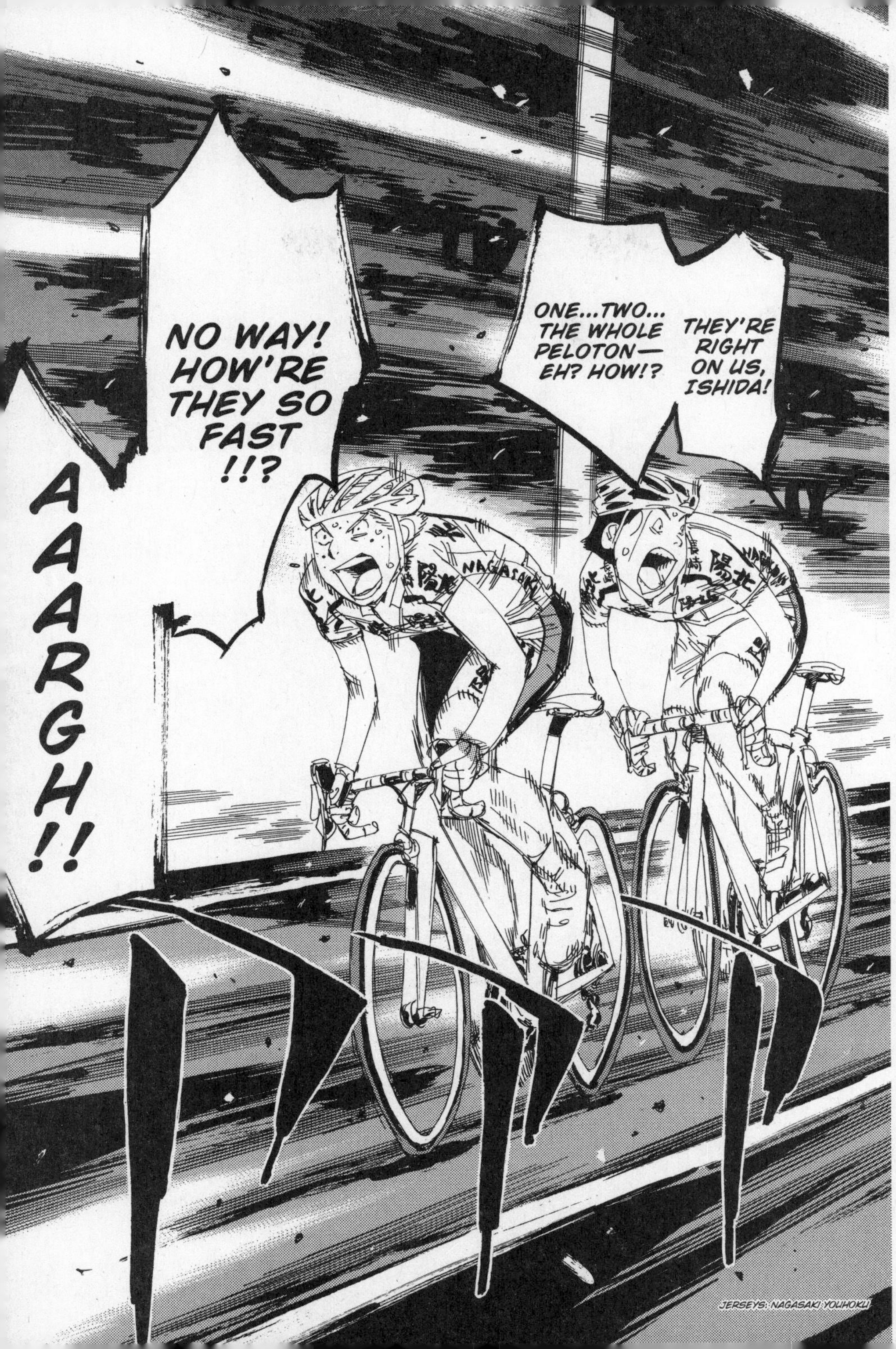
THEY'RE RIGHT ON US, ISHIDA!
ONE...TWO... THE WHOLE PELOTON— EH? HOW!?
NO WAY! HOW'RE THEY SO FAST!!?
AAAARGH!!
JERSEYS: NAGASAKI YOUHOKU

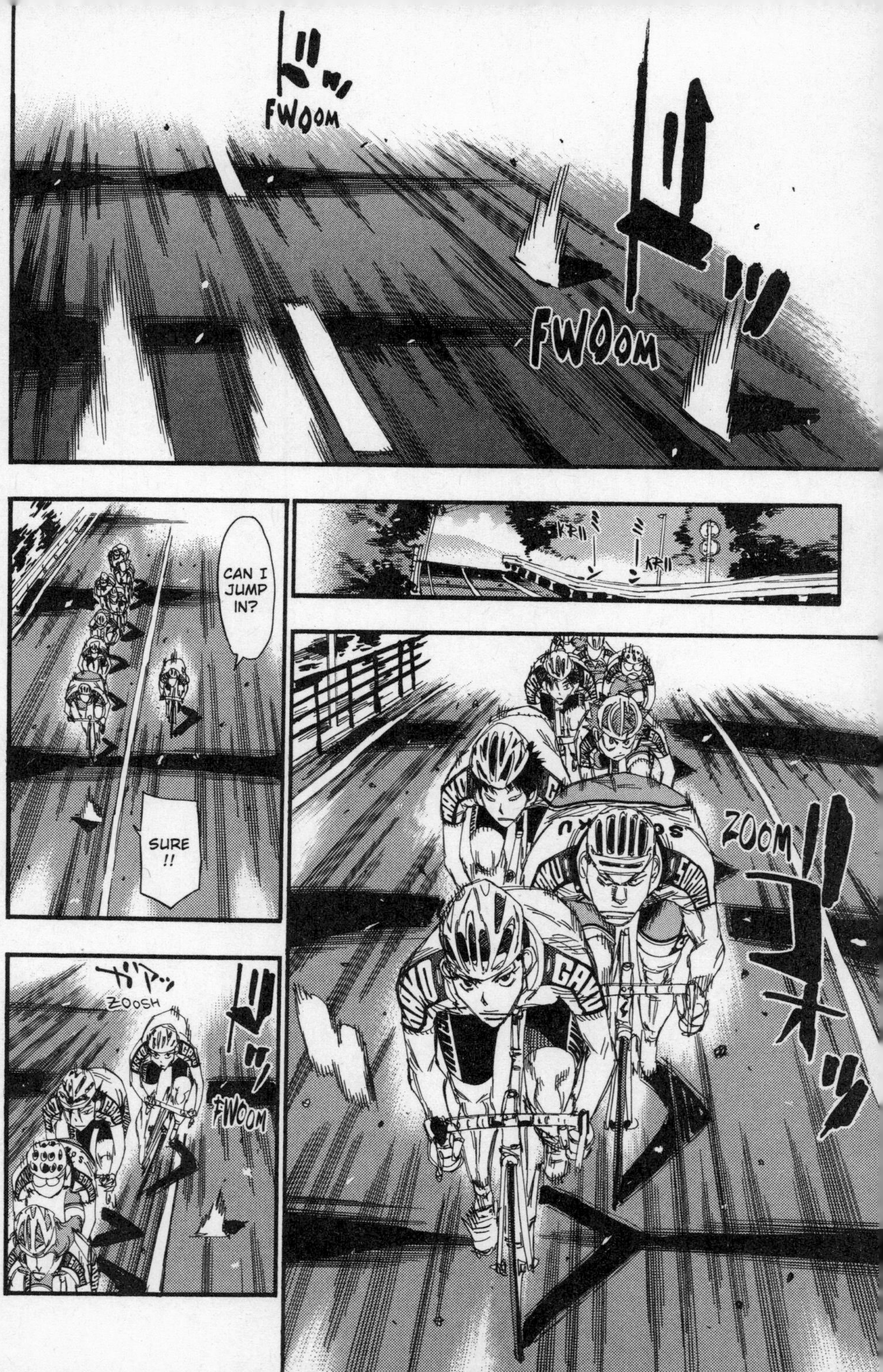
FWOOM
FWOOM
KRII
KRII
ZOOM
CAN I JUMP IN?
SURE !!
ZOOSH
FWOOM

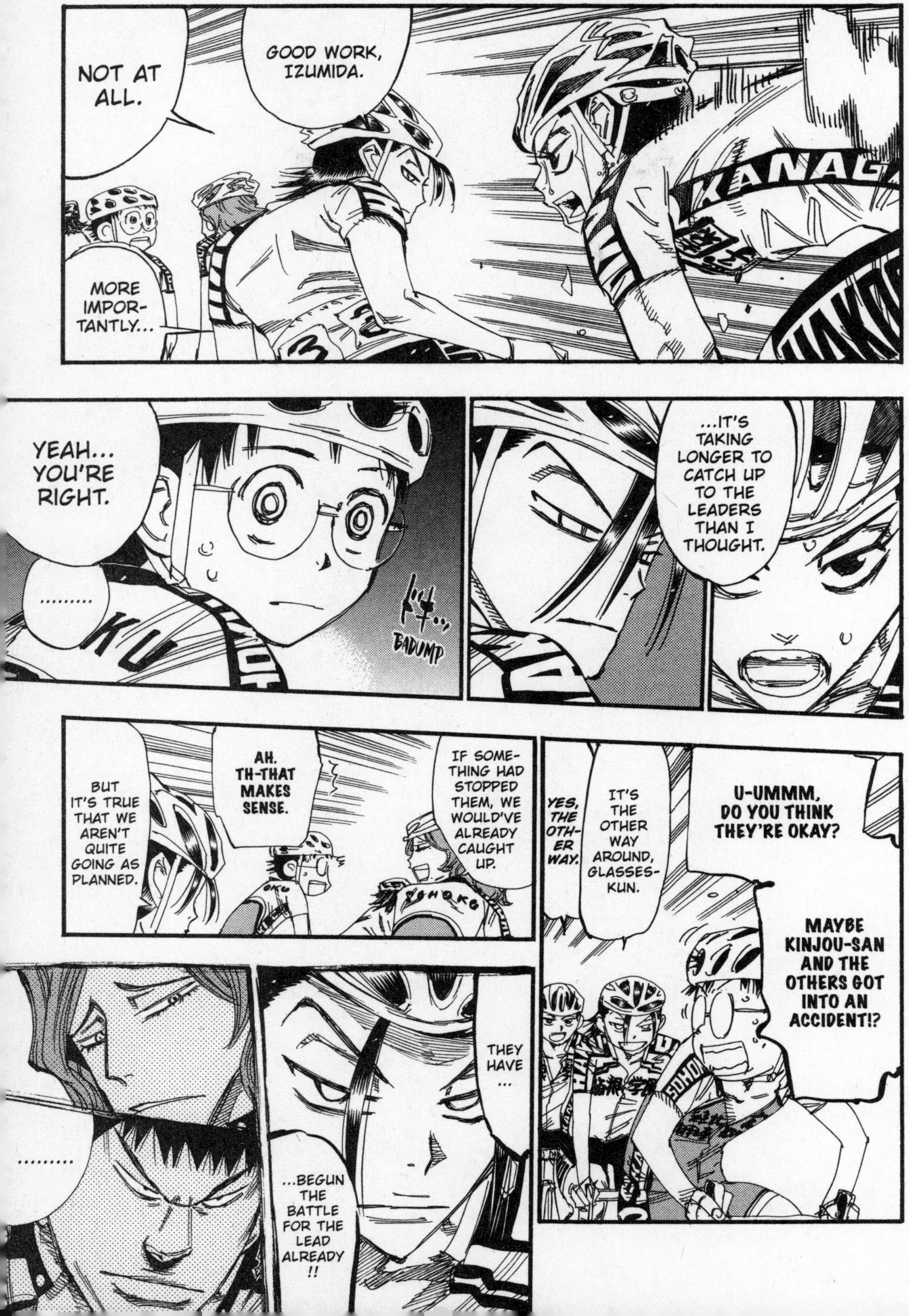
GOOD WORK, IZUMIDA.
NOT AT ALL.
MORE IMPORTANTLY...
...IT'S TAKING LONGER TO CATCH UP TO THE LEADERS THAN I THOUGHT.
YEAH... YOU'RE RIGHT.
....
BADUMP
U-UMMM, DO YOU THINK THEY'RE OKAY?
MAYBE KINJOU-SAN AND THE OTHERS GOT INTO AN ACCIDENT!?
IT'S THE OTHER WAY AROUND, GLASSES-KUN.
YES, THE OTHER WAY.
IF SOMETHING HAD STOPPED THEM, WE WOULD'VE ALREADY CAUGHT UP.
AH. TH-THAT MAKES SENSE.
BUT IT'S TRUE THAT WE AREN'T QUITE GOING AS PLANNED.
THEY HAVE...
...BEGUN THE BATTLE FOR THE LEAD ALREADY!!
....

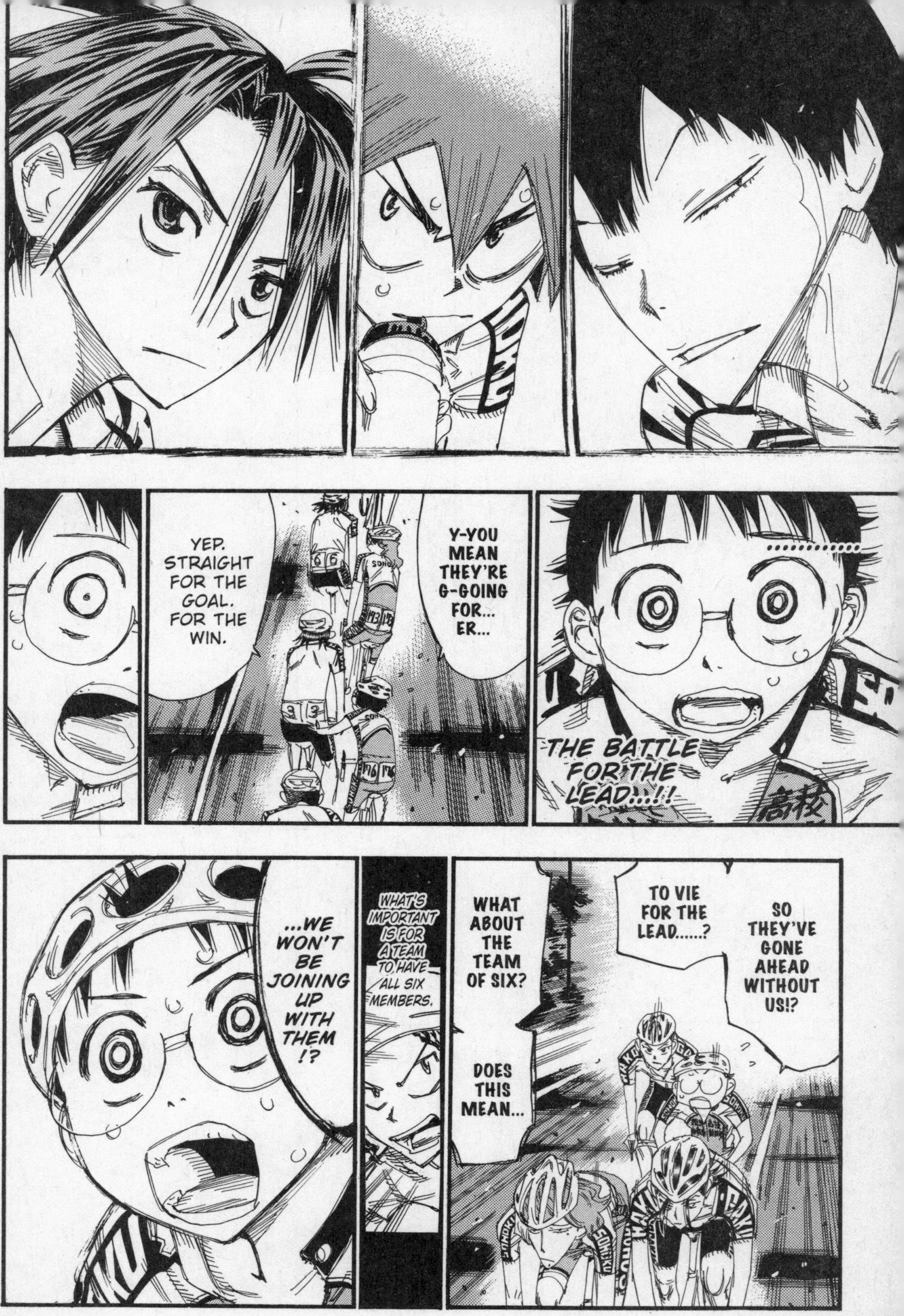

....
THE BATTLE FOR THE LEAD...!!
Y-YOU MEAN THEY'RE G-GOING FOR... ER...
YEP. STRAIGHT FOR THE GOAL. FOR THE WIN.
SO THEY'VE GONE AHEAD WITHOUT US!?
TO VIE FOR THE LEAD......?
WHAT ABOUT THE TEAM OF SIX?
DOES THIS MEAN...
WHAT'S IMPORTANT IS FOR A TEAM TO HAVE ALL SIX MEMBERS.
...WE WON'T BE JOINING UP WITH THEM!?

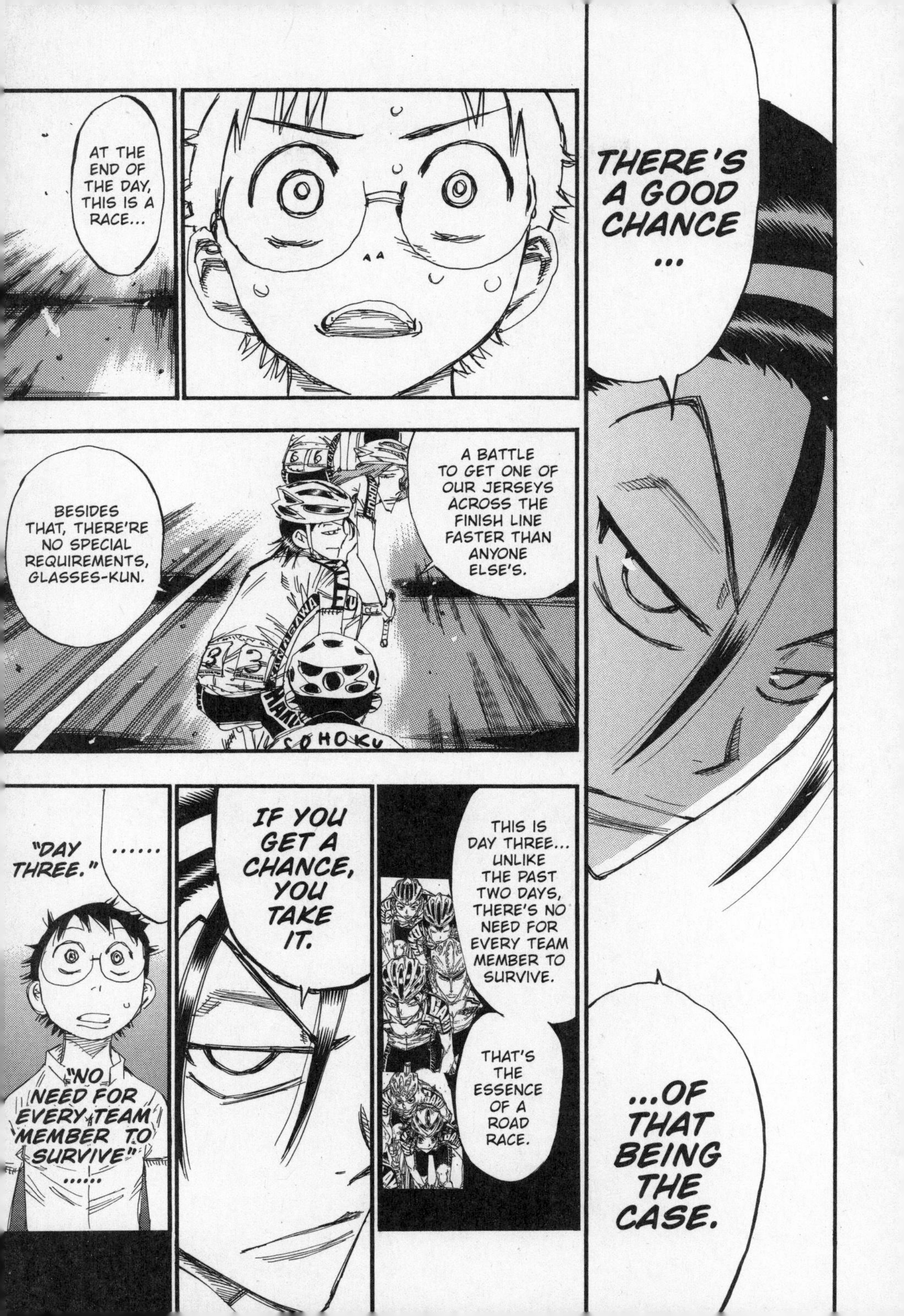
THERE'S A GOOD CHANCE ...
...OF THAT BEING THE CASE.
AT THE END OF THE DAY, THIS IS A RACE...
A BATTLE TO GET ONE OF OUR JERSEYS ACROSS THE FINISH LINE FASTER THAN ANYONE ELSE'S.
BESIDES THAT, THERE'RE NO SPECIAL REQUIREMENTS, GLASSES-KUN.
SOHOKU
THIS IS DAY THREE... UNLIKE THE PAST TWO DAYS, THERE'S NO NEED FOR EVERY TEAM MEMBER TO SURVIVE.
THAT'S THE ESSENCE OF A ROAD RACE.
IF YOU GET A CHANCE, YOU TAKE IT.
......
"DAY THREE."
"NO NEED FOR EVERY TEAM MEMBER TO SURVIVE" ......

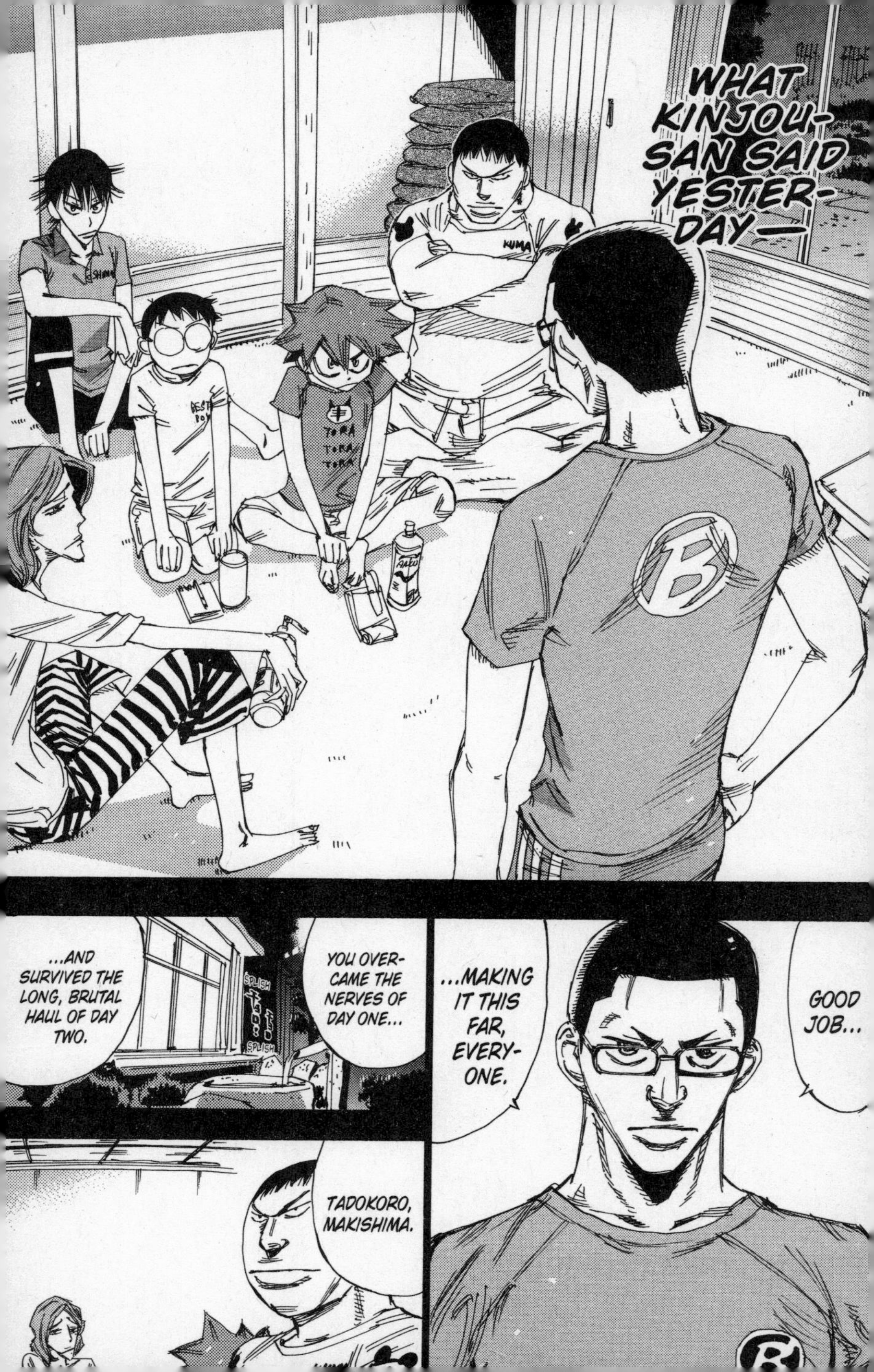
WHAT KINJOU-SAN SAID YESTER-DAY—
GOOD JOB...
...MAKING IT THIS FAR, EVERY-ONE.
YOU OVER-CAME THE NERVES OF DAY ONE...
...AND SURVIVED THE LONG, BRUTAL HAUL OF DAY TWO.
SPLISH
SPLISH
TADOKORO, MAKISHIMA.

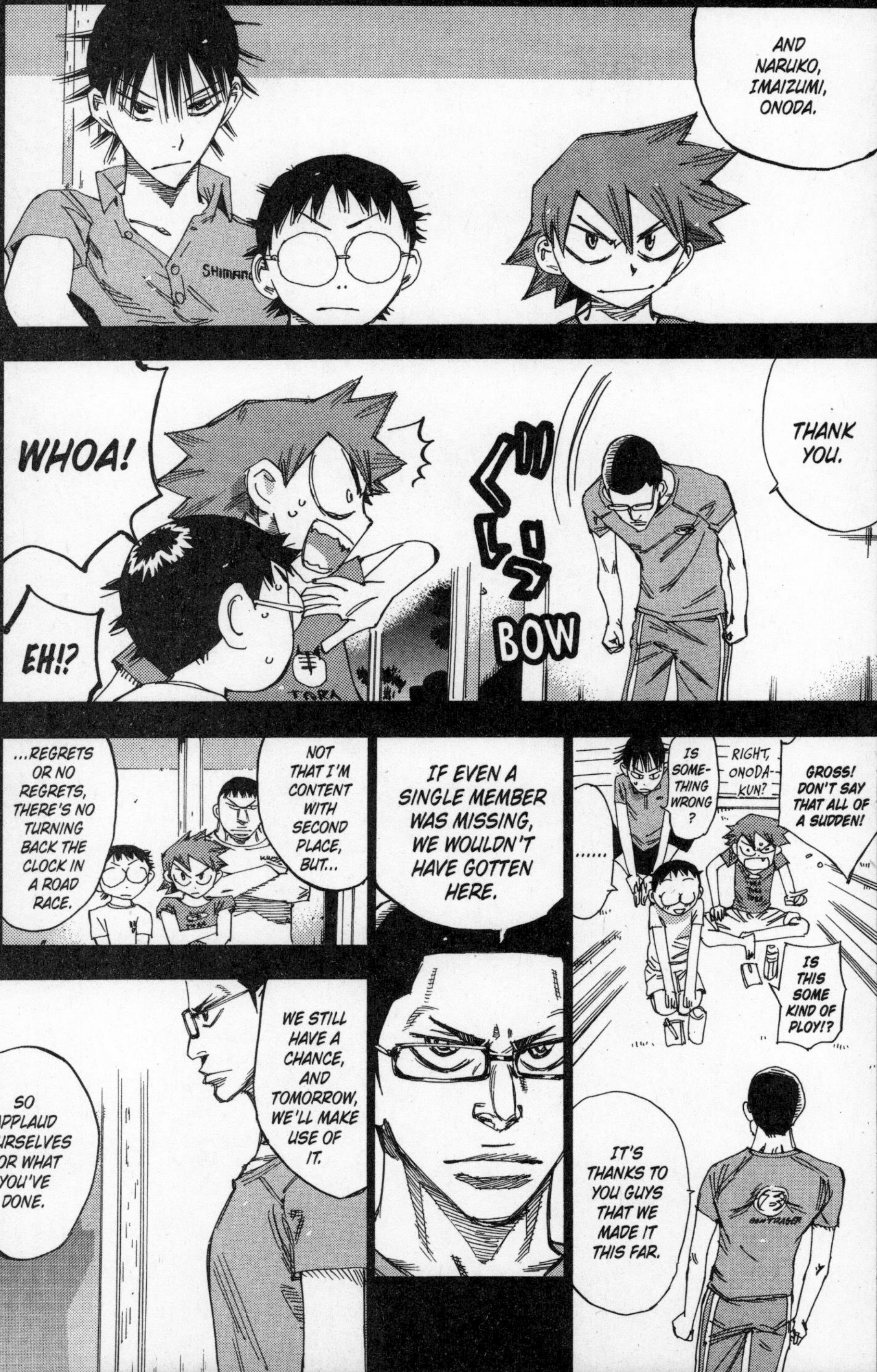
AND NARUKO, IMAIZUMI, ONODA.
THANK YOU.
BOW
WHOA!
EH!?
GROSS! DON'T SAY THAT ALL OF A SUDDEN!
RIGHT, ONODA-KUN?
IS SOMETHING WRONG?
......
IS THIS SOME KIND OF PLOY!?
IT'S THANKS TO YOU GUYS THAT WE MADE IT THIS FAR.
IF EVEN A SINGLE MEMBER WAS MISSING, WE WOULDN'T HAVE GOTTEN HERE.
NOT THAT I'M CONTENT WITH SECOND PLACE, BUT...
...REGRETS OR NO REGRETS, THERE'S NO TURNING BACK THE CLOCK IN A ROAD RACE.
WE STILL HAVE A CHANCE, AND TOMORROW, WE'LL MAKE USE OF IT.
SO APPLAUD YOURSELVES FOR WHAT YOU'VE DONE.

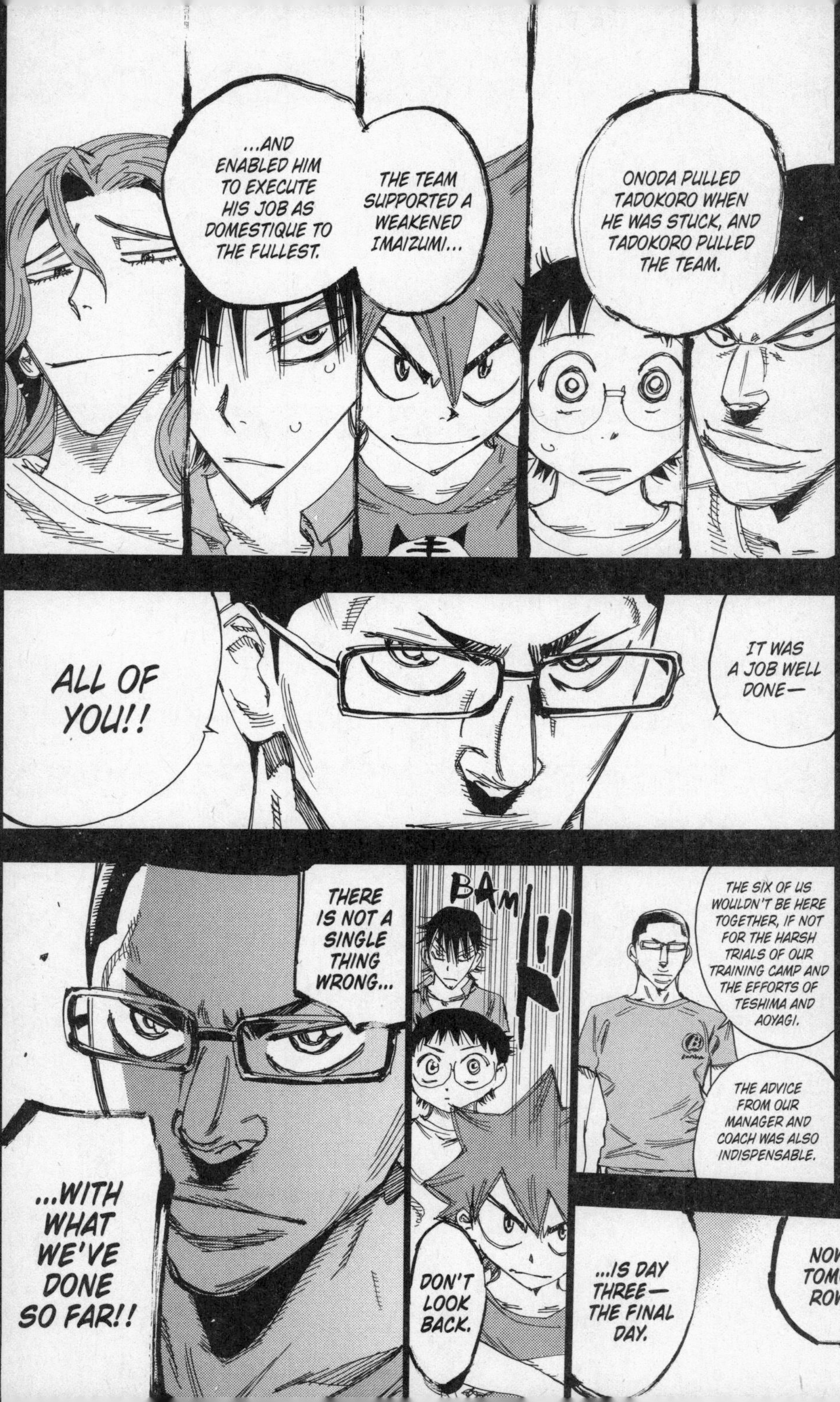

ONODA PULLED TADOKORO WHEN HE WAS STUCK, AND TADOKORO PULLED THE TEAM.
THE TEAM SUPPORTED A WEAKENED IMAIZUMI...
...AND ENABLED HIM TO EXECUTE HIS JOB AS DOMESTIQUE TO THE FULLEST.
IT WAS A JOB WELL DONE—
ALL OF YOU!!
THE SIX OF US WOULDN'T BE HERE TOGETHER, IF NOT FOR THE HARSH TRIALS OF OUR TRAINING CAMP AND THE EFFORTS OF TESHIMA AND AOYAGI.
THE ADVICE FROM OUR MANAGER AND COACH WAS ALSO INDISPENSABLE.
NOW... TOMOR-ROW...
...IS DAY THREE— THE FINAL DAY.
BAM!!
THERE IS NOT A SINGLE THING WRONG...
DON'T LOOK BACK.
...WITH WHAT WE'VE DONE SO FAR!!

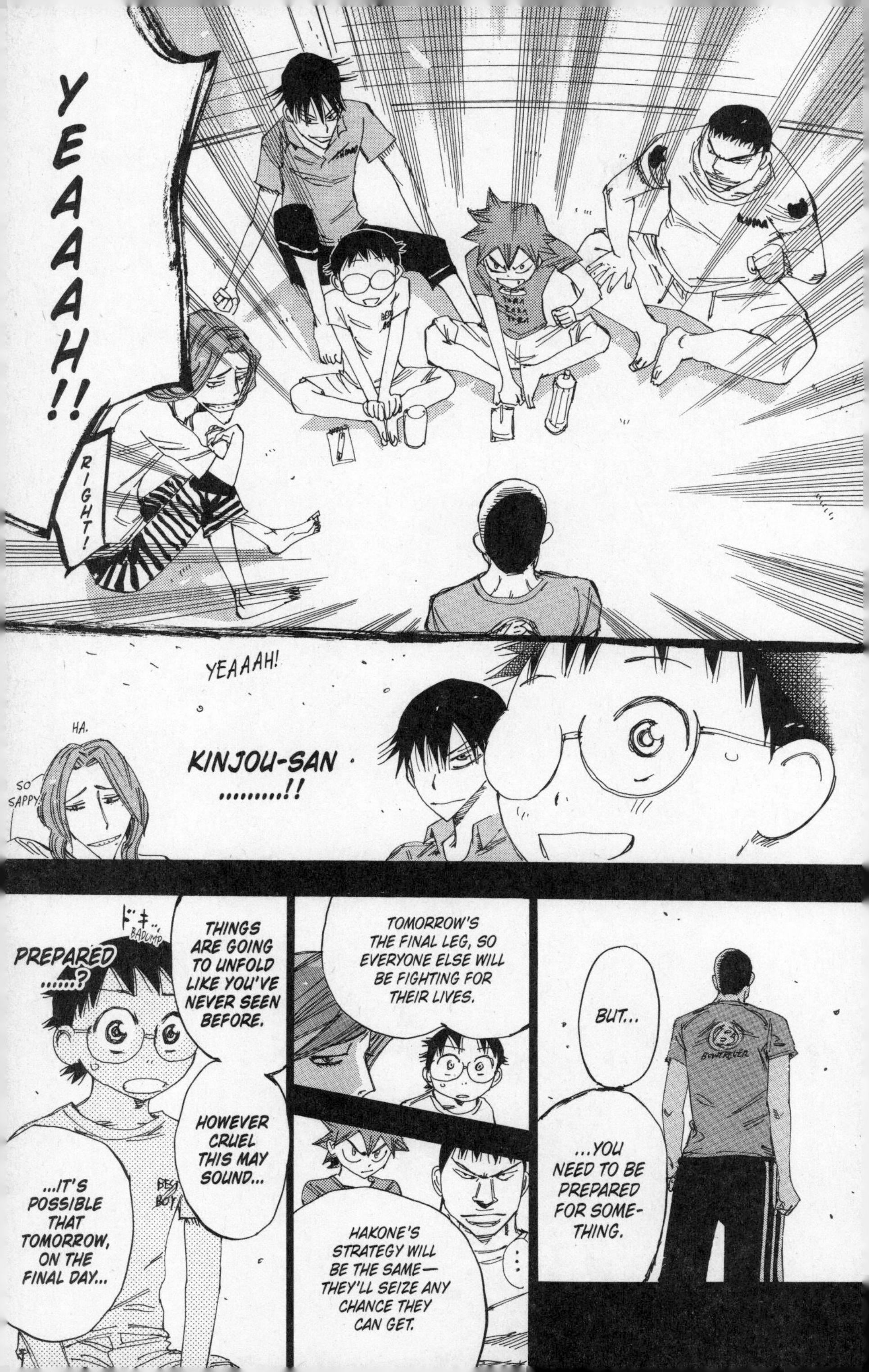
YEAAAAH!!
RIGHT!
KINJOU-SAN ....!!
YEAAAH!
HA.
SO SAPPY!
BUT...
...YOU NEED TO BE PREPARED FOR SOME-THING.
TOMORROW'S THE FINAL LEG, SO EVERYONE ELSE WILL BE FIGHTING FOR THEIR LIVES.
HAKONE'S STRATEGY WILL BE THE SAME—THEY'LL SEIZE ANY CHANCE THEY CAN GET.
...
THINGS ARE GOING TO UNFOLD LIKE YOU'VE NEVER SEEN BEFORE.
HOWEVER CRUEL THIS MAY SOUND...
...IT'S POSSIBLE THAT TOMORROW, ON THE FINAL DAY...
ドキ..
BADUMP
PREPARED ......?

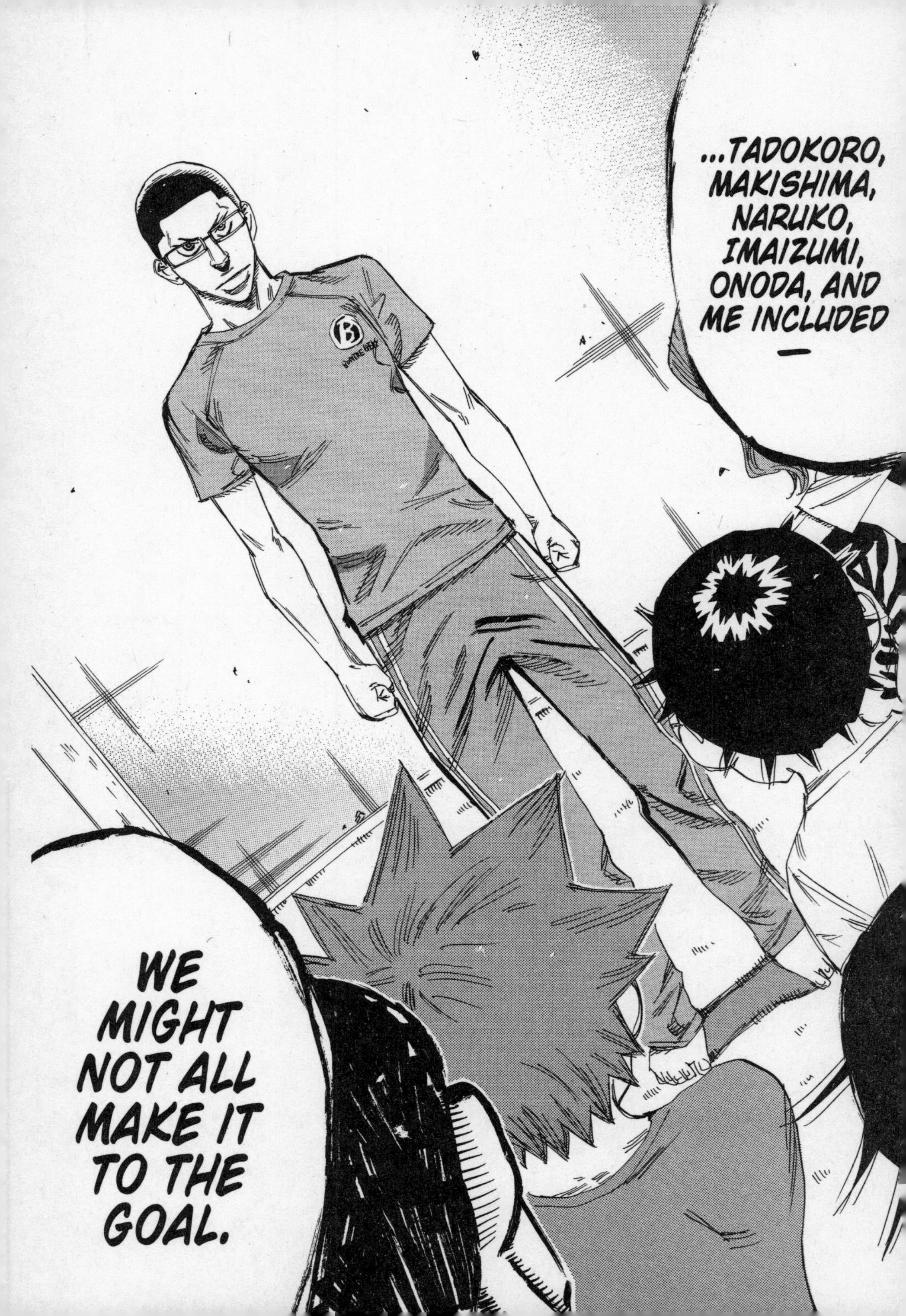
...TADOKORO, MAKISHIMA, NARUKO, IMAIZUMI, ONODA, AND ME INCLUDED—
WE MIGHT NOT ALL MAKE IT TO THE GOAL.

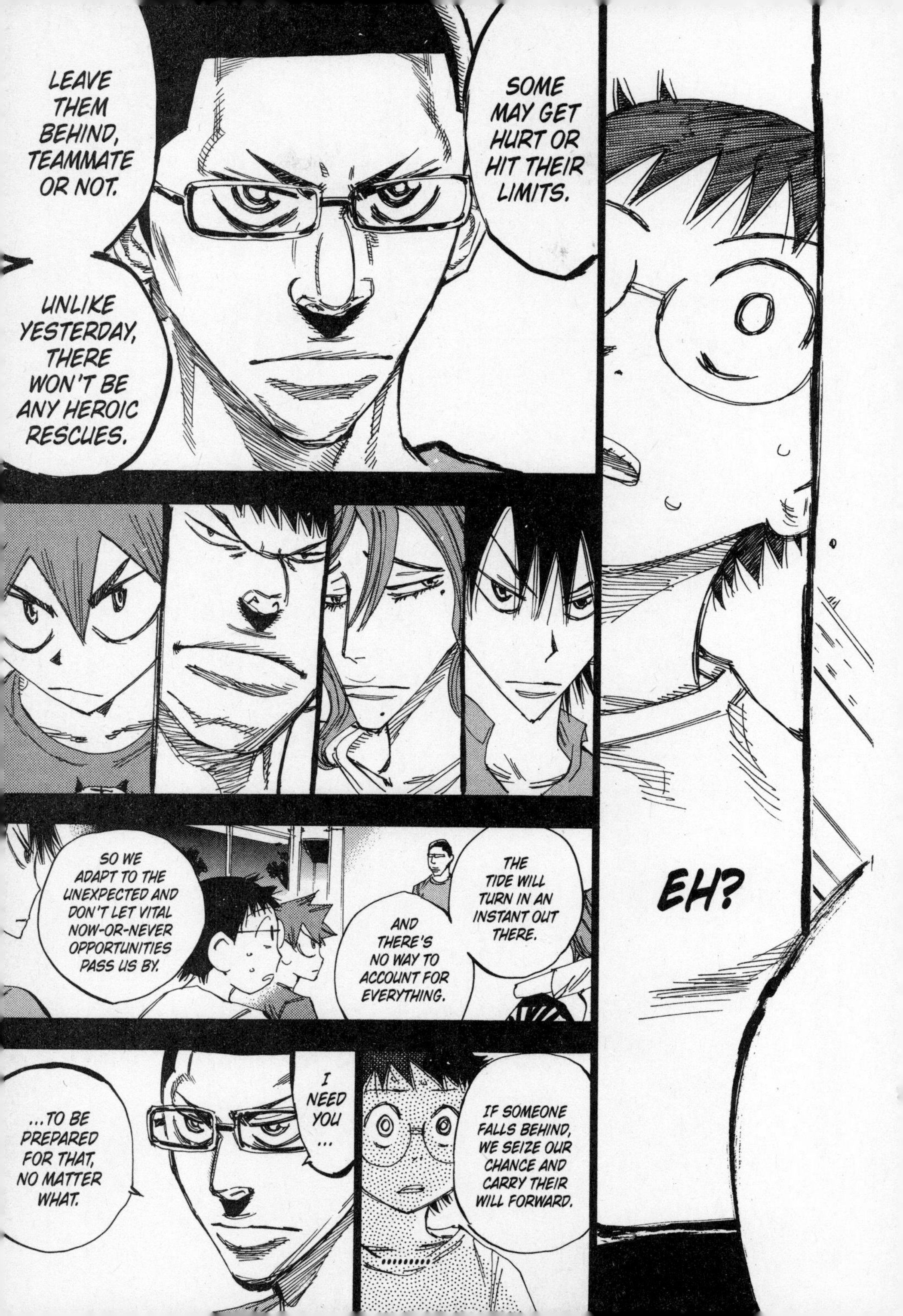
EH?
SOME MAY GET HURT OR HIT THEIR LIMITS.
LEAVE THEM BEHIND, TEAMMATE OR NOT.
UNLIKE YESTERDAY, THERE WON'T BE ANY HEROIC RESCUES.
THE TIDE WILL TURN IN AN INSTANT OUT THERE.
AND THERE'S NO WAY TO ACCOUNT FOR EVERYTHING.
SO WE ADAPT TO THE UNEXPECTED AND DON'T LET VITAL NOW-OR-NEVER OPPORTUNITIES PASS US BY.
IF SOMEONE FALLS BEHIND, WE SEIZE OUR CHANCE AND CARRY THEIR WILL FORWARD.
I NEED YOU ...
...TO BE PREPARED FOR THAT, NO MATTER WHAT.

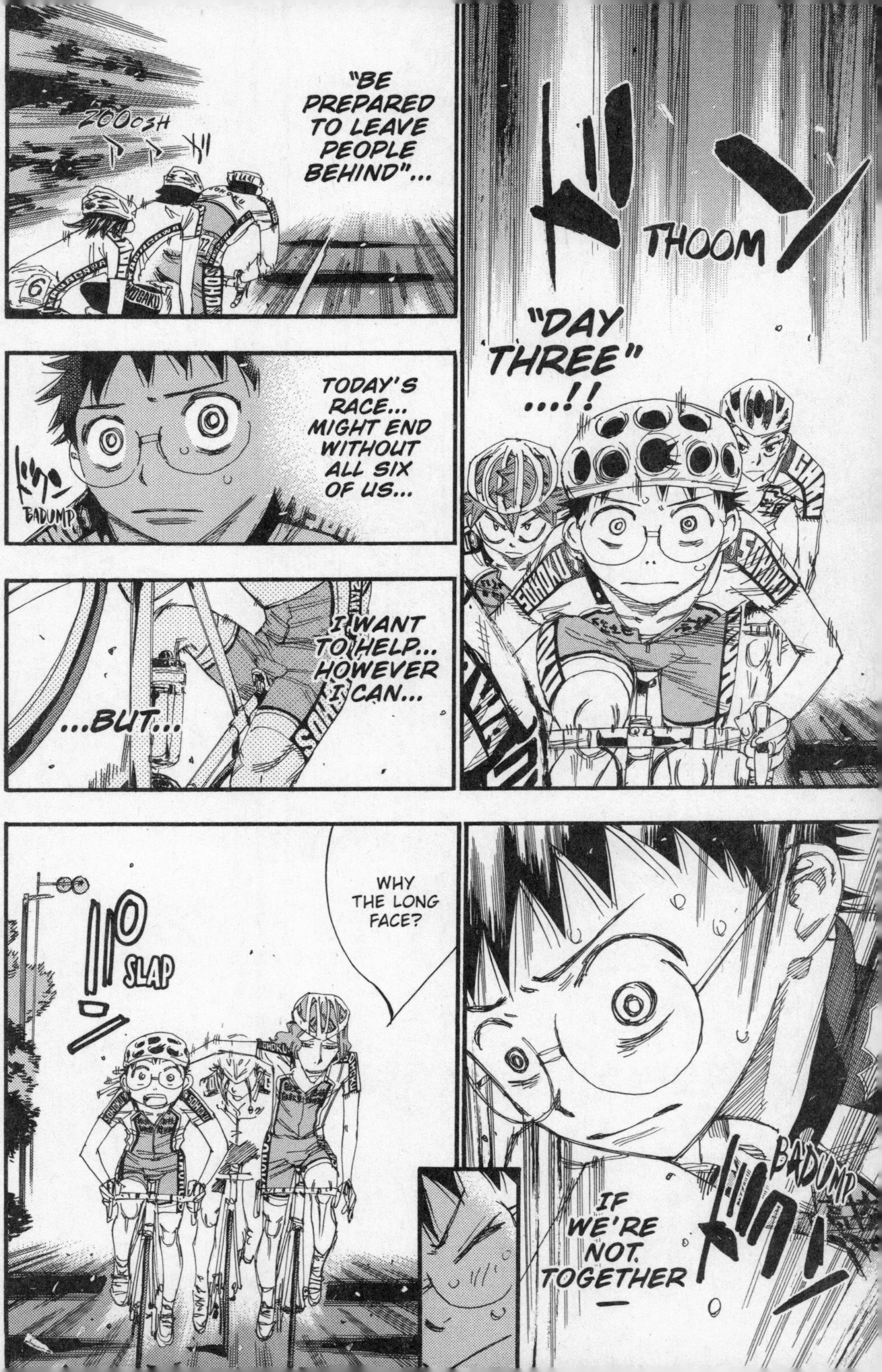
THOOM
"DAY THREE" ...!!
"BE PREPARED TO LEAVE PEOPLE BEHIND"...
ZOOOSH
TODAY'S RACE... MIGHT END WITHOUT ALL SIX OF US...
BADUMP
I WANT TO HELP... HOWEVER I CAN...
...BUT...
BADUMP
IF WE'RE NOT TOGETHER —
WHY THE LONG FACE?
SLAP

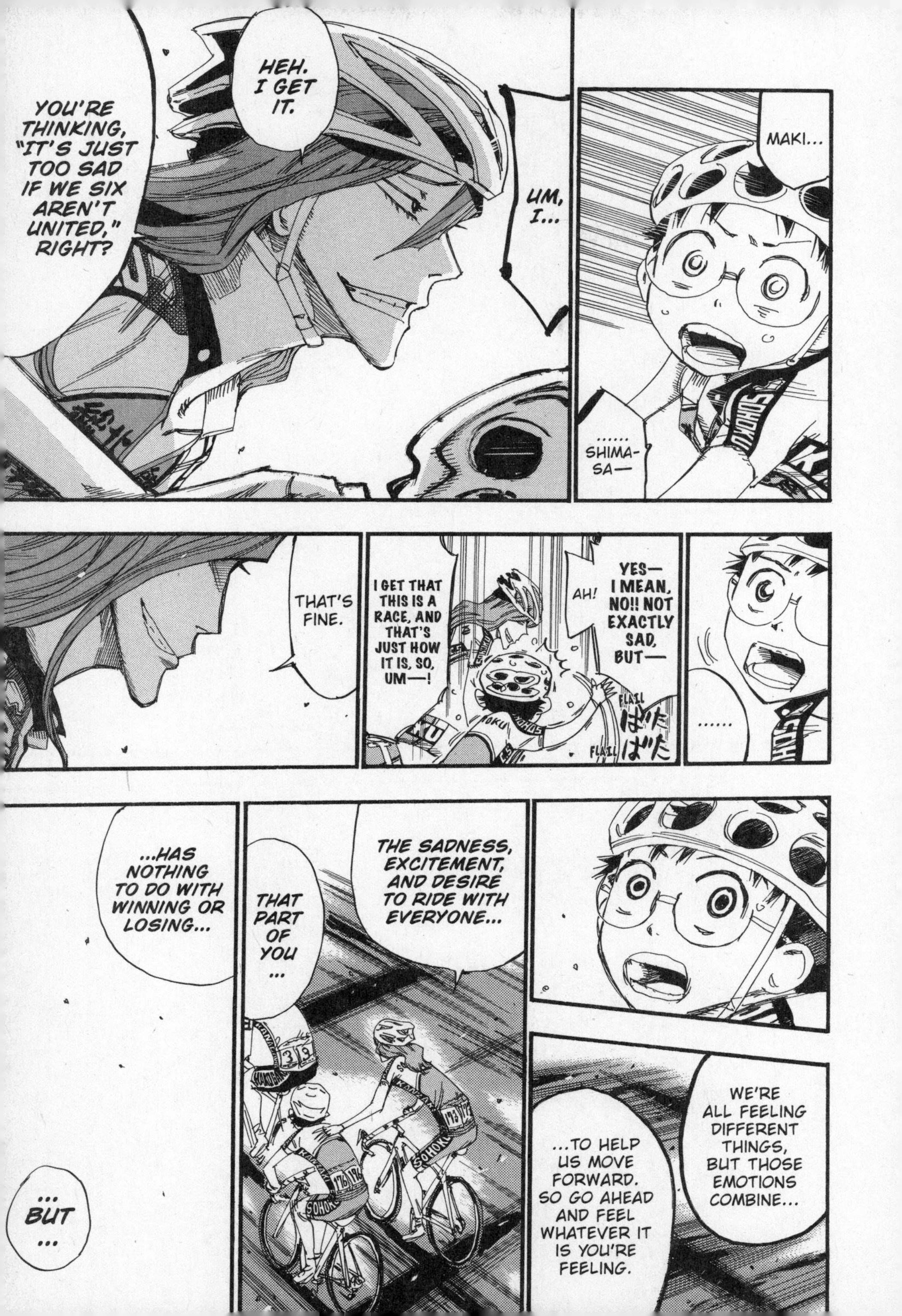
MAKI...
......SHIMA-SA—
UM, I...
HEH. I GET IT.
YOU'RE THINKING, "IT'S JUST TOO SAD IF WE SIX AREN'T UNITED," RIGHT?
......
YES— I MEAN, NO!! NOT EXACTLY SAD, BUT—
AH!
FLAIL ぱた
FLAIL ぱた
I GET THAT THIS IS A RACE, AND THAT'S JUST HOW IT IS, SO, UM—!
THAT'S FINE.
THE SADNESS, EXCITEMENT, AND DESIRE TO RIDE WITH EVERYONE...
THAT PART OF YOU ...
...HAS NOTHING TO DO WITH WINNING OR LOSING...
... BUT ...
WE'RE ALL FEELING DIFFERENT THINGS, BUT THOSE EMOTIONS COMBINE...
...TO HELP US MOVE FORWARD. SO GO AHEAD AND FEEL WHATEVER IT IS YOU'RE FEELING.

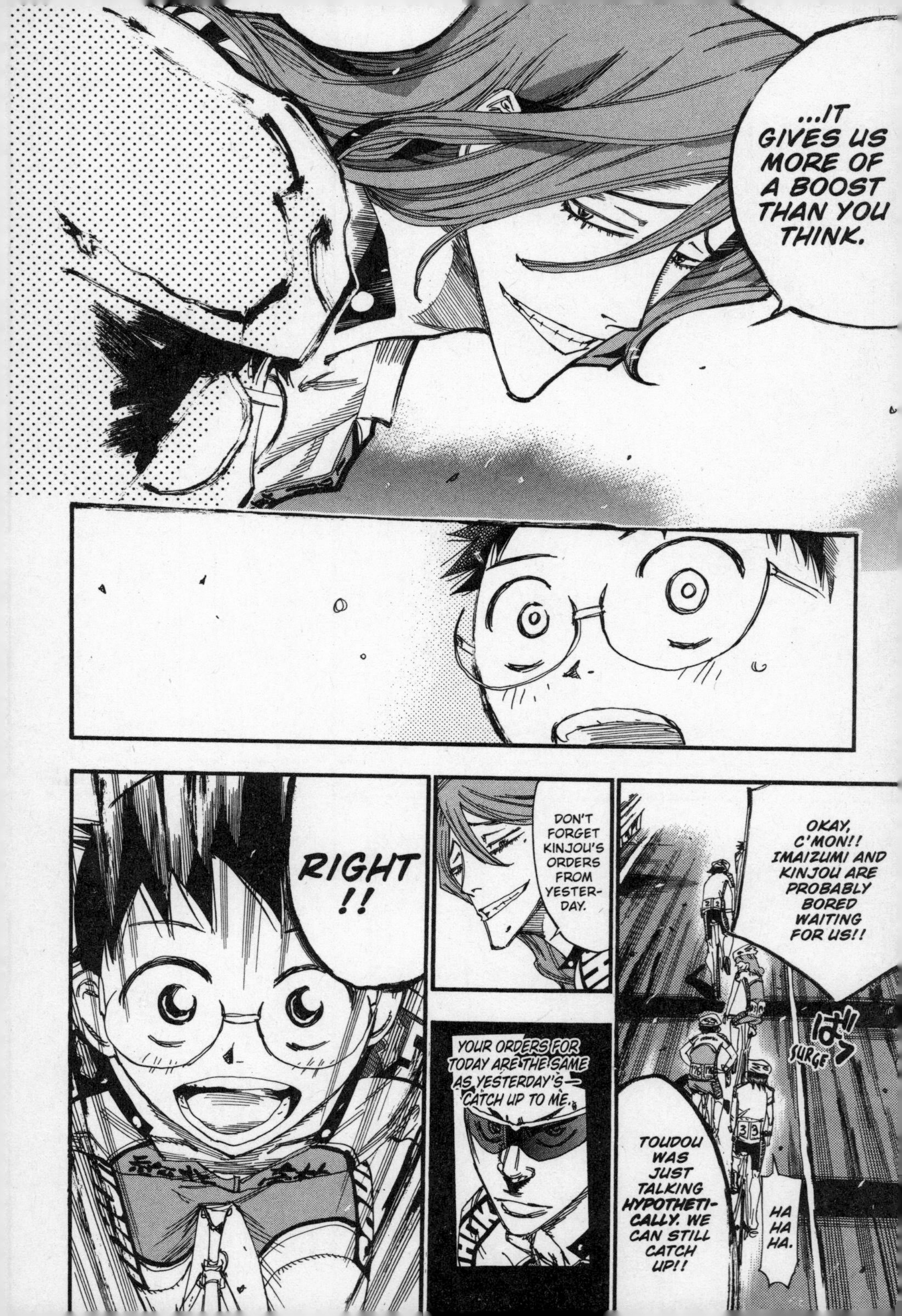
...IT GIVES US MORE OF A BOOST THAN YOU THINK.
OKAY, C'MON!! IMAIZUMI AND KINJOU ARE PROBABLY BORED WAITING FOR US!!
ぱっ
SURGE
TOUDOU WAS JUST TALKING HYPOTHETICALLY. WE CAN STILL CATCH UP!!
HA HA HA.
DON'T FORGET KINJOU'S ORDERS FROM YESTERDAY.
YOUR ORDERS FOR TODAY ARE THE SAME AS YESTERDAY'S— CATCH UP TO ME.
RIGHT!!

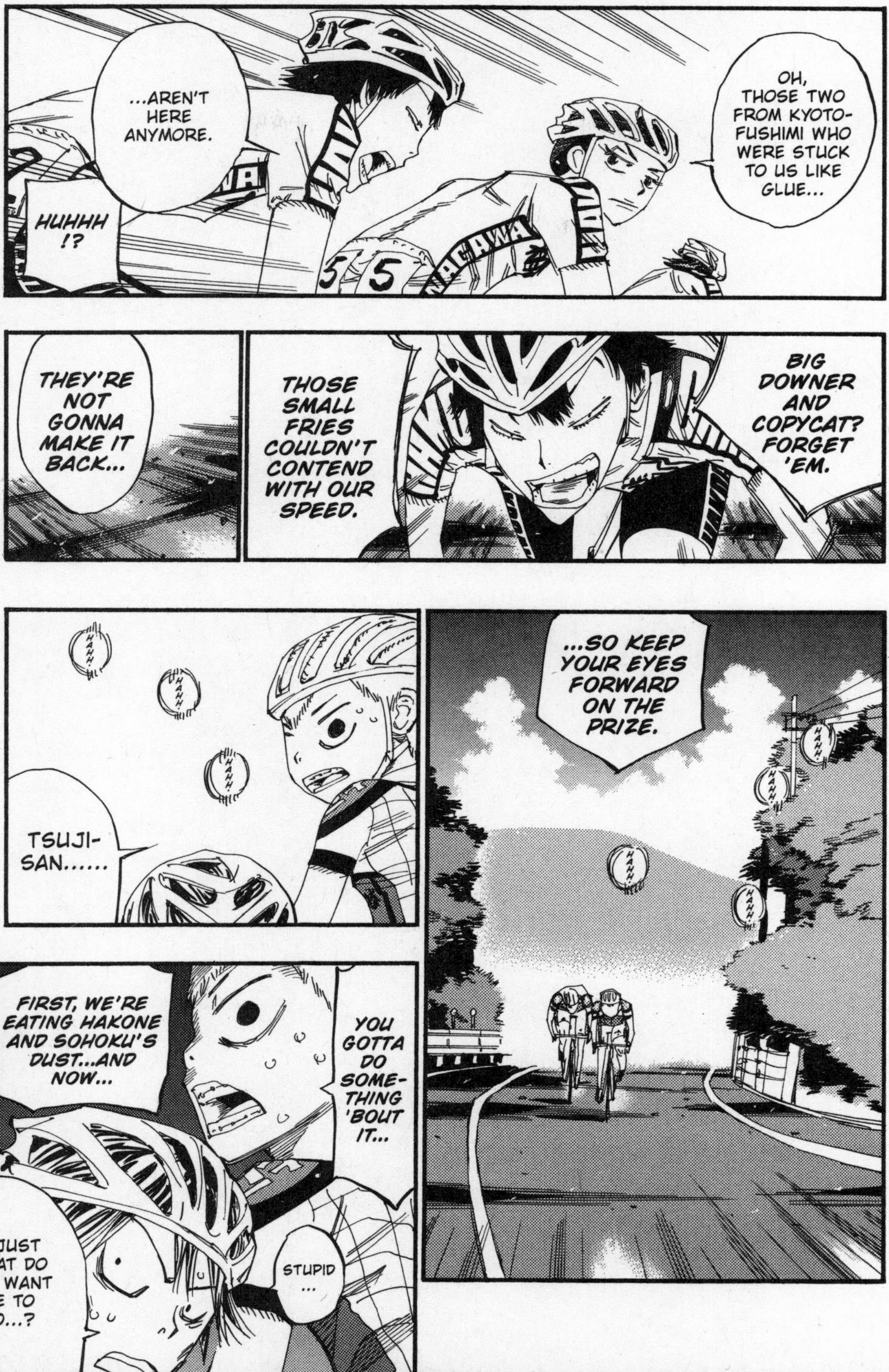
OH, THOSE TWO FROM KYOTO-FUSHIMI WHO WERE STUCK TO US LIKE GLUE...
...AREN'T HERE ANYMORE.
HUHHH!?
BIG DOWNER AND COPYCAT? FORGET 'EM.
THOSE SMALL FRIES COULDN'T CONTEND WITH OUR SPEED.
THEY'RE NOT GONNA MAKE IT BACK...
...SO KEEP YOUR EYES FORWARD ON THE PRIZE.
TSUJI-SAN......
YOU GOTTA DO SOMETHING 'BOUT IT...
FIRST, WE'RE EATING HAKONE AND SOHOKU'S DUST...AND NOW...
STUPID...
...JUST WHAT DO YOU WANT ME TO DO...?

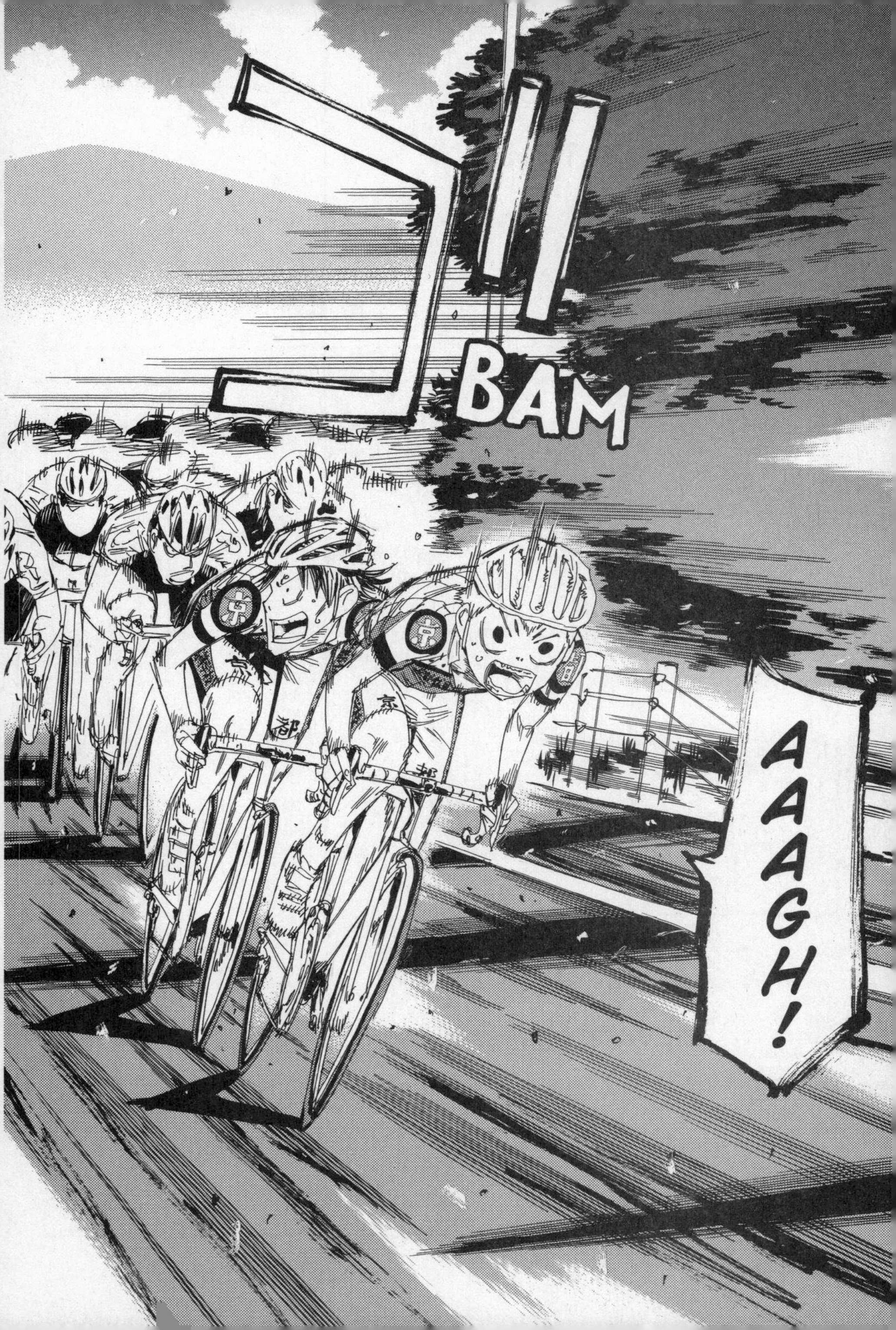
BAM
AAAGH!

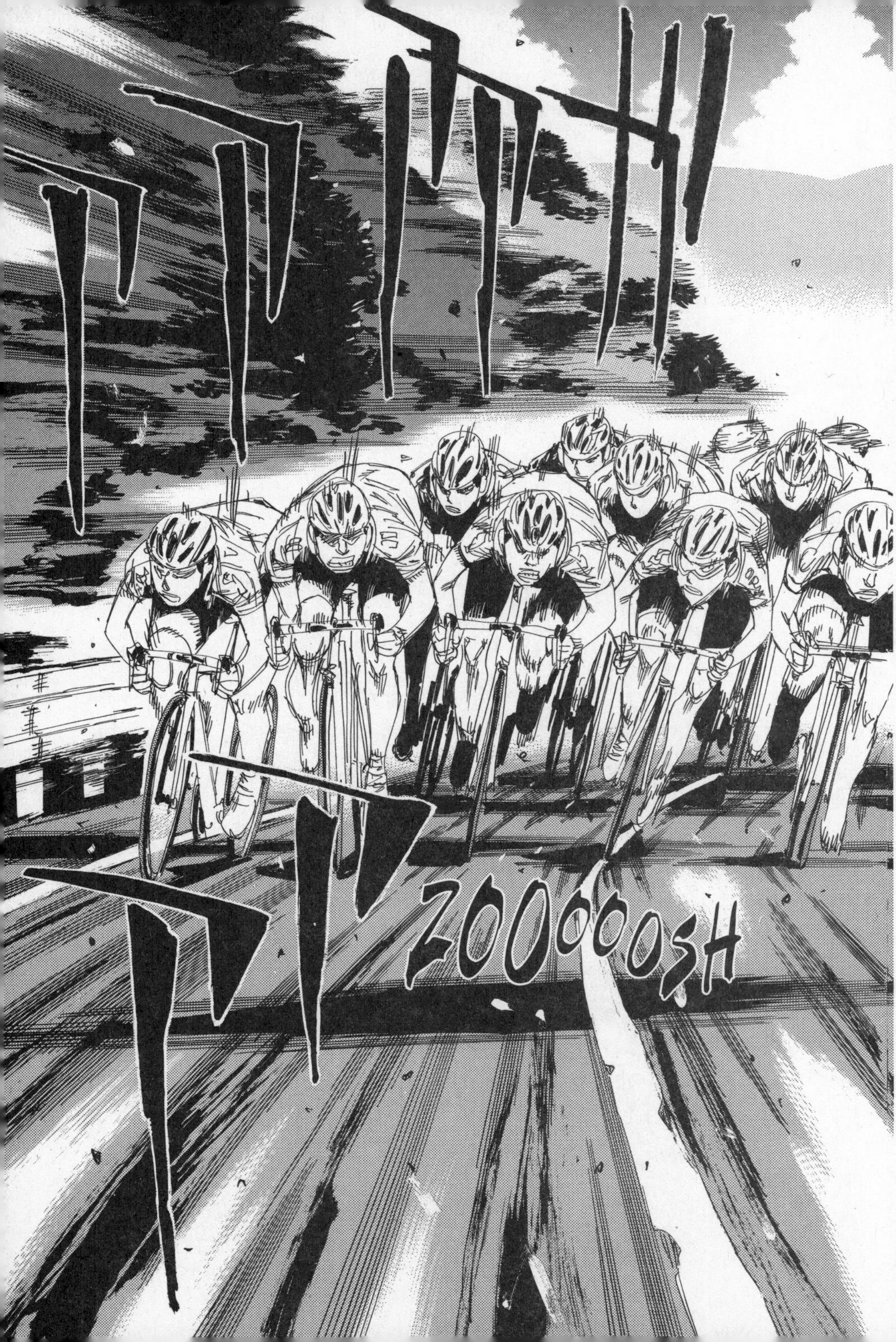
ZOOOOOSH

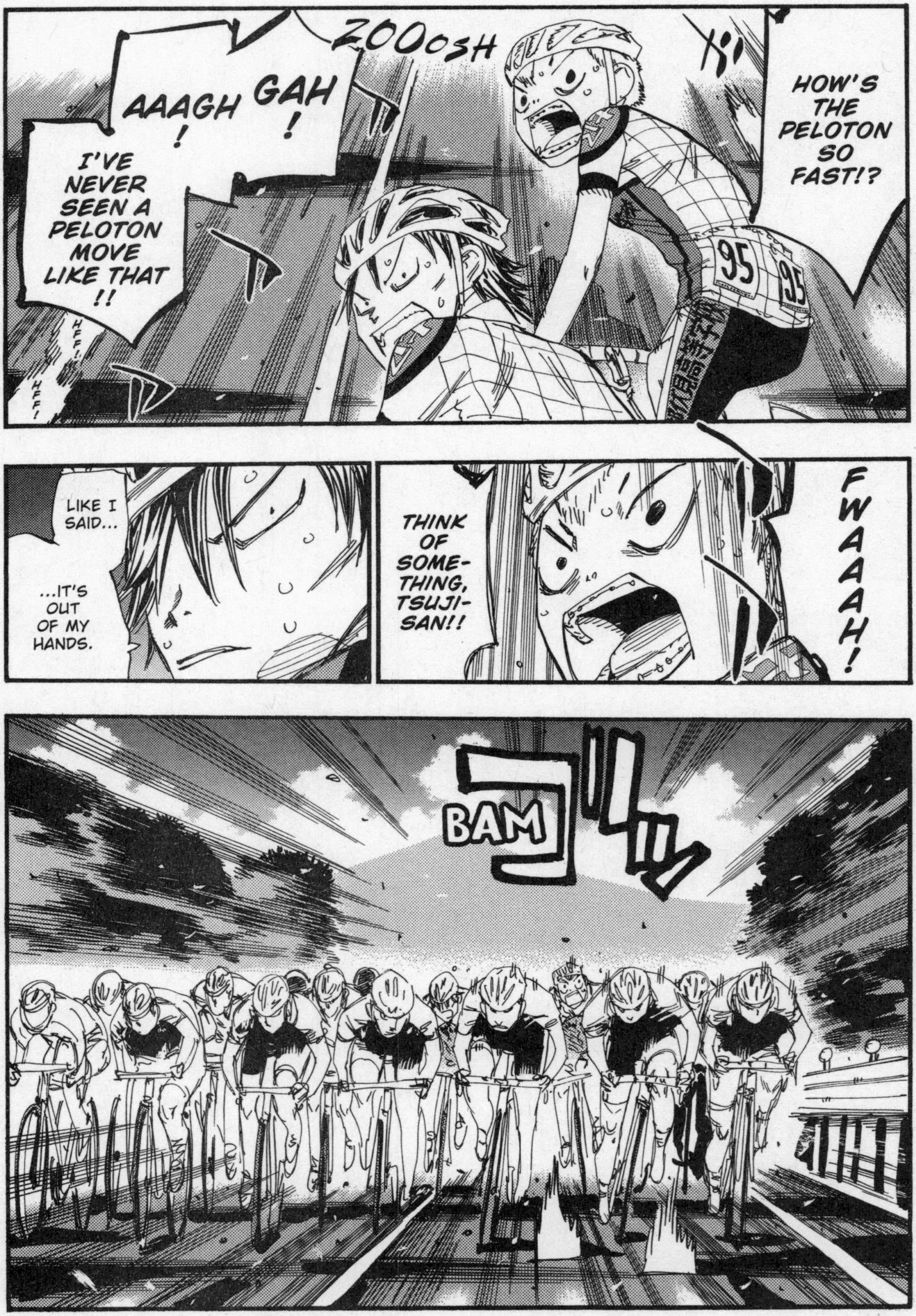
HOW'S THE PELOTON SO FAST!?
ZOOOOSH
GAH!
AAAGH!
I'VE NEVER SEEN A PELOTON MOVE LIKE THAT!!
HFF! HFF!
FWAAAH!
THINK OF SOME-THING, TSUJI-SAN!!
LIKE I SAID...
...IT'S OUT OF MY HANDS.
BAM

RIDE.165 HIROSHIMA'S KUREMINAMI

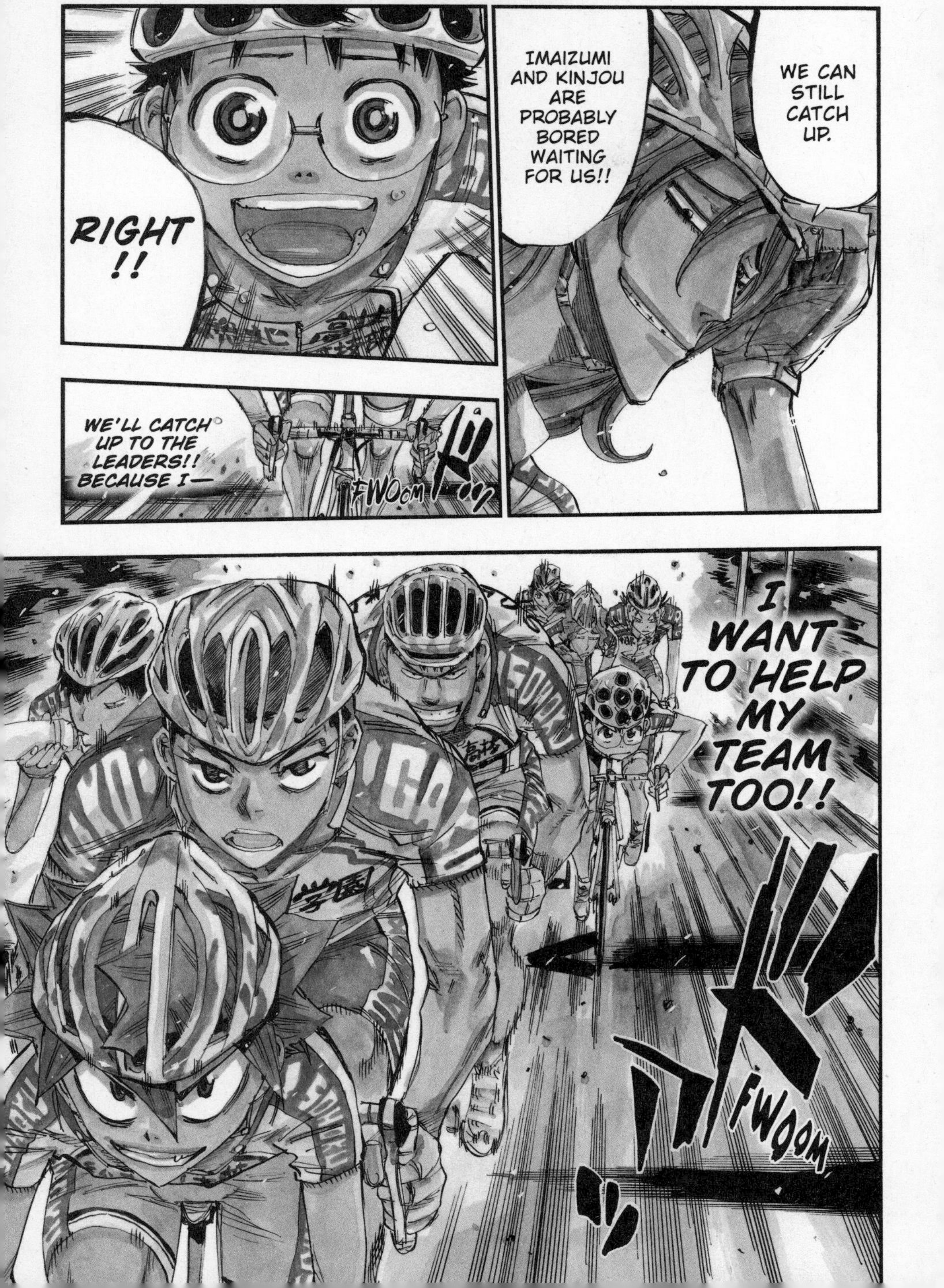
WE CAN STILL CATCH UP.
IMAIZUMI AND KINJOU ARE PROBABLY BORED WAITING FOR US!!
RIGHT!!
WE'LL CATCH UP TO THE LEADERS!! BECAUSE I—
FWOOM
I WANT TO HELP MY TEAM TOO!!
FWOOM

RIDE.165 HIROSHIMA'S KUREMINAMI

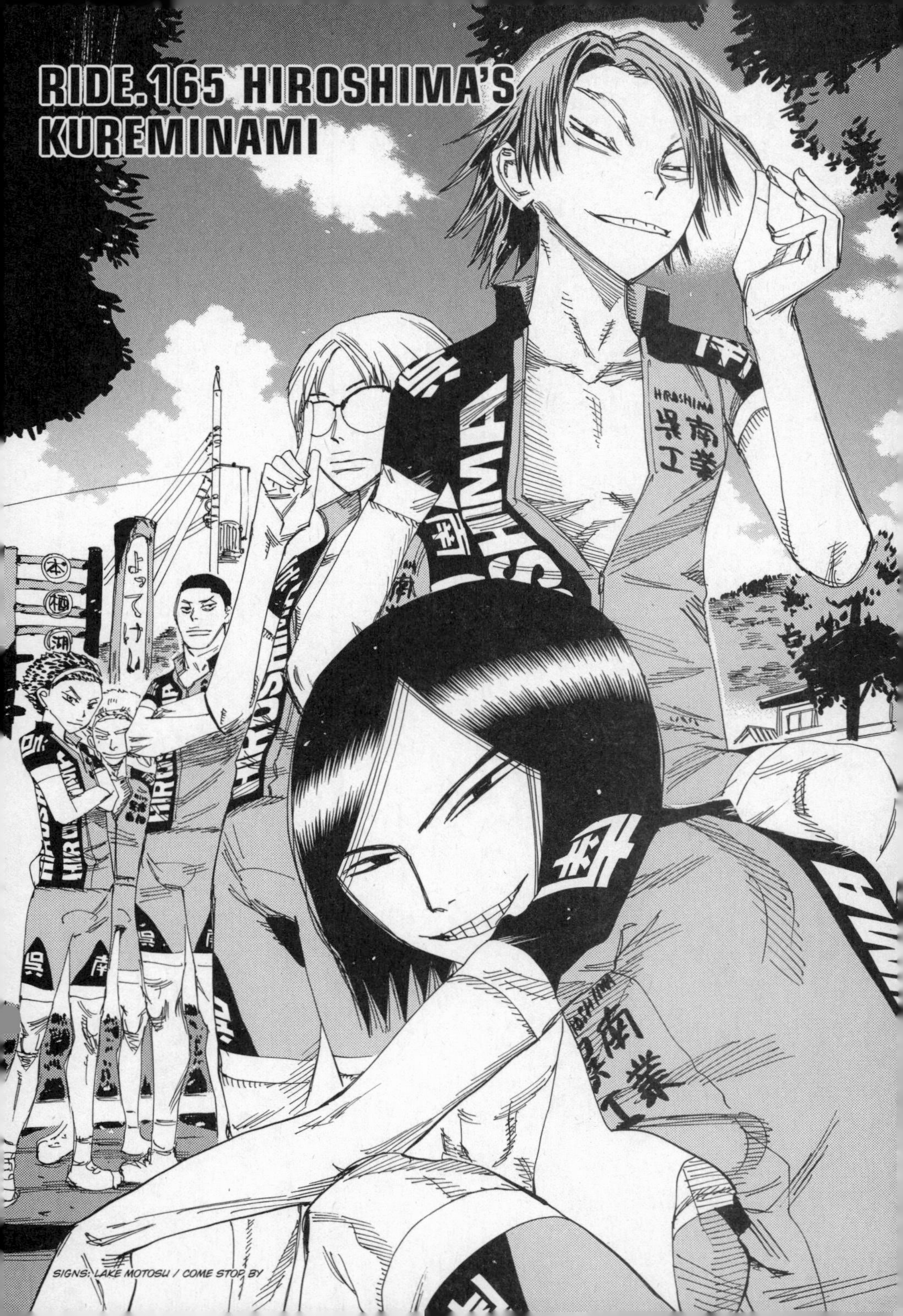
本栖湖
よってけし
HIROSHIMA
呉南工業
SIGNS: LAKE MOTOSU / COME STOP BY

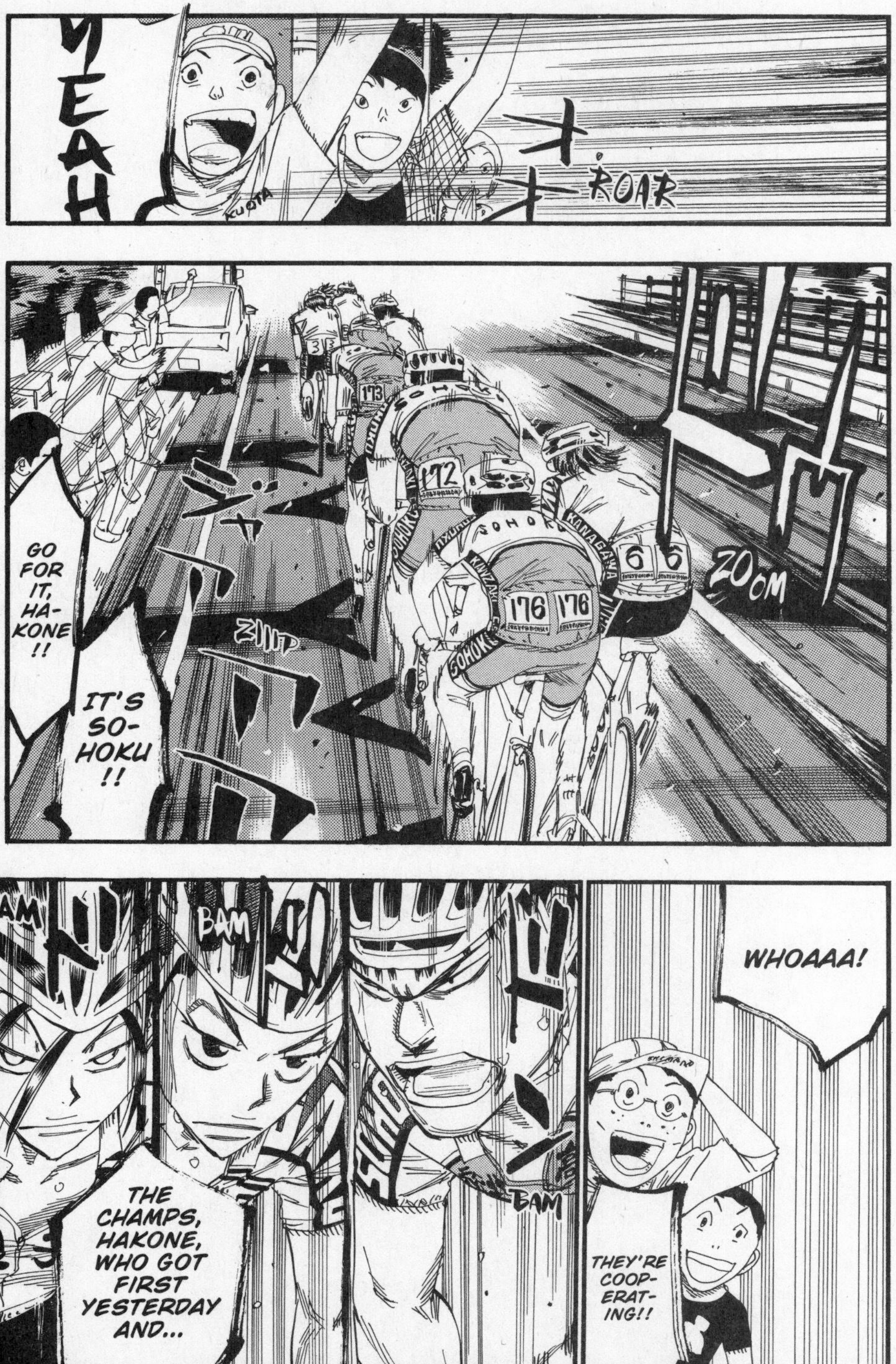
ROAR
MEAH
ZOOM
ZIIIP
GO FOR IT, HAKONE!!
IT'S SOHOKU!!
WHOAAA!
THEY'RE COOPERATING!!
BAM
THE CHAMPS, HAKONE, WHO GOT FIRST YESTERDAY AND...
BAM
BAM

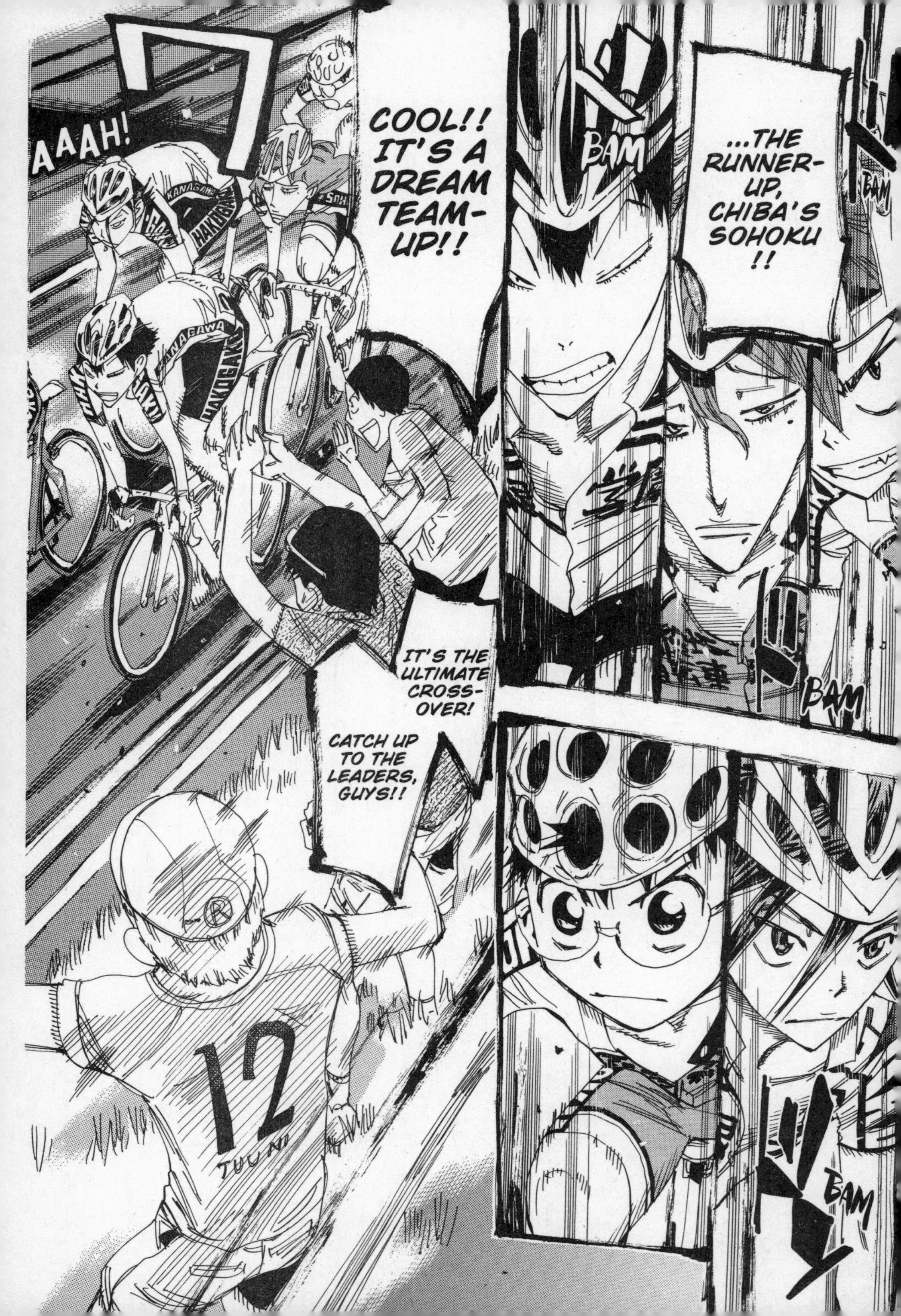
...THE RUNNER-UP, CHIBA'S SOHOKU!!
BAM
BAM
BAM
BAM
COOL!! IT'S A DREAM TEAM-UP!!
AAAH!
IT'S THE ULTIMATE CROSS-OVER!
CATCH UP TO THE LEADERS, GUYS!!
12

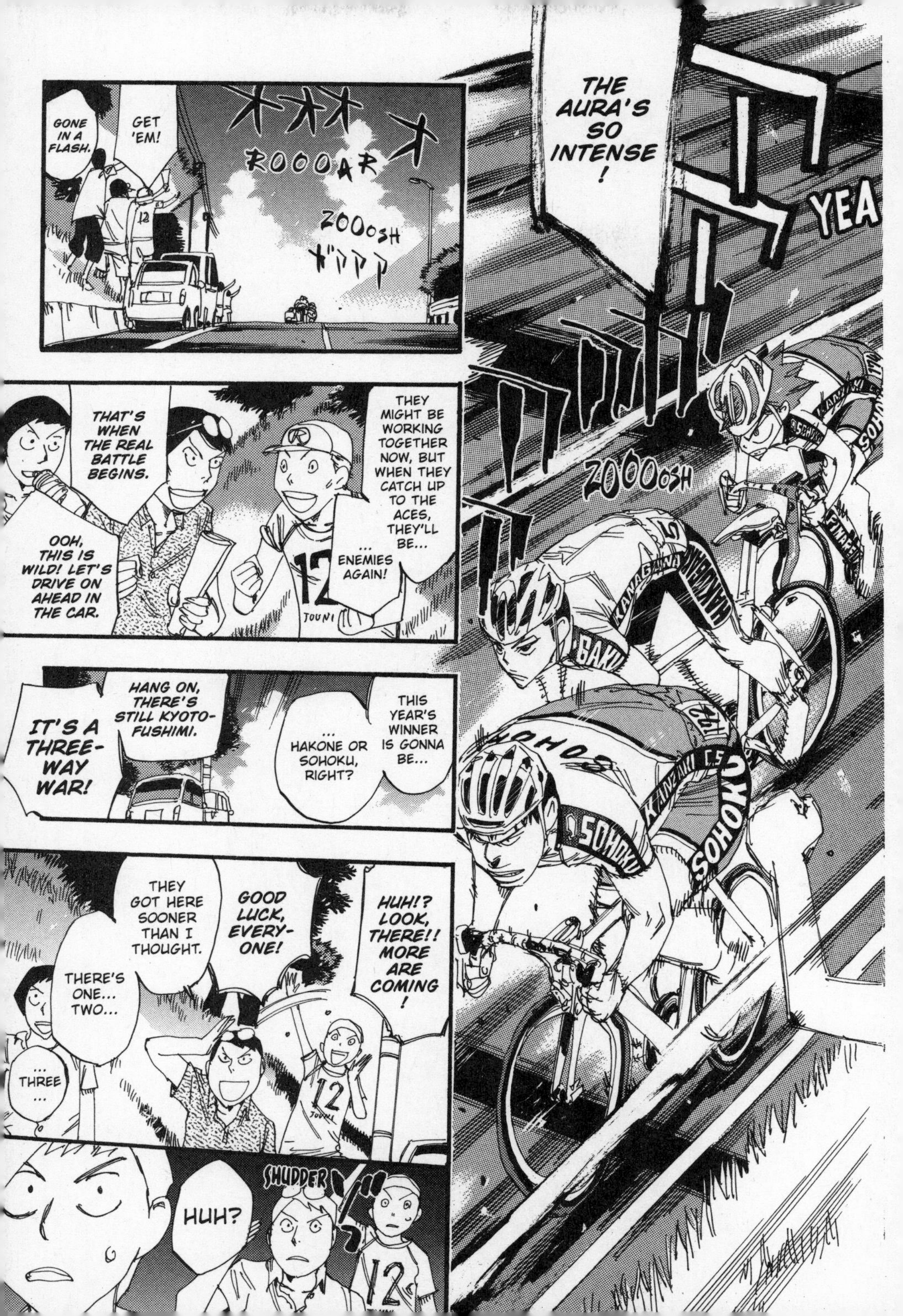
THE AURA'S SO INTENSE!
YEA
ZOOOosh
ROOOAR
GET 'EM!
GONE IN A FLASH.
ZOOOsh
THEY MIGHT BE WORKING TOGETHER NOW, BUT WHEN THEY CATCH UP TO THE ACES, THEY'LL BE...
...ENEMIES AGAIN!
THAT'S WHEN THE REAL BATTLE BEGINS.
OOH, THIS IS WILD! LET'S DRIVE ON AHEAD IN THE CAR.
THIS YEAR'S WINNER IS GONNA BE...
...HAKONE OR SOHOKU, RIGHT?
HANG ON, THERE'S STILL KYOTO-FUSHIMI.
IT'S A THREE-WAY WAR!
HUH!? LOOK, THERE!! MORE ARE COMING!
GOOD LUCK, EVERYONE!
THEY GOT HERE SOONER THAN I THOUGHT.
THERE'S ONE... TWO...
...THREE...
SHUDDER
HUH?

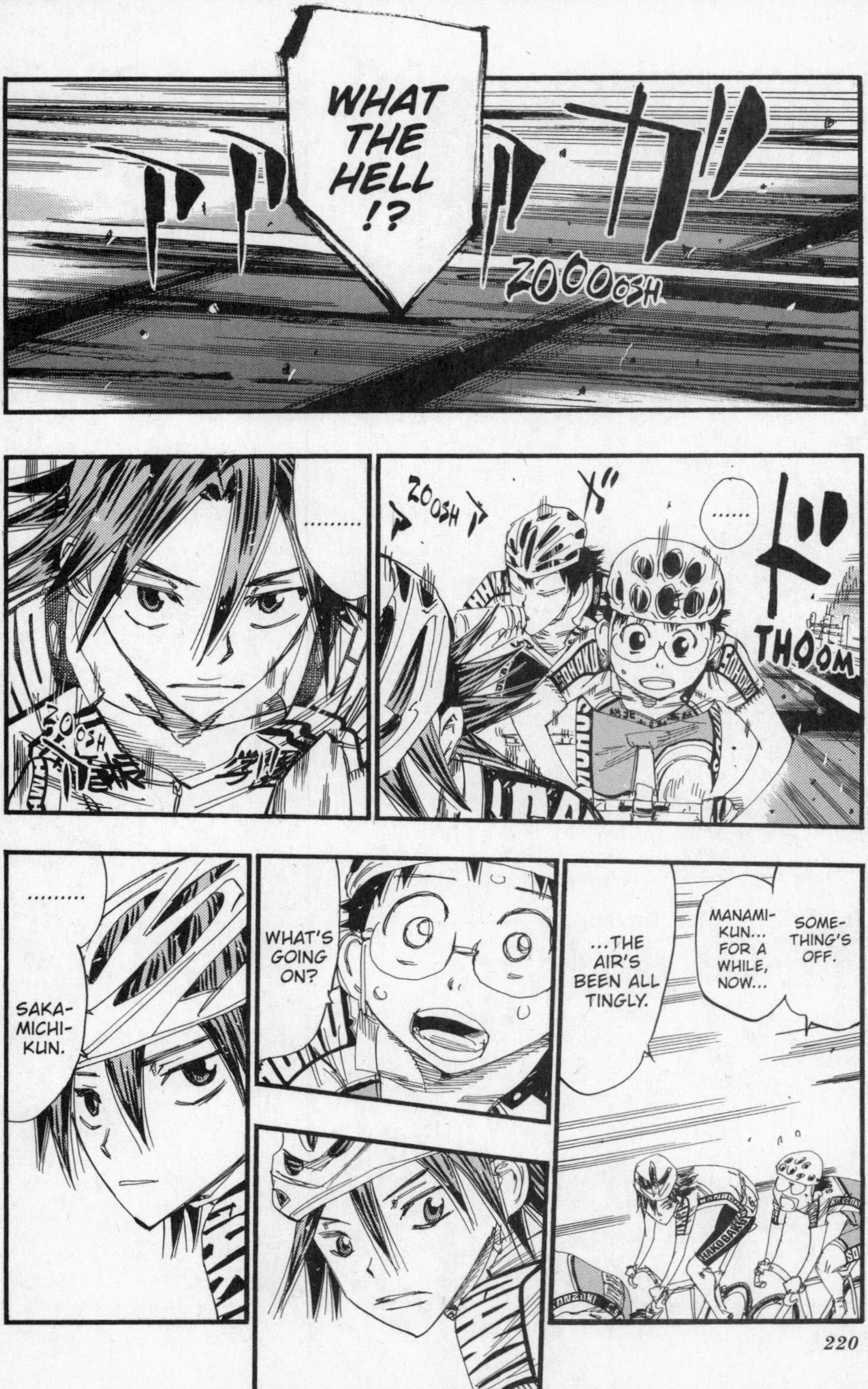
WHAT THE HELL !?
ZOOOOOSH
ZOOSH
......
THOOM
ZOOSH
....
SOME-THING'S OFF.
MANAMI-KUN... FOR A WHILE, NOW...
...THE AIR'S BEEN ALL TINGLY.
WHAT'S GOING ON?
....
SAKA-MICHI-KUN.

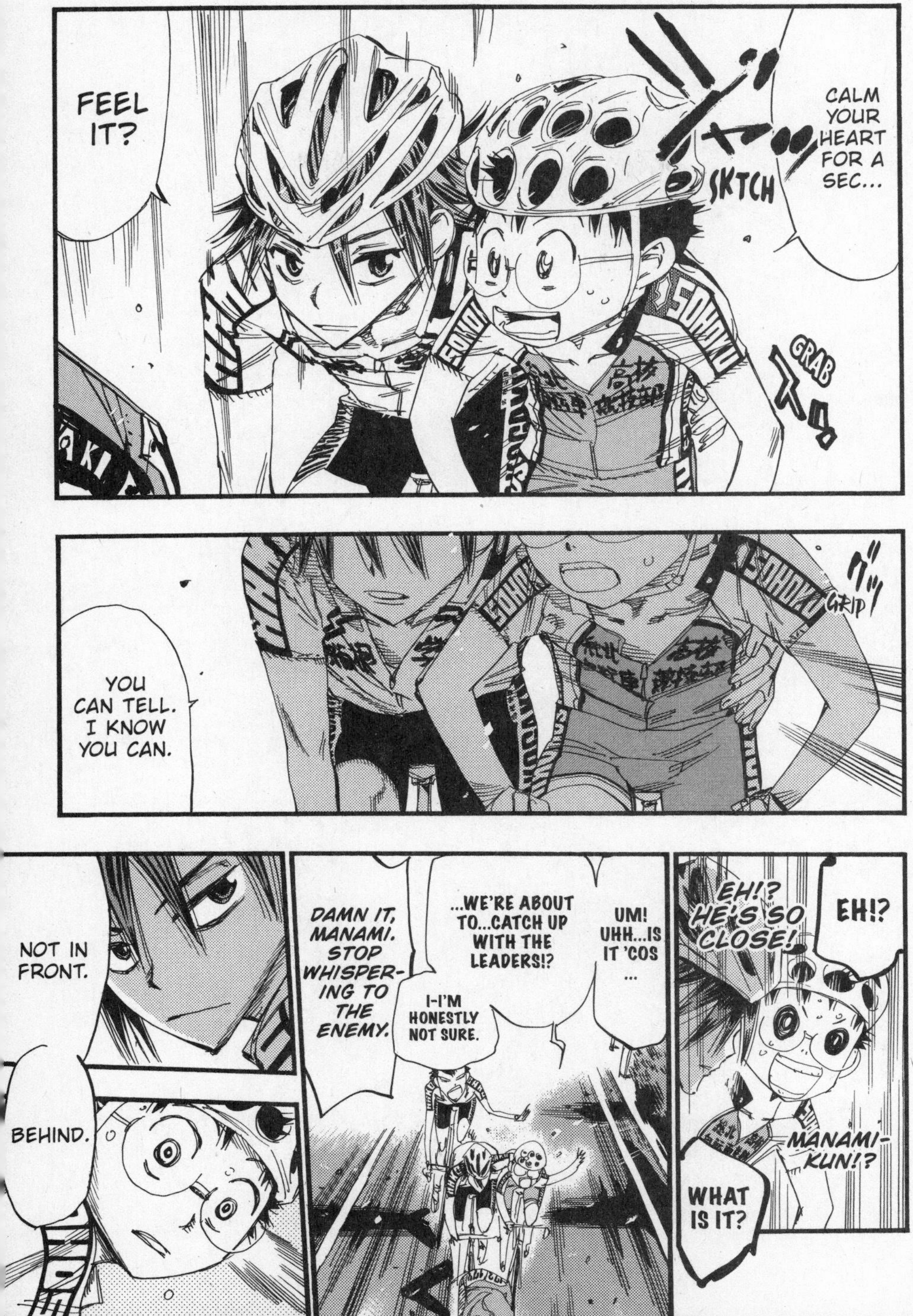
CALM YOUR HEART FOR A SEC...
SKTCH
GRAB
FEEL IT?
GRIP
YOU CAN TELL. I KNOW YOU CAN.
EH!?
EH!? HE'S SO CLOSE!
MANAMI-KUN!?
WHAT IS IT?
UM! UHH...IS IT 'COS ...
...WE'RE ABOUT TO...CATCH UP WITH THE LEADERS!?
DAMN IT, MANAMI. STOP WHISPER-ING TO THE ENEMY.
I-I'M HONESTLY NOT SURE.
NOT IN FRONT.
BEHIND.

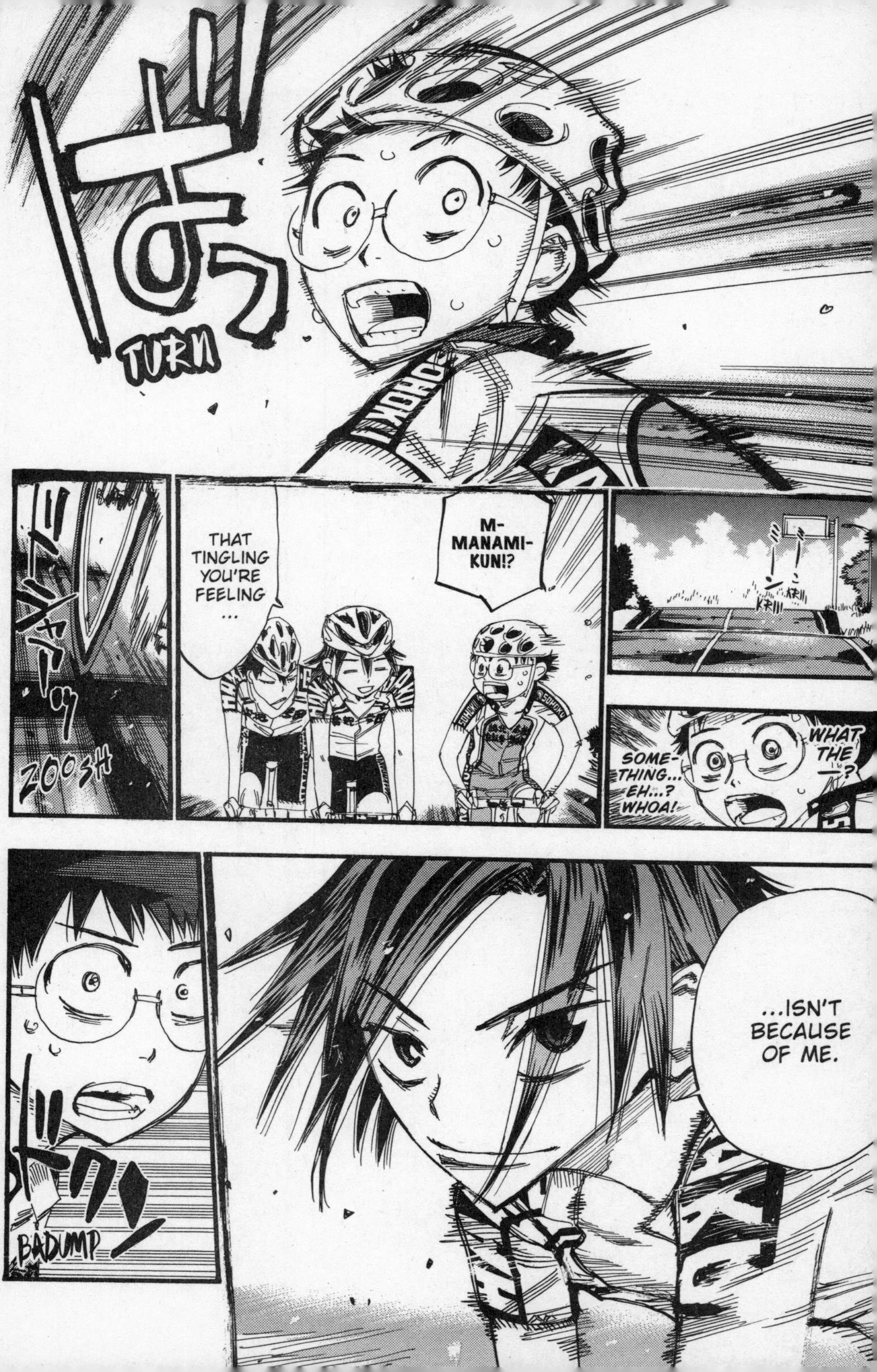
TURN
WHAT THE—?
SOME-THING... EH...? WHOA!
M-MANAMI-KUN!?
THAT TINGLING YOU'RE FEELING ...
ZOOSH
...ISN'T BECAUSE OF ME.
BADUMP

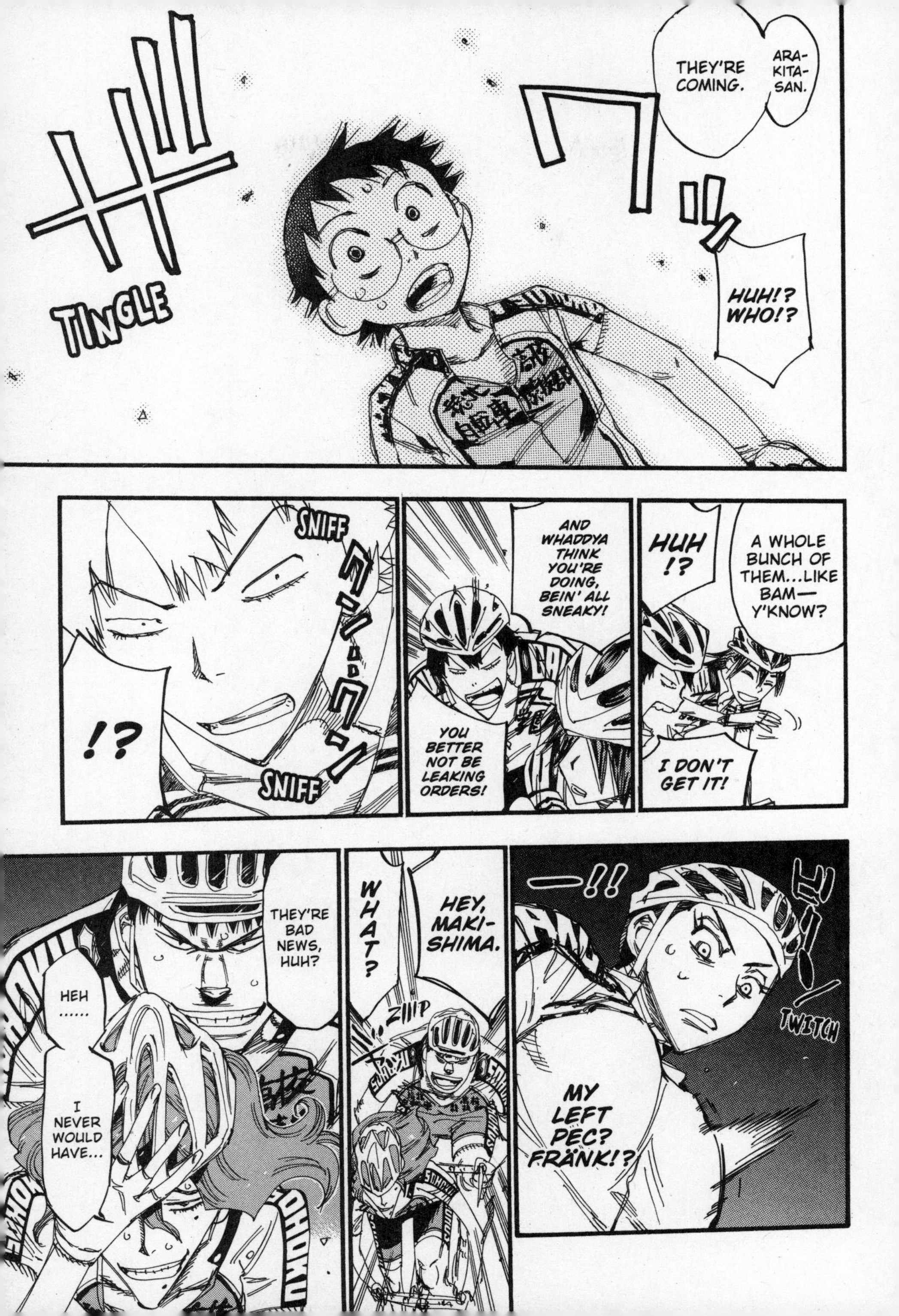
ARA-KITA-SAN.
THEY'RE COMING.
HUH!? WHO!?
TINGLE
A WHOLE BUNCH OF THEM...LIKE BAM— Y'KNOW?
HUH!?
I DON'T GET IT!
AND WHADDYA THINK YOU'RE DOING, BEIN' ALL SNEAKY!
YOU BETTER NOT BE LEAKING ORDERS!
SNIFF
SNIFF
!?
—!!
TWITCH
MY LEFT PEC? FRANK!?
HEY, MAKI-SHIMA.
WHAT?
ZIIIP
THEY'RE BAD NEWS, HUH?
HEH ......
I NEVER WOULD HAVE...

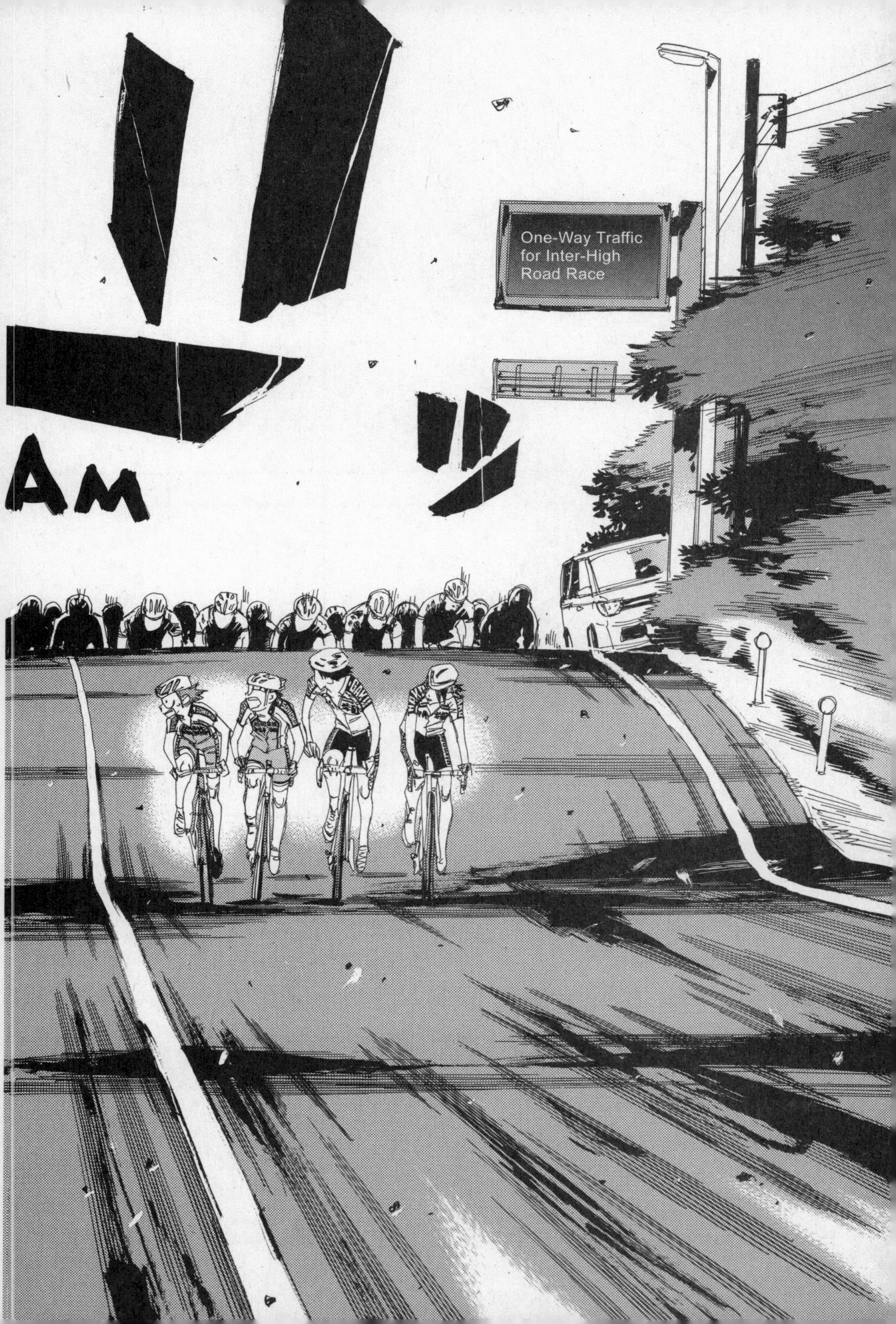
One-Way Traffic for Inter-High Road Race
AM

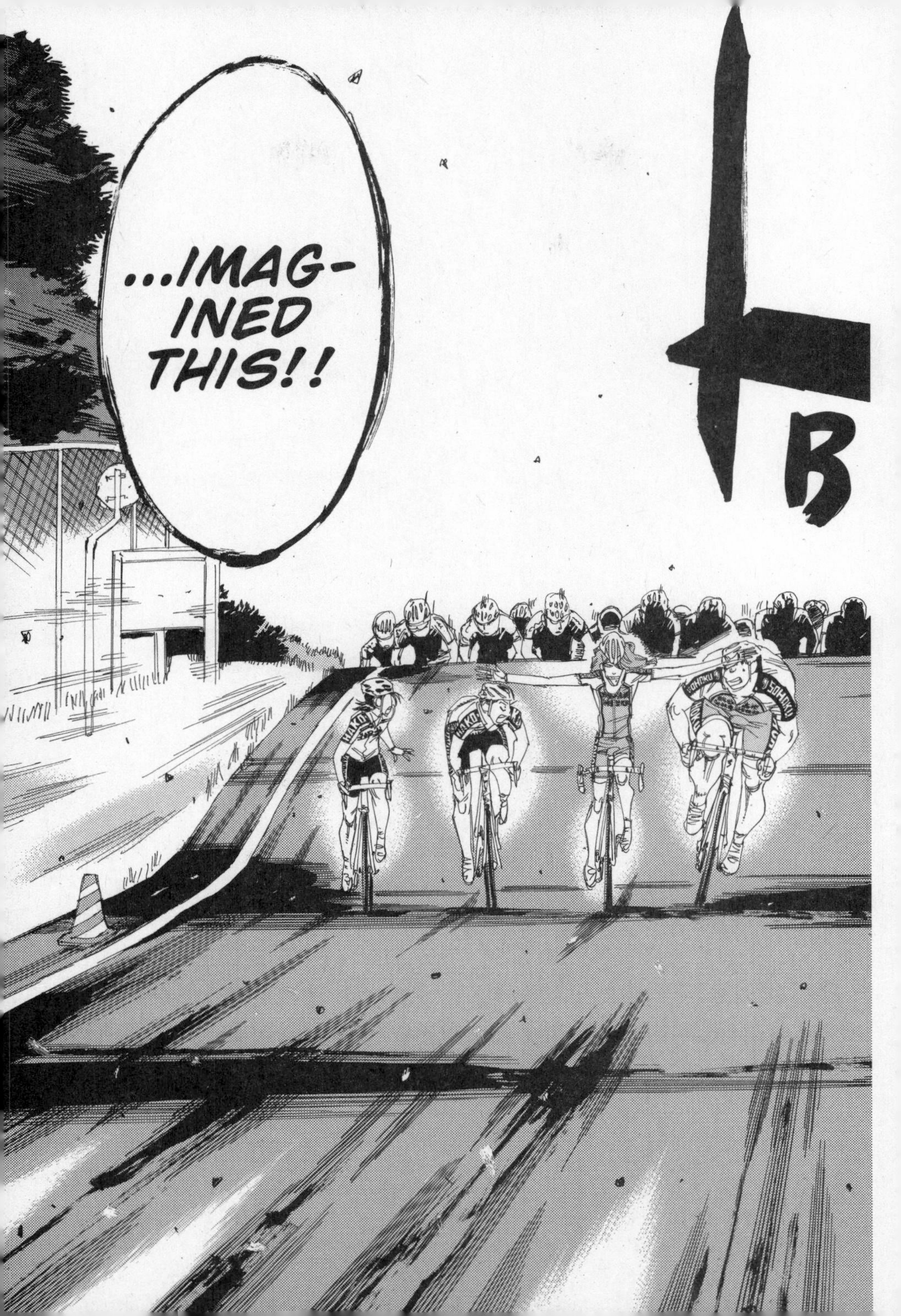
...IMAG-INED THIS!!

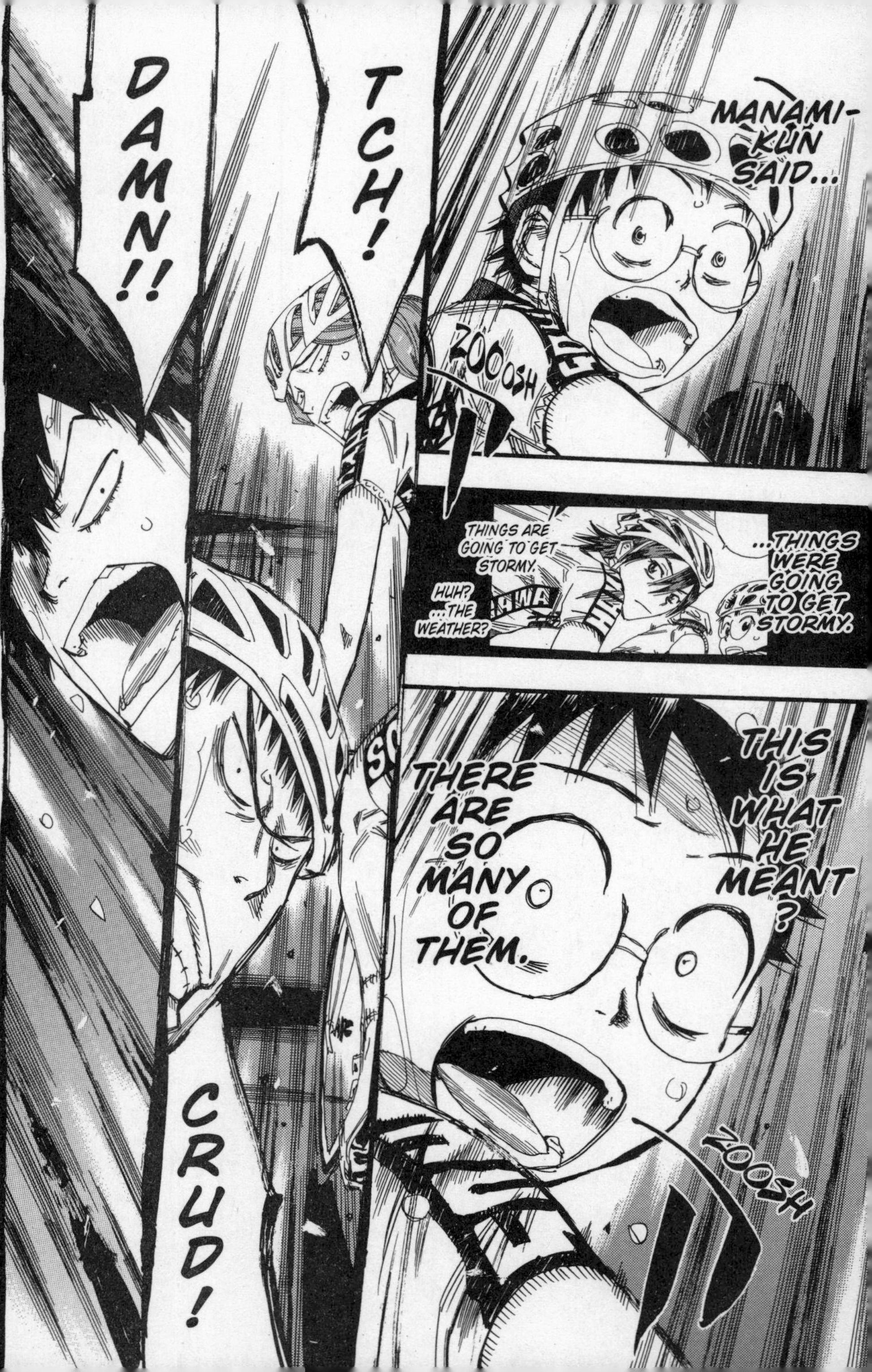
MANAMI-KUN SAID...
ZOOOSH
...THINGS WERE GOING TO GET STORMY.
THINGS ARE GOING TO GET STORMY.
HUH? ...THE WEATHER?
THIS IS WHAT HE MEANT?
THERE ARE SO MANY OF THEM.
ZOOOSH
TCH!
DAMN!!
CRUD!

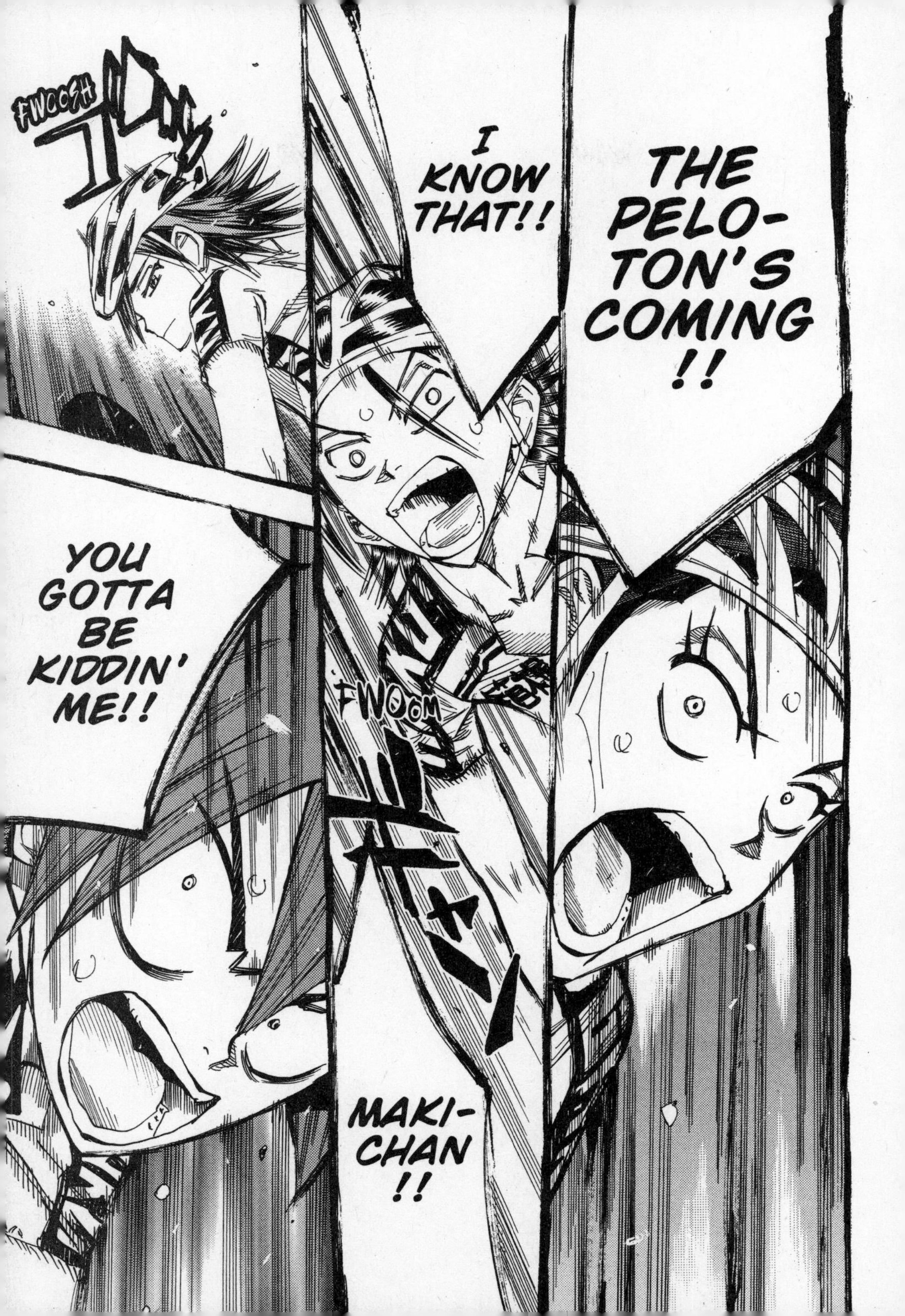
THE PELO-TON'S COMING!!
I KNOW THAT!!
FWOOM
MAKI-CHAN!!
FWOOSH
YOU GOTTA BE KIDDIN' ME!!

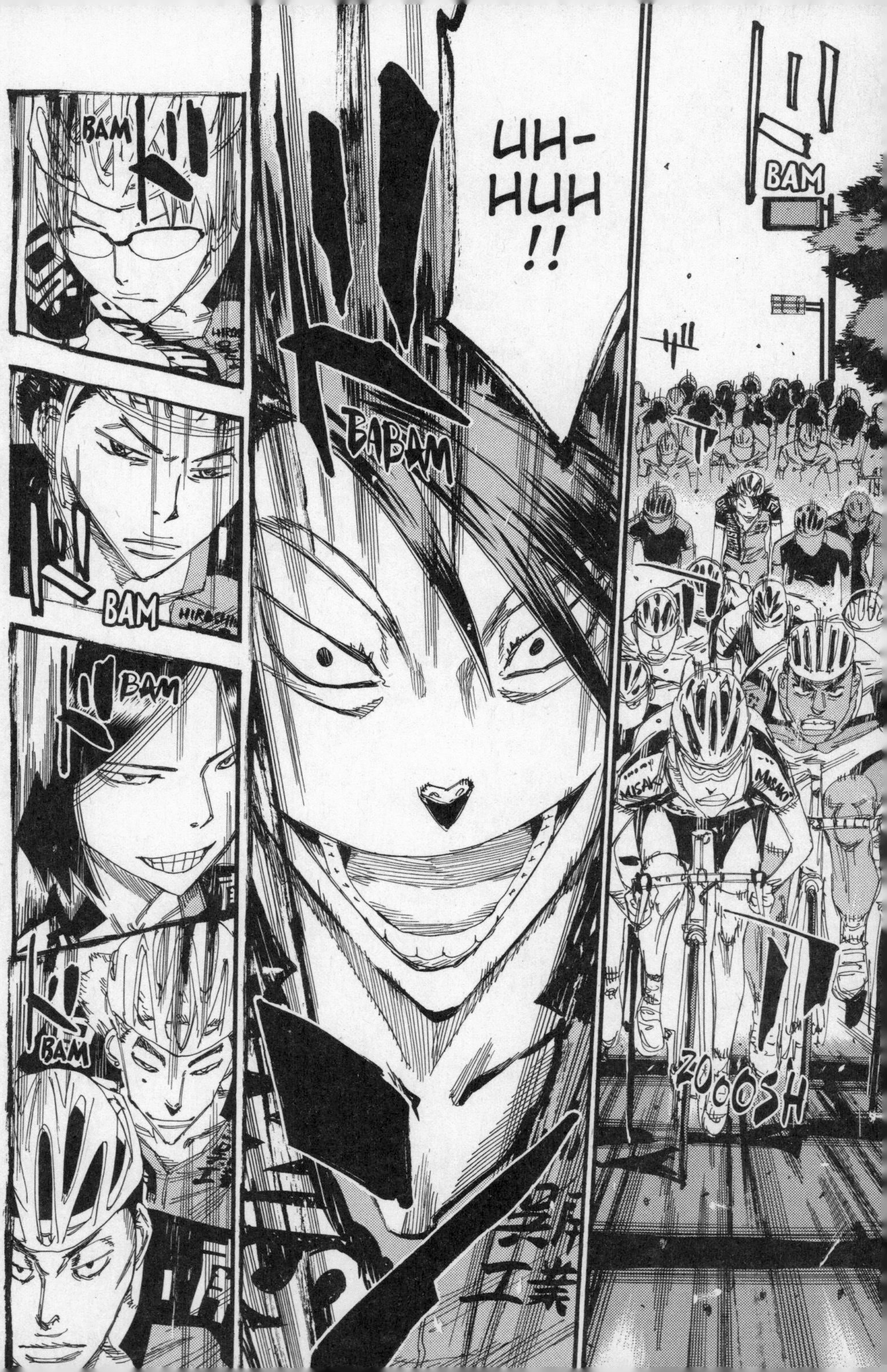
BAM
ZOOOSH
UH-HUH!!
BABAM
BAM
BAM
BAM
BAM

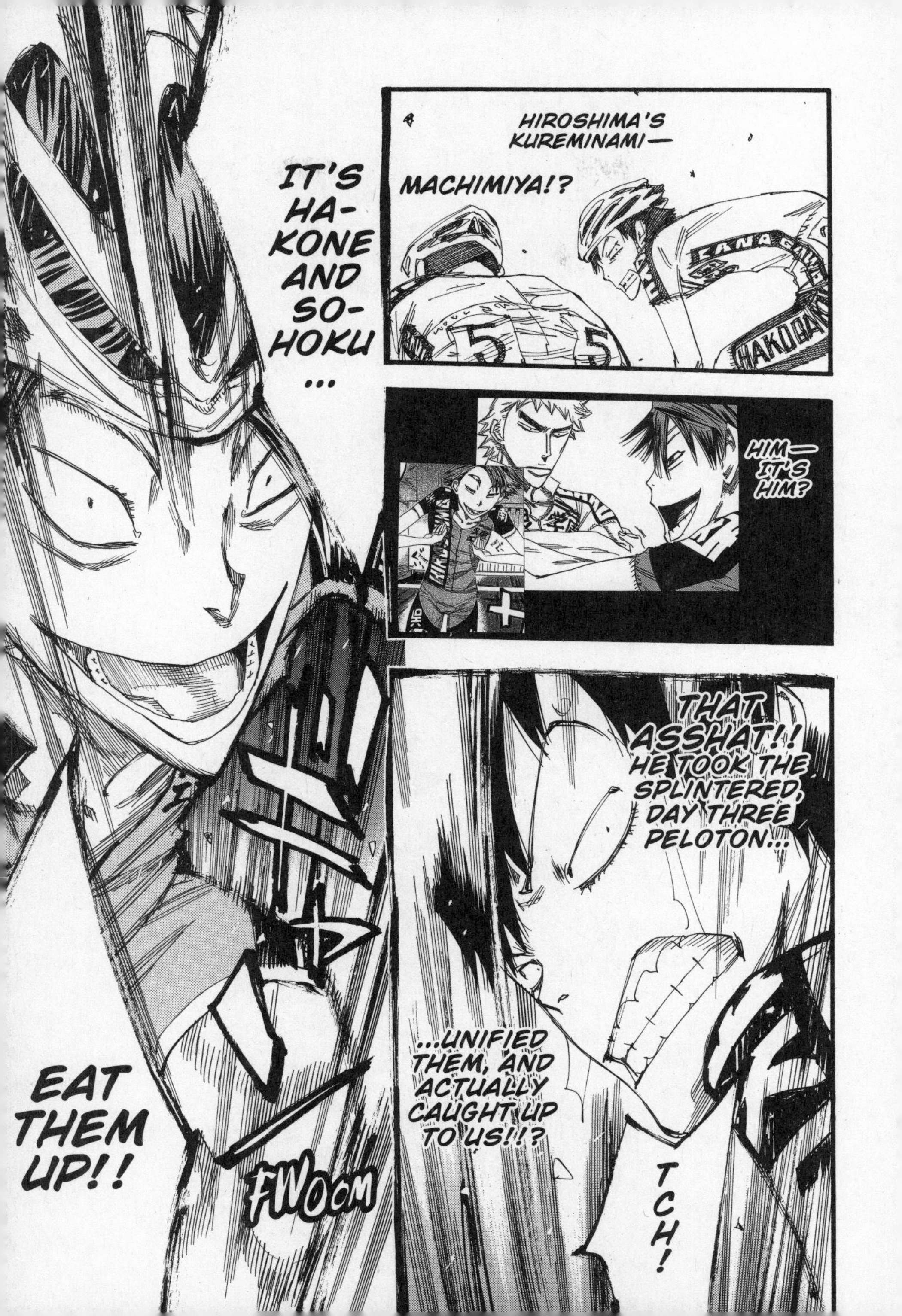
HIROSHIMA'S KUREMINAMI—
MACHIMIYA!?
HIM— IT'S HIM?
THAT ASSHAT!! HE TOOK THE SPLINTERED, DAY THREE PELOTON...
...UNIFIED THEM, AND ACTUALLY CAUGHT UP TO US!!?
TCH!
IT'S HA-KONE AND SO-HOKU...
EAT THEM UP!!
FWOOM

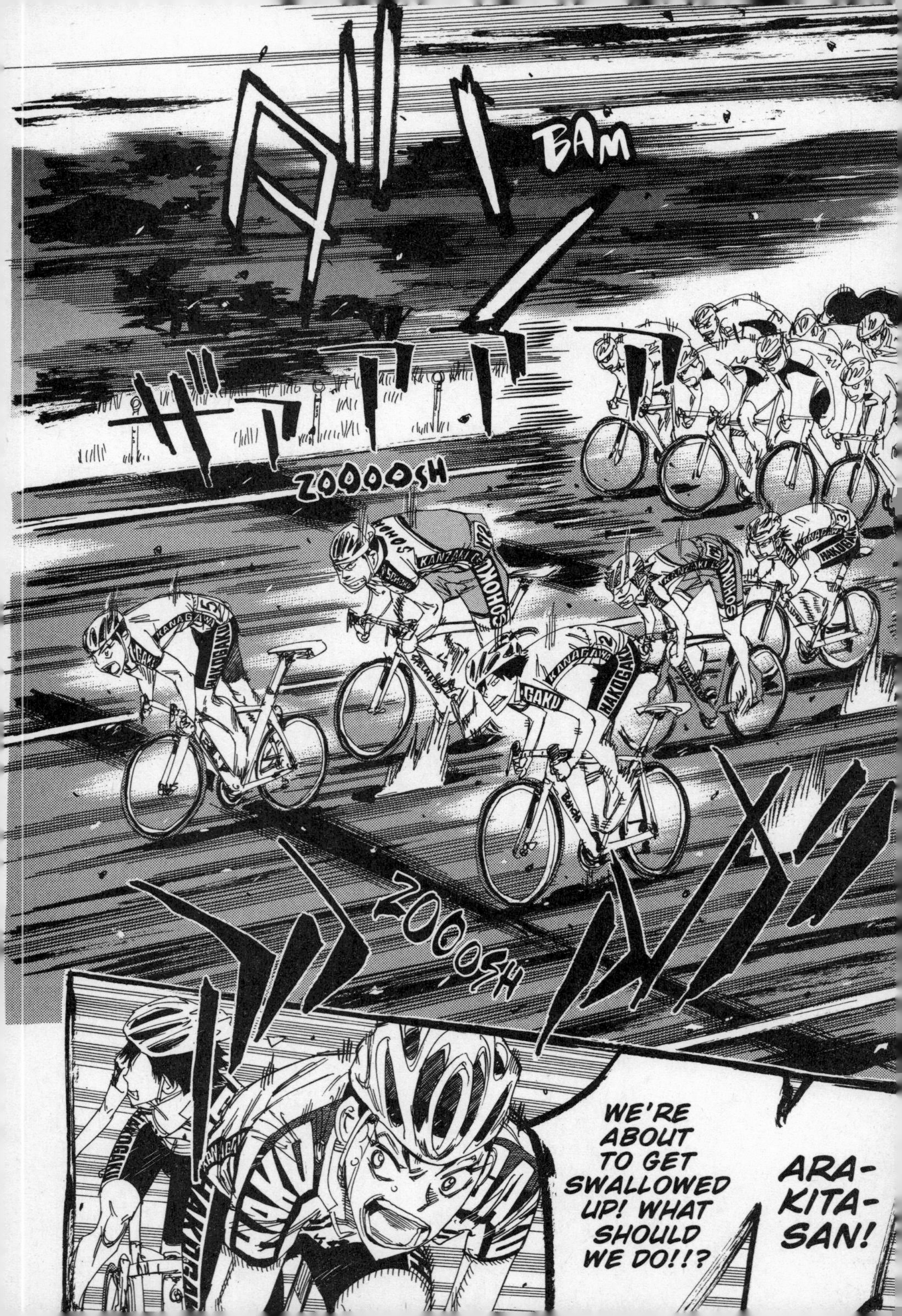
BAM
ZOOOOSH
ZOOOOSH
ARA-KITA-SAN!
WE'RE ABOUT TO GET SWALLOWED UP! WHAT SHOULD WE DO!!?

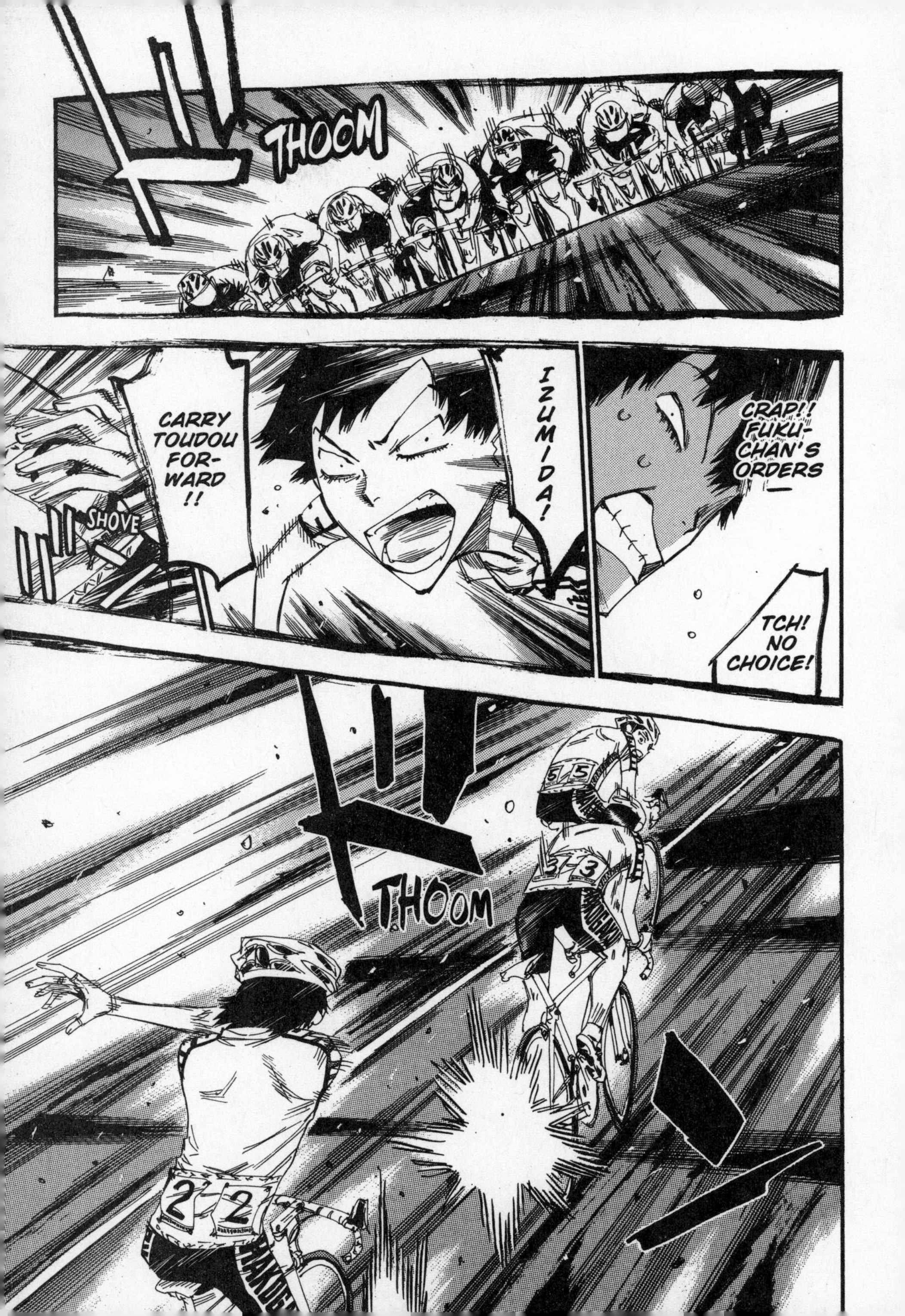
THOOM
CRAP!! FUKU-CHAN'S ORDERS—
TCH! NO CHOICE!
IZUMIDA!
CARRY TOUDOU FOR-WARD!!
SHOVE
THOOM

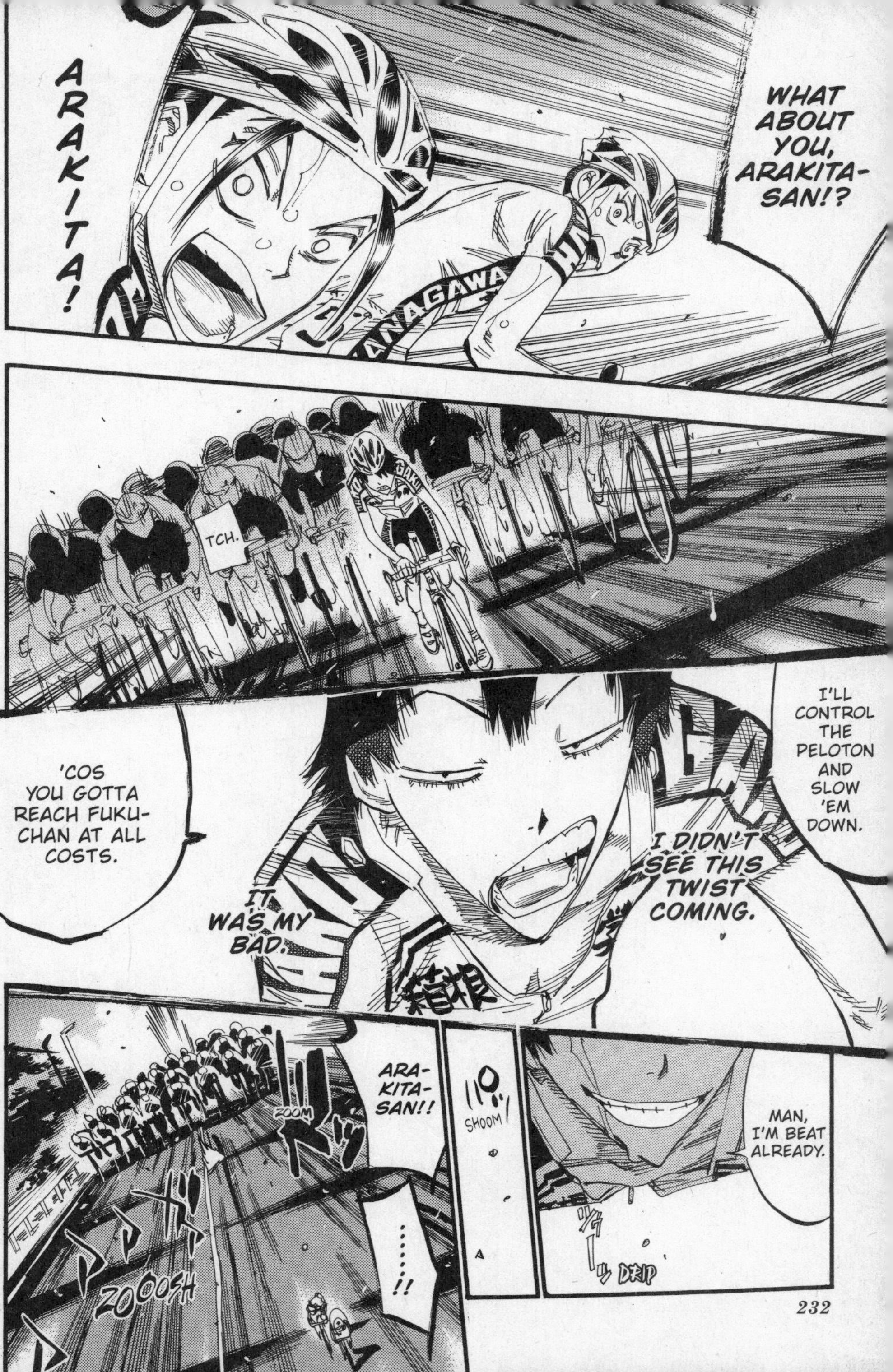
WHAT ABOUT YOU, ARAKITA-SAN!?
ARAKITA!
TCH.
I'LL CONTROL THE PELOTON AND SLOW 'EM DOWN.
I DIDN'T SEE THIS TWIST COMING.
IT WAS MY BAD.
'COS YOU GOTTA REACH FUKU-CHAN AT ALL COSTS.
箱根
MAN, I'M BEAT ALREADY.
DRIP
SHOOM
ARA-KITA-SAN!!
ZOOM
......!!
ZOOOSH

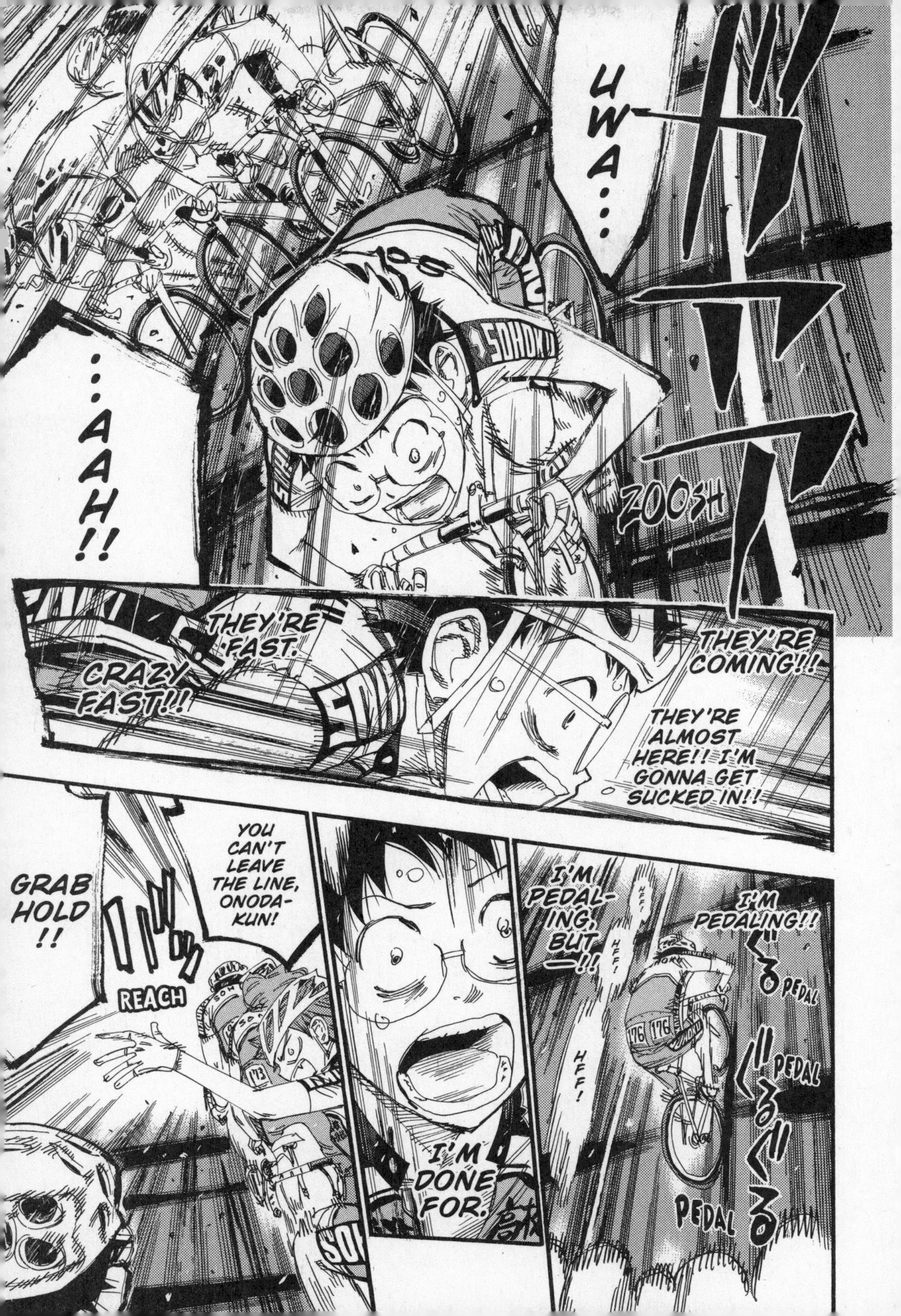
UWA...
ZOOSH
...AAAH!!
THEY'RE COMING!!
THEY'RE ALMOST HERE!! I'M GONNA GET SUCKED IN!!
THEY'RE FAST.
CRAZY FAST!!
I'M PEDALING!!
PEDAL
PEDAL
PEDAL
I'M PEDAL-ING, BUT—!!
HFF!
HFF!
HFF!
I'M DONE FOR.
YOU CAN'T LEAVE THE LINE, ONODA-KUN!
GRAB HOLD!!
REACH

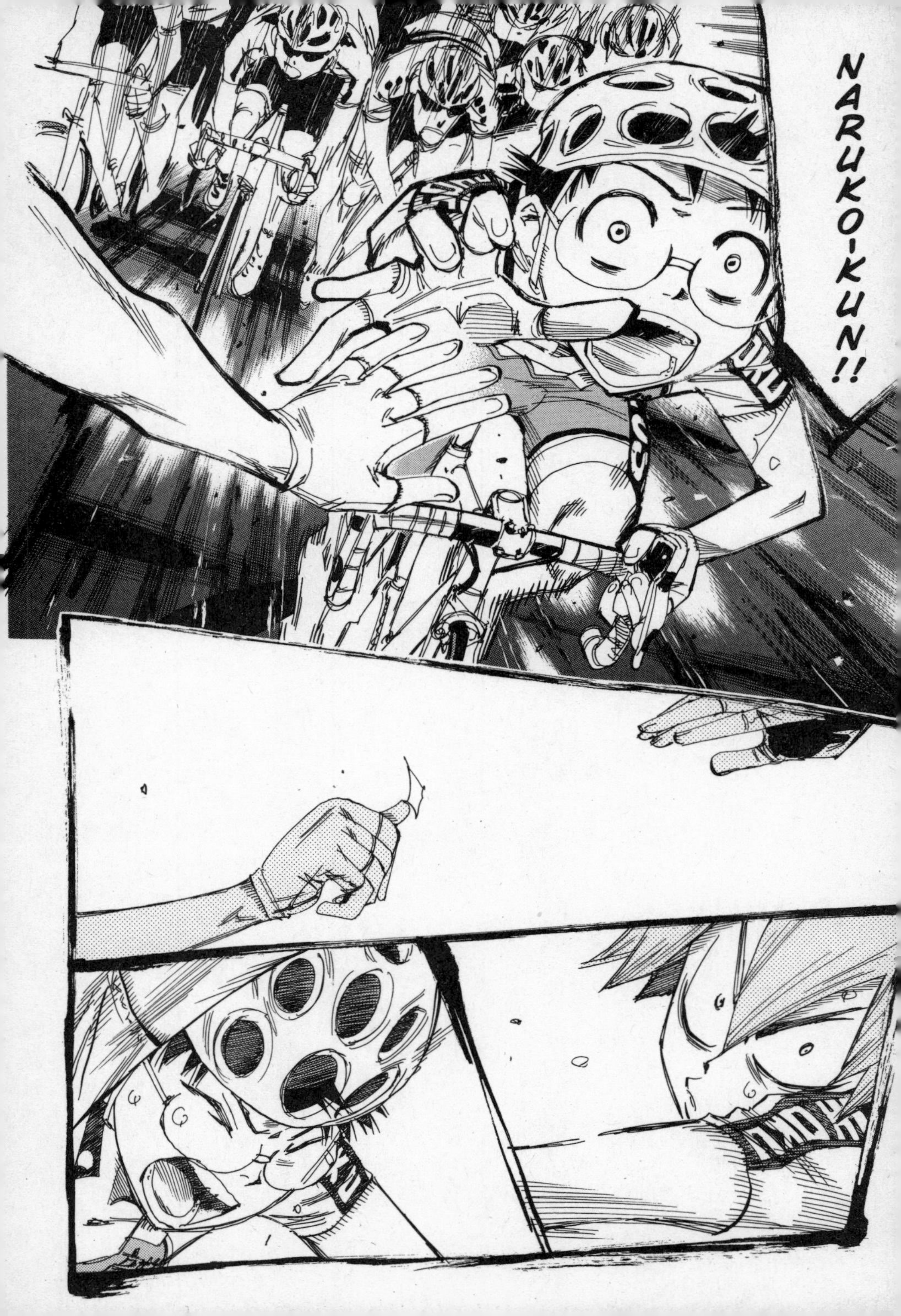
NARUKO-KUN!!

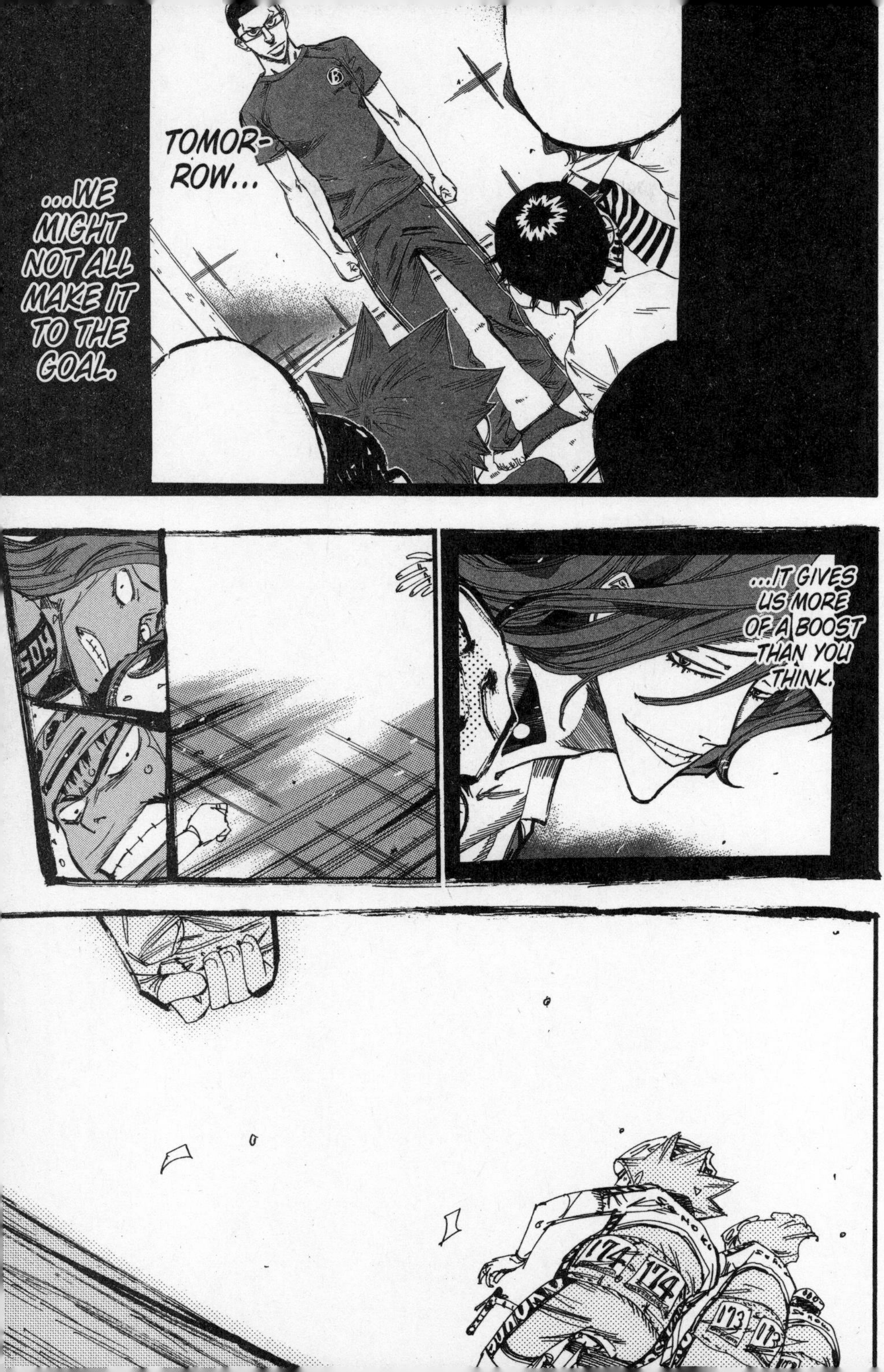
TOMOR-ROW...
...WE MIGHT NOT ALL MAKE IT TO THE GOAL.
...IT GIVES US MORE OF A BOOST THAN YOU THINK.

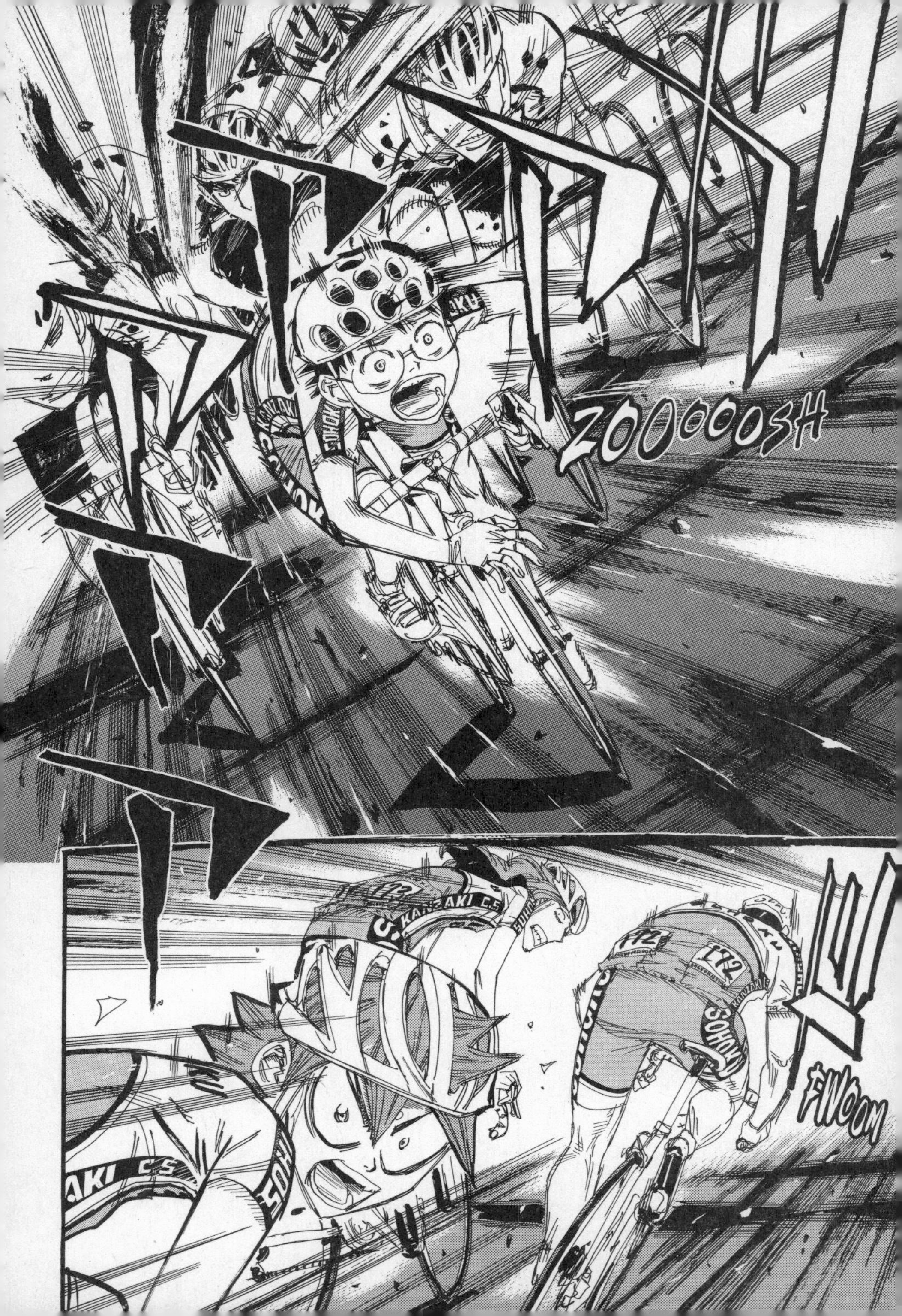
ZOOOOOSH
FWOOM

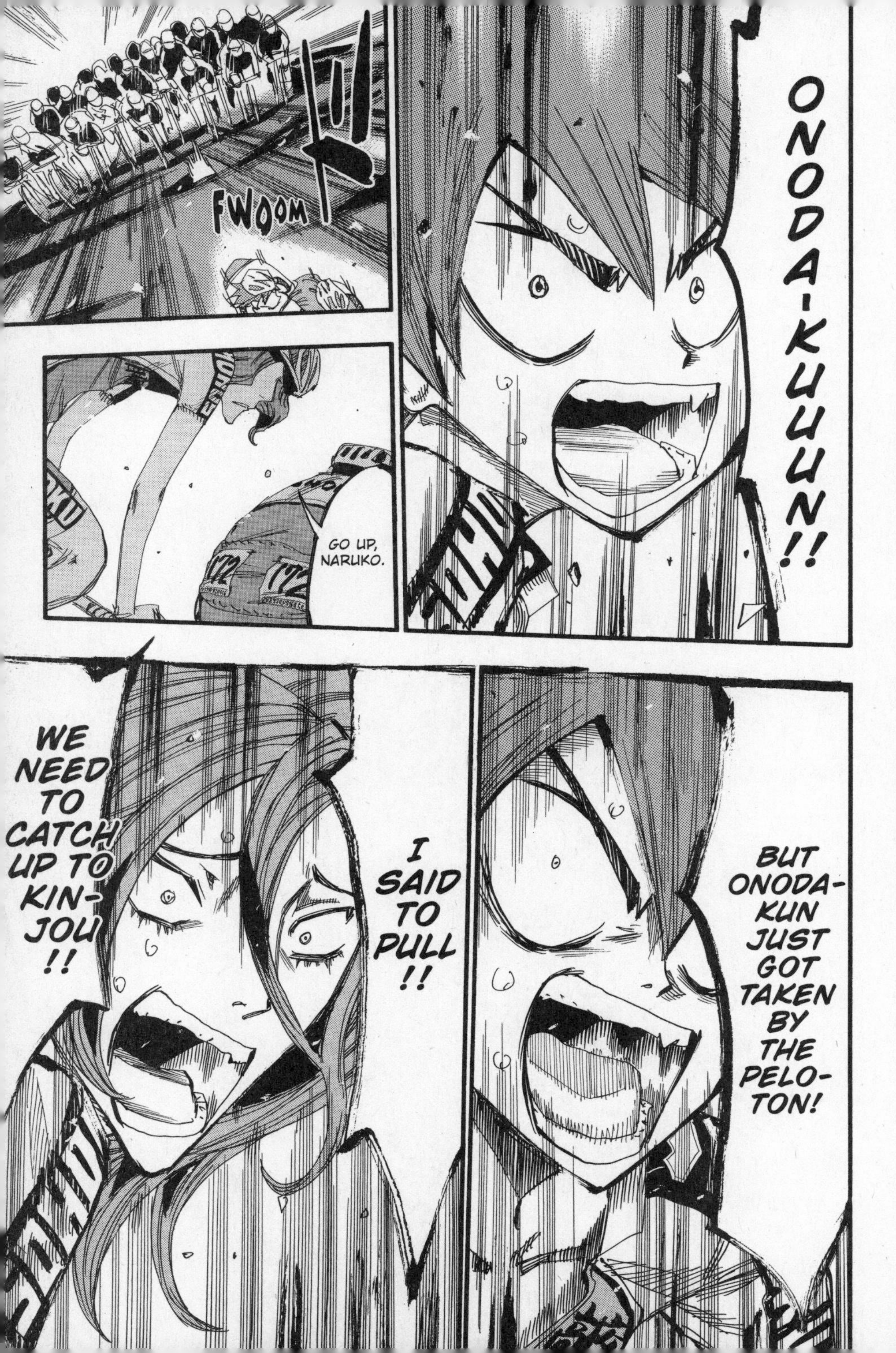
ONODA-KUUUUN!!
FWOOM
GO UP, NARUKO.
BUT ONODA-KUN JUST GOT TAKEN BY THE PELOTON!
I SAID TO PULL!!
WE NEED TO CATCH UP TO KINJOU!!

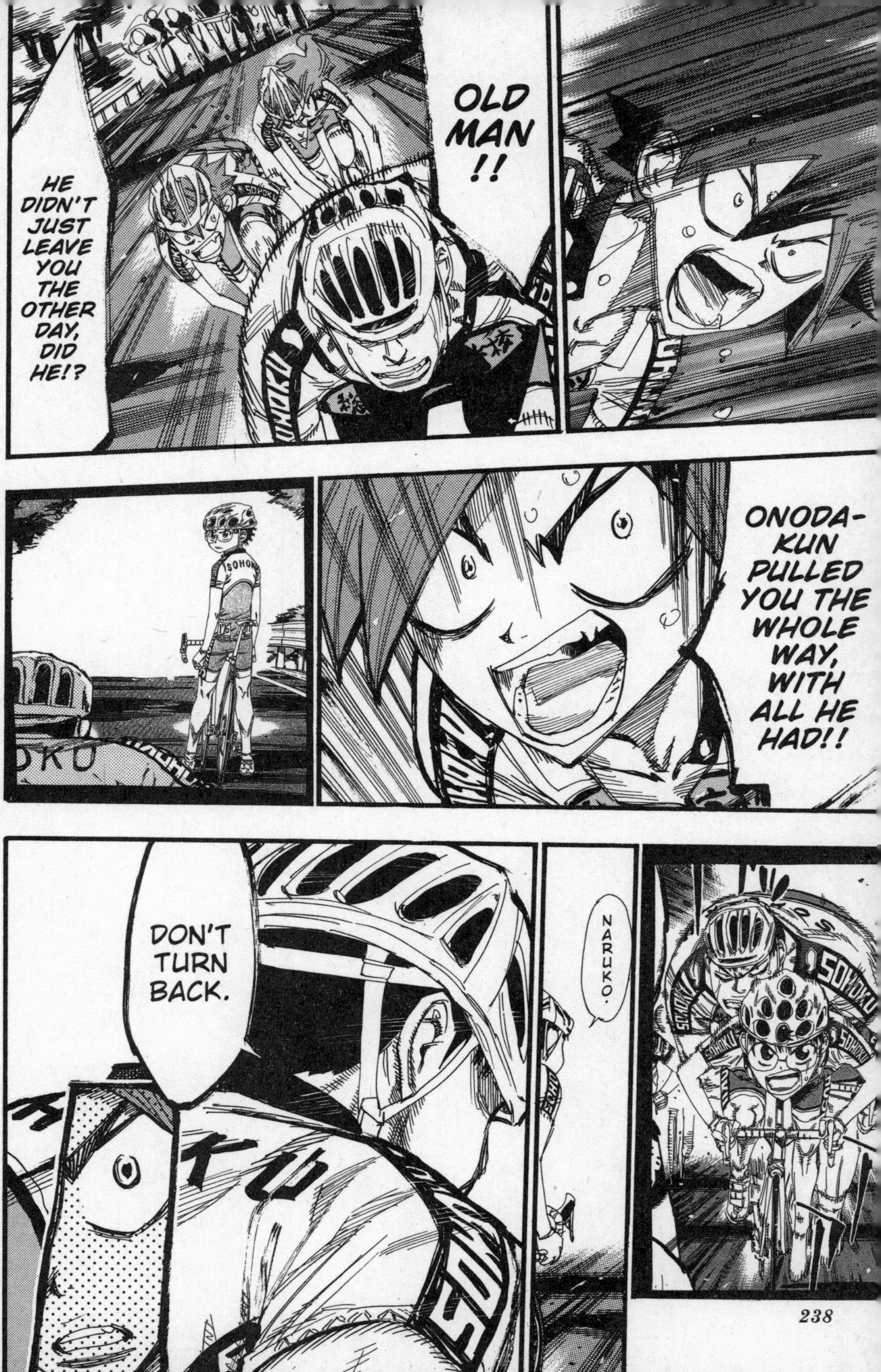
OLD MAN!!
HE DIDN'T JUST LEAVE YOU THE OTHER DAY, DID HE!?
ONODA-KUN PULLED YOU THE WHOLE WAY, WITH ALL HE HAD!!
NARUKO.
DON'T TURN BACK.

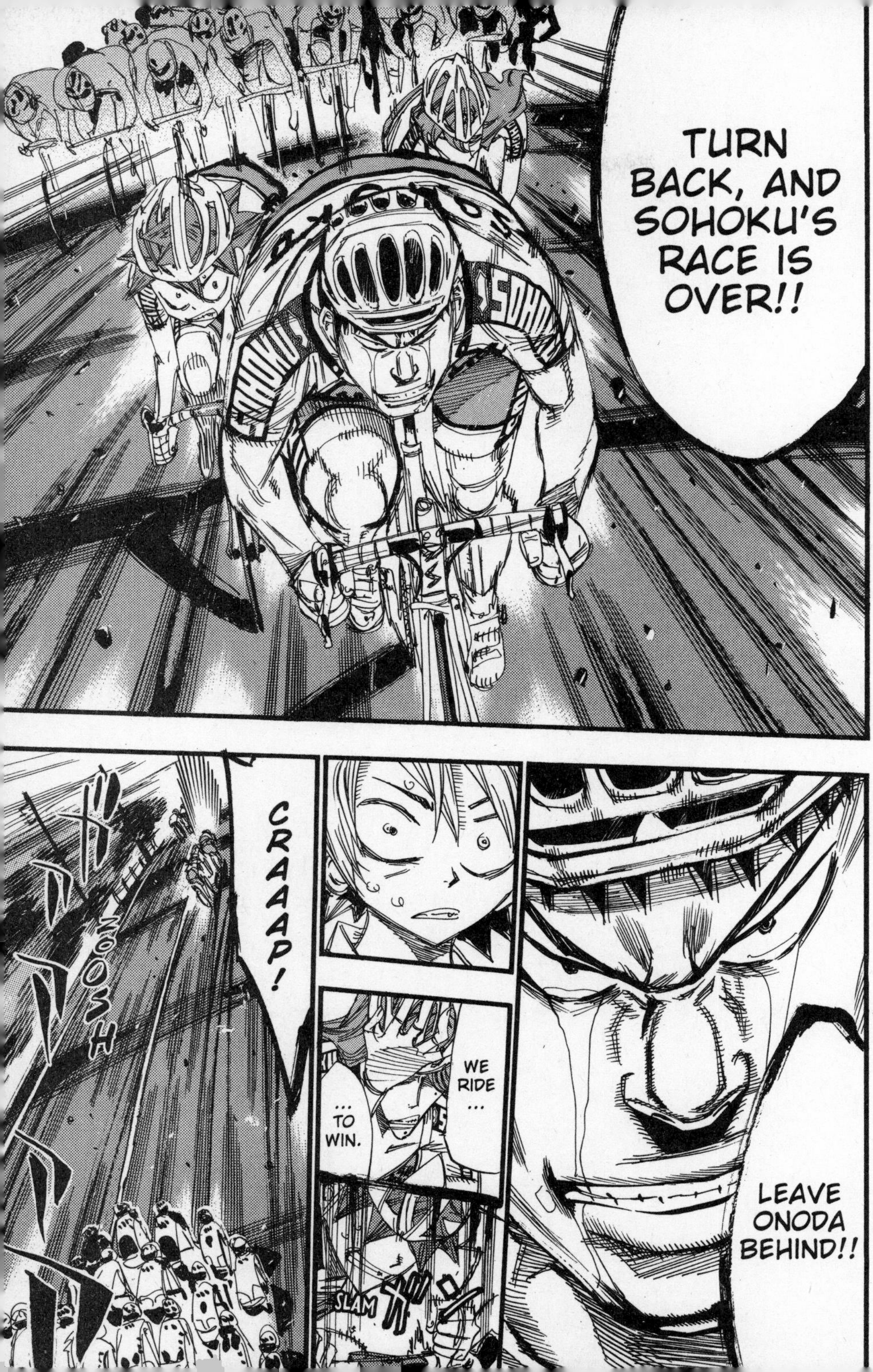
TURN BACK, AND SOHOKU'S RACE IS OVER!!
LEAVE ONODA BEHIND!!
WE RIDE...
...TO WIN.
SLAM
CRAAAAP!
WHOOSH

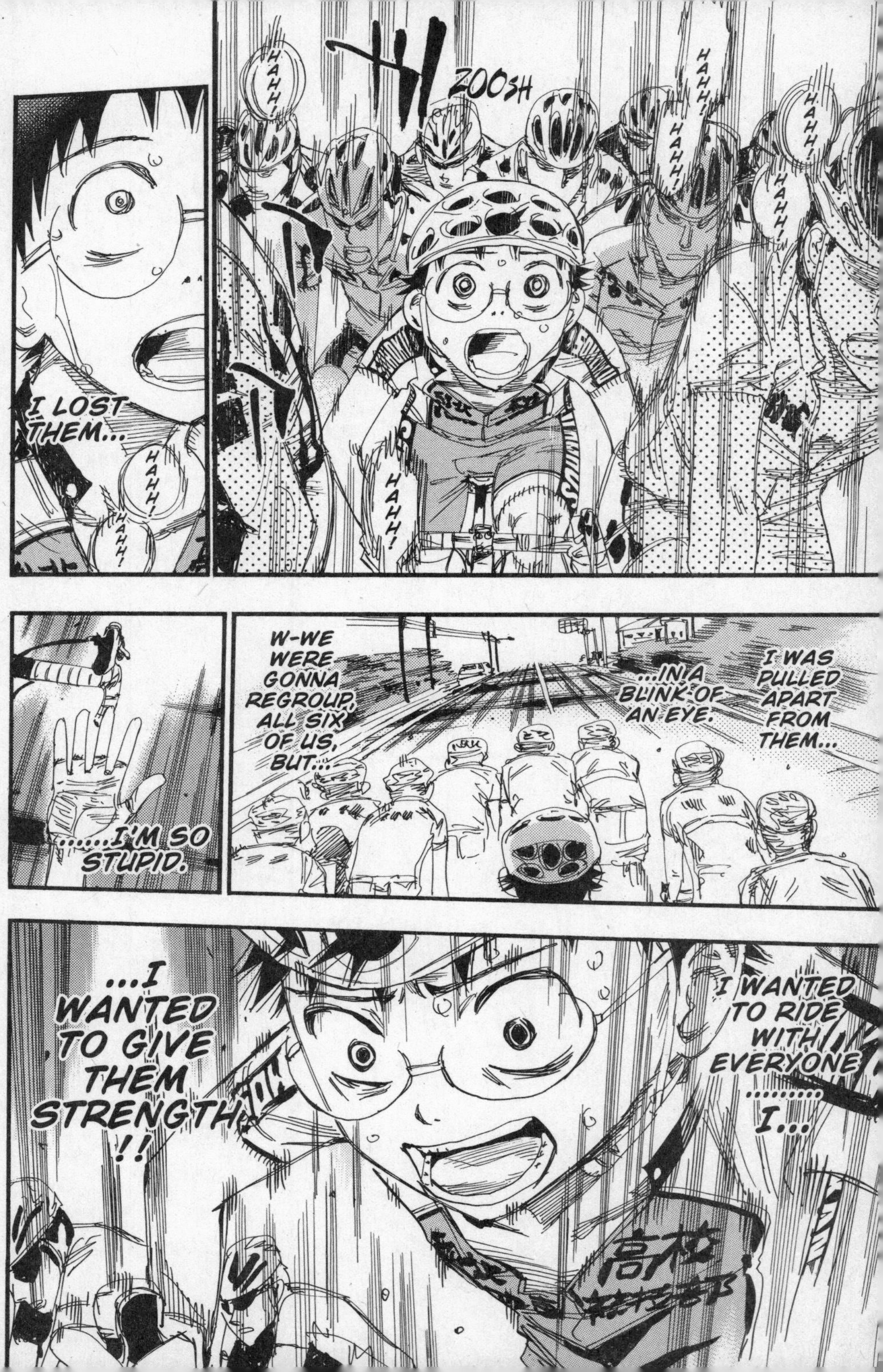
ZOOSH
HAHH!
HAHH!
HAHH!
HAHH!
HAHH!
HAHH!
HAHH!
I LOST THEM...
HAHH!
HAHH!
I WAS PULLED APART FROM THEM...
...IN A BLINK OF AN EYE.
W-WE WERE GONNA REGROUP, ALL SIX OF US, BUT...
......I'M SO STUPID.
I WANTED TO RIDE WITH EVERYONE......... I...
...I WANTED TO GIVE THEM STRENGTH!!

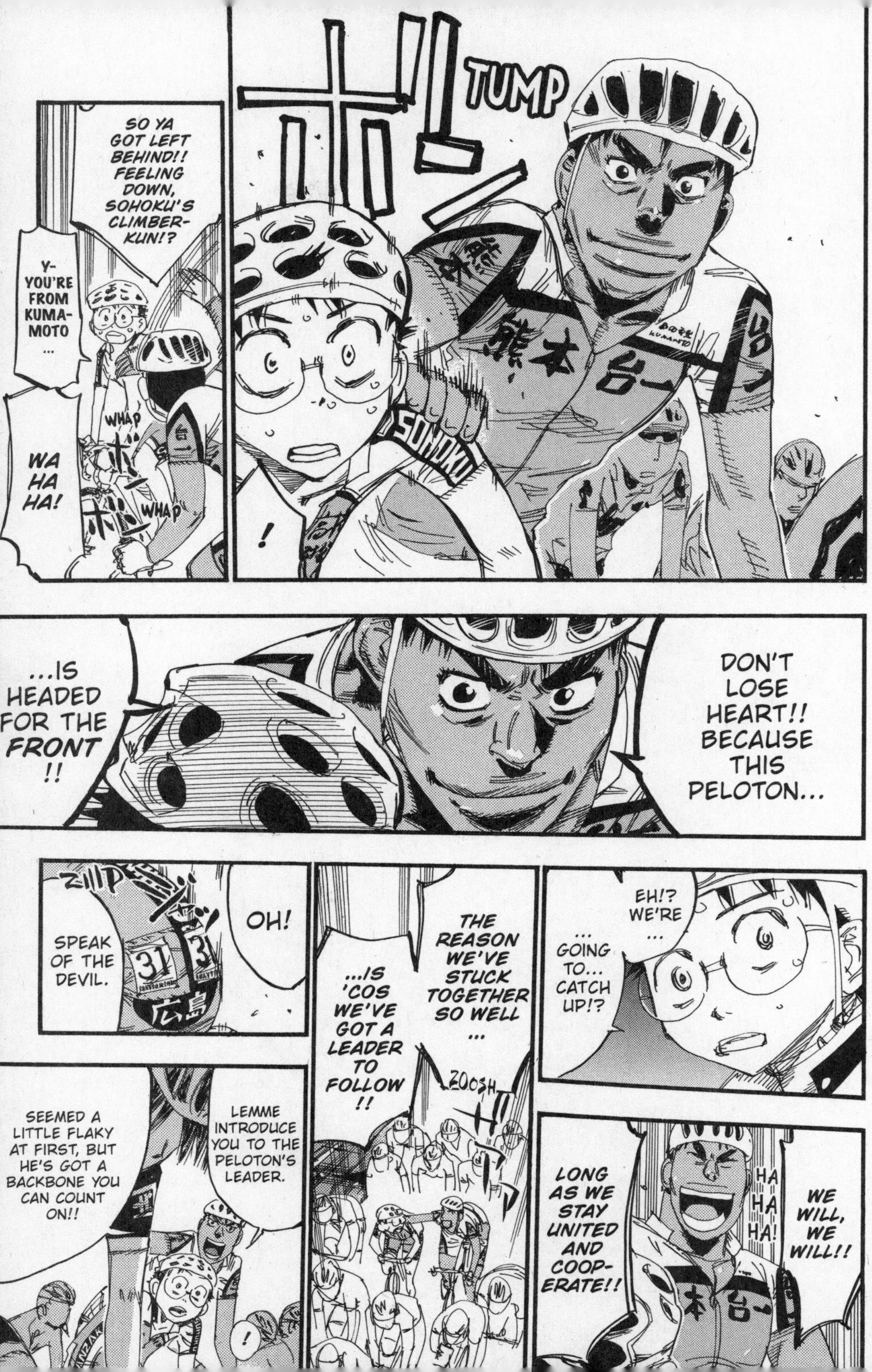
TUMP
SOHOKU
!
SO YA GOT LEFT BEHIND!! FEELING DOWN, SOHOKU'S CLIMBER-KUN!?
Y-YOU'RE FROM KUMAMOTO ...
WHAP
WA HA HA!
WHAP
DON'T LOSE HEART!! BECAUSE THIS PELOTON...
...IS HEADED FOR THE FRONT!!
EH!? WE'RE ...
... GOING TO... CATCH UP!?
WE WILL, WE WILL!!
HA HA HA!
LONG AS WE STAY UNITED AND COOP-ERATE!!
THE REASON WE'VE STUCK TOGETHER SO WELL ...
...IS 'COS WE'VE GOT A LEADER TO FOLLOW!!
ZOOSH
OH!
ZIIIP
SPEAK OF THE DEVIL.
LEMME INTRODUCE YOU TO THE PELOTON'S LEADER.
SEEMED A LITTLE FLAKY AT FIRST, BUT HE'S GOT A BACKBONE YOU CAN COUNT ON!!
!

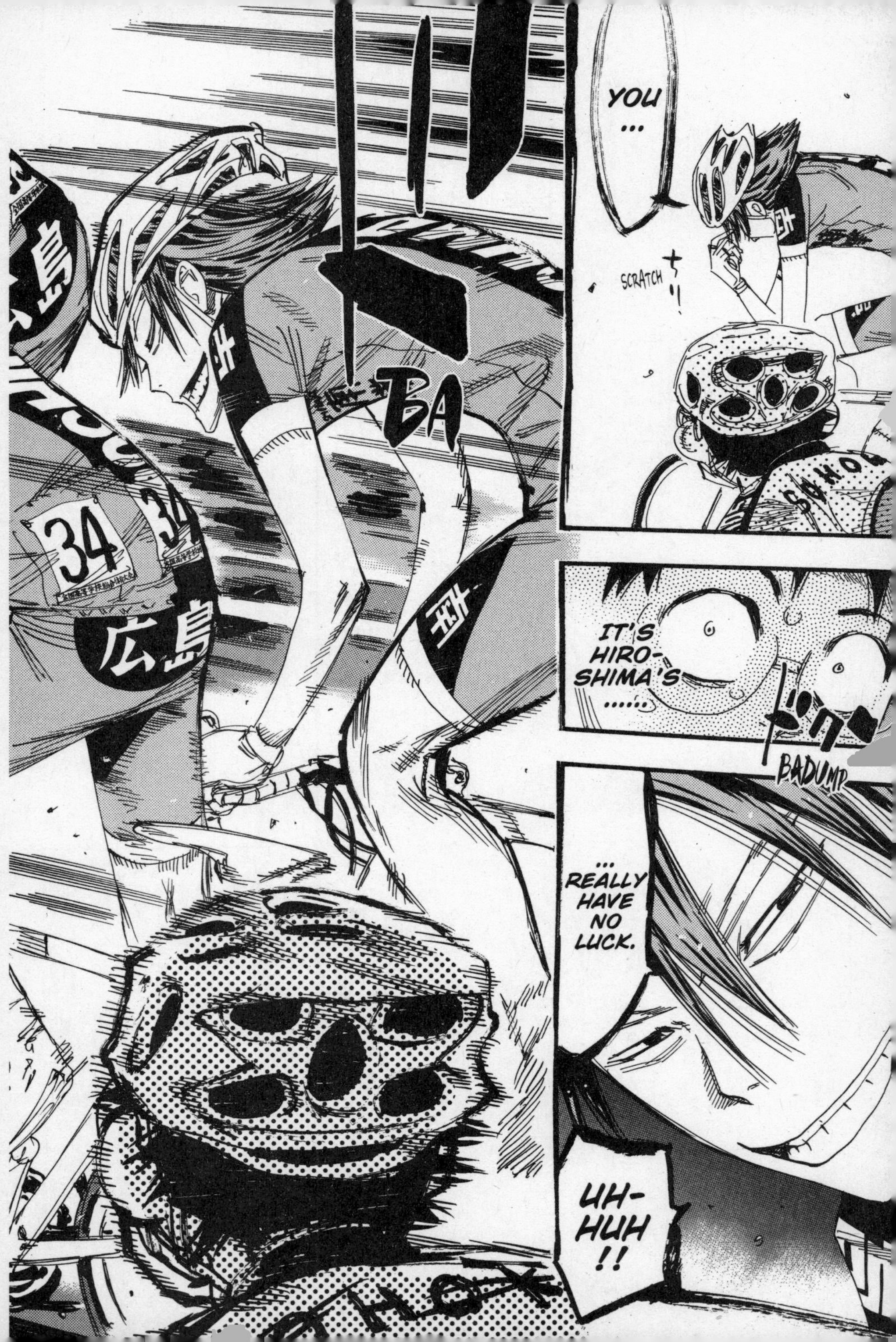
YOU ...
SCRATCH
IT'S HIRO-SHIMA'S ......
BADUMP
... REALLY HAVE NO LUCK.
UH-HUH !!
BA

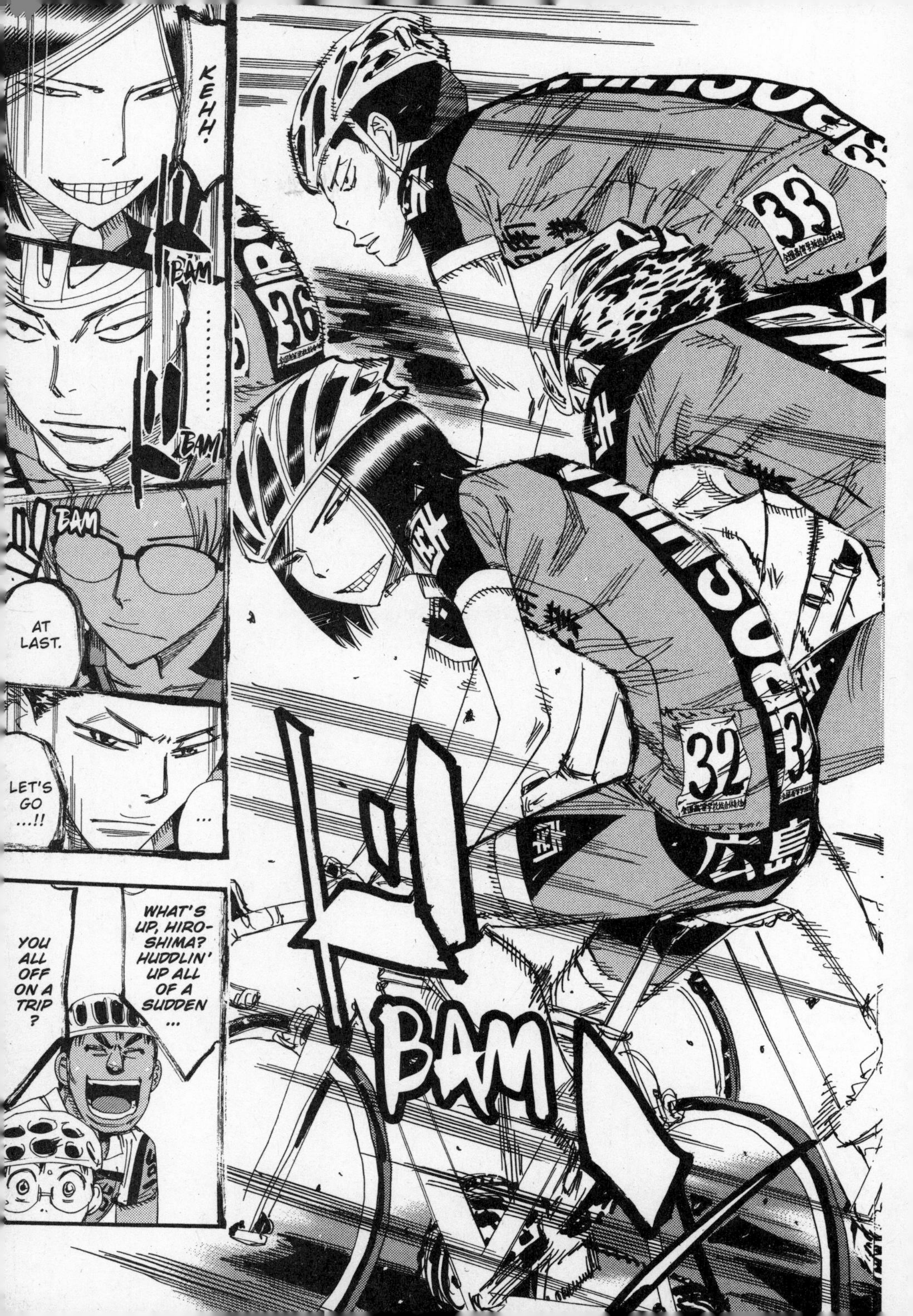
33
36
32
広島
BAM
KEHH!
BAM
......
BAM
BAM
AT LAST.
LET'S GO ...!!
...
WHAT'S UP, HIROSHIMA? HUDDLIN' UP ALL OF A SUDDEN ...
YOU ALL OFF ON A TRIP?

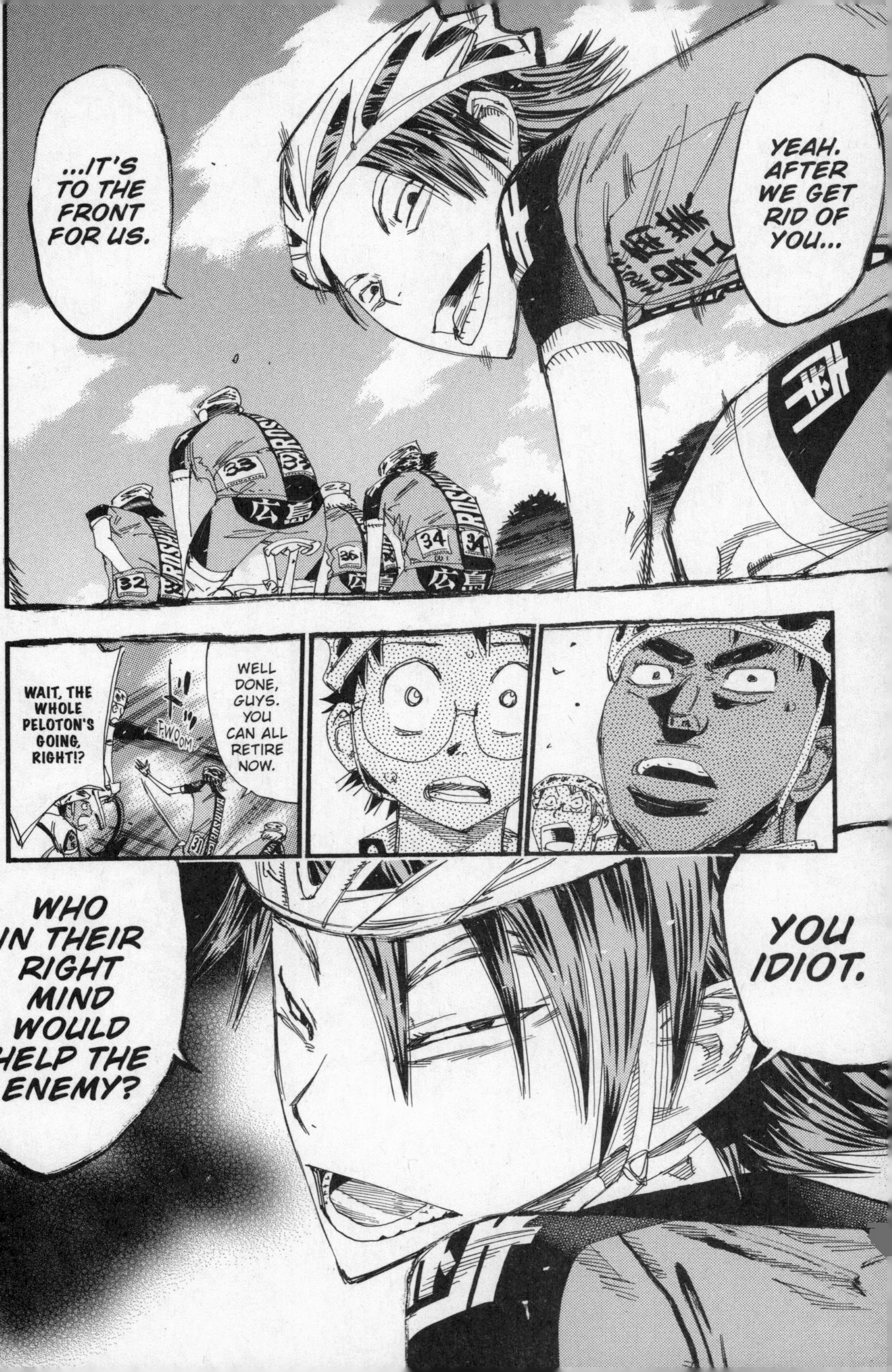
YEAH. AFTER WE GET RID OF YOU...
...IT'S TO THE FRONT FOR US.
WELL DONE, GUYS. YOU CAN ALL RETIRE NOW.
F-WOOM
WAIT, THE WHOLE PELOTON'S GOING, RIGHT!?
YOU IDIOT.
WHO IN THEIR RIGHT MIND WOULD HELP THE ENEMY?

RIDE.166: THE TERROR OF MACHIMIYA

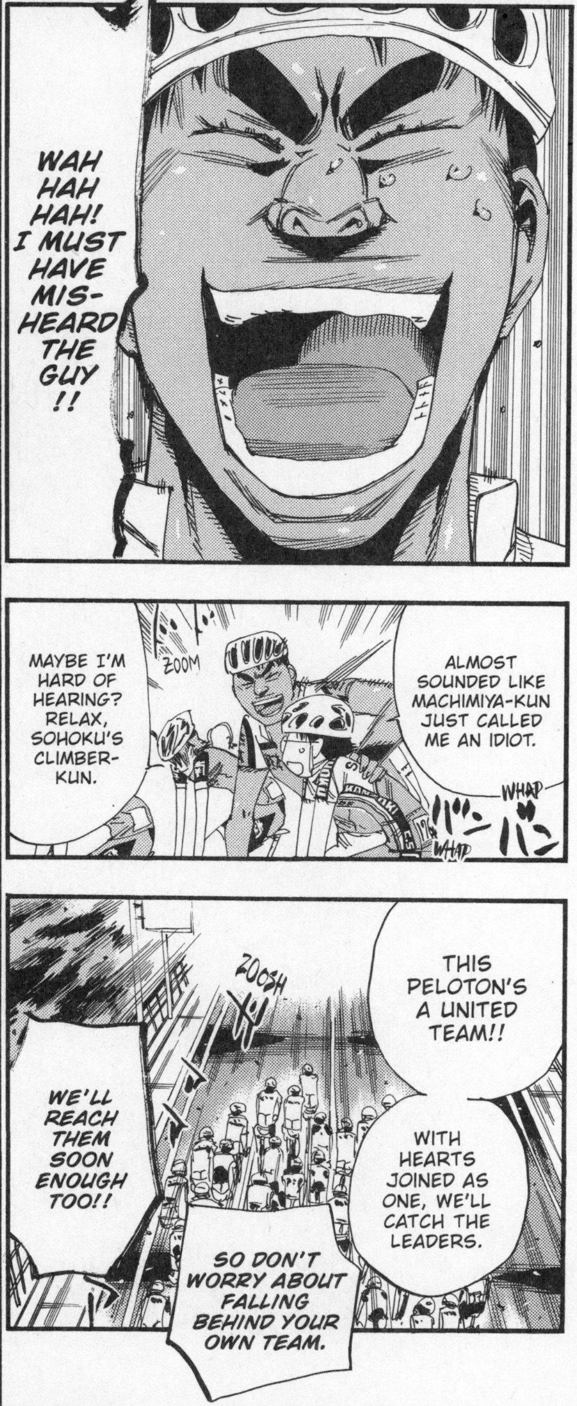
WAH HAH HAH! I MUST HAVE MIS-HEARD THE GUY!!
ALMOST SOUNDED LIKE MACHIMIYA-KUN JUST CALLED ME AN IDIOT.
ZOOM
MAYBE I'M HARD OF HEARING? RELAX, SOHOKU'S CLIMBER-KUN.
WHAP
WHAP
THIS PELOTON'S A UNITED TEAM!!
WITH HEARTS JOINED AS ONE, WE'LL CATCH THE LEADERS.
ZOOSH
WE'LL REACH THEM SOON ENOUGH TOO!!
SO DON'T WORRY ABOUT FALLING BEHIND YOUR OWN TEAM.

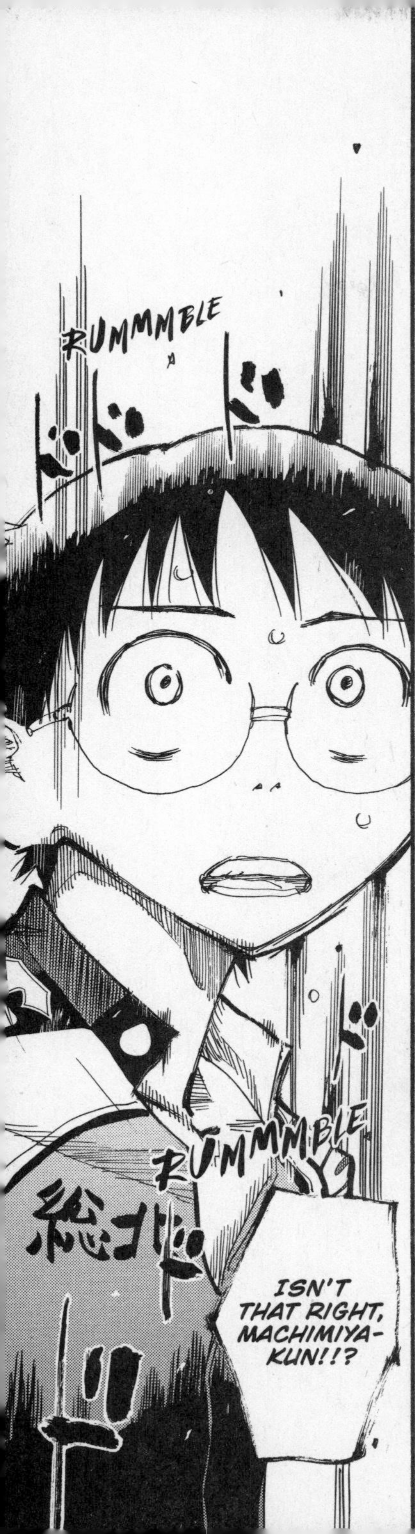
RUMMMBLE
RUMMMBLE
ISN'T THAT RIGHT, MACHIMIYA-KUN!!?

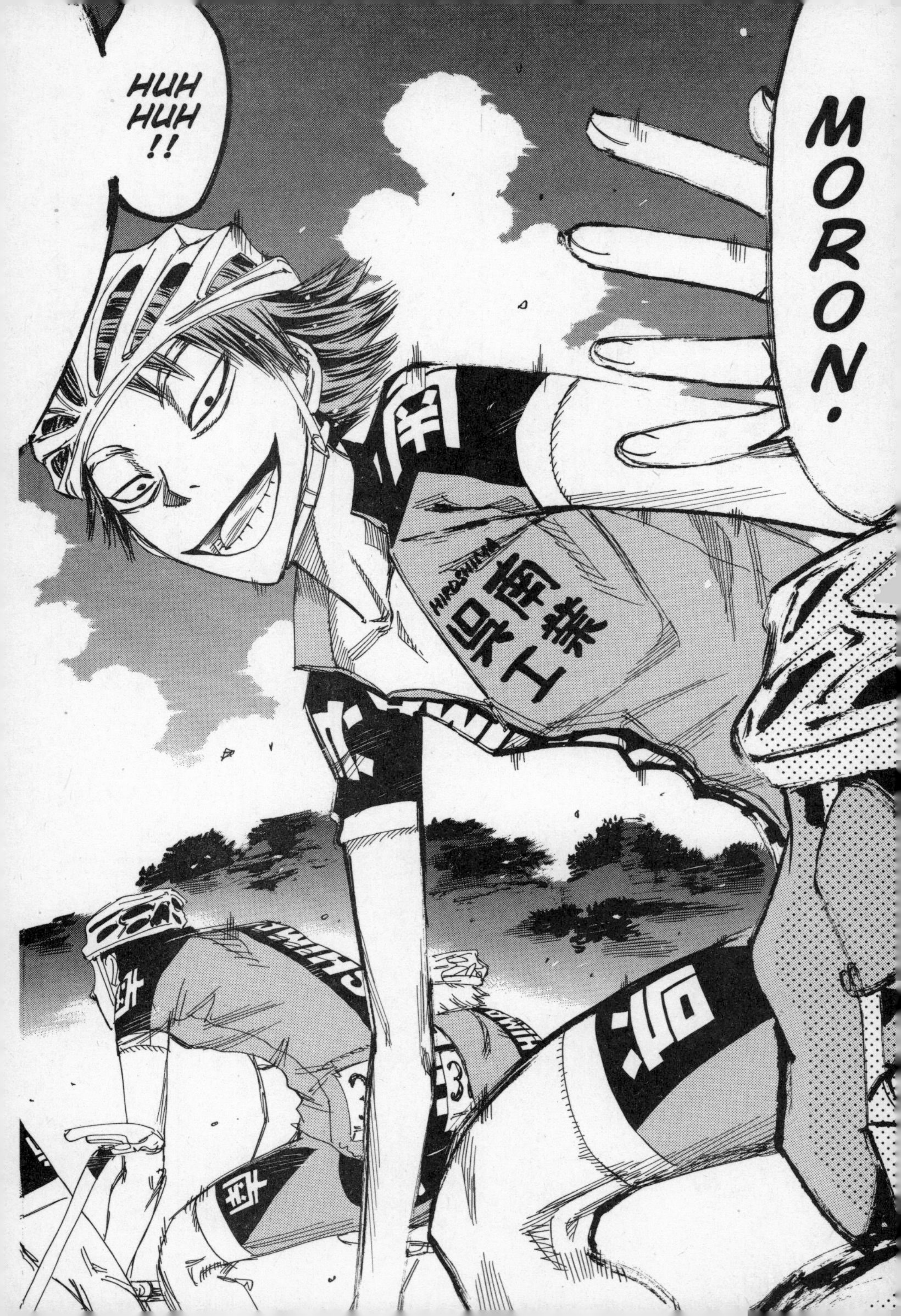
MORON.
HUH HUH!!

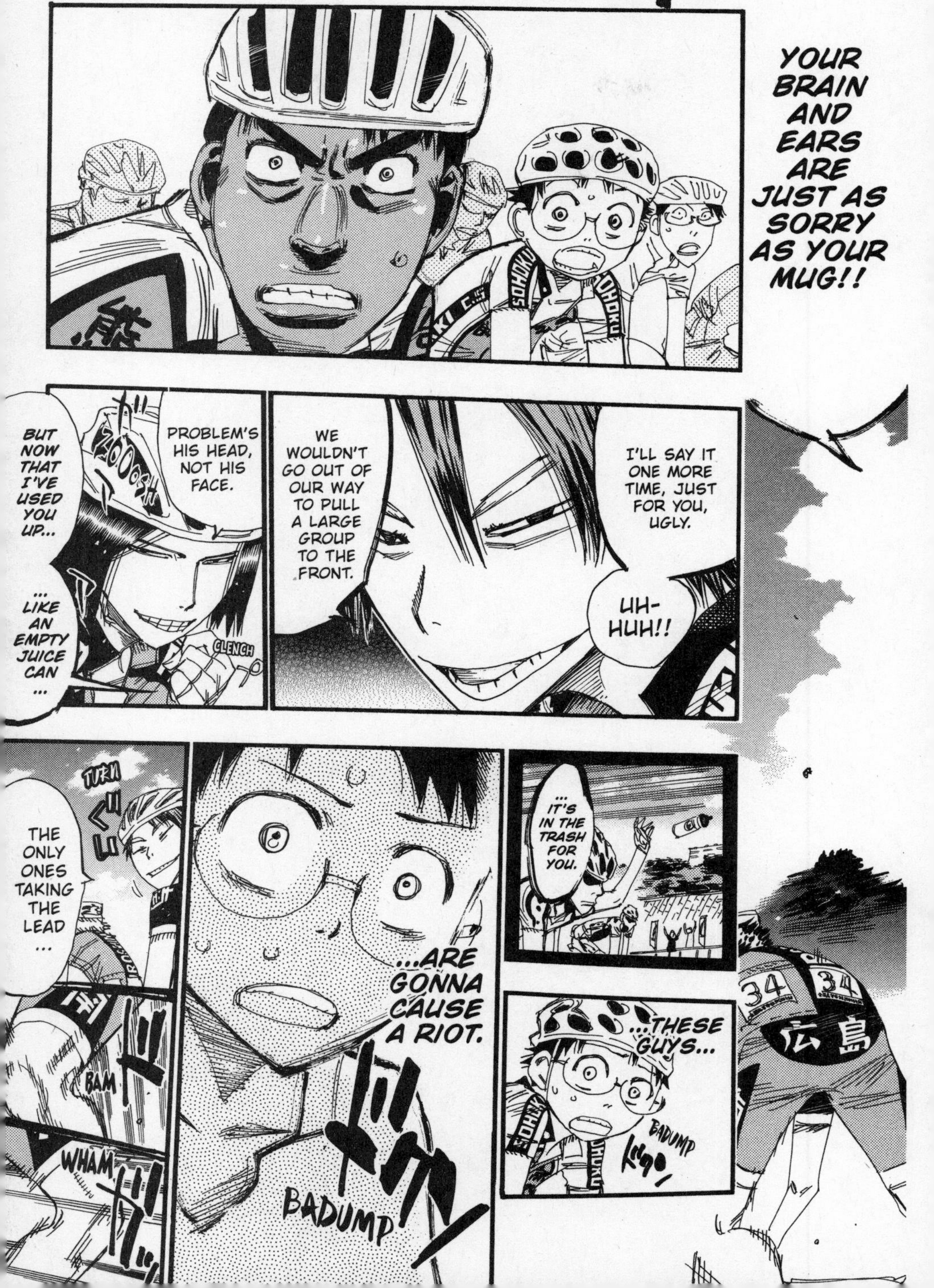
YOUR BRAIN AND EARS ARE JUST AS SORRY AS YOUR MUG!!
I'LL SAY IT ONE MORE TIME, JUST FOR YOU, UGLY.
UH-HUH!!
WE WOULDN'T GO OUT OF OUR WAY TO PULL A LARGE GROUP TO THE FRONT.
PROBLEM'S HIS HEAD, NOT HIS FACE.
BUT NOW THAT I'VE USED YOU UP...
...LIKE AN EMPTY JUICE CAN ...
CLENCH
...IT'S IN THE TRASH FOR YOU.
...THESE GUYS...
BADUMP
TURN
THE ONLY ONES TAKING THE LEAD ...
...ARE GONNA CAUSE A RIOT.
BADUMP
BAM
WHAM

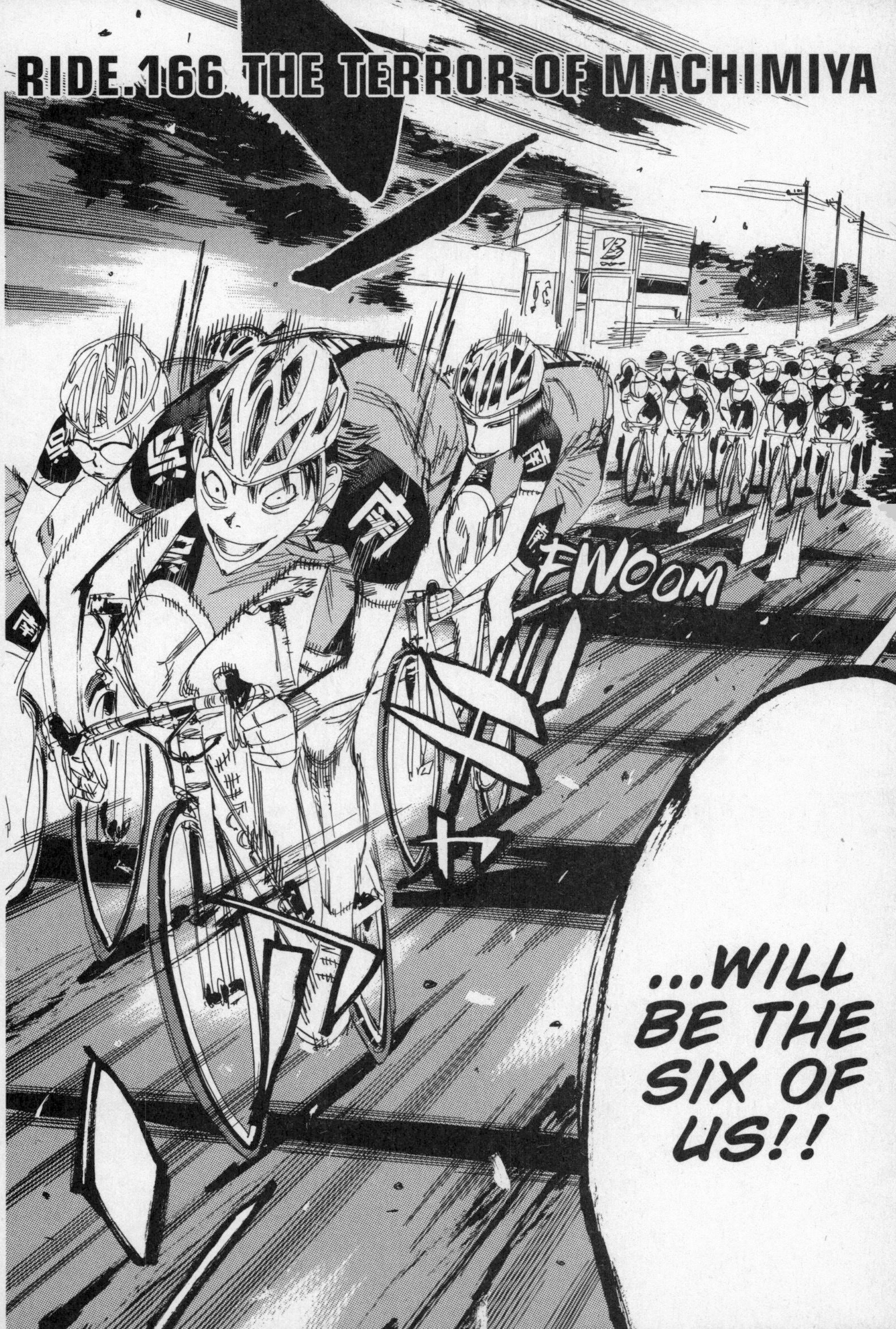
RIDE.166 THE TERROR OF MACHIMIYA
FWOOM
...WILL BE THE SIX OF US!!

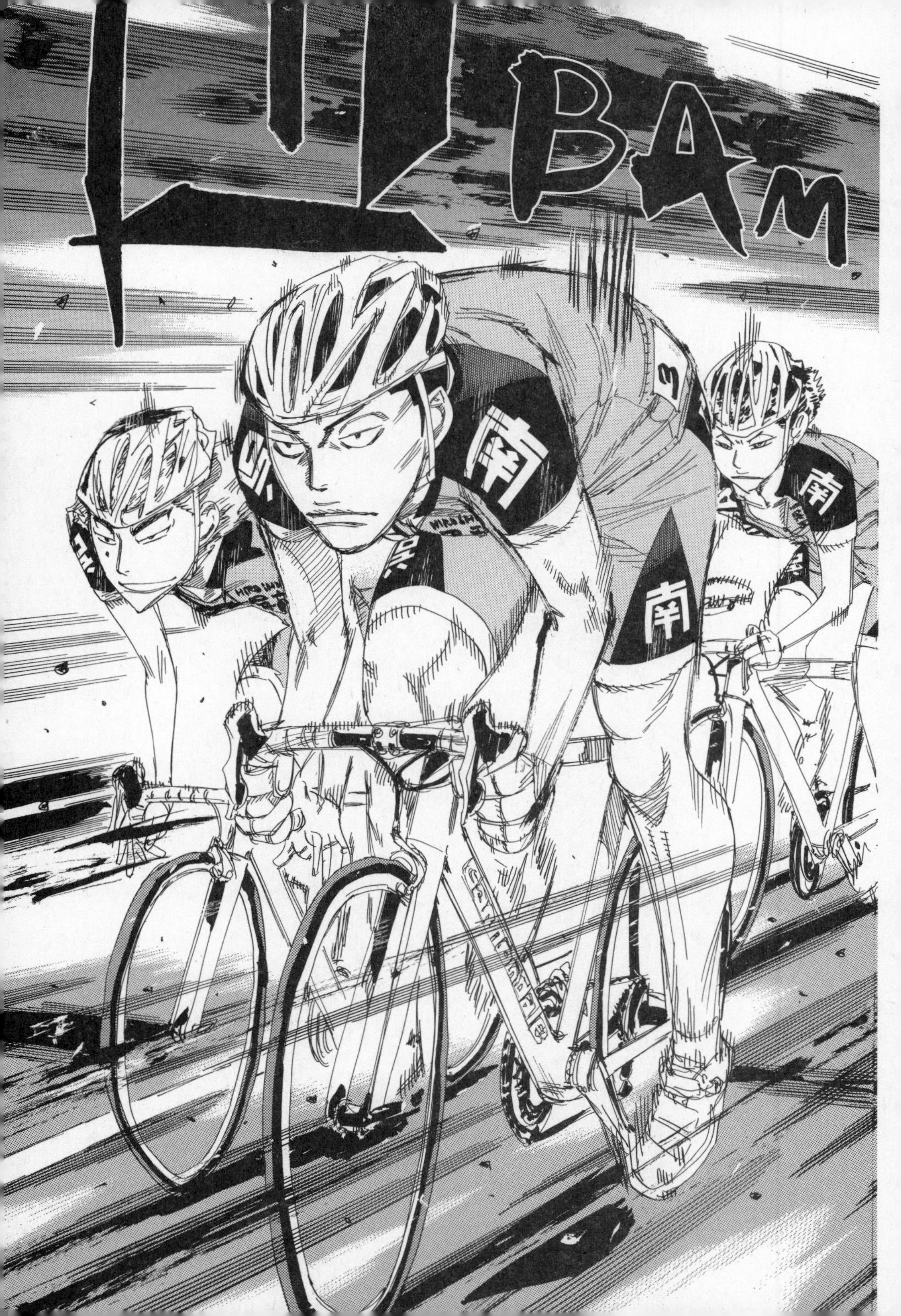
BAM

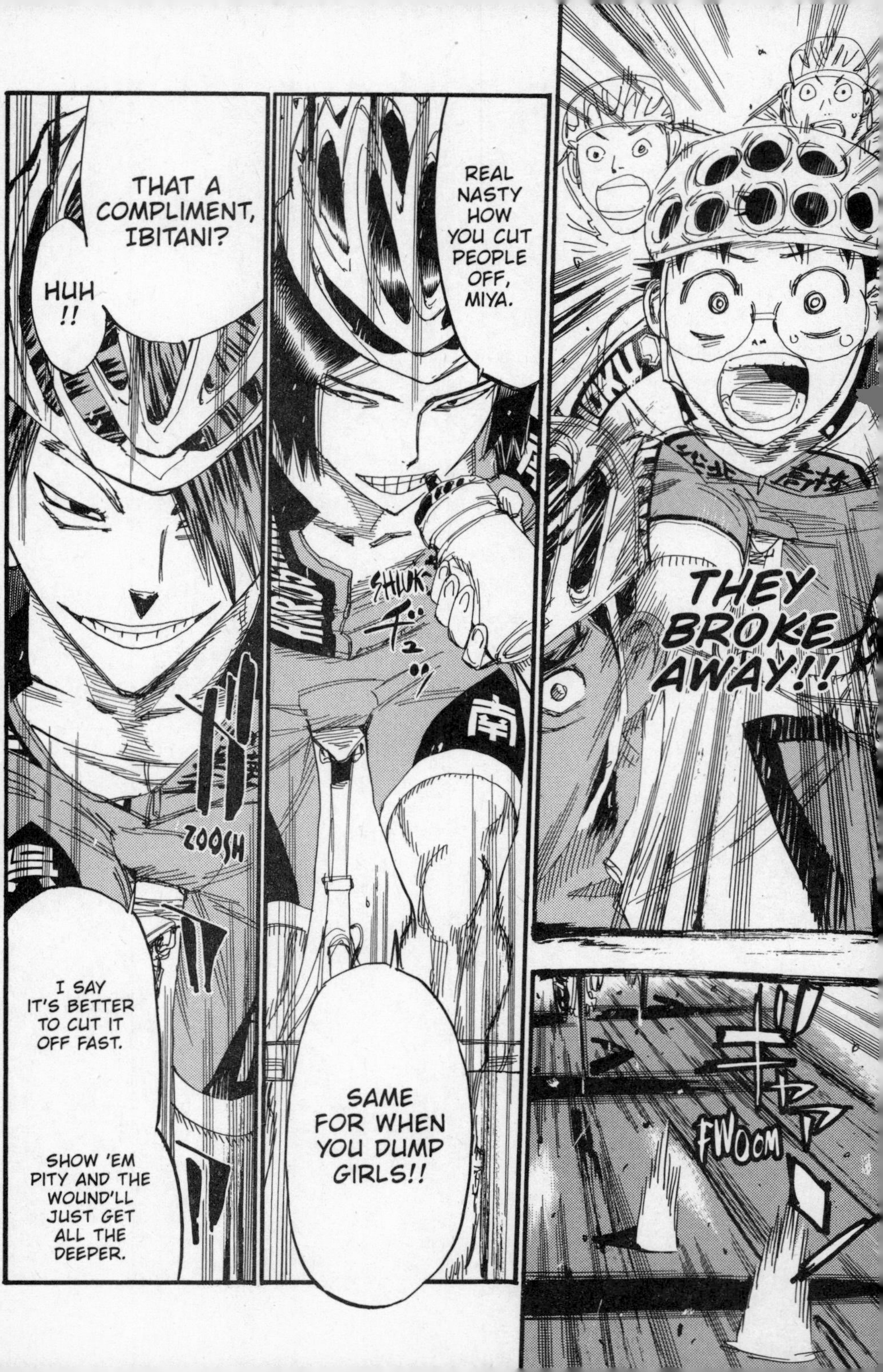
THEY BROKE AWAY!!
FWOOM
REAL NASTY HOW YOU CUT PEOPLE OFF, MIYA.
SHLUK
SAME FOR WHEN YOU DUMP GIRLS!!
THAT A COMPLIMENT, IBITANI?
HUH!!
ZOOSH
I SAY IT'S BETTER TO CUT IT OFF FAST.
SHOW 'EM PITY AND THE WOUND'LL JUST GET ALL THE DEEPER.

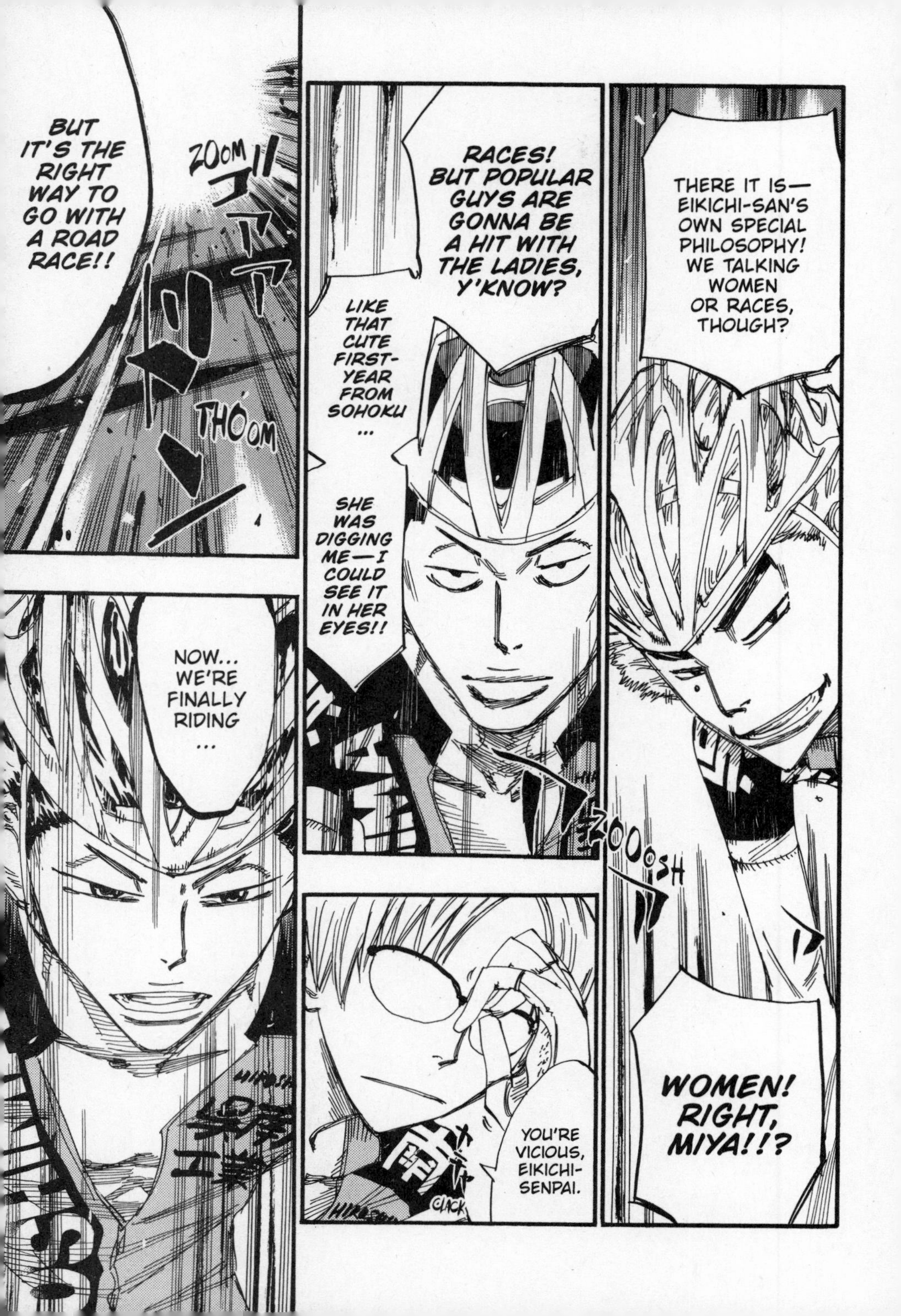
THERE IT IS—EIKICHI-SAN'S OWN SPECIAL PHILOSOPHY! WE TALKING WOMEN OR RACES, THOUGH?
WOMEN! RIGHT, MIYA!!?
ZOOOSH
RACES! BUT POPULAR GUYS ARE GONNA BE A HIT WITH THE LADIES, Y'KNOW?
LIKE THAT CUTE FIRST-YEAR FROM SOHOKU...
SHE WAS DIGGING ME—I COULD SEE IT IN HER EYES!!
YOU'RE VICIOUS, EIKICHI-SENPAI.
CLACK
BUT IT'S THE RIGHT WAY TO GO WITH A ROAD RACE!!
ZOOM
THOOM
NOW... WE'RE FINALLY RIDING...

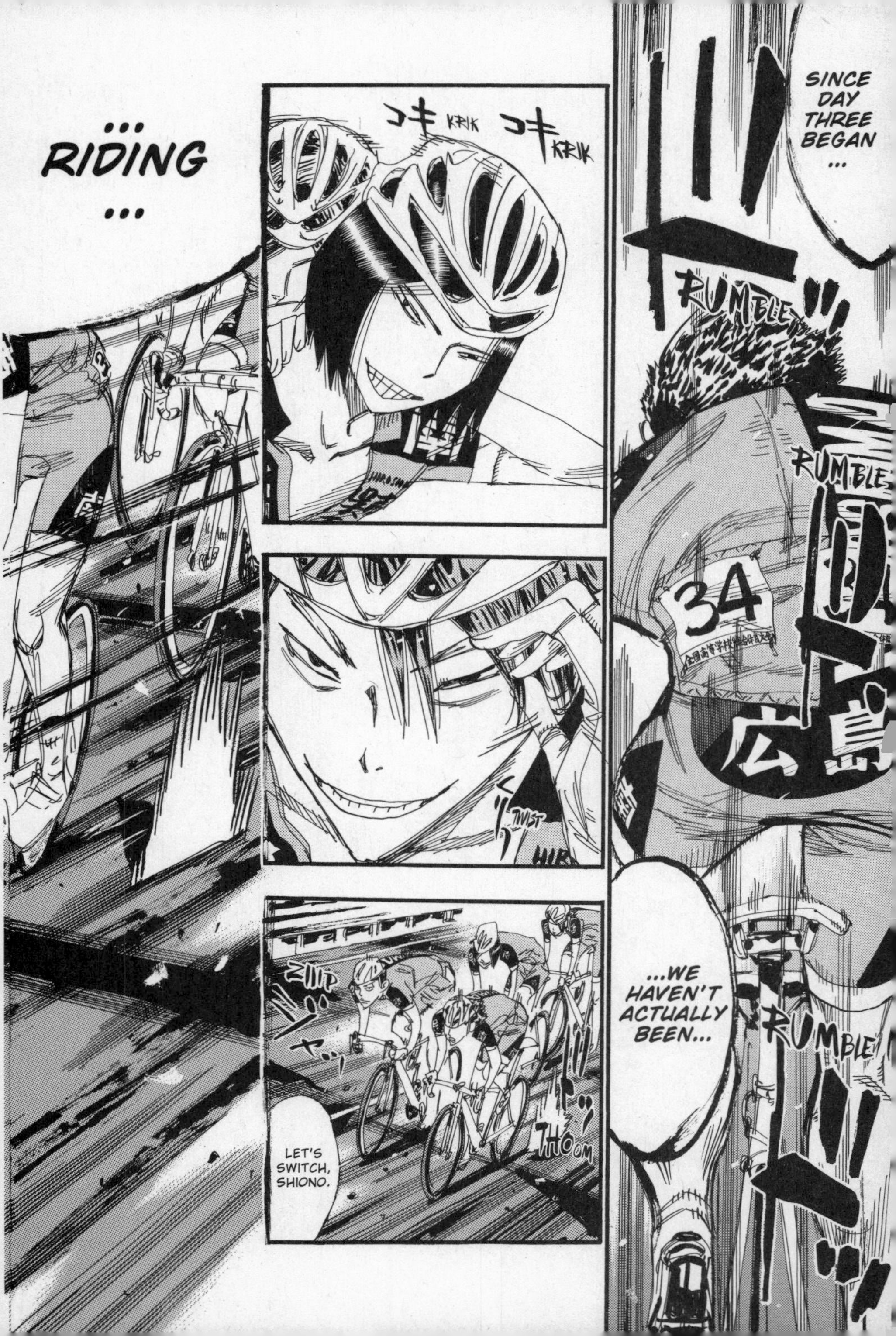
SINCE DAY THREE BEGAN ...
RUMBLE
RUMBLE
34
...WE HAVEN'T ACTUALLY BEEN...
RUMBLE
コキ KRIK
コキ KRIK
TWIST
ZHIP
LET'S SWITCH, SHIONO.
THOOM
... RIDING ...

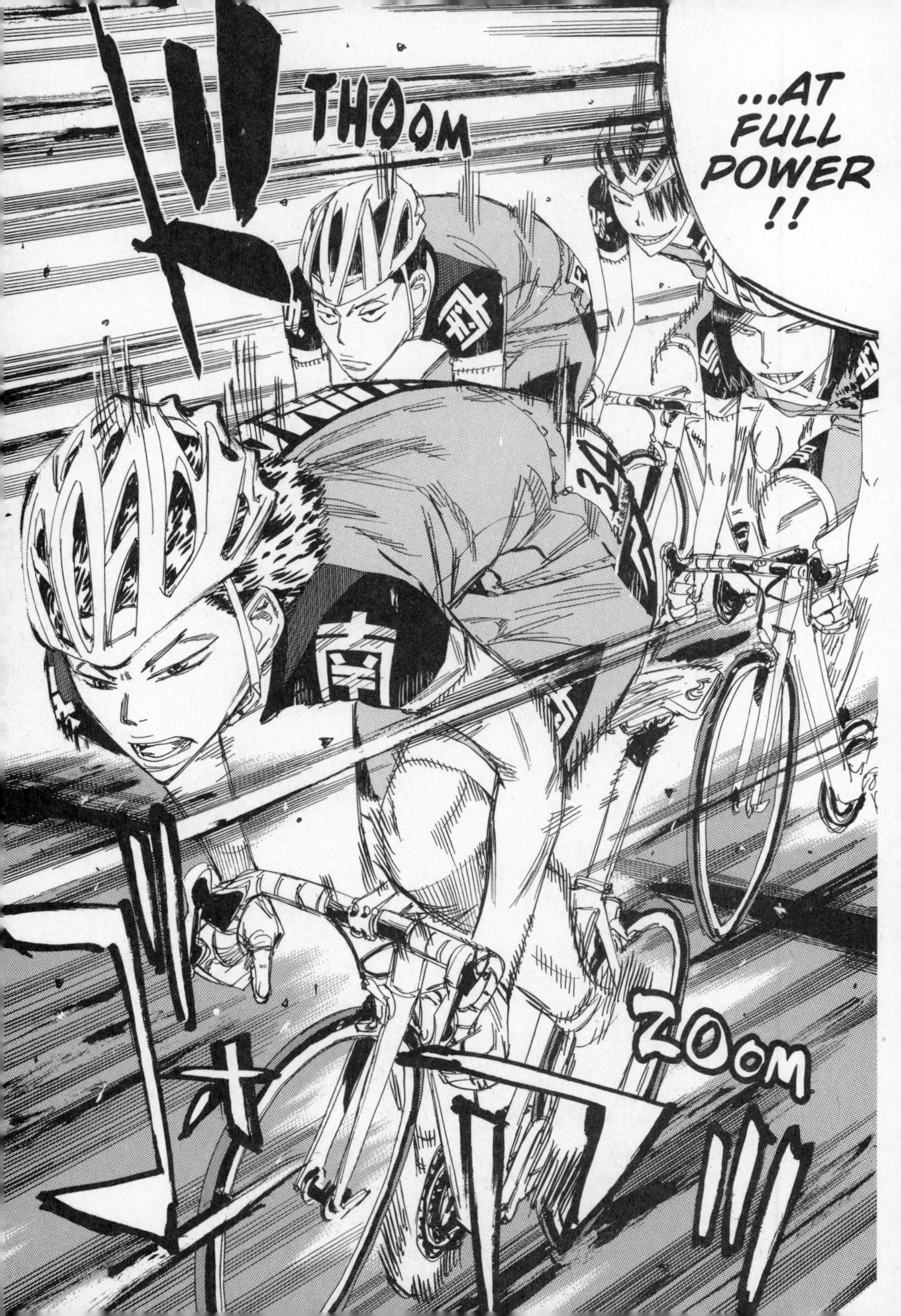
...AT FULL POWER!!
THOOM
ZOOM

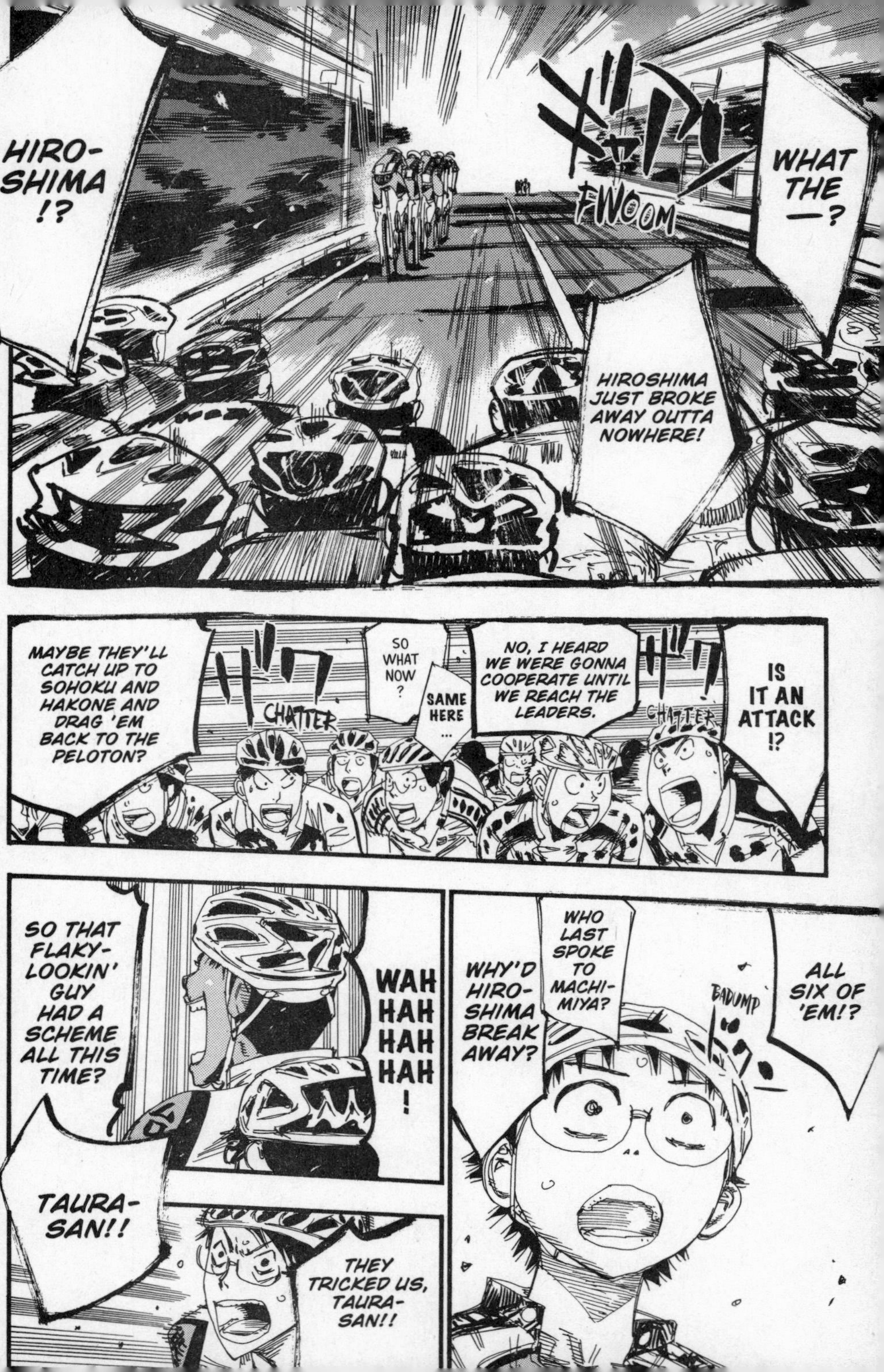
WHAT THE—?
FWOOM
HIROSHIMA JUST BROKE AWAY OUTTA NOWHERE!
HIRO-SHIMA!?
IS IT AN ATTACK!?
CHATTER
NO, I HEARD WE WERE GONNA COOPERATE UNTIL WE REACH THE LEADERS.
SAME HERE...
SO WHAT NOW?
CHATTER
MAYBE THEY'LL CATCH UP TO SOHOKU AND HAKONE AND DRAG 'EM BACK TO THE PELOTON?
ALL SIX OF 'EM!?
BADUMP
WHO LAST SPOKE TO MACHIMIYA?
WHY'D HIROSHIMA BREAK AWAY?
WAH HAH HAH HAH!
SO THAT FLAKY-LOOKIN' GUY HAD A SCHEME ALL THIS TIME?
TAURA-SAN!!
THEY TRICKED US, TAURA-SAN!!

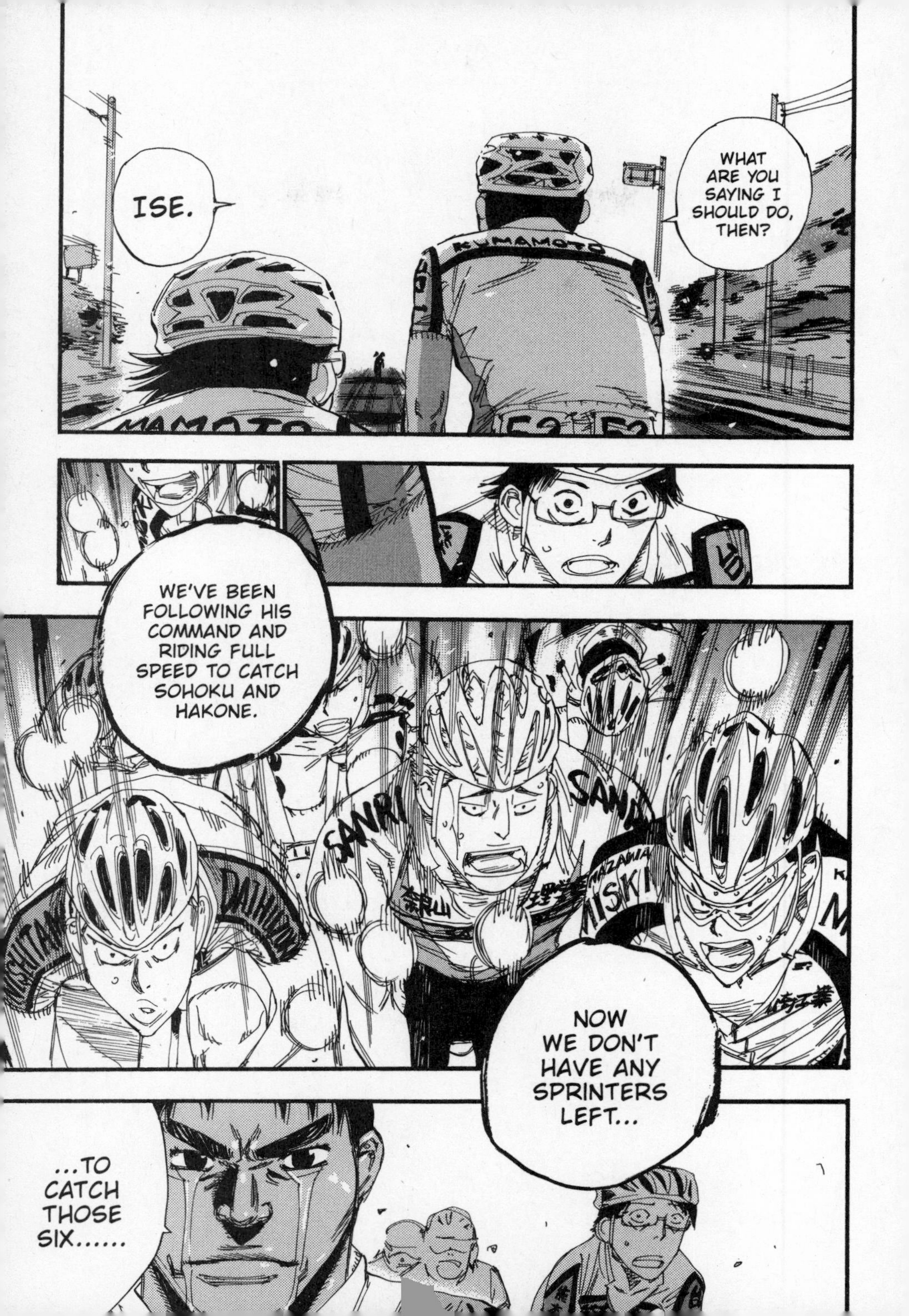
WHAT ARE YOU SAYING I SHOULD DO, THEN?
ISE.
WE'VE BEEN FOLLOWING HIS COMMAND AND RIDING FULL SPEED TO CATCH SOHOKU AND HAKONE.
NOW WE DON'T HAVE ANY SPRINTERS LEFT...
...TO CATCH THOSE SIX.......

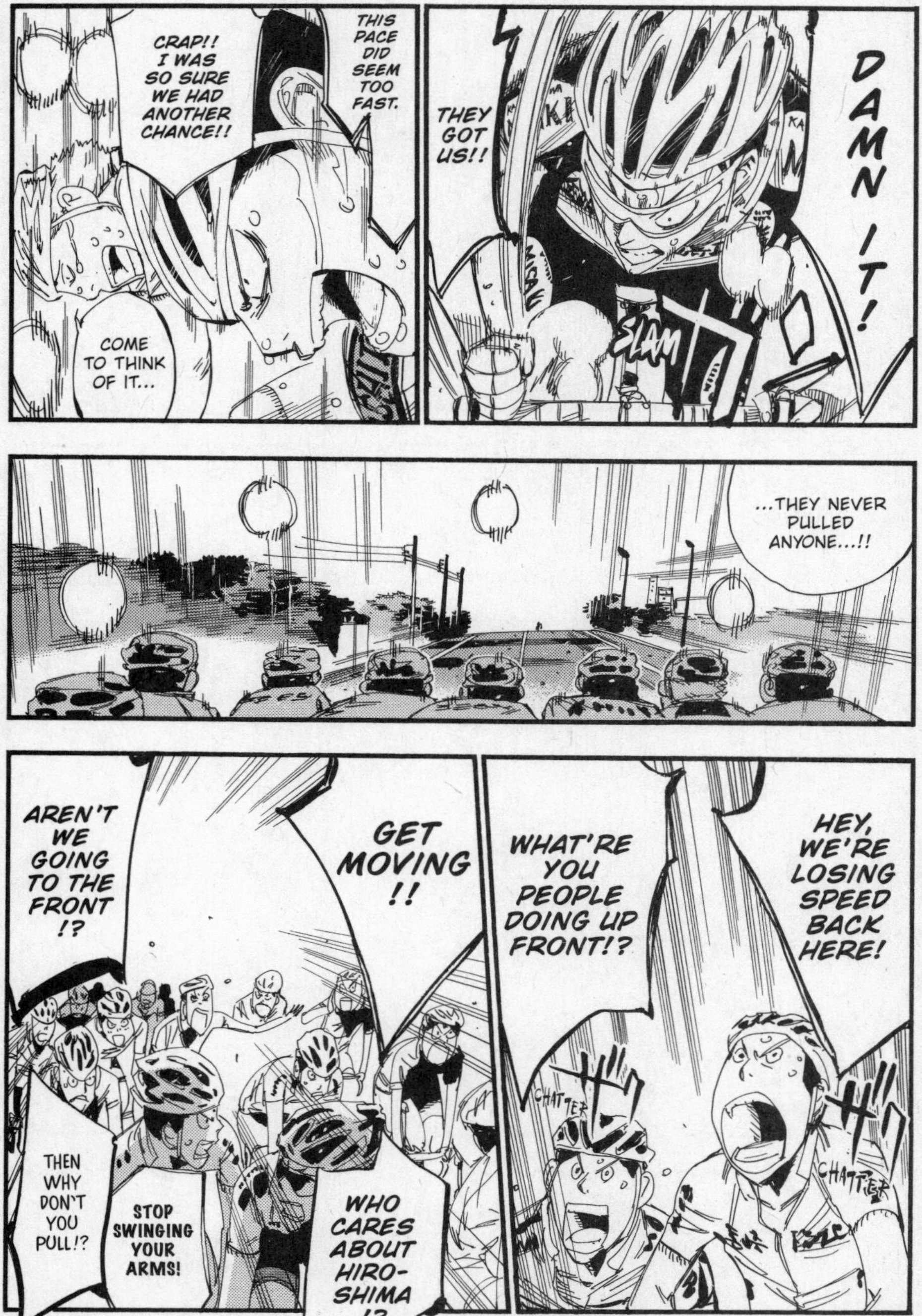
DAMN IT!
THEY GOT US!!
SLAM
THIS PACE DID SEEM TOO FAST.
CRAP!! I WAS SO SURE WE HAD ANOTHER CHANCE!!
COME TO THINK OF IT...
...THEY NEVER PULLED ANYONE...!!
HEY, WE'RE LOSING SPEED BACK HERE!
WHAT'RE YOU PEOPLE DOING UP FRONT!?
CHATTER
CHATTER
GET MOVING!!
AREN'T WE GOING TO THE FRONT!?
WHO CARES ABOUT HIRO-SHIMA!?
STOP SWINGING YOUR ARMS!
THEN WHY DON'T YOU PULL!?

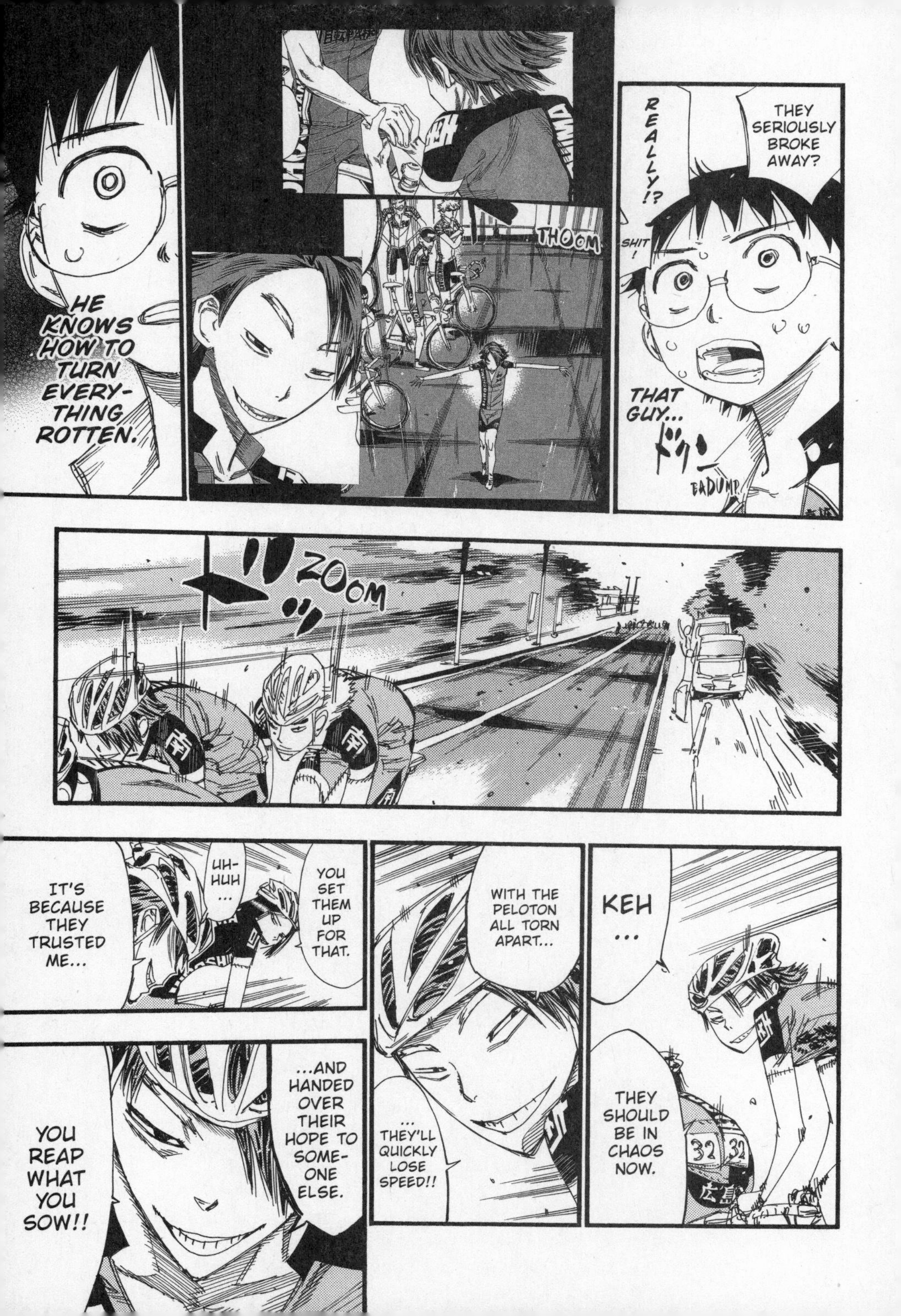
THEY SERIOUSLY BROKE AWAY?
REALLY!?
SHIT!
THAT GUY...
ドクン
BADUMP
THOOM
HE KNOWS HOW TO TURN EVERY-THING ROTTEN.
ZOOM
KEH...
THEY SHOULD BE IN CHAOS NOW.
WITH THE PELOTON ALL TORN APART...
...THEY'LL QUICKLY LOSE SPEED!!
YOU SET THEM UP FOR THAT.
UH-HUH...
IT'S BECAUSE THEY TRUSTED ME...
...AND HANDED OVER THEIR HOPE TO SOME-ONE ELSE.
YOU REAP WHAT YOU SOW!!

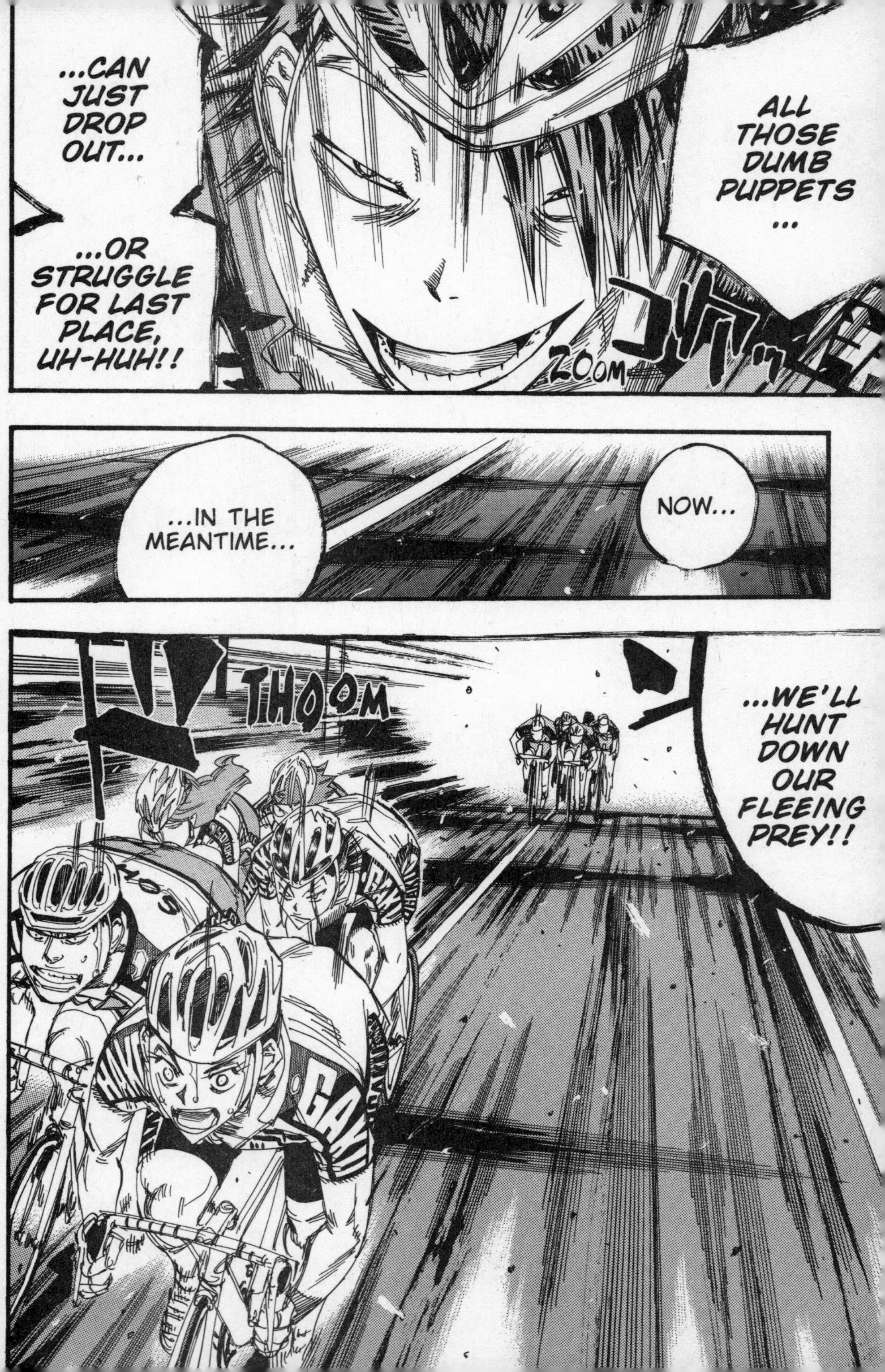
ALL THOSE DUMB PUPPETS...
...CAN JUST DROP OUT...
...OR STRUGGLE FOR LAST PLACE, UH-HUH!!
ZOOM
NOW...
...IN THE MEANTIME...
...WE'LL HUNT DOWN OUR FLEEING PREY!!
THOOM

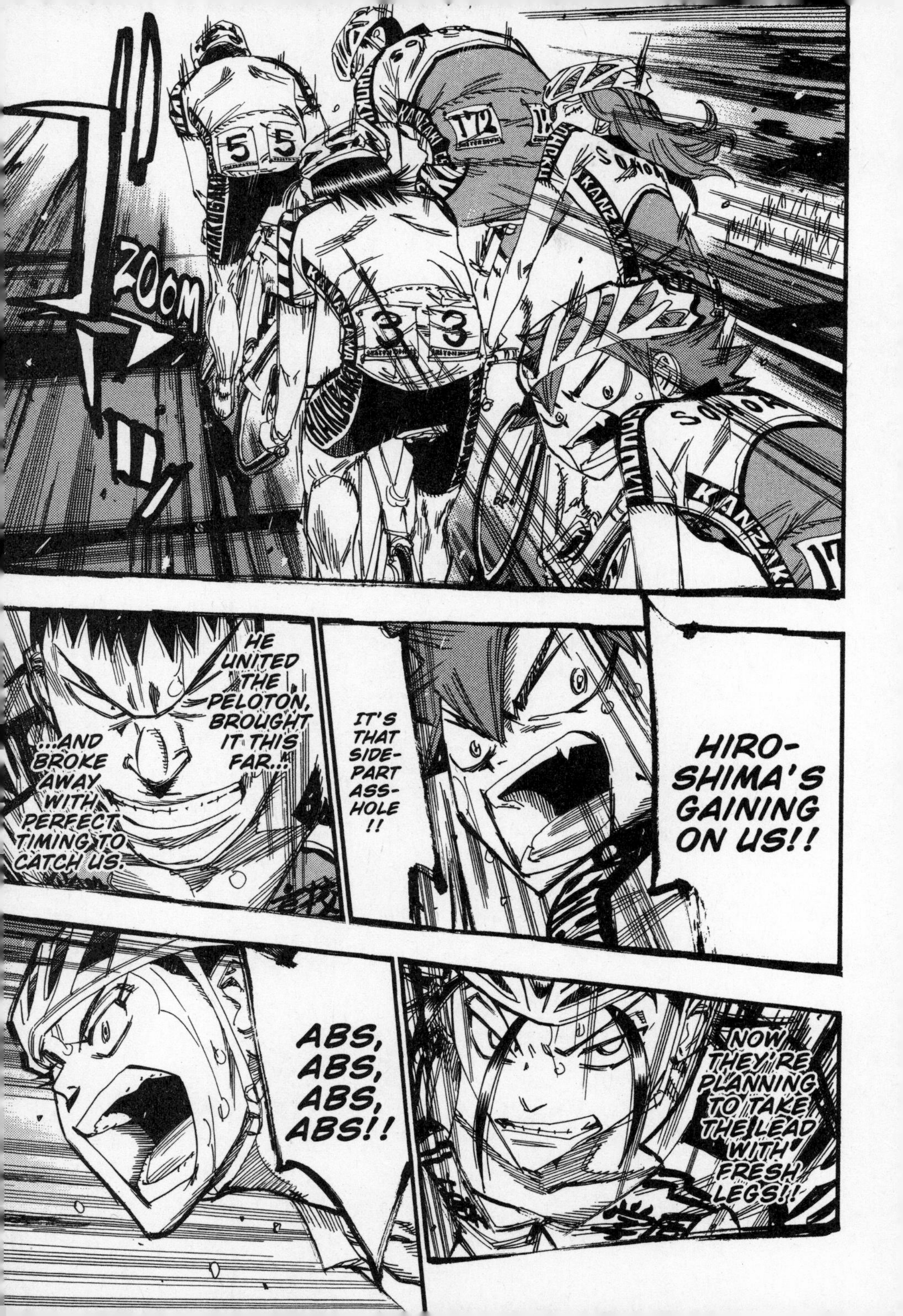
ZOOM
HIROSHIMA'S GAINING ON US!!
IT'S THAT SIDE-PART ASSHOLE!!
HE UNITED THE PELOTON, BROUGHT IT THIS FAR...
...AND BROKE AWAY WITH PERFECT TIMING TO CATCH US.
NOW THEY'RE PLANNING TO TAKE THE LEAD WITH FRESH LEGS!!
ABS, ABS, ABS, ABS!!

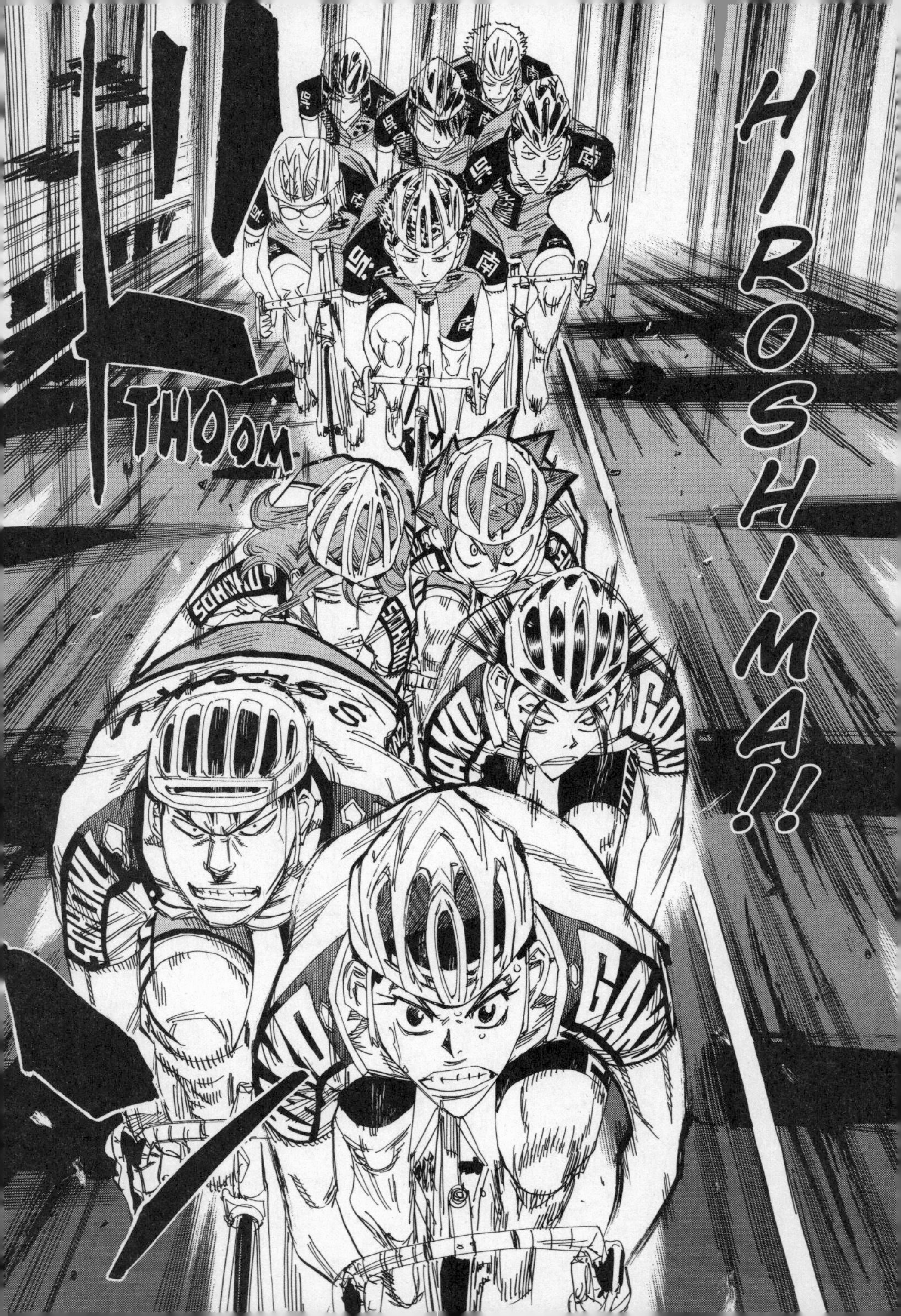
HIROSHIMA!!
THOOM

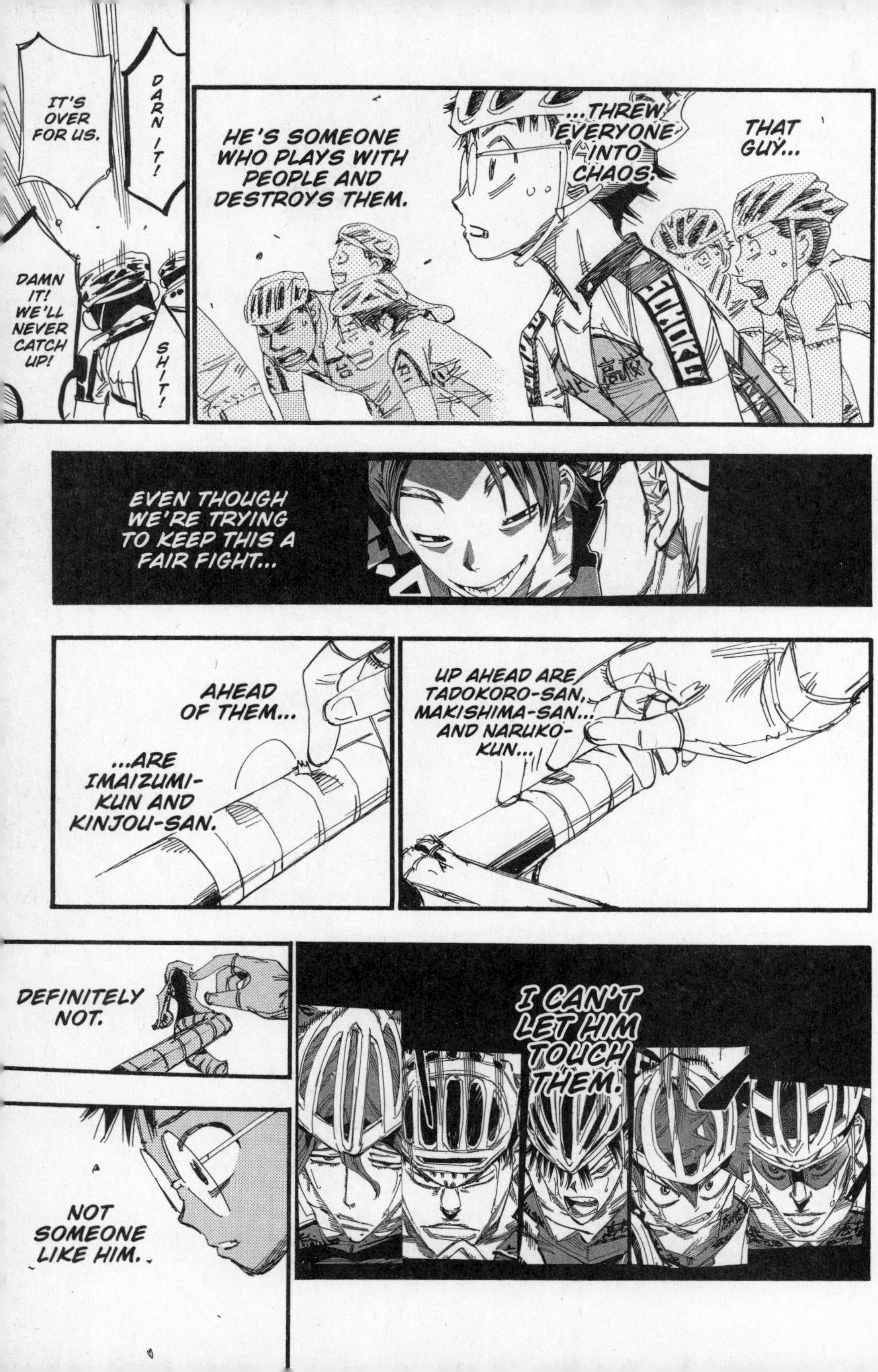
THAT GUY...
...THREW EVERYONE INTO CHAOS.
HE'S SOMEONE WHO PLAYS WITH PEOPLE AND DESTROYS THEM.
DARN IT!
IT'S OVER FOR US.
SHIT!
DAMN IT! WE'LL NEVER CATCH UP!
EVEN THOUGH WE'RE TRYING TO KEEP THIS A FAIR FIGHT...
UP AHEAD ARE TADOKORO-SAN, MAKISHIMA-SAN... AND NARUKO-KUN...
AHEAD OF THEM...
...ARE IMAIZUMI-KUN AND KINJOU-SAN.
I CAN'T LET HIM TOUCH THEM.
DEFINITELY NOT.
NOT SOMEONE LIKE HIM.

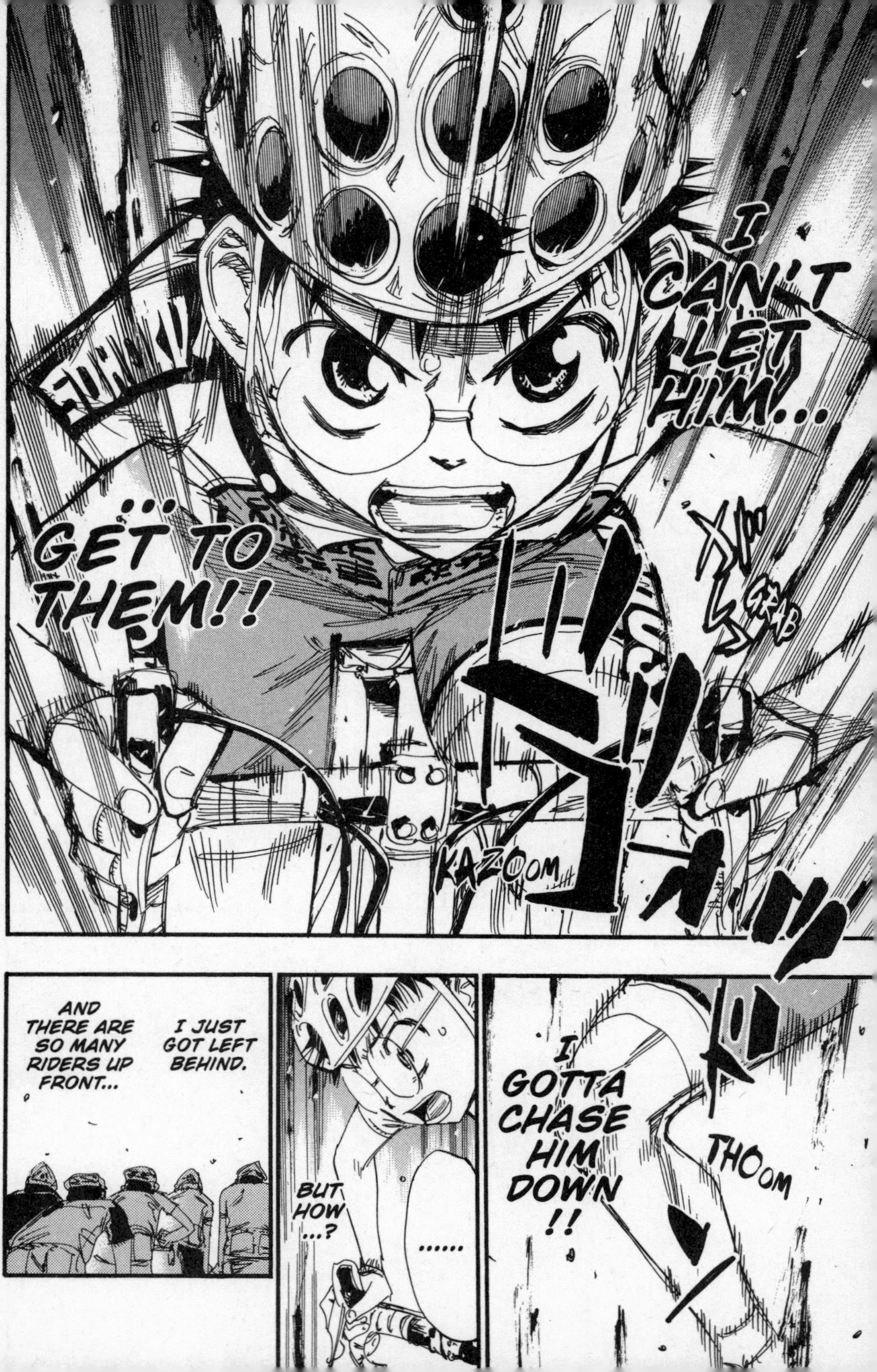
I CAN'T LET HIM...
...GET TO THEM!!
GRAB
KAZOOM
I GOTTA CHASE HIM DOWN!!
THOOM
BUT HOW...?
......
I JUST GOT LEFT BEHIND.
AND THERE ARE SO MANY RIDERS UP FRONT...

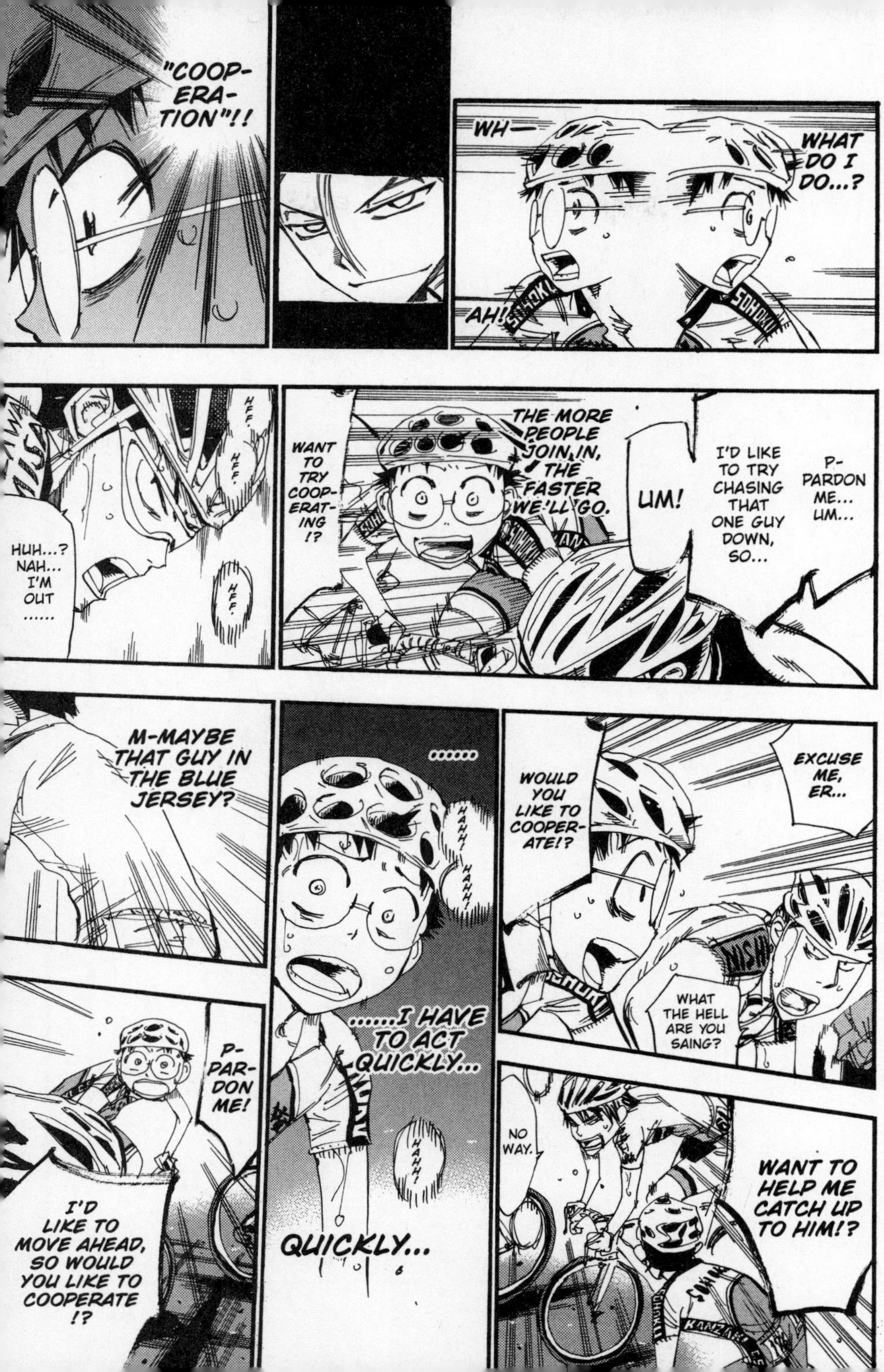
WH—
WHAT DO I DO...?
AH!
"COOPERATION"!!
P-PARDON ME... UM...
I'D LIKE TO TRY CHASING THAT ONE GUY DOWN, SO...
UM!
THE MORE PEOPLE JOIN IN, THE FASTER WE'LL GO.
WANT TO TRY COOPERATING!?
HFF. HFF. HFF.
HUH...? NAH... I'M OUT ......
EXCUSE ME, ER...
WOULD YOU LIKE TO COOPERATE!?
WHAT THE HELL ARE YOU SAING?
WANT TO HELP ME CATCH UP TO HIM!?
NO WAY.
......
HAHH! HAHH!
......I HAVE TO ACT QUICKLY...
HAHH!
QUICKLY...
M-MAYBE THAT GUY IN THE BLUE JERSEY?
P-PARDON ME!
I'D LIKE TO MOVE AHEAD, SO WOULD YOU LIKE TO COOPERATE!?

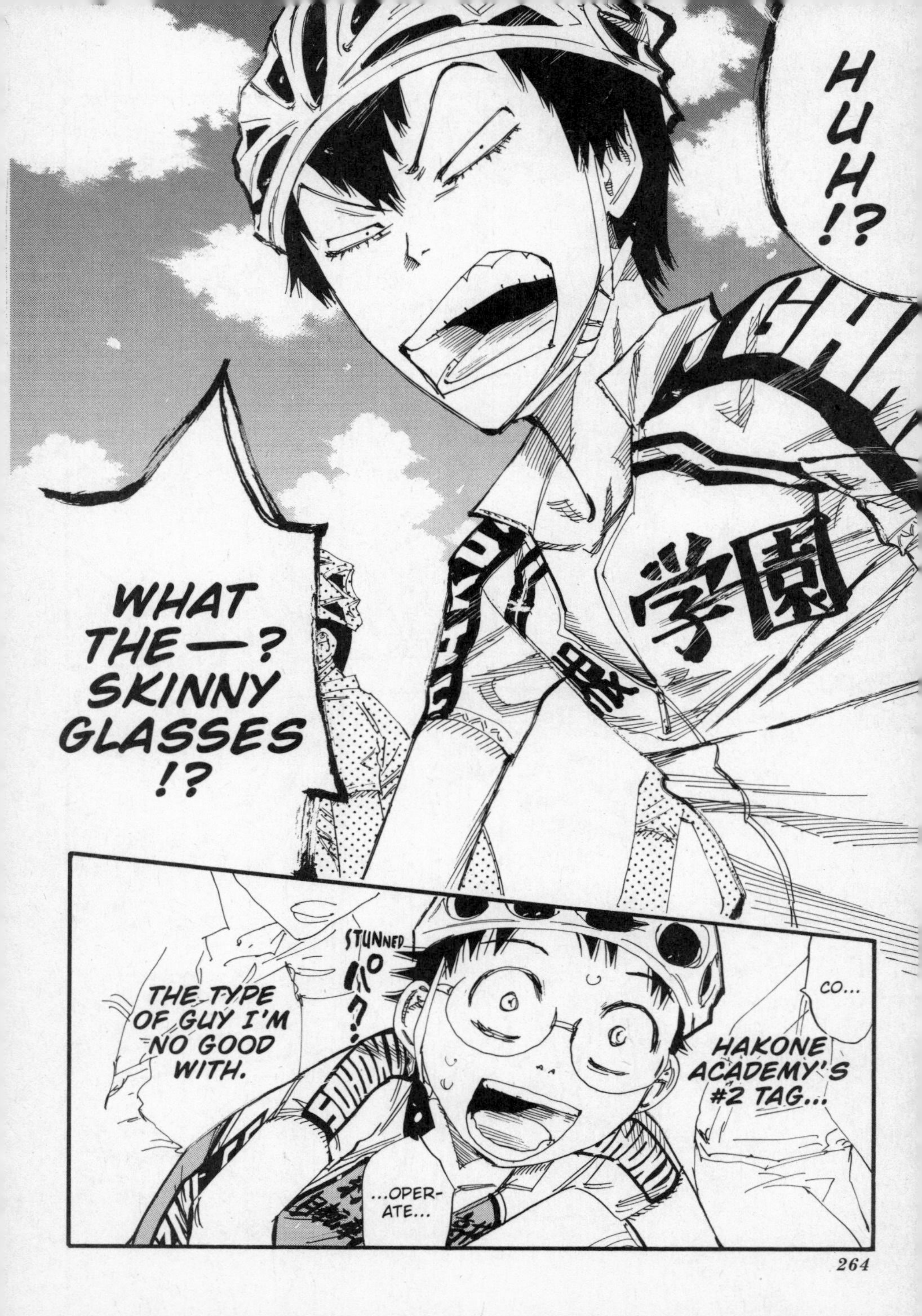
HUH!?
WHAT THE—? SKINNY GLASSES!?
CO...
HAKONE ACADEMY'S #2 TAG...
STUNNED
パ?
THE TYPE OF GUY I'M NO GOOD WITH.
...OPER-ATE...

RIDE.167 ARAKITA

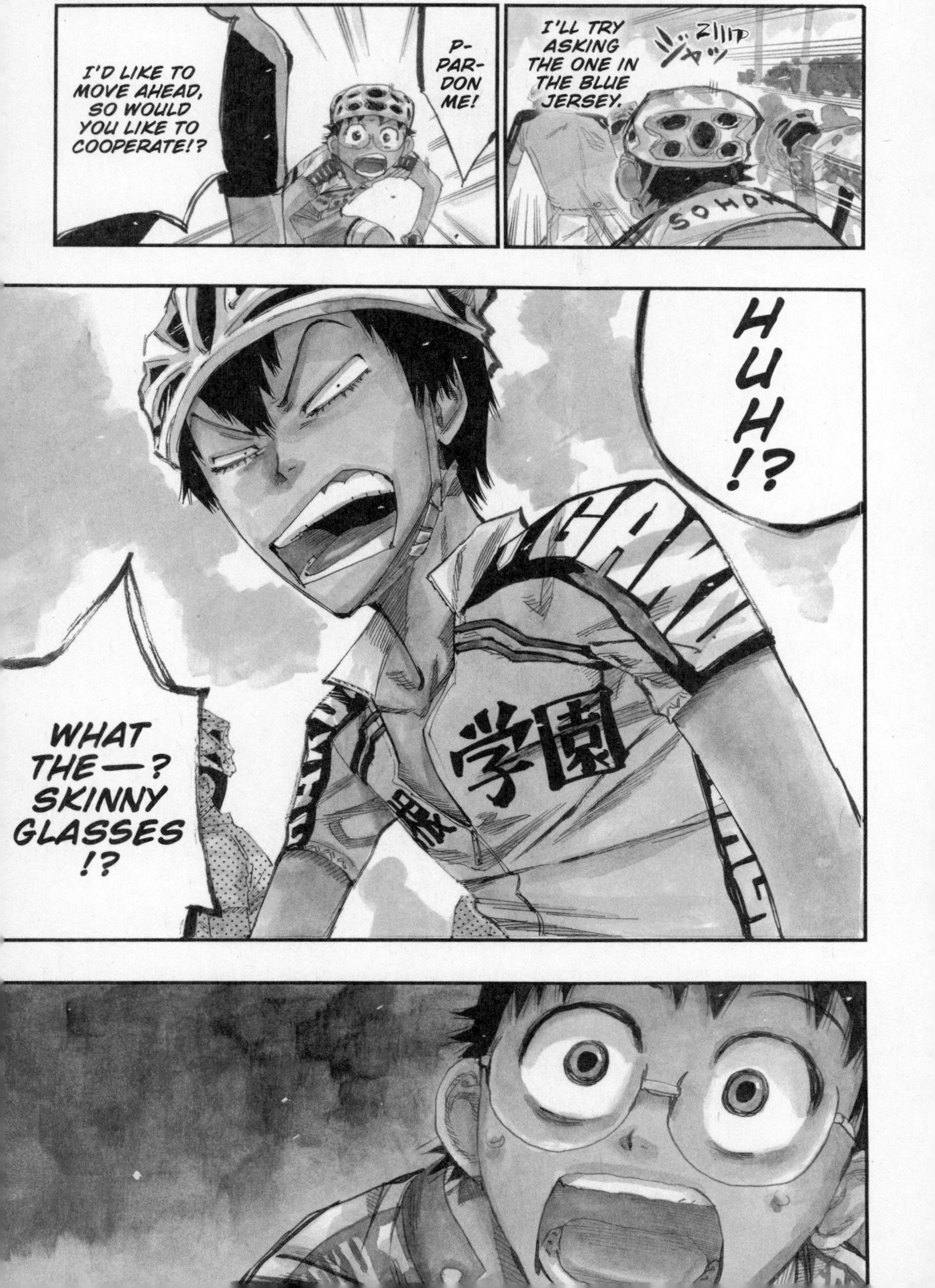
I'LL TRY ASKING THE ONE IN THE BLUE JERSEY.
ZIIIP
ジャッ
SOHOK
P-PARDON ME!
I'D LIKE TO MOVE AHEAD, SO WOULD YOU LIKE TO COOPERATE!?
HUH!?
WHAT THE—? SKINNY GLASSES!?
学園

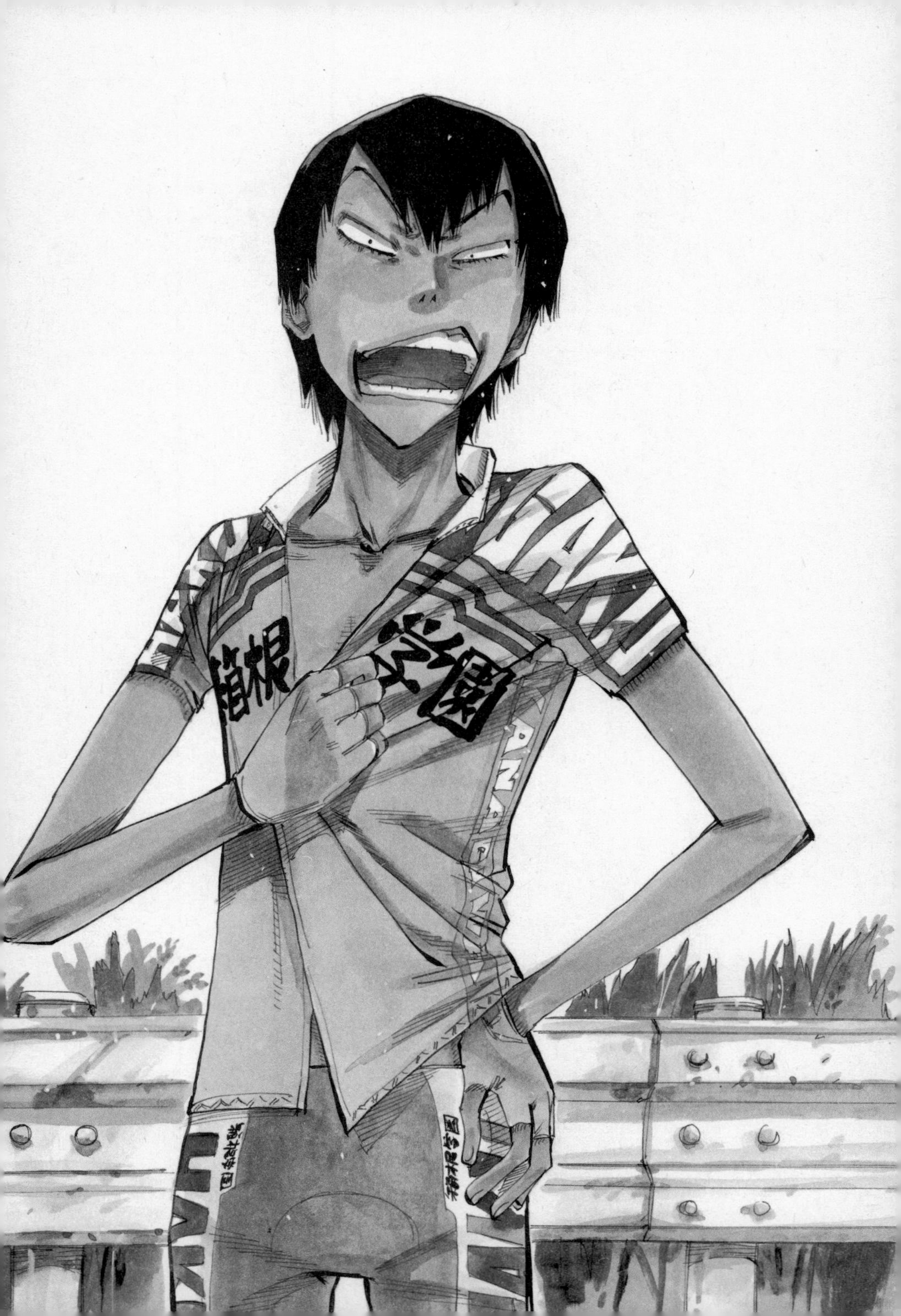
箱根学園

RIDE.167 ARAKITA

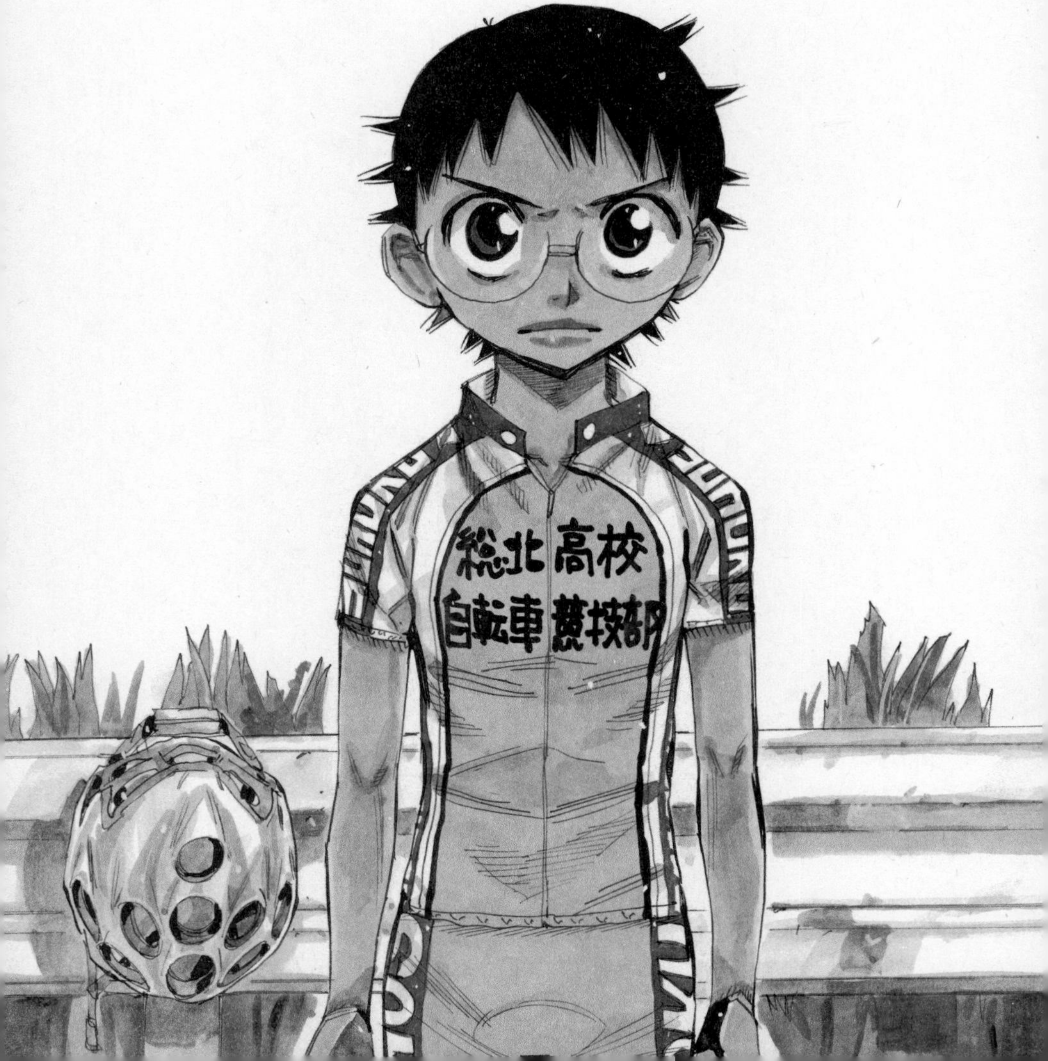
総北高校
自転車競技部

SAKAMICHI ONODA

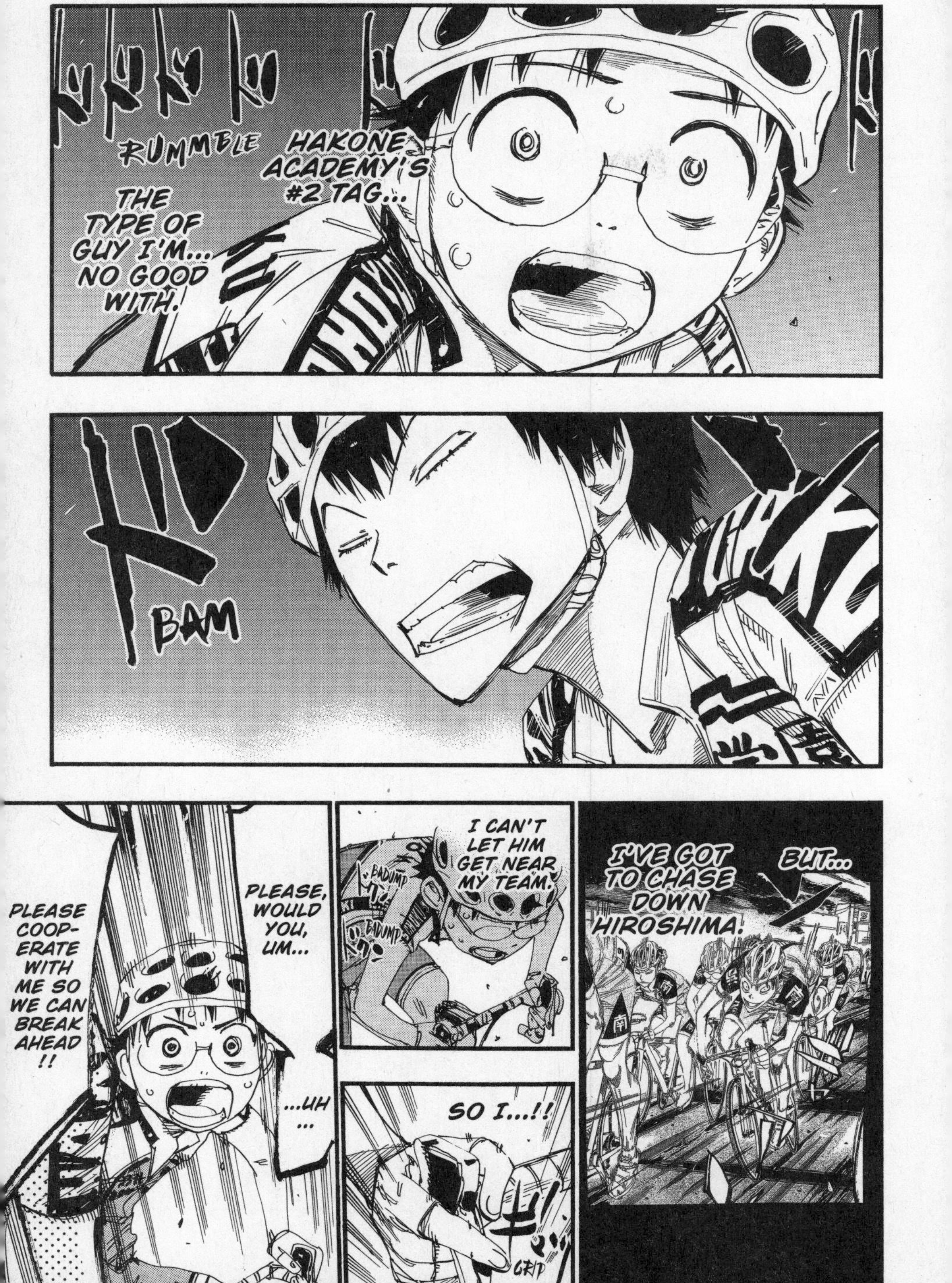
HAKONE ACADEMY'S #2 TAG...
THE TYPE OF GUY I'M... NO GOOD WITH.
RUMMBLE
BAM
BUT...
I'VE GOT TO CHASE DOWN HIROSHIMA.
I CAN'T LET HIM GET NEAR MY TEAM.
BADUMP
BADUMP
SO I...!!
GRIP
PLEASE, WOULD YOU, UM...
...UH ...
PLEASE COOP-ERATE WITH ME SO WE CAN BREAK AHEAD !!

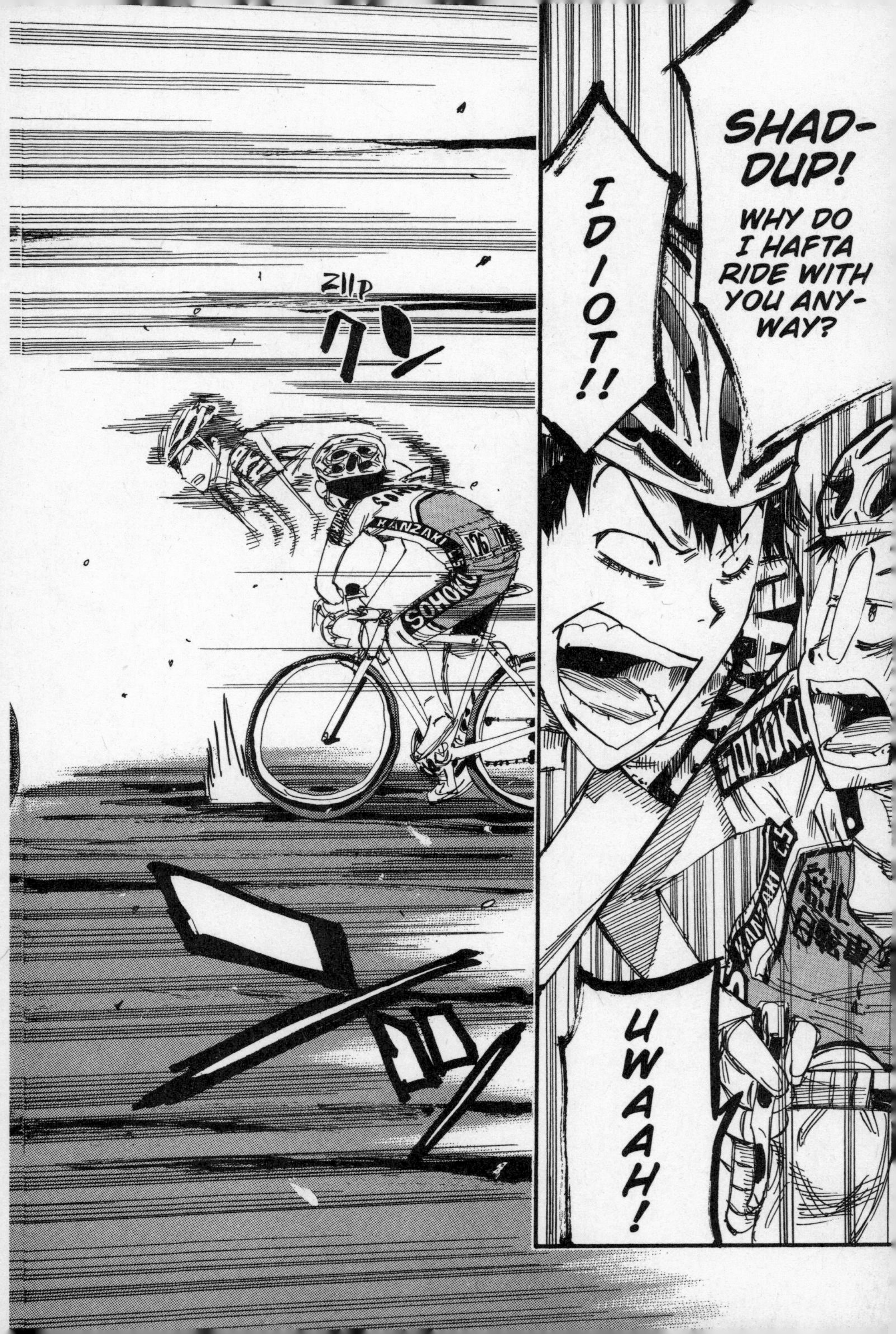
SHAD-DUP! WHY DO I HAFTA RIDE WITH YOU ANYWAY?
IDIOT!!
UWAAAH!
ZIP

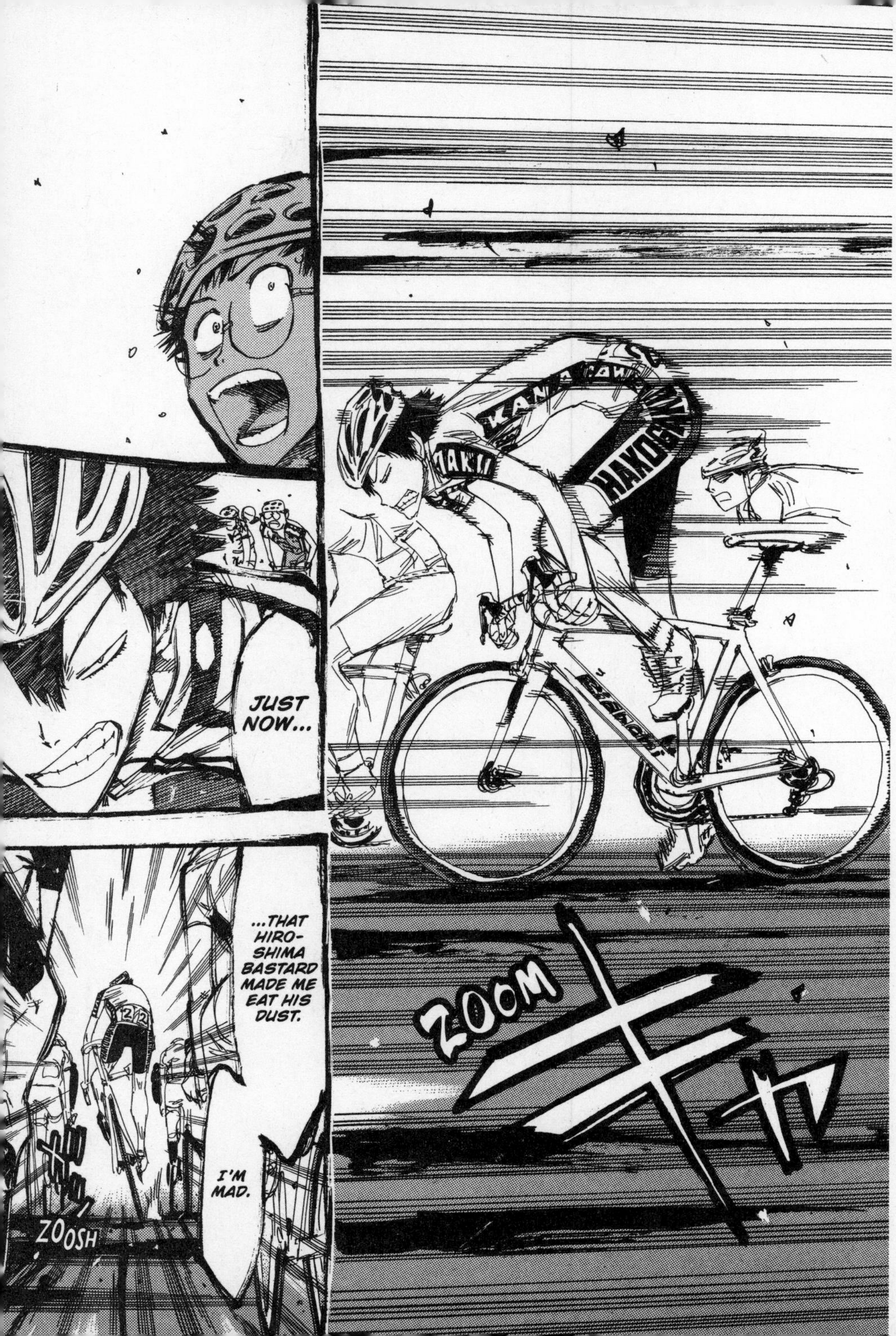
ZOOM
JUST NOW...
...THAT HIROSHIMA BASTARD MADE ME EAT HIS DUST.
I'M MAD.
ZOOSH

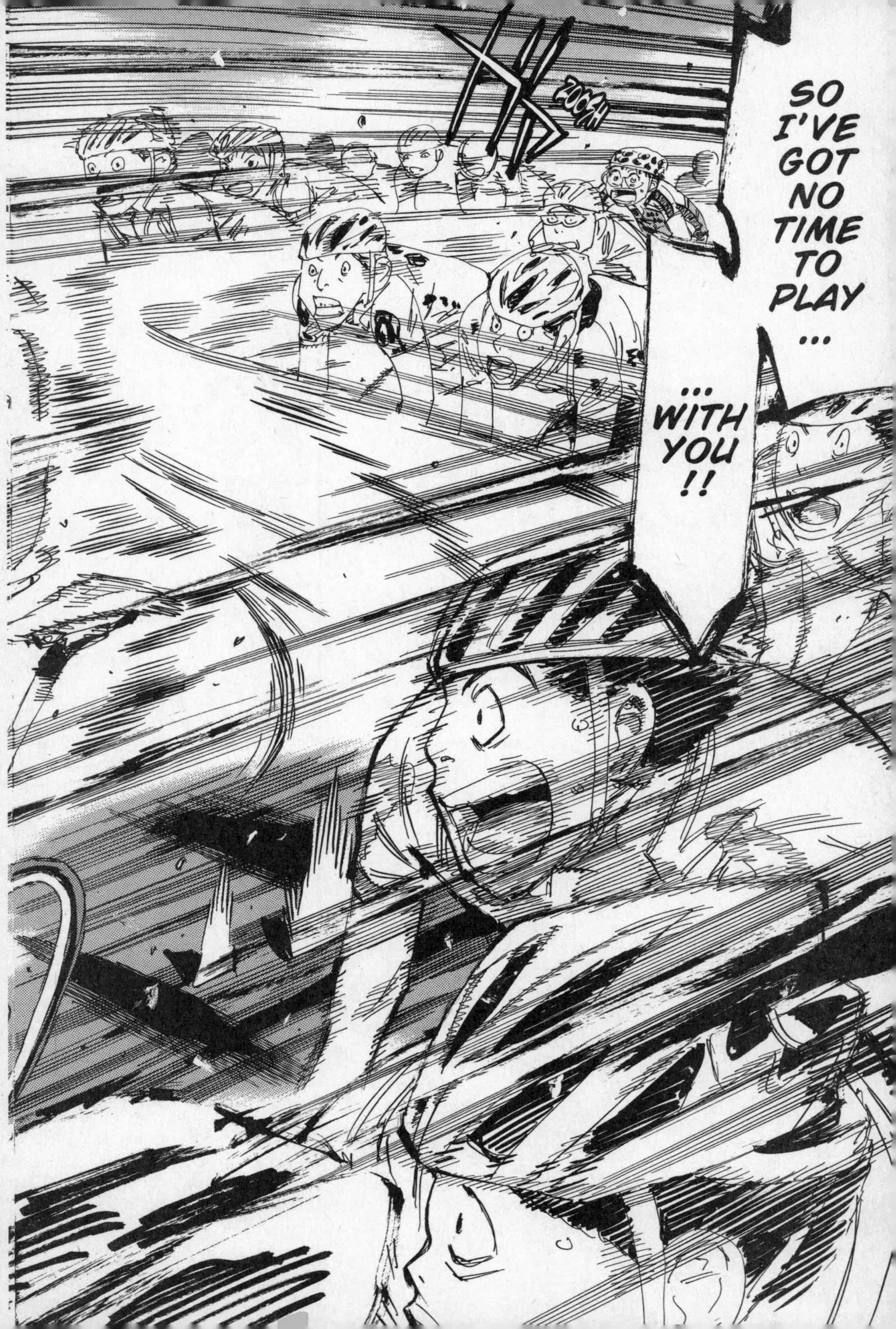
ZOOSH
SO I'VE GOT NO TIME TO PLAY...
...WITH YOU!!

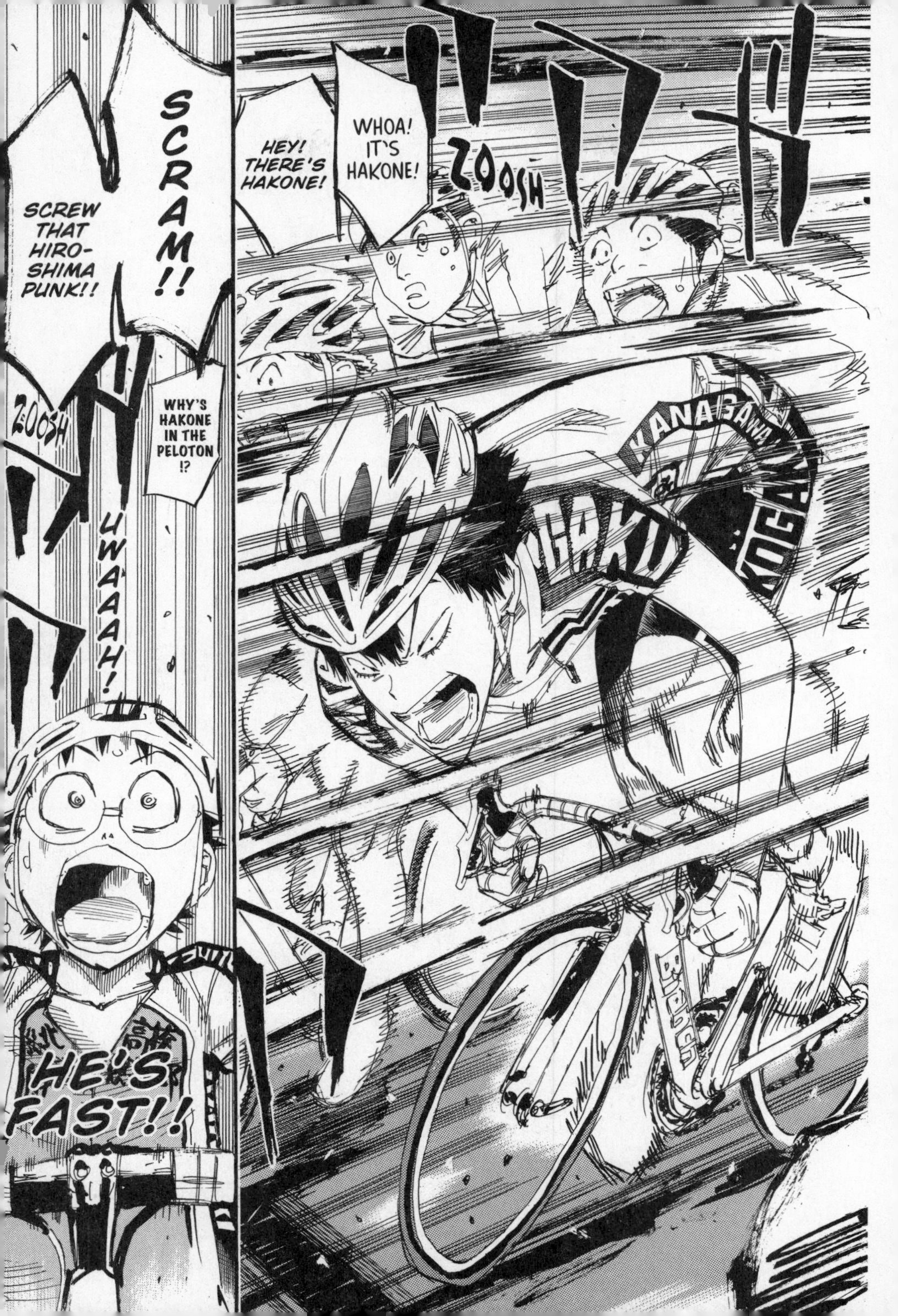
ZOOSH
WHOA! IT'S HAKONE!
HEY! THERE'S HAKONE!
SCRAM!!
SCREW THAT HIRO-SHIMA PUNK!!
WHY'S HAKONE IN THE PELOTON !?
ZOOSH
UWAAAAAH!
HE'S FAST!!

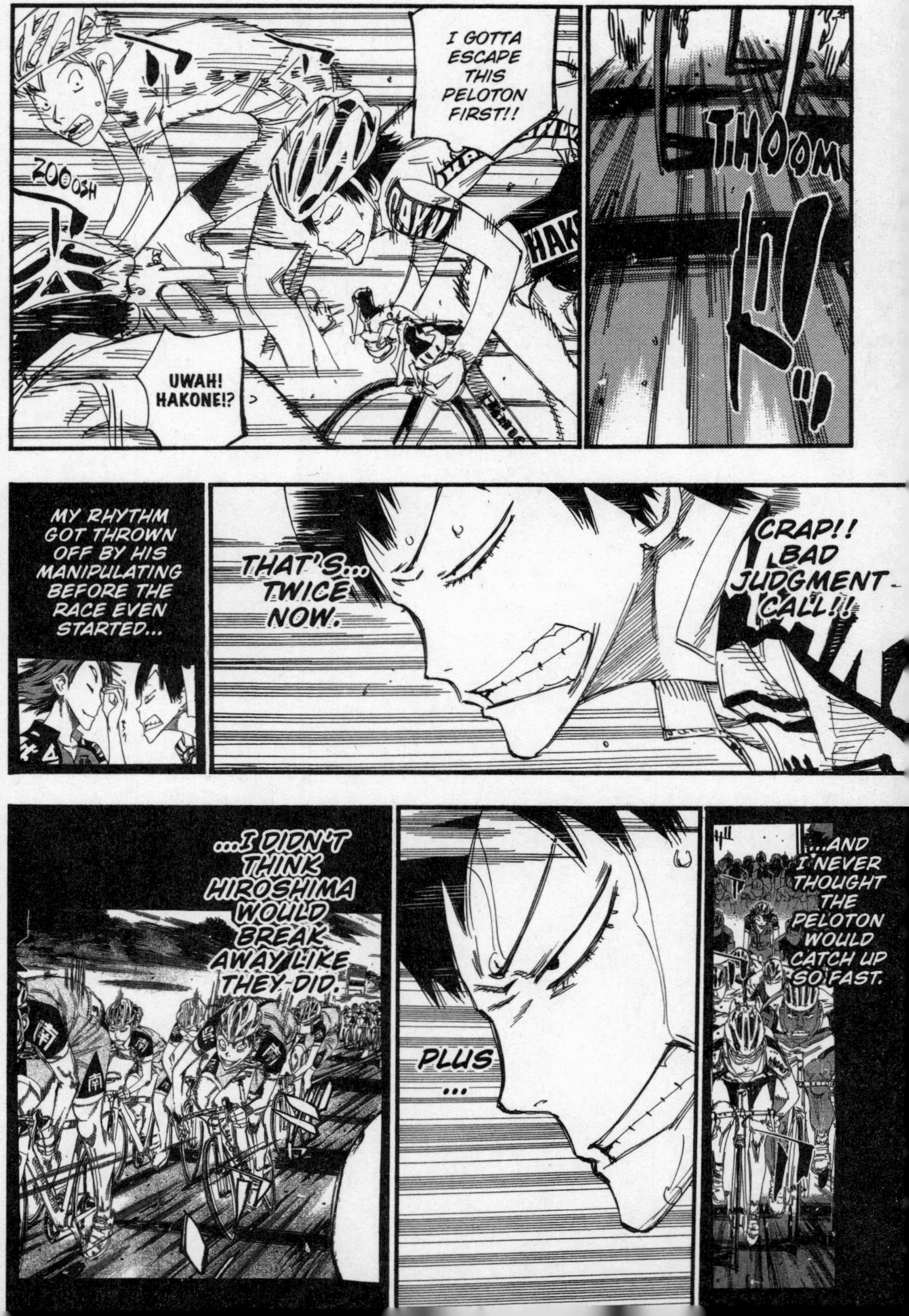
THOOM
I GOTTA ESCAPE THIS PELOTON FIRST!!
ZOOOSH
UWAH! HAKONE!?
CRAP!! BAD JUDGMENT CALL!!
THAT'S... TWICE NOW.
MY RHYTHM GOT THROWN OFF BY HIS MANIPULATING BEFORE THE RACE EVEN STARTED...
...AND I NEVER THOUGHT THE PELOTON WOULD CATCH UP SO FAST.
PLUS...
...I DIDN'T THINK HIROSHIMA WOULD BREAK AWAY LIKE THEY DID.

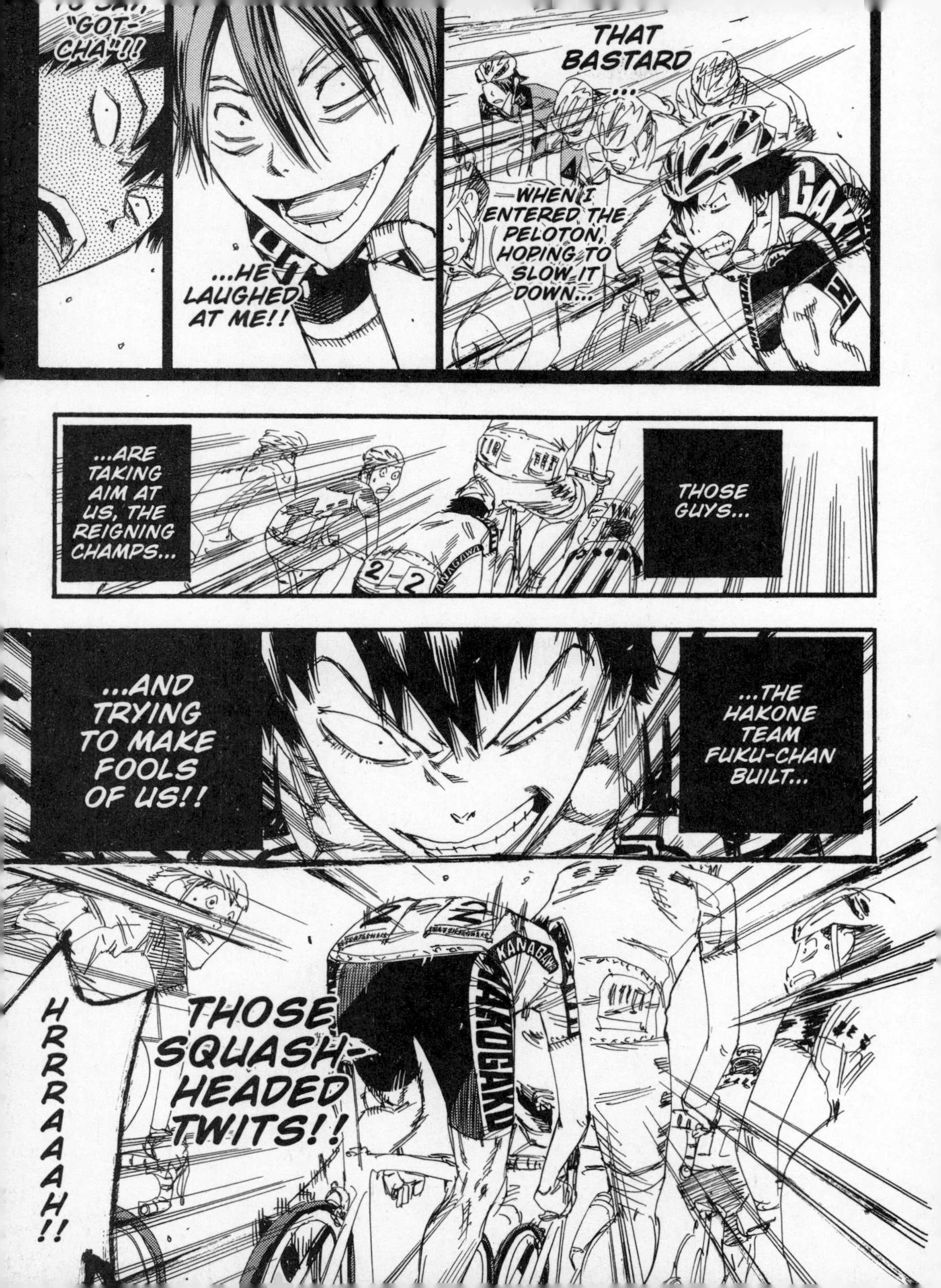
THAT BASTARD...
WHEN I ENTERED THE PELOTON, HOPING TO SLOW IT DOWN...
...HE LAUGHED AT ME!!
"GOT-CHA"!!
THOSE GUYS...
...ARE TAKING AIM AT US, THE REIGNING CHAMPS...
...THE HAKONE TEAM FUKU-CHAN BUILT...
...AND TRYING TO MAKE FOOLS OF US!!
THOSE SQUASH-HEADED TWITS!!
HRRRAAAH!!

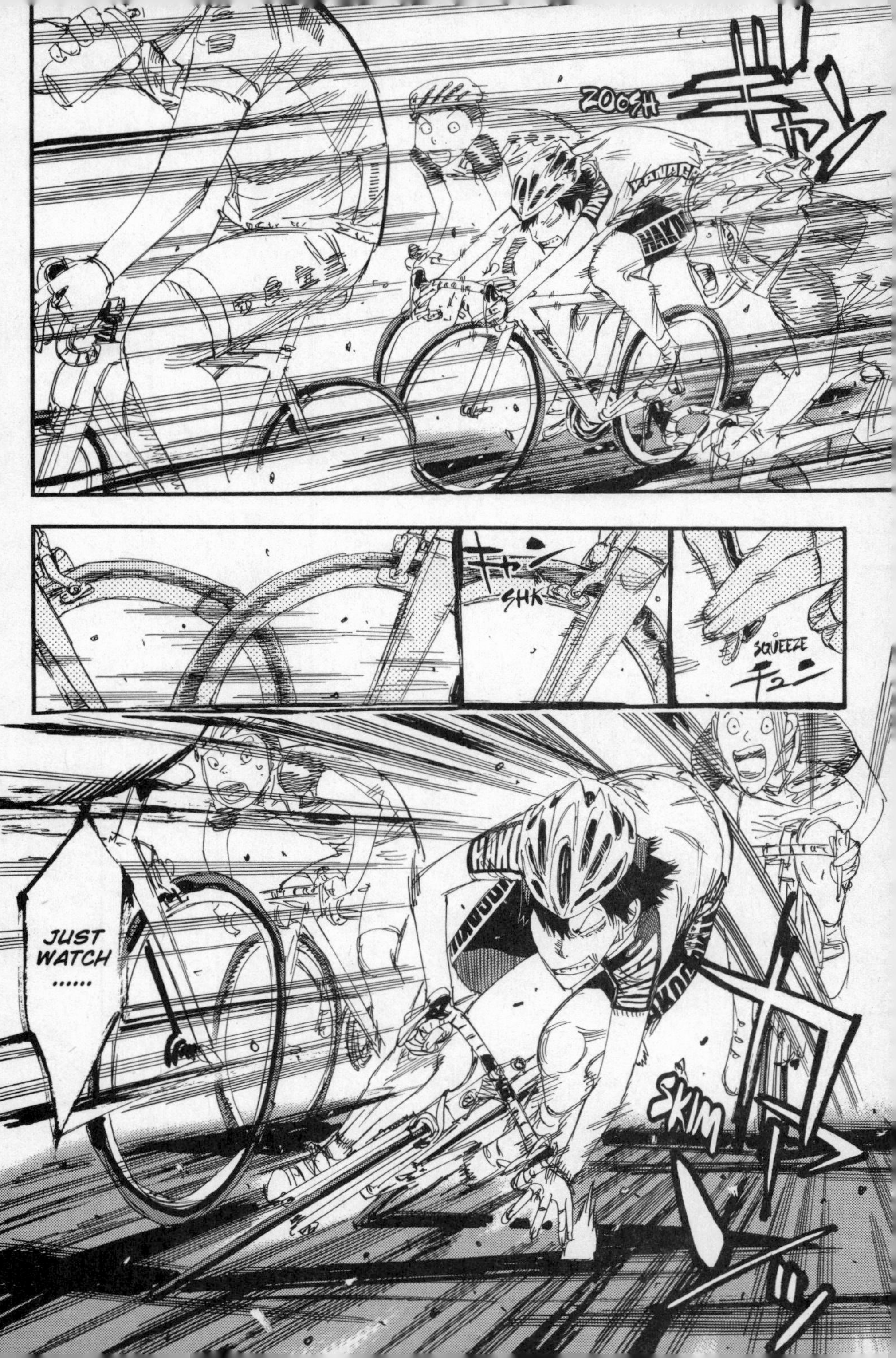
ZOOSH
SQUEEZE
SHK
JUST WATCH
......
SKIM

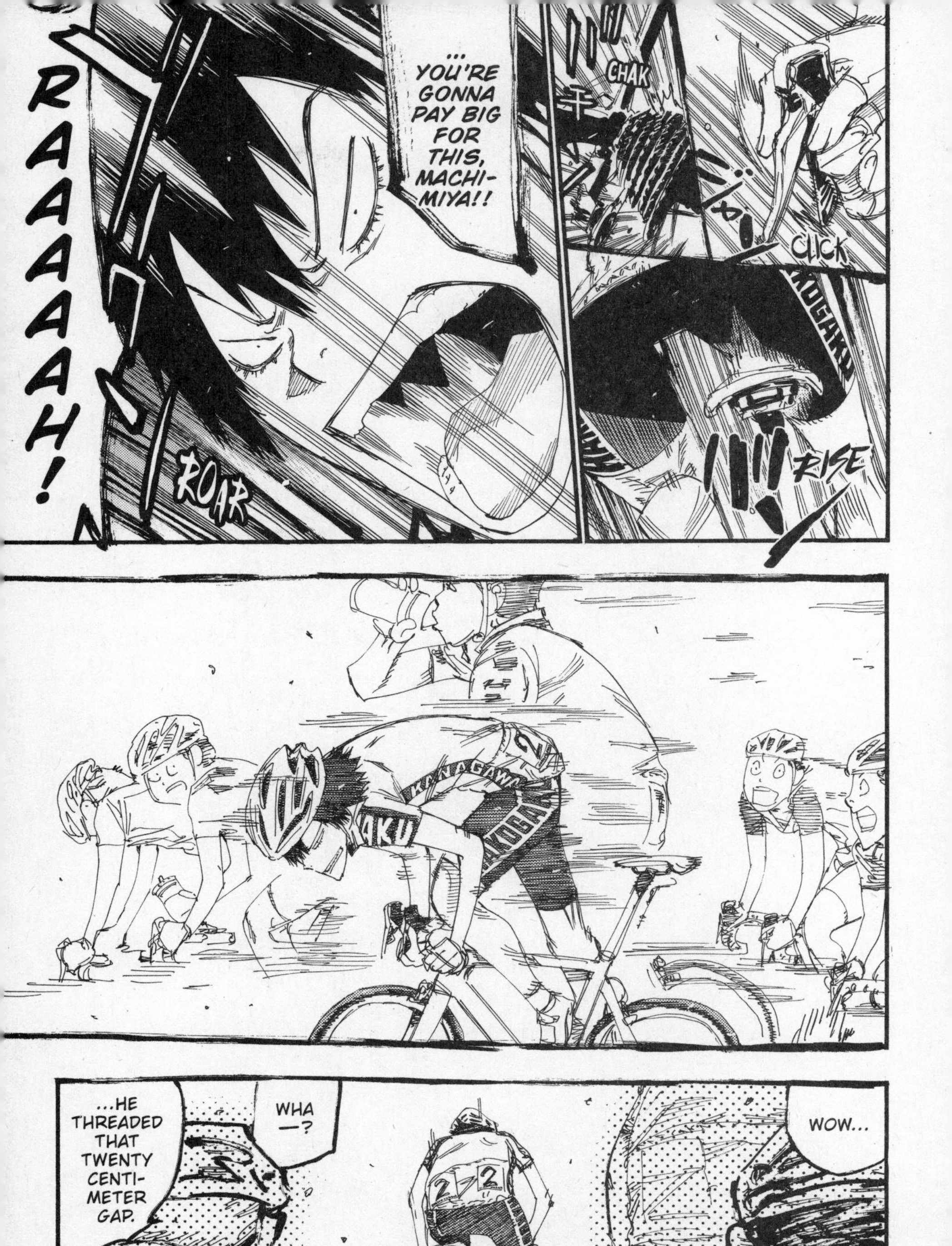
CHAK
CLICK
RISE
... YOU'RE GONNA PAY BIG FOR THIS, MACHI-MIYA!!
RAAAAAAH!
ROAR
WOW...
WHA —?
...HE THREADED THAT TWENTY CENTI-METER GAP.

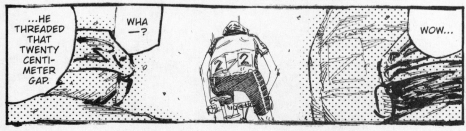

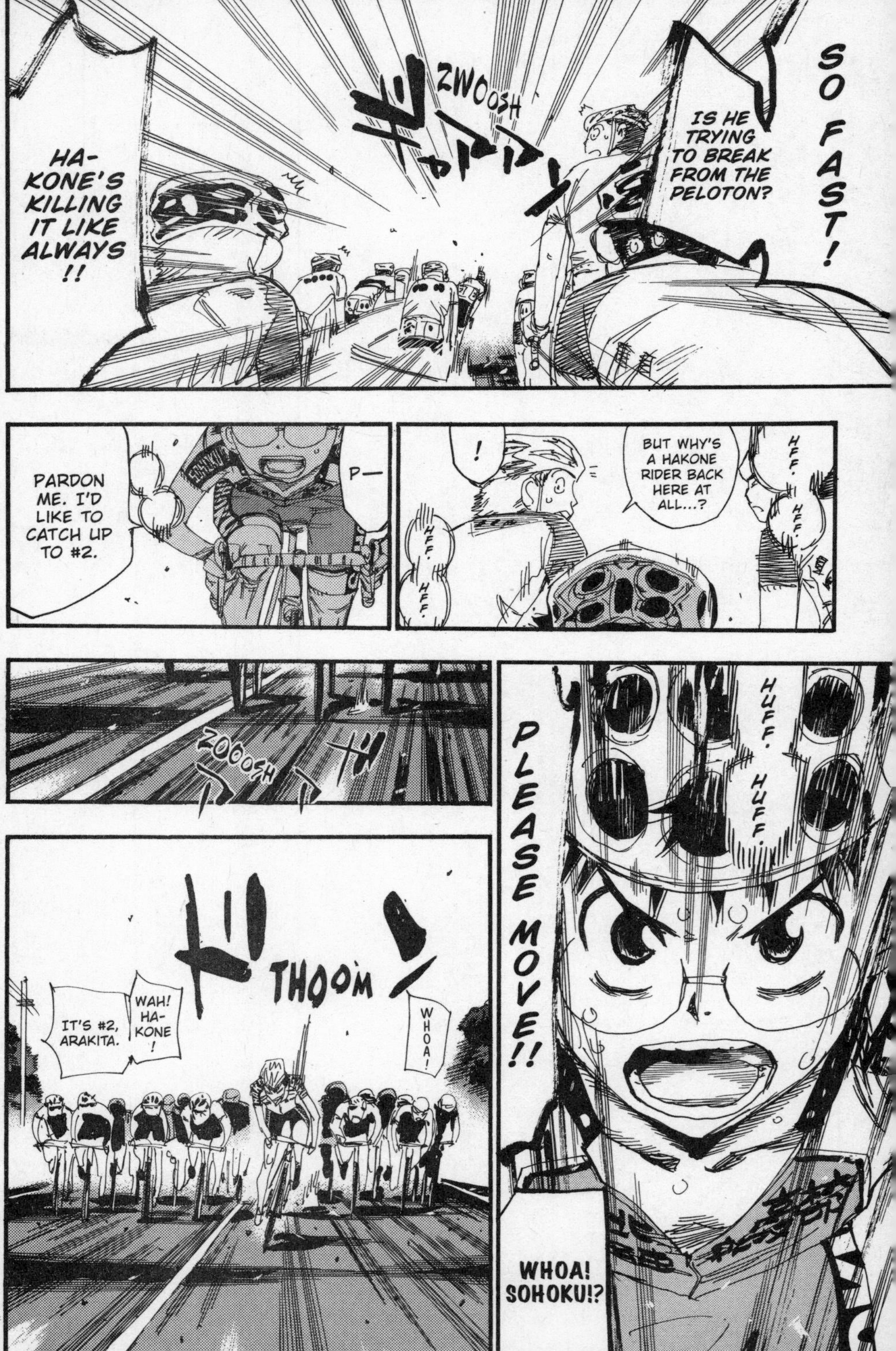
SO FAST!
IS HE TRYING TO BREAK FROM THE PELOTON?
ZWOOSH
HA-KONE'S KILLING IT LIKE ALWAYS!!
HFF. HFF.
BUT WHY'S A HAKONE RIDER BACK HERE AT ALL...?
!
HFF. HFF.
P—
PARDON ME. I'D LIKE TO CATCH UP TO #2.
HUFF. HUFF.
PLEASE MOVE!!
WHOA! SOHOKU!?
ZOOOSH
THOOM
WHOA!
WAH! HA-KONE!
IT'S #2, ARAKITA.

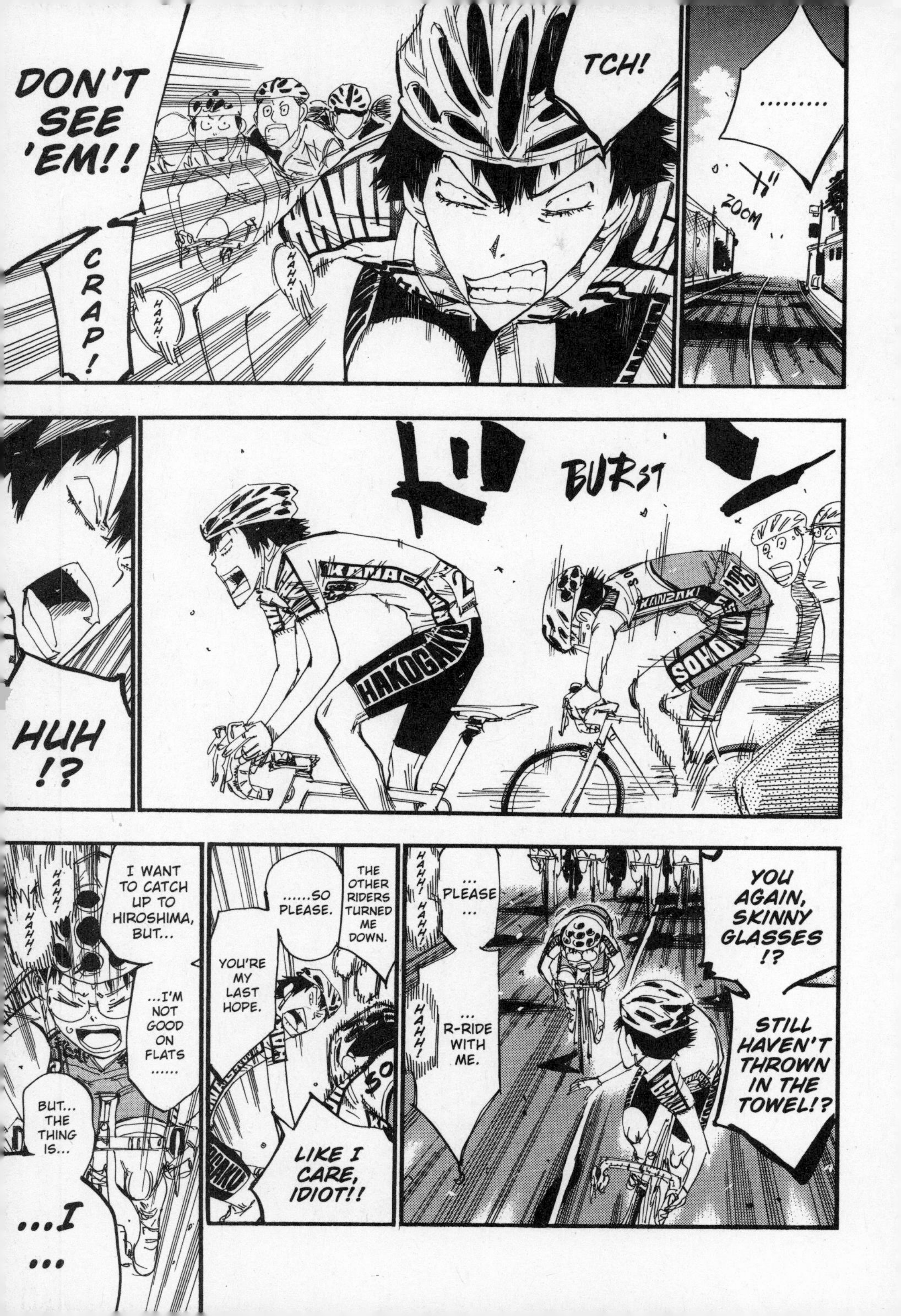
....
ZOOM
TCH!
DON'T SEE 'EM!!
HAHH!
HAHH!
CRAP!
BURST
HUH!?
YOU AGAIN, SKINNY GLASSES!?
STILL HAVEN'T THROWN IN THE TOWEL!?
... PLEASE ...
... R-RIDE WITH ME.
HAHH! HAHH!
HAHH!
THE OTHER RIDERS TURNED ME DOWN.
......SO PLEASE.
YOU'RE MY LAST HOPE.
LIKE I CARE, IDIOT!!
I WANT TO CATCH UP TO HIROSHIMA, BUT...
...I'M NOT GOOD ON FLATS ......
BUT... THE THING IS...
...I ...
HAHH!
HAHH!

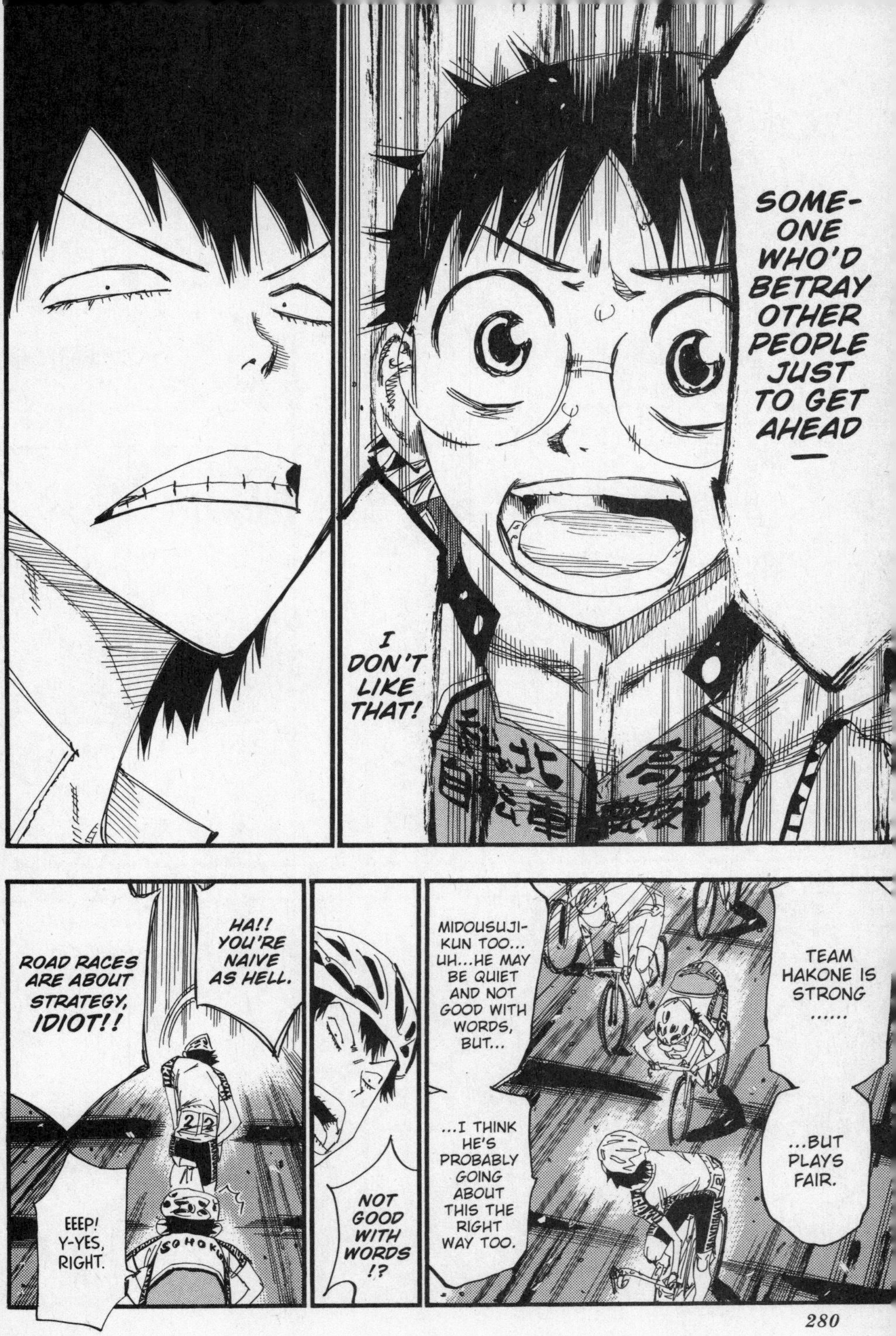
SOME-ONE WHO'D BETRAY OTHER PEOPLE JUST TO GET AHEAD—
I DON'T LIKE THAT!
TEAM HAKONE IS STRONG......
...BUT PLAYS FAIR.
MIDOUSUJI-KUN TOO... UH...HE MAY BE QUIET AND NOT GOOD WITH WORDS, BUT...
...I THINK HE'S PROBABLY GOING ABOUT THIS THE RIGHT WAY TOO.
NOT GOOD WITH WORDS!?
HA!! YOU'RE NAIVE AS HELL.
ROAD RACES ARE ABOUT STRATEGY, IDIOT!!
EEEP! Y-YES, RIGHT.

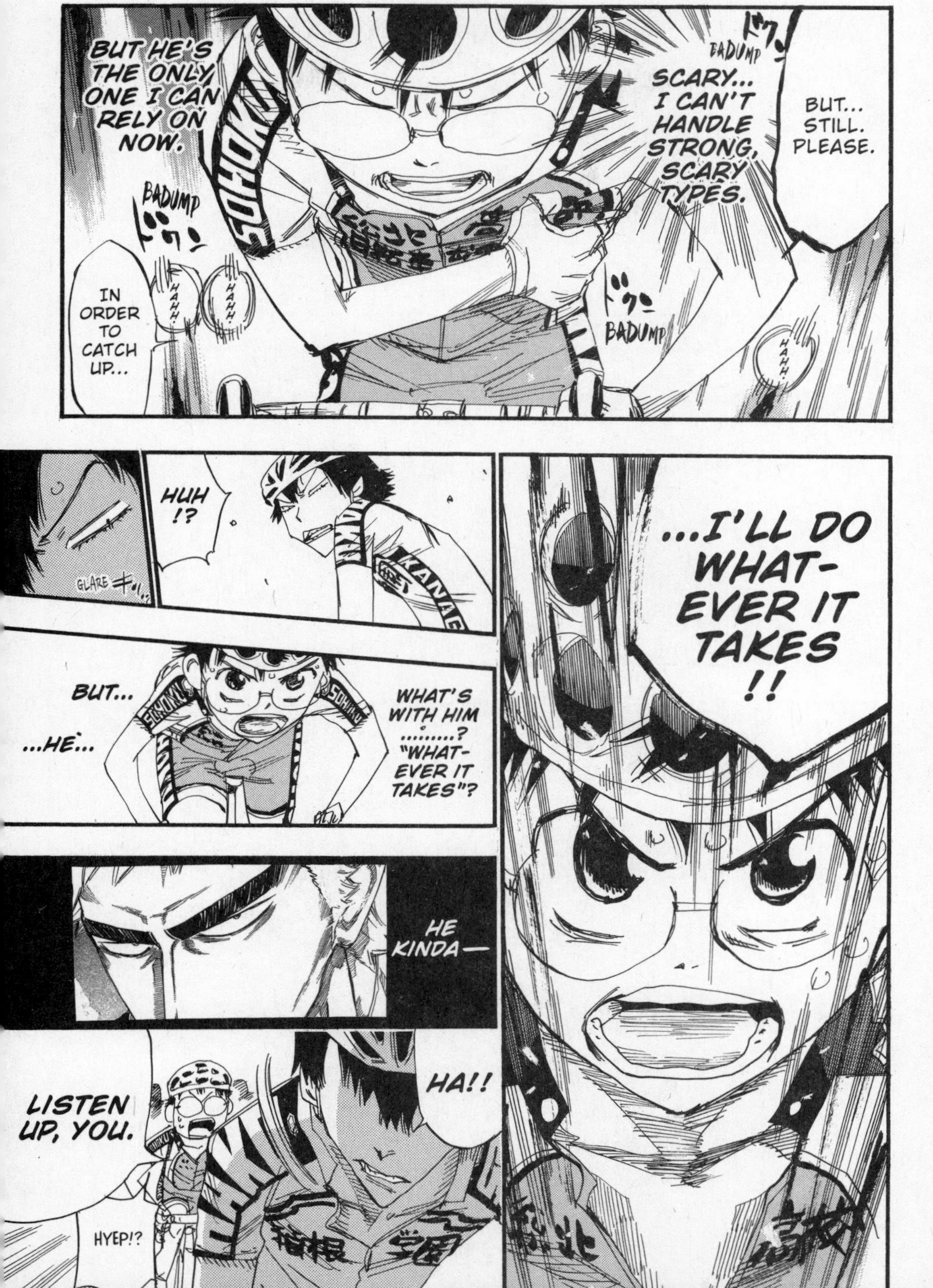
BUT... STILL. PLEASE.
BADUMP
SCARY... I CAN'T HANDLE STRONG, SCARY TYPES.
BADUMP
BUT HE'S THE ONLY ONE I CAN RELY ON NOW.
BADUMP
HAHH
HAHH
HAHH
IN ORDER TO CATCH UP...
...I'LL DO WHAT-EVER IT TAKES!!
HUH!?
GLARE
WHAT'S WITH HIM ....? "WHAT-EVER IT TAKES"?
BUT...
...HE...
HE KINDA—
HA!!
LISTEN UP, YOU.
HYEP!?

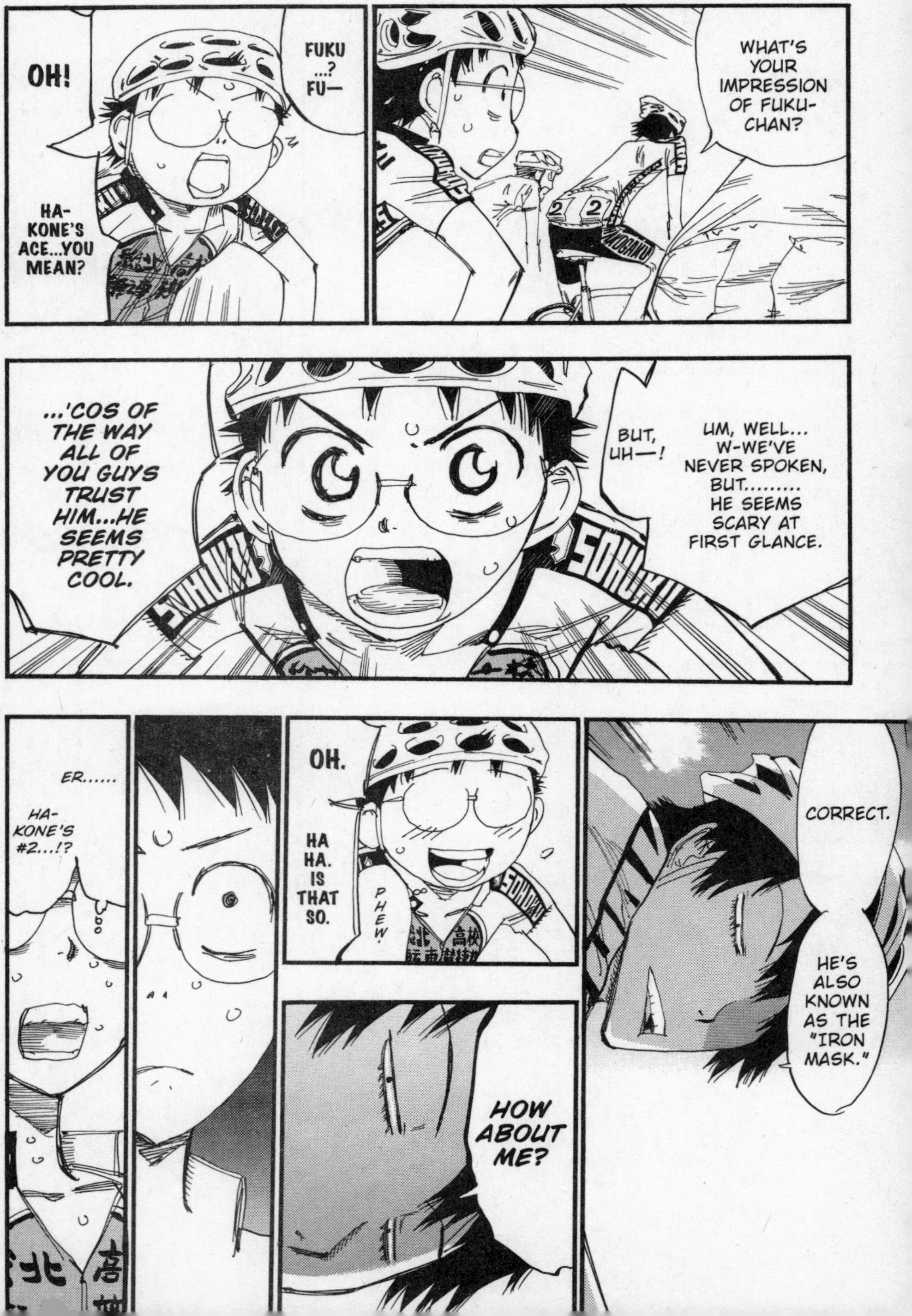
WHAT'S YOUR IMPRESSION OF FUKU-CHAN?
FUKU ...? FU—
OH!
HA-KONE'S ACE...YOU MEAN?
UM, WELL... W-WE'VE NEVER SPOKEN, BUT......... HE SEEMS SCARY AT FIRST GLANCE.
BUT, UH—!
...'COS OF THE WAY ALL OF YOU GUYS TRUST HIM...HE SEEMS PRETTY COOL.
CORRECT.
HE'S ALSO KNOWN AS THE "IRON MASK."
OH.
HA HA. IS THAT SO.
PHEW
HOW ABOUT ME?
ER......
HA-KONE'S #2...!?

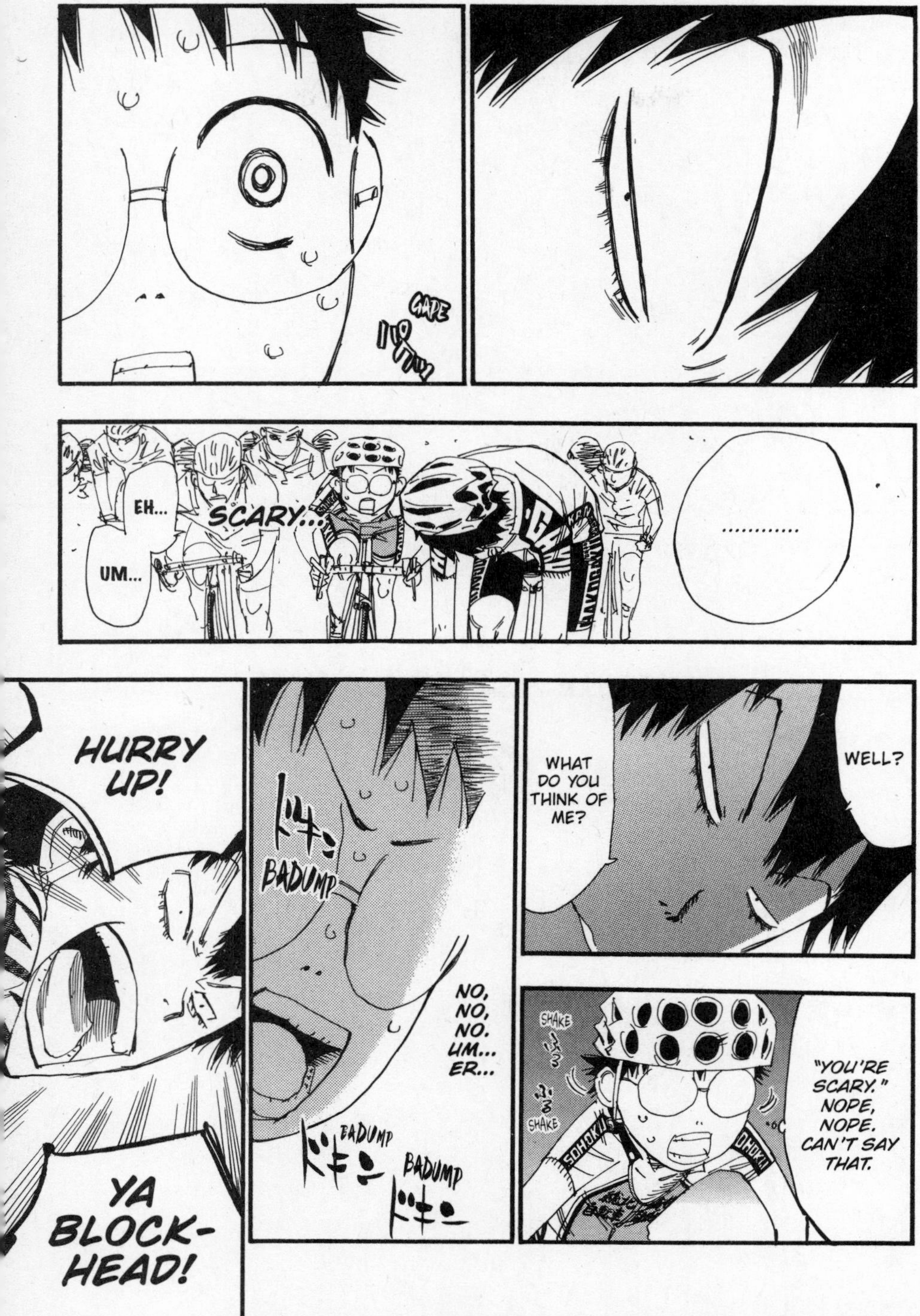
GAPE
....
SCARY...
EH...
UM...
WELL?
WHAT DO YOU THINK OF ME?
"YOU'RE SCARY." NOPE, NOPE. CAN'T SAY THAT.
SHAKE
SHAKE
BADUMP
NO, NO, NO. UM... ER...
BADUMP
BADUMP
HURRY UP!
YA BLOCK-HEAD!

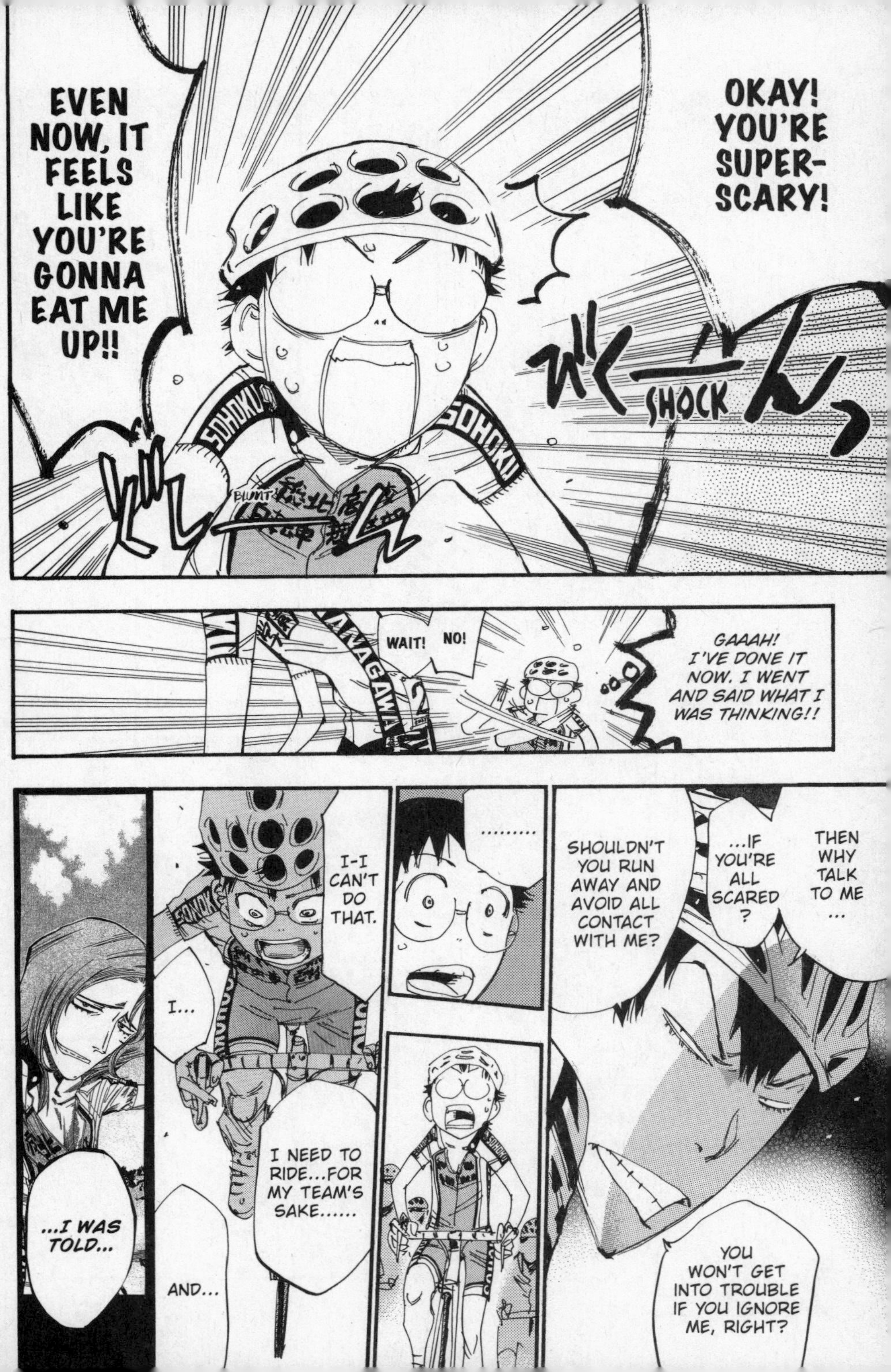
OKAY! YOU'RE SUPER-SCARY!
EVEN NOW, IT FEELS LIKE YOU'RE GONNA EAT ME UP!!
SHOCK
BLUNT
GAAAH! I'VE DONE IT NOW. I WENT AND SAID WHAT I WAS THINKING!!
NO!
WAIT!
THEN WHY TALK TO ME ...
...IF YOU'RE ALL SCARED ?
SHOULDN'T YOU RUN AWAY AND AVOID ALL CONTACT WITH ME?
YOU WON'T GET INTO TROUBLE IF YOU IGNORE ME, RIGHT?
....
I-I CAN'T DO THAT.
I...
...I WAS TOLD...
AND...
I NEED TO RIDE...FOR MY TEAM'S SAKE......

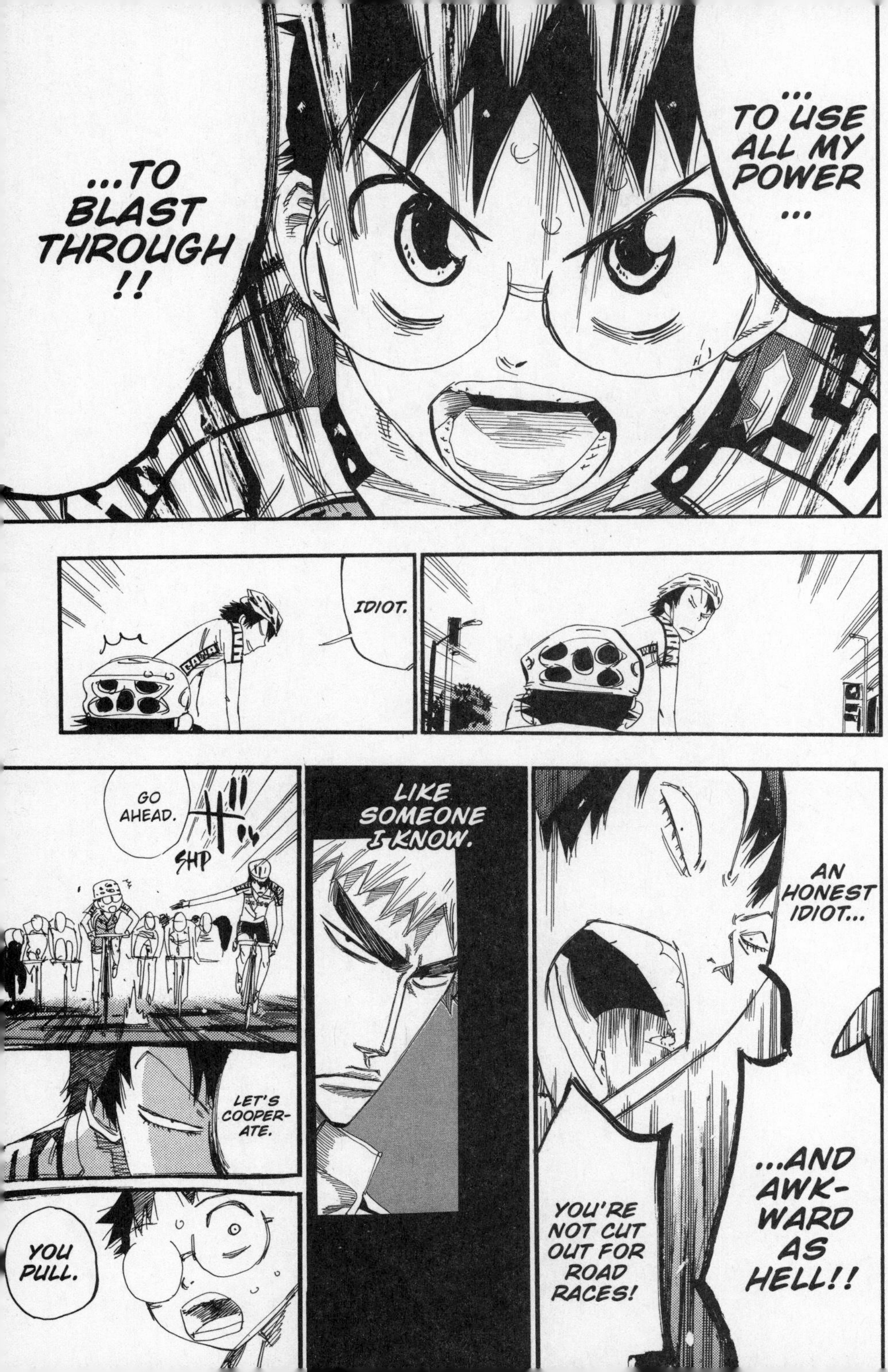
...TO USE ALL MY POWER...
...TO BLAST THROUGH!!
IDIOT.
AN HONEST IDIOT...
...AND AWK-WARD AS HELL!!
YOU'RE NOT CUT OUT FOR ROAD RACES!
LIKE SOMEONE I KNOW.
GO AHEAD.
SHP
LET'S COOPER-ATE.
YOU PULL.

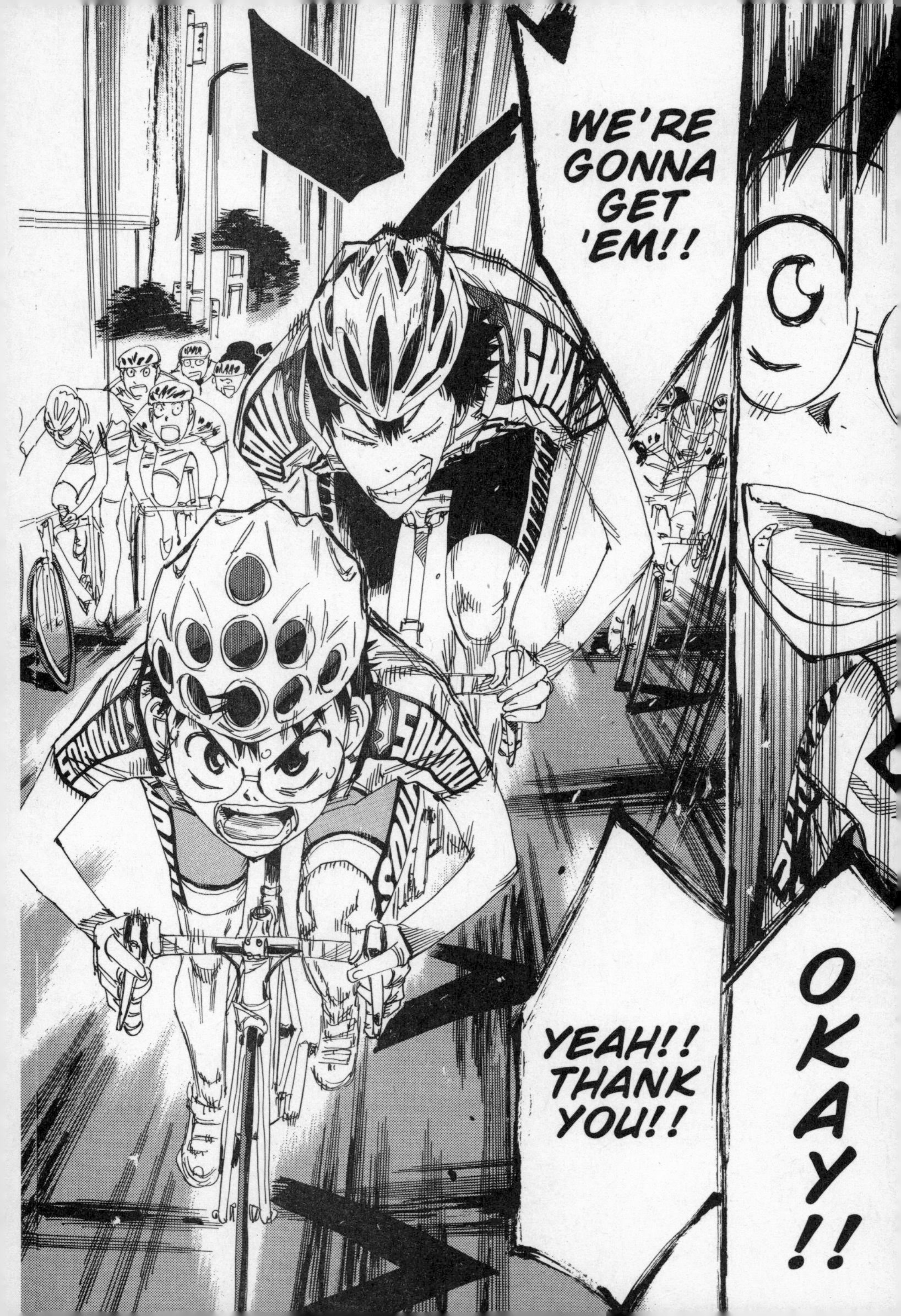
WE'RE GONNA GET 'EM!!
OKAY!!
YEAH!! THANK YOU!!

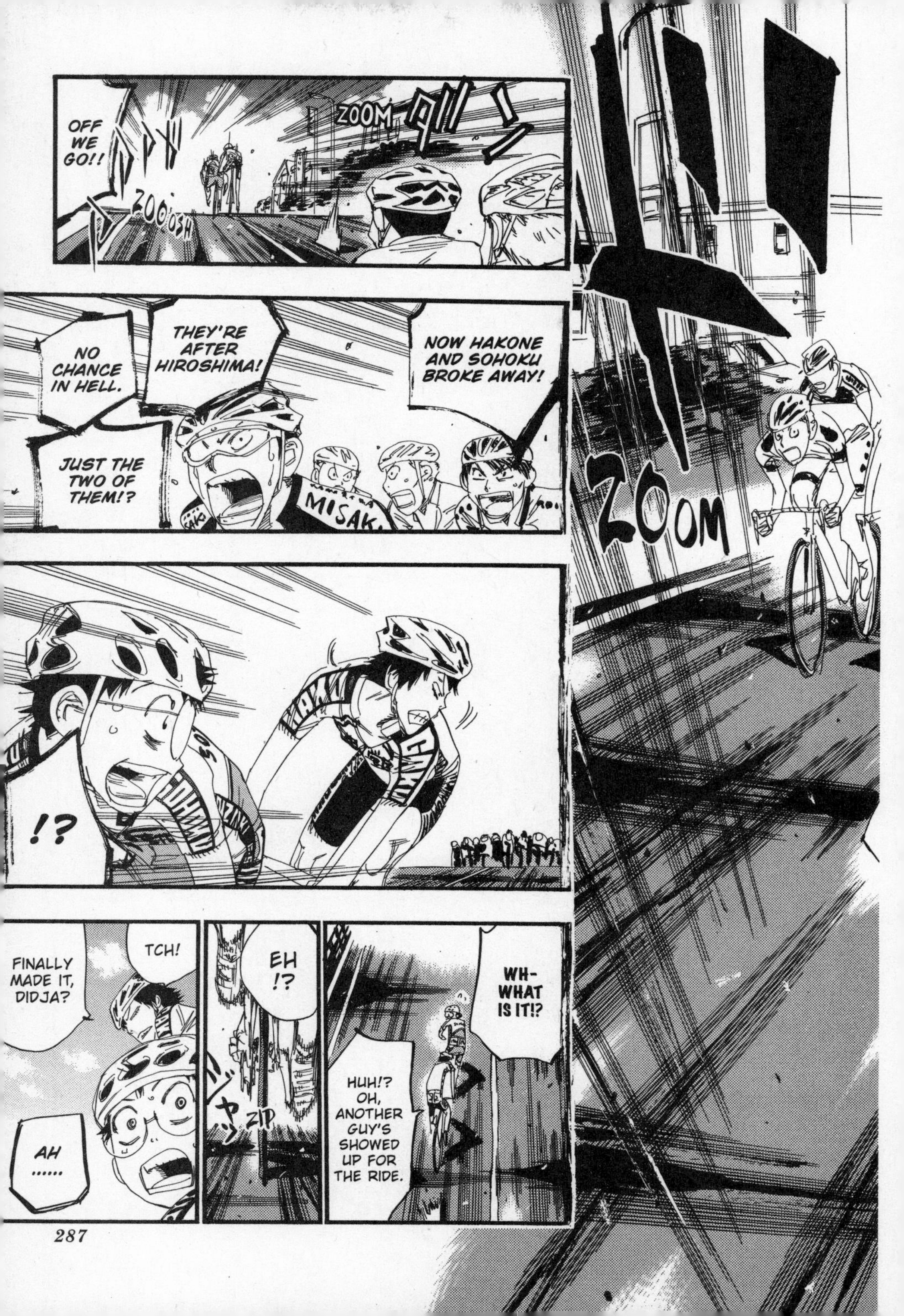
ZOOM
ZOOM
OFF WE GO!!
ZOOOSH
NOW HAKONE AND SOHOKU BROKE AWAY!
THEY'RE AFTER HIROSHIMA!
NO CHANCE IN HELL.
JUST THE TWO OF THEM!?
!?
WH- WHAT IS IT!?
HUH!? OH, ANOTHER GUY'S SHOWED UP FOR THE RIDE.
EH !?
ZIP
TCH!
FINALLY MADE IT, DIDJA?
AH ......

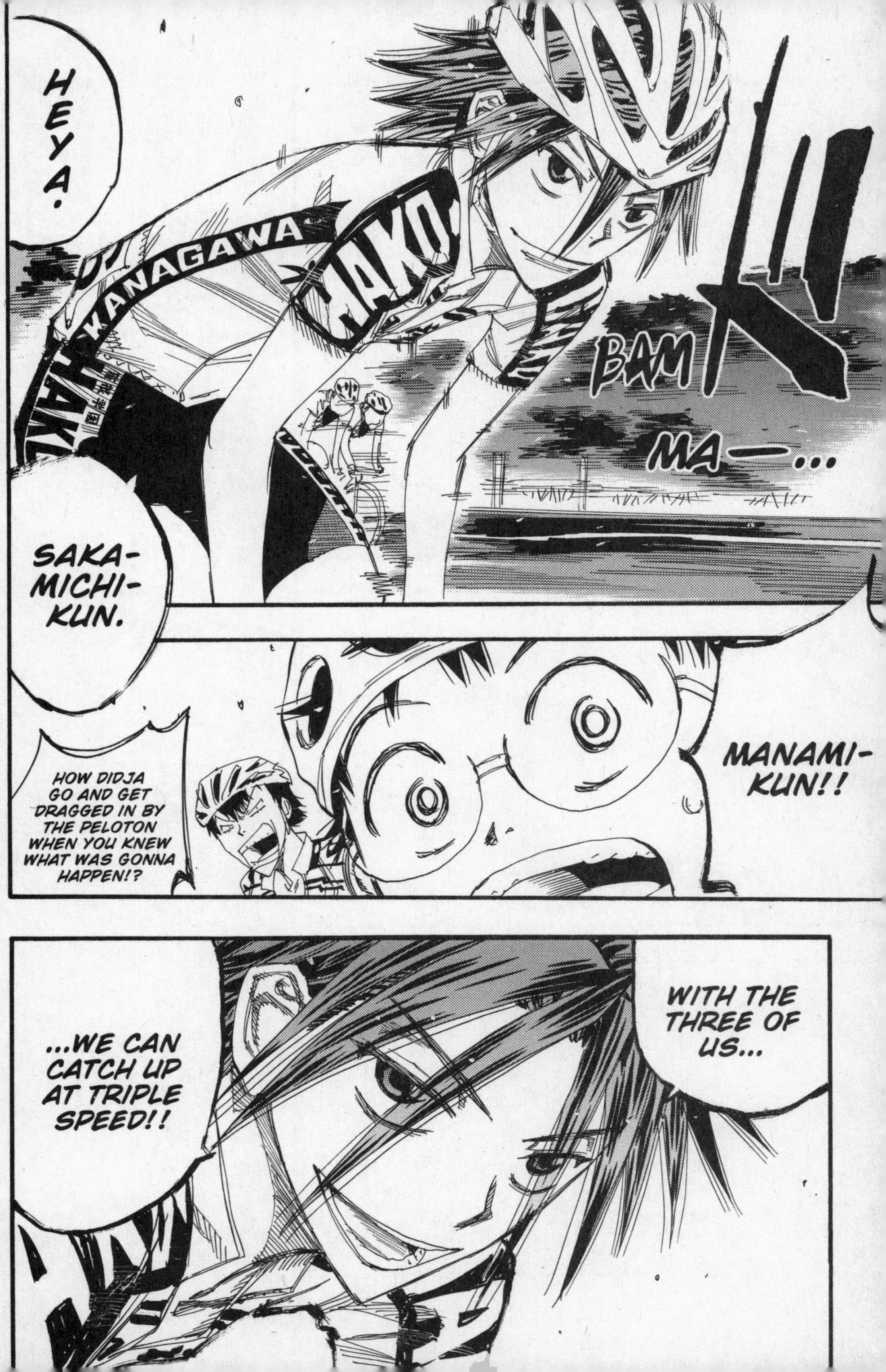
BAM
MA—...
HEYA.
KANAGAWA
SAKA-MICHI-KUN.
MANAMI-KUN!!
HOW DIDJA GO AND GET DRAGGED IN BY THE PELOTON WHEN YOU KNEW WHAT WAS GONNA HAPPEN!?
WITH THE THREE OF US...
...WE CAN CATCH UP AT TRIPLE SPEED!!

RIDE.168 THE TRIO CHASE!!

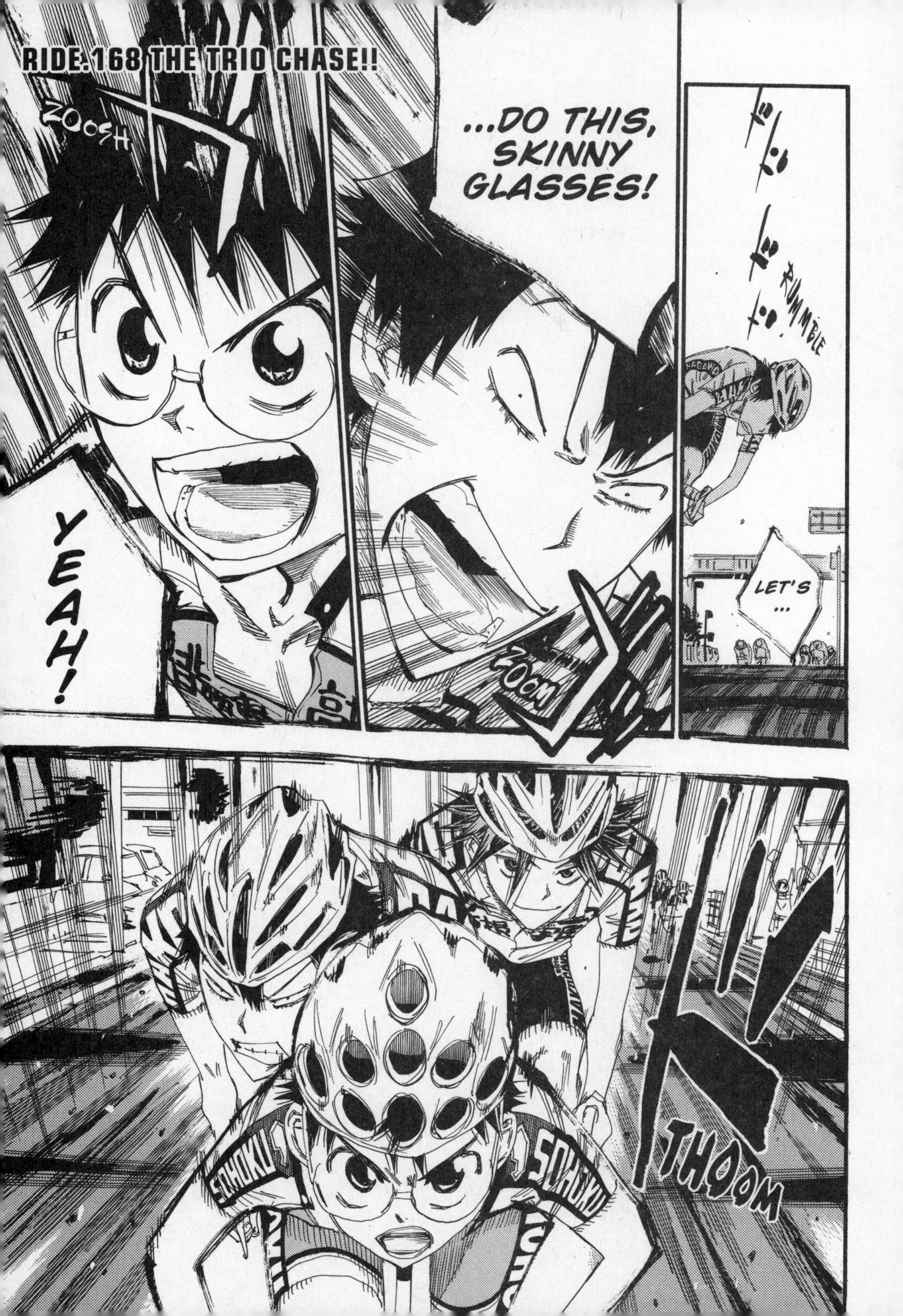
RUMMBLE
LET'S ...
...DO THIS, SKINNY GLASSES!
ZOOM
ZOOSH
YEAH!
THOOM

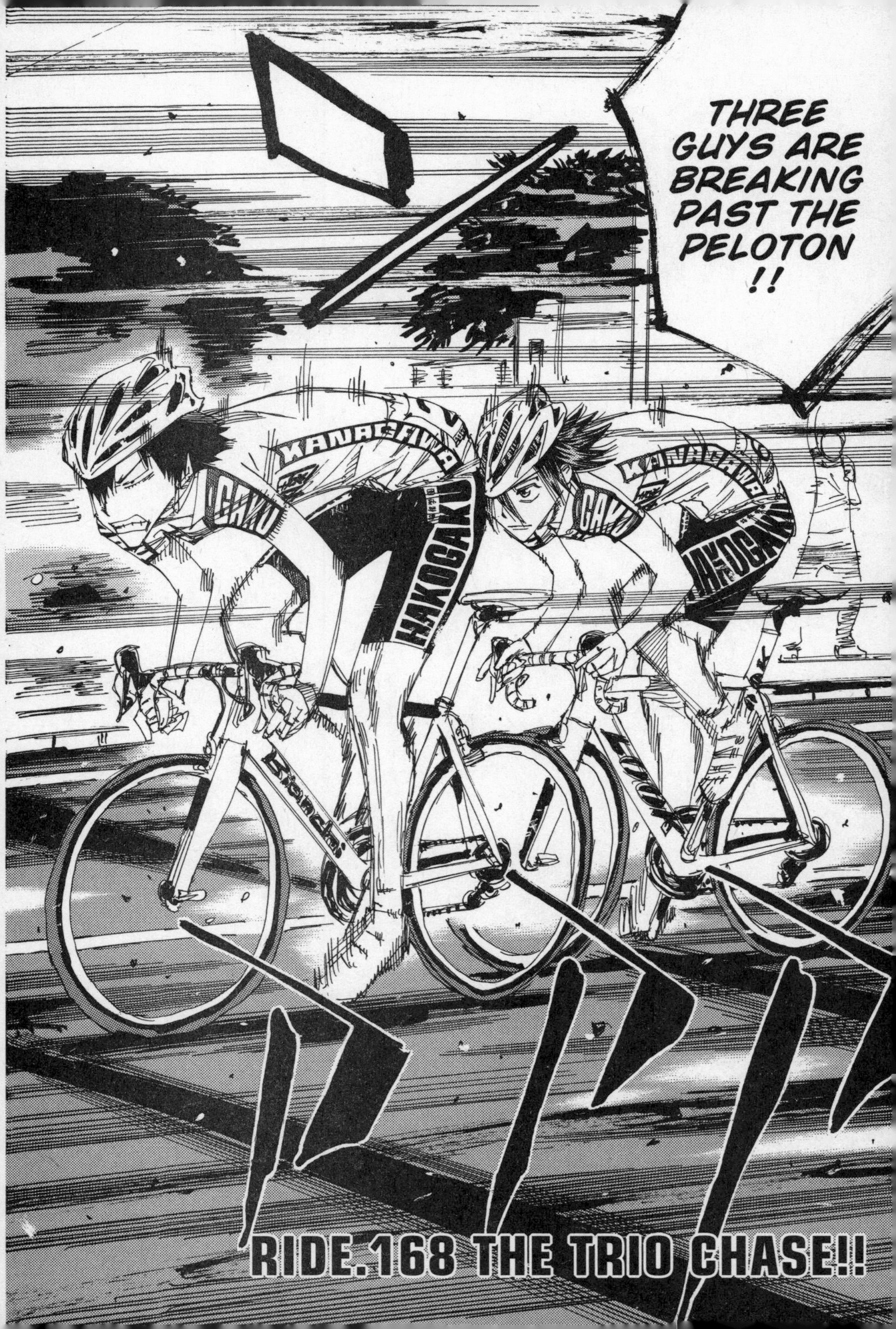
THREE GUYS ARE BREAKING PAST THE PELOTON !!
RIDE.168 THE TRIO CHASE!!

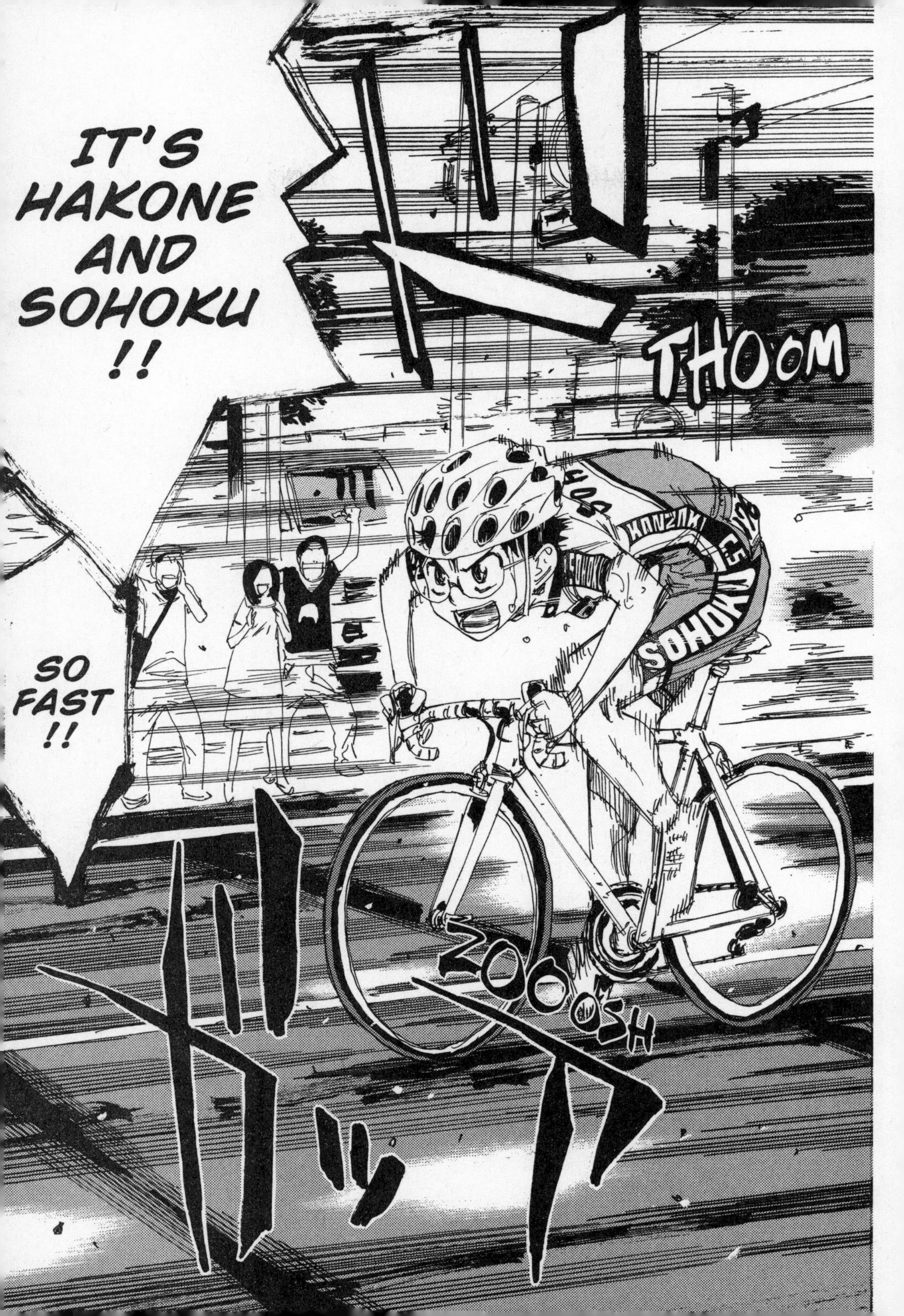
IT'S HAKONE AND SOHOKU!!
THOOM
SO FAST!!
ZOOOOSH

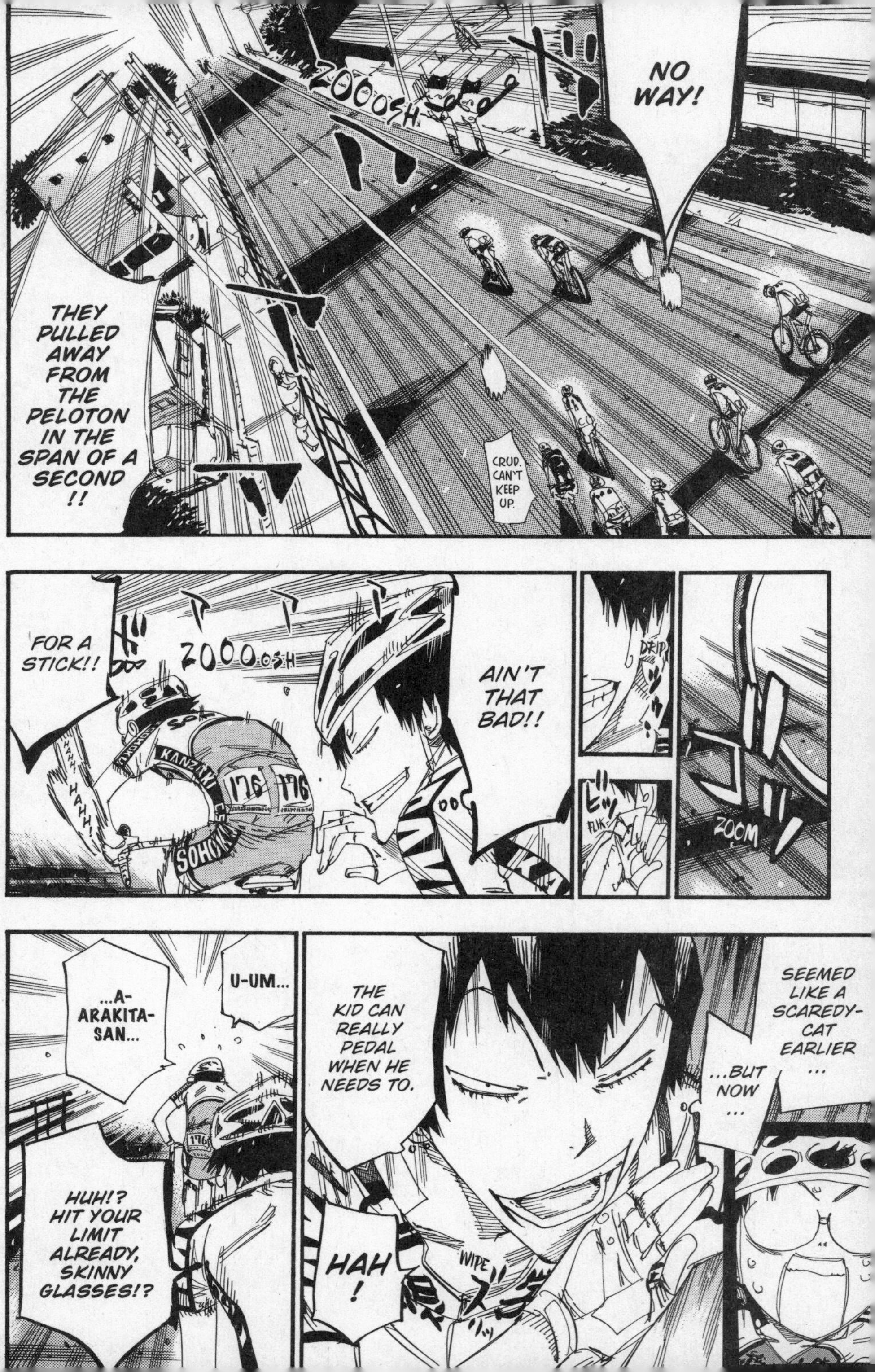
NO WAY!
ZOOOSH
CRUD. CAN'T KEEP UP.
THEY PULLED AWAY FROM THE PELOTON IN THE SPAN OF A SECOND!!
ZOOM
DRIP
FLIK
AIN'T THAT BAD!!
ZOOOOSH
FOR A STICK!!
HAHH! HAHH! HAHH!
SEEMED LIKE A SCAREDY-CAT EARLIER...
...BUT NOW...
THE KID CAN REALLY PEDAL WHEN HE NEEDS TO.
HAH!
WIPE
U-UM...
...A-ARAKITA-SAN...
HUH!? HIT YOUR LIMIT ALREADY, SKINNY GLASSES!?

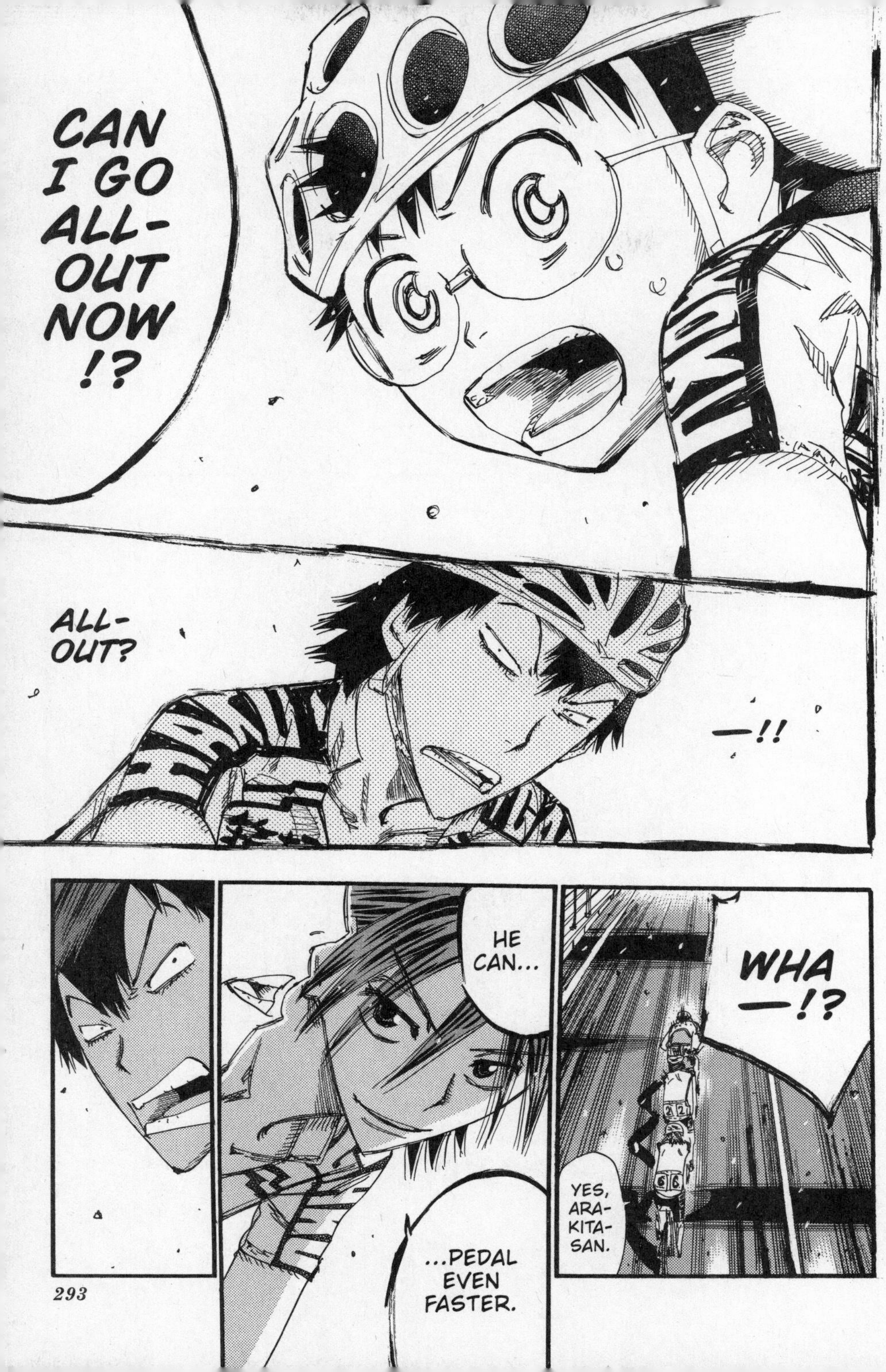
CAN I GO ALL-OUT NOW!?
ALL-OUT?
—!!
WHA—!?
YES, ARA-KITA-SAN.
HE CAN...
...PEDAL EVEN FASTER.

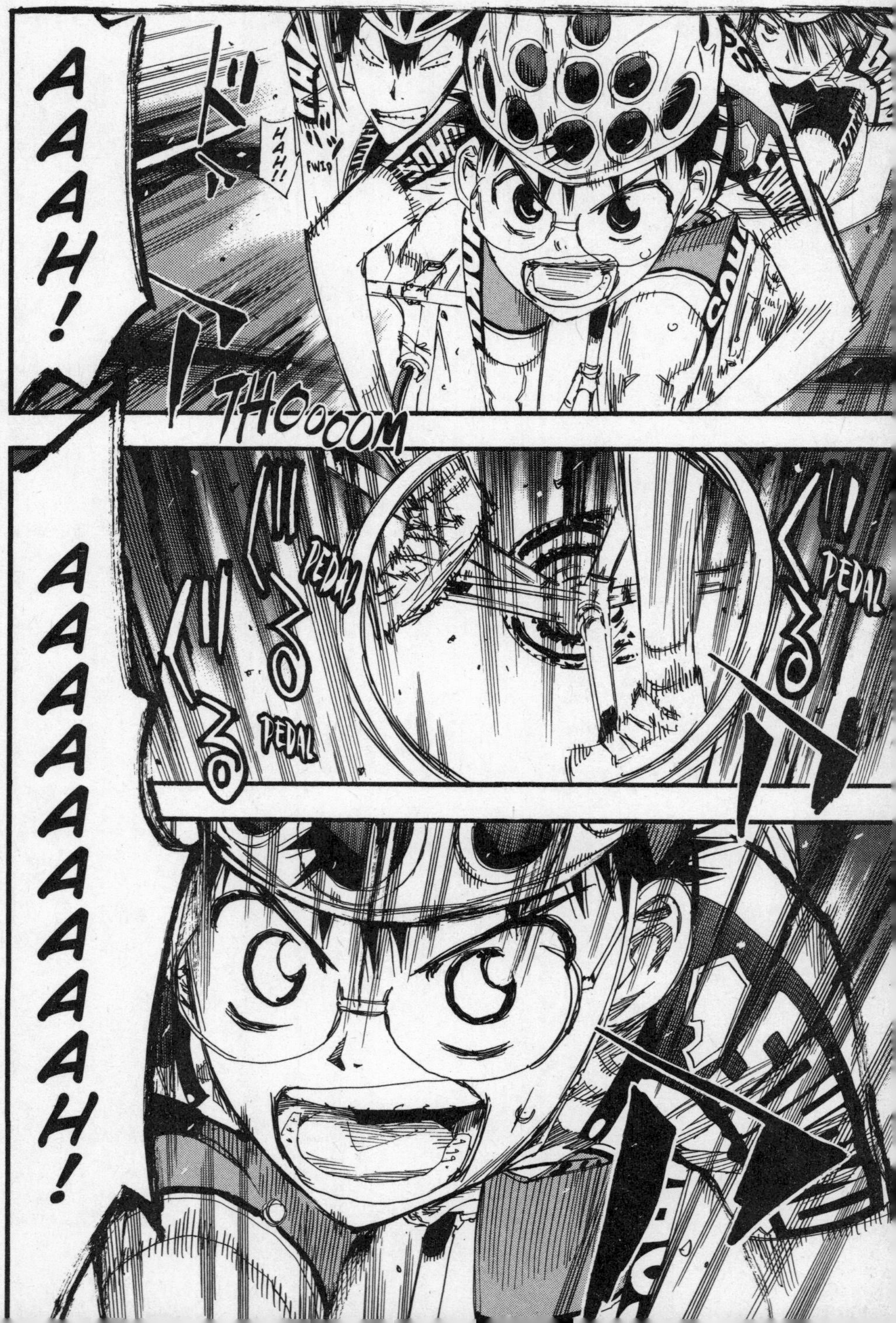
HAH HAH!!
FWIP
THOOOOM
AAAAH!
PEDAL
PEDAL
PEDAL
AAAAAAAAAAAH!

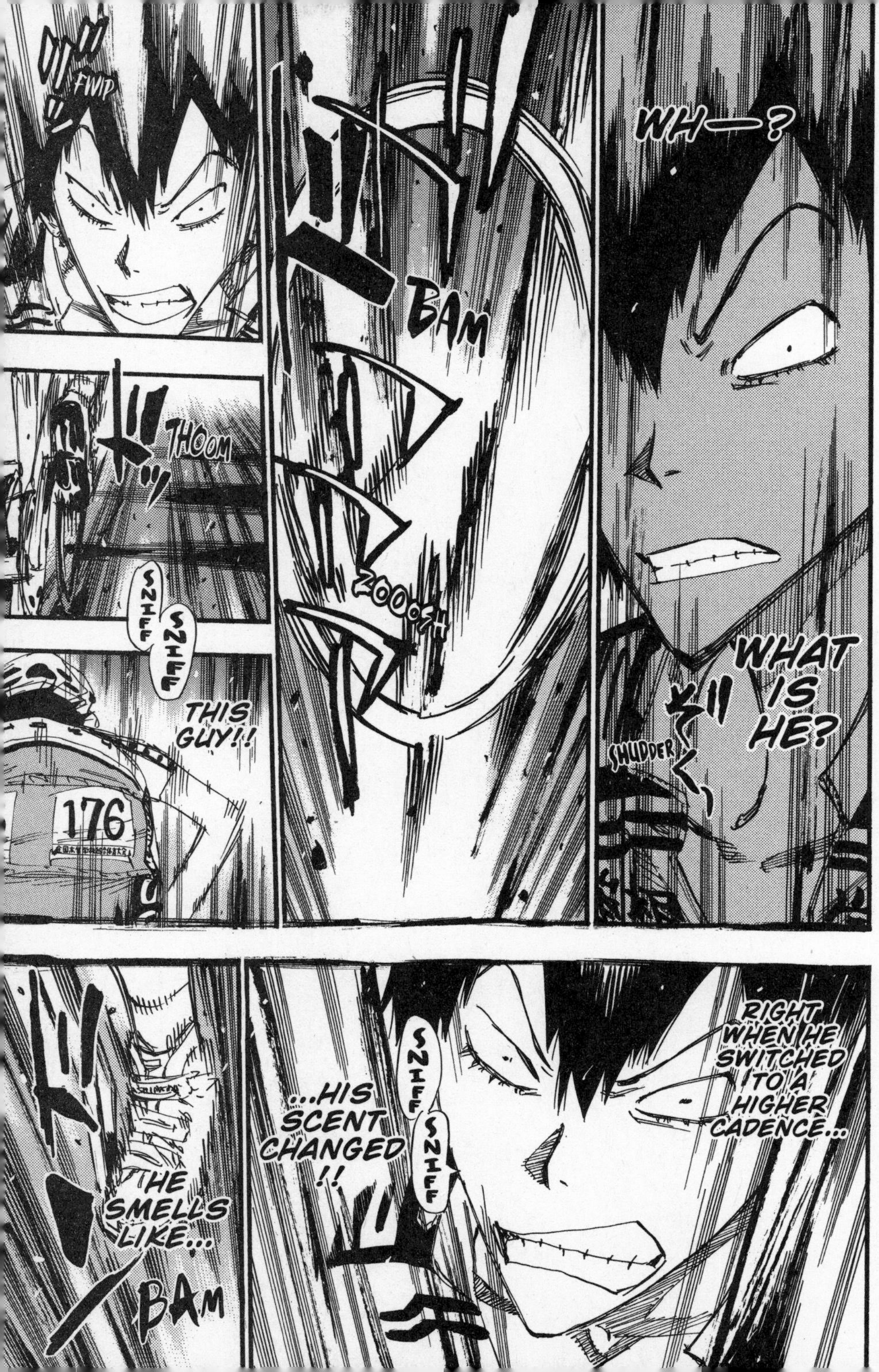
WH—?
WHAT IS HE?
SHUDDER
BAM
ZOOOSH
FWIP
THOOM
SNIFF
SNIFF
THIS GUY!!
176
RIGHT WHEN HE SWITCHED TO A HIGHER CADENCE...
...HIS SCENT CHANGED!!
SNIFF
SNIFF
HE SMELLS LIKE...
BAM

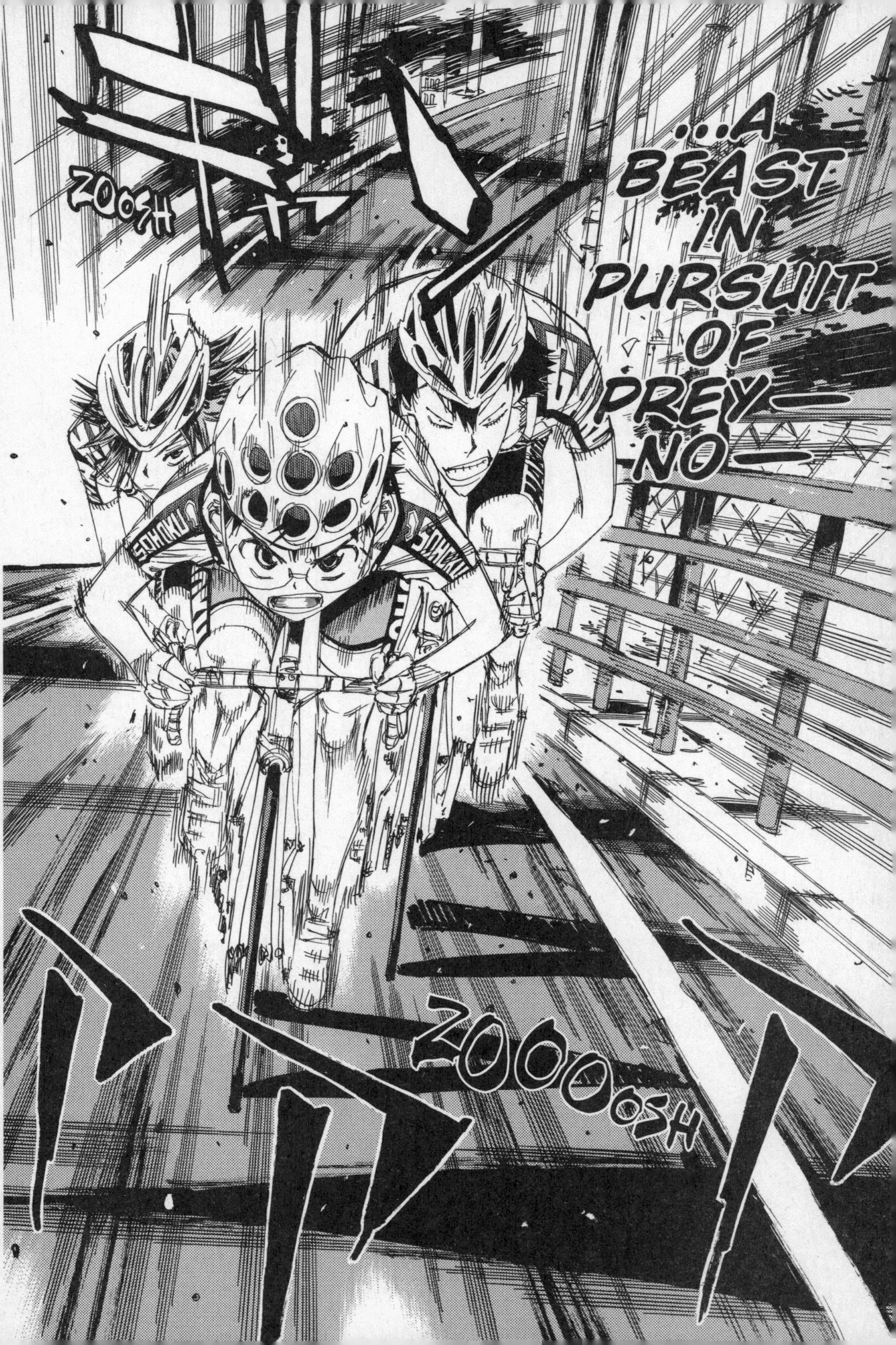
...A BEAST IN PURSUIT OF PREY—
NO—
ZOOSH
ZOOOOOSH

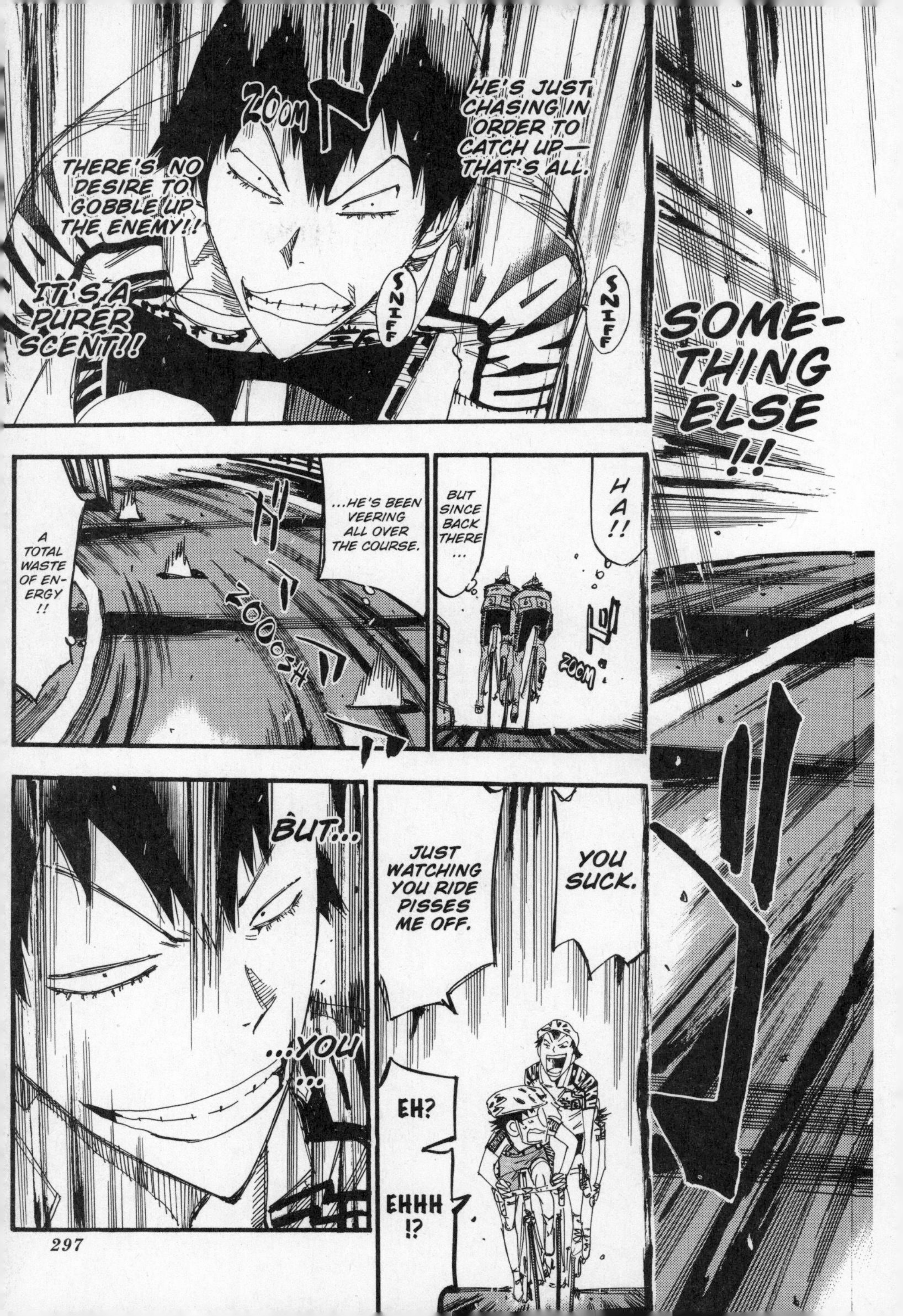
ZOOM
HE'S JUST CHASING IN ORDER TO CATCH UP—THAT'S ALL.
THERE'S NO DESIRE TO GOBBLE UP THE ENEMY!!
IT'S A PURER SCENT!!
SNIFF
SNIFF
SOME-THING ELSE!!
HA!!
BUT SINCE BACK THERE...
ZOOM
...HE'S BEEN VEERING ALL OVER THE COURSE.
A TOTAL WASTE OF EN-ERGY!!
ZOOOSH
YOU SUCK.
JUST WATCHING YOU RIDE PISSES ME OFF.
EH?
EHHH!?
BUT...
...YOU...

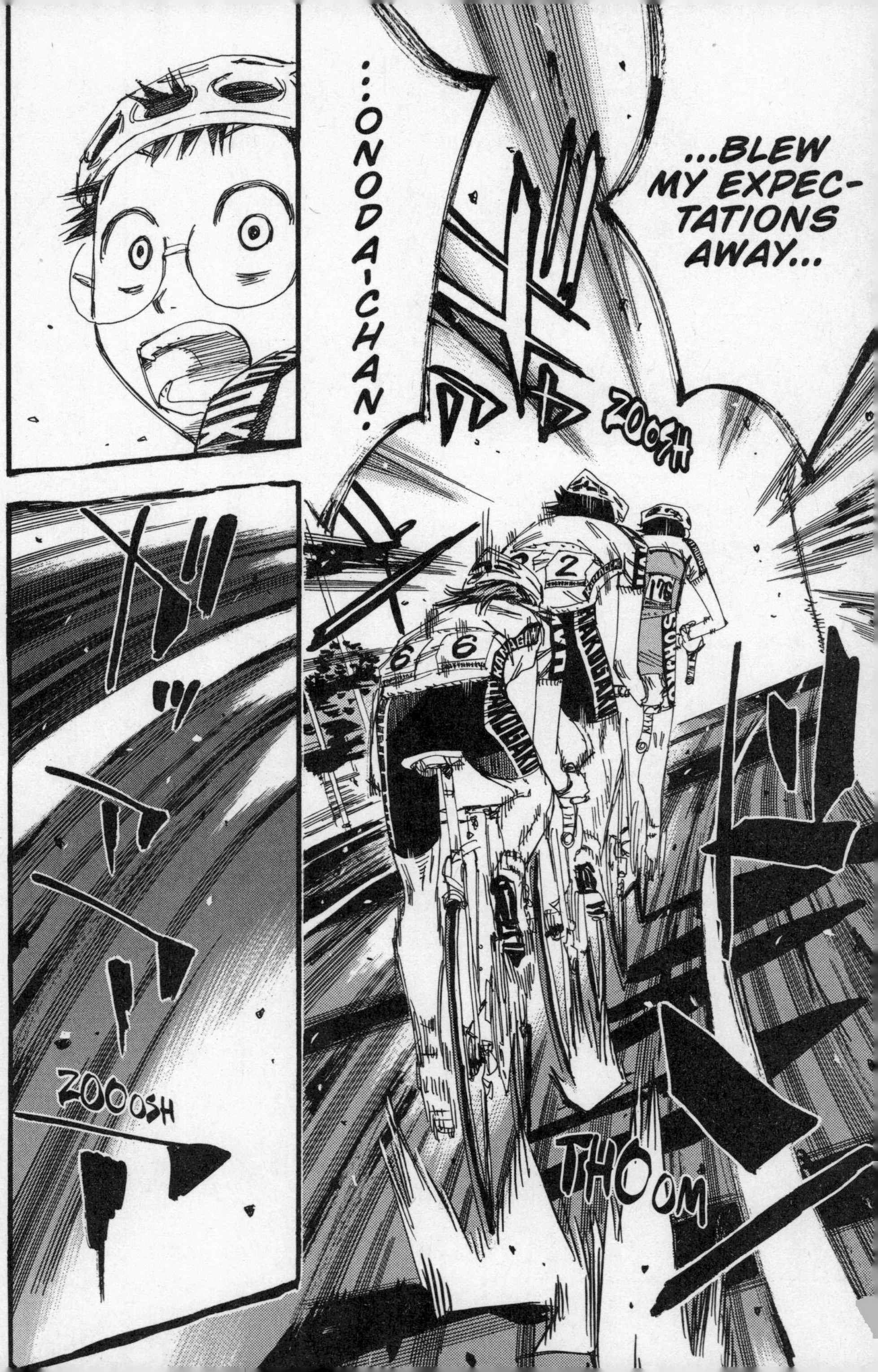
...BLEW MY EXPECTATIONS AWAY...
...ONODA-CHAN!
ZOOSH
THOOM
ZOOOSH

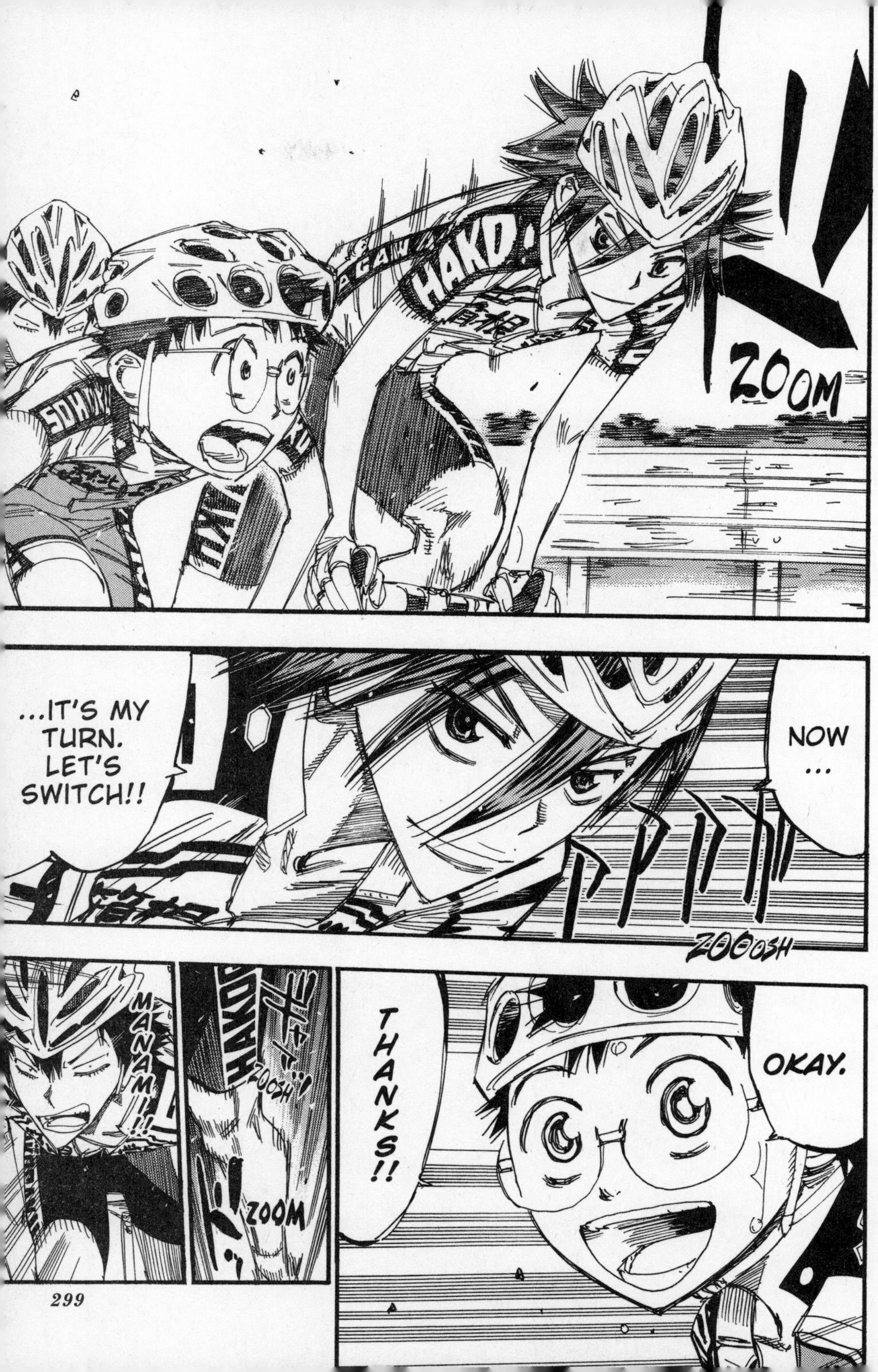
ZOOM
NOW ...
...IT'S MY TURN. LET'S SWITCH!!
ZOOOSH
OKAY.
THANKS!!
ZOOSH
ZOOM
MANAMI!!

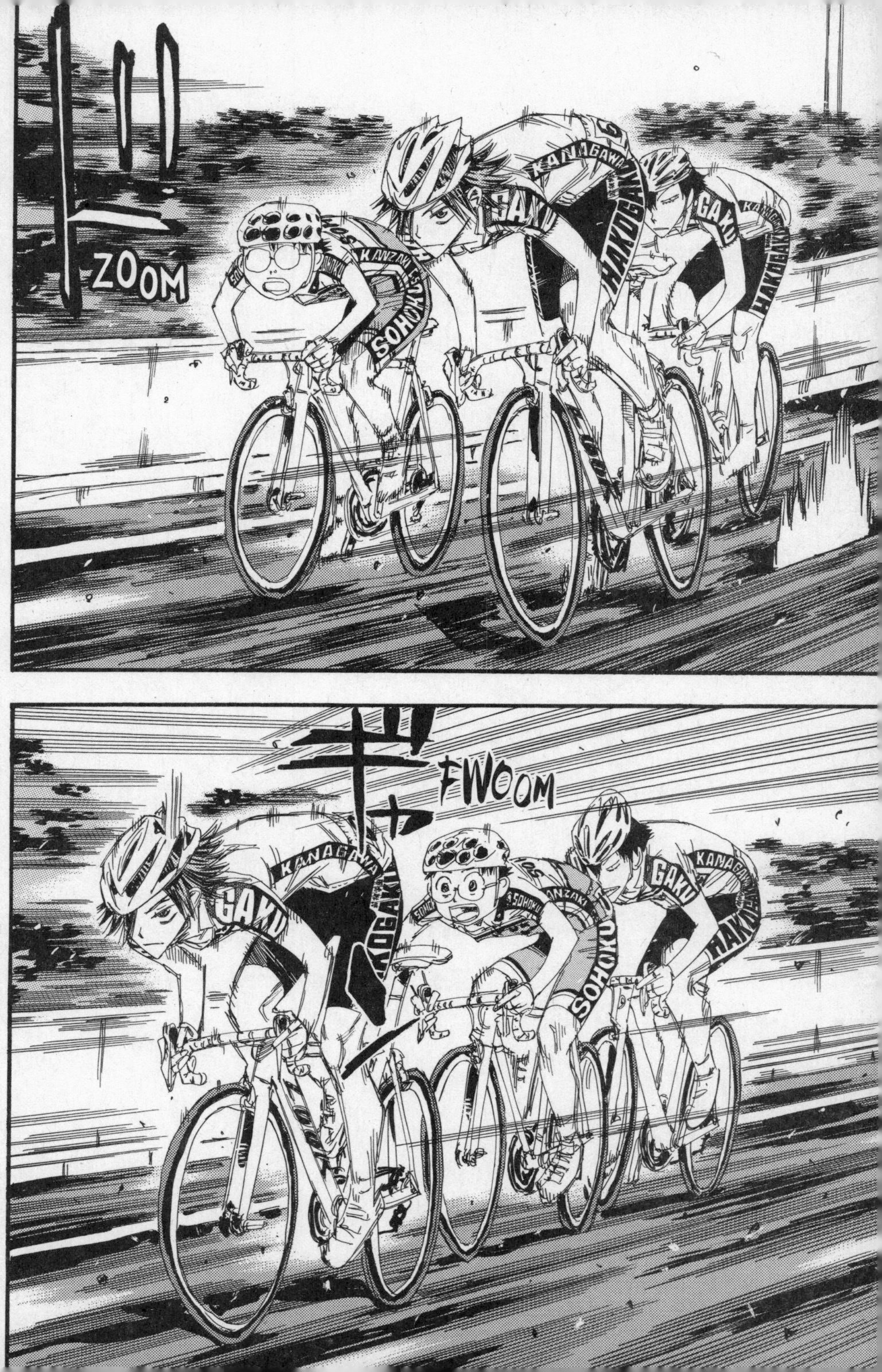
ZOOM
FWOOM

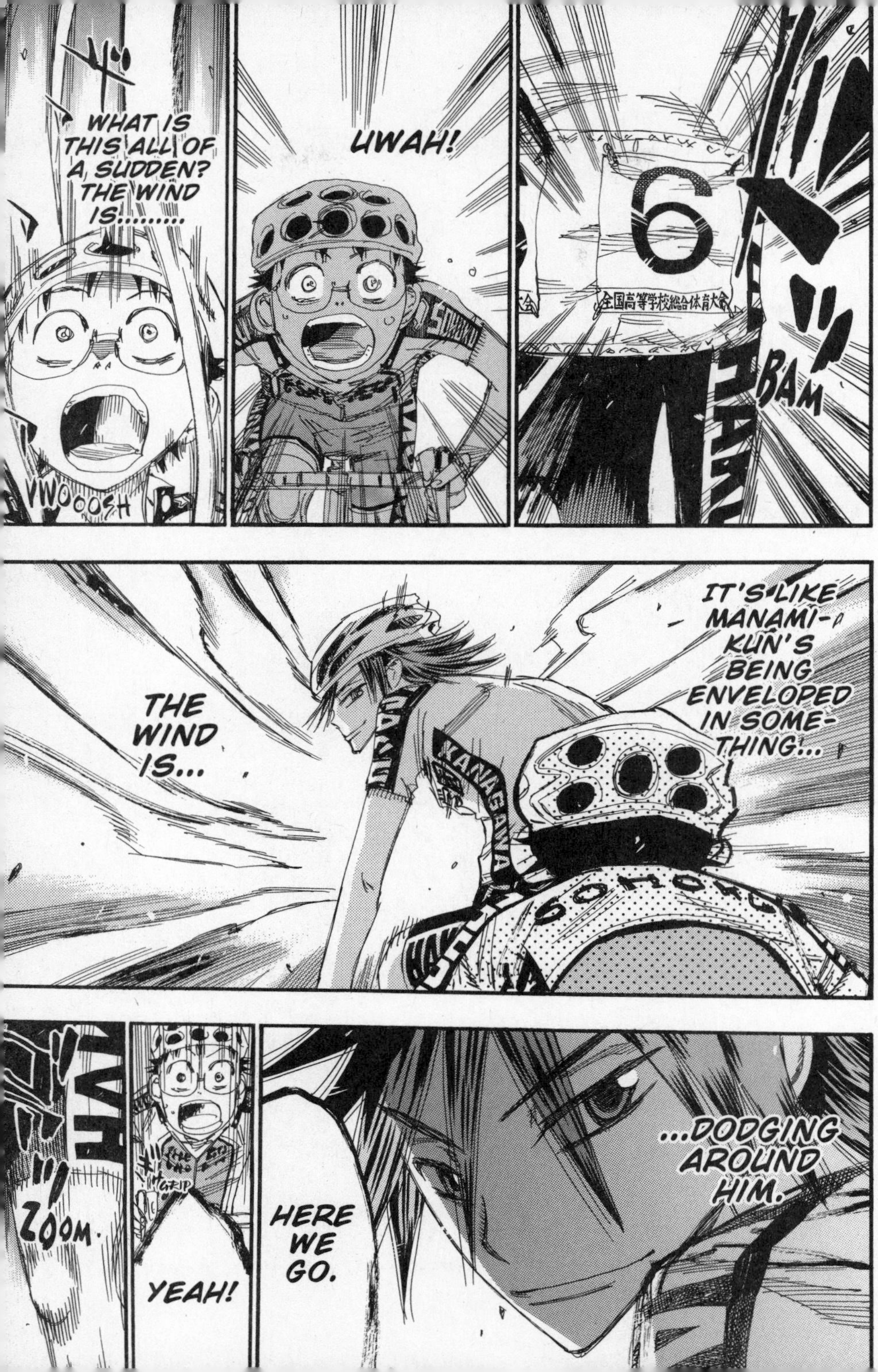
6
全国高等学校総合体育大会
BAM
UWAH!
WHAT IS THIS ALL OF A SUDDEN? THE WIND IS.........
VWOOOSH
IT'S LIKE MANAMI-KUN'S BEING ENVELOPED IN SOME-THING...
THE WIND IS...
KANAGAWA
SOHOKU
...DODGING AROUND HIM.
HERE WE GO.
GRIP
YEAH!
ZOOM

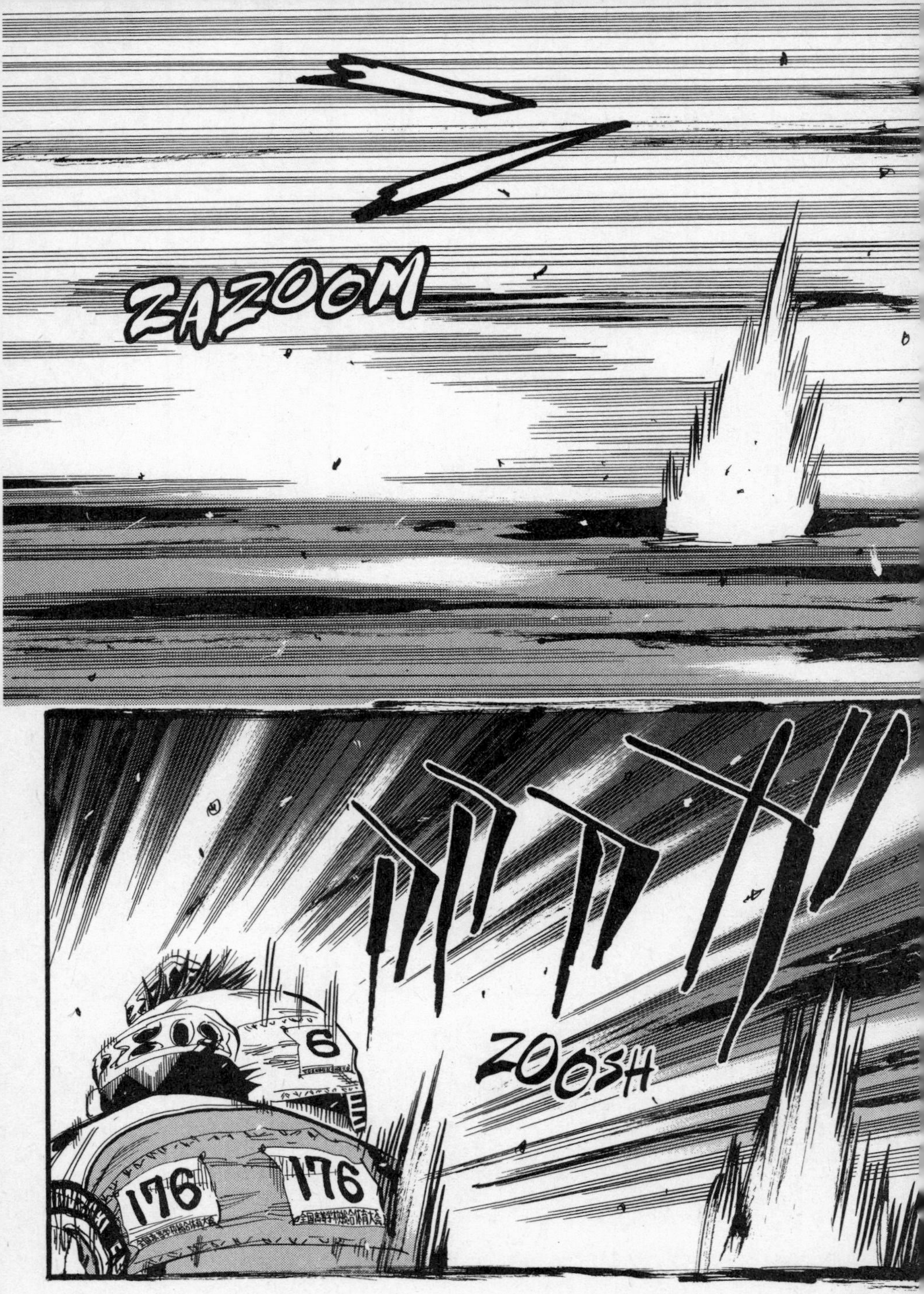
ZAZOOM
ZOOSH
6
176
176

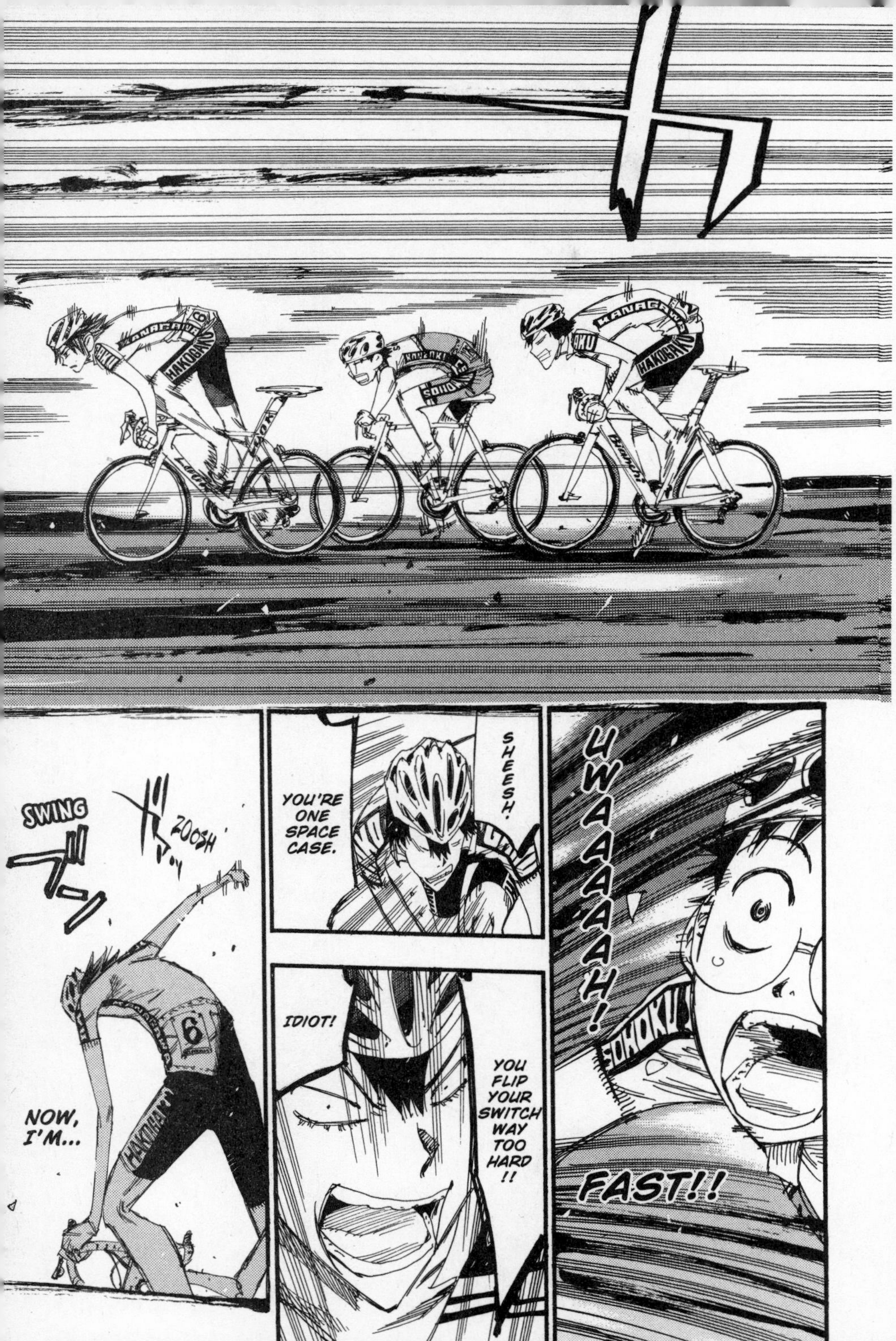
UWAAAAAAAH!
FAST!!
SHEESH!
YOU'RE ONE SPACE CASE.
IDIOT!
YOU FLIP YOUR SWITCH WAY TOO HARD!!
SWING
ZOOSH
NOW, I'M...

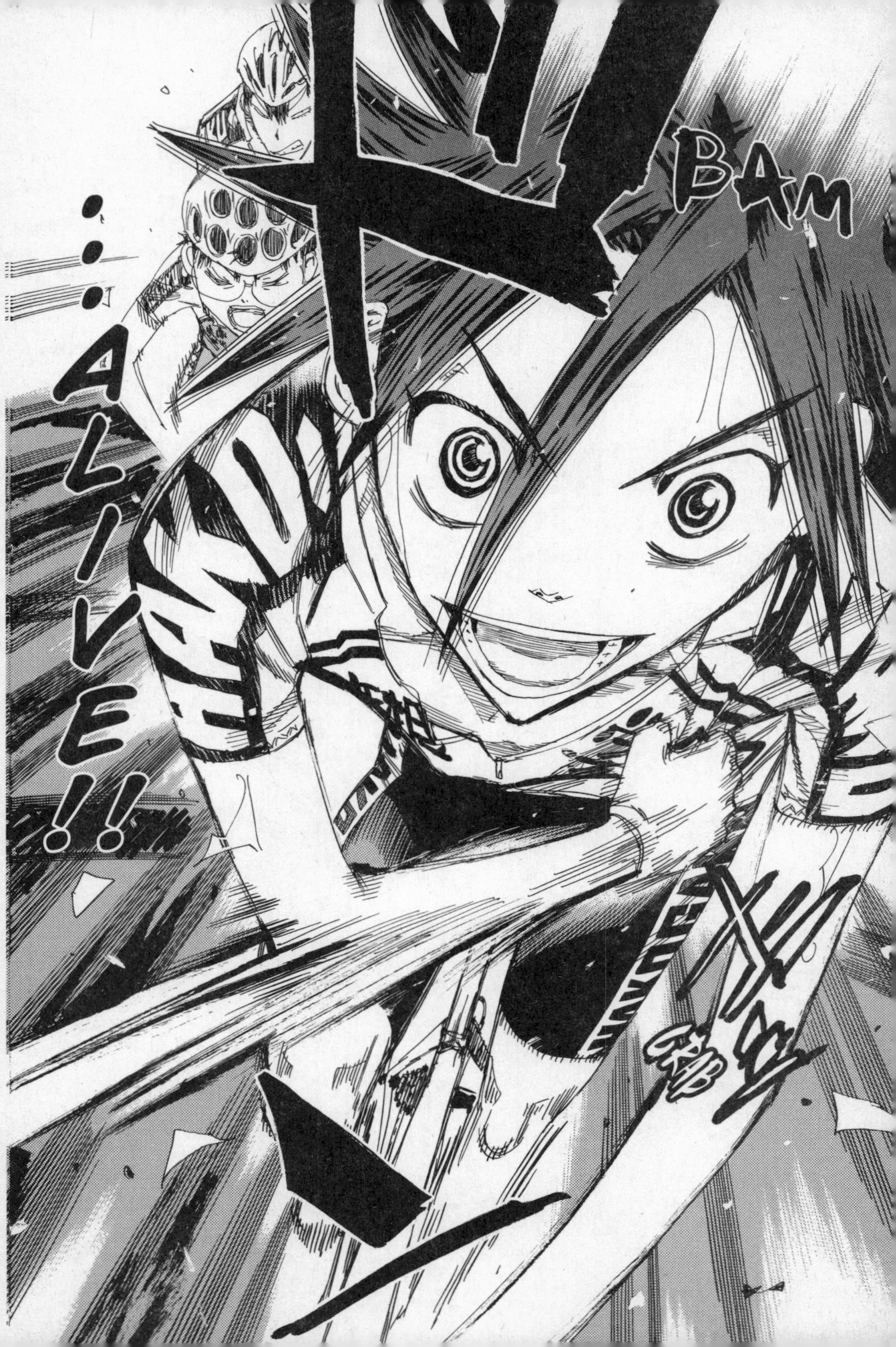
BAM
...ALIVE!!
GRAB

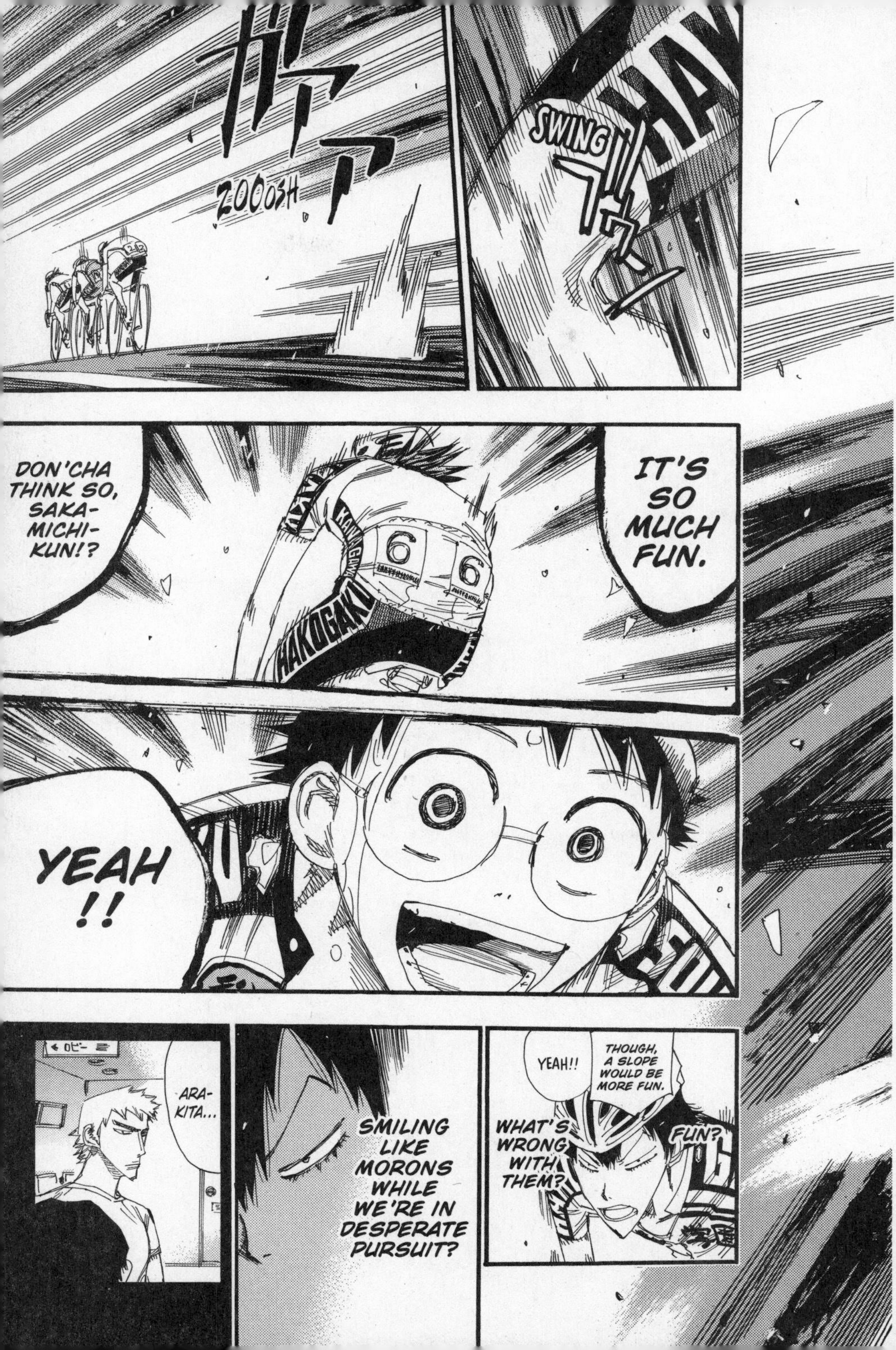
SWING
ZOOOSH
IT'S SO MUCH FUN.
DON'CHA THINK SO, SAKAMICHI-KUN!?
YEAH!!
THOUGH, A SLOPE WOULD BE MORE FUN.
YEAH!!
FUN?
WHAT'S WRONG WITH THEM?
SMILING LIKE MORONS WHILE WE'RE IN DESPERATE PURSUIT?
ARA-KITA...
ロビー

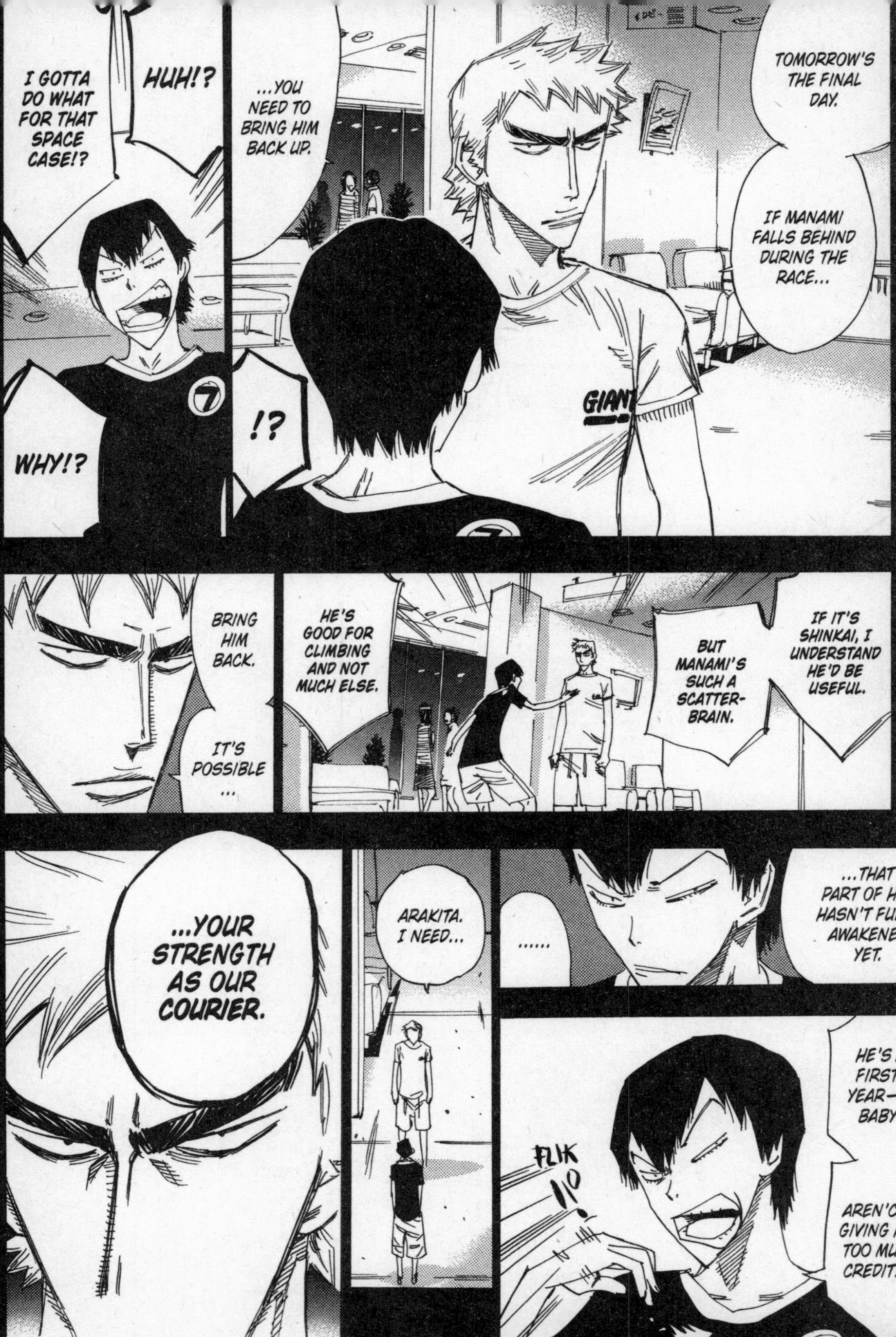
TOMORROW'S THE FINAL DAY.
IF MANAMI FALLS BEHIND DURING THE RACE...
...YOU NEED TO BRING HIM BACK UP.
!?
HUH!?
I GOTTA DO WHAT FOR THAT SPACE CASE!?
WHY!?
IF IT'S SHINKAI, I UNDERSTAND HE'D BE USEFUL.
BUT MANAMI'S SUCH A SCATTER-BRAIN.
HE'S GOOD FOR CLIMBING AND NOT MUCH ELSE.
BRING HIM BACK.
IT'S POSSIBLE ...
...THAT PART OF HIM HASN'T FULLY AWAKENED YET.
......
HE'S A FIRST-YEAR—A BABY!
AREN'CHA GIVING HIM TOO MUCH CREDIT!!?
FLIK
!!
ARAKITA. I NEED...
...YOUR STRENGTH AS OUR COURIER.

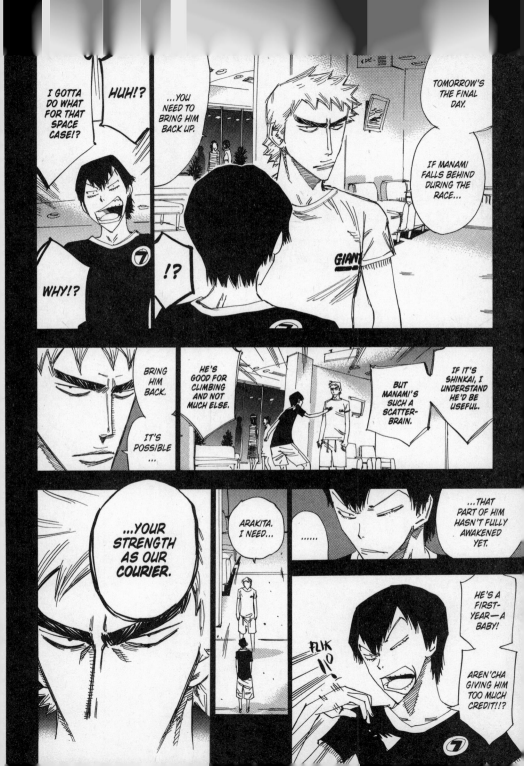

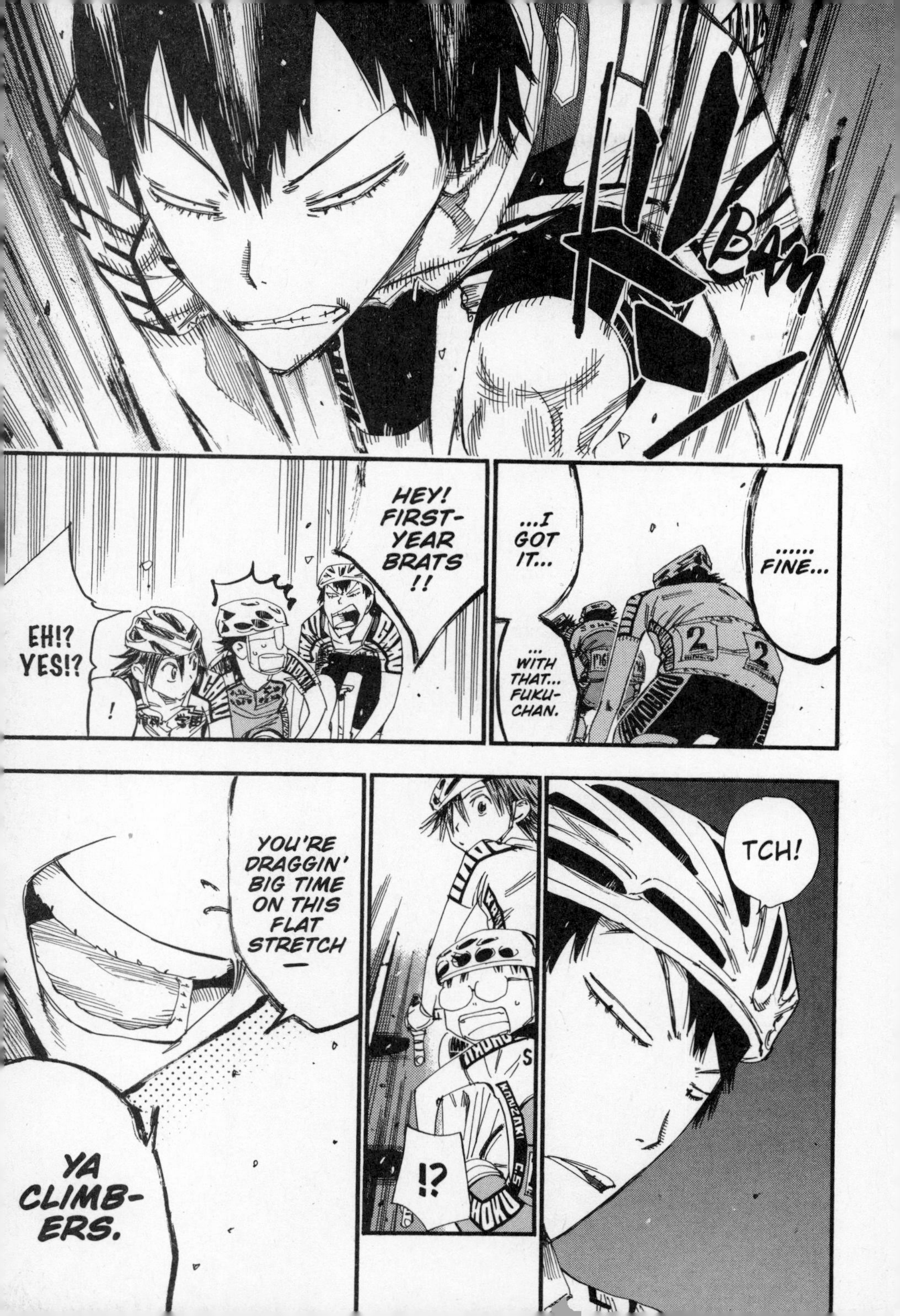
BAM
......FINE...
...I GOT IT...
...WITH THAT... FUKU-CHAN.
HEY! FIRST-YEAR BRATS!!
EH!? YES!?
!
TCH!
!?
YOU'RE DRAGGIN' BIG TIME ON THIS FLAT STRETCH—
YA CLIMBERS.

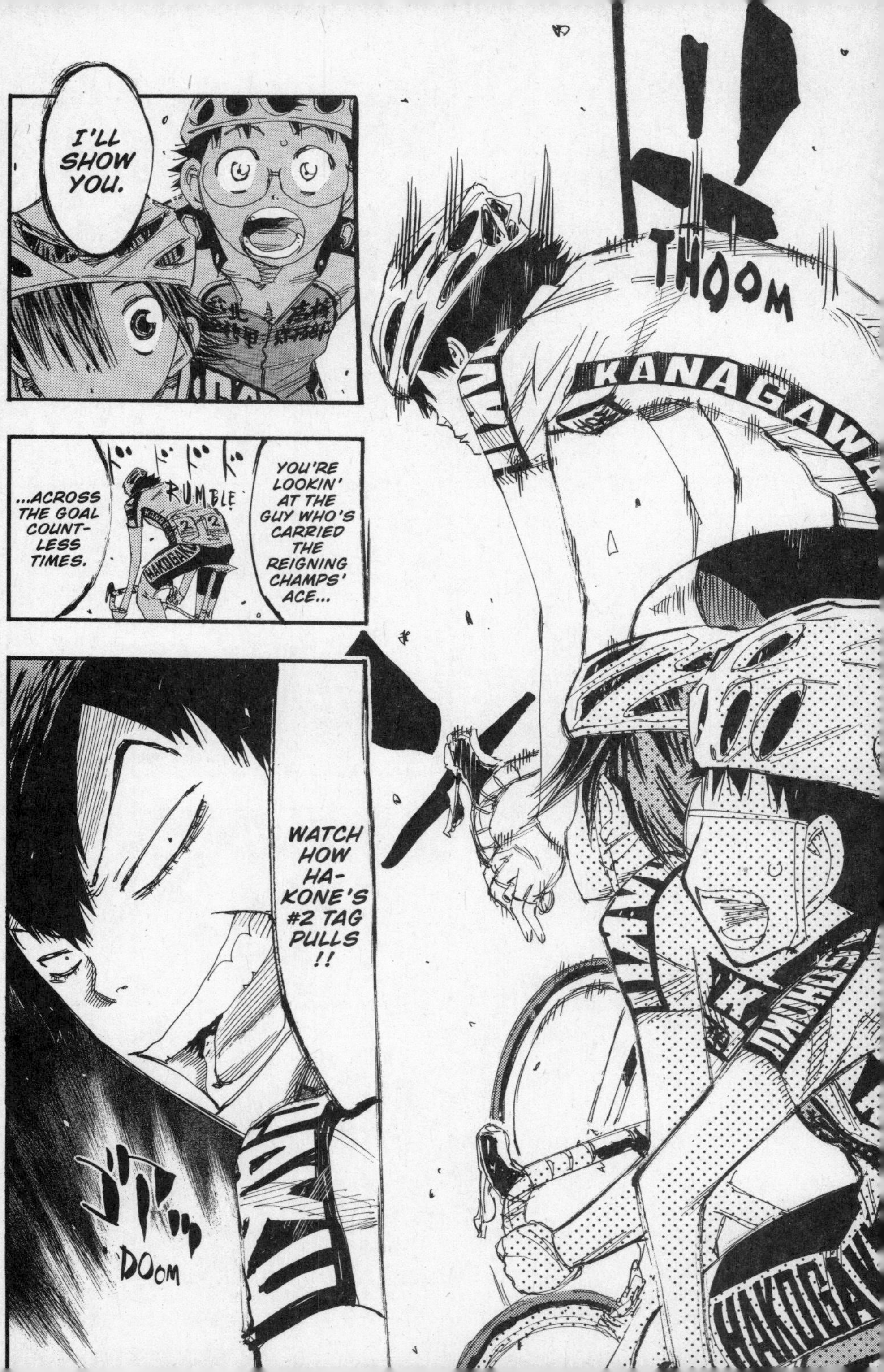
THOOM
KANAGAWA
I'LL SHOW YOU.
YOU'RE LOOKIN' AT THE GUY WHO'S CARRIED THE REIGNING CHAMPS' ACE...
RUMBLE
...ACROSS THE GOAL COUNT-LESS TIMES.
WATCH HOW HA-KONE'S #2 TAG PULLS !!
DOOM

RIDE.169 ROLLER COASTER RIDE

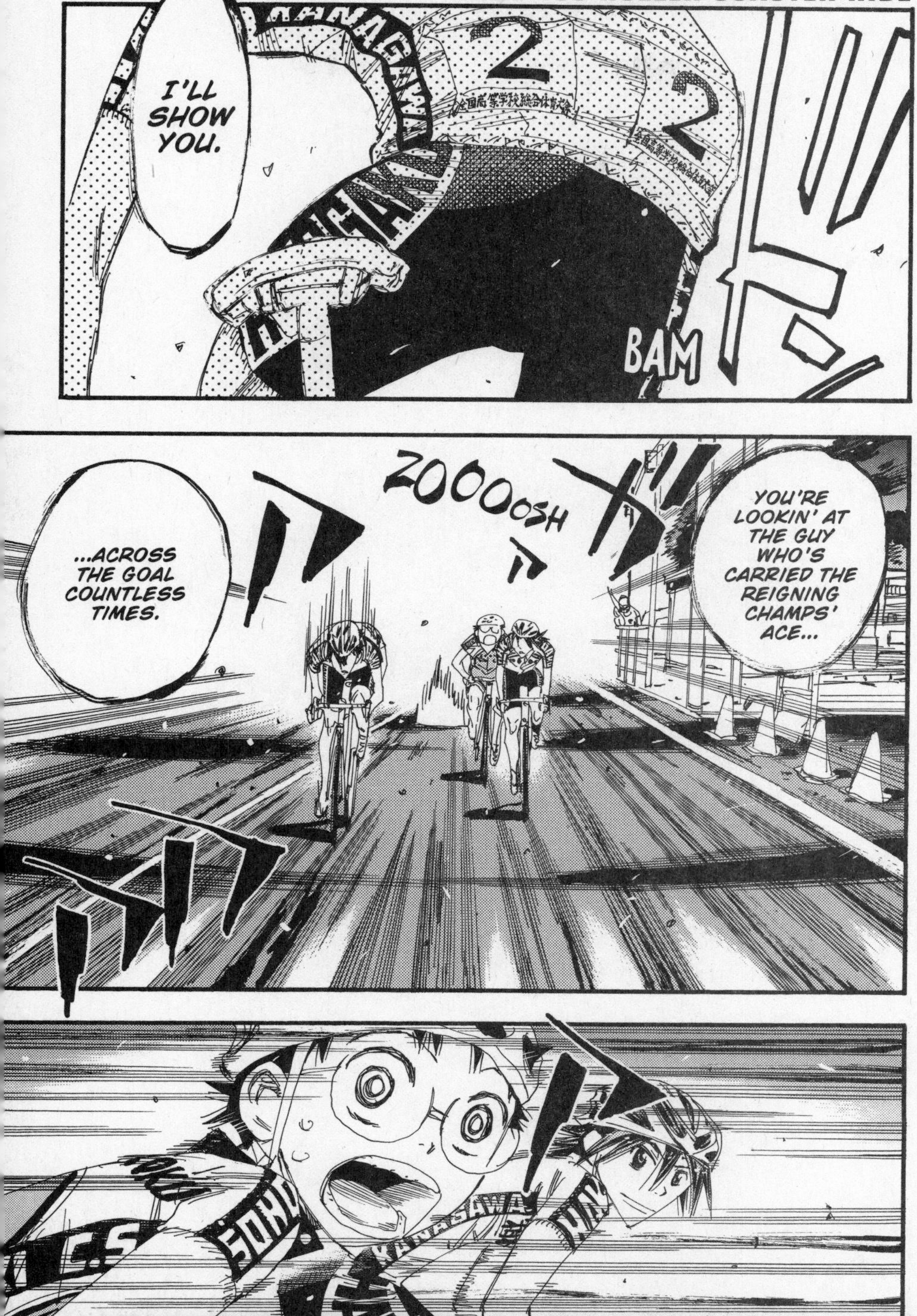
I'LL SHOW YOU.
BAM
YOU'RE LOOKIN' AT THE GUY WHO'S CARRIED THE REIGNING CHAMPS' ACE...
ZOOOOOSH
...ACROSS THE GOAL COUNTLESS TIMES.

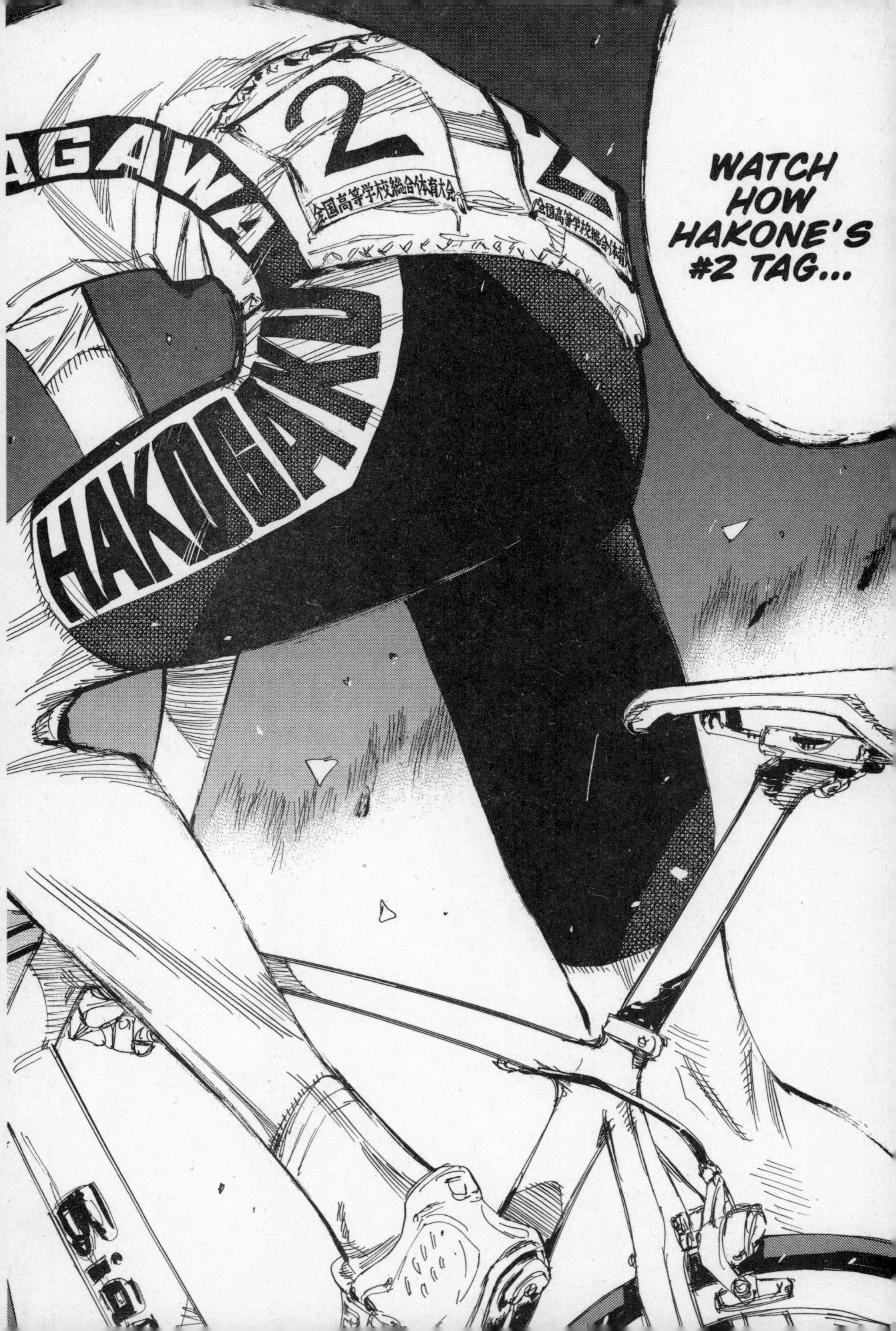
WATCH HOW HAKONE'S #2 TAG...
2
全国高等学校総合体育大会
HAKOGAKU

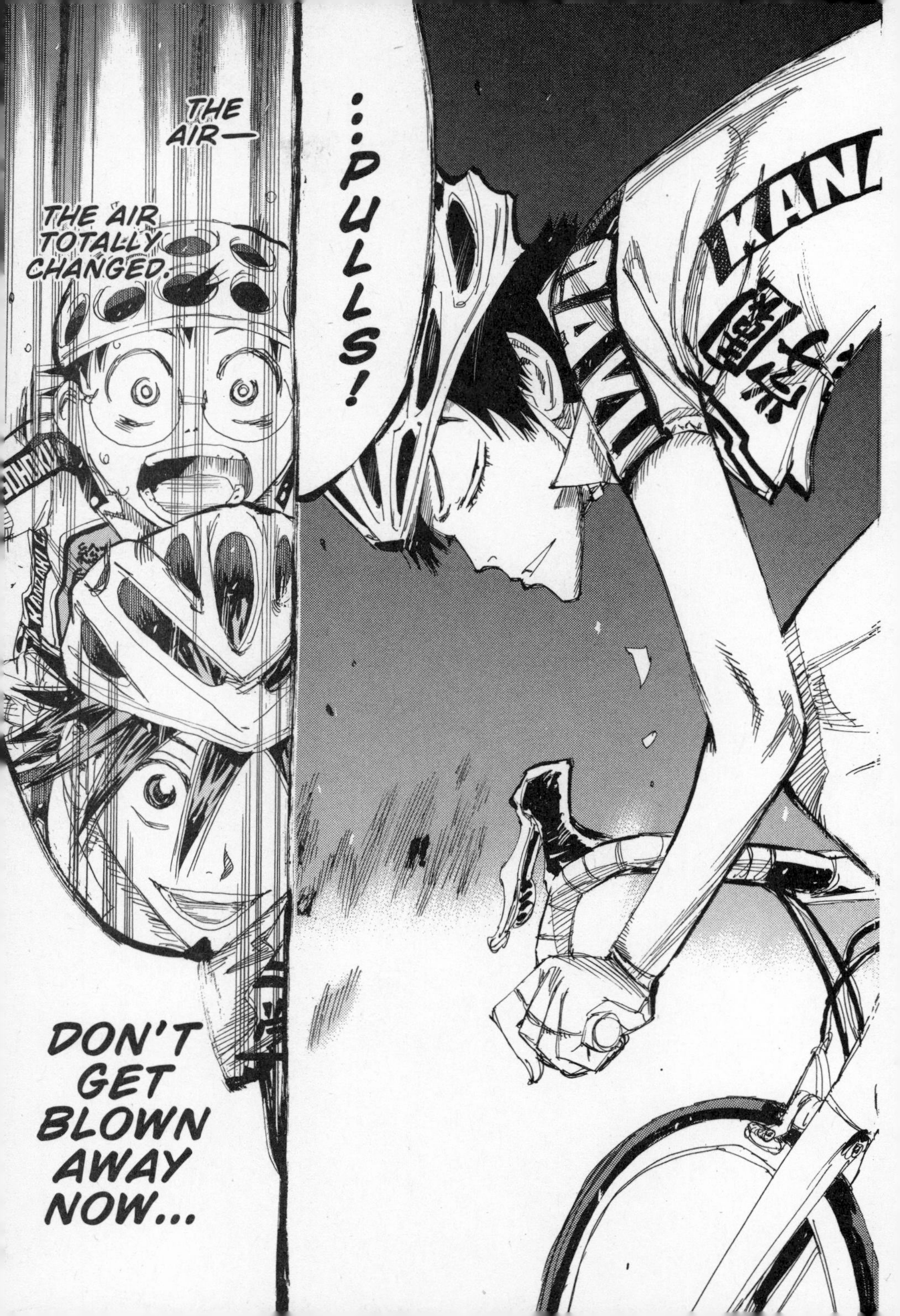
...PULLS!
THE AIR—
THE AIR TOTALLY CHANGED.
DON'T GET BLOWN AWAY NOW...

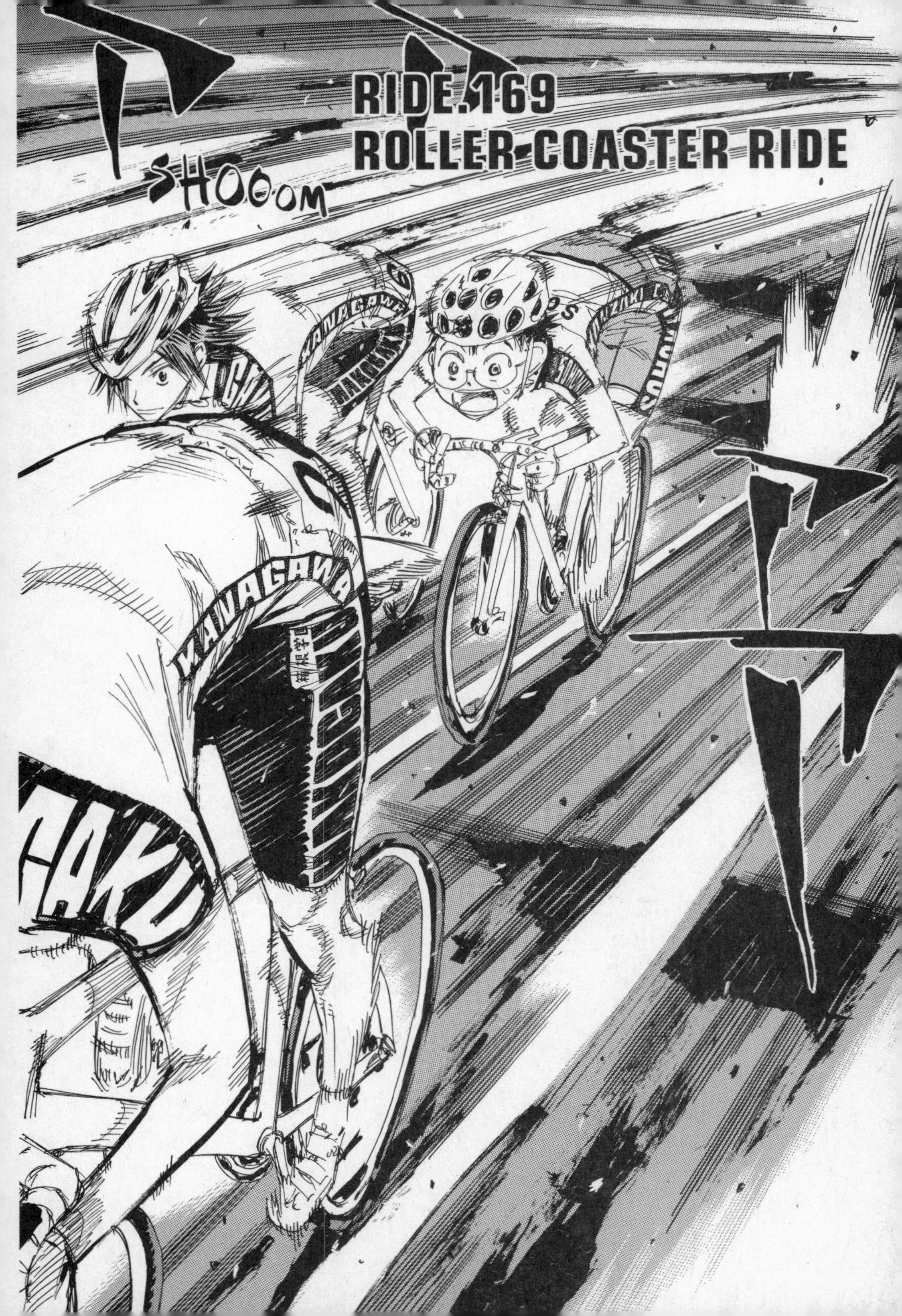
RIDE.169
ROLLER-COASTER RIDE
SHOOOM
KANAGAWA

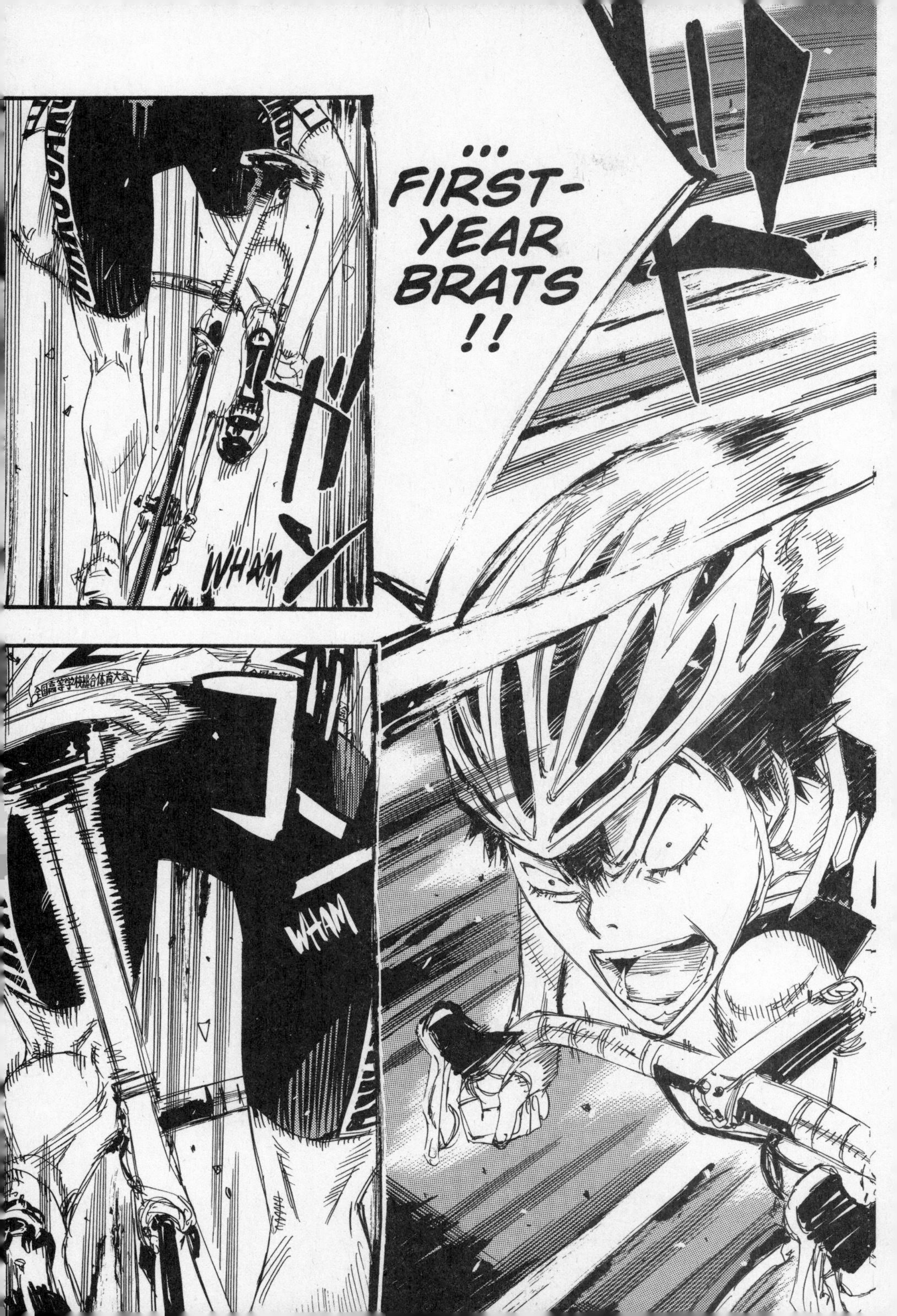
...FIRST-YEAR BRATS!!
WHAM
全国高等学校総合体育大会
WHAM

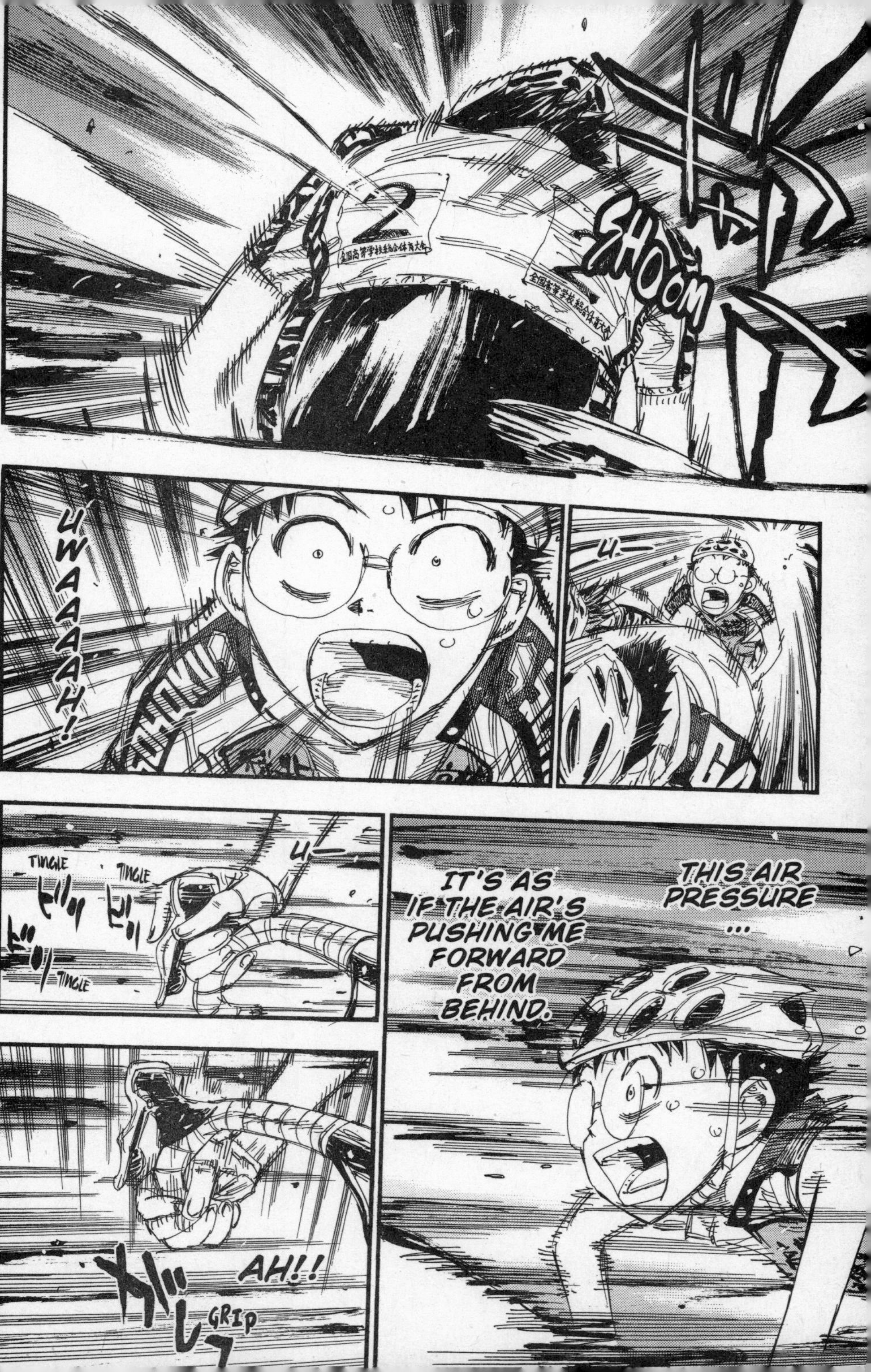
SHOOM
U—
UWAAAAAAH!
THIS AIR PRESSURE ...
IT'S AS IF THE AIR'S PUSHING ME FORWARD FROM BEHIND.
U—
TINGLE
TINGLE
TINGLE
AH!!
GRIP

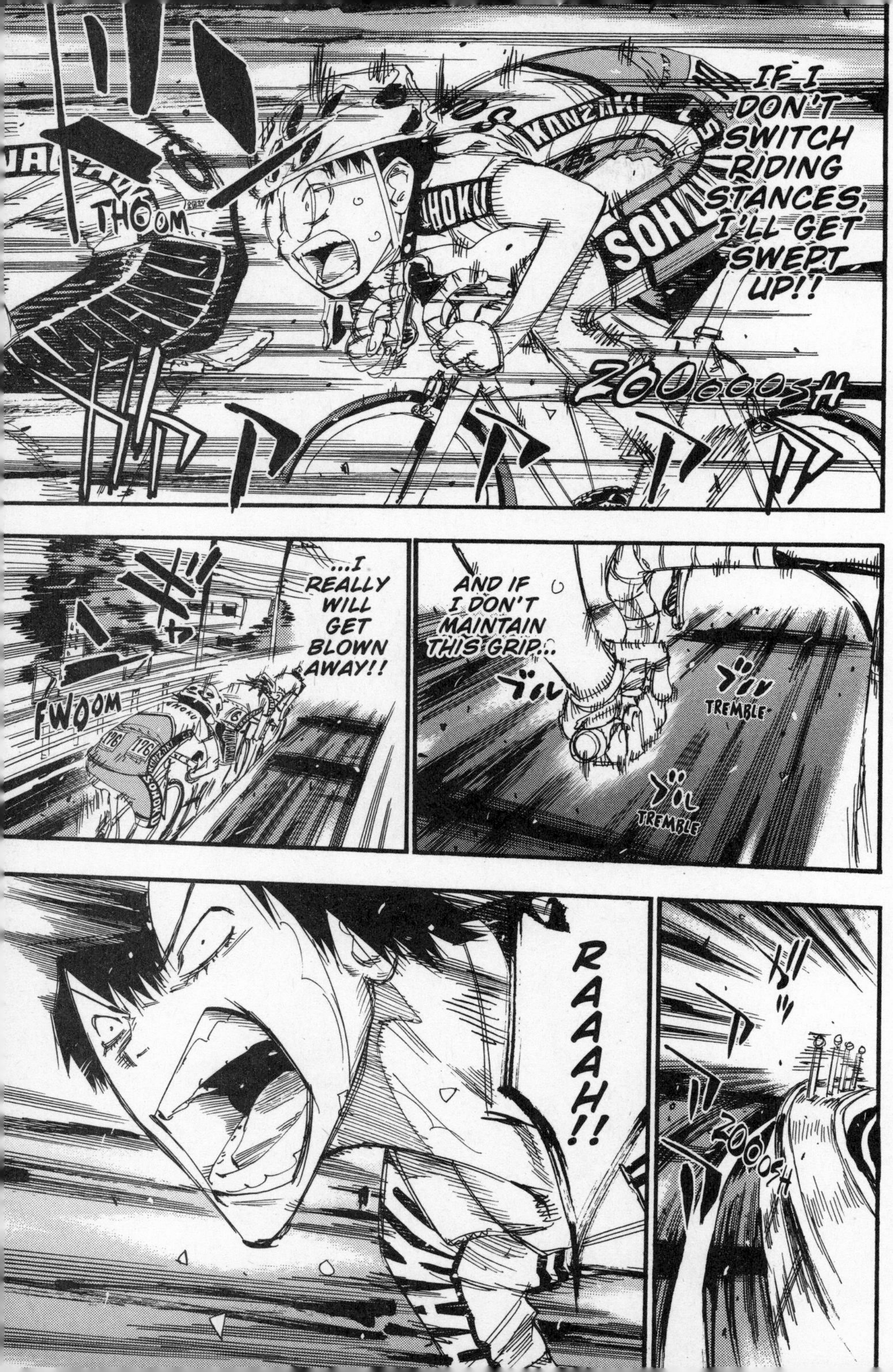
IF I DON'T SWITCH RIDING STANCES, I'LL GET SWEPT UP!!
THOOM
ZOOOOOOSH
AND IF I DON'T MAINTAIN THIS GRIP...
TREMBLE
TREMBLE
...I REALLY WILL GET BLOWN AWAY!!
FWOOM
ZOOOSH
RAAAAH!!

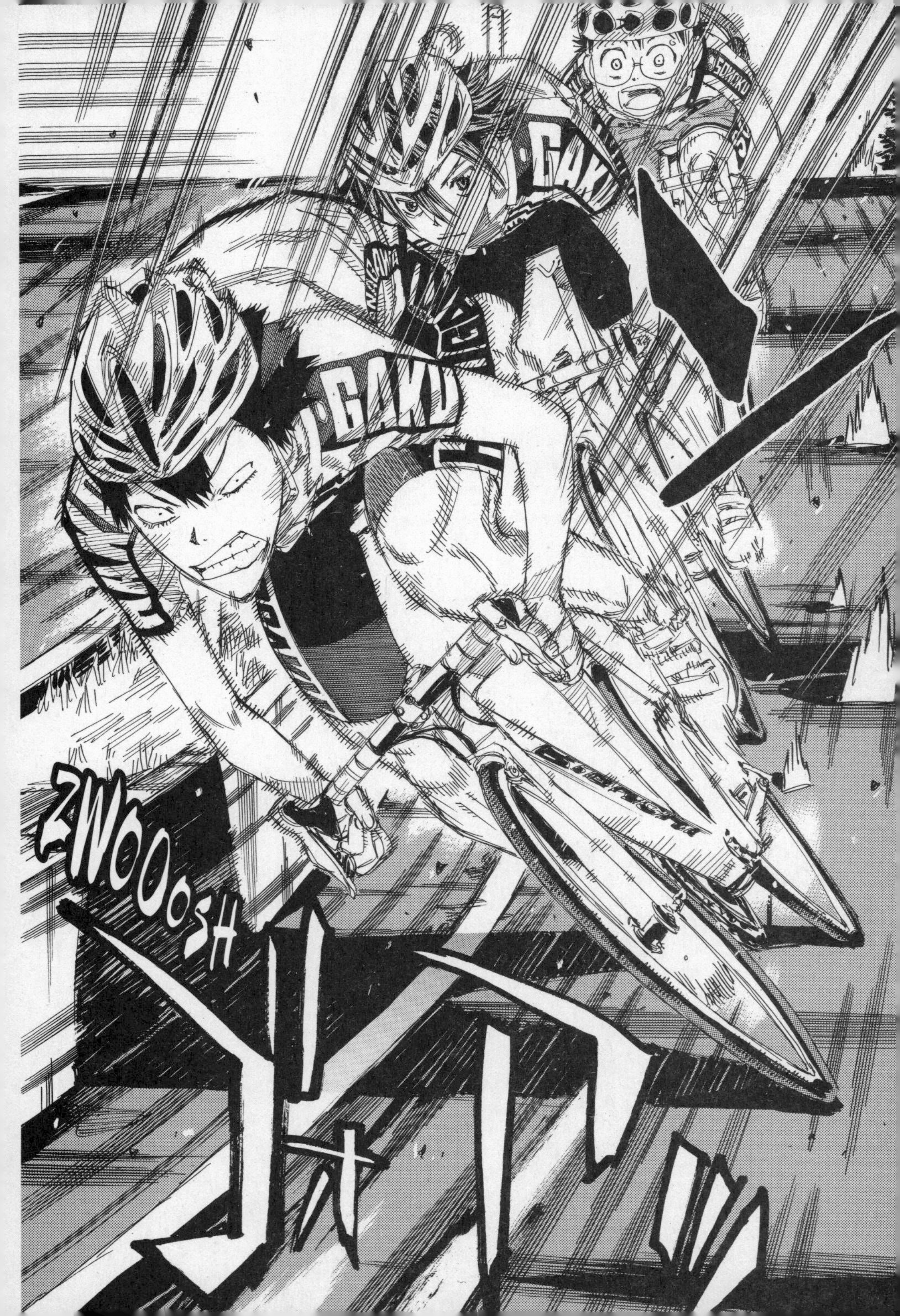
ZWOOOSH

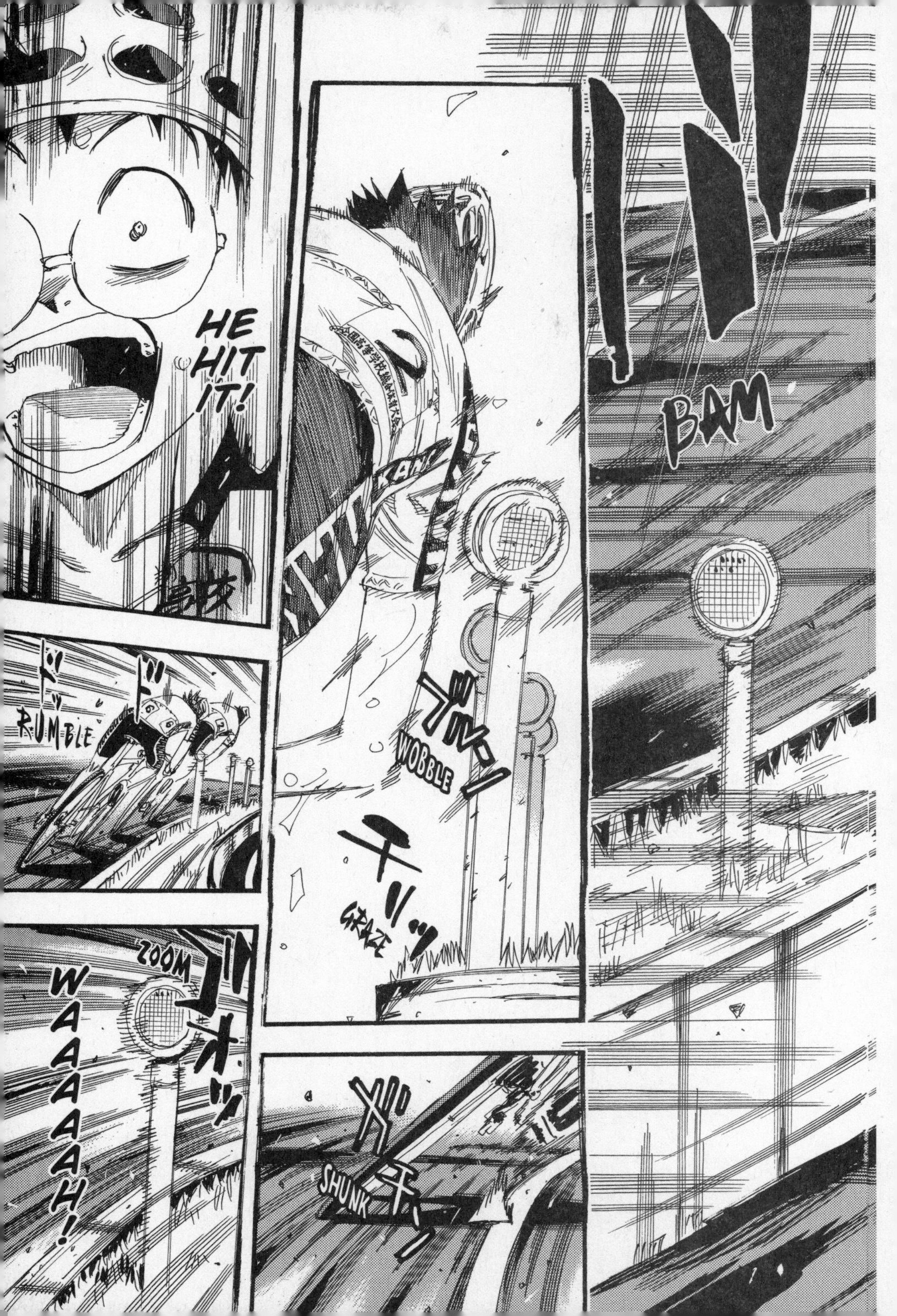
BAM
WOBBLE
GRAZE
HE HIT IT!
RUMBLE
SHUNK
ZOOM
WAAAAAAH!

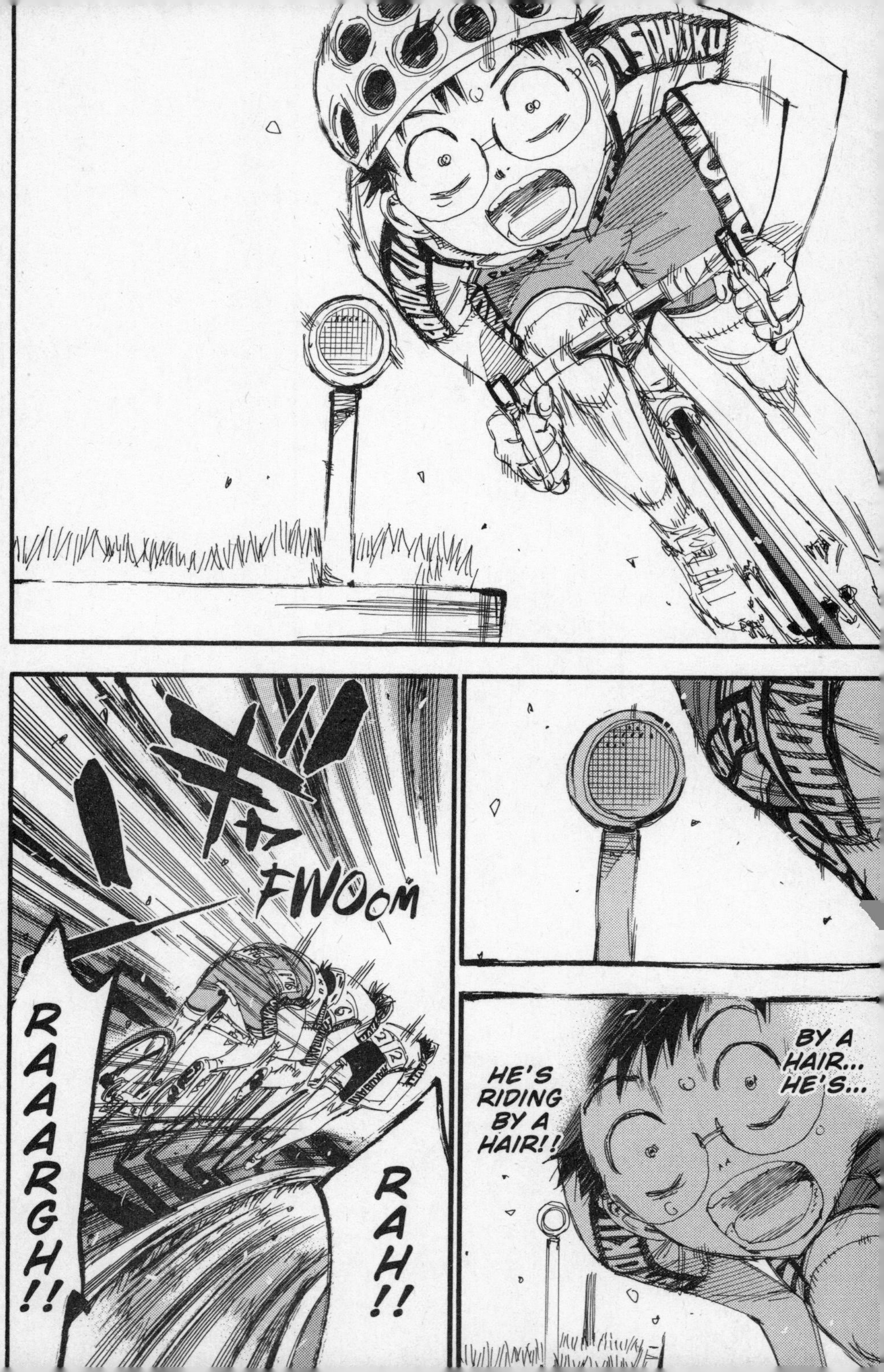
BY A HAIR... HE'S...
HE'S RIDING BY A HAIR!!
FWOOM
RAH!!
RAAAARGH!!

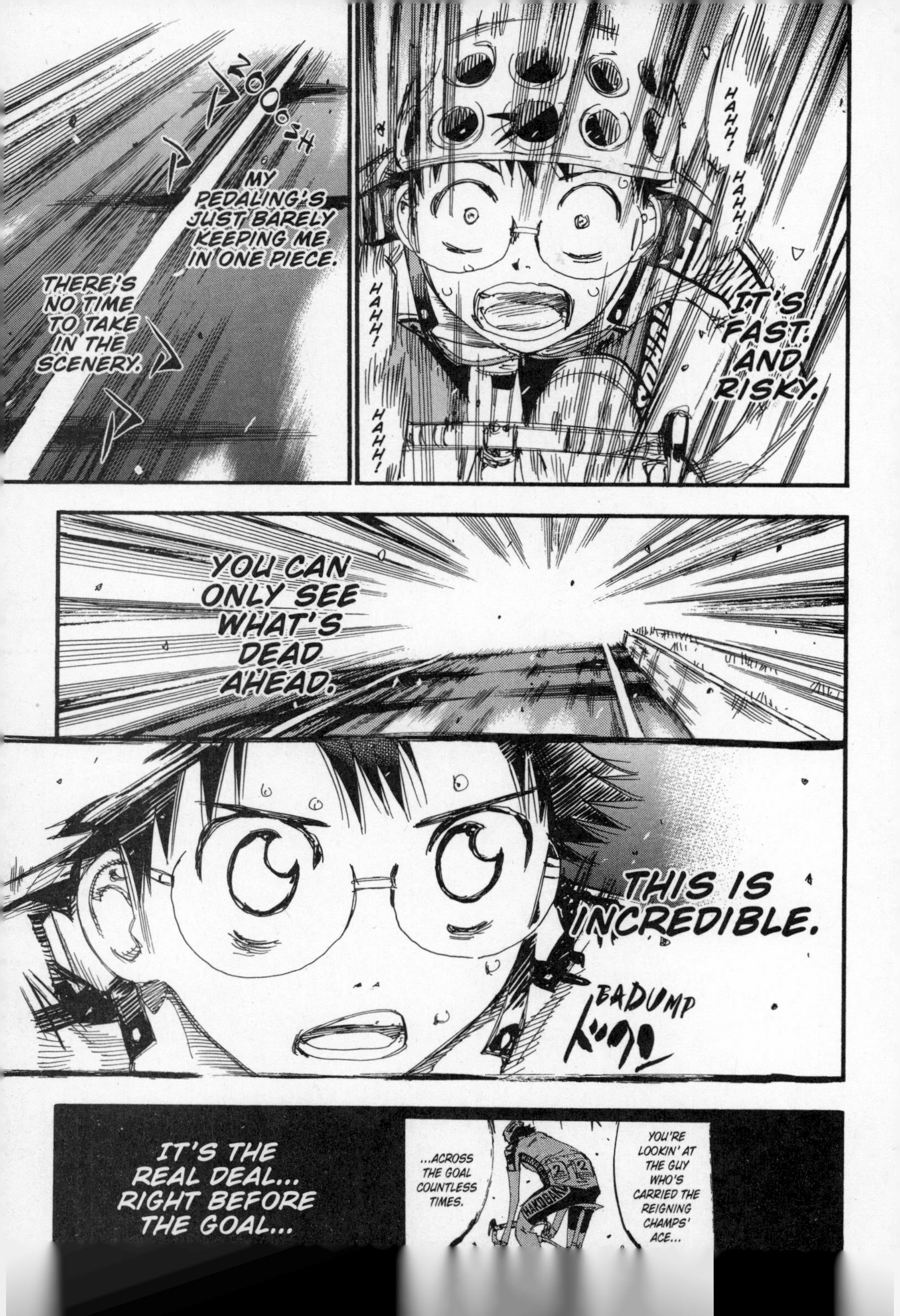
HAHH! HAHH!
HAHH!
HAHH!
IT'S FAST. AND RISKY.
ZOOOOSH
MY PEDALING'S JUST BARELY KEEPING ME IN ONE PIECE.
THERE'S NO TIME TO TAKE IN THE SCENERY.
YOU CAN ONLY SEE WHAT'S DEAD AHEAD.
THIS IS INCREDIBLE.
BADUMP
YOU'RE LOOKIN' AT THE GUY WHO'S CARRIED THE REIGNING CHAMPS' ACE...
...ACROSS THE GOAL COUNTLESS TIMES.
IT'S THE REAL DEAL... RIGHT BEFORE THE GOAL...

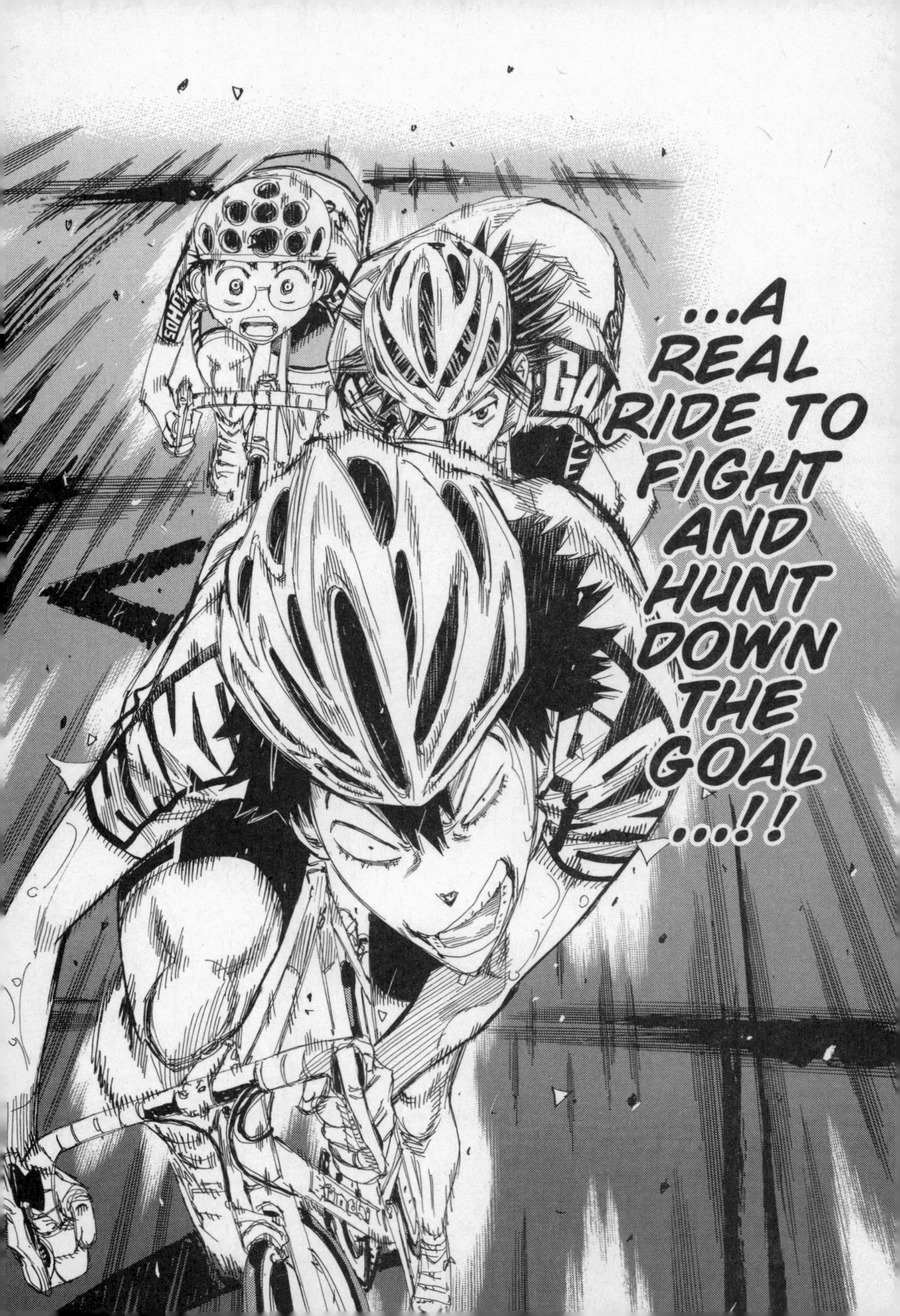
...A REAL RIDE TO FIGHT AND HUNT DOWN THE GOAL ...!!

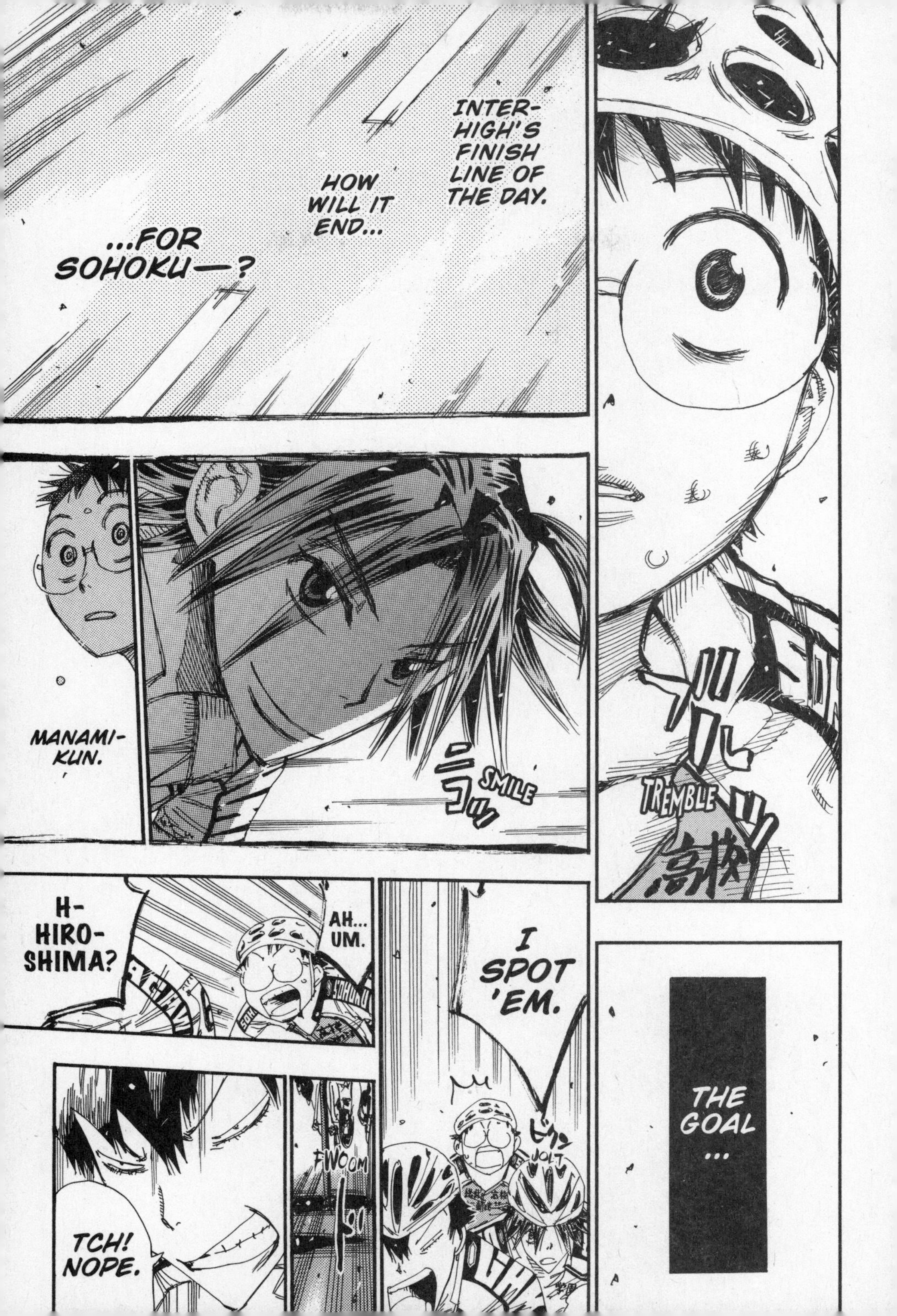
TREMBLE
INTER-HIGH'S FINISH LINE OF THE DAY.
HOW WILL IT END...
...FOR SOHOKU—?
SMILE
MANAMI-KUN.
THE GOAL...
I SPOT 'EM.
JOLT
AH... UM.
H-HIROSHIMA?
FWOOM
TCH! NOPE.

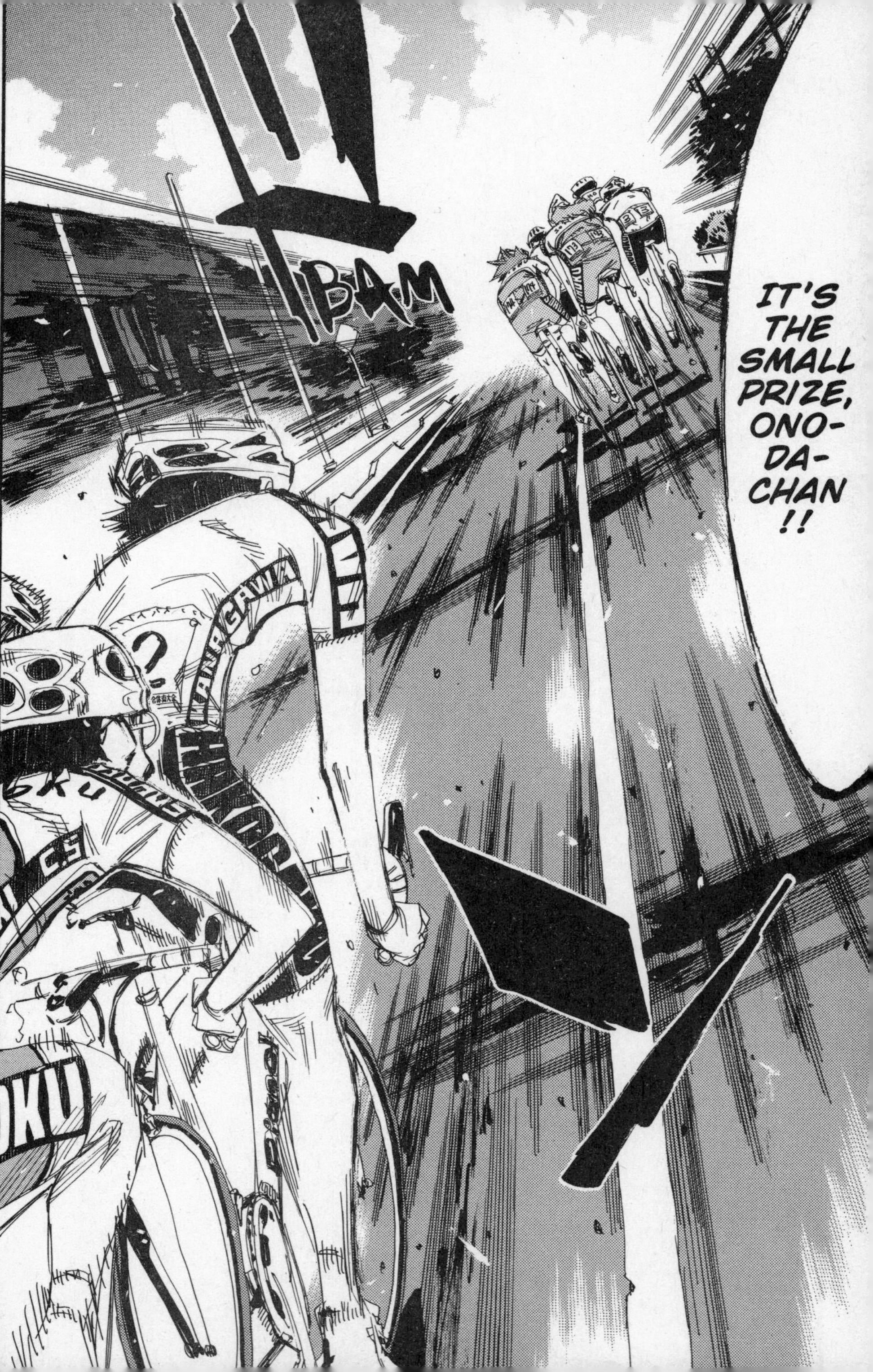
IT'S THE SMALL PRIZE, ONODA-CHAN!!
BAM

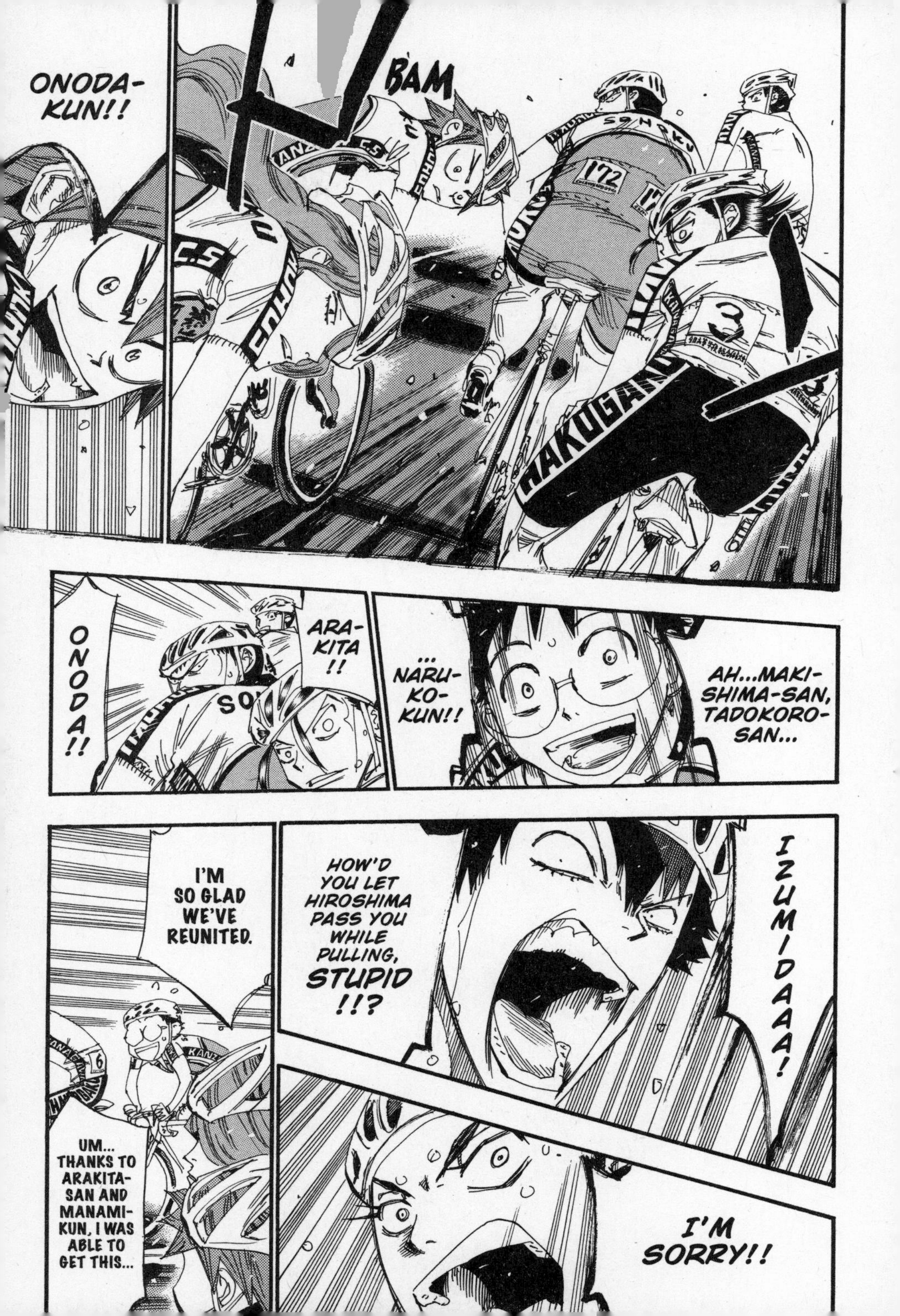
BAM
ONODA-KUN!!
AH...MAKI-SHIMA-SAN, TADOKORO-SAN...
...NARU-KO-KUN!!
ARA-KITA!!
ONODA!!
IZUMIDAAAA!
HOW'D YOU LET HIROSHIMA PASS YOU WHILE PULLING, STUPID!!?
I'M SORRY!!
I'M SO GLAD WE'VE REUNITED.
UM... THANKS TO ARAKITA-SAN AND MANAMI-KUN, I WAS ABLE TO GET THIS...

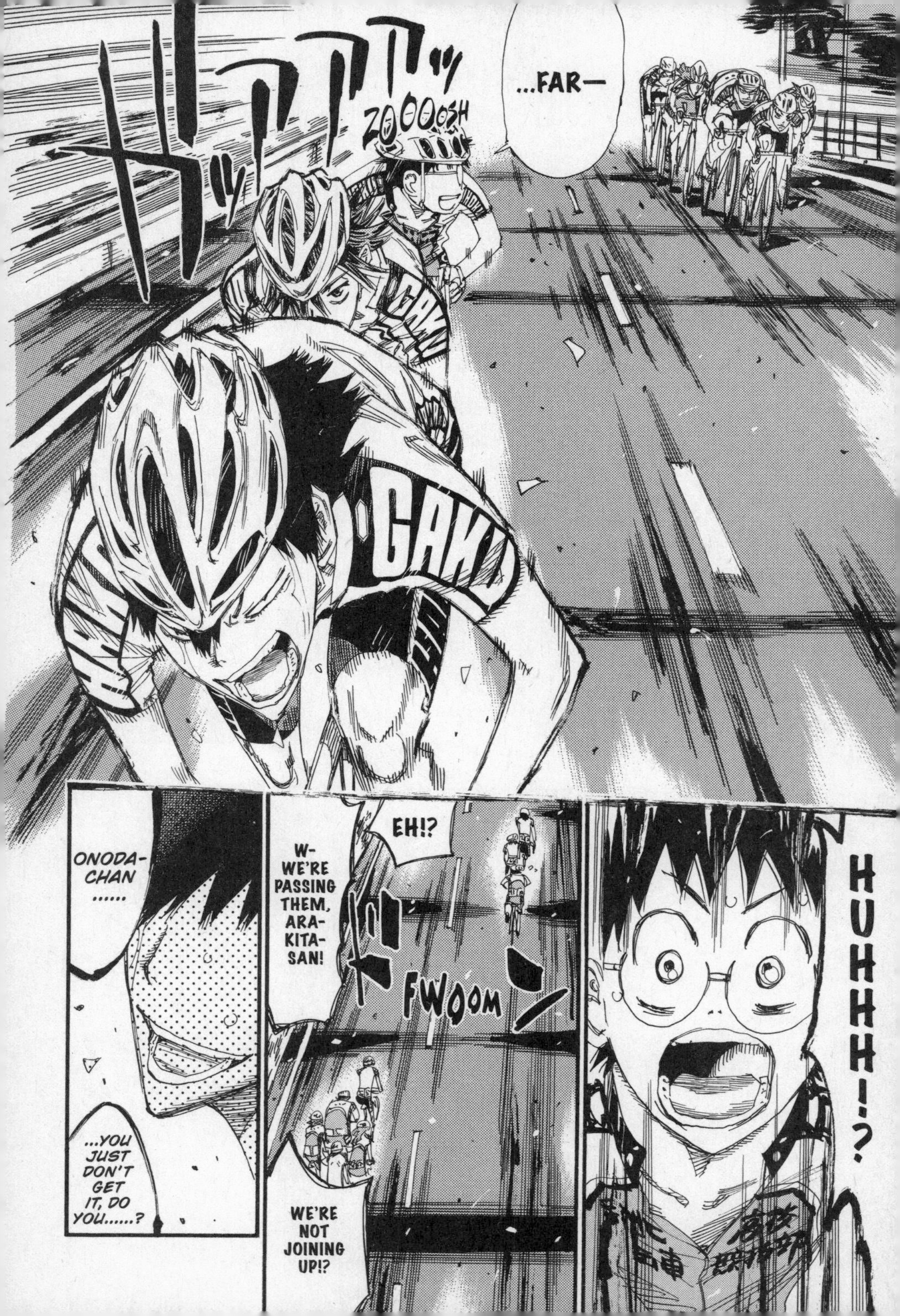
...FAR—
ZOOOOSH
HUHHHH!?
EH!?
W-WE'RE PASSING THEM, ARAKITA-SAN!
FWOOM
WE'RE NOT JOINING UP!?
ONODA-CHAN ......
...YOU JUST DON'T GET IT, DO YOU......?

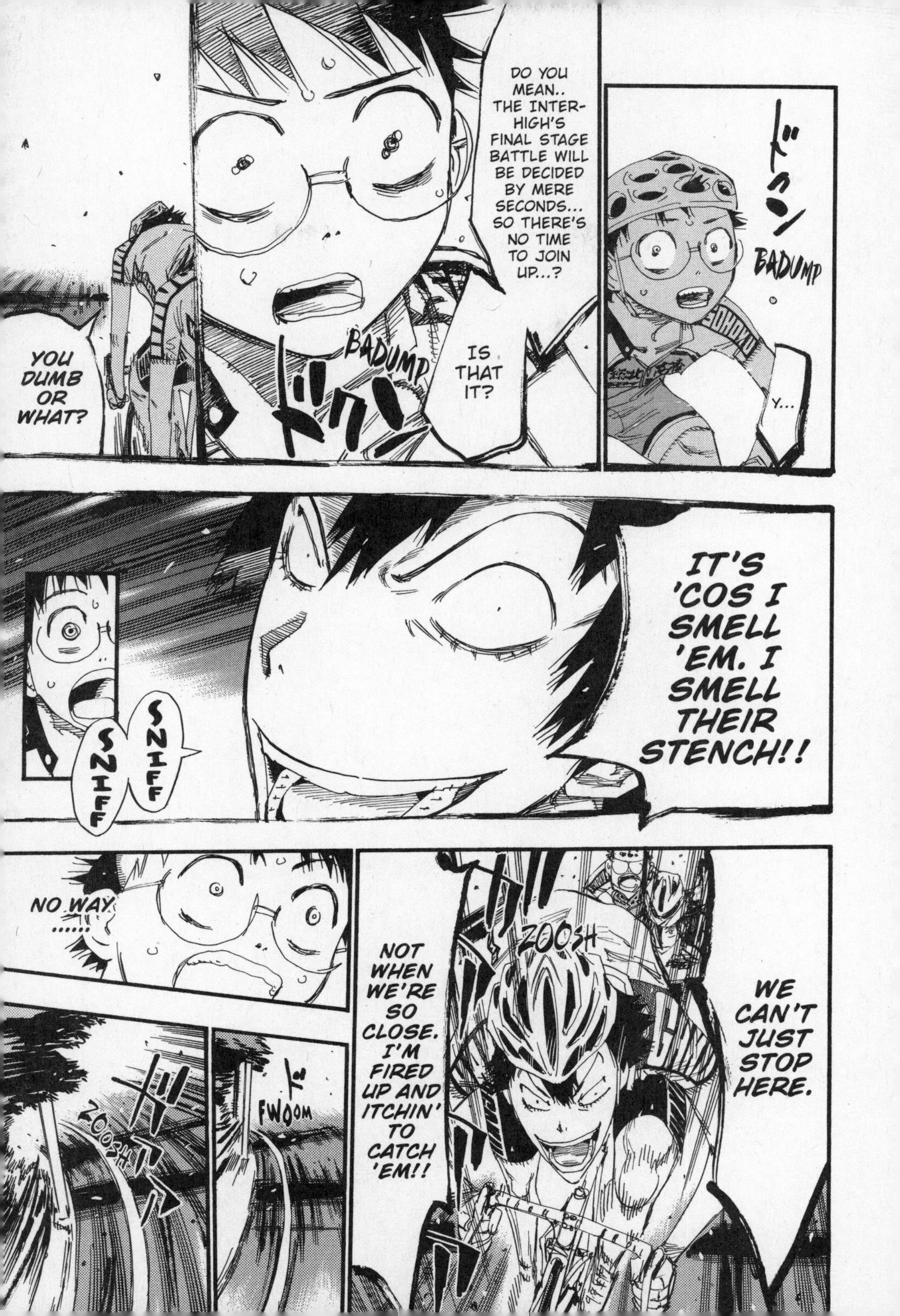
BADUMP
Y...
DO YOU MEAN.. THE INTER-HIGH'S FINAL STAGE BATTLE WILL BE DECIDED BY MERE SECONDS... SO THERE'S NO TIME TO JOIN UP...?
IS THAT IT?
BADUMP
YOU DUMB OR WHAT?
IT'S 'COS I SMELL 'EM. I SMELL THEIR STENCH!!
SNIFF SNIFF
WE CAN'T JUST STOP HERE.
NOT WHEN WE'RE SO CLOSE. I'M FIRED UP AND ITCHIN' TO CATCH 'EM!!
ZOOSH
NO WAY ......
FWOOM
ZOOSH

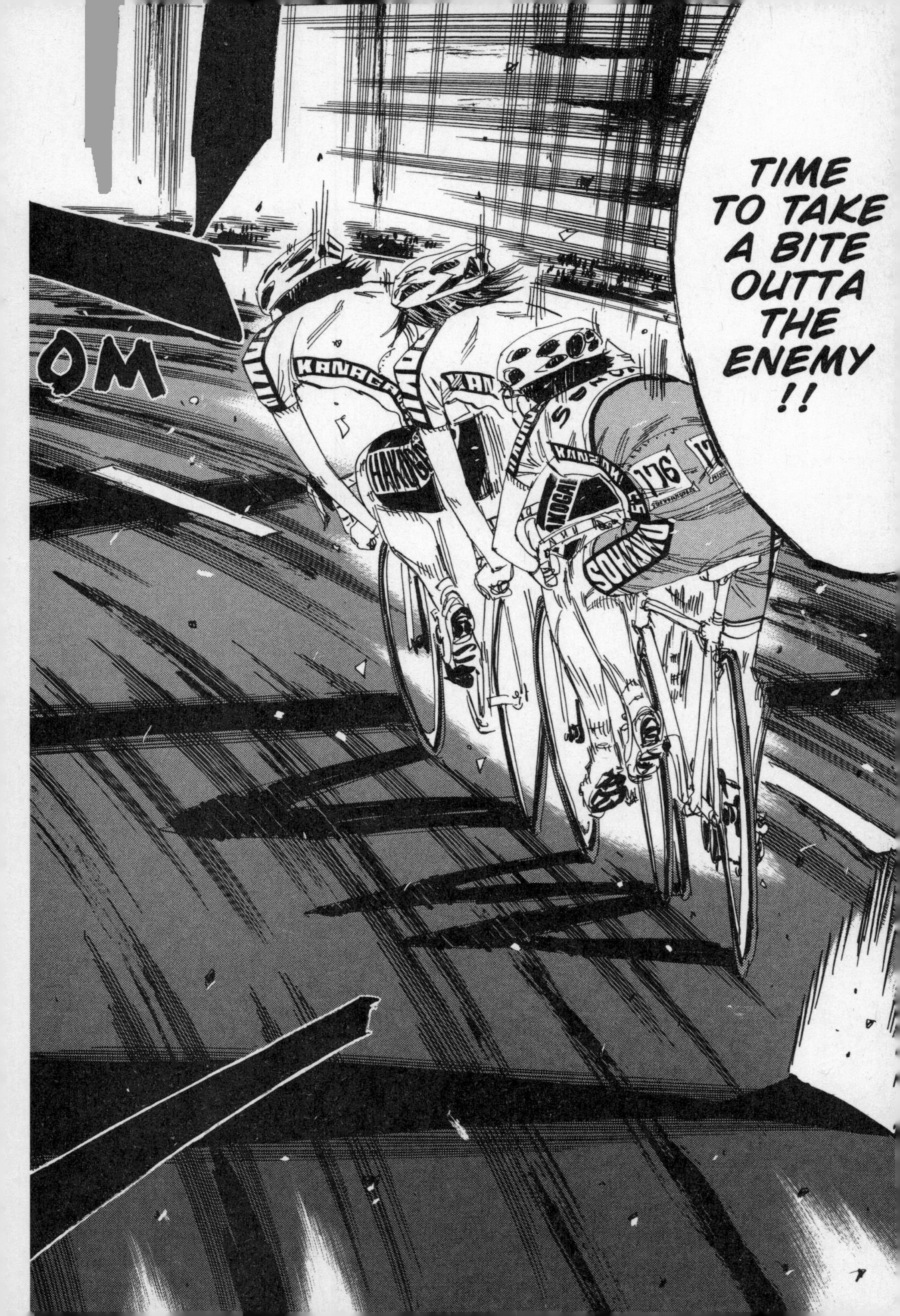
TIME TO TAKE A BITE OUTTA THE ENEMY !!
OM

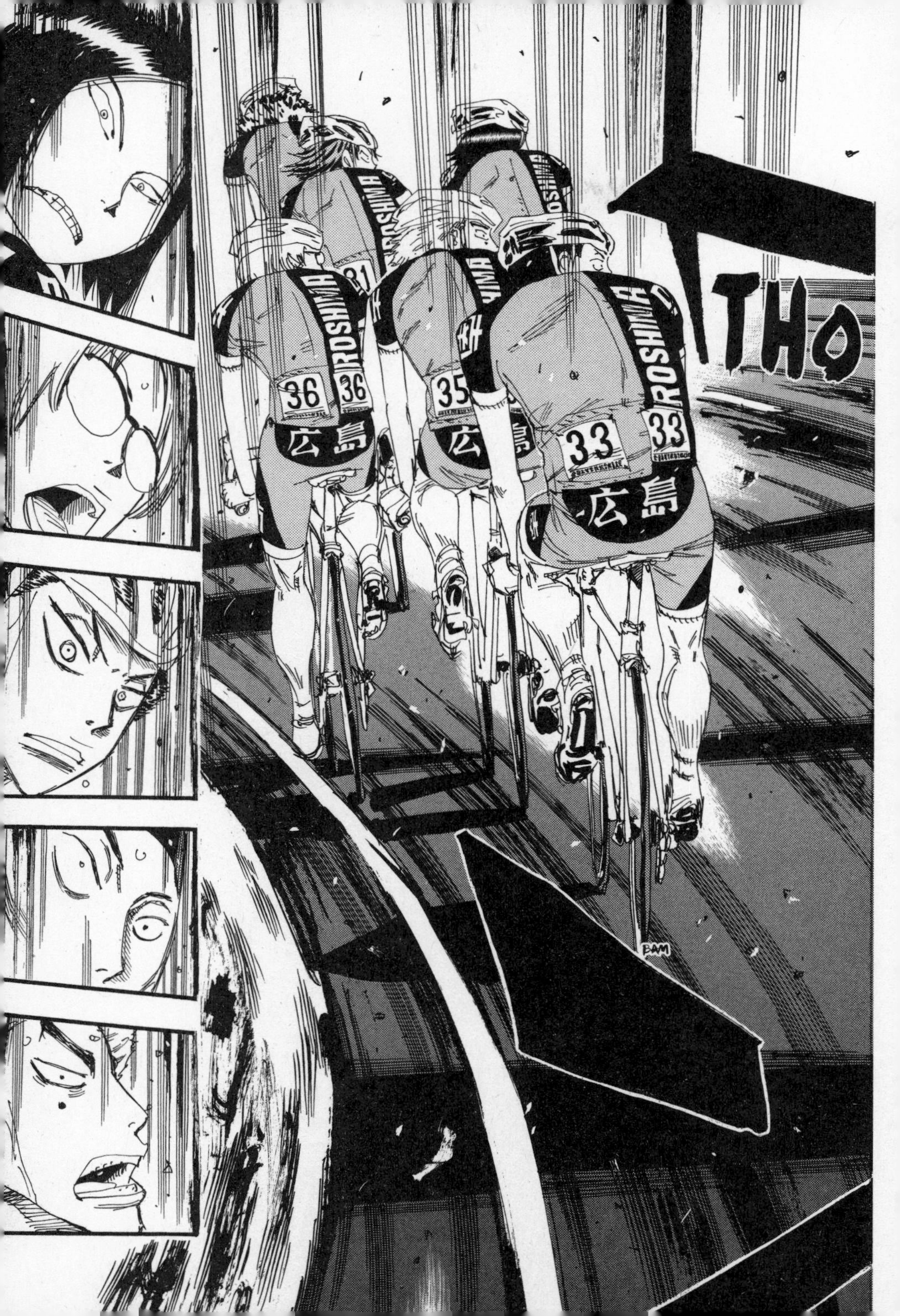
THO
BAM

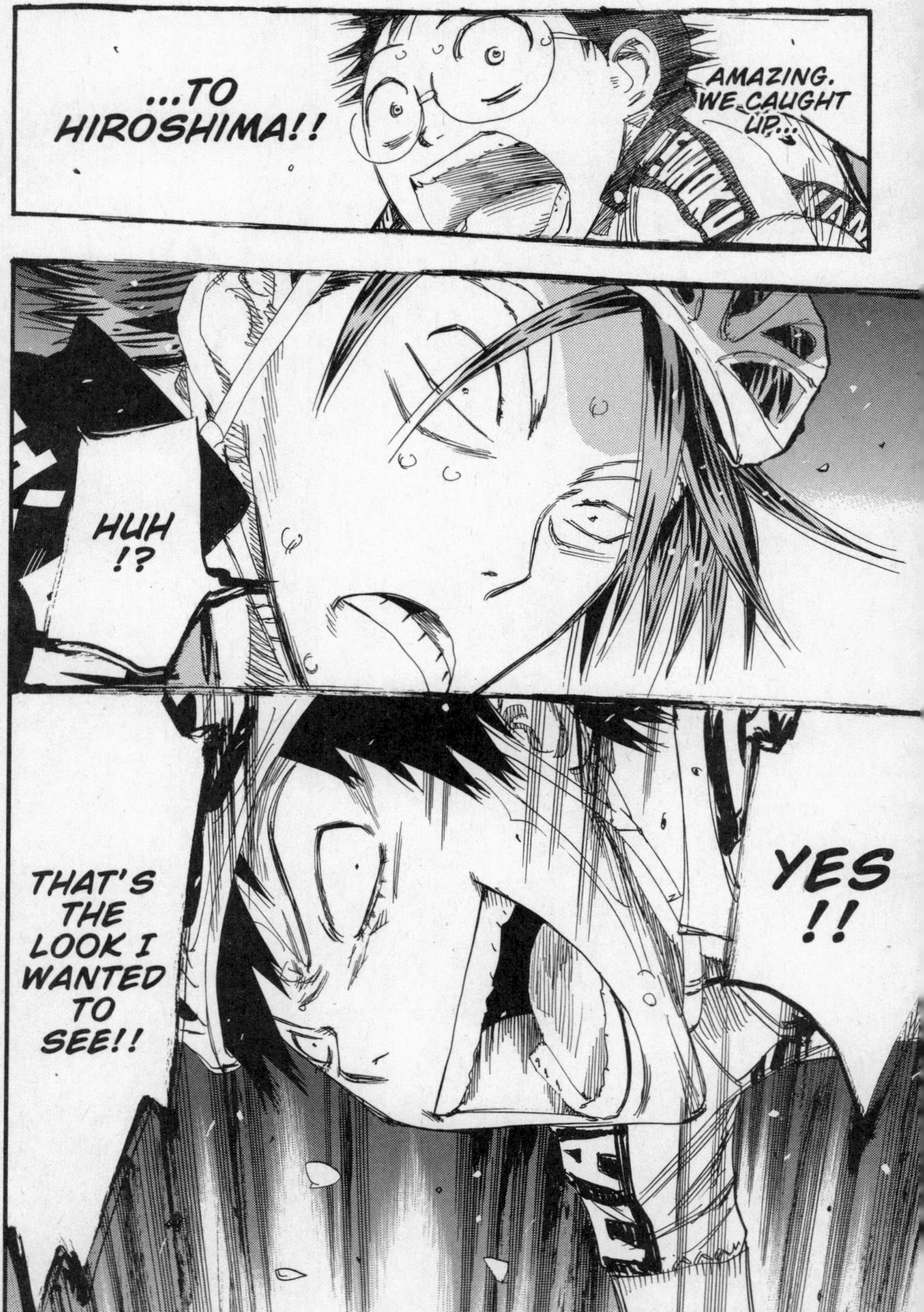
AMAZING. WE CAUGHT UP...
...TO HIROSHIMA!!
HUH!?
YES!!
THAT'S THE LOOK I WANTED TO SEE!!

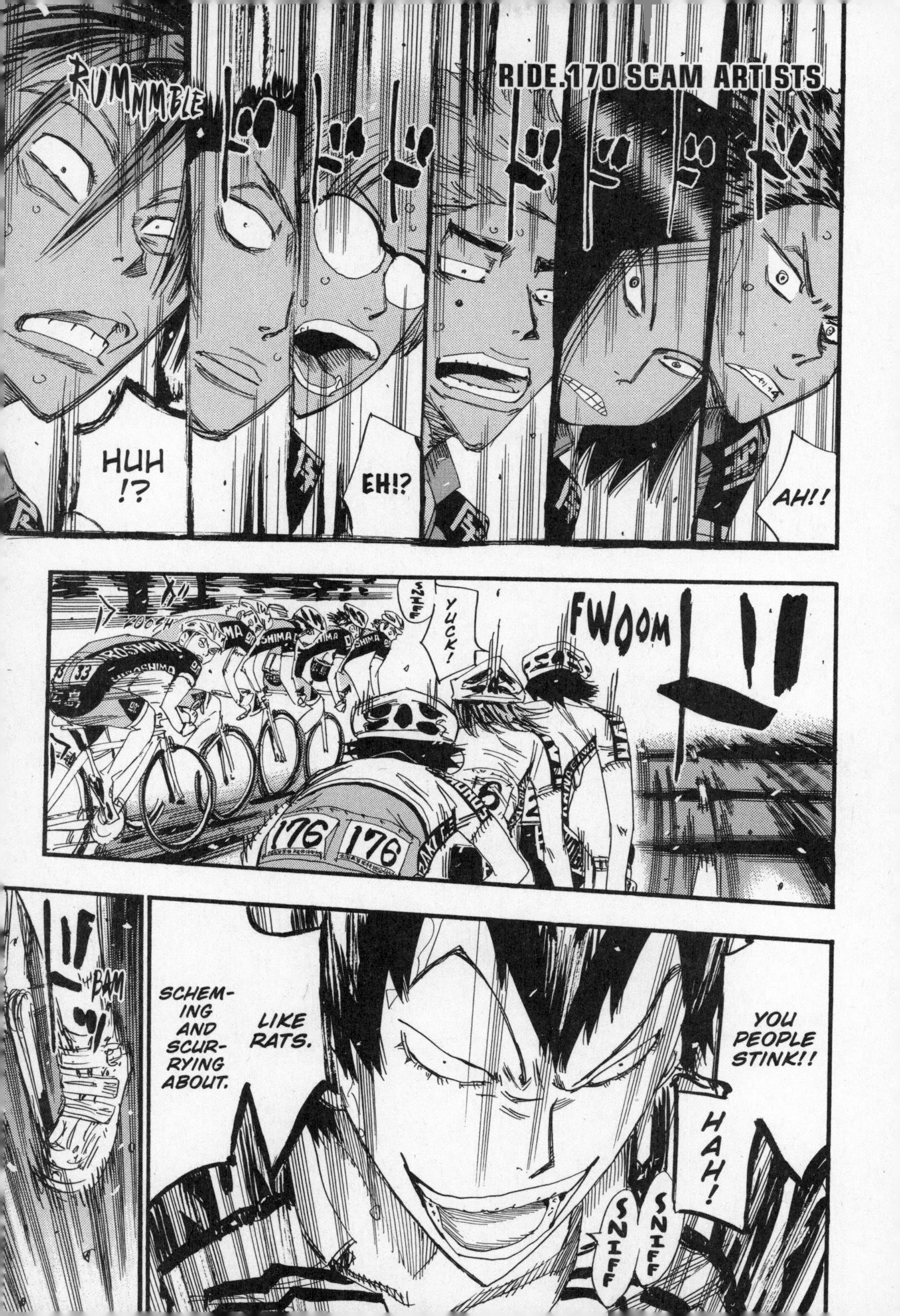
RIDE.170 SCAM ARTISTS
RUMMMMBLE
AH!!
EH!?
HUH !?
FWOOM
YUCK!
SNIFF
ZOOSH
YOU PEOPLE STINK!!
HAH!
SNIFF
SNIFF
LIKE RATS.
SCHEM-ING AND SCUR-RYING ABOUT.
BAM

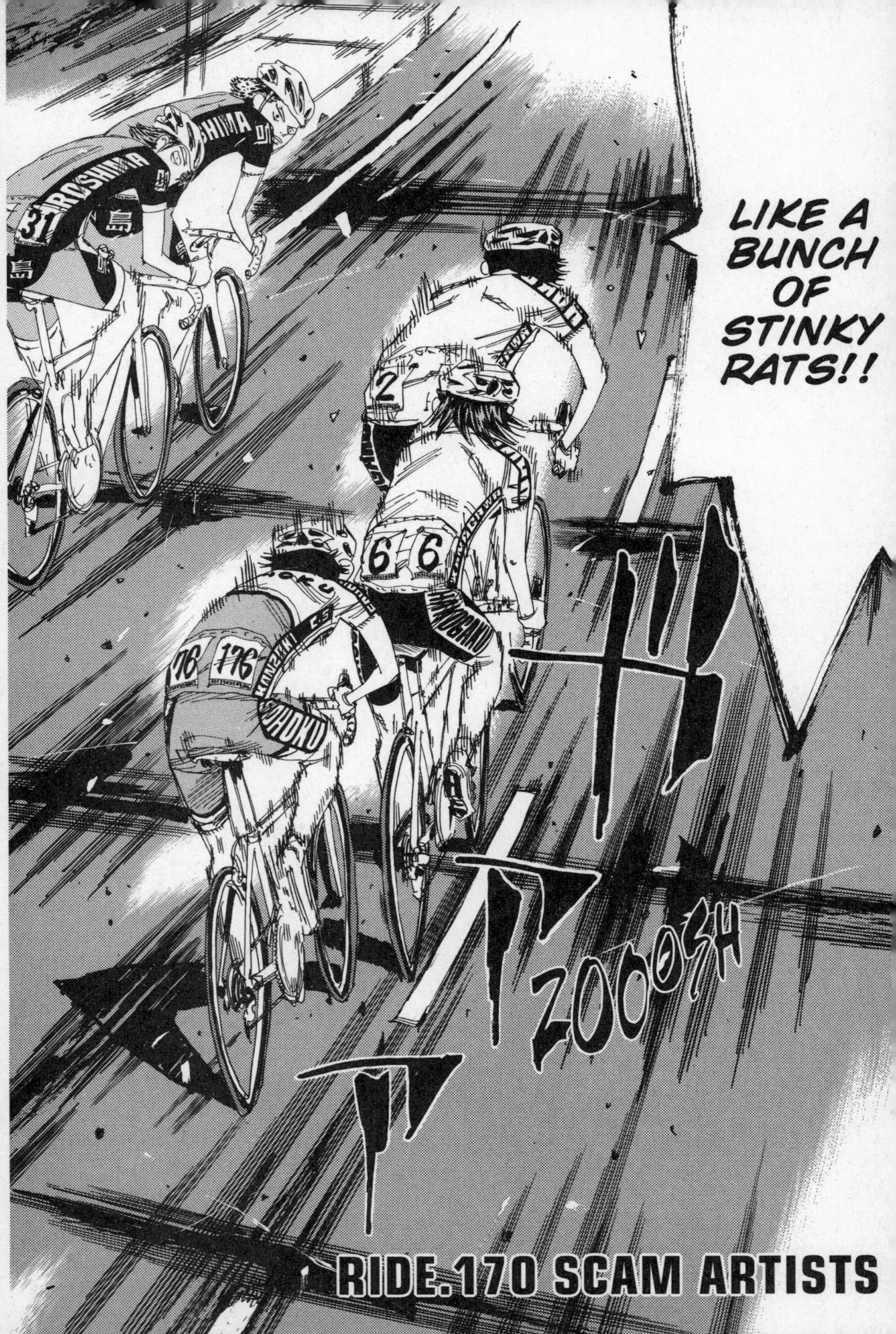
LIKE A BUNCH OF STINKY RATS!!
ZOOOSH

RIDE.170 SCAM ARTISTS

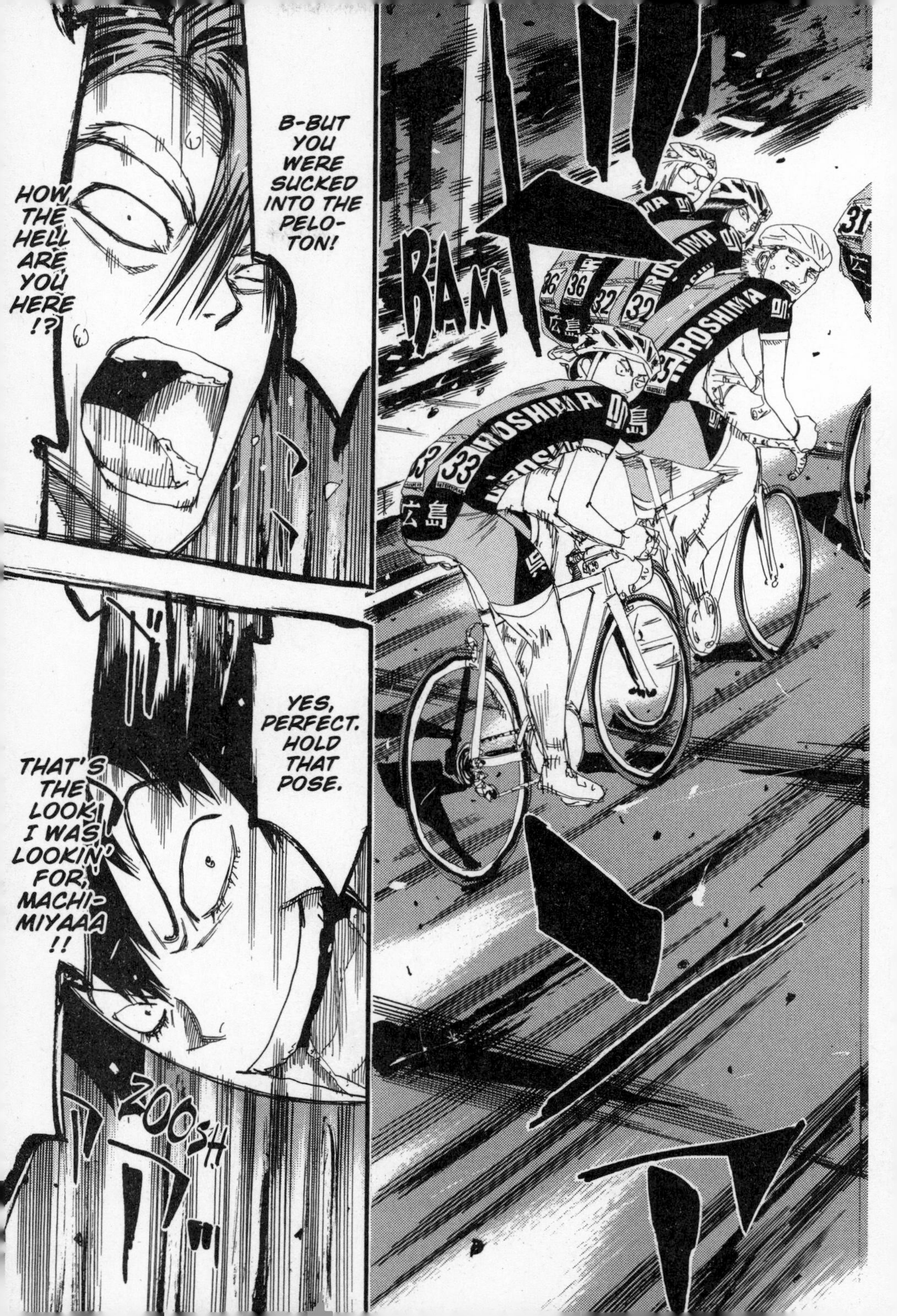
BAM
B-BUT YOU WERE SUCKED INTO THE PELOTON!
HOW THE HELL ARE YOU HERE!?
YES, PERFECT. HOLD THAT POSE.
THAT'S THE LOOK I WAS LOOKIN' FOR, MACHIMIYAAA!!
ZOOSH

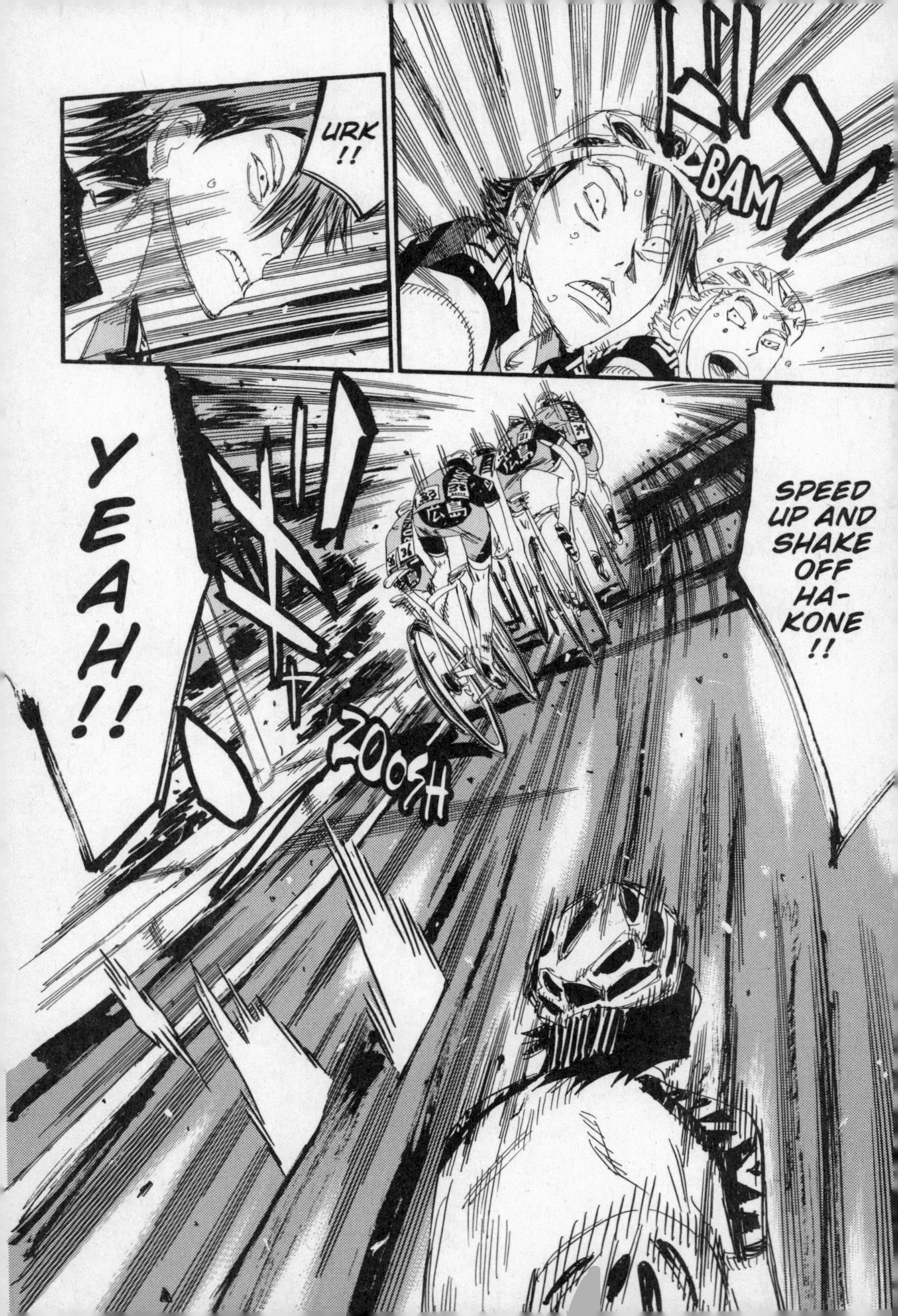
BAM
URK !!
SPEED UP AND SHAKE OFF HA-KONE !!
YEAH!!
ZOOSH

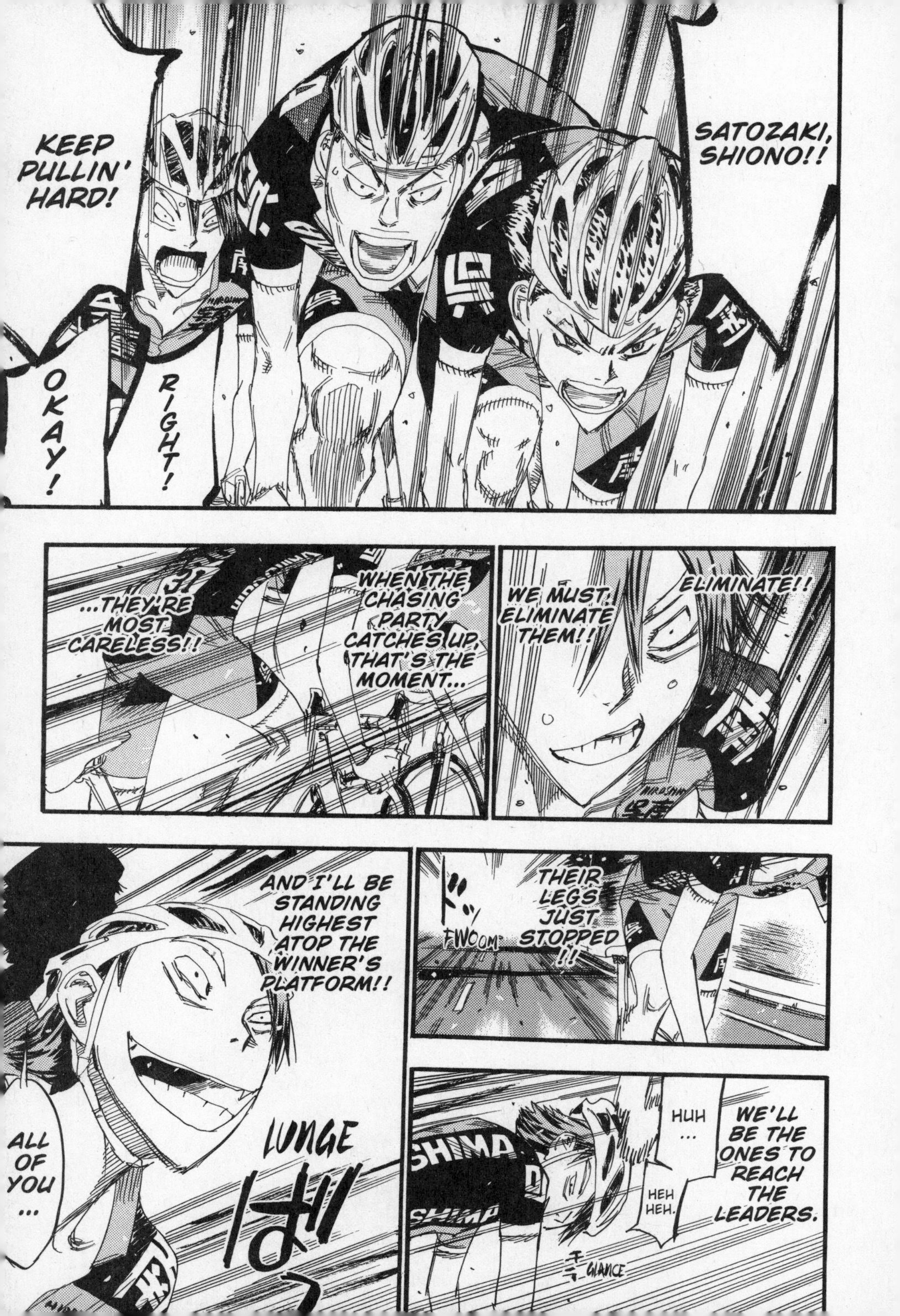
SATOZAKI, SHIONO!!
KEEP PULLIN' HARD!
RIGHT!
OKAY!
ELIMINATE!!
WE MUST ELIMINATE THEM!!
WHEN THE CHASING PARTY CATCHES UP, THAT'S THE MOMENT...
...THEY'RE MOST CARELESS!!
THEIR LEGS JUST STOPPED!!
ドッ
FWOOM
WE'LL BE THE ONES TO REACH THE LEADERS.
HUH...
HEH HEH.
GLANCE
AND I'LL BE STANDING HIGHEST ATOP THE WINNER'S PLATFORM!!
LUNGE
ばっ
ALL OF YOU...

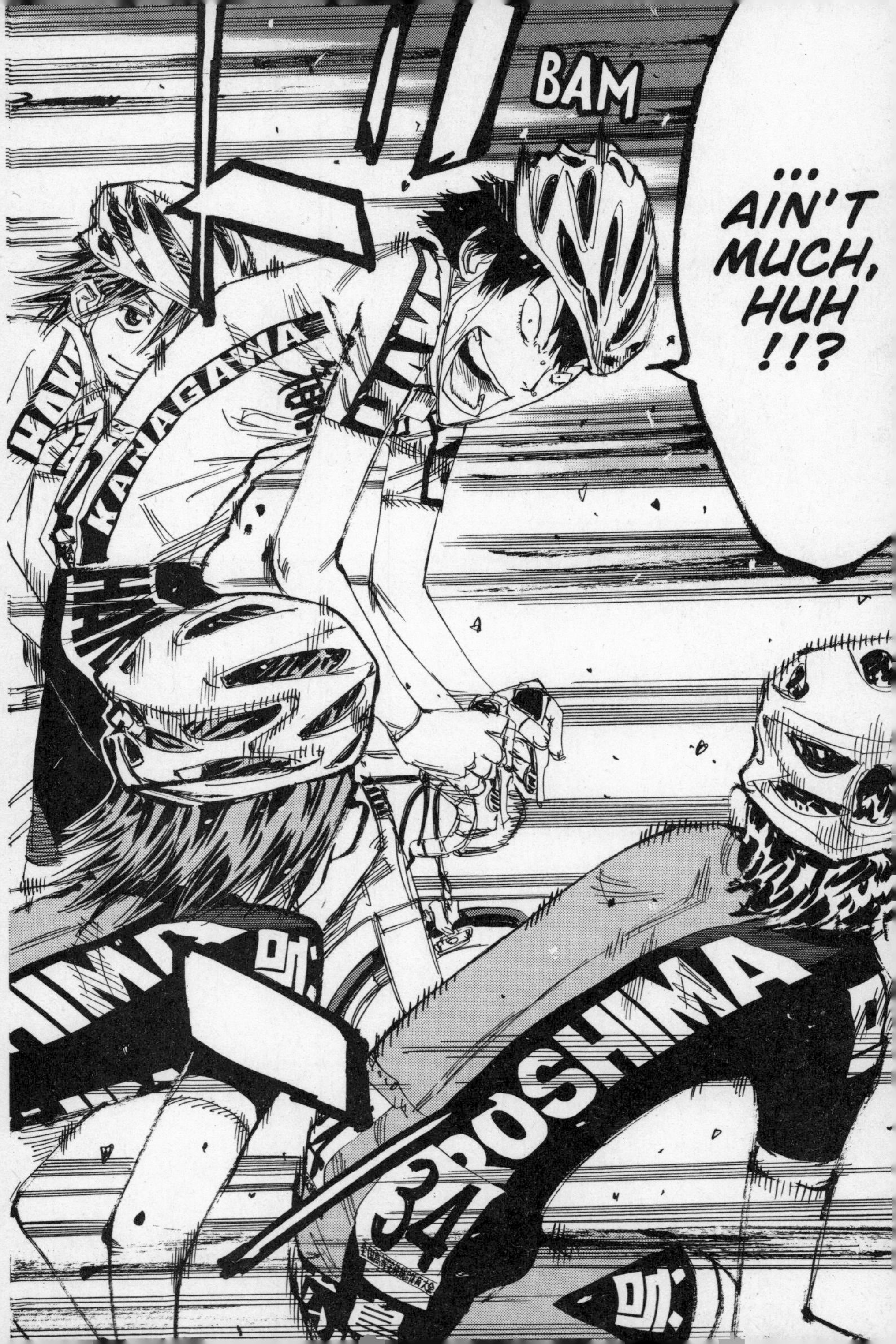
BAM
... AIN'T MUCH, HUH !!?
HAK
KANAGAWA
HAK
ROSHIMA
34

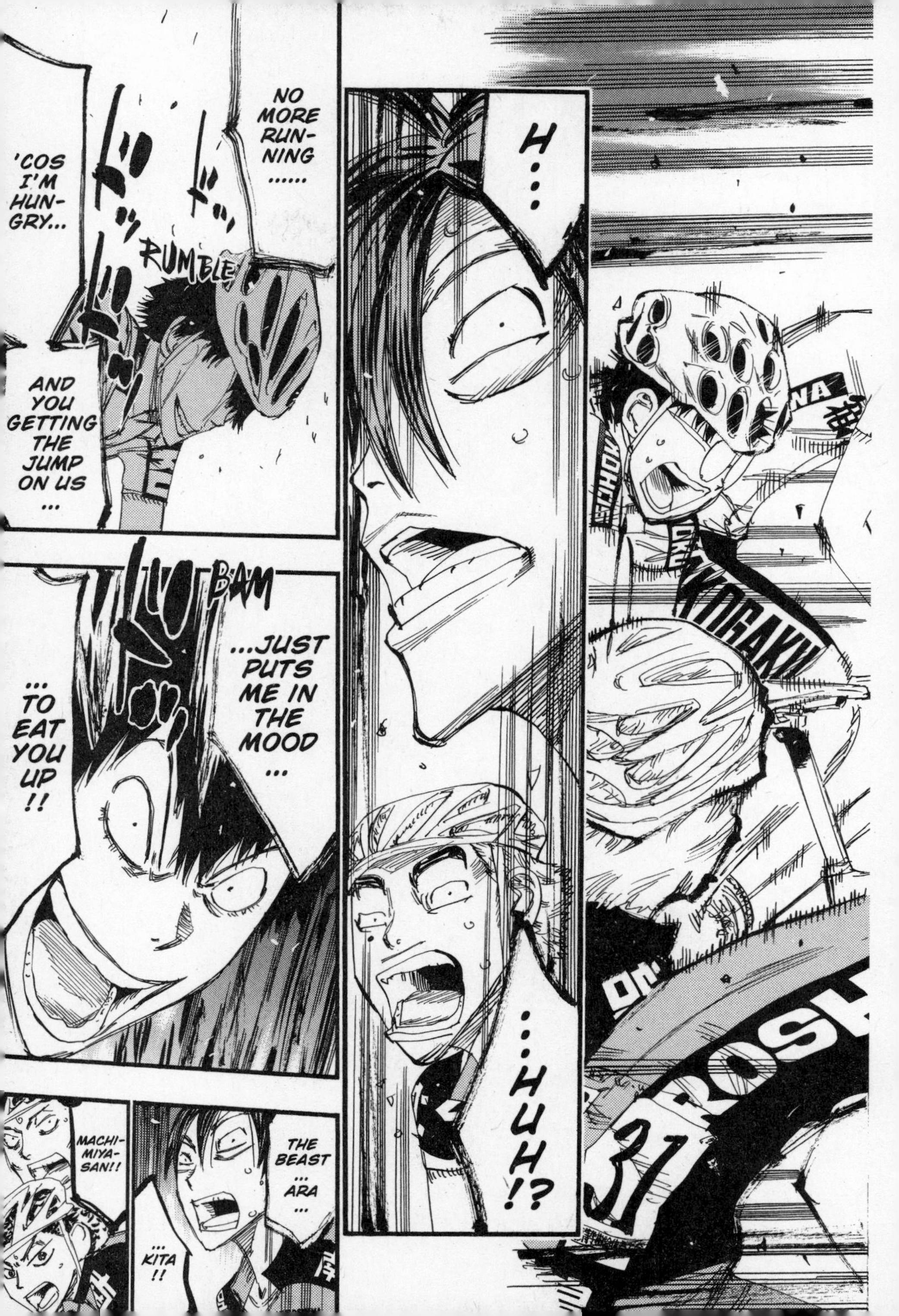
H...
...HUH!?
NO MORE RUN-NING ......
'COS I'M HUN-GRY...
RUMBLE
AND YOU GETTING THE JUMP ON US ...
BAM
...JUST PUTS ME IN THE MOOD ...
... TO EAT YOU UP !!
THE BEAST ... ARA ...
... KITA !!
MACHI-MIYA-SAN!!

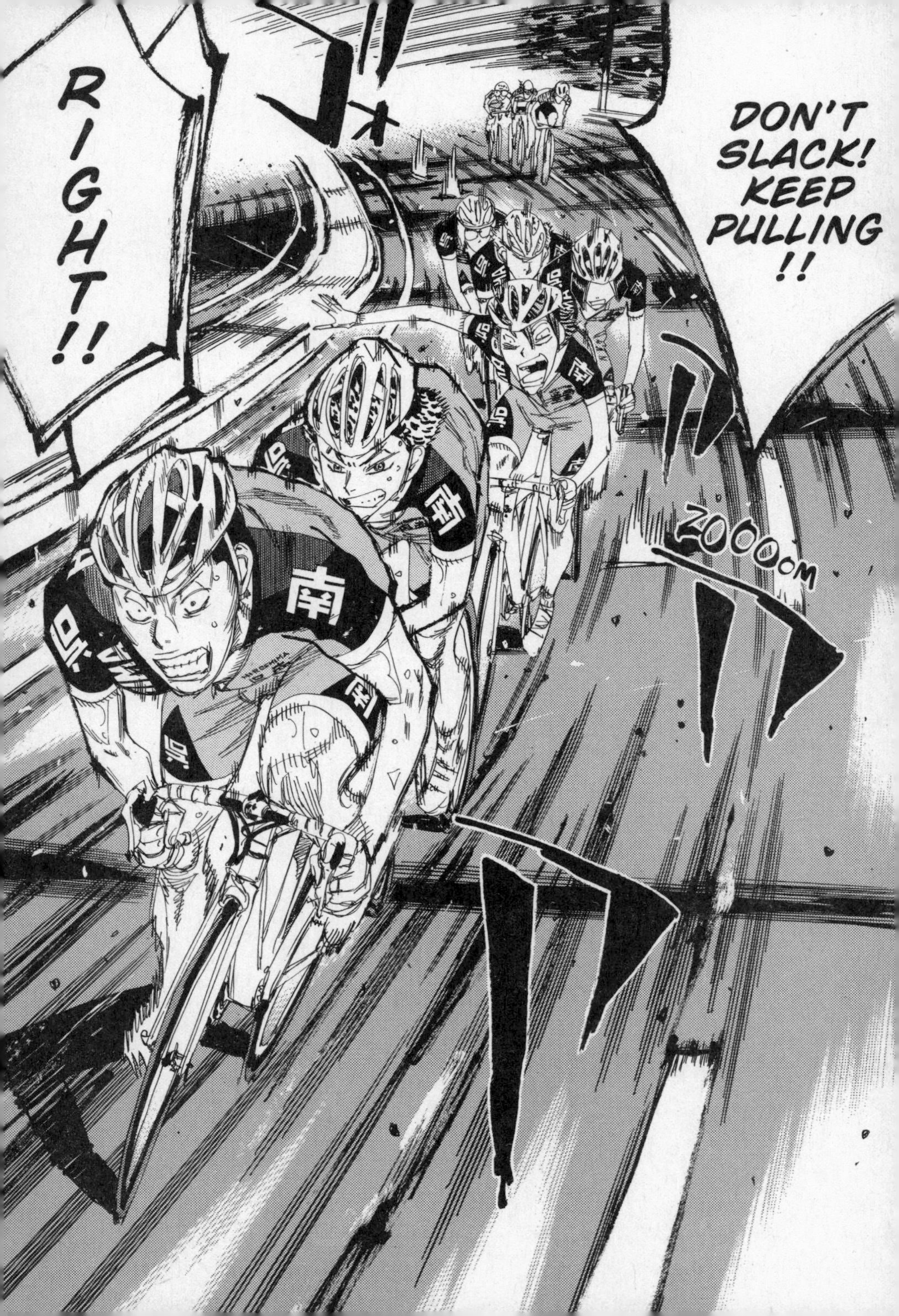

DON'T SLACK! KEEP PULLING!!
RIGHT!!
ゴォ
ZOOOOM

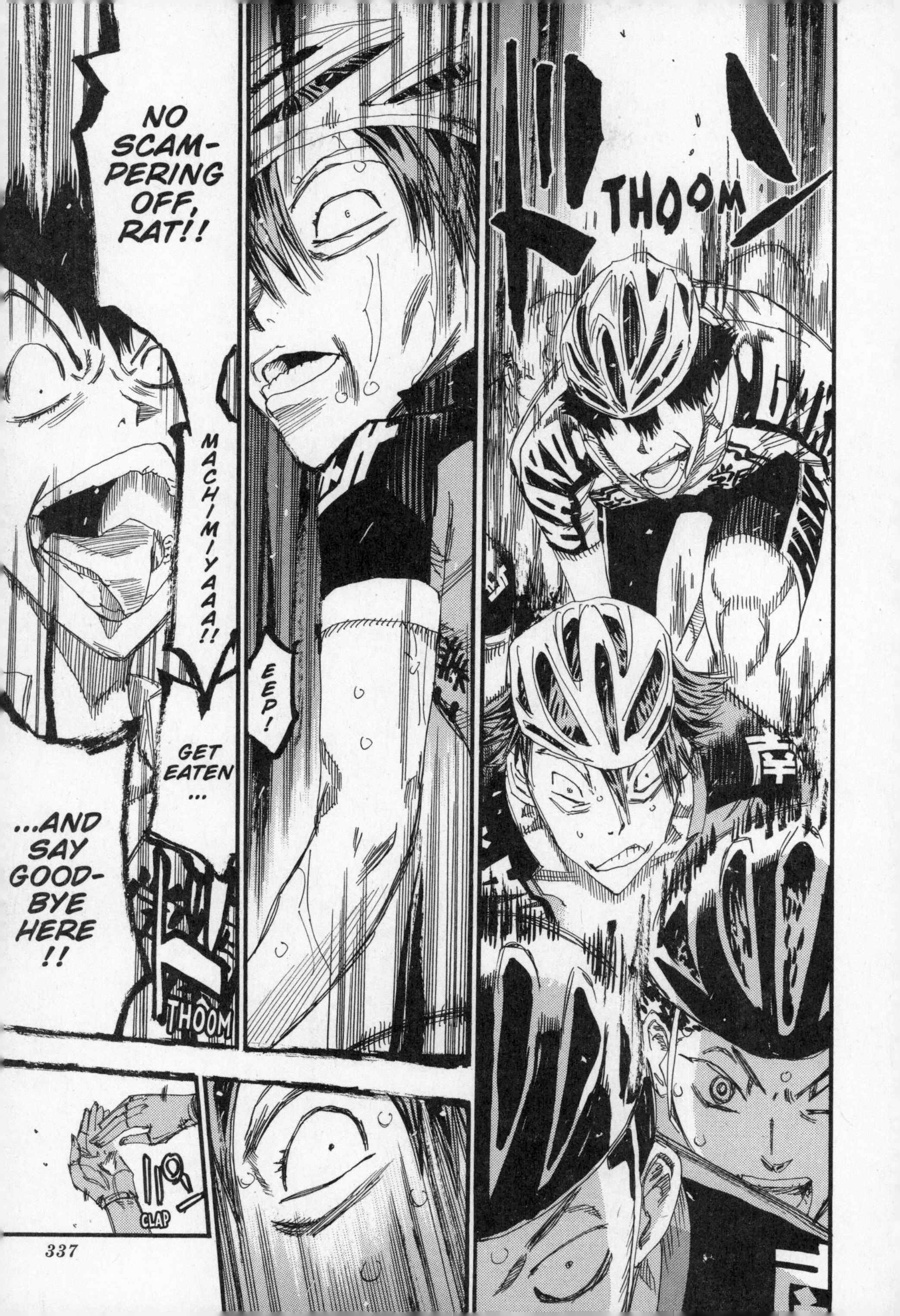
THOOM
EEP!
NO SCAMPERING OFF, RAT!!
MACHIMIYAAAA!!
GET EATEN...
...AND SAY GOODBYE HERE!!
THOOM
CLAP

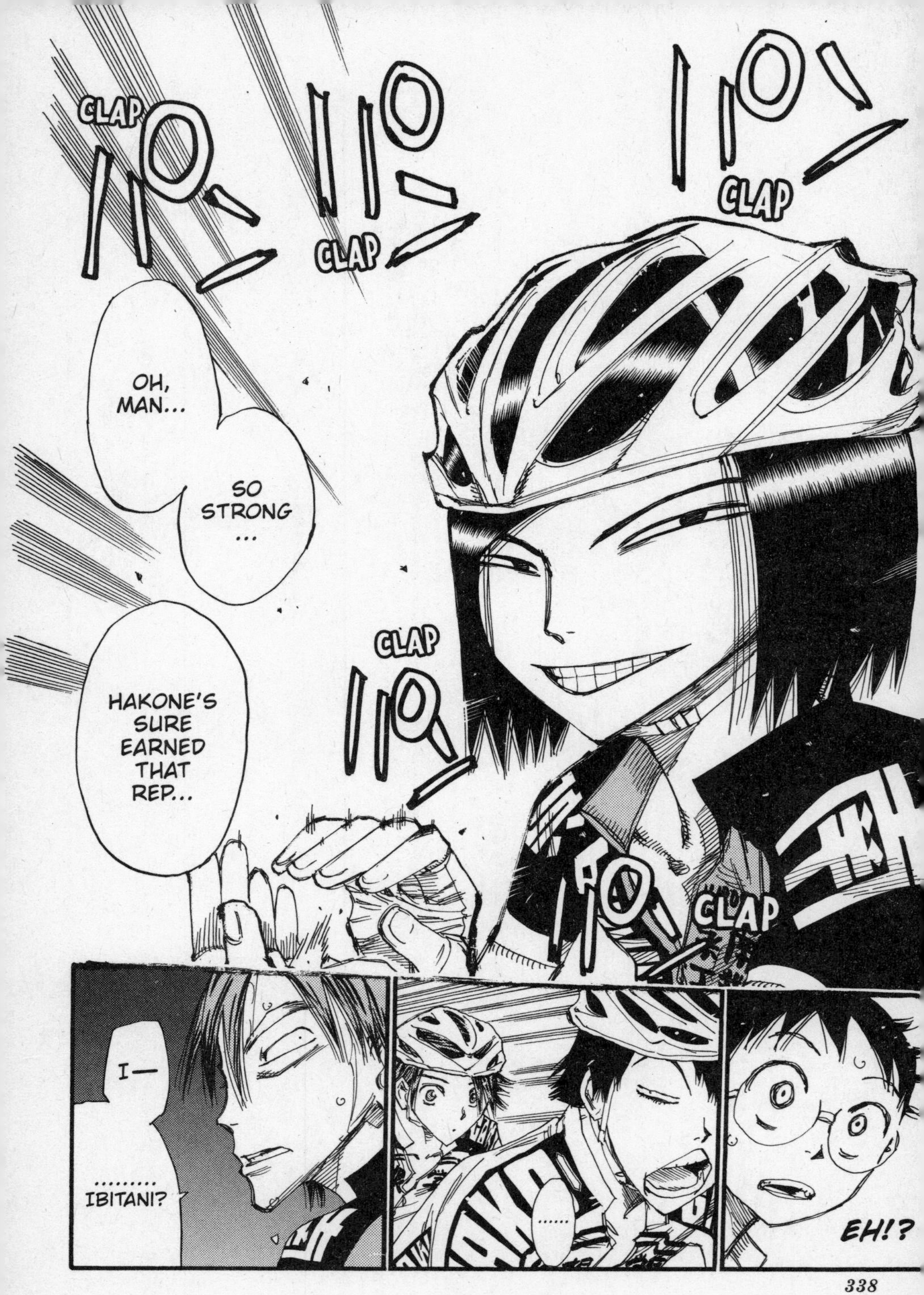

CLAP
CLAP
CLAP
OH, MAN...
SO STRONG ...
CLAP
HAKONE'S SURE EARNED THAT REP...
CLAP
EH!?
......
I—
.... IBITANI?

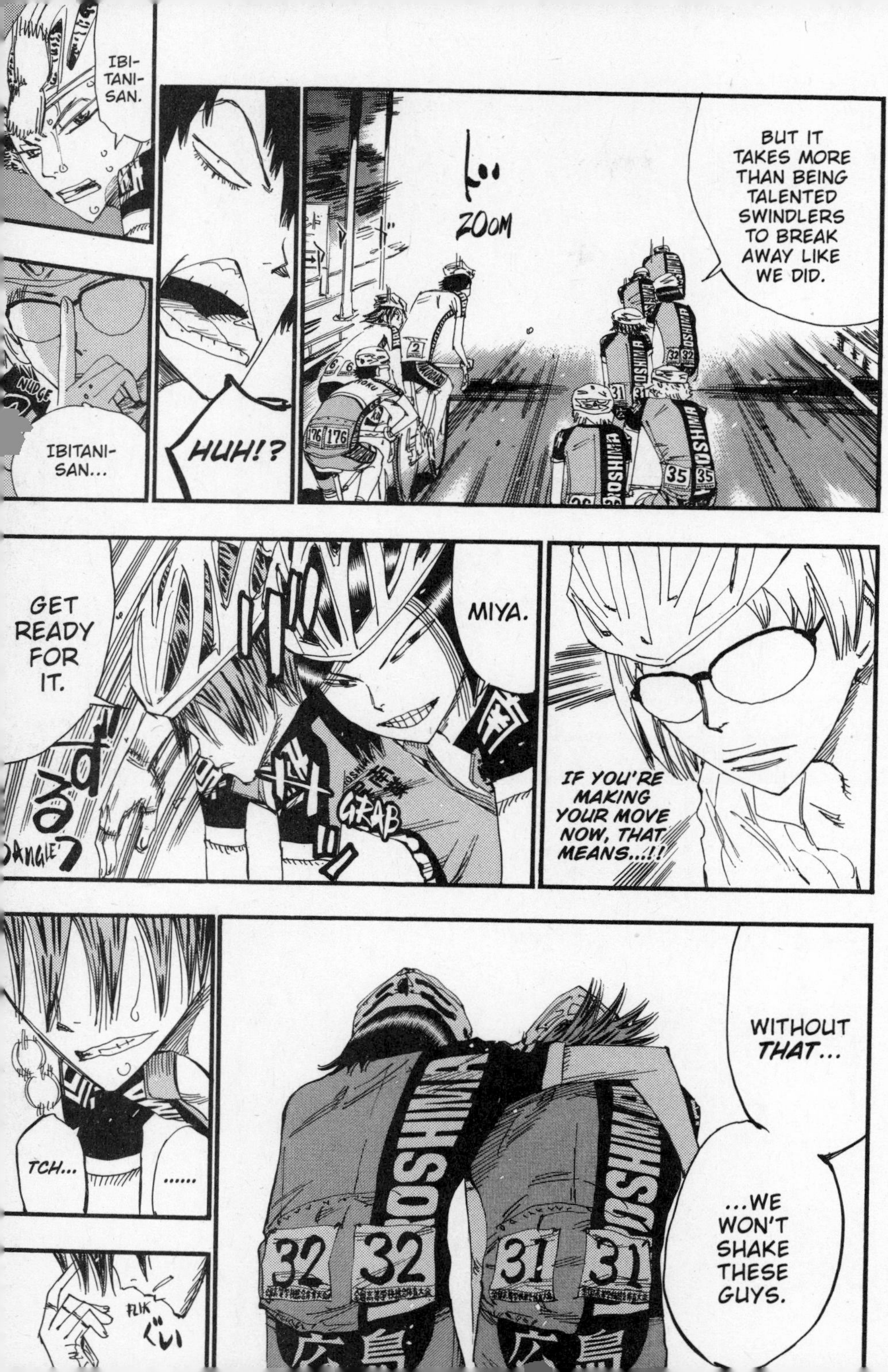
ZOOM
BUT IT TAKES MORE THAN BEING TALENTED SWINDLERS TO BREAK AWAY LIKE WE DID.
HUH!?
IBITANI-SAN.
NUDGE
IBITANI-SAN...
IF YOU'RE MAKING YOUR MOVE NOW, THAT MEANS...!!!
MIYA.
GET READY FOR IT.
GRAB
DANGLE
WITHOUT THAT...
...WE WON'T SHAKE THESE GUYS.
TCH...
......
FLIK

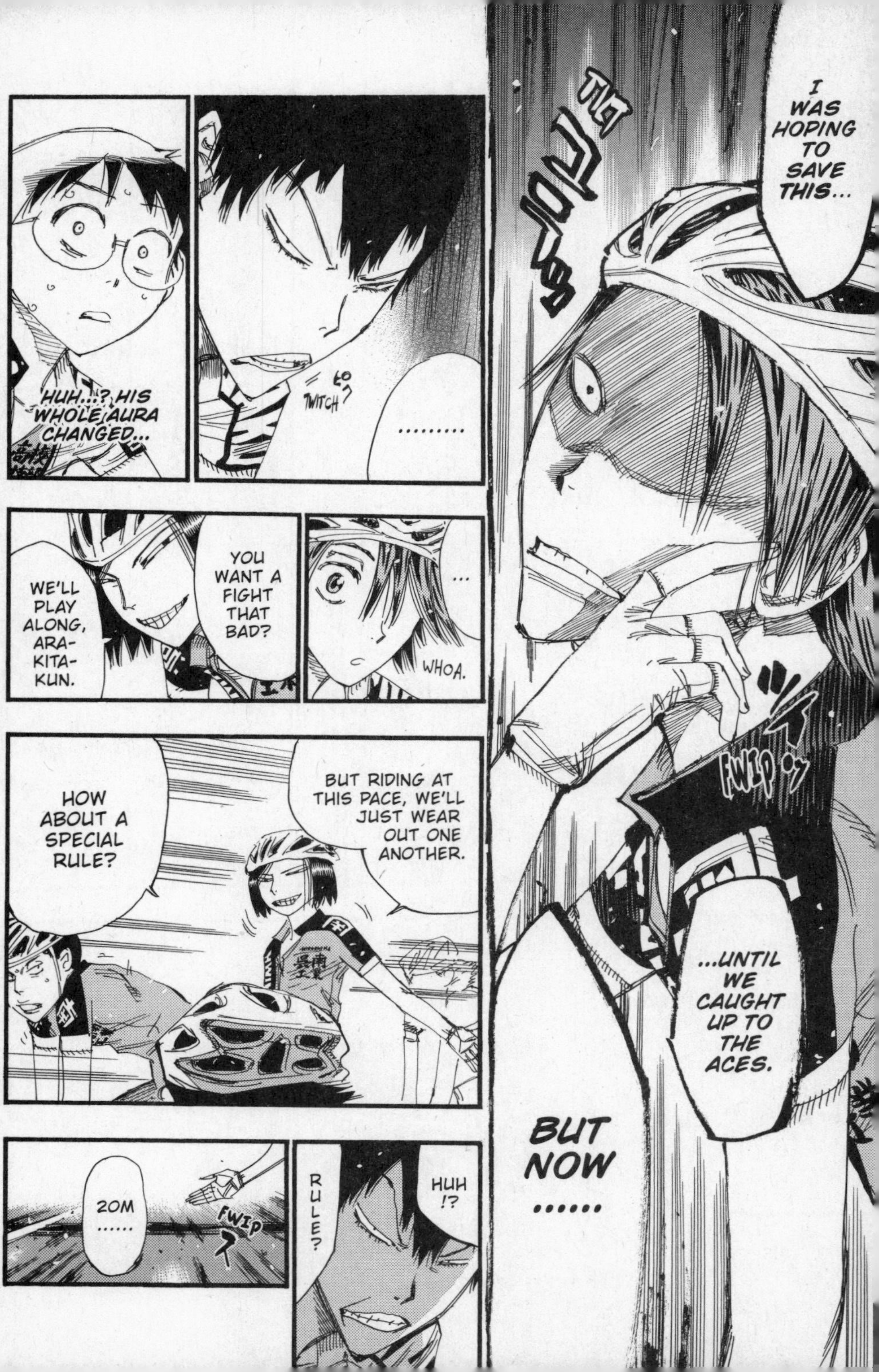
I WAS HOPING TO SAVE THIS...
FWIP
...UNTIL WE CAUGHT UP TO THE ACES.
BUT NOW ......
TWITCH
....
HUH...? HIS WHOLE AURA CHANGED...
...
WHOA.
YOU WANT A FIGHT THAT BAD?
WE'LL PLAY ALONG, ARA-KITA-KUN.
BUT RIDING AT THIS PACE, WE'LL JUST WEAR OUT ONE ANOTHER.
HOW ABOUT A SPECIAL RULE?
HUH!?
RULE?
FWIP
20M ......

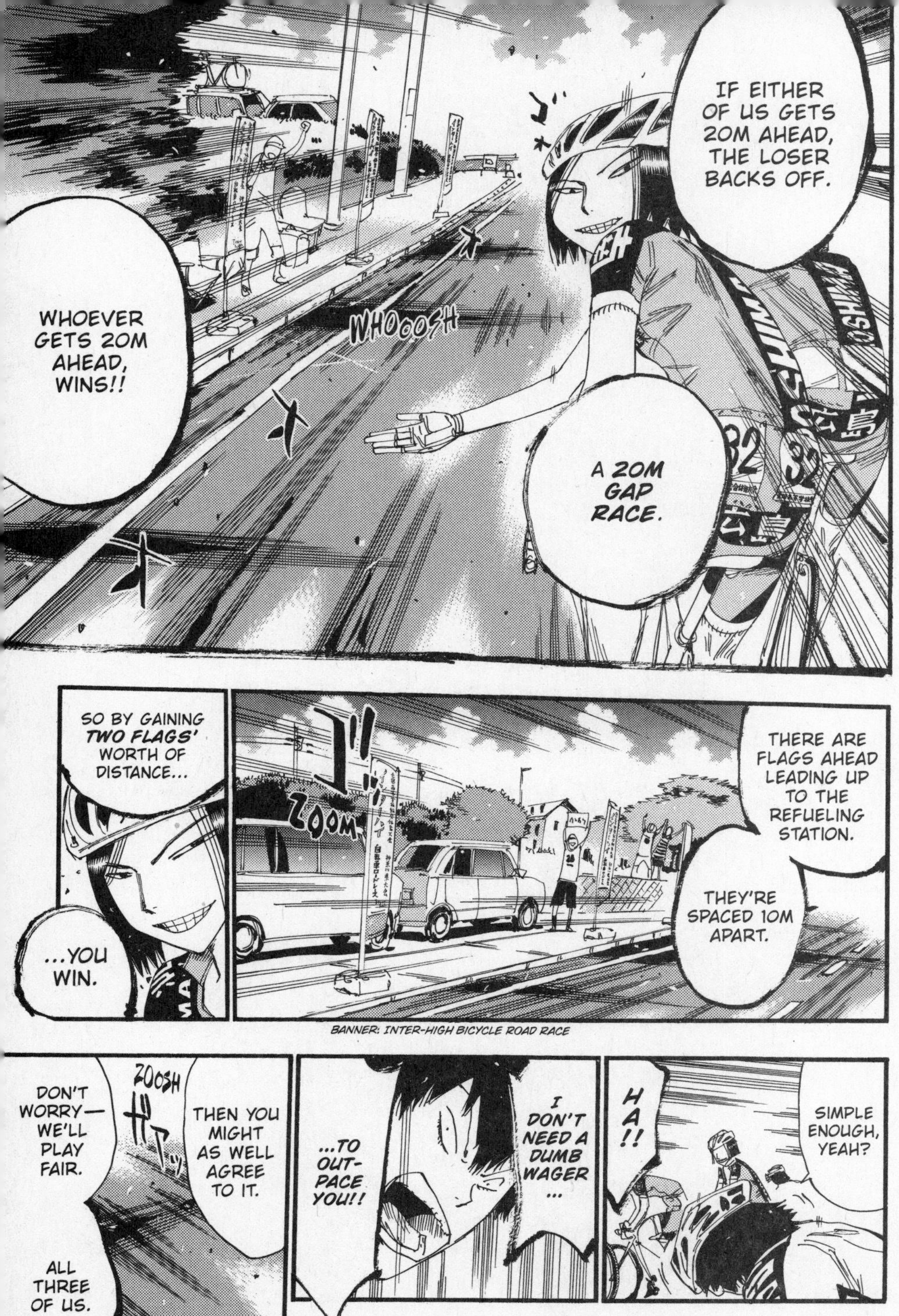
IF EITHER OF US GETS 20M AHEAD, THE LOSER BACKS OFF.
A 20M GAP RACE.
WHOEVER GETS 20M AHEAD, WINS!!
WHOOOSH
THERE ARE FLAGS AHEAD LEADING UP TO THE REFUELING STATION.
THEY'RE SPACED 10M APART.
ZOOM
SO BY GAINING *TWO FLAGS'* WORTH OF DISTANCE...
...YOU WIN.
BANNER: INTER-HIGH BICYCLE ROAD RACE
HA!!
SIMPLE ENOUGH, YEAH?
I DON'T NEED A DUMB WAGER...
...TO OUTPACE YOU!!
THEN YOU MIGHT AS WELL AGREE TO IT.
DON'T WORRY—WE'LL PLAY FAIR.
ZOOSH
ALL THREE OF US.

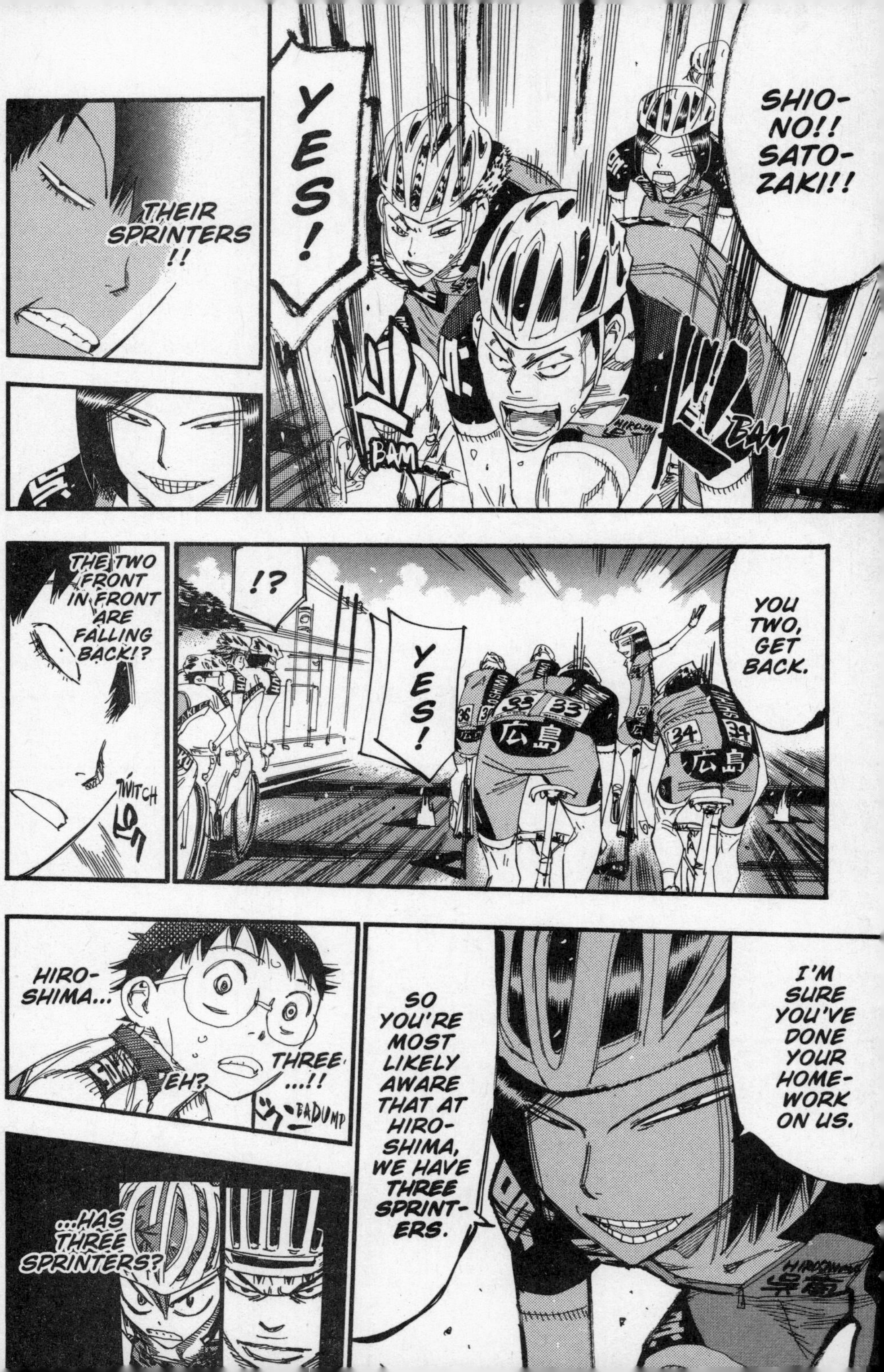
SHIONO!! SATOZAKI!!
YES!
BAM
BAM
THEIR SPRINTERS!!
YOU TWO, GET BACK.
YES!
!?
THE TWO FRONT IN FRONT ARE FALLING BACK!?
TWITCH
I'M SURE YOU'VE DONE YOUR HOMEWORK ON US.
SO YOU'RE MOST LIKELY AWARE THAT AT HIROSHIMA, WE HAVE THREE SPRINTERS.
HIROSHIMA...
THREE...!!
EH?
BADUMP
...HAS THREE SPRINTERS?

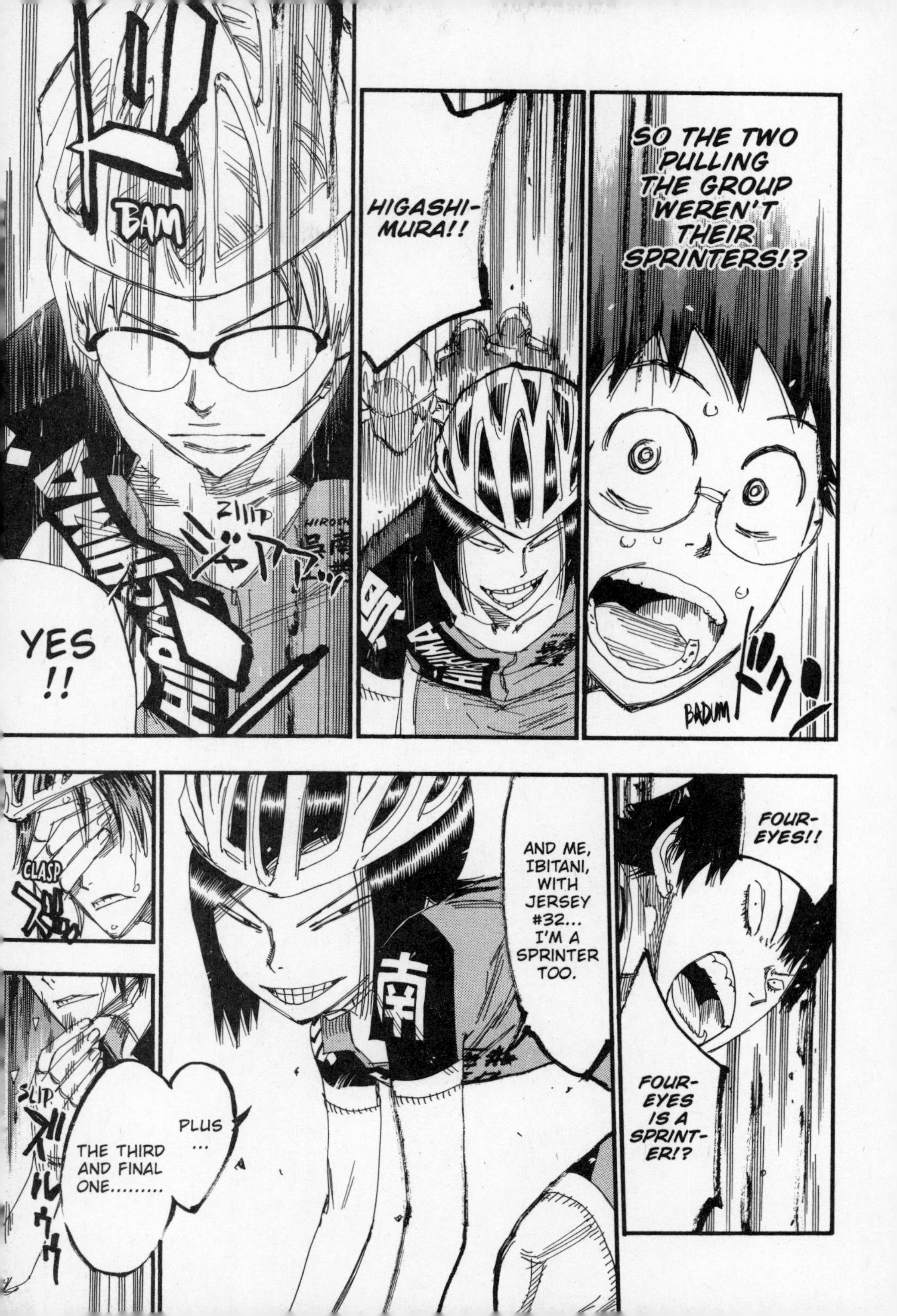
SO THE TWO PULLING THE GROUP WEREN'T THEIR SPRINTERS!?
BADUM
HIGASHI-MURA!!
BAM
ZIIIP
YES!!
FOUR-EYES!!
FOUR-EYES IS A SPRINT-ER!?
AND ME, IBITANI, WITH JERSEY #32... I'M A SPRINTER TOO.
PLUS ...
THE THIRD AND FINAL ONE.........
CLASP
SLIP

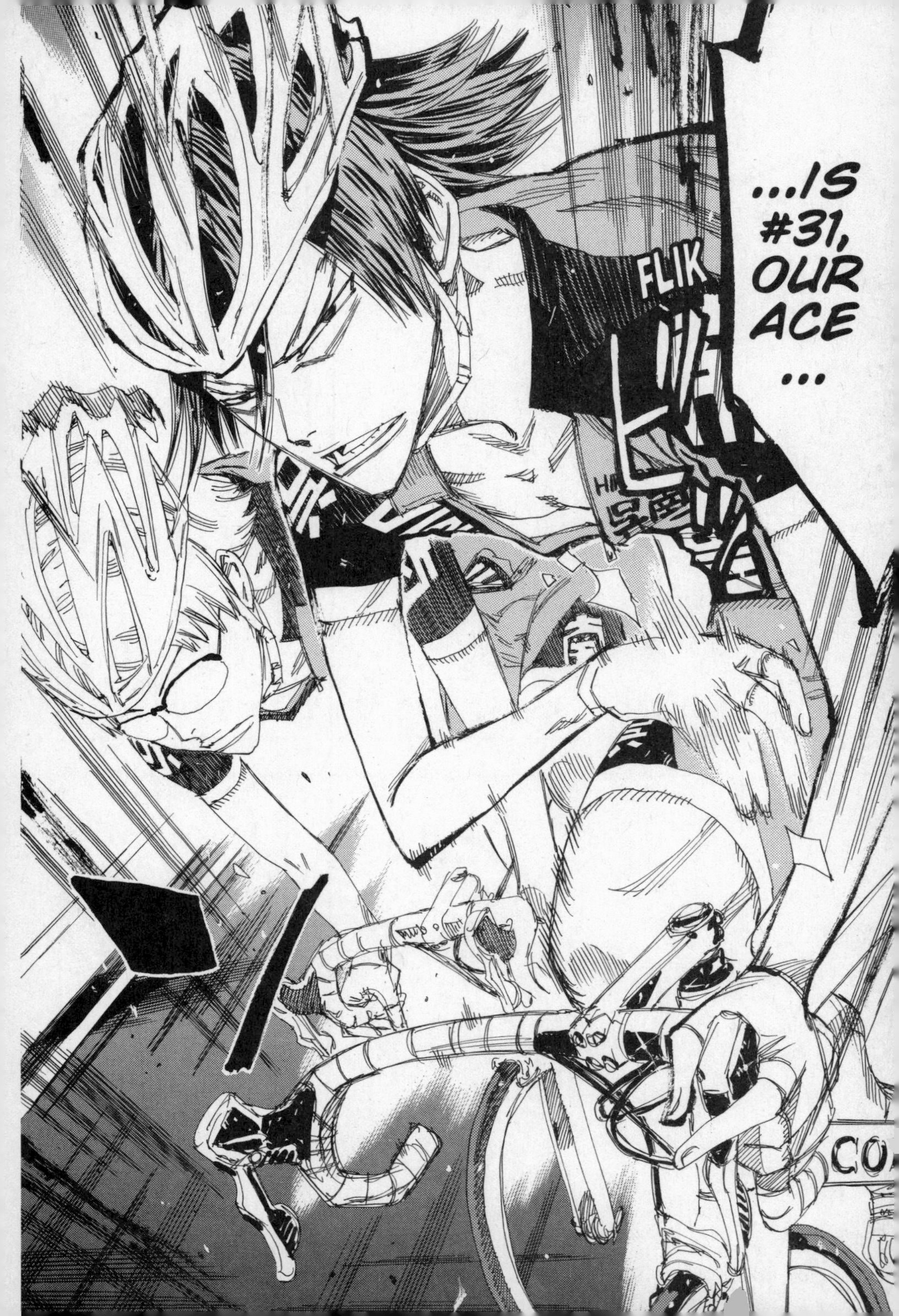
...IS #31, OUR ACE ...
FLIK

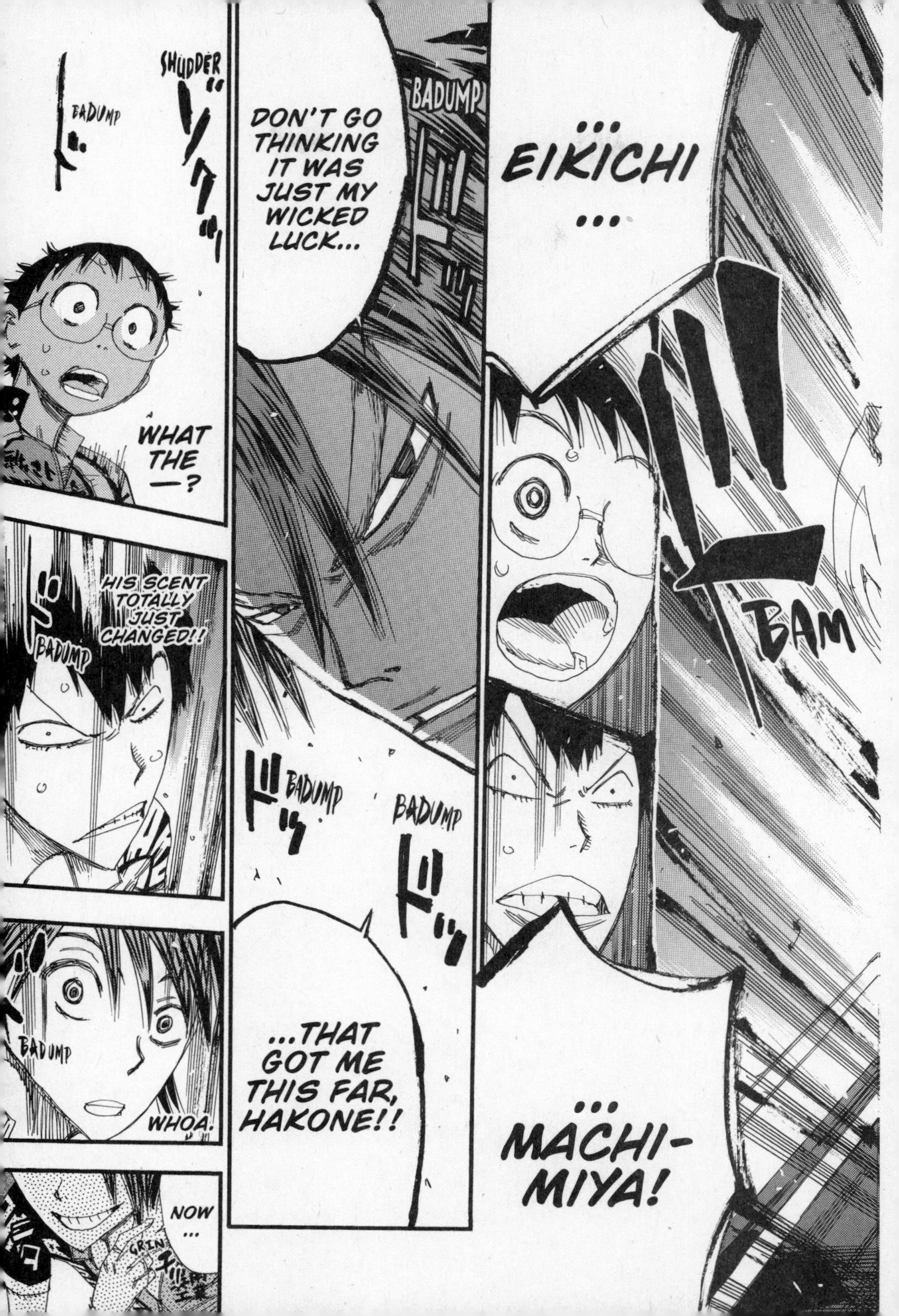
...EIKICHI...
BAM
...MACHI-MIYA!
BADUMP
DON'T GO THINKING IT WAS JUST MY WICKED LUCK...
BADUMP
BADUMP
...THAT GOT ME THIS FAR, HAKONE!!
SHUDDER
BADUMP
WHAT THE—?
HIS SCENT TOTALLY JUST CHANGED!!
BADUMP
BADUMP
WHOA.
NOW...
GRIN

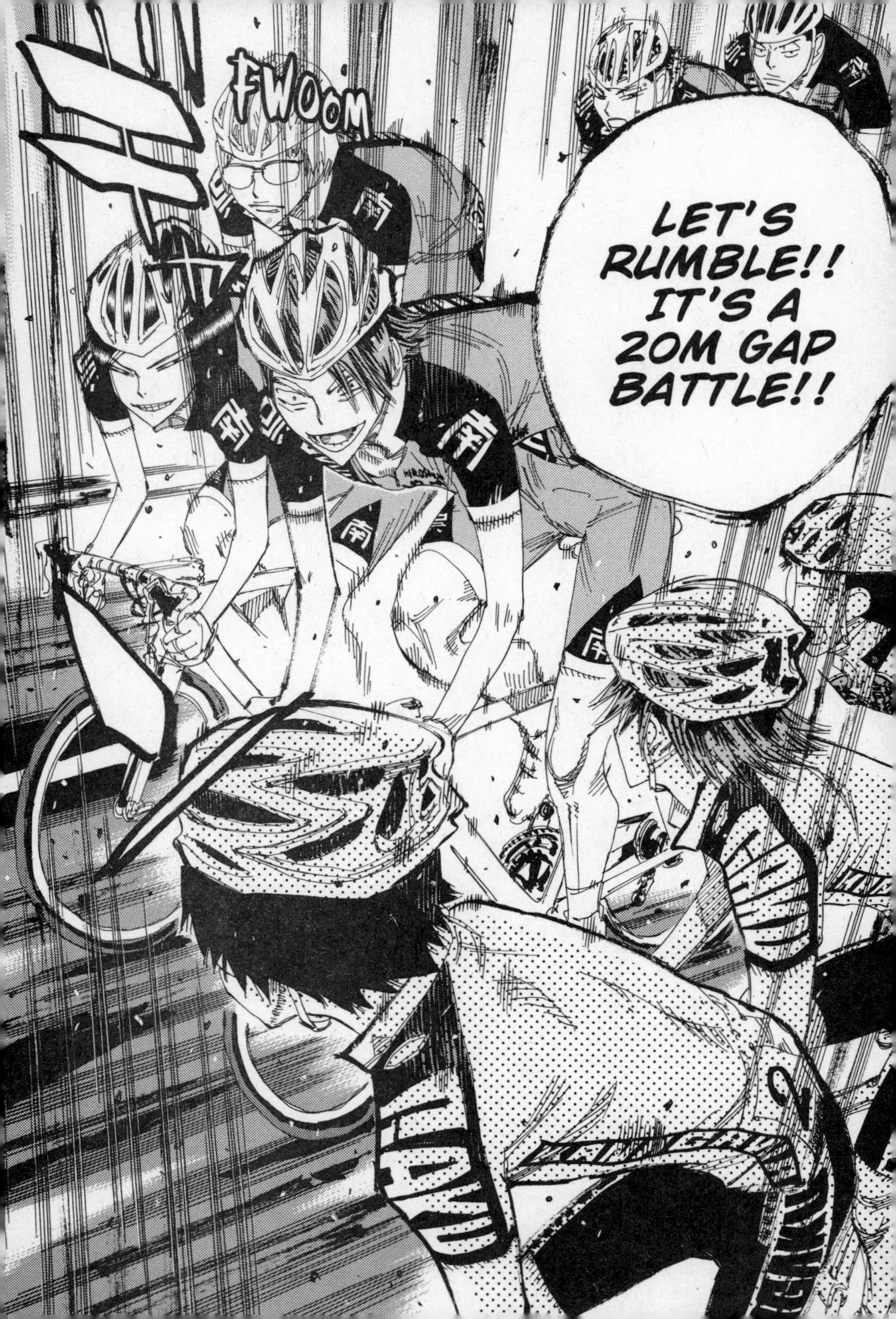
FWOOM
LET'S RUMBLE!! IT'S A 20M GAP BATTLE!!

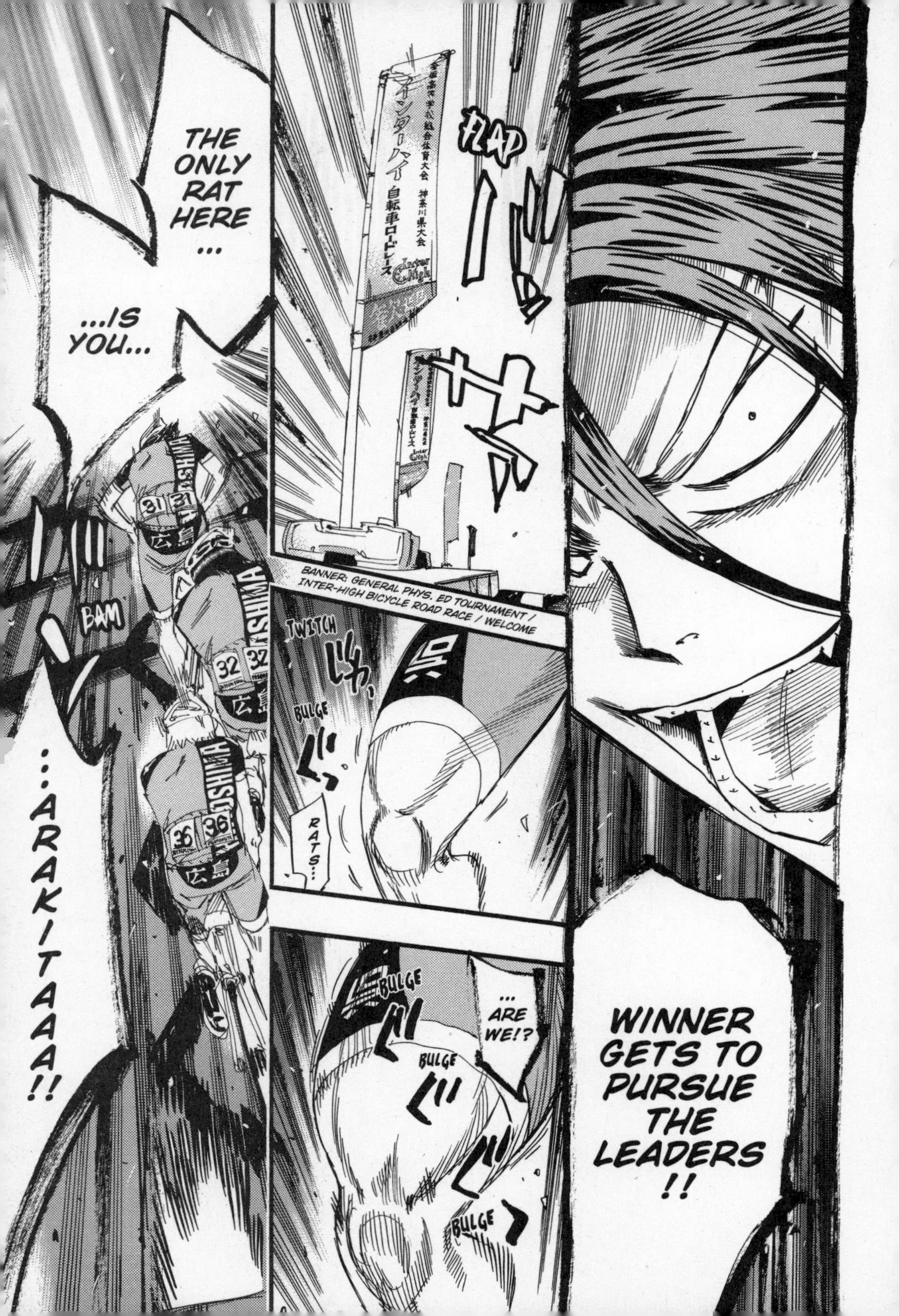
WINNER GETS TO PURSUE THE LEADERS!!
FLAP
BANNER: GENERAL PHYS. ED TOURNAMENT / INTER-HIGH BICYCLE ROAD RACE / WELCOME
TWITCH
BULGE
RATS...
BULGE
...ARE WE!?
BULGE
BULGE
THE ONLY RAT HERE...
...IS YOU...
BAM
...ARAKITAAAA!!

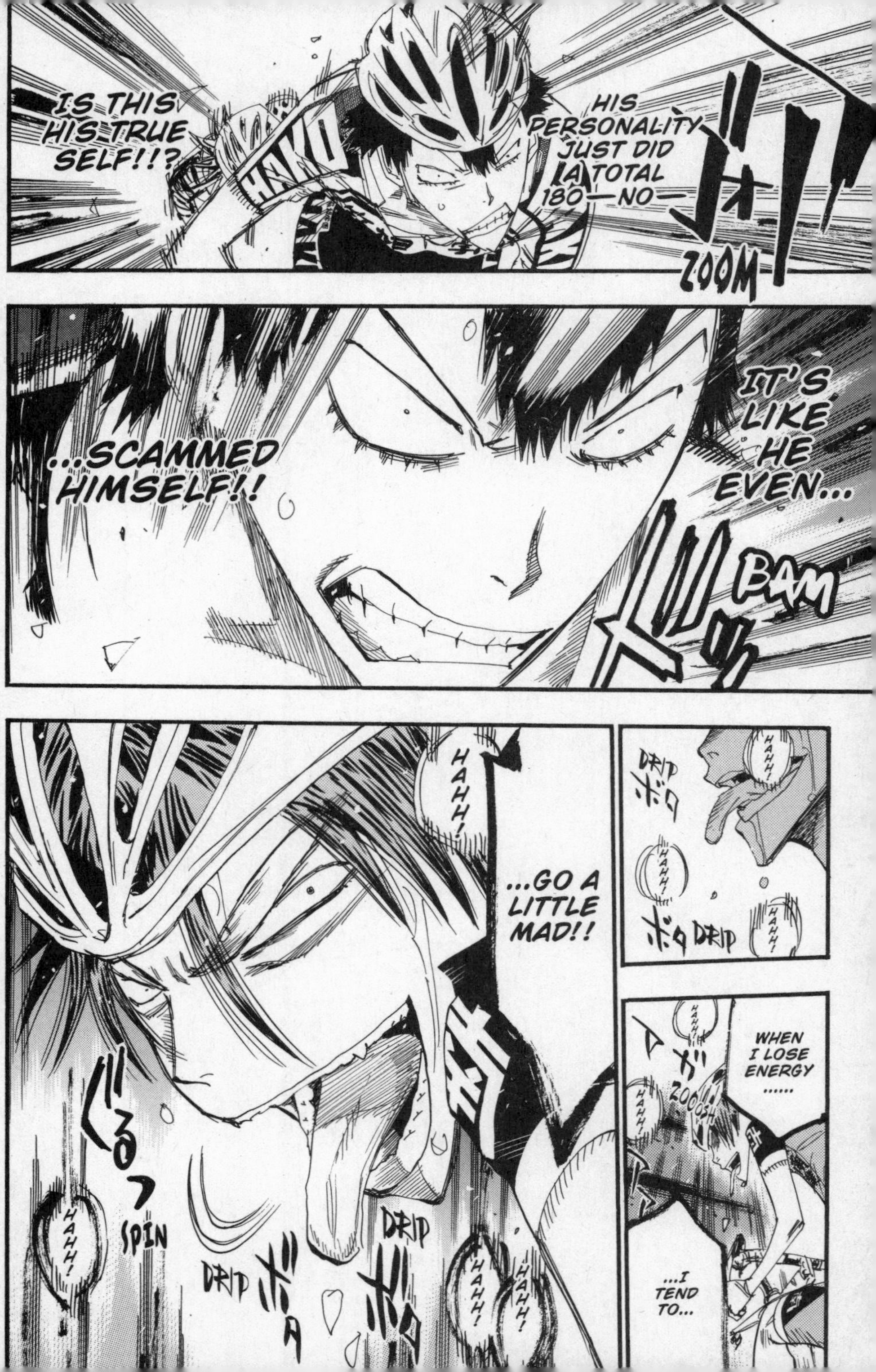
ZOOM
HIS PERSONALITY JUST DID A TOTAL 180—NO—
IS THIS HIS TRUE SELF!!?
IT'S LIKE HE EVEN...
BAM
...SCAMMED HIMSELF!!
HAHH!
DRIP
ボタ
HAHH!
HAHH!
ボタ DRIP
WHEN I LOSE ENERGY ......
HAHH!
ガ
ZOOOSH
HAHH!
...I TEND TO...
HAHH!
...GO A LITTLE MAD!!
ぐるっ
SPIN
HAHH!
DRIP
ボタ
DRIP
ボタ
HAHH!
HAHH!

RIDE.171 PIT DOG OF KURE

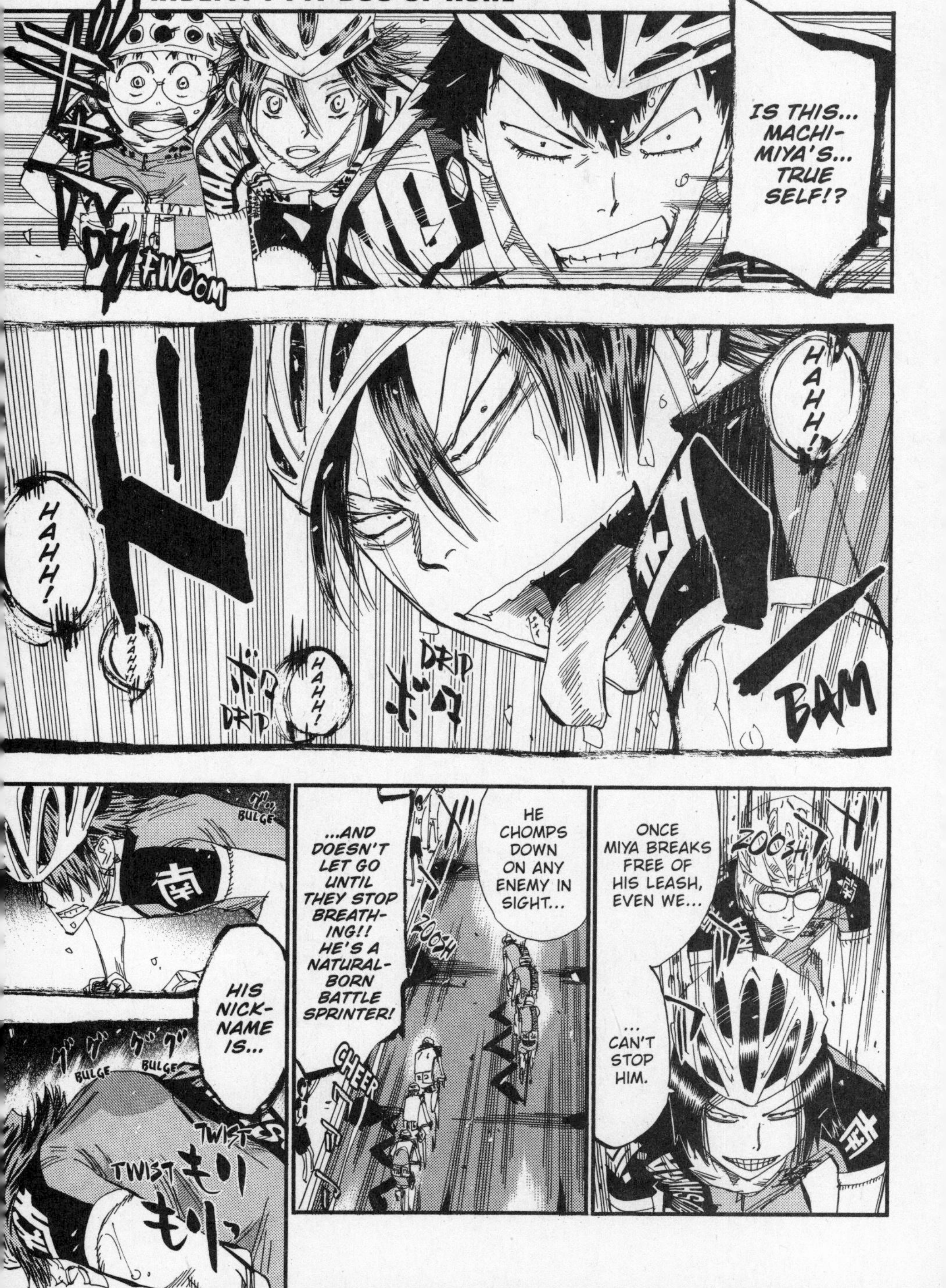
IS THIS... MACHI-MIYA'S... TRUE SELF!?
FWOOM
HAHH!
HAHH!
HAHH!
HAHH!
DRIP
DRIP
BAM
ONCE MIYA BREAKS FREE OF HIS LEASH, EVEN WE...
ZOOSH
... CAN'T STOP HIM.
HE CHOMPS DOWN ON ANY ENEMY IN SIGHT...
...AND DOESN'T LET GO UNTIL THEY STOP BREATHING!! HE'S A NATURAL-BORN BATTLE SPRINTER!
ZOOSH
CHEER
BULGE
HIS NICK-NAME IS...
BULGE
BULGE
TWIST
TWIST

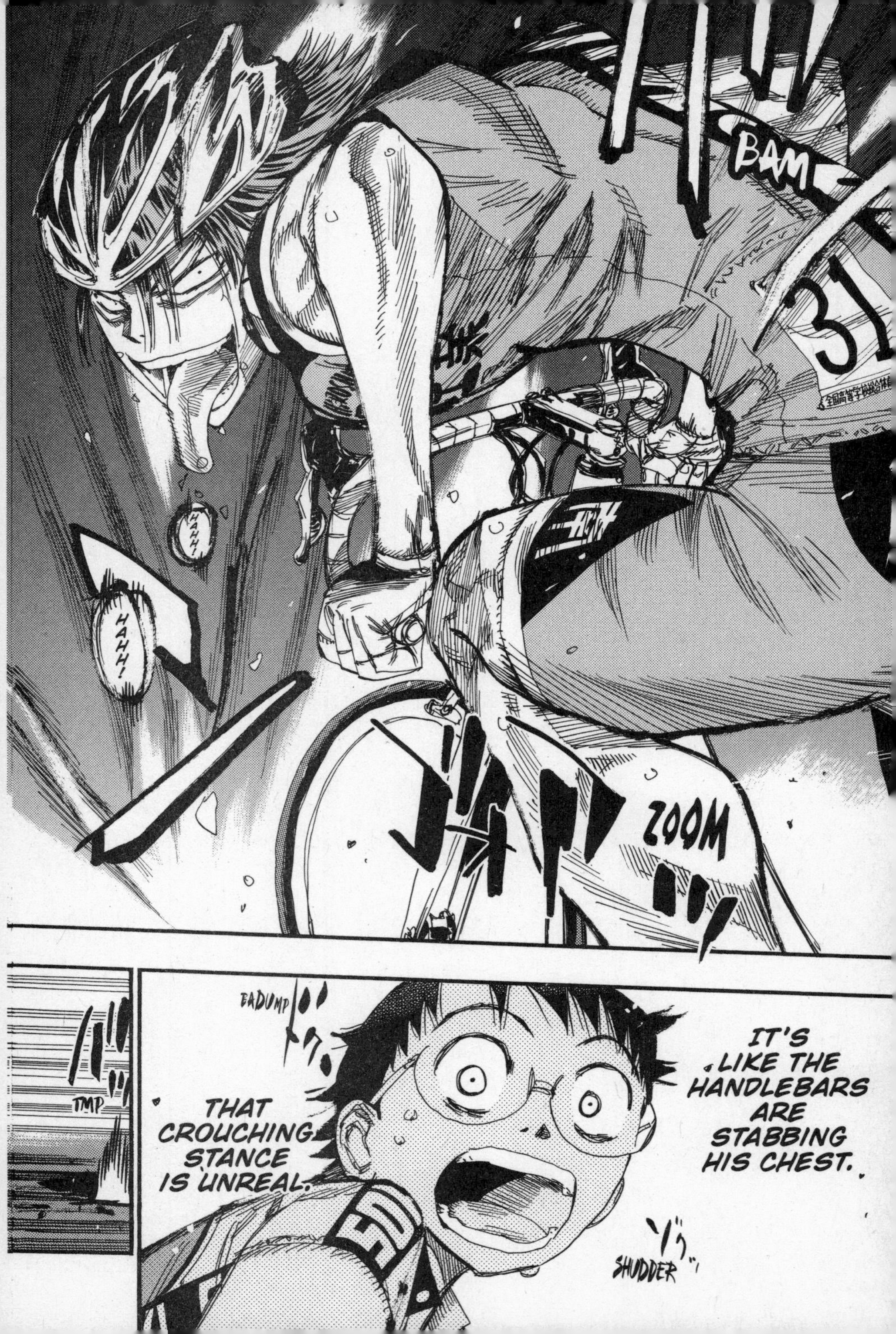
BAM
31
HAHH!
HAHH!
ZOOM
BADUMP
IT'S LIKE THE HANDLEBARS ARE STABBING HIS CHEST.
THAT CROUCHING STANCE IS UNREAL.
SHUDDER
TMP

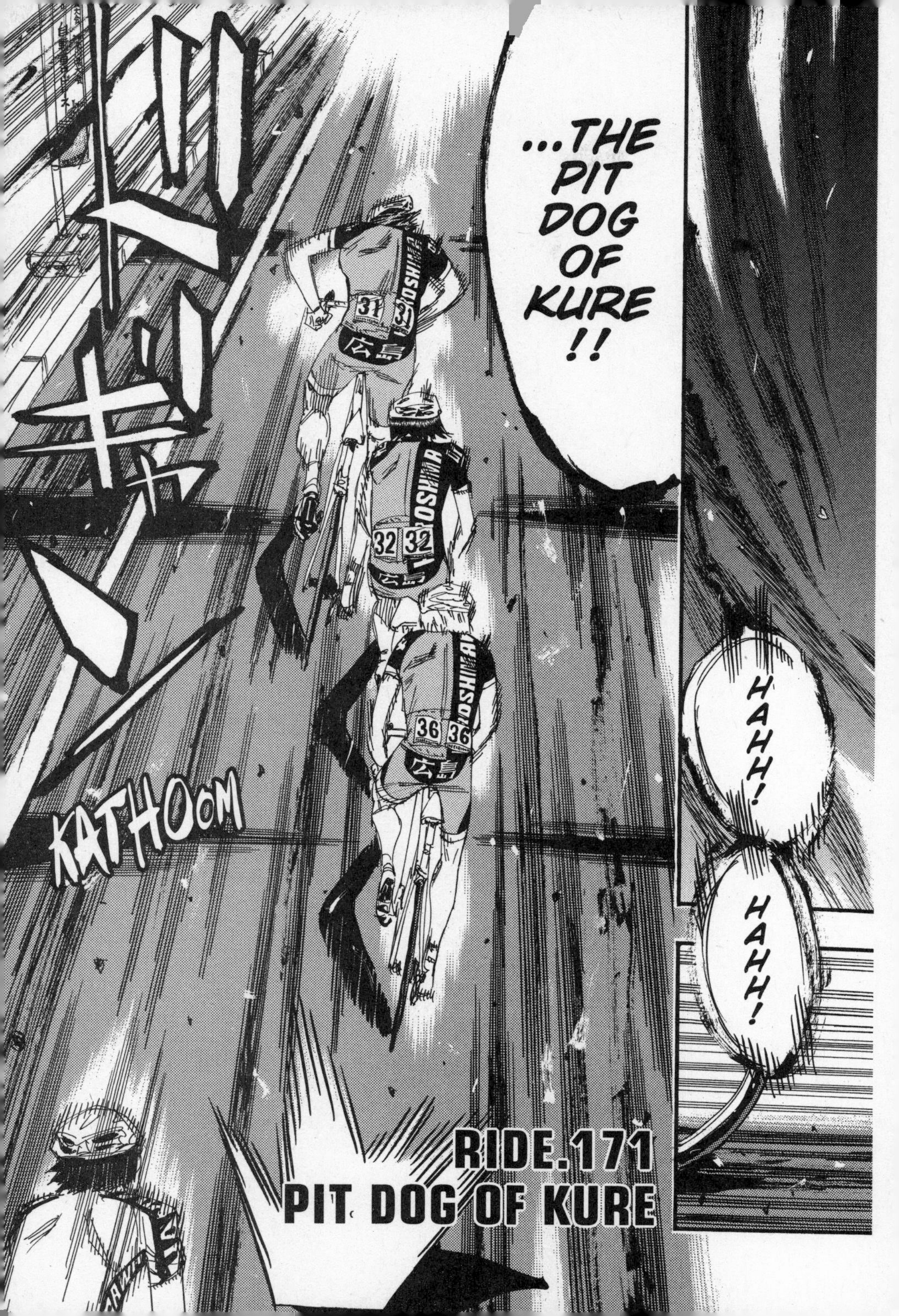
...THE PIT DOG OF KURE!!
HAHH!
HAHH!
KATHOOM
RIDE.171
PIT DOG OF KURE

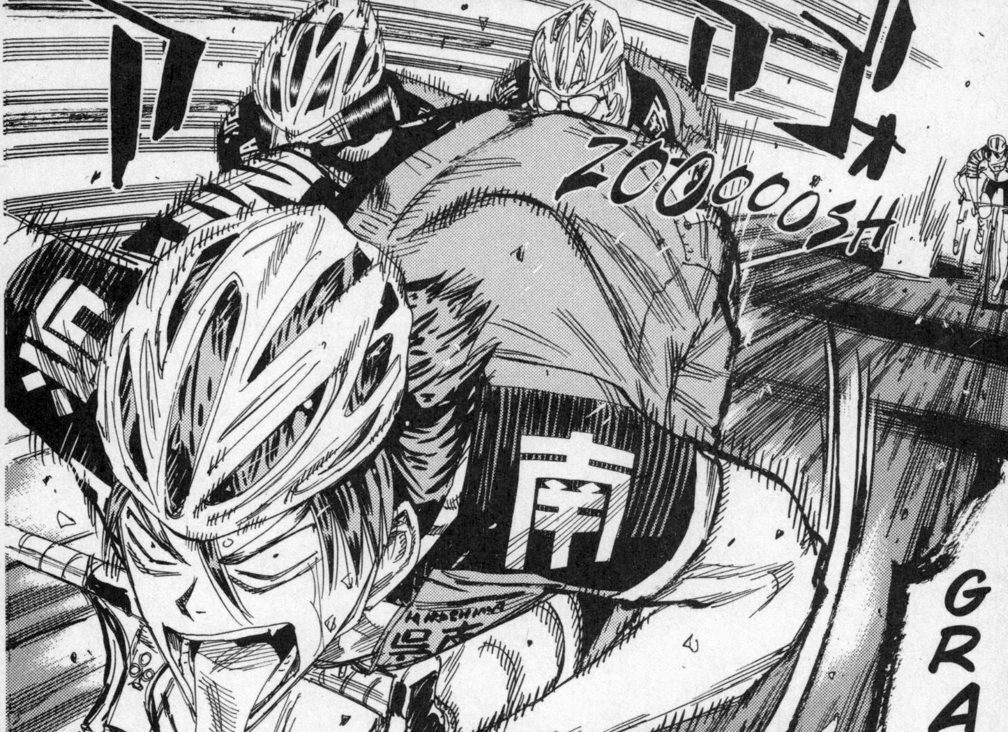
ZOOOOOSH
GRAAAAAH!

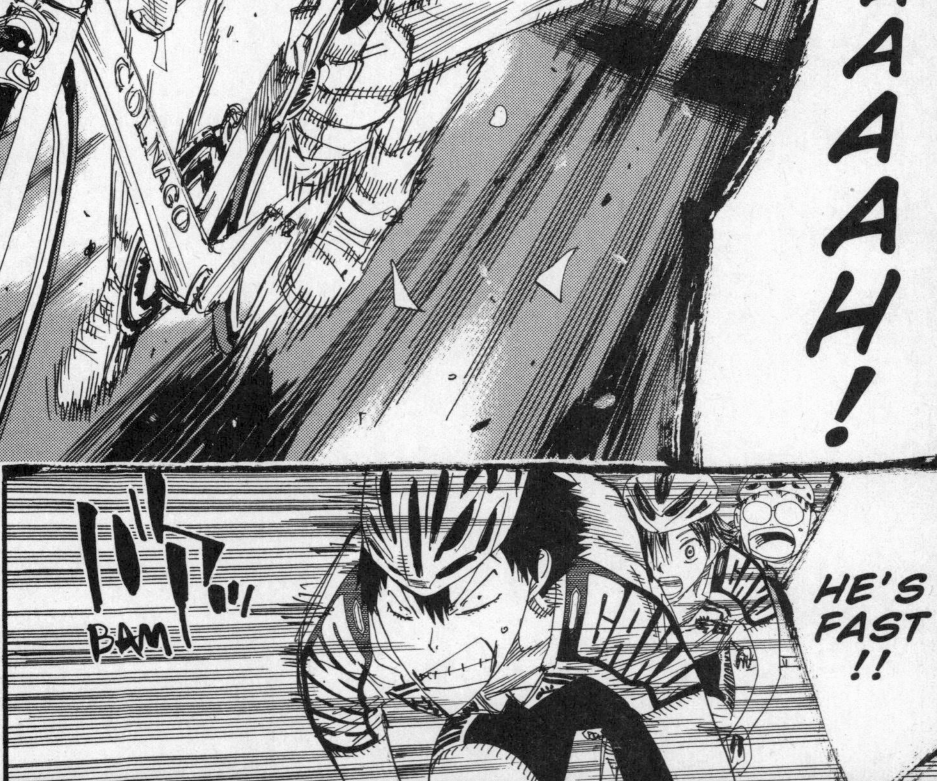
BAM
HE'S FAST!!

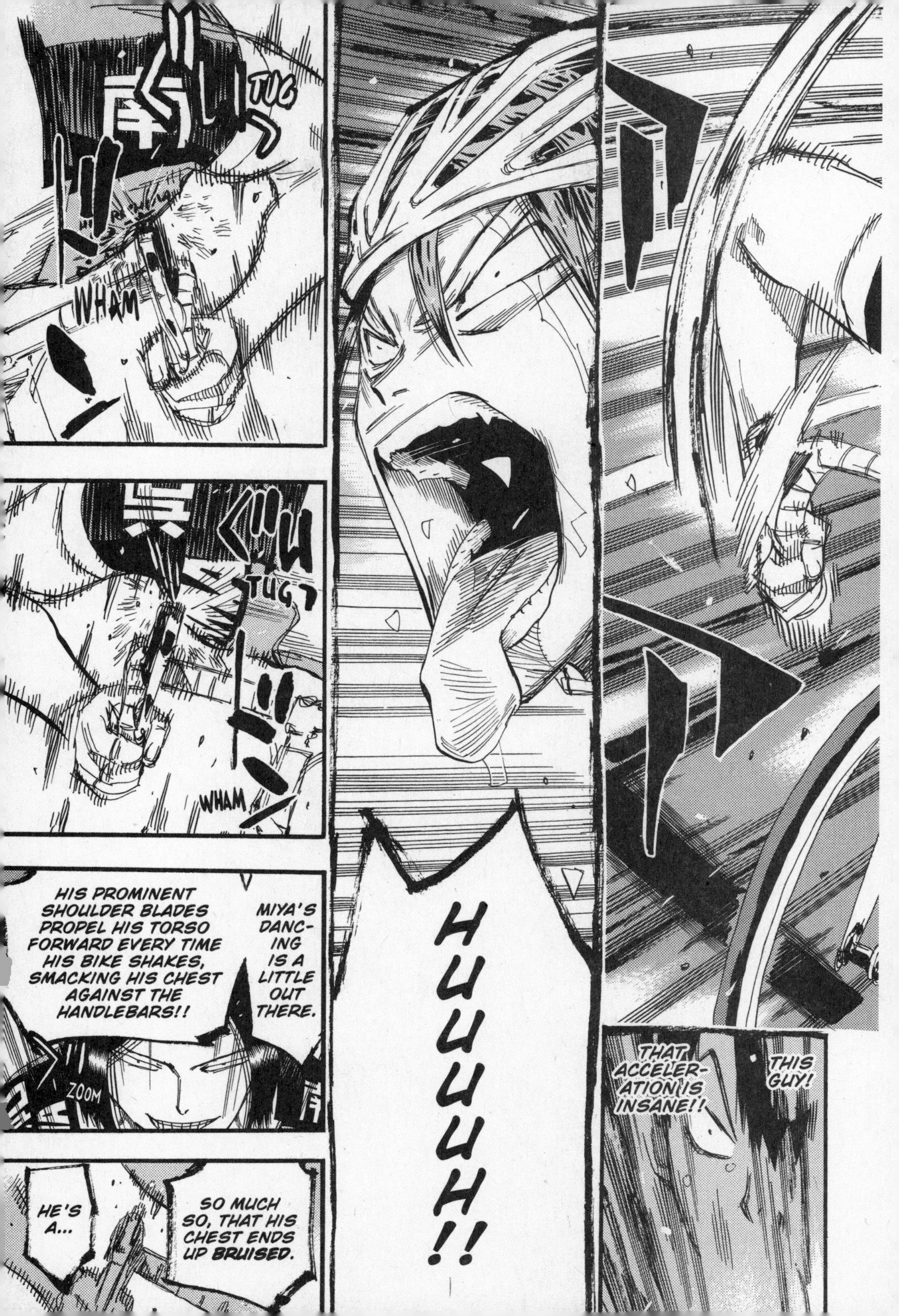

THIS GUY!
THAT ACCELERATION IS INSANE!!
HUUUUH!!
TUG
WHAM
TUG
WHAM
MIYA'S DANCING IS A LITTLE OUT THERE.
HIS PROMINENT SHOULDER BLADES PROPEL HIS TORSO FORWARD EVERY TIME HIS BIKE SHAKES, SMACKING HIS CHEST AGAINST THE HANDLEBARS!!
ZOOM
SO MUCH SO, THAT HIS CHEST ENDS UP BRUISED.
HE'S A...

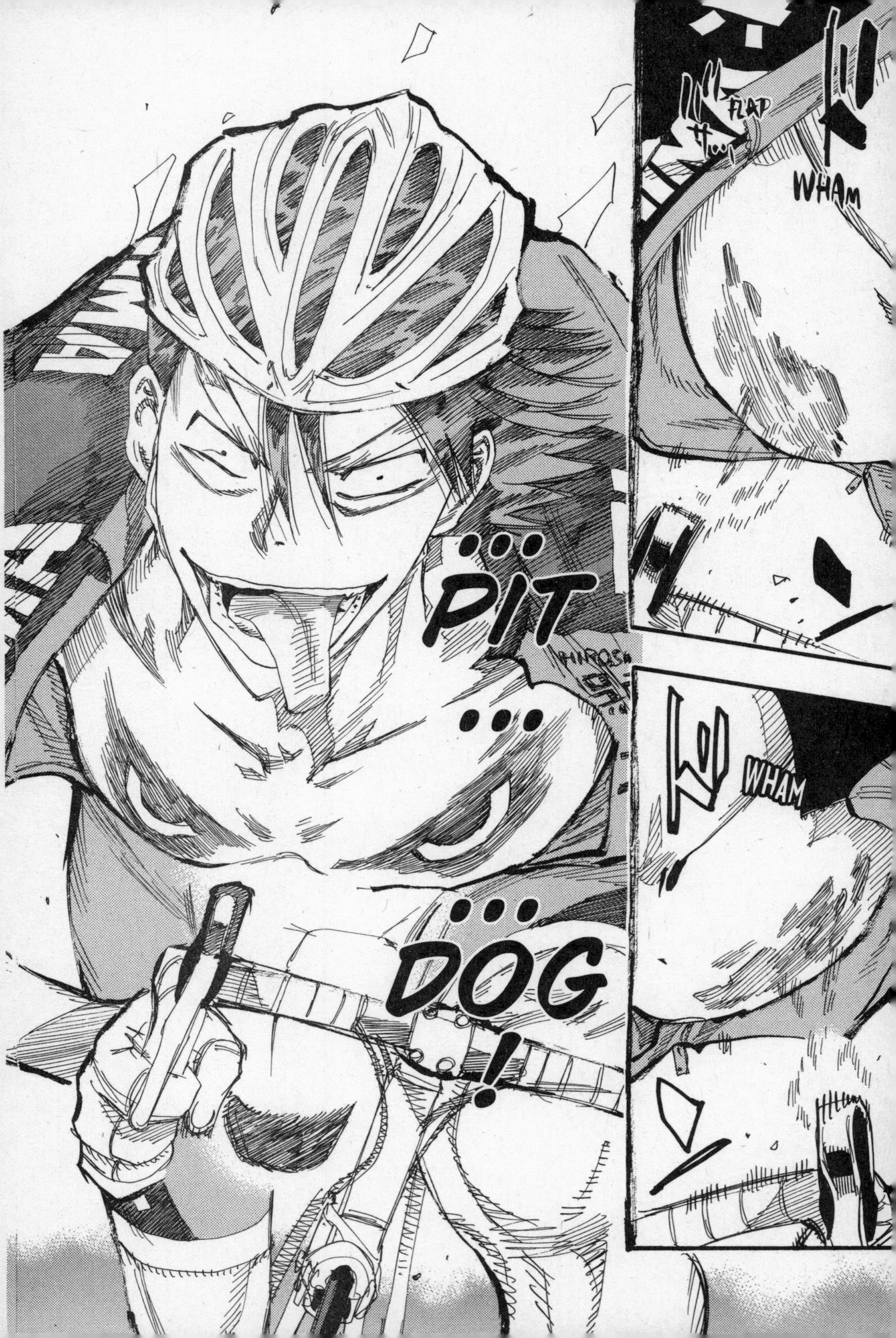
FLAP
WHAM
WHAM
...PIT...
...DOG!

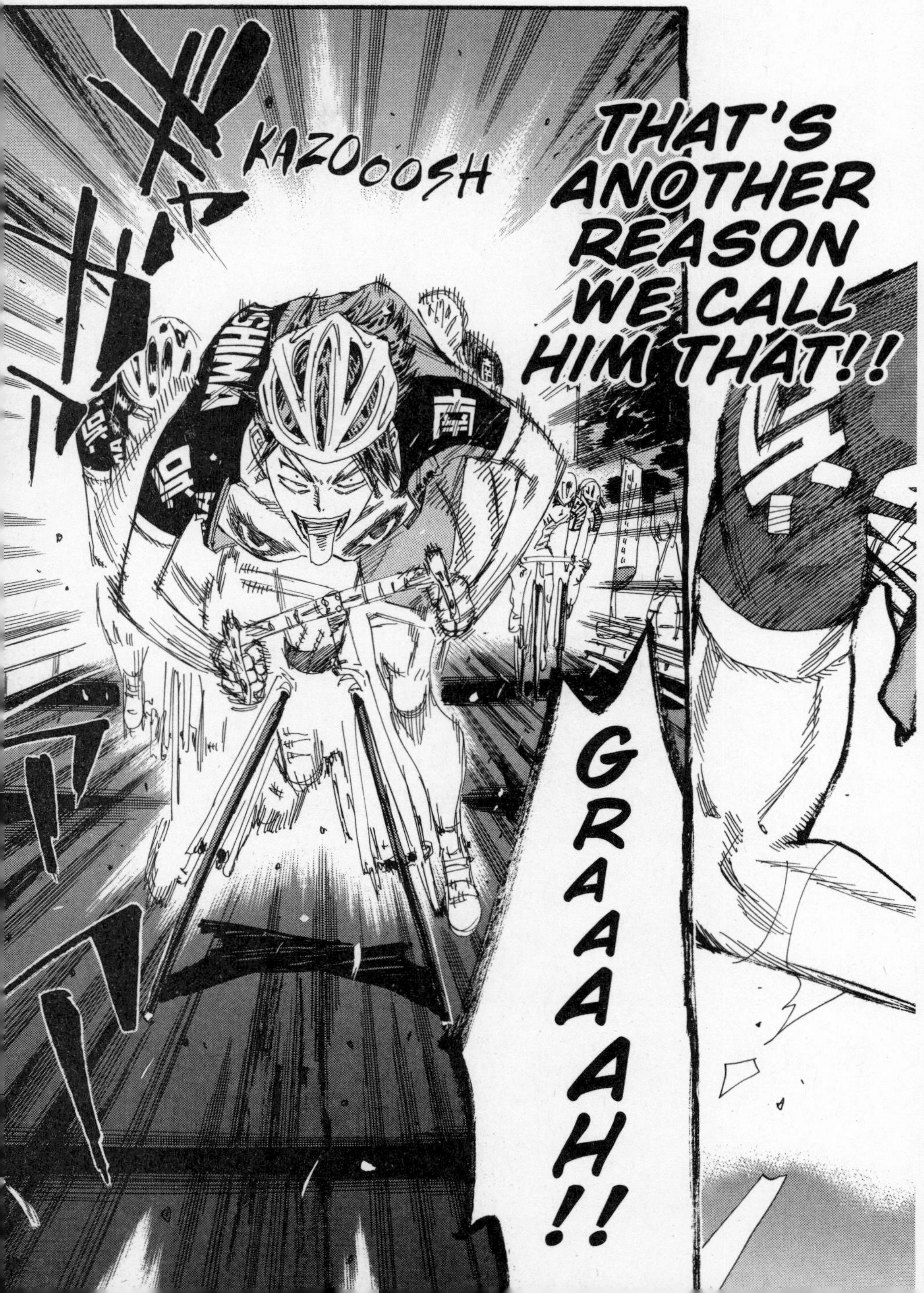
THAT'S ANOTHER REASON WE CALL HIM THAT!!
KAZOOOOSH
GRAAAAAH!!

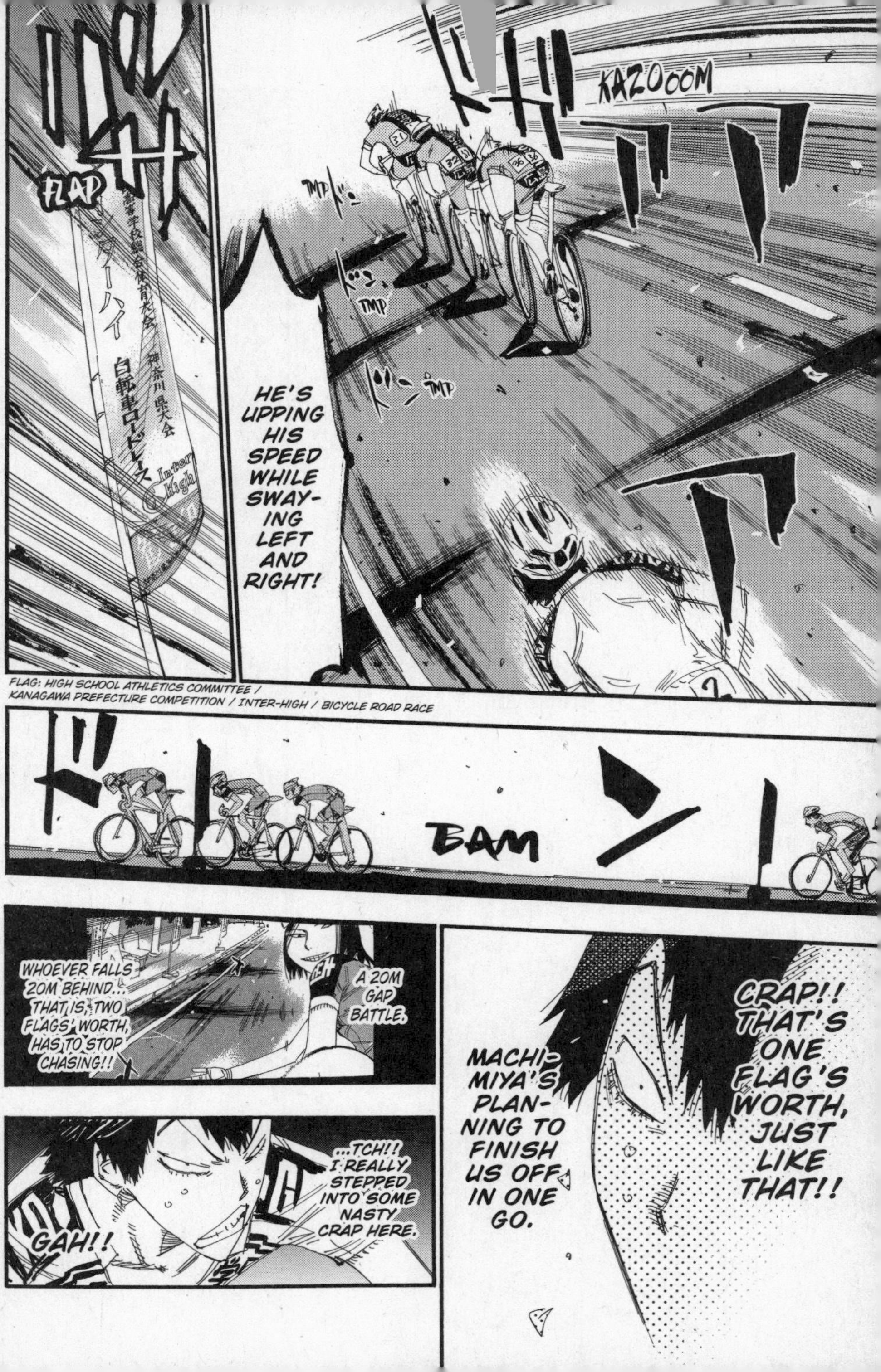
KAZOOOM
TMP
TMP
TMP
HE'S UPPING HIS SPEED WHILE SWAYING LEFT AND RIGHT!
FLAP
FLAG: HIGH SCHOOL ATHLETICS COMMITTEE / KANAGAWA PREFECTURE COMPETITION / INTER-HIGH / BICYCLE ROAD RACE
BAM
CRAP!! THAT'S ONE FLAG'S WORTH, JUST LIKE THAT!!
MACHIMIYA'S PLANNING TO FINISH US OFF IN ONE GO.
A 20M GAP BATTLE.
WHOEVER FALLS 20M BEHIND... THAT IS, TWO FLAGS' WORTH, HAS TO STOP CHASING!!
...TCH!! I REALLY STEPPED INTO SOME NASTY CRAP HERE.
GAH!!

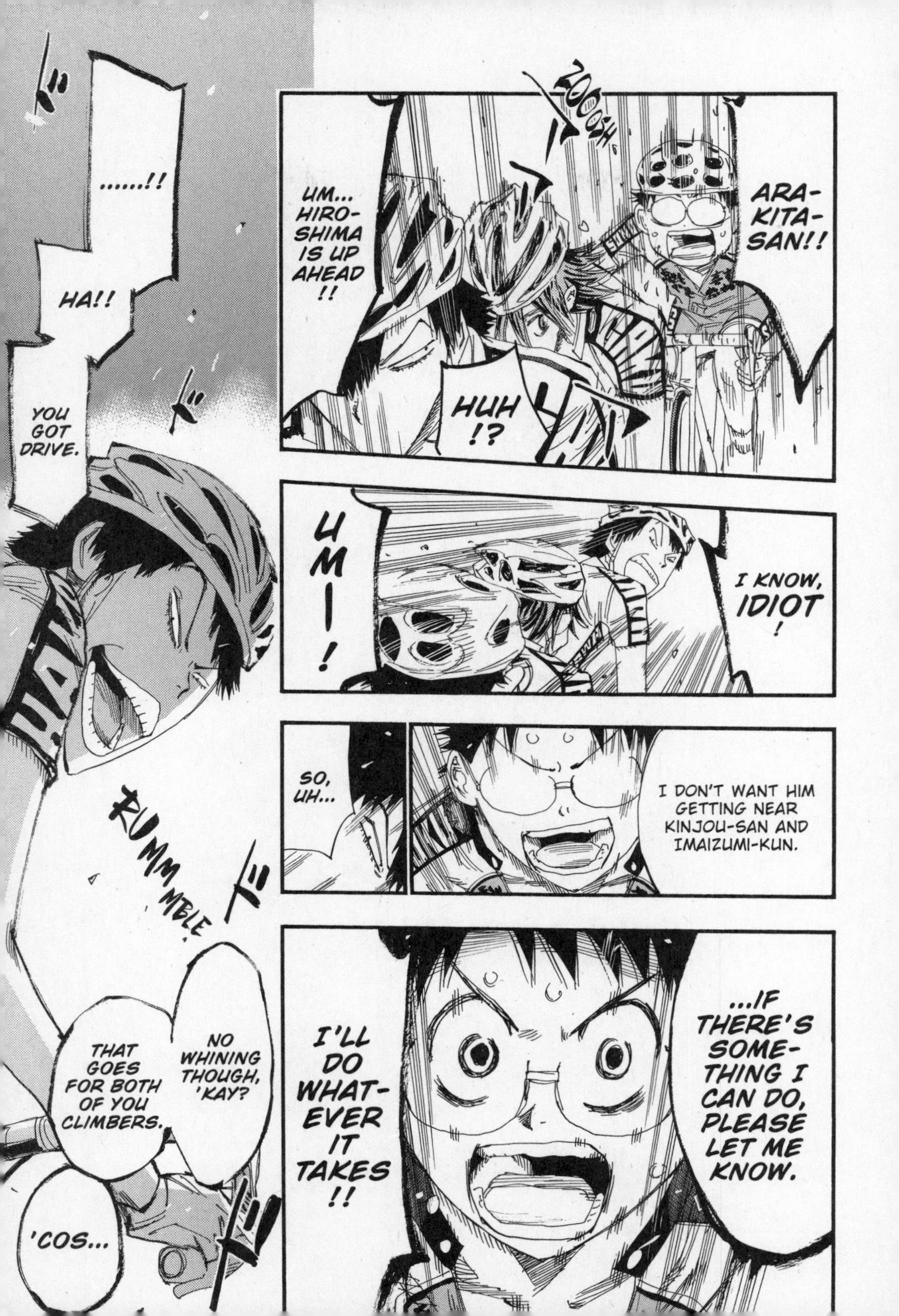

ZOOOSH
ARA-KITA-SAN!!
UM... HIROSHIMA IS UP AHEAD!!
HUH!?
I KNOW, IDIOT!
UMI-!
I DON'T WANT HIM GETTING NEAR KINJOU-SAN AND IMAIZUMI-KUN.
SO, UH...
...IF THERE'S SOMETHING I CAN DO, PLEASE LET ME KNOW.
I'LL DO WHATEVER IT TAKES!!
......!!
HA!!
YOU GOT DRIVE.
RUMMMBLE
NO WHINING THOUGH, 'KAY?
THAT GOES FOR BOTH OF YOU CLIMBERS.
'COS...

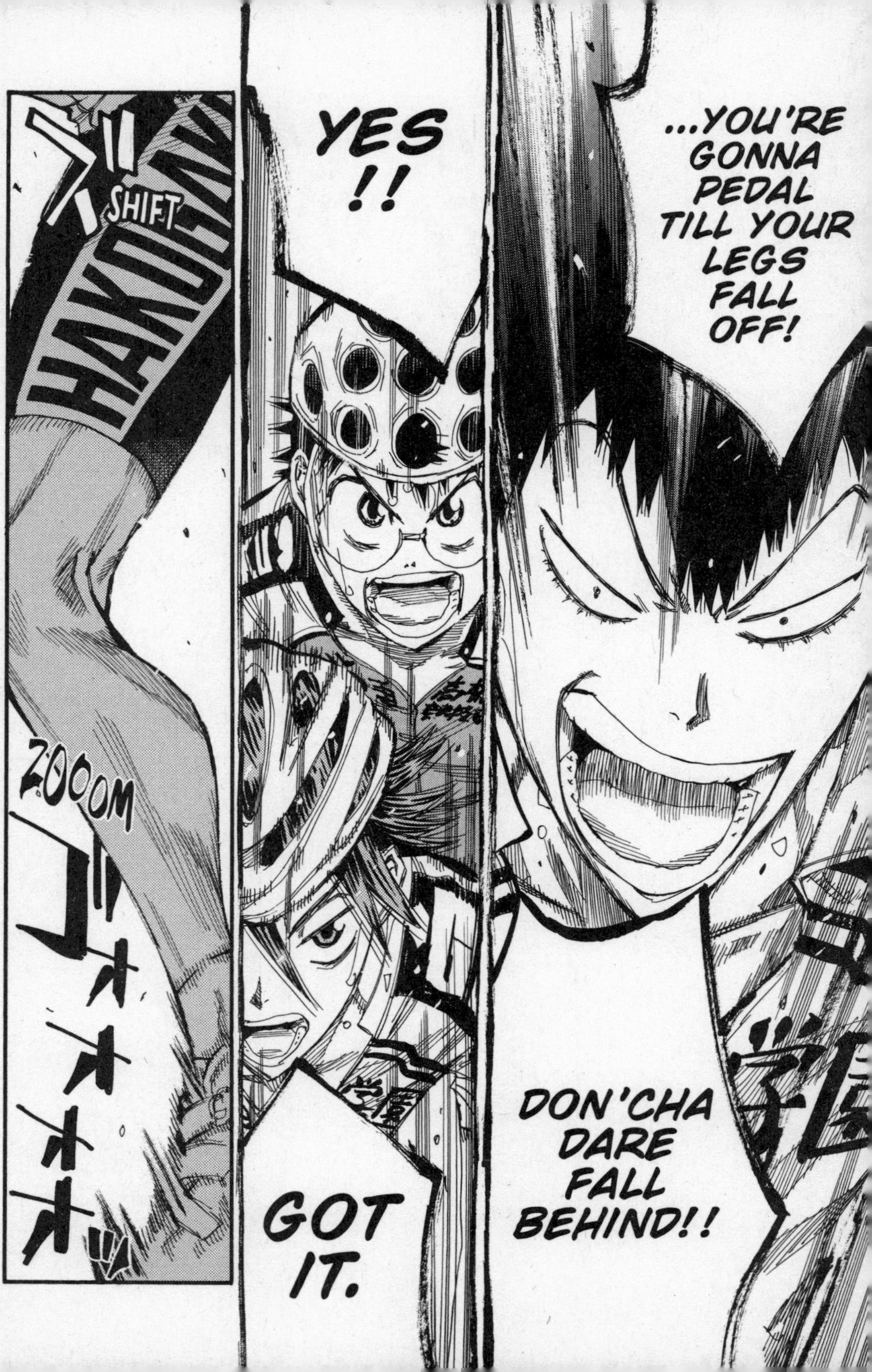
...YOU'RE GONNA PEDAL TILL YOUR LEGS FALL OFF!
DON'CHA DARE FALL BEHIND!!
YES!!
GOT IT.
SHIFT
ZOOOM

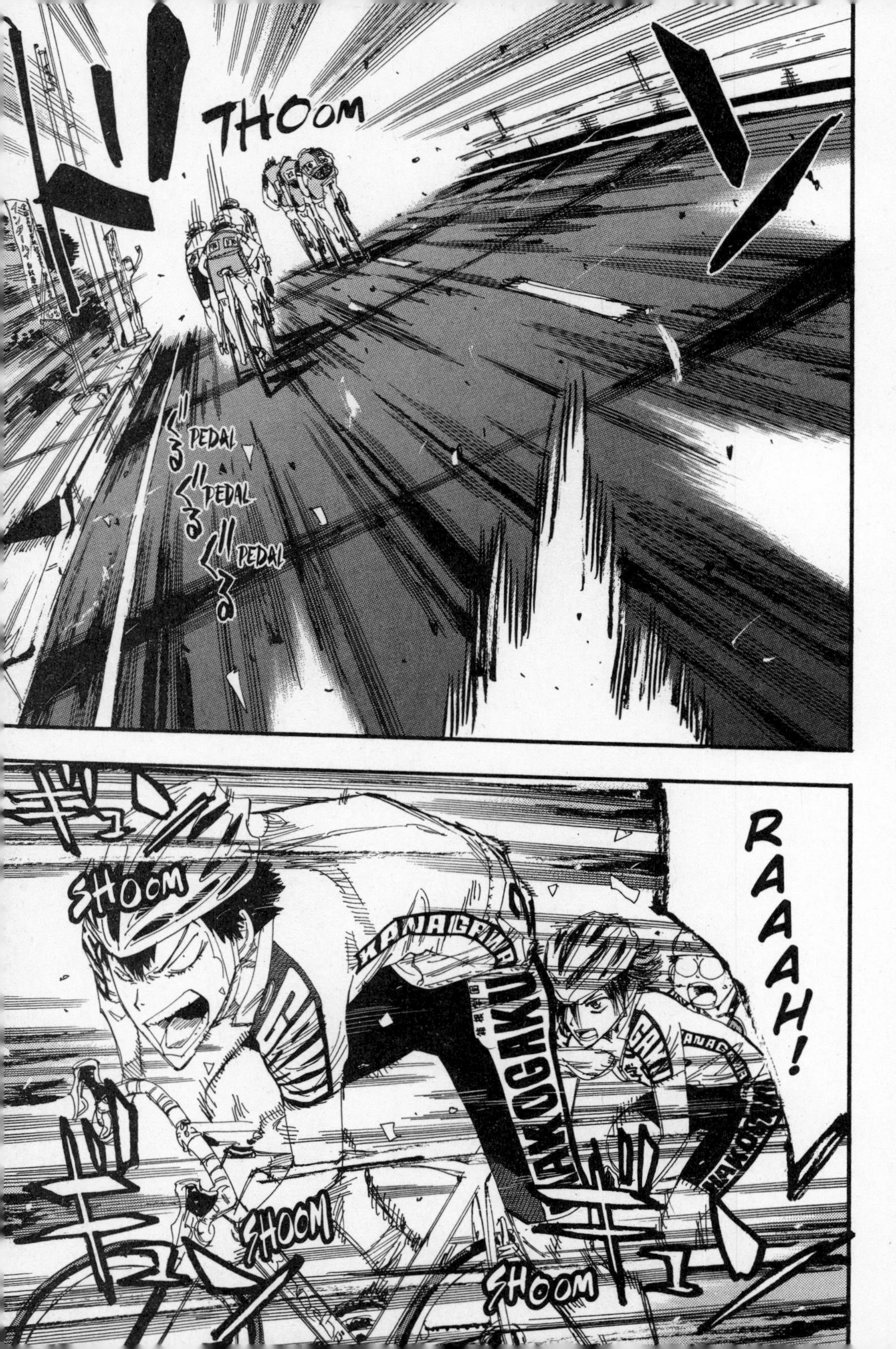
THOOM
PEDAL
PEDAL
PEDAL
RAAAAH!
SHOOM
SHOOM
SHOOM

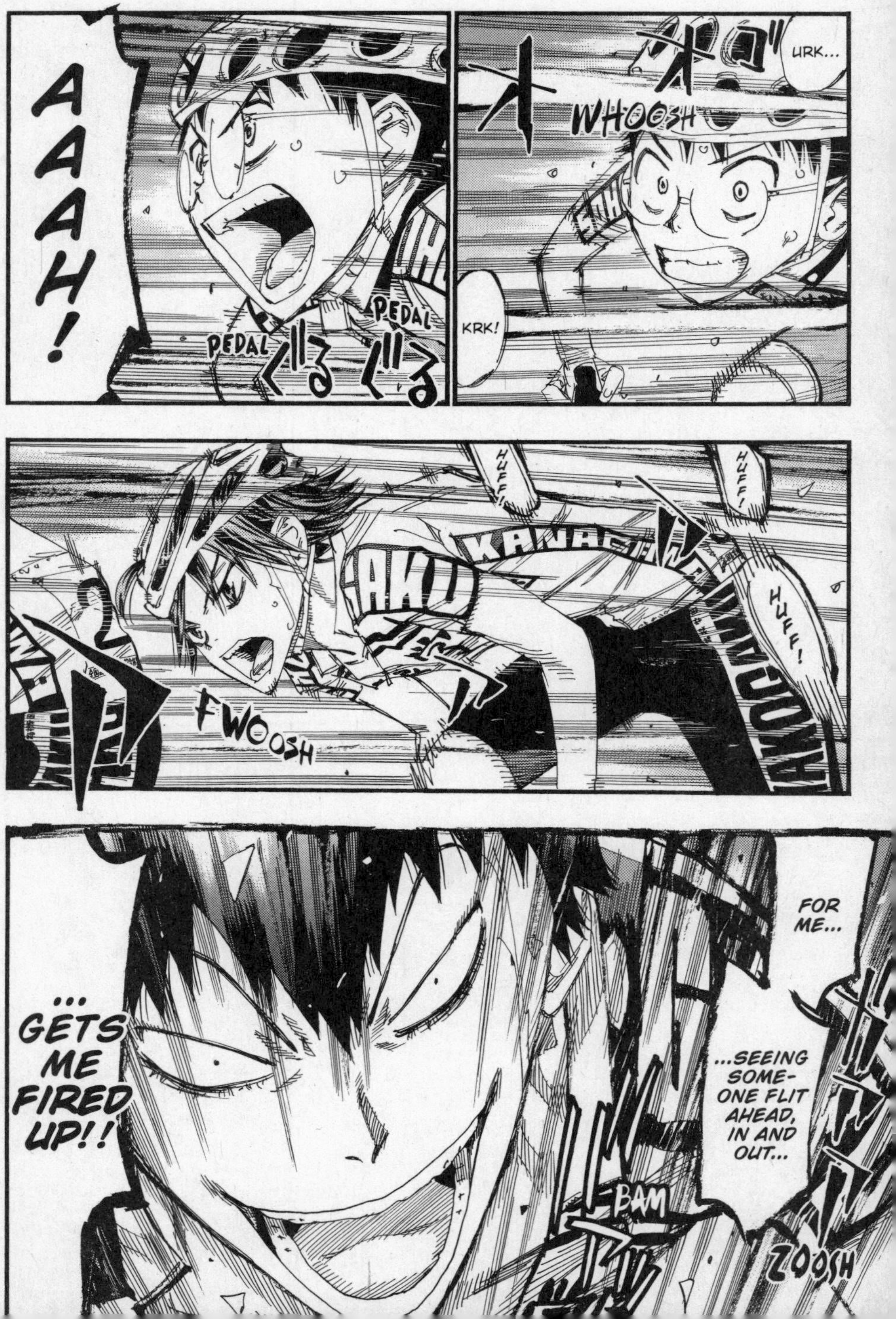
URK...
WHOOSH
KRK!
AAAAH!
PEDAL
PEDAL
HUFF!
HUFF!
HUFF!
FWOOSH
FOR ME...
...SEEING SOME-ONE FLIT AHEAD, IN AND OUT...
...GETS ME FIRED UP!!
BAM
ZOOSH

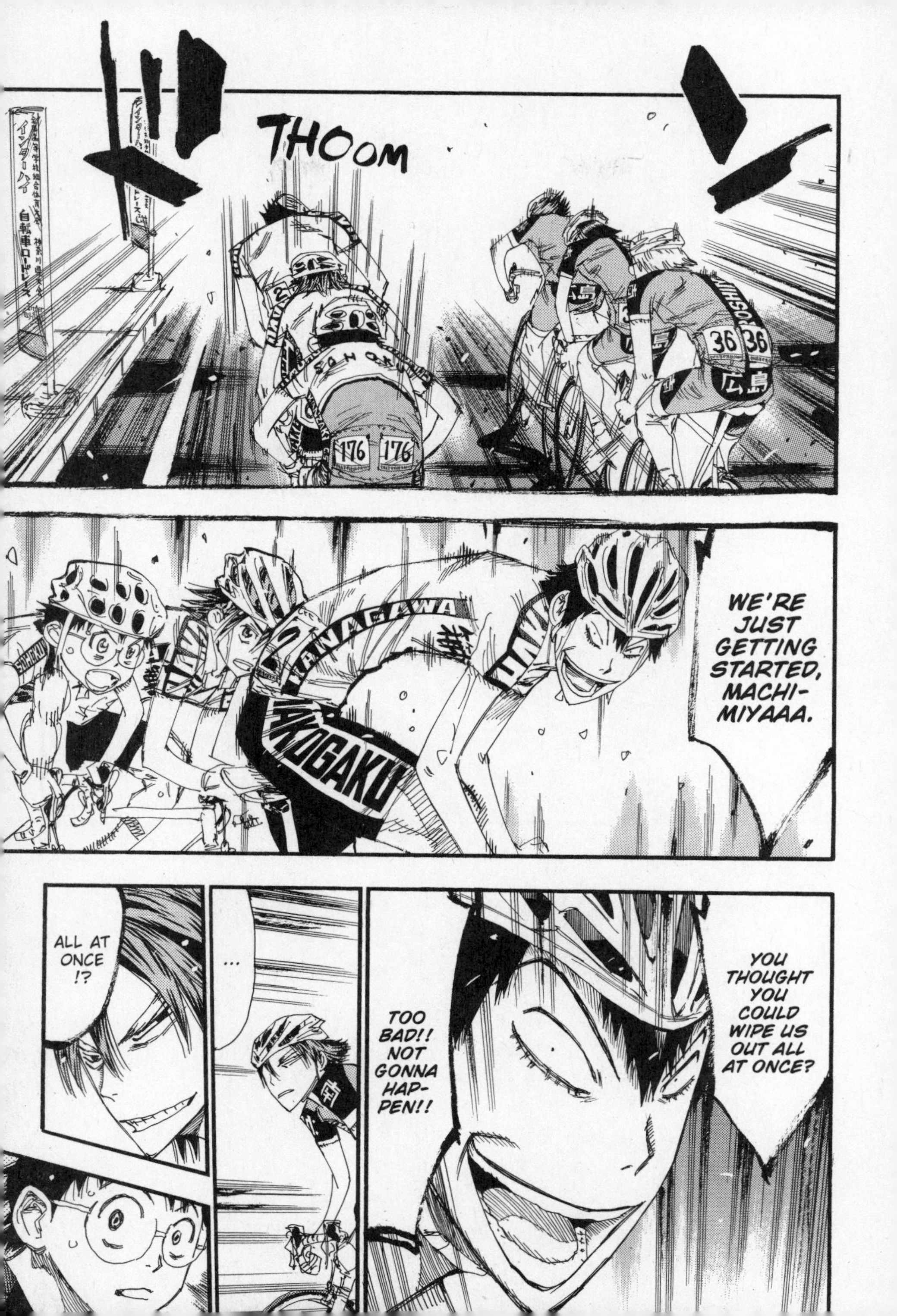
THOOM
WE'RE JUST GETTING STARTED, MACHI-MIYAAA.
YOU THOUGHT YOU COULD WIPE US OUT ALL AT ONCE?
TOO BAD!! NOT GONNA HAP-PEN!!
...
ALL AT ONCE !?

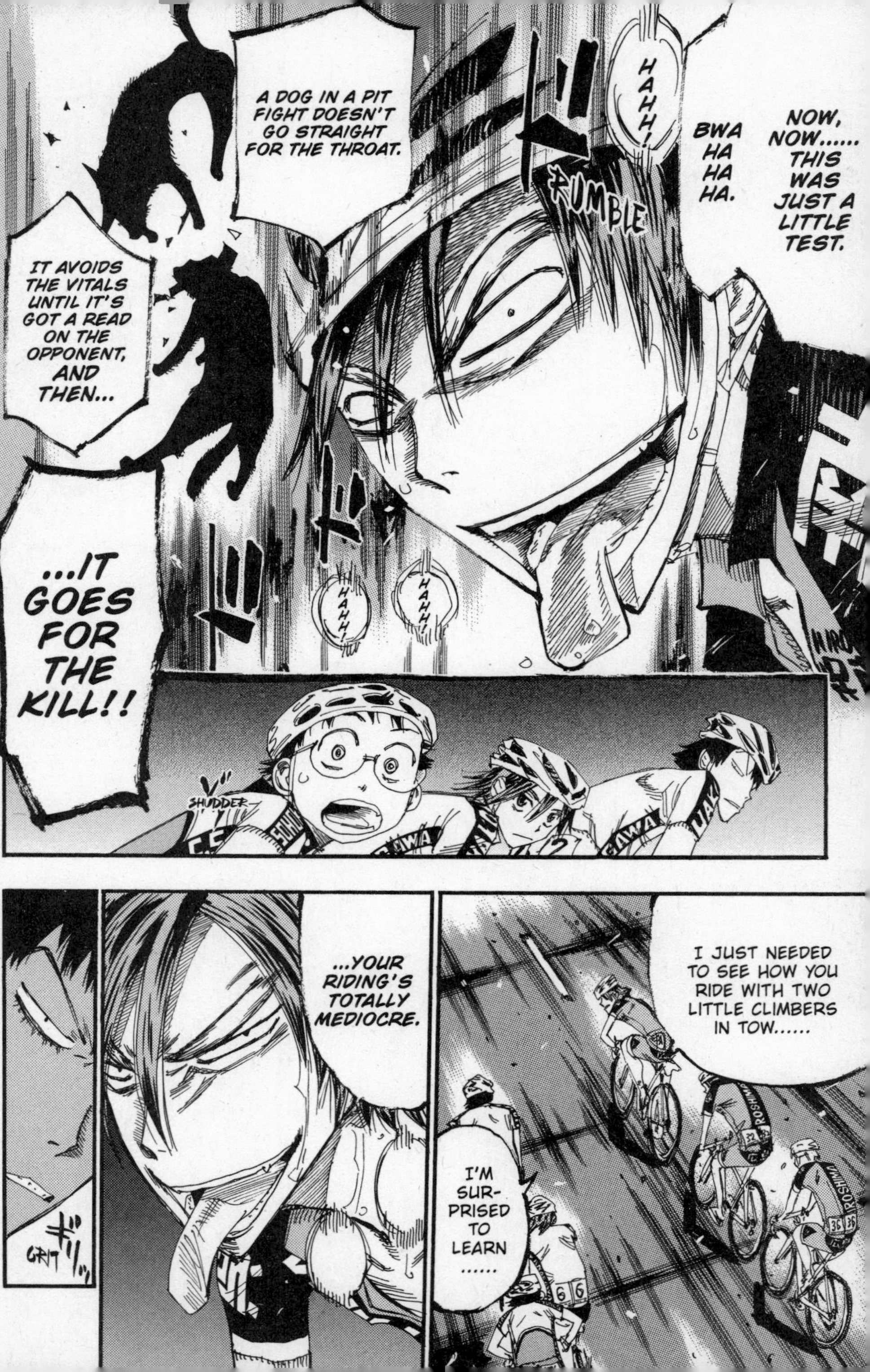
NOW, NOW...... THIS WAS JUST A LITTLE TEST.
BWA HA HA HA.
HAHH!
RUMBLE
A DOG IN A PIT FIGHT DOESN'T GO STRAIGHT FOR THE THROAT.
IT AVOIDS THE VITALS UNTIL IT'S GOT A READ ON THE OPPONENT, AND THEN...
HAHH!
HAHH!
...IT GOES FOR THE KILL!!
SHUDDER
I JUST NEEDED TO SEE HOW YOU RIDE WITH TWO LITTLE CLIMBERS IN TOW......
I'M SUR-PRISED TO LEARN ......
...YOUR RIDING'S TOTALLY MEDIOCRE.
GRIT

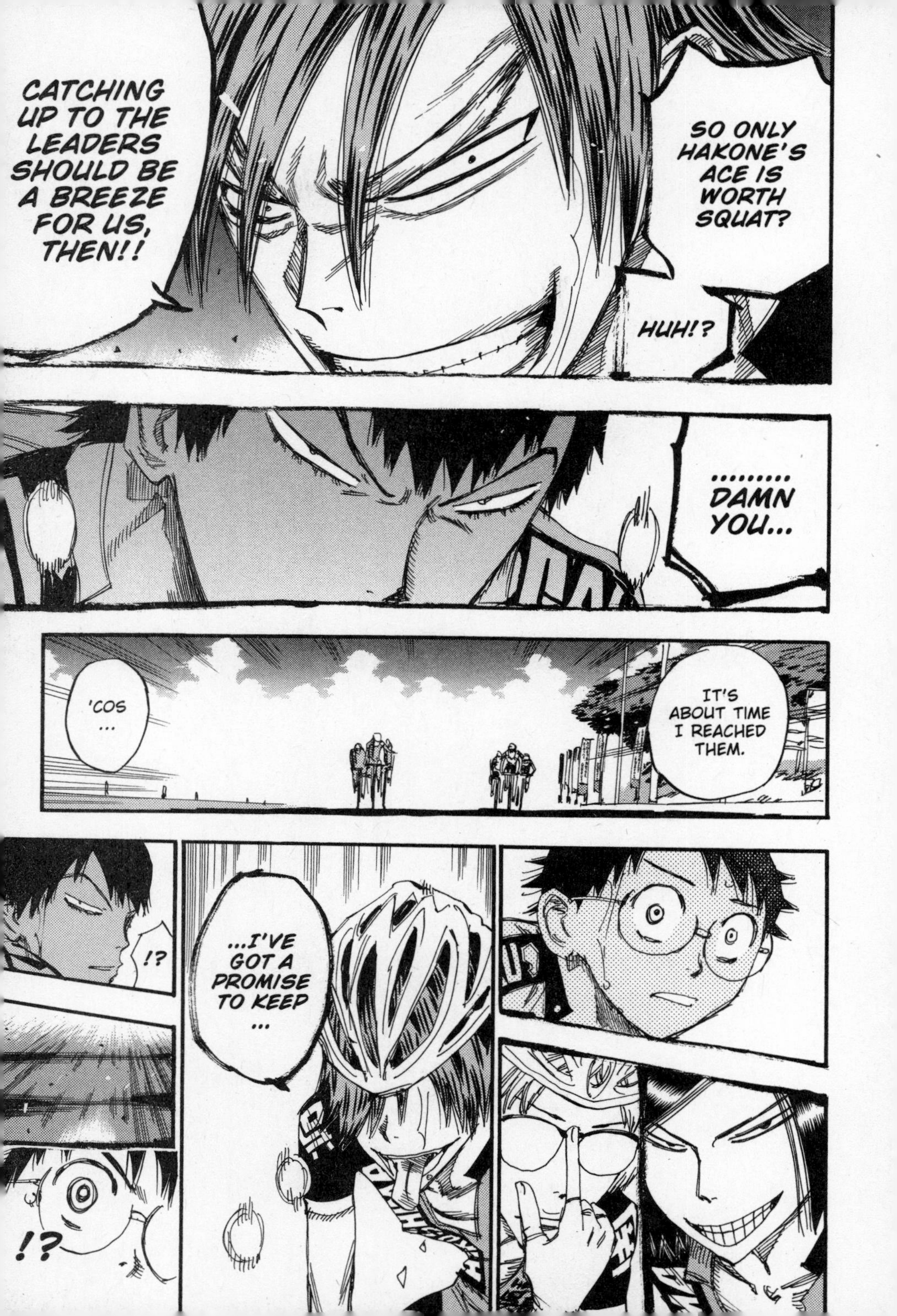
SO ONLY HAKONE'S ACE IS WORTH SQUAT?
HUH!?
CATCHING UP TO THE LEADERS SHOULD BE A BREEZE FOR US, THEN!!
.... DAMN YOU...
IT'S ABOUT TIME I REACHED THEM.
'COS ...
...I'VE GOT A PROMISE TO KEEP ...
!?
!?

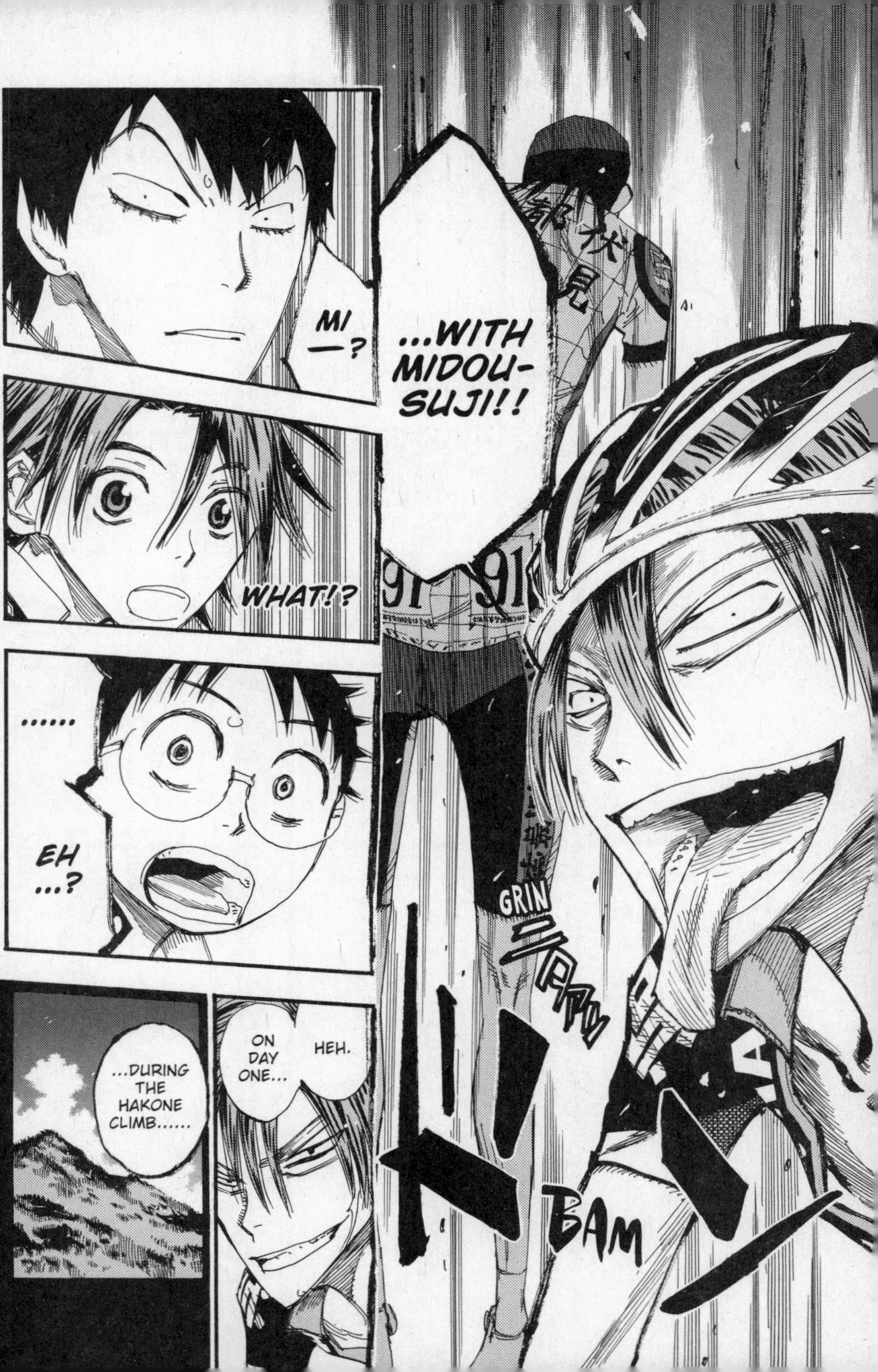
...WITH MIDOU-SUJI!!
GRIN
BAM
MI—?
WHAT!?
......
EH ...?
HEH.
ON DAY ONE...
...DURING THE HAKONE CLIMB......

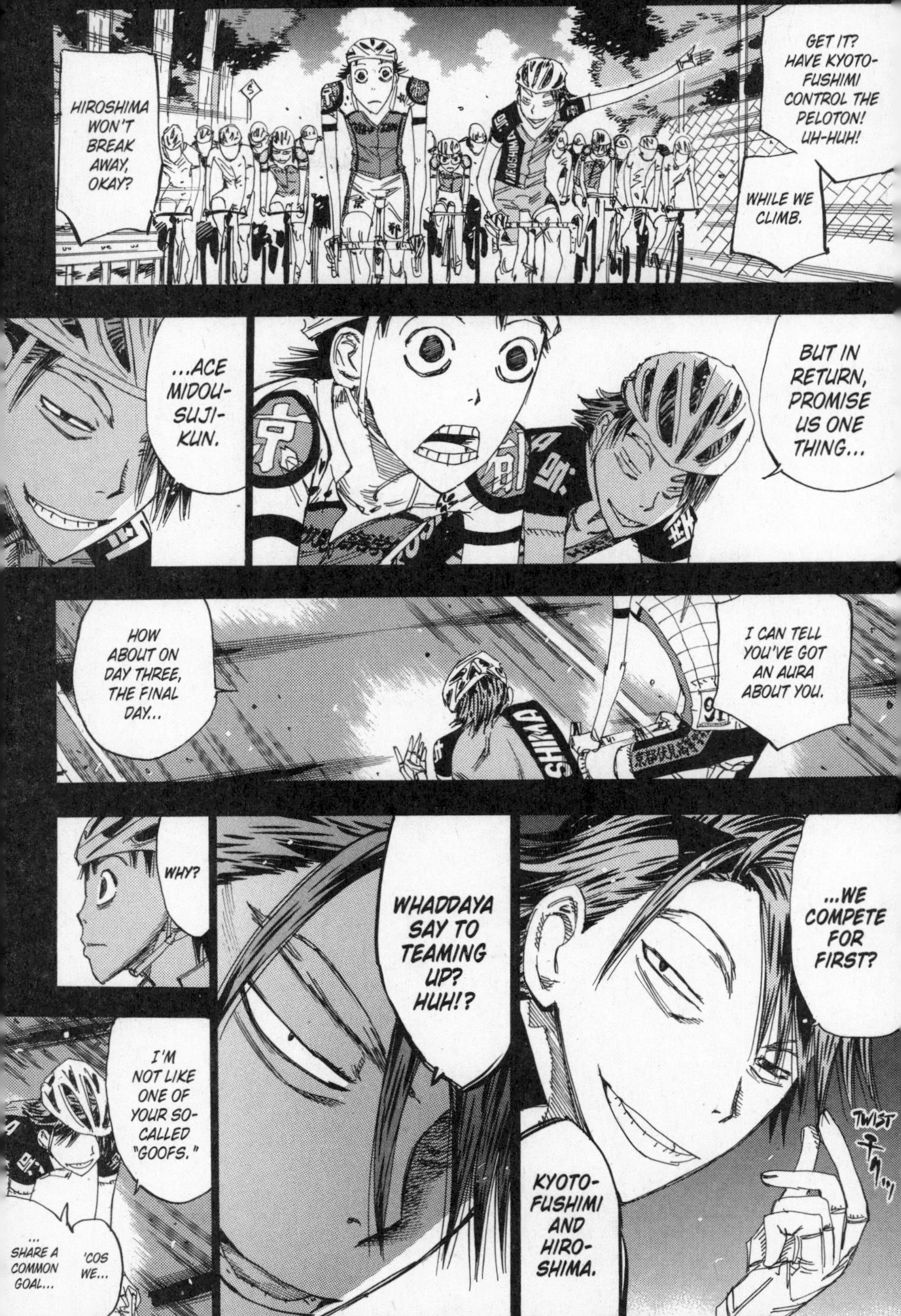
GET IT? HAVE KYOTO-FUSHIMI CONTROL THE PELOTON! UH-HUH!
WHILE WE CLIMB.
HIROSHIMA WON'T BREAK AWAY, OKAY?
BUT IN RETURN, PROMISE US ONE THING...
...ACE MIDOU-SUJI-KUN.
I CAN TELL YOU'VE GOT AN AURA ABOUT YOU.
HOW ABOUT ON DAY THREE, THE FINAL DAY...
...WE COMPETE FOR FIRST?
TWIST
KYOTO-FUSHIMI AND HIRO-SHIMA.
WHADDAYA SAY TO TEAMING UP? HUH!?
WHY?
I'M NOT LIKE ONE OF YOUR SO-CALLED "GOOFS."
'COS WE...
...SHARE A COMMON GOAL...

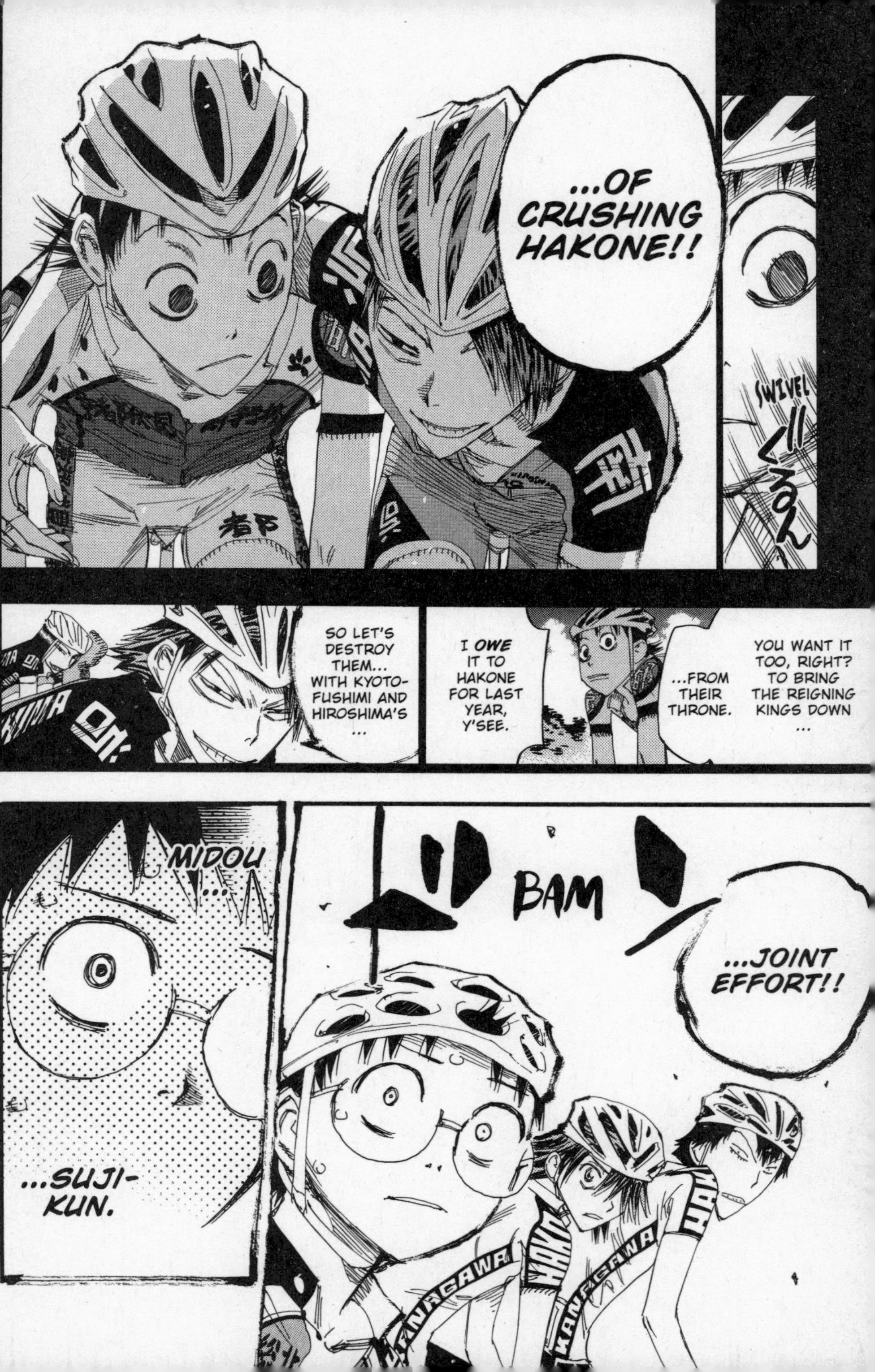
SWIVEL
くるん
...OF CRUSHING HAKONE!!
YOU WANT IT TOO, RIGHT? TO BRING THE REIGNING KINGS DOWN ...
...FROM THEIR THRONE.
I *OWE* IT TO HAKONE FOR LAST YEAR, Y'SEE.
SO LET'S DESTROY THEM... WITH KYOTO-FUSHIMI AND HIROSHIMA'S ...
BAM
...JOINT EFFORT!!
MIDOU ...
...SUJI-KUN.

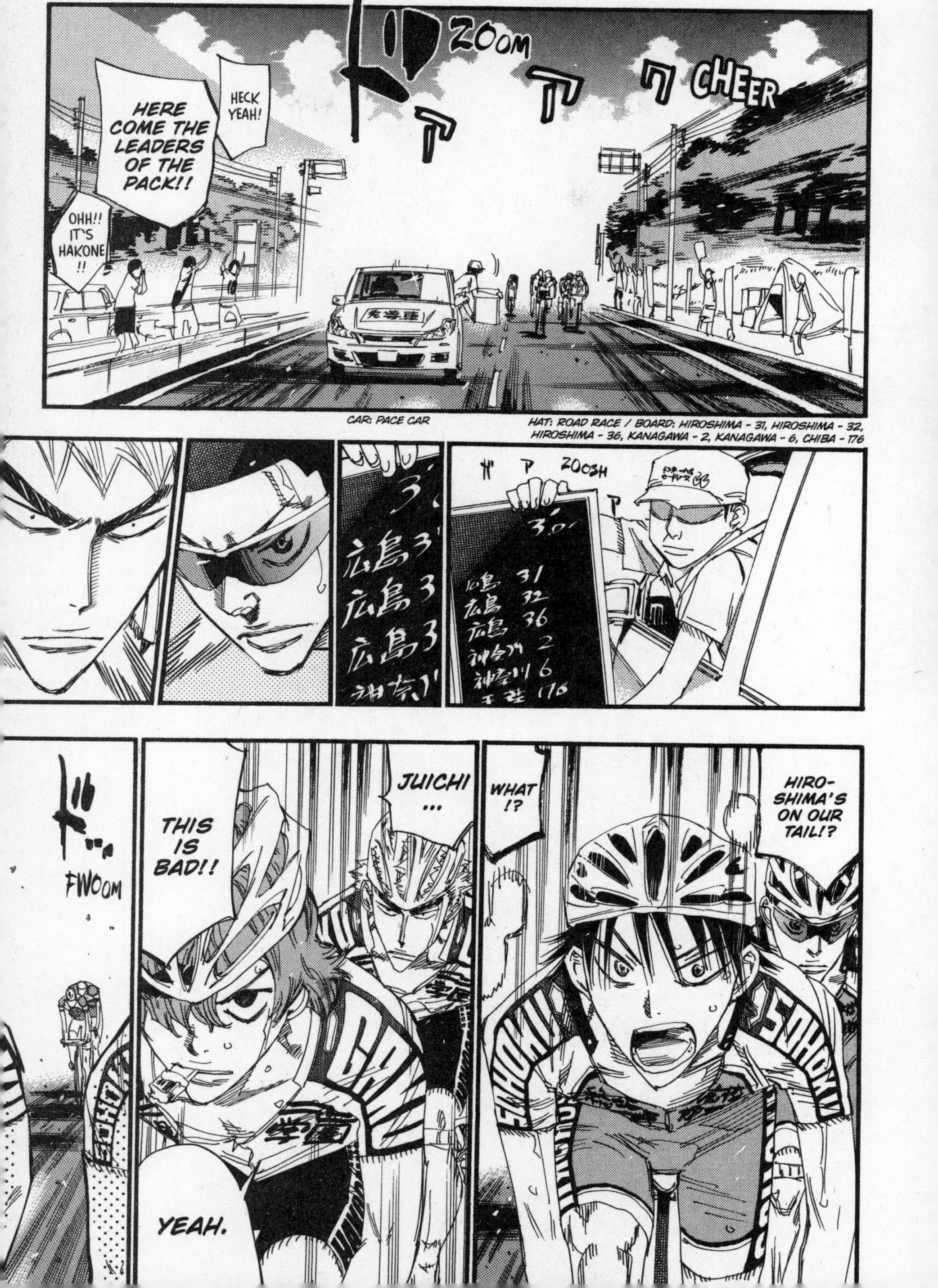
CHEER
ZOOM
HECK YEAH!
HERE COME THE LEADERS OF THE PACK!!
OHH!! IT'S HAKONE!!
CAR: PACE CAR
HAT: ROAD RACE / BOARD: HIROSHIMA - 31, HIROSHIMA - 32, HIROSHIMA - 36, KANAGAWA - 2, KANAGAWA - 6, CHIBA - 176
ZOOSH
HIRO-SHIMA'S ON OUR TAIL!?
WHAT!?
JUICHI...
THIS IS BAD!!
YEAH.
FWOOM

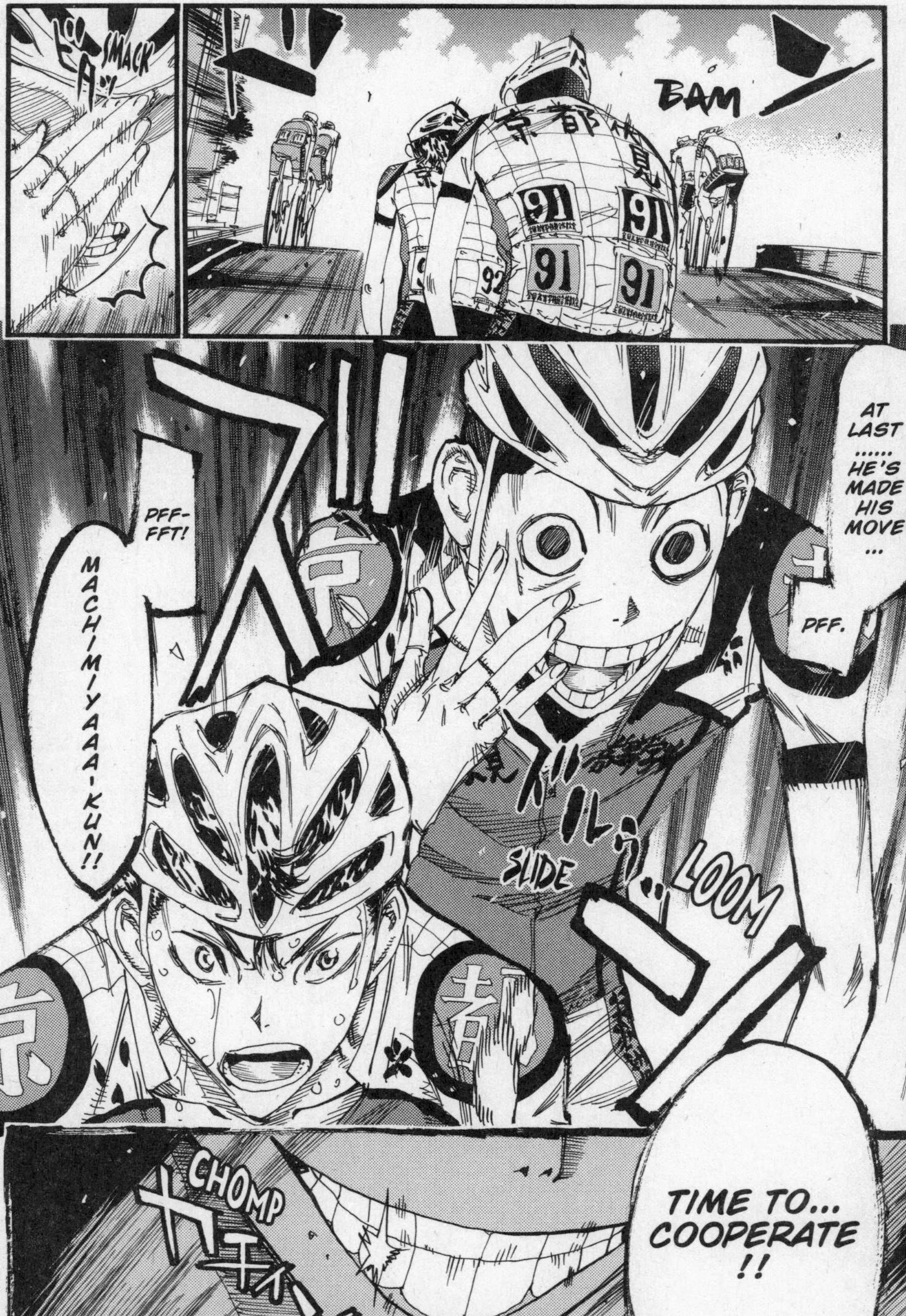

BAM
SMACK
AT LAST ...... HE'S MADE HIS MOVE ...
PFF.
PFF-FFT!
MACHIMIYAAAA-KUN!!
SLIDE
LOOM
TIME TO... COOPERATE !!
CHOMP

RIDE.172 THE PIT DOG'S HOWL!

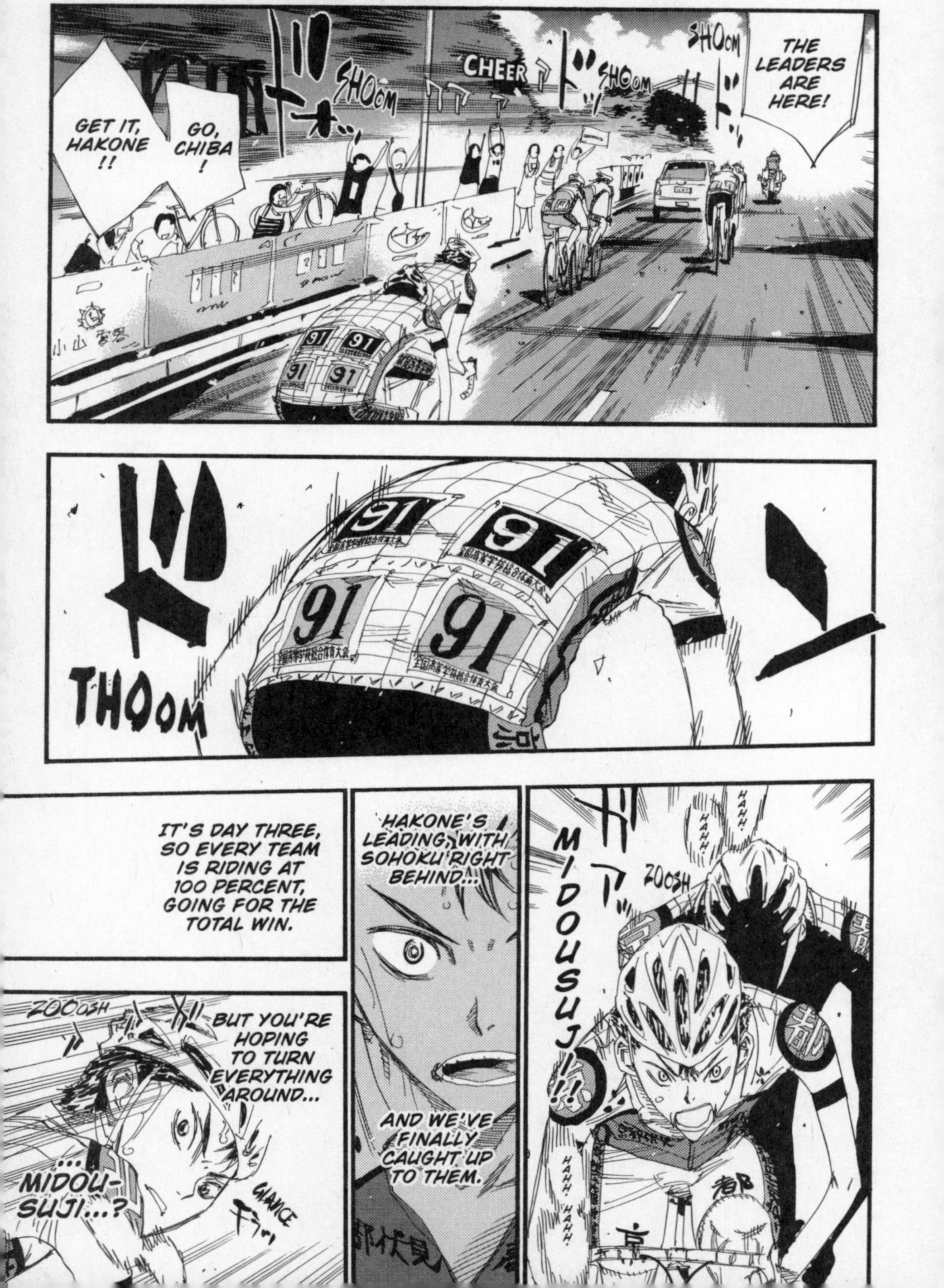
THE LEADERS ARE HERE!
SHOOM
SHOOM
CHEER
SHOOM
GO, CHIBA!
GET IT, HAKONE!!
THOOM
HAHH
HAHH
HAHH
MIDOUSUJI!!!
ZOOSH
HAHH
HAHH
HAKONE'S LEADING, WITH SOHOKU RIGHT BEHIND...
AND WE'VE FINALLY CAUGHT UP TO THEM.
IT'S DAY THREE, SO EVERY TEAM IS RIDING AT 100 PERCENT, GOING FOR THE TOTAL WIN.
ZOOOSH
BUT YOU'RE HOPING TO TURN EVERYTHING AROUND...
...MIDOU-SUJI...?
GLANCE

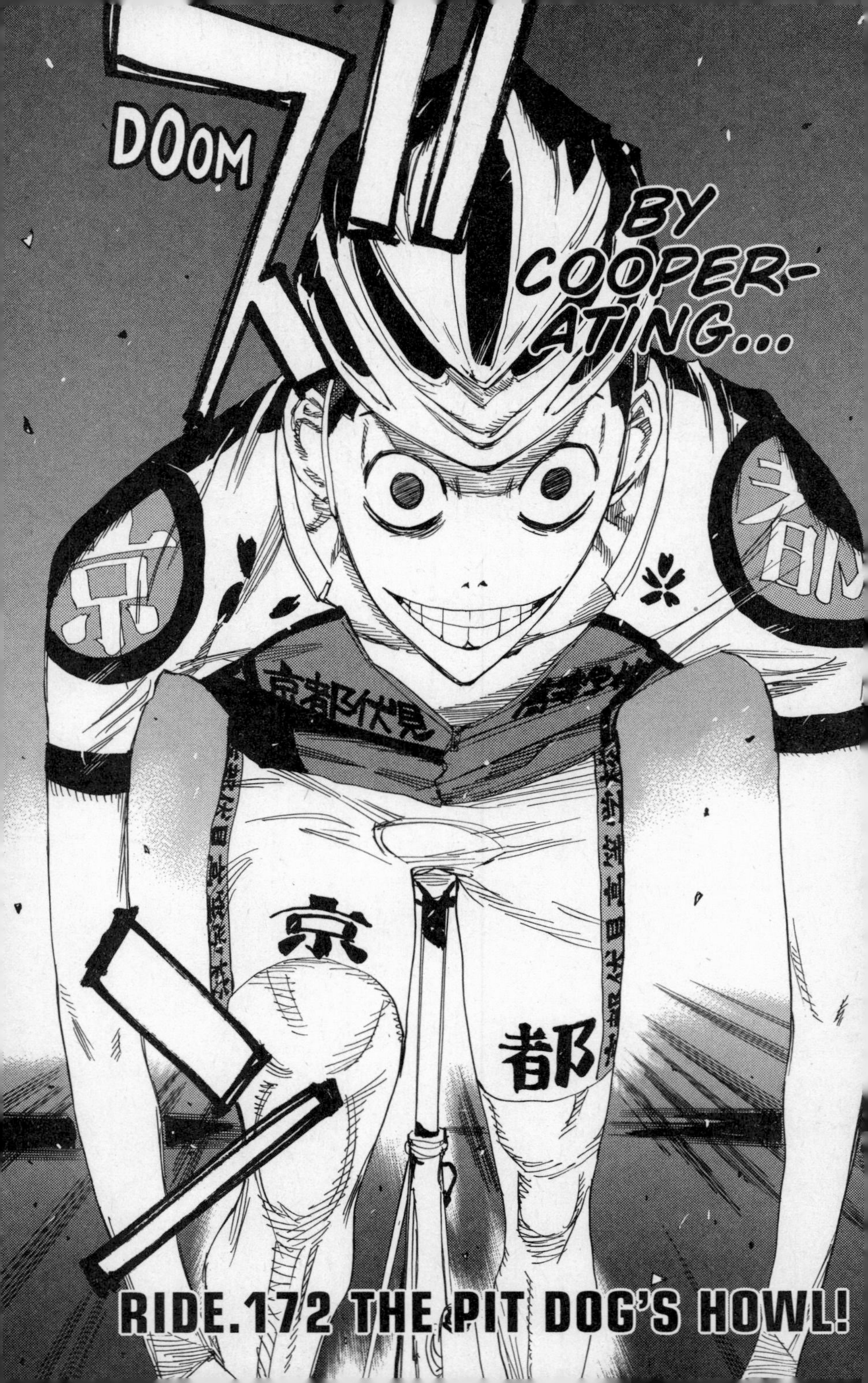

RIDE.172 THE PIT DOG'S HOWL!

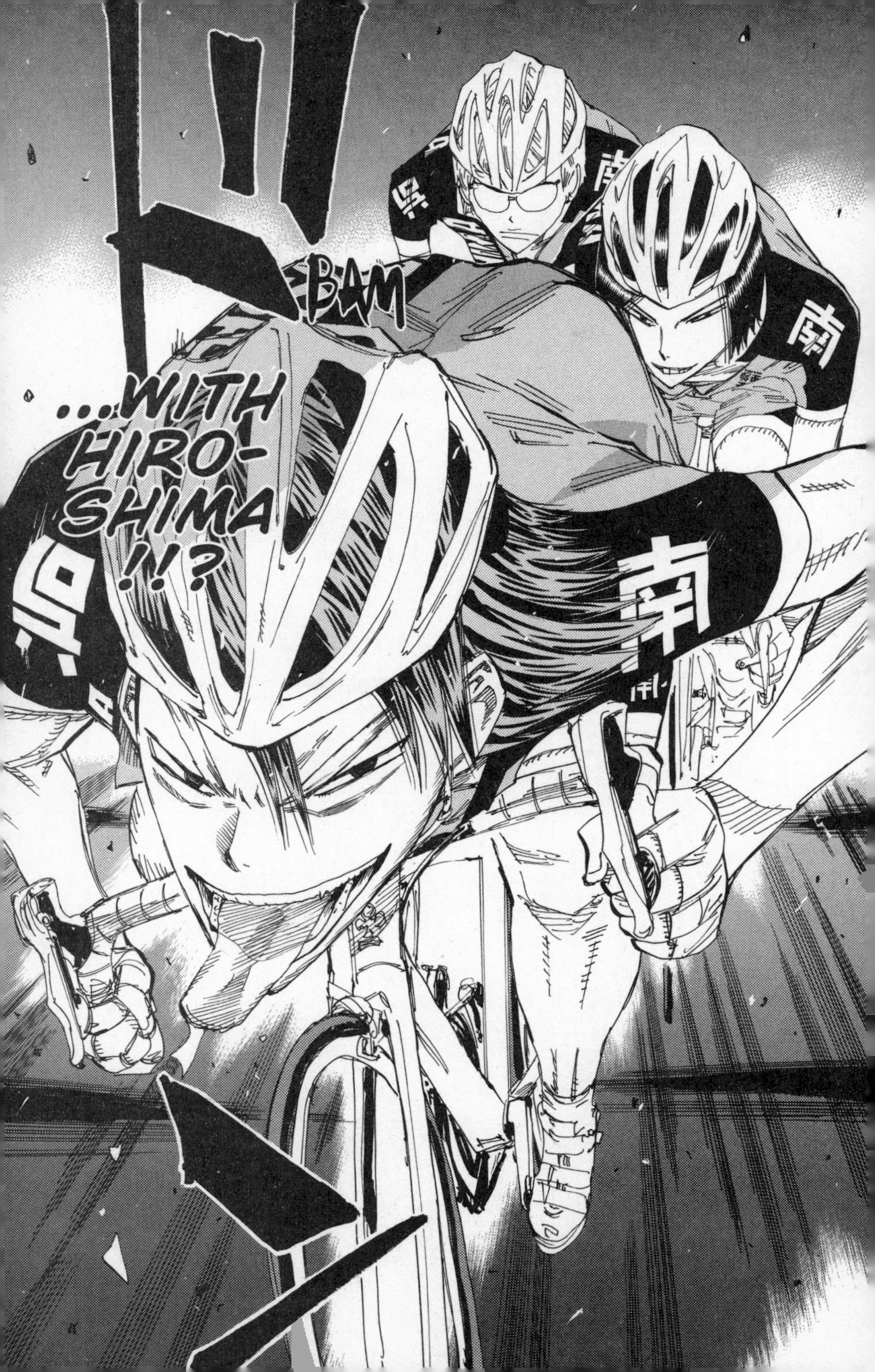
BAM
...WITH HIRO-SHIMA !!?

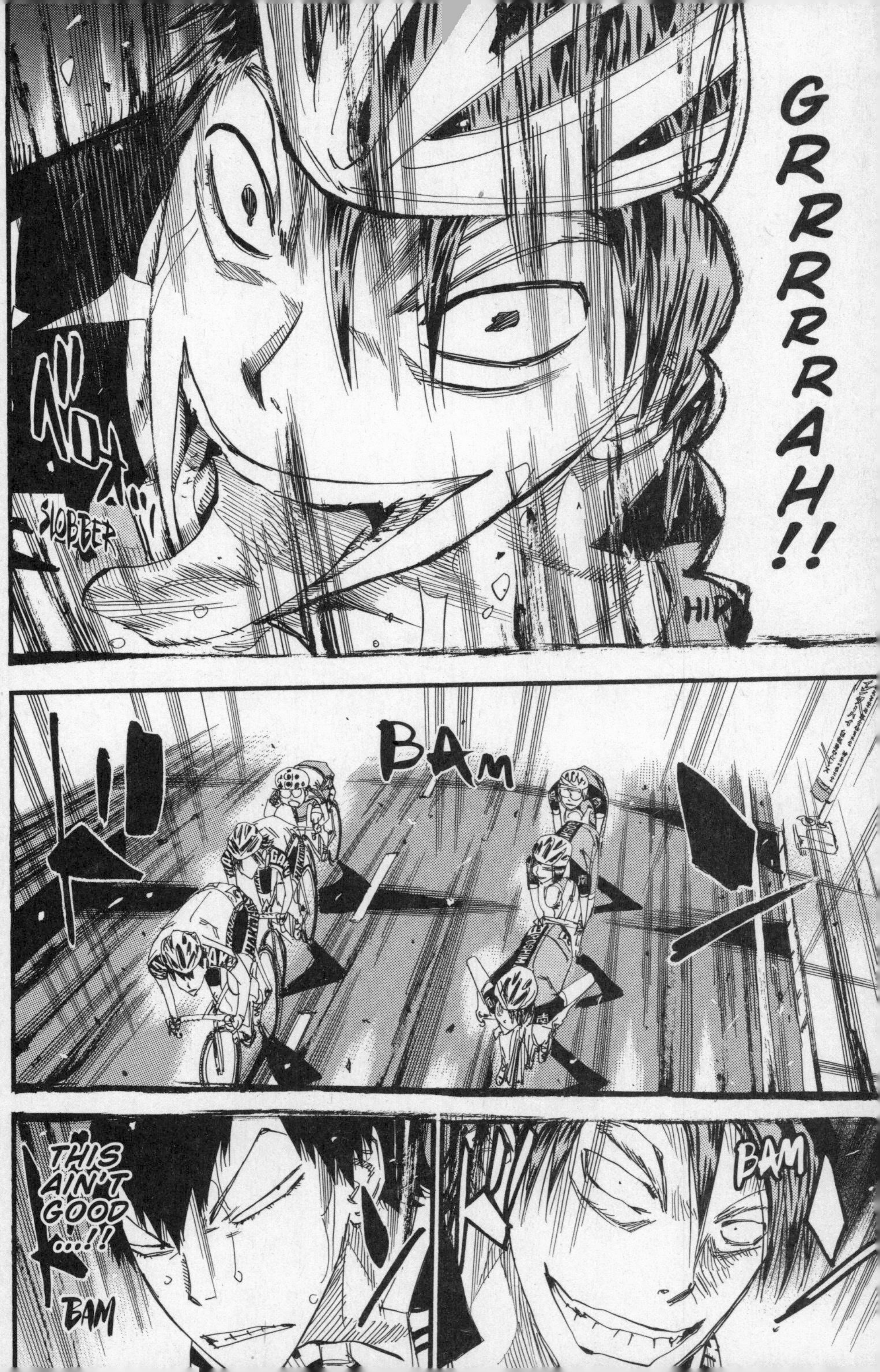
GRRRRRAH!!
HIR
SLOBBER
BAM
BAM
THIS AIN'T GOOD ...!!
BAM

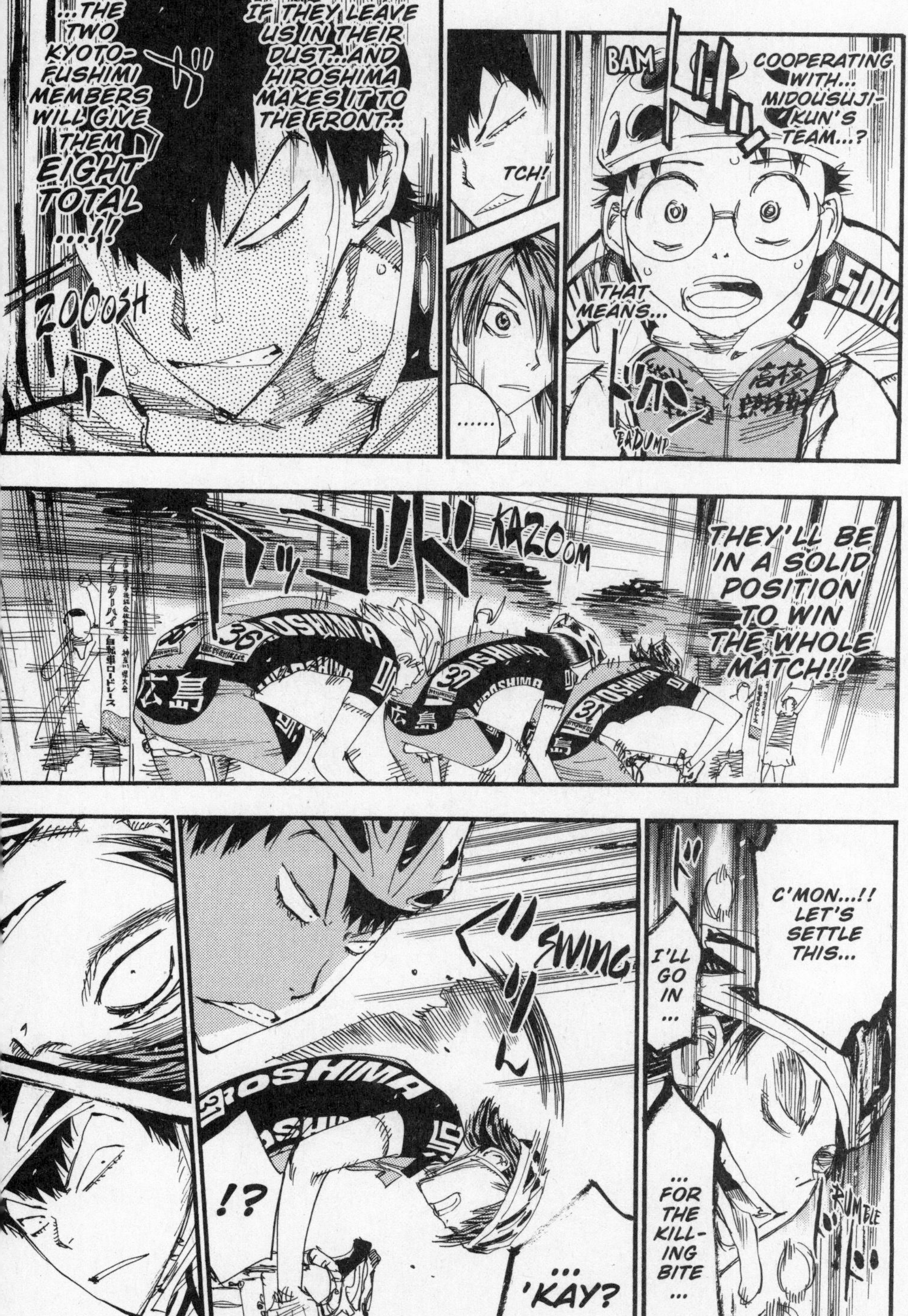
BAM
COOPERATING WITH... MIDOUSUJI-KUN'S TEAM...?
THAT MEANS...
BADUMP
TCH!
......
IF THEY LEAVE US IN THEIR DUST... AND HIROSHIMA MAKES IT TO THE FRONT...
...THE TWO KYOTO-FUSHIMI MEMBERS WILL GIVE THEM EIGHT TOTAL...!!
ZOOOSH
THEY'LL BE IN A SOLID POSITION TO WIN THE WHOLE MATCH!!
KAZOOM
C'MON...!! LET'S SETTLE THIS...
I'LL GO IN...
...FOR THE KILLING BITE...
RUMBLE
SWING
!?
...'KAY?

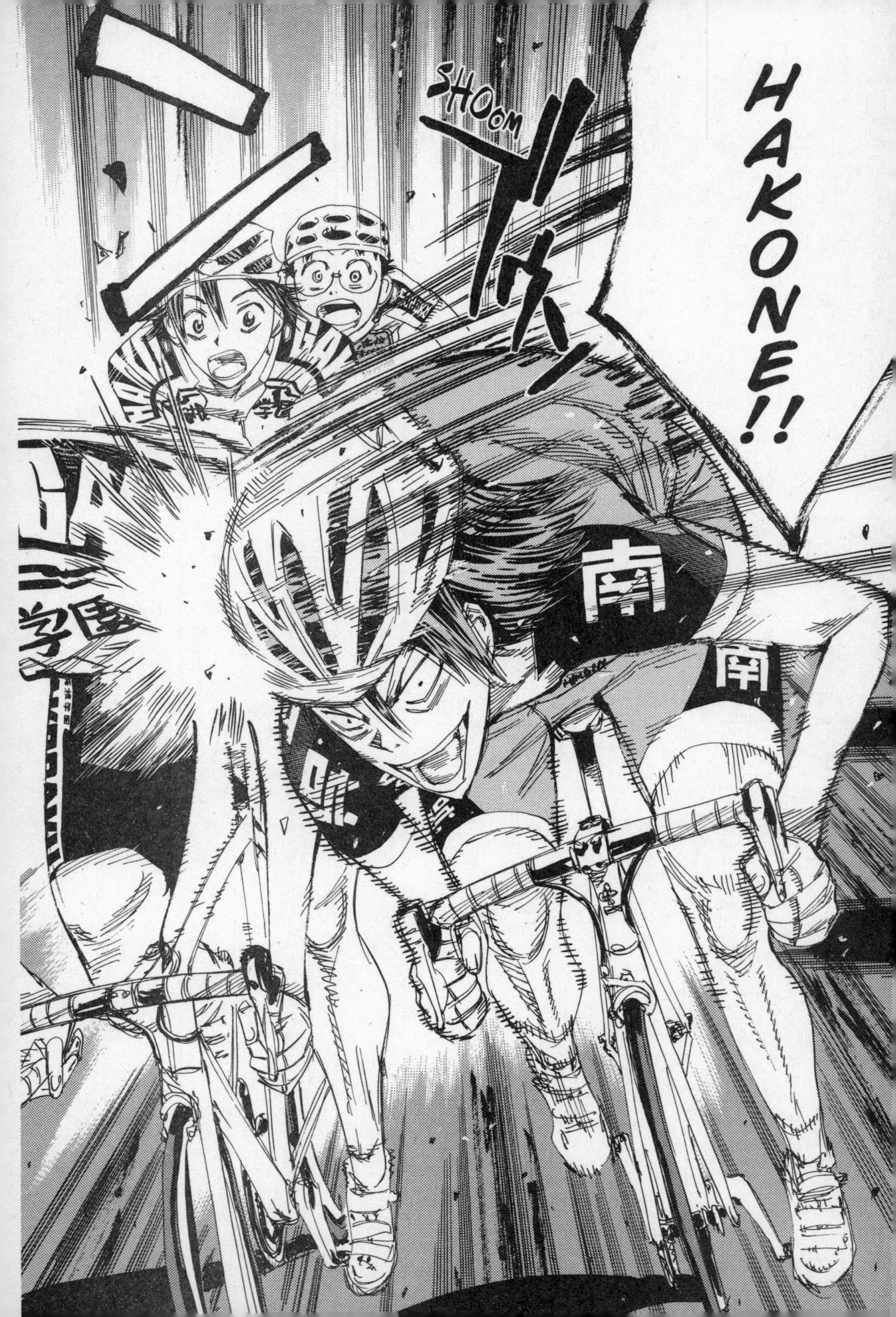
HAKONE!!
SHOOM

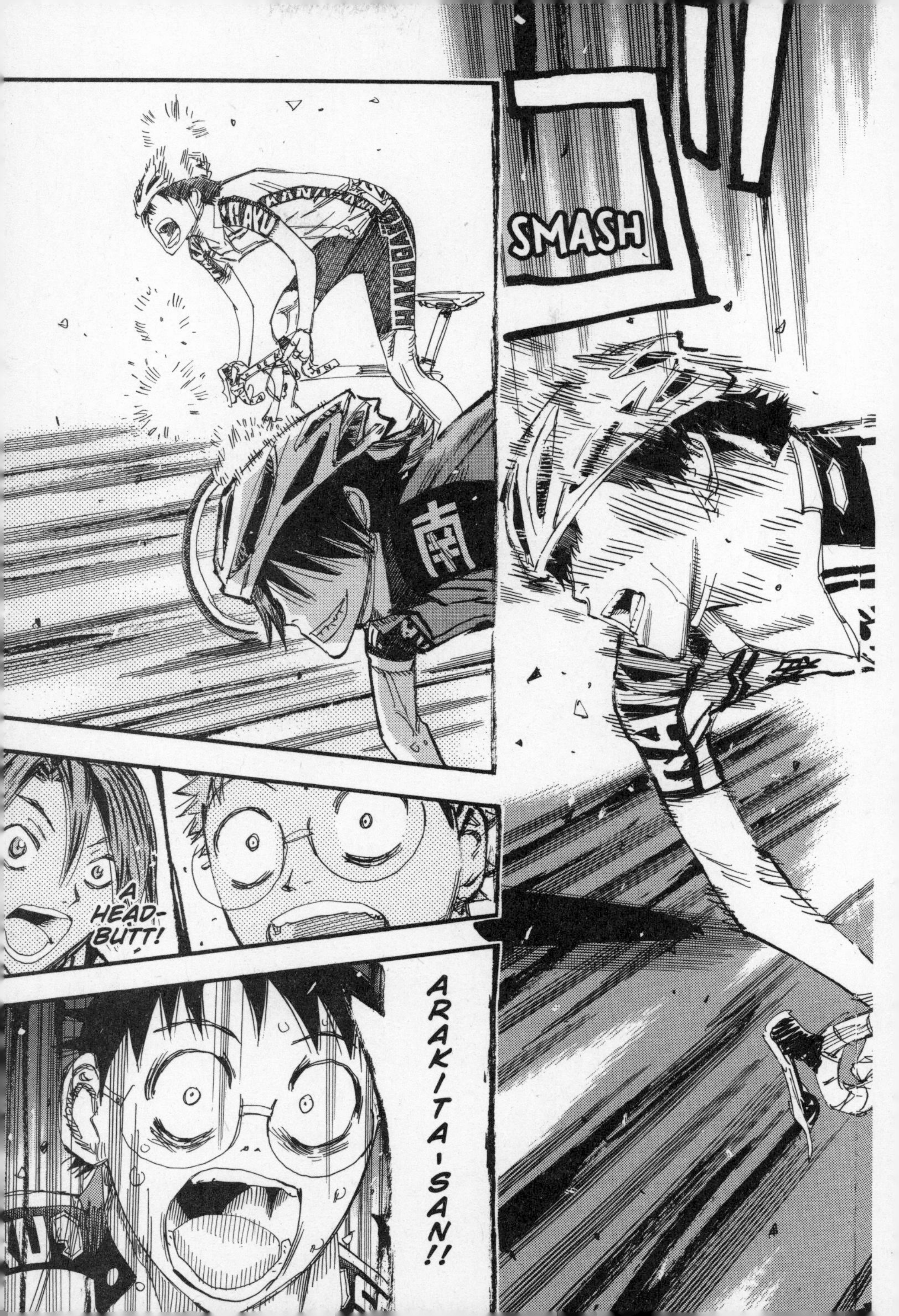
SMASH
A HEAD-BUTT!
ARAKITA-SAN!!

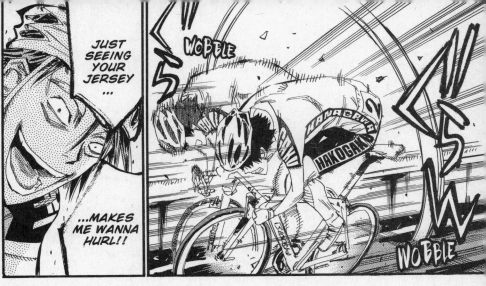

JUST SEEING YOUR JERSEY...

...MAKES ME WANNA HURL!!

WOBBLE

WOBBLE

PUTS ME IN THE WORST MOOD, I TELL YA!!

CHAK

CLICK

TH-THAT WAS CLOSE... THANK GOD...

HAHH! HAHH

BAM

....

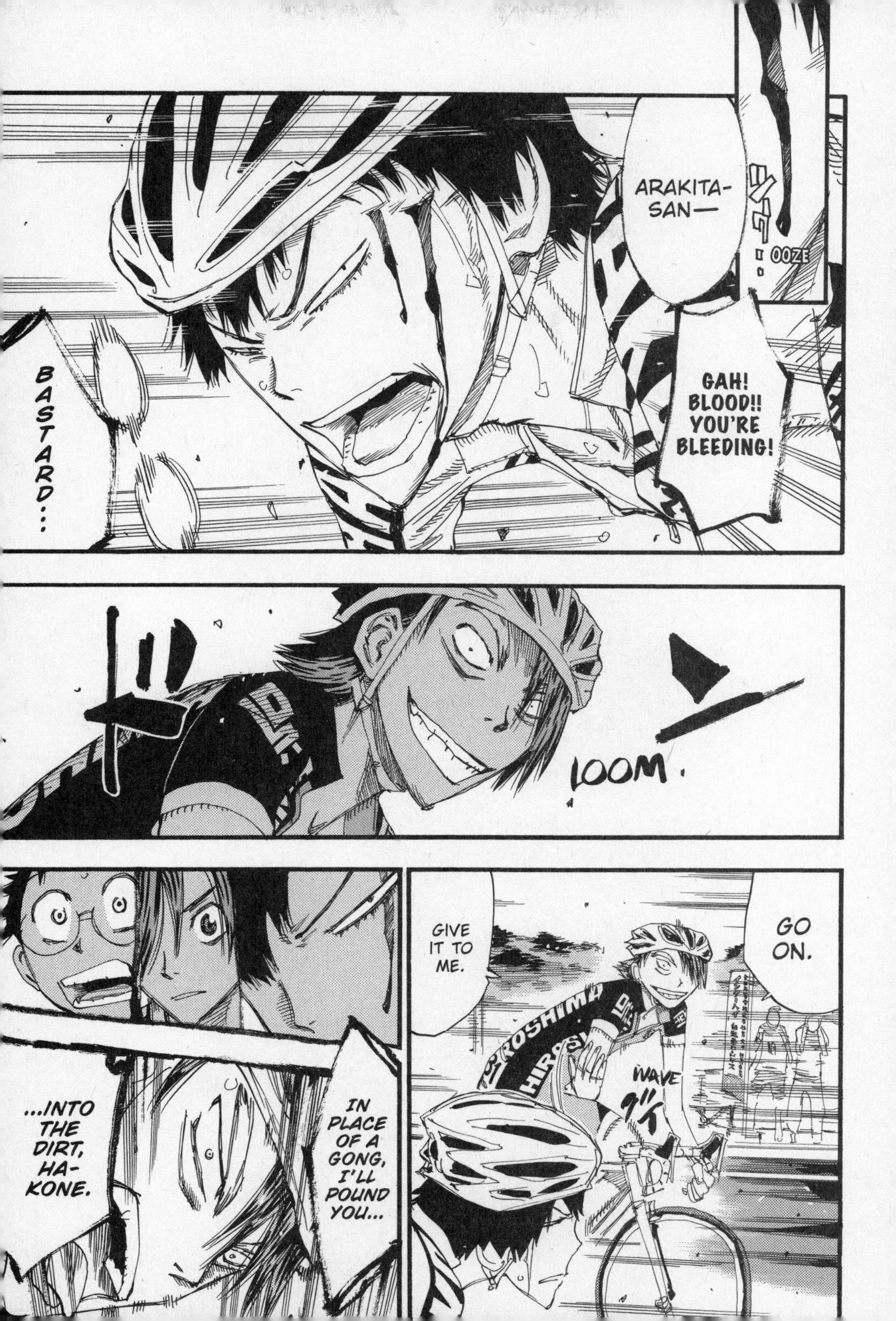
ARAKITA-SAN—
OOZE
GAH! BLOOD!! YOU'RE BLEEDING!
BASTARD...
LOOM
GO ON.
GIVE IT TO ME.
WAVE
IN PLACE OF A GONG, I'LL POUND YOU...
...INTO THE DIRT, HAKONE.

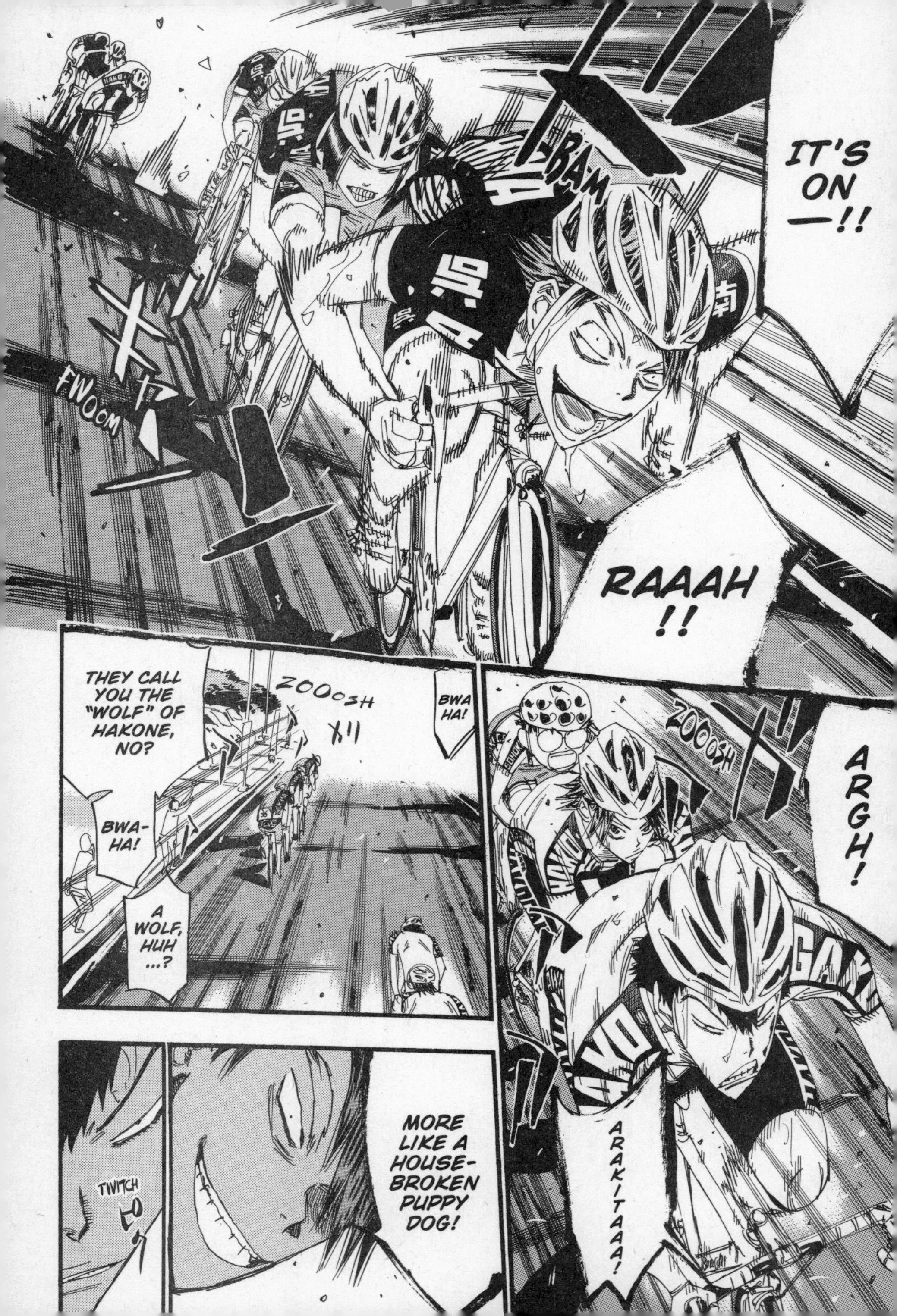
IT'S ON—!!
BAM
RAAAH !!
FWOOM
ARGH!
ZOOOSH
ARAKITAAA!
BWA HA!
ZOOOSH
THEY CALL YOU THE "WOLF" OF HAKONE, NO?
BWA-HA!
A WOLF, HUH ...?
MORE LIKE A HOUSE-BROKEN PUPPY DOG!
TWITCH

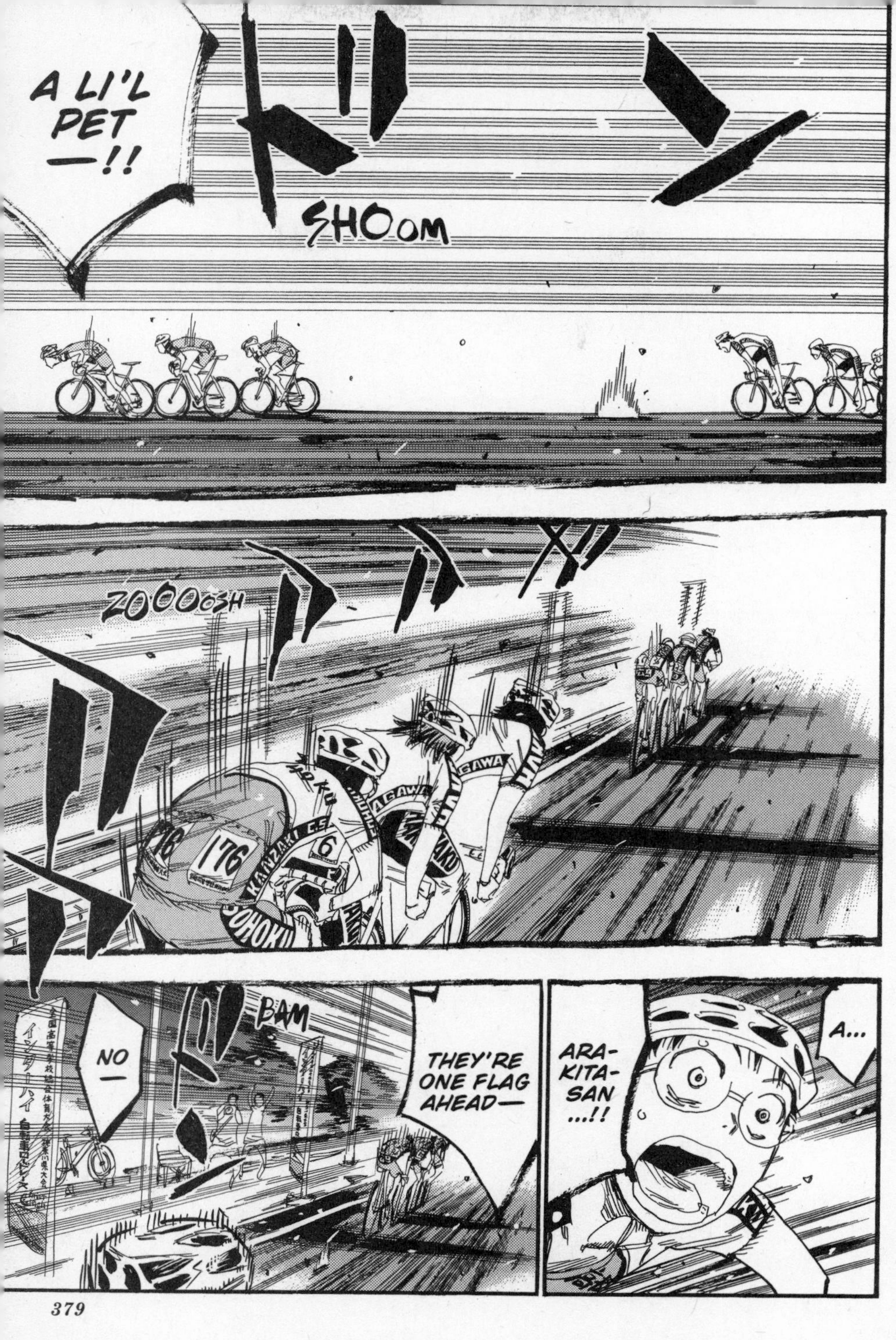
A LI'L PET—!!
SHOOM
ZOOOOOSH
A...
ARA-KITA-SAN...!!
THEY'RE ONE FLAG AHEAD—
BAM
NO—

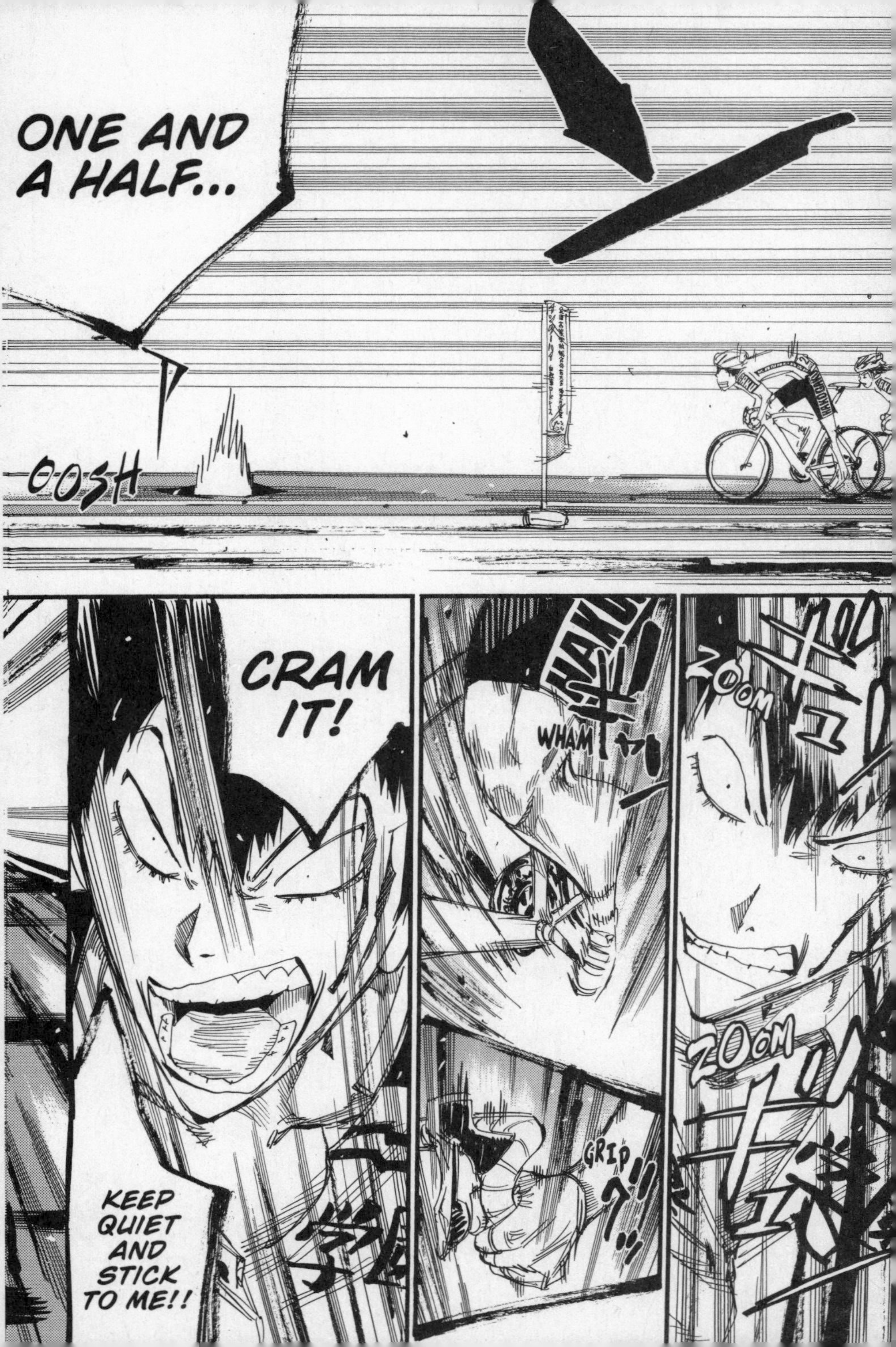
ONE AND A HALF...
OOSH
ZOOM
ZOOM
WHAM
GRIP
CRAM IT!
KEEP QUIET AND STICK TO ME!!

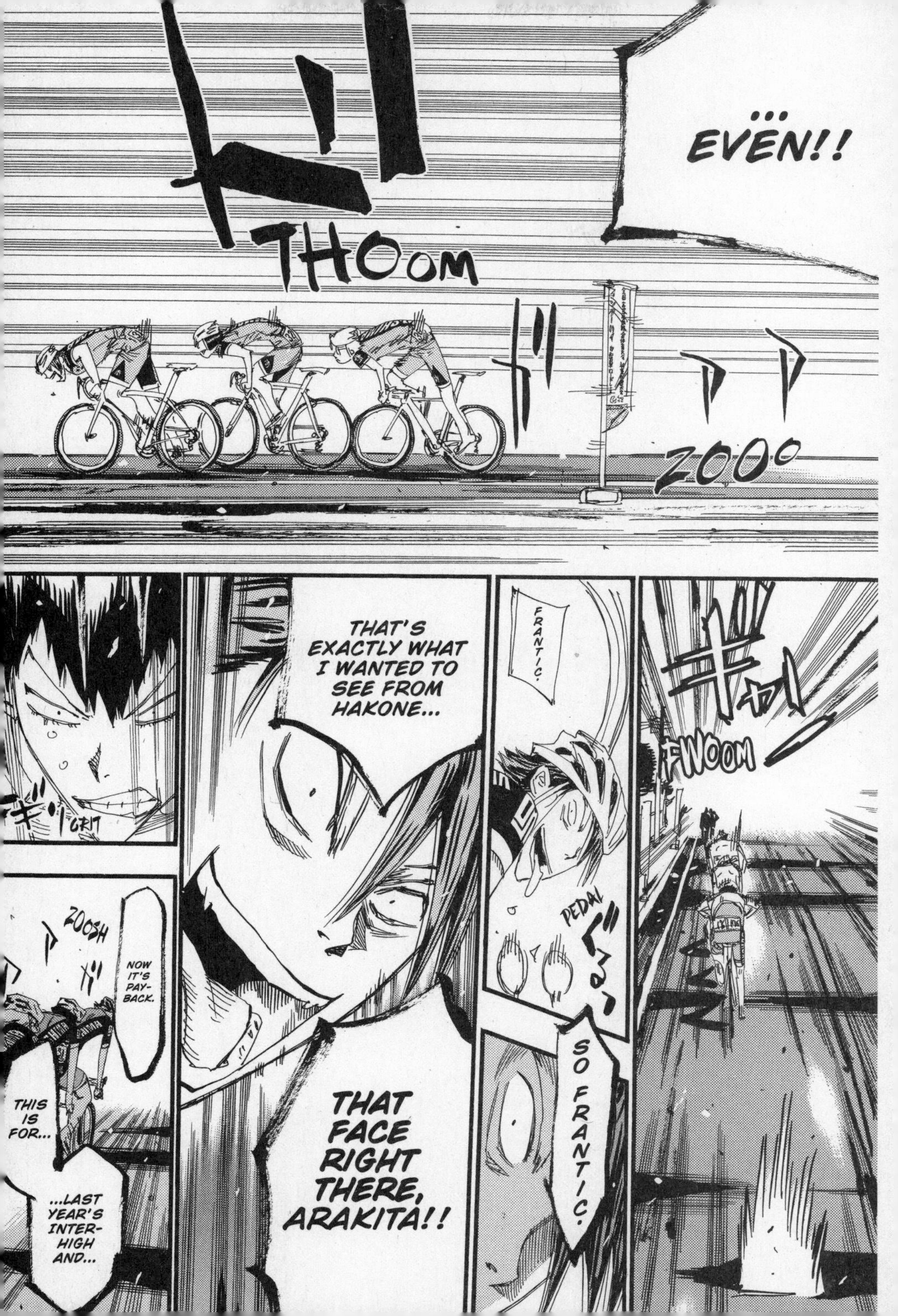

...EVEN!!
THOOM
ZOOO
FWOOM
FRANTIC.
PEDAL
SO FRANTIC.
THAT'S EXACTLY WHAT I WANTED TO SEE FROM HAKONE...
THAT FACE RIGHT THERE, ARAKITA!!
GRIT
ZOOSH
NOW IT'S PAY-BACK.
THIS IS FOR...
...LAST YEAR'S INTER-HIGH AND...

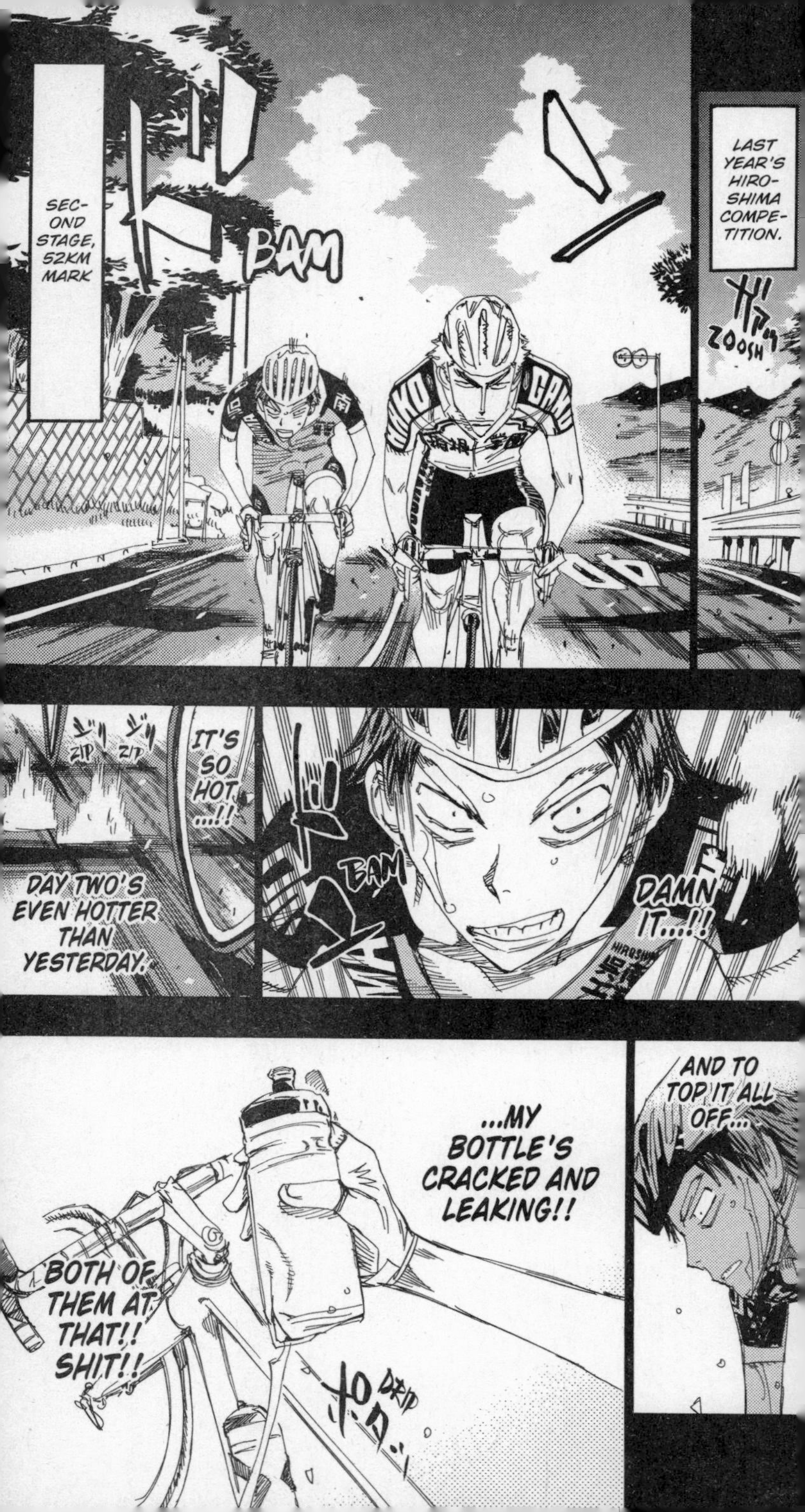
LAST YEAR'S HIRO-SHIMA COMPE-TITION.
ZOOSH
SEC-OND STAGE, 52KM MARK
BAM
BAM
DAMN IT...!!
IT'S SO HOT...!!
ZIP ZIP
DAY TWO'S EVEN HOTTER THAN YESTERDAY.
AND TO TOP IT ALL OFF...
...MY BOTTLE'S CRACKED AND LEAKING!!
BOTH OF THEM AT THAT!! SHIT!!
DRIP

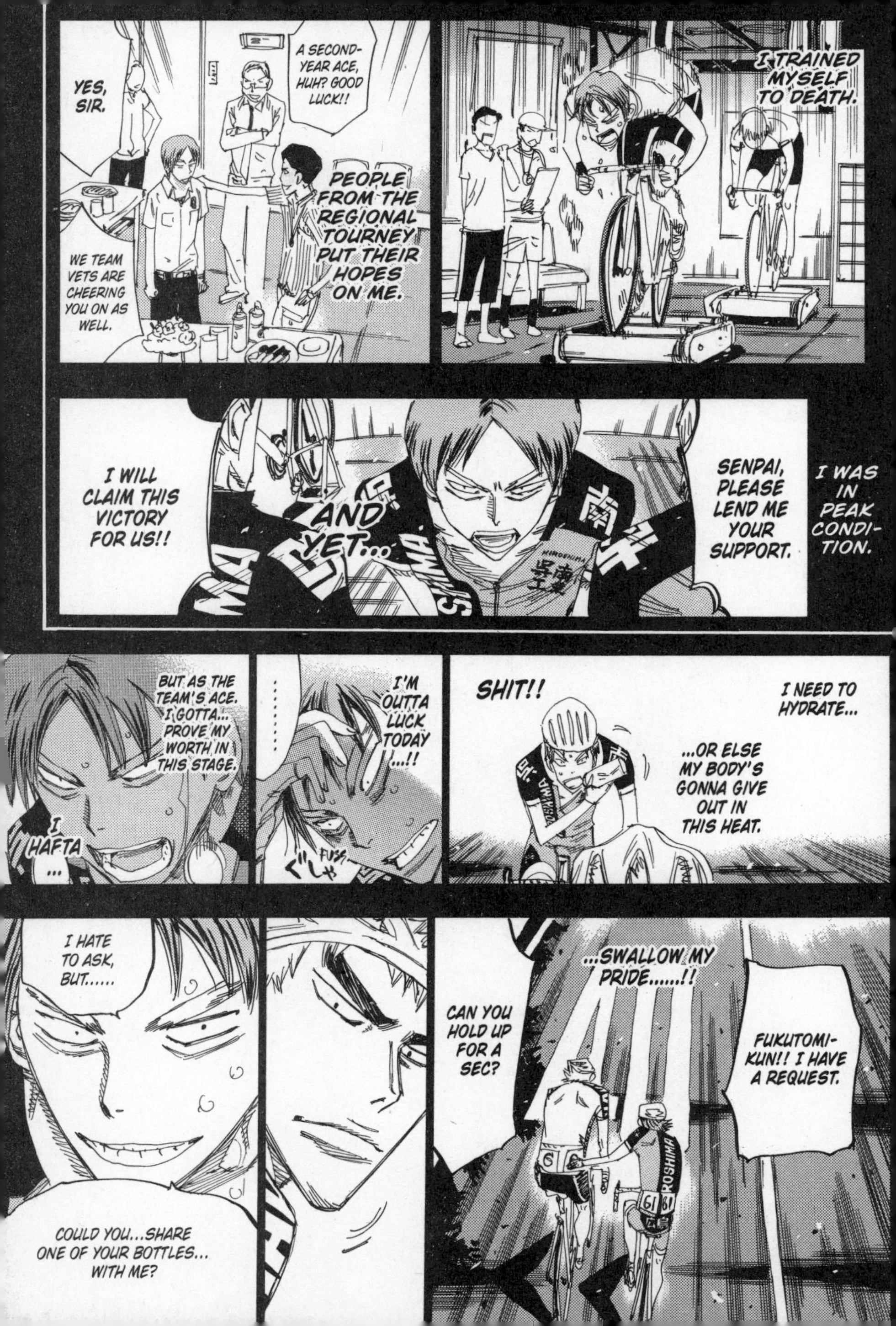

I TRAINED MYSELF TO DEATH.
A SECOND-YEAR ACE, HUH? GOOD LUCK!!
PEOPLE FROM THE REGIONAL TOURNEY PUT THEIR HOPES ON ME.
YES, SIR.
WE TEAM VETS ARE CHEERING YOU ON AS WELL.
I WAS IN PEAK CONDITION.
SENPAI, PLEASE LEND ME YOUR SUPPORT.
AND YET...
I WILL CLAIM THIS VICTORY FOR US!!
I NEED TO HYDRATE...
SHIT!!
...OR ELSE MY BODY'S GONNA GIVE OUT IN THIS HEAT.
I'M OUTTA LUCK TODAY...!!
......
FUSS ぐしゃ
BUT AS THE TEAM'S ACE, I GOTTA... PROVE MY WORTH IN THIS STAGE.
I HAFTA...
FUKUTOMI-KUN!! I HAVE A REQUEST.
...SWALLOW MY PRIDE......!!
CAN YOU HOLD UP FOR A SEC?
I HATE TO ASK, BUT......
COULD YOU...SHARE ONE OF YOUR BOTTLES... WITH ME?

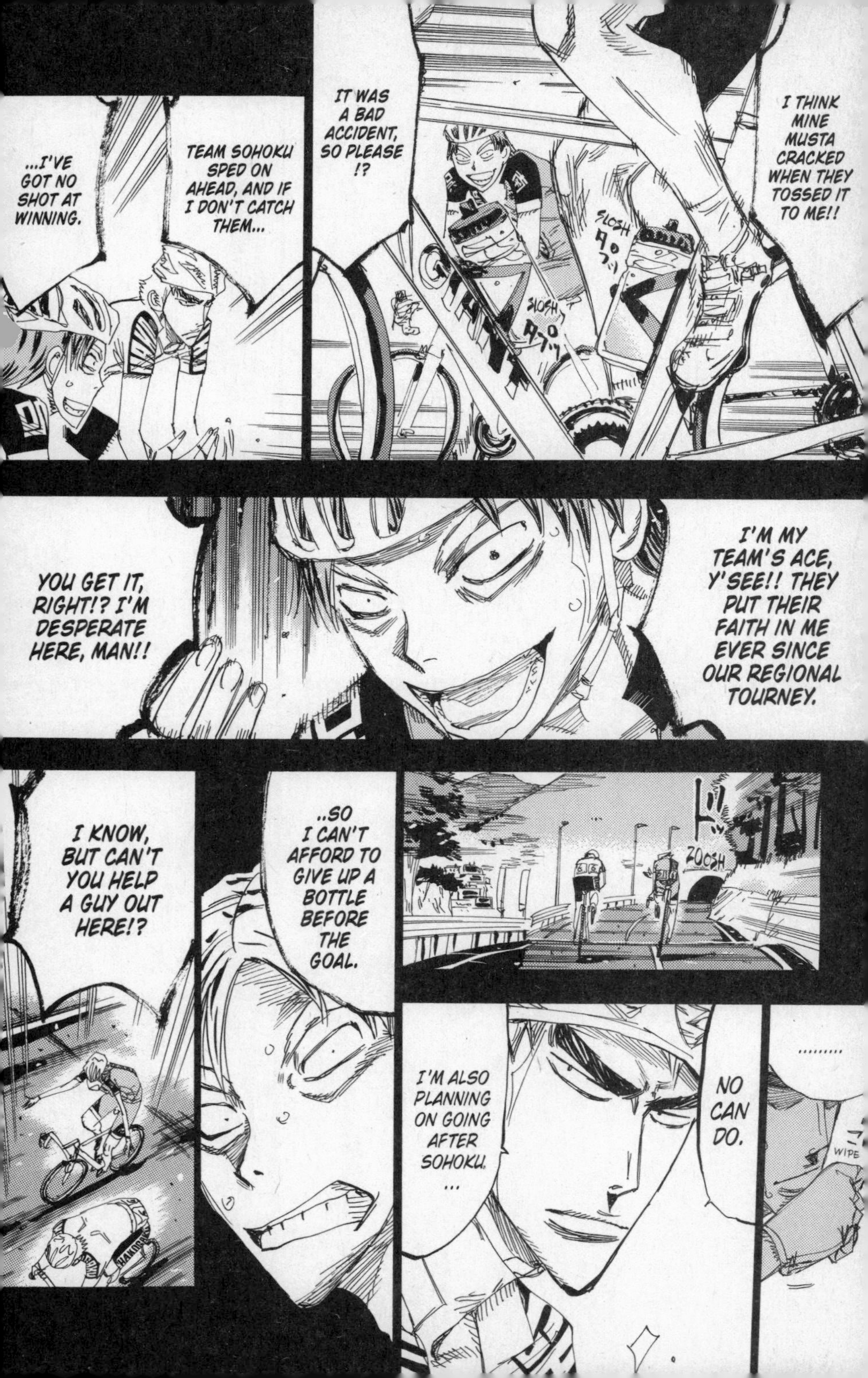
I THINK MINE MUSTA CRACKED WHEN THEY TOSSED IT TO ME!!
SLOSH
SLOSH
IT WAS A BAD ACCIDENT, SO PLEASE !?
TEAM SOHOKU SPED ON AHEAD, AND IF I DON'T CATCH THEM...
...I'VE GOT NO SHOT AT WINNING.
I'M MY TEAM'S ACE, Y'SEE!! THEY PUT THEIR FAITH IN ME EVER SINCE OUR REGIONAL TOURNEY.
YOU GET IT, RIGHT!? I'M DESPERATE HERE, MAN!!
ZOOSH
....
WIPE
NO CAN DO.
I'M ALSO PLANNING ON GOING AFTER SOHOKU. ...
..SO I CAN'T AFFORD TO GIVE UP A BOTTLE BEFORE THE GOAL.
I KNOW, BUT CAN'T YOU HELP A GUY OUT HERE!?

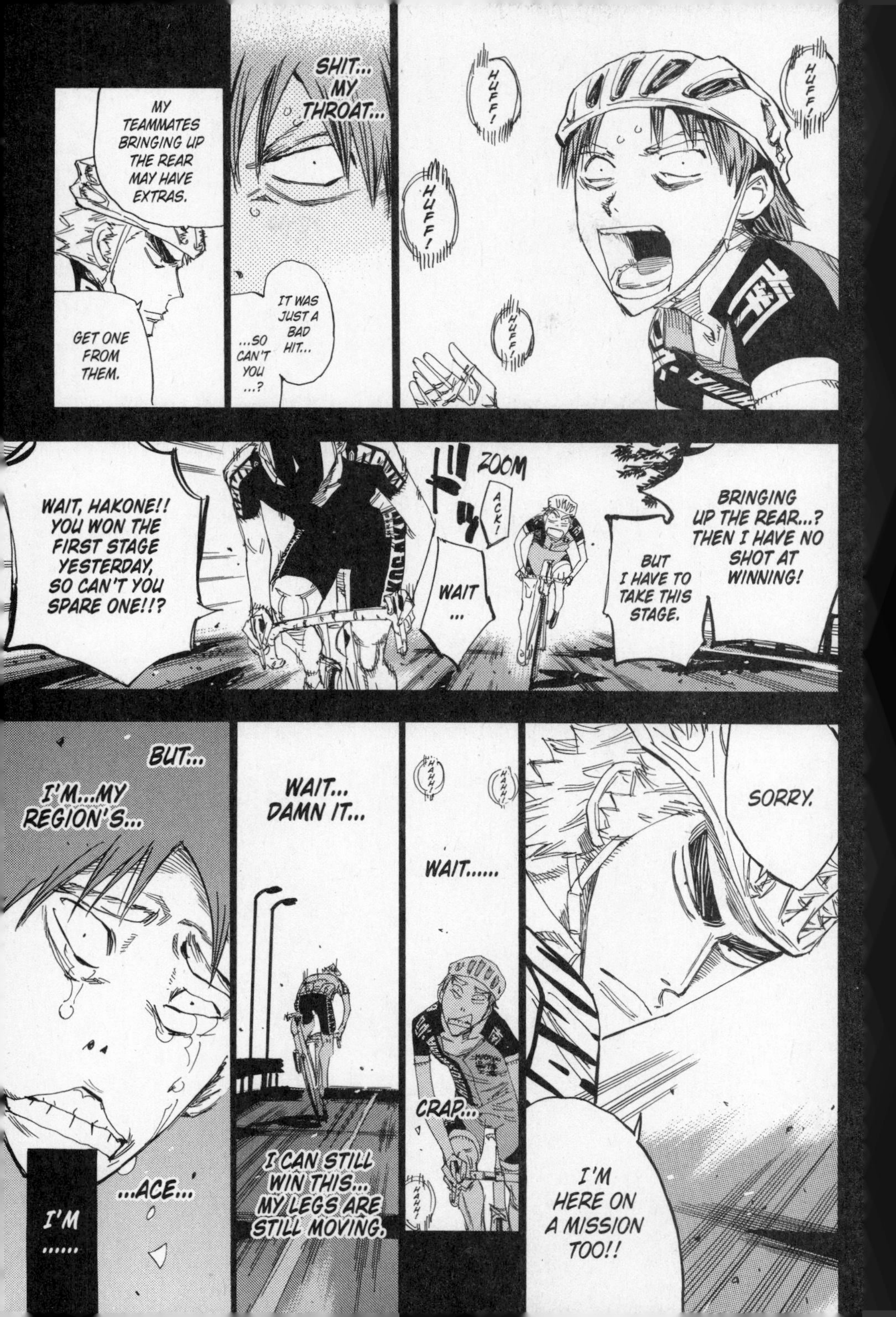
HUFF!
HUFF!
HUFF!
HUFF!
SHIT... MY THROAT...
IT WAS JUST A BAD HIT...
...SO CAN'T YOU ...?
MY TEAMMATES BRINGING UP THE REAR MAY HAVE EXTRAS.
GET ONE FROM THEM.
BRINGING UP THE REAR...? THEN I HAVE NO SHOT AT WINNING!
BUT I HAVE TO TAKE THIS STAGE.
ZOOM
ACK!
WAIT ...
WAIT, HAKONE!! YOU WON THE FIRST STAGE YESTERDAY, SO CAN'T YOU SPARE ONE!!?
SORRY.
I'M HERE ON A MISSION TOO!!
HAHH
HAHH
WAIT......
CRAP...
HAHH
WAIT... DAMN IT...
I CAN STILL WIN THIS... MY LEGS ARE STILL MOVING.
BUT...
I'M...MY REGION'S...
...ACE...
I'M ......

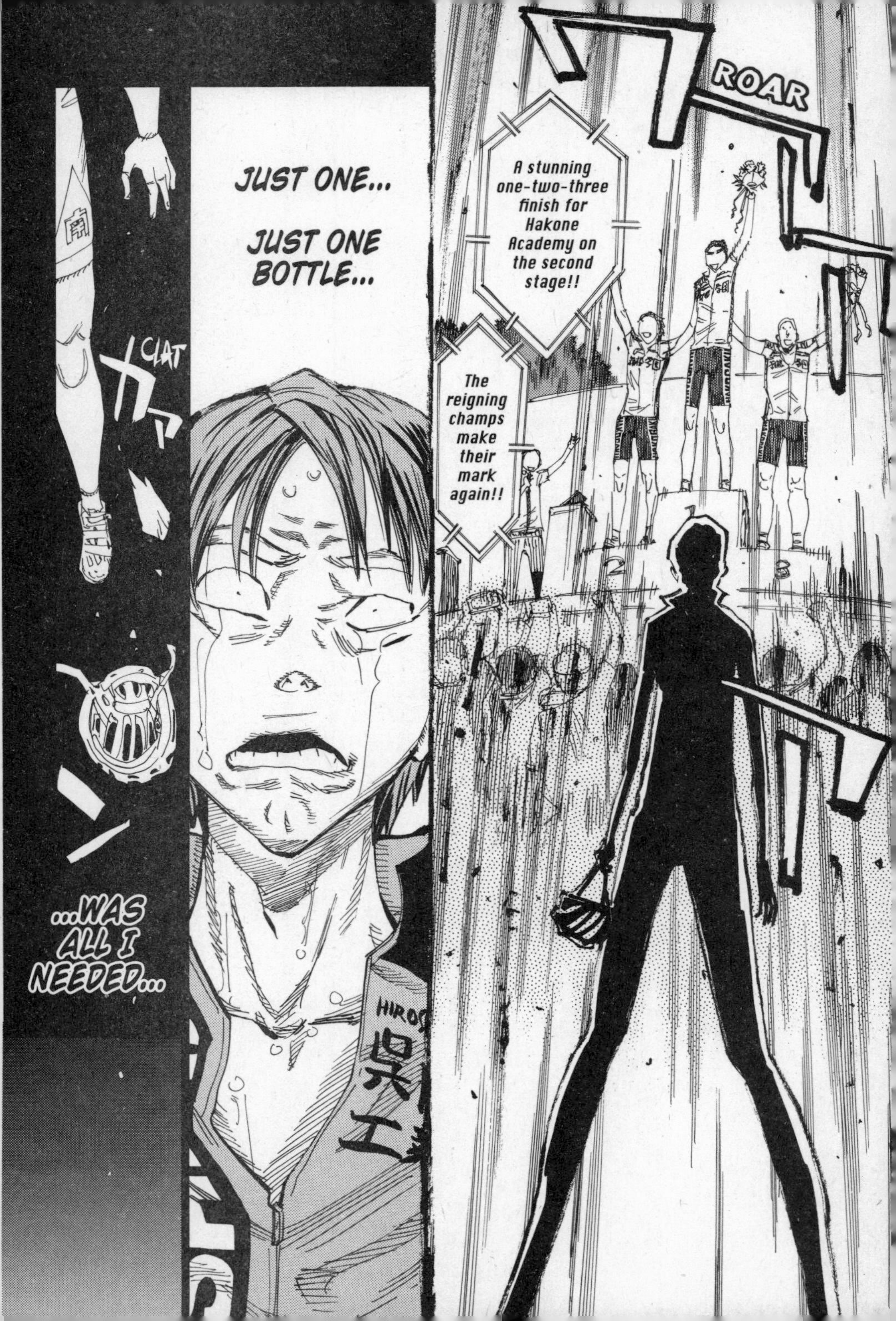
ROAR
A stunning one-two-three finish for Hakone Academy on the second stage!!
The reigning champs make their mark again!!
JUST ONE...
JUST ONE BOTTLE...
CLAT
...WAS ALL I NEEDED...

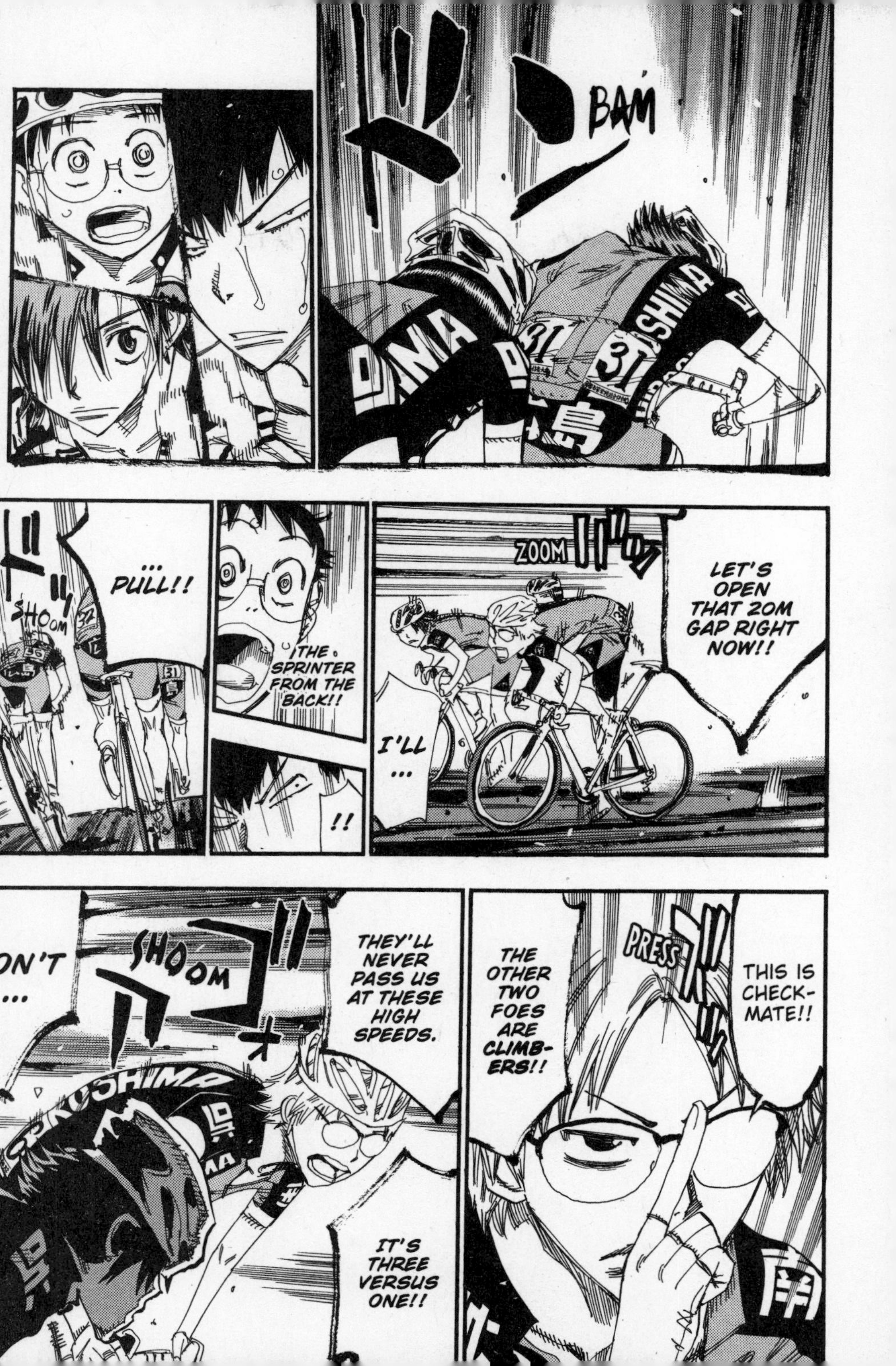
BAM
ZOOM
LET'S OPEN THAT 20M GAP RIGHT NOW!!
I'LL ...
THE SPRINTER FROM THE BACK!!
!!
... PULL!!
SHOOM
PRESS
THIS IS CHECK-MATE!!
THE OTHER TWO FOES ARE CLIMB-ERS!!
THEY'LL NEVER PASS US AT THESE HIGH SPEEDS.
SHOOM
DON'T ...
IT'S THREE VERSUS ONE!!

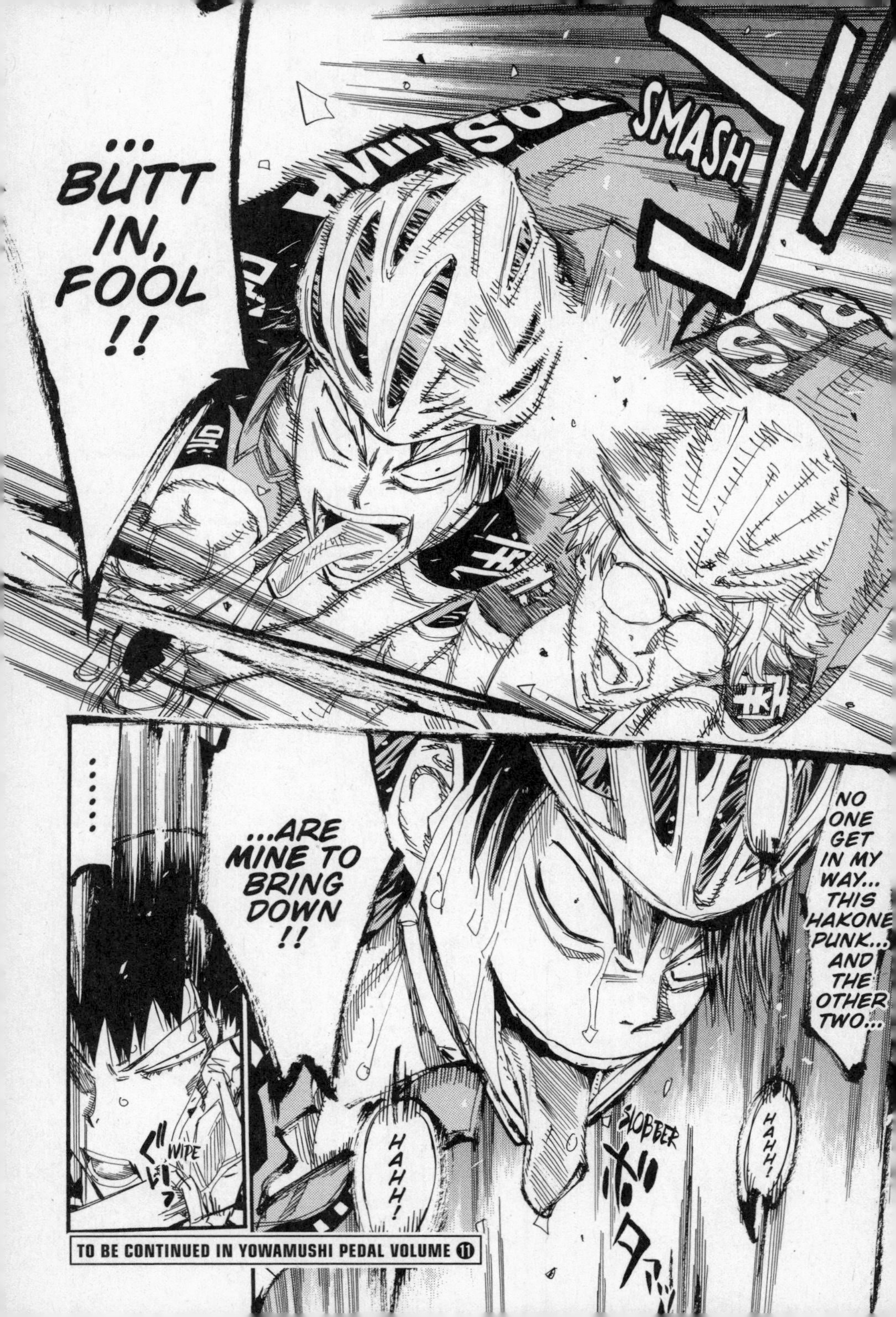
SMASH
...BÜTT IN, FOOL!!
NO ONE GET IN MY WAY... THIS HAKONE PUNK... AND THE OTHER TWO...
HAHH!
SLOBBER
...ARE MINE TO BRING DOWN!!
HAHH!
......
WIPE
TO BE CONTINUED IN YOWAMUSHI PEDAL VOLUME 11

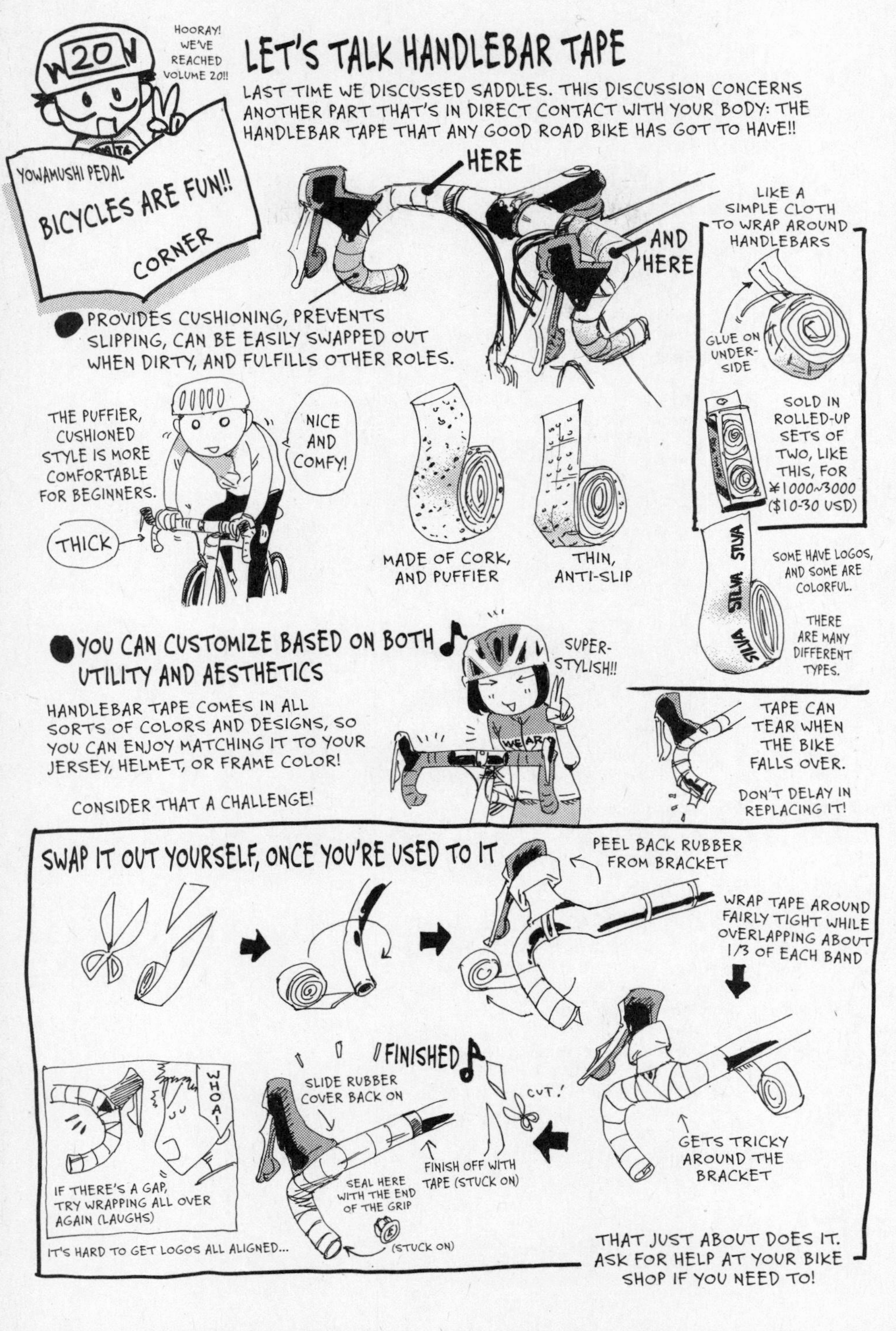
HOORAY! WE'VE REACHED VOLUME 20!!
20
YOWAMUSHI PEDAL
BICYCLES ARE FUN!!
CORNER
LET'S TALK HANDLEBAR TAPE
LAST TIME WE DISCUSSED SADDLES. THIS DISCUSSION CONCERNS ANOTHER PART THAT'S IN DIRECT CONTACT WITH YOUR BODY: THE HANDLEBAR TAPE THAT ANY GOOD ROAD BIKE HAS GOT TO HAVE!!
HERE
AND HERE
LIKE A SIMPLE CLOTH TO WRAP AROUND HANDLEBARS
GLUE ON UNDER-SIDE
SOLD IN ROLLED-UP SETS OF TWO, LIKE THIS, FOR ¥1000~3000 ($10-30 USD)
PROVIDES CUSHIONING, PREVENTS SLIPPING, CAN BE EASILY SWAPPED OUT WHEN DIRTY, AND FULFILLS OTHER ROLES.
THE PUFFIER, CUSHIONED STYLE IS MORE COMFORTABLE FOR BEGINNERS.
NICE AND COMFY!
THICK
MADE OF CORK, AND PUFFIER
THIN, ANTI-SLIP
SILVA
SOME HAVE LOGOS, AND SOME ARE COLORFUL.
THERE ARE MANY DIFFERENT TYPES.
YOU CAN CUSTOMIZE BASED ON BOTH UTILITY AND AESTHETICS
SUPER-STYLISH!!
HANDLEBAR TAPE COMES IN ALL SORTS OF COLORS AND DESIGNS, SO YOU CAN ENJOY MATCHING IT TO YOUR JERSEY, HELMET, OR FRAME COLOR!
CONSIDER THAT A CHALLENGE!
TAPE CAN TEAR WHEN THE BIKE FALLS OVER.
DON'T DELAY IN REPLACING IT!
SWAP IT OUT YOURSELF, ONCE YOU'RE USED TO IT
PEEL BACK RUBBER FROM BRACKET
WRAP TAPE AROUND FAIRLY TIGHT WHILE OVERLAPPING ABOUT 1/3 OF EACH BAND
GETS TRICKY AROUND THE BRACKET
CUT!
FINISHED
SLIDE RUBBER COVER BACK ON
FINISH OFF WITH TAPE (STUCK ON)
SEAL HERE WITH THE END OF THE GRIP
(STUCK ON)
WHOA!
IF THERE'S A GAP, TRY WRAPPING ALL OVER AGAIN (LAUGHS)
IT'S HARD TO GET LOGOS ALL ALIGNED...
THAT JUST ABOUT DOES IT. ASK FOR HELP AT YOUR BIKE SHOP IF YOU NEED TO!

Translation Notes

Common Honorifics
-san: The Japanese equivalent of Mr./Mrs./Miss. If a situation calls for politeness, this is the fail-safe honorific.
-kun: Used most often when referring to boys, this indicates affection or familiarity. Occasionally used by older men among their peers, but it may also be used by anyone referring to a person of lower standing.
-chan: An affectionate honorific indicating familiarity used mostly in reference to girls; also used in reference to cute persons or animals of either gender.
-senpai: A suffix used to address upperclassmen or more experienced co-workers.
-shi: A more formal version of san common to written Japanese, it's the default honorific used in newspapers.
no honorific: Indicates familiarity or closeness; if used without permission or reason, addressing someone in this manner would constitute an insult.

A kilometer is approximately .6 of a mile.

PAGE 9
Hakone: A town located in a mountainous area of Kanagawa Prefecture, it's popular among tourists for its scenic views and hot springs.

Kyoto: Former capital of Japan located in the Kansai region. It's known for its plethora of traditional Japanese architecture, having come out of World War II relatively unscathed.

PAGE 15
Domestique: A cyclist on a competitive team who focuses on helping the team and the ace over winning the race themselves.

PAGE 40
Chiba: A prefecture in the Kantou region of Japan. Chiba has both long stretches of mountains and large areas of flat plains, and it is known for having mild summers and winters.

PAGE 42
Gouf: Midousuji uses the term zaku in the Japanese version, which means "assorted vegetables for sukiyaki hot pot" but is also the name of the common enemy robot in the anime Mobile Suit Gundam. In previous volumes of the English translation, Midousuji has used the term "Goof," as both Zakus and Goufs [sic] are weapons of the opposing Zeon forces.

Crimson Commander Type: This is a veiled reference to Gundam antagonist Char Aznable and his use of red mobile suits.

Royal Force: A title reminiscent of the Studio Gainax anime Royal Space Force: The Wings of the Honnêamise.

PAGE 44
Humanoid Weapon Unit-02: This is suggestive of the red EVA Unit-02 from the anime Neon Genesis Evangelion, another Gainax series.

PAGE 89

Hiroshima: A populous city located on the island of Honshu, Japan. The city was the target of the first atomic bombing of World War II, which led to major devastation in its infrastructure and the deaths of thousands of innocent civilians. It is known for its peace memorial, which stands a remaining marker of the war.

Odawara: Once ruled by a feudal lord, the town is located in Kanagawa Prefecture and is bordered by the mountains of Hakone. It is known for Odawara Castle, a fortress that served as a defensive base during Japan's earlier war era.

PAGE 150

Peloton: A cycling term for the "pack," or the main group of riders in a race.

PAGE 151

Kumamoto: The capital of Kumamoto Prefecture in Kyushu, known for its frequent rain. Home of Kumamoto Castle—the largest complete castle in Japan.

PAGE 157

Persist: Taura shouts, "*Higo Mokkosu!*" which is a motto that expresses the unyielding spirit of Kumamoto. *Higo* was an old province that occupied the area of present-day Kumamoto.

PAGE 174

Bottom bracket motor: A motor usually placed in the bottom bracket or rear hub of an electric bike. It is possible to turn a regular road bike into an e-bike or add a concealed motor to it.

YOWAMUSHI PEDAL *VOLUME 11*

Read on for a sneak peek of Volume 11, available April 2019!

RIDE.173 GRUDGE-POWERED BOOST

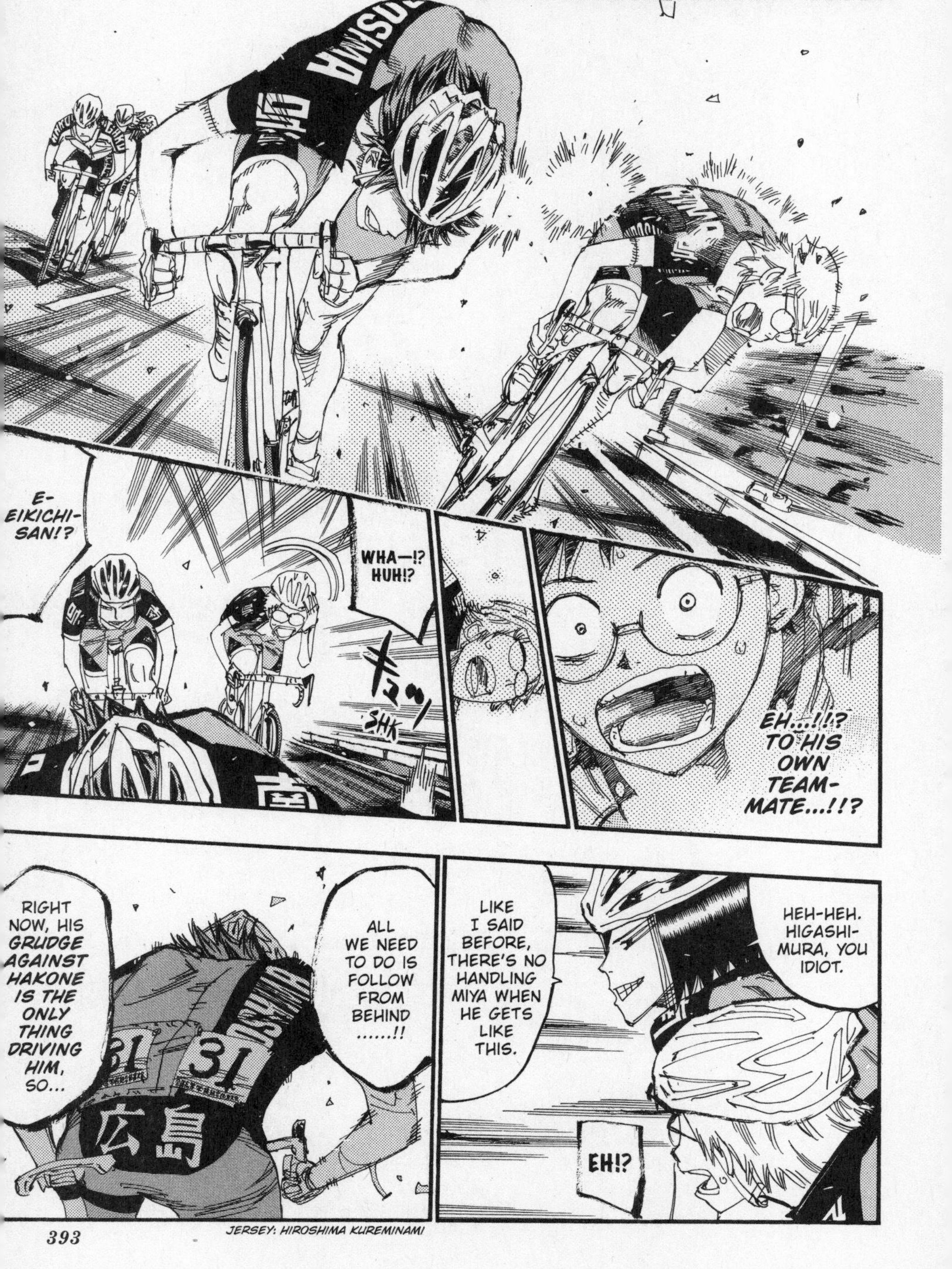
EH...!!? TO HIS OWN TEAM-MATE...!!?
WHA—!? HUH!?
SHK
E-EIKICHI-SAN!?
HEH-HEH. HIGASHIMURA, YOU IDIOT.
LIKE I SAID BEFORE, THERE'S NO HANDLING MIYA WHEN HE GETS LIKE THIS.
EH!?
ALL WE NEED TO DO IS FOLLOW FROM BEHIND ......!!
RIGHT NOW, HIS GRUDGE AGAINST HAKONE IS THE ONLY THING DRIVING HIM, SO...

JERSEY: HIROSHIMA KUREMINAMI

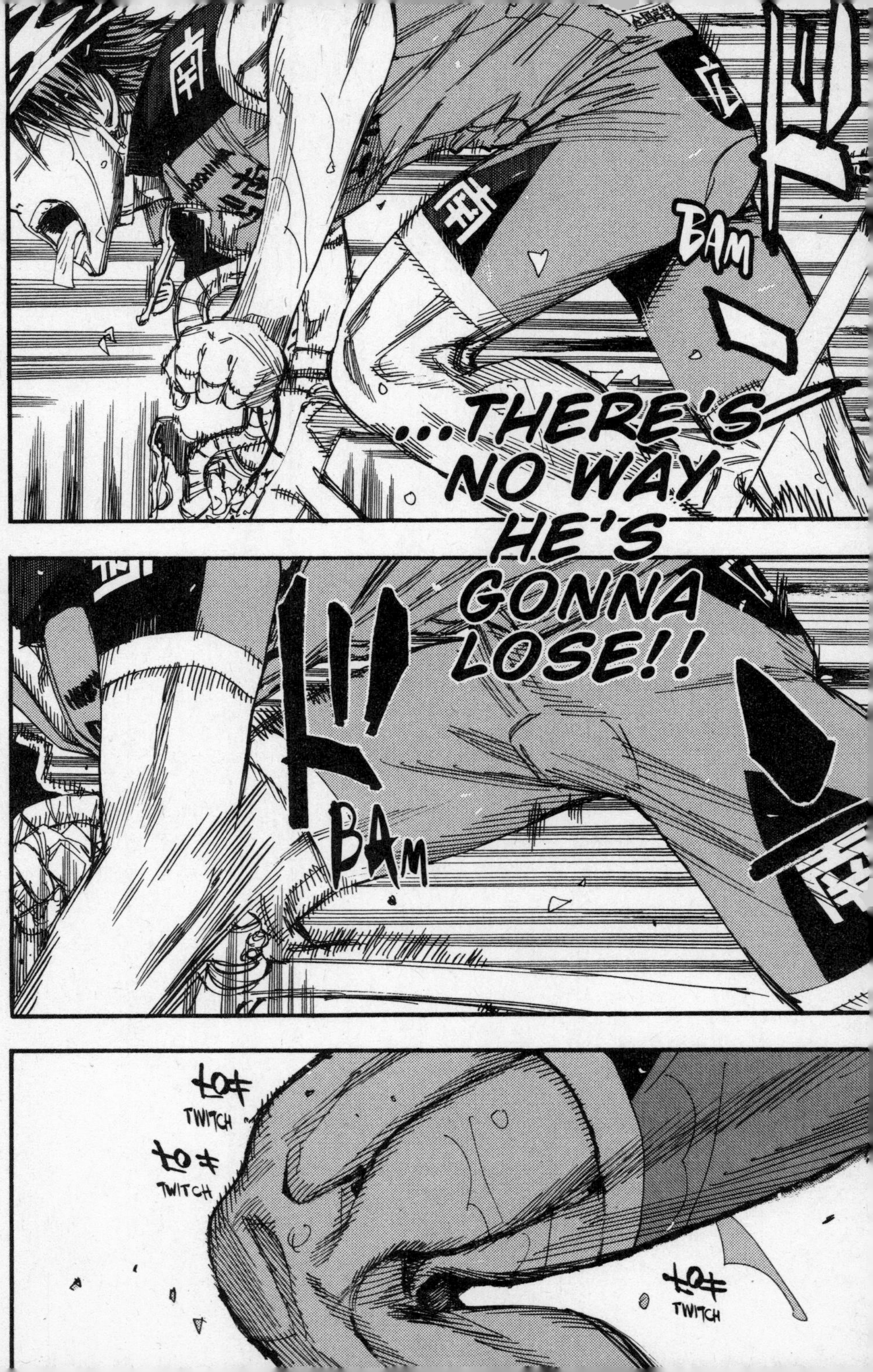
BAM
...THERE'S NO WAY HE'S GONNA LOSE!!
BAM
TWITCH
TWITCH
TWITCH

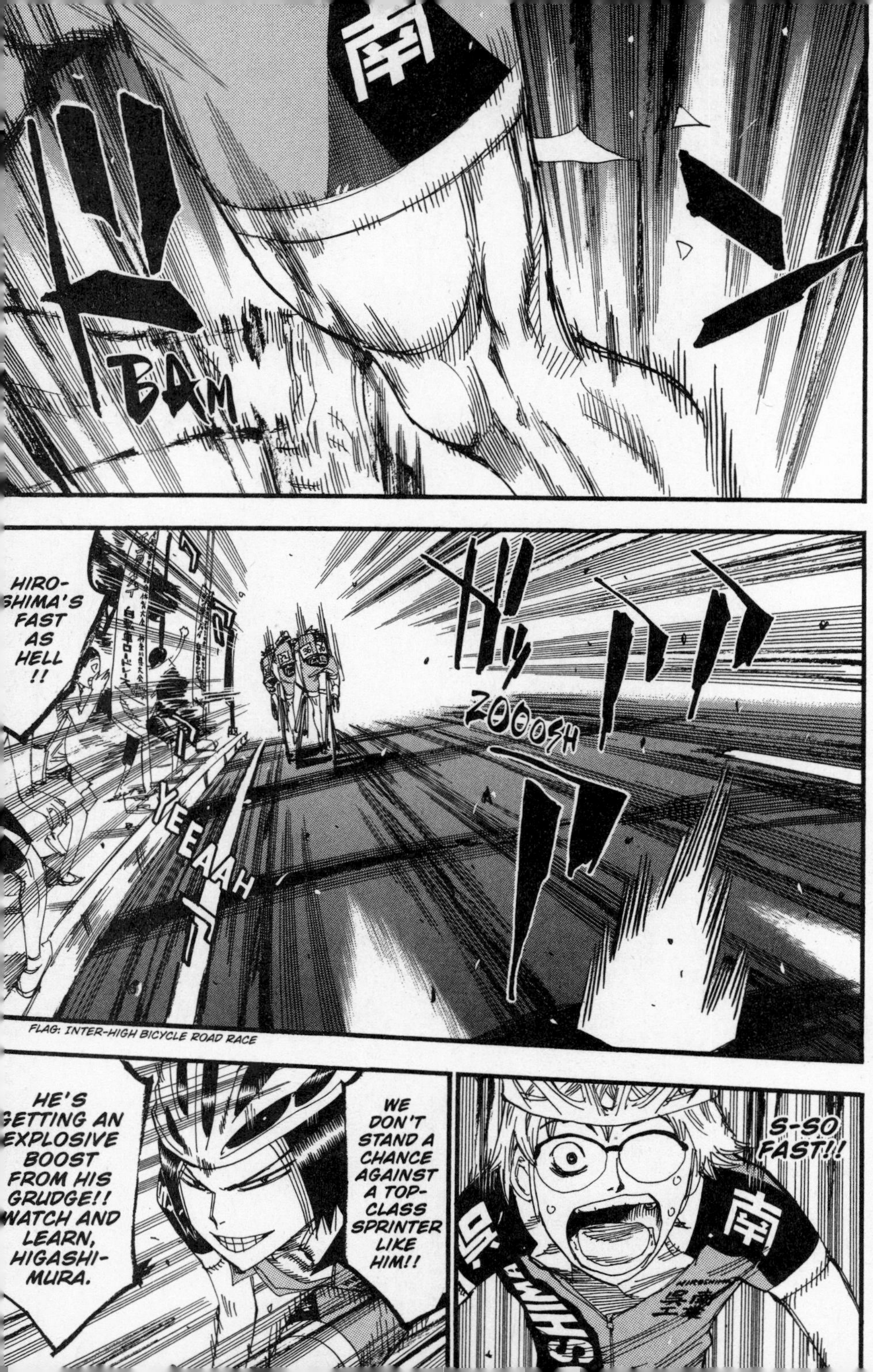
BAM
ZOOOSH
YEEAAH
HIRO-SHIMA'S FAST AS HELL!!
FLAG: INTER-HIGH BICYCLE ROAD RACE
S-SO FAST!!
WE DON'T STAND A CHANCE AGAINST A TOP-CLASS SPRINTER LIKE HIM!!
HE'S GETTING AN EXPLOSIVE BOOST FROM HIS GRUDGE!! WATCH AND LEARN, HIGASHI-MURA.

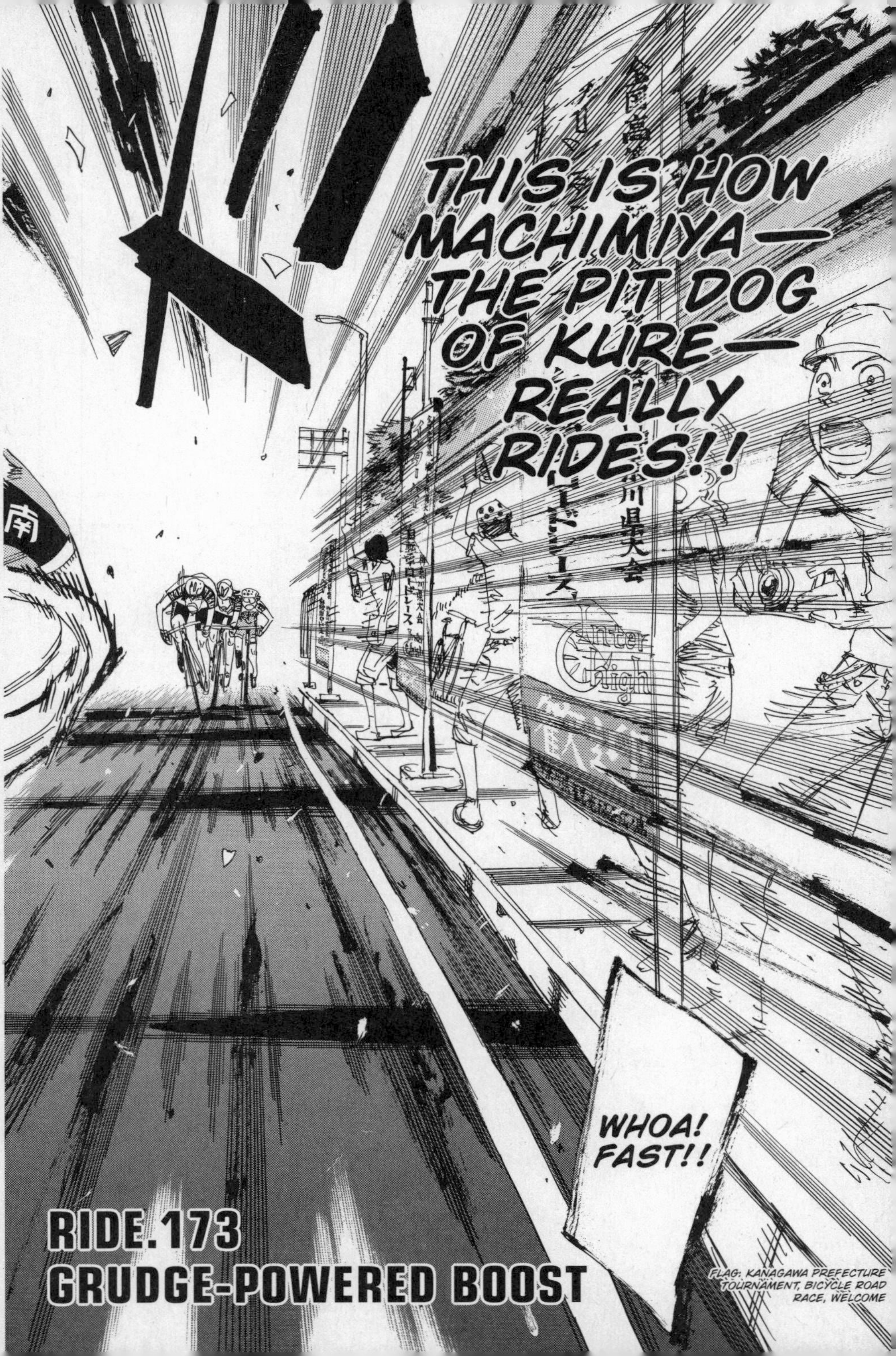
THIS IS HOW MACHIMIYA— THE PIT DOG OF KURE— REALLY RIDES!!
WHOA! FAST!!
RIDE.173
GRUDGE-POWERED BOOST
FLAG: KANAGAWA PREFECTURE TOURNAMENT, BICYCLE ROAD RACE, WELCOME

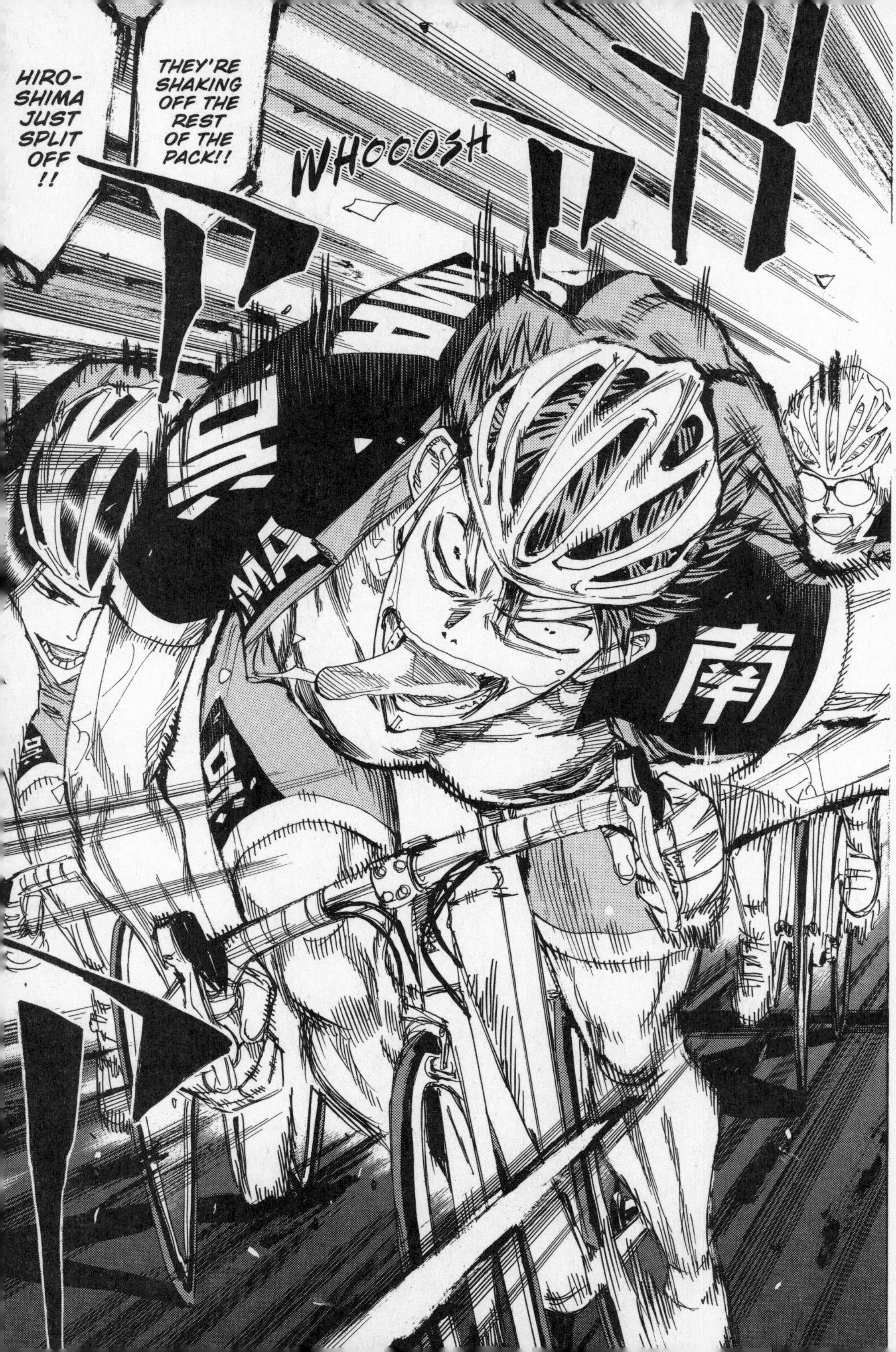
THEY'RE SHAKING OFF THE REST OF THE PACK!!
HIRO-SHIMA JUST SPLIT OFF!!
WHOOOSH

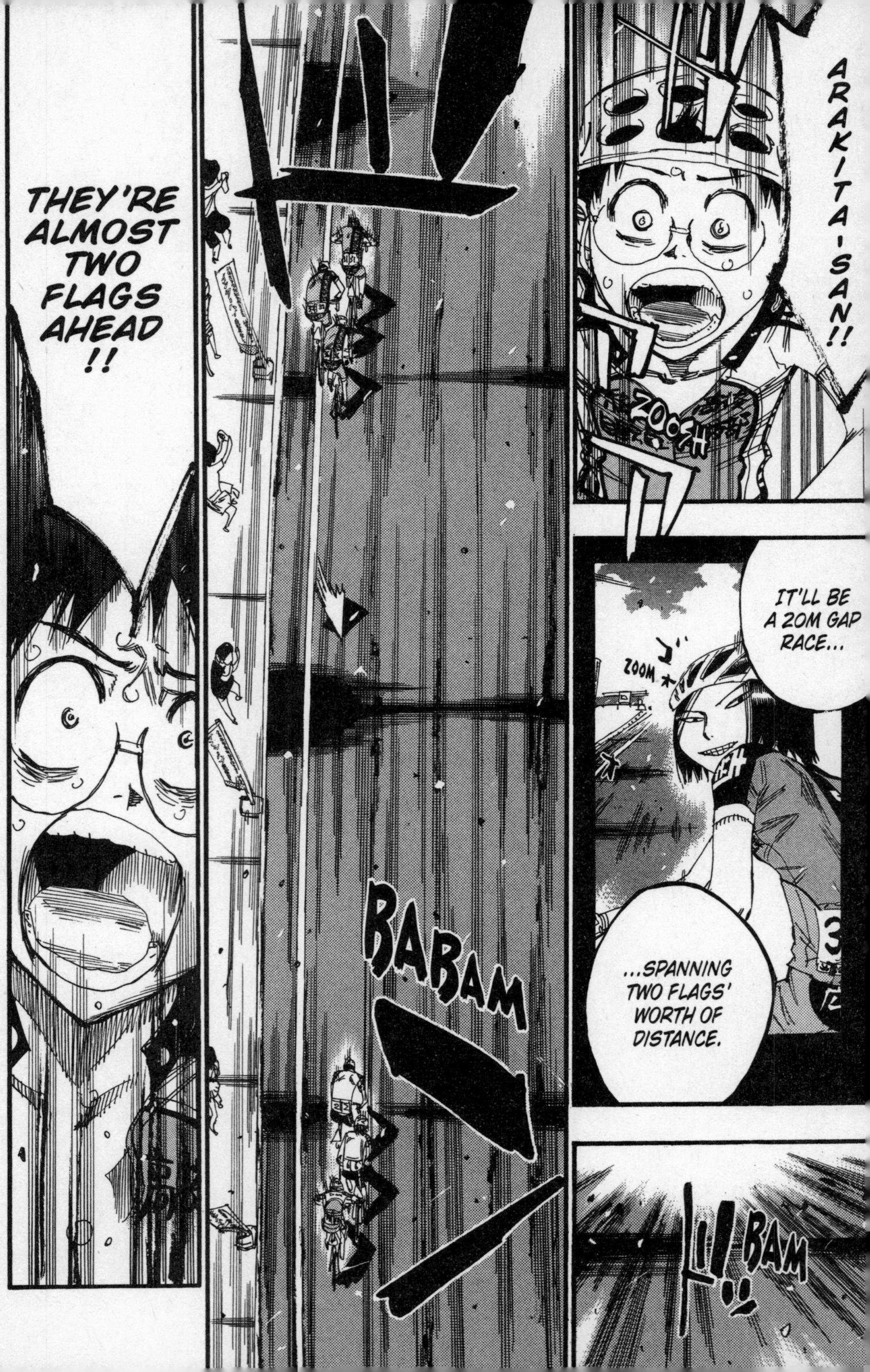
ARAKITA-SAN!!
ZOOSH
IT'LL BE A 20M GAP RACE...
ZOOM
...SPANNING TWO FLAGS' WORTH OF DISTANCE.
BAM
BABAM
THEY'RE ALMOST TWO FLAGS AHEAD!!

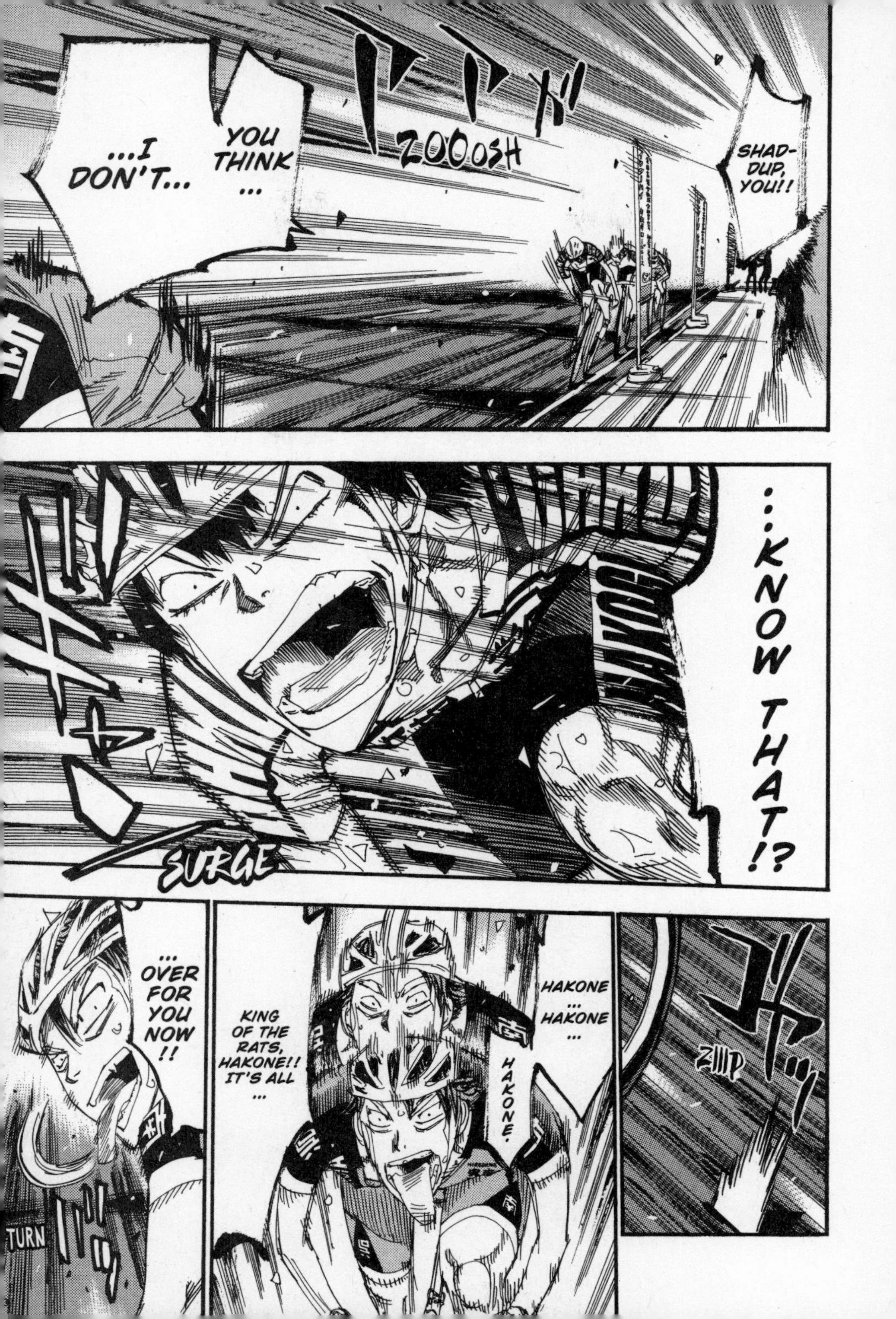
SHAD-DUP, YOU!!
ZOOOSH
YOU THINK ...
...I DON'T...
...KNOW THAT!?
SURGE
ZIIIP
HAKONE ... HAKONE ...
HAKONE.
KING OF THE RATS, HAKONE!! IT'S ALL ...
... OVER FOR YOU NOW !!
TURN

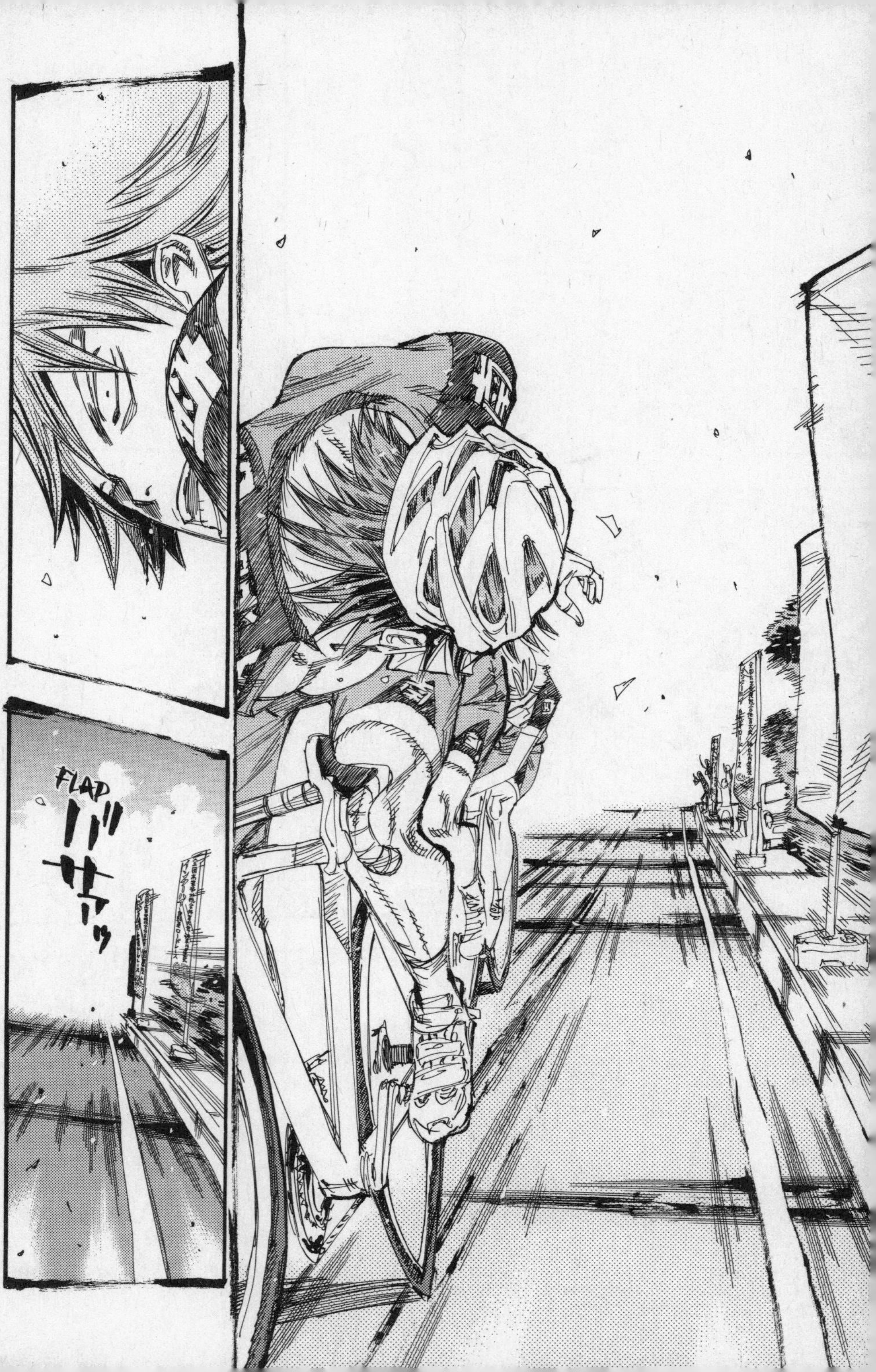
FLAP
バサァッ

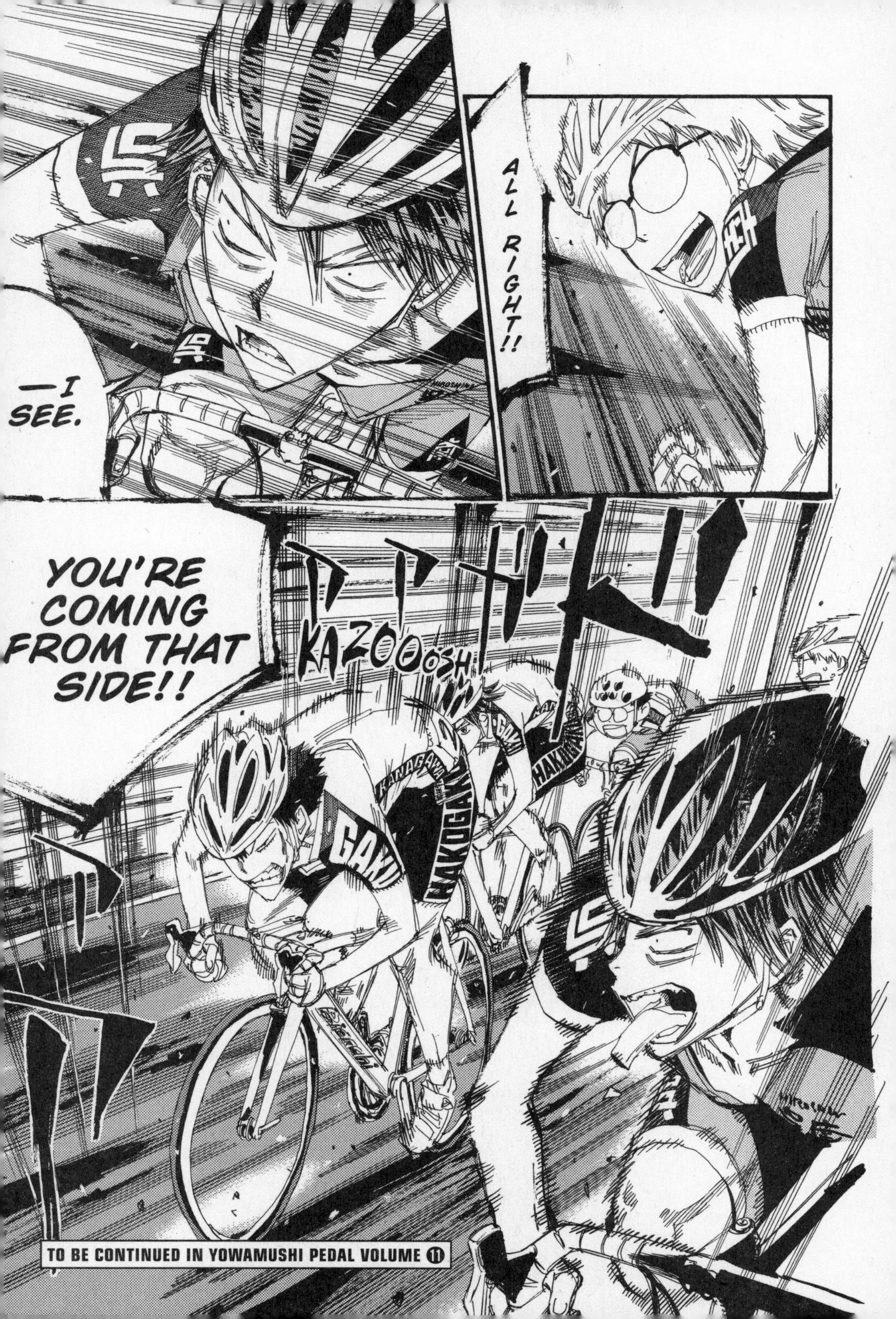
ALL RIGHT!!
—I SEE.
YOU'RE COMING FROM THAT SIDE!!
KAZOOOOSH
TO BE CONTINUED IN YOWAMUSHI PEDAL VOLUME 11

YOWAMUSHI PEDAL ⑩

WATARU WATANABE

Translation: Su Mon Han, Caleb D. Cook

Lettering: Lys Blakeslee, Rachel J. Pierce

YOWAMUSHI PEDAL Volume 19, 20
© 2011 Wataru Watanabe
All rights reserved.
First published in Japan in 2011 by Akita Publishing Co., Ltd., Tokyo.
English translation rights arranged with Akita Publishing Co., Ltd. through Tuttle-Mori Agency, Inc., Tokyo.

English translation © 2018 by Yen Press, LLC

Yen Press
1290 Avenue of the Americas
New York, NY 10104

Visit us at yenpress.com
facebook.com/yenpress
twitter.com/yenpress
yenpress.tumblr.com
instagram.com/yenpress

First Yen Press Edition: December 2018

Library of Congress Control Number: 2015960124

ISBNs: 978-0-316-52091-1 (paperback)
       978-0-316-52092-8 (ebook)

10 9 8 7 6 5 4 3 2 1

WOR

Printed in the United States of America